VIDEOGAME ARCHITECTURE

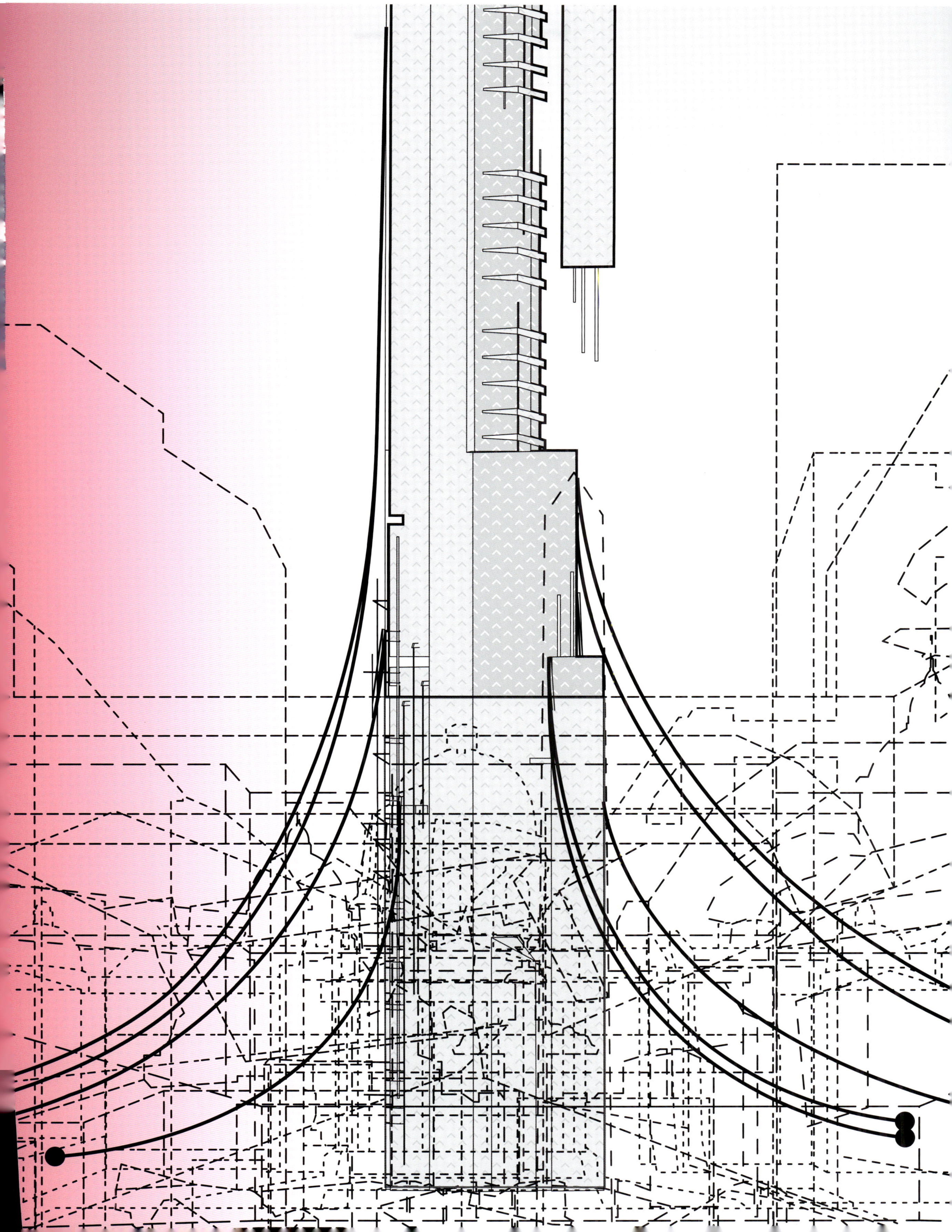

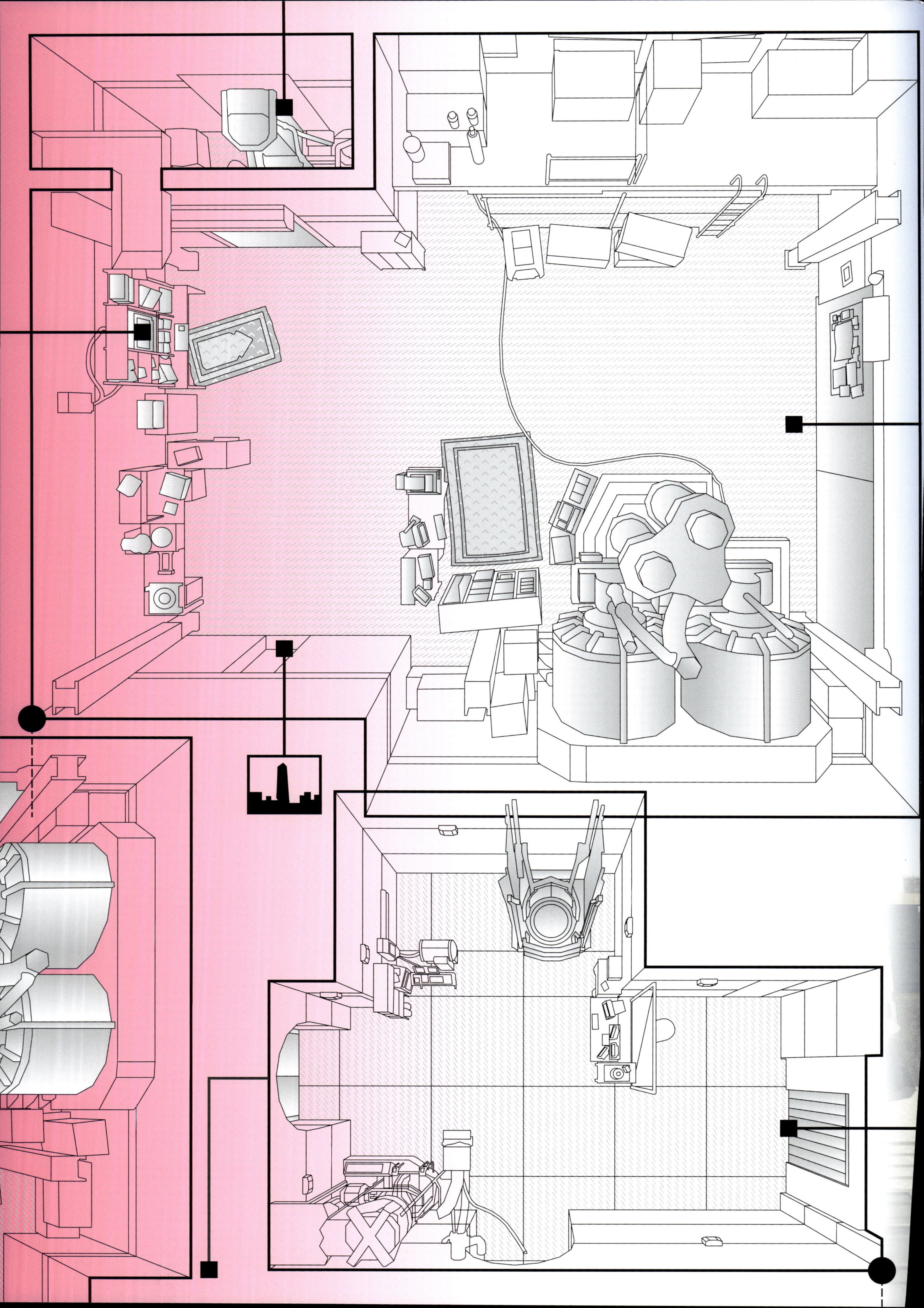

VIDEOGAME ARCHITECTURE

BUILDING VIRTUAL SPACES

Luke Caspar Pearson
Sandra Youkhana

T&H

Foreword by John Romero

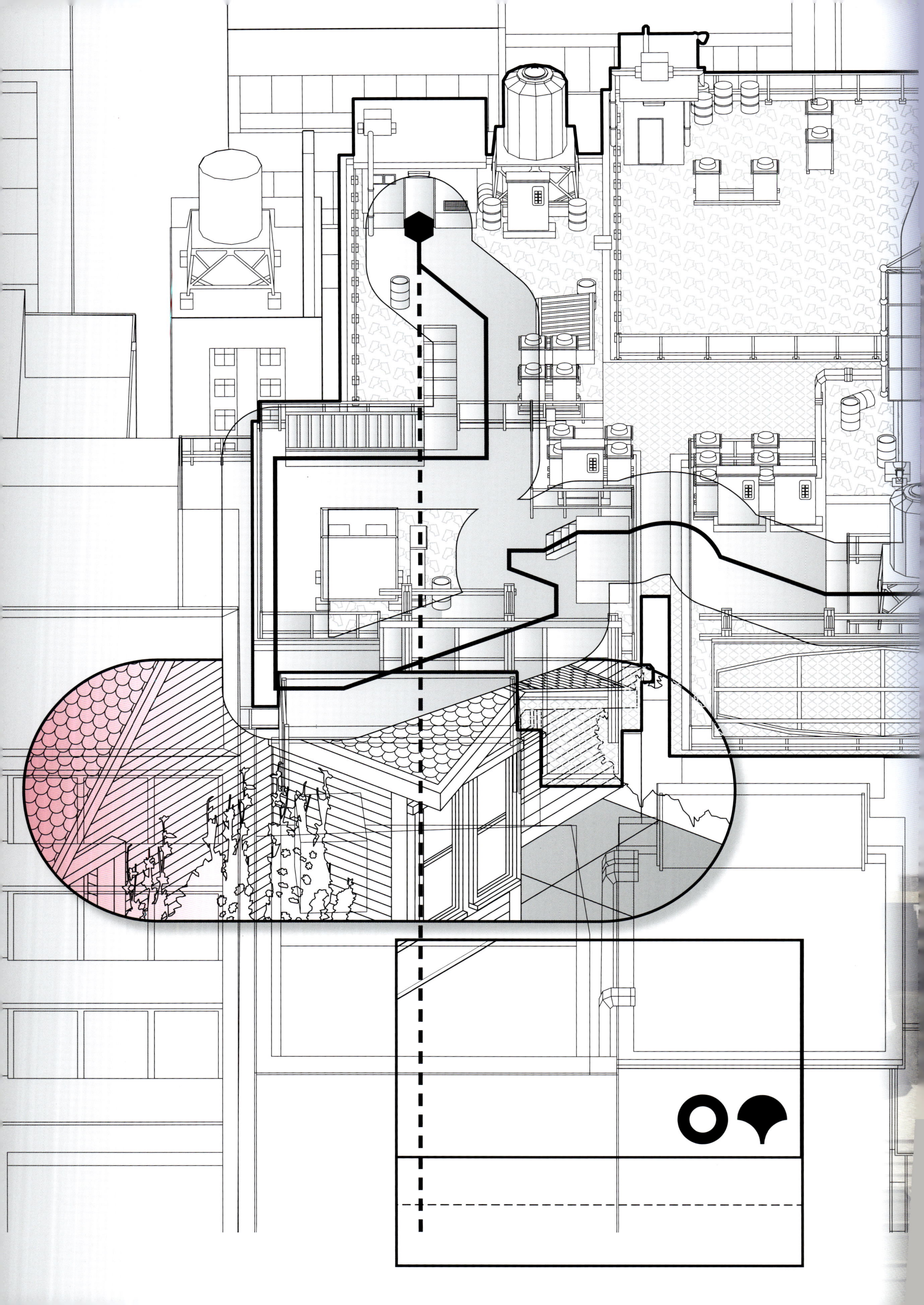

TABLE OF CONTENTS

FOREWORD BY JOHN ROMERO

CO-FOUNDER OF ID SOFTWARE AND DESIGNER OF *DOOM*

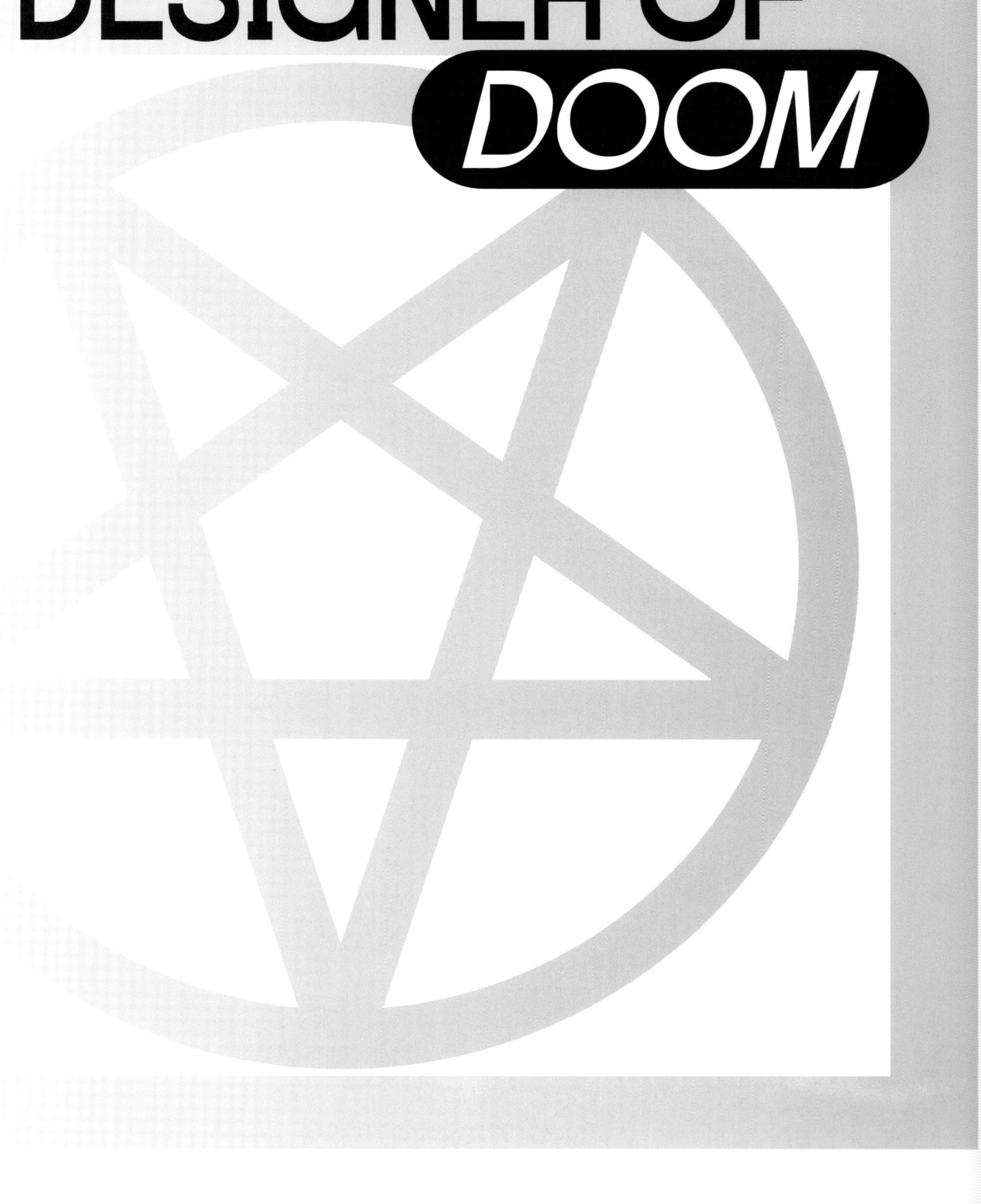

There was a tipping point in game development when 3D space stopped looking like a maze drawn with a ruler. Early environments were locked to right angles and flat planes. They worked, but they felt constrained. Then things opened up. Floors rose and fell with intention. Light and shadow became design tools. Levels looped back on themselves. Space started to feel authored rather than assembled.

DOOM sits right on that fault line.

People often focus on the technology or the controversy, but what really matters is how it handled space. The speed of movement, the flow of the layouts, the contrast between tight corridors and open arenas – all of it was deliberate. The player was tearing through architecture rather than creeping through it, and that speed changes everything. When players move that fast, space has to be readable at a glance. It has to create tension through layout, not cutscenes.

When we built levels for *Wolfenstein 3D*, *DOOM* and later *Quake*, we were constantly pushing against technical limits. At first, you worked within strict geometric rules. You couldn't stack rooms freely. You couldn't do everything you imagined. When those restrictions started to lift, it felt like real freedom. Verticality became expressive. Spaces could interlock. You could surprise players in ways that weren't possible before. But more freedom also meant you had to be more disciplined. The tools don't make the design good, they just remove excuses.

Videogame architecture is fundamentally different from real-world architecture. Real buildings deal with gravity, structure, budgets and safety. Game spaces deal with perception, mechanics and player behavior. A wall might block movement, trigger an event, hide a secret or control how enemies react. The geometry itself is part of the gameplay, creating action rather than simply containing it.

Movement speed is one of the most important design variables we have. In *DOOM* and *Quake*, players move faster than any real person could. That speed turns corridors into sprints and arenas into combat puzzles. You're not designing for someone strolling through a building. You're designing for someone who can strafe, circle and rocket-jump through it. The architecture has to support that energy.

This book takes that idea seriously. It looks at games as constructed spaces with rules, material languages and spatial logic. By analysing titles like *DOOM* through architectural drawings and diagrams, it shows how much thought goes into places that millions of players have moved through at full speed. It's a reminder that videogame worlds are designed environments, and that the craft of building them deserves to be studied with the same care as any other form of architecture.

INTRODUCTION

Many of the most experimental and strange pieces of architecture we encounter today are not, and never will be, physically built. These are the spaces of *Videogame Architecture*, where millions of people find meaning in curious domains that must be experienced through a screen, yet give us a deep sense of place. Where else could we jump between floating islands that each have their own planetary gravity, or battle mythical gods in a tiled world that changes each time we die? These are environments made to bunny-hop and spin through, where the precise positioning of our body can unlock secret spaces, and where we can literally drag and drop pieces of world beneath us. These are also sites where communities grow and share knowledge, and players gain new identities through avatars. As games become ever more realistic-looking, they naturally become more connected to our conceptions of the 'real world.' The software used by game designers in the virtual and architects in the physical is increasingly similar, suggesting that future designers may slip seamlessly between realms. Yet many of the most beloved game worlds are stylized, cartoonish or abstract in appearance and still exist as deep and coherent places. As this book demonstrates, game spaces can resonate with reality in meaningful ways whatever number of pixels are contained on the screen.

This is the power of architecture in videogames: that however realistic or not the world may appear, they are worlds designed for people to interact with and their playability fundamentally affects the form that the environment takes. Making the world playable involves twisting, magnifying and erasing elements and concepts from the physical to create the virtual. These divergences combine to form the new alternate reality of the game world, allowing for players to assume new personas or gain improbable abilities. As such, the presence of a player, a virtual camera and game mechanisms are key to fully understanding how architecture operates in videogames. But by deviating from our 'real world', games implicitly connect to it. Exposing the process of transforming places, structures and narrative into Videogame Architecture leads us to find many traces and establish new links to how we think about and analyse 'reality'.

We consider videogame architecture holistically, not only discussing the levels in which gameplay takes place, but also the edges of the world that provide contextual details and information. This focuses on how these virtual spaces translate the physical world into new architectural forms, perhaps subjecting real places to terrible imaginary events, sinking cities underwater and floating them into the air, or clashing architectural styles together with cultural tropes from cinema or folklore. We take each game world and assess them as they are shown to the player, examining them as architects do.

The analysis in the following chapters builds on theories and design research practices that we have developed over the last decade in our studio You+Pea, including our previous book *Videogame Atlas: Mapping Interactive Worlds*[1], which can be read as a companion piece to *Videogame Architecture*. These unique methods apply analytical techniques from architecture to generate new understandings of videogame worlds. Architectural drawing is key to this, including familiar forms of projection such as maps, floorplans, details, cross sections and 'exploded' isometric diagrams, used to unravel the complexity of these virtual spaces. We delve into historical and experimental forms of drawing to find other methods of visual analysis, adopting centuries-old styles such as *analytique* or *oblique* drawings to showcase virtual architecture in a new light. We also apply contemporary computational techniques such as data analysis, hacking and glitching to uncover the form of these worlds. Our research takes inspiration from the books and surveys of other architects who scrutinize the world around them. Architects have surveyed the casinos of Las Vegas,[2] the design strategies of Disneyland[3], or buildings that look like robots,[4] meaning that investigating *Videogame Architecture* has some likeminded parallels to draw from. However, the interactivity and sheer diversity of the games we cover reveals that the worlds we discuss are always changing around us – as do our methods of analysis.

We have played many hundreds of hours of games, often in very strange ways, to understand the extents and complexity of each game world. This has also produced thousands of screenshots that we use to create our visual analysis. Our findings are presented through well over 100 design research drawings, examining each game in fine detail. We also include selected screenshot 'photographs' from our journeys of each world, using the virtual camera to frame the architectural landscape. Embodying the spirit and process of real-world architectural photographers allows us to put these worlds into a new visual context alongside the drawings. From diving into the culture of sharing suburban house designs, to punching our way around Japanese cities and piecing together buildings from 30-year-old rendered graphics, each chapter has taken us on unexpected journeys into well-known games. The processes of playing, recording, drawing and writing have combined to generate new readings and understandings of these beloved places.

This work could not be done without all the tools that each game's community has developed, whether for modding or simply the pleasure of understanding game worlds in more detail. Camera mods have been key for our screenshots, while other tools have allowed us to view models and export worlds to architectural design software for closer analysis. Aside from these software tools, we draw from many 'folksonomies'[5] and archives of community knowledge. They demonstrate players' desires to fully comprehend the logic and design of these digital environments, whether that is for the purposes of walkthroughs, speed running or generating fan fiction. While these may not be traditional forms of academic source, they are essential to understanding game worlds. A full list of these can be found in the Community Resources section at the end of this book and we advise investigating them further.

AN ARCHITECTURAL ANTHOLOGY

Each game is as unique as its community. When we discuss games, we are also speaking of all the technologies, art styles and mechanics that underpin them. In *Videogame Architecture* we have analysed titles that treat space in radically different ways. We see these differences as productive – demonstrating a broad range of means by which videogame architecture can function. Despite their variation, each game allows us to establish deep and foundational connections to the history and theory of architecture and spatial design.

In the *Baldur's Gate 3* chapter, we explore the diverse architectural inspirations behind the world, discussing how the game creates an 'anachronistic' landscape, combining buildings from different eras and styles. We examine how the game's architecture is shaped by its relationship to (turn-based) time, light and dark, and varying conceptions of scale. In comparison, our discussion of *BioShock* focusses on the specific reference point of Art Deco architecture and the architects that shaped the style in cities like New York. We employ several techniques to calculate the depth, dimensions and density of Rapture, finding that it may not be so different to the city that inspired it, though would be impossible to build.

Disco Elysium's isometric viewpoint becomes the basis for studying its world, by taking advantage of a representational style common to both games and architecture. This enables us to examine the game's 'chaotic mix' of architecture, relationships between the inside and outside of buildings, and critique one of the game's central questions: *where did the shot come from?* In *DOOM* we explore how John Romero's level design rules shape the world, and how this establishes a fiendish relationship between floorplans and the player's experience of space. Key to this is our study into the role of lines, which both define the geometry of *DOOM*'s levels and encode all the logic and behaviour that makes the levels come to life.

We consider the rich symbolism of *Elden Ring*'s world, and the way the game alludes to real-world buildings while manipulating the scale of architecture to fantastical proportions. The game channels ideas of the *picturesque* and its design principles, producing architectural forms that are visually arresting, yet demonstrate complex and thoughtful approaches to the circulation of buildings. Examining *Genshin Impact*, we see how the world is shaped through 'regionalism', where cities and urban space become symbols of the cultures that inspired them. We demonstrate how the game's urbanism creates a sense of place even as it funnels players towards the completion of tasks.

Our discussion of *Gravity Rush 2* enables us to lose the shackles of physics and investigate the architecture of a floating world, where cities can be navigated from any angle. We use *gravity shifting* to measure cities designed to be perpetually viewed from the air, and explore how the architectural and urban form of these places communicates a strict social hierarchy. The world of *Grim Fandango*, by contrast, is fixed to pre-rendered viewpoints, so we use 3D reconstruction to investigate the architectural design of its Art Deco environment. We place the Land of the Dead's design in a new light by connecting the game's Mexican iconography to trends in 20th-century architectural discourse that promoted Mayan and Aztec forms as 'true American' building blocks.

Half-Life 2's urban environments underpin a discussion on the relationship between Eastern European architecture and the parasitic spatial insertions of the Combine. By analysing the density of spaces that Gordon Freeman travels to, we show how architectural design is a key driver in the game's narrative, taking us from dense urban spaces to hinterlands beyond and back again. We also tackle the question that has fascinated gamers since they first saw City 17 – just how big is the Citadel? *The Last of Us Part 1* also shows cities under duress, this time through the forces of the cordyceps virus and the social breakdown it causes. Here we examine the curious romantic beauty of American urbanism overtaken by nature becoming a new form of 'frontier'. By exploring the prevalence of domestic space and everyday objects, we analyse how small and personal moments express the enormity of what has happened.

Taking the domestic in a different direction, our study of *The Sims 4* looks at how this suburban simulation has been transformed by the game's community. From 'shell' challenges to viral building hacks, we reveal ways in which budding architectural designers from around the globe have pushed the game's systems to generate new forms of living virtually, with strange spaces to match. Finally, in *Yakuza Kiwami*, we compare the digital district of Kamurochō to its real-world equivalent, Tokyo's Kabukichō. Through comparative mappings, we discuss how the real and virtual connect and diverge. We map their shared architectural language of signs, exuberant building façades and hostess bars, while also demonstrating how *Yakuza* tweaks the design of streets to better facilitate combat. Ultimately, we see the shared spaces of cocktail bars, cabaret clubs and ramen joints as an illustration of how close real world and videogame architecture can be.

Each chapter of this book employs a different approach to its analysis because each game provides us with a site-specific world for investigation. Many connections we make and discuss may not have been the original intentions of the designers. Just as a real-world architect or urban planner cannot fully dictate the way their buildings and cities will be used in the future, each of these game worlds takes on a new life when played critically, observed carefully and peeled apart through our drawings and analysis. In seeing these videogame worlds as real worlds, we believe they should be treated as thoughtfully and thoroughly as we would analyse any place on Earth, 'cementing' videogame architecture as an ever-changing, transformative spatial typology as good as any other.

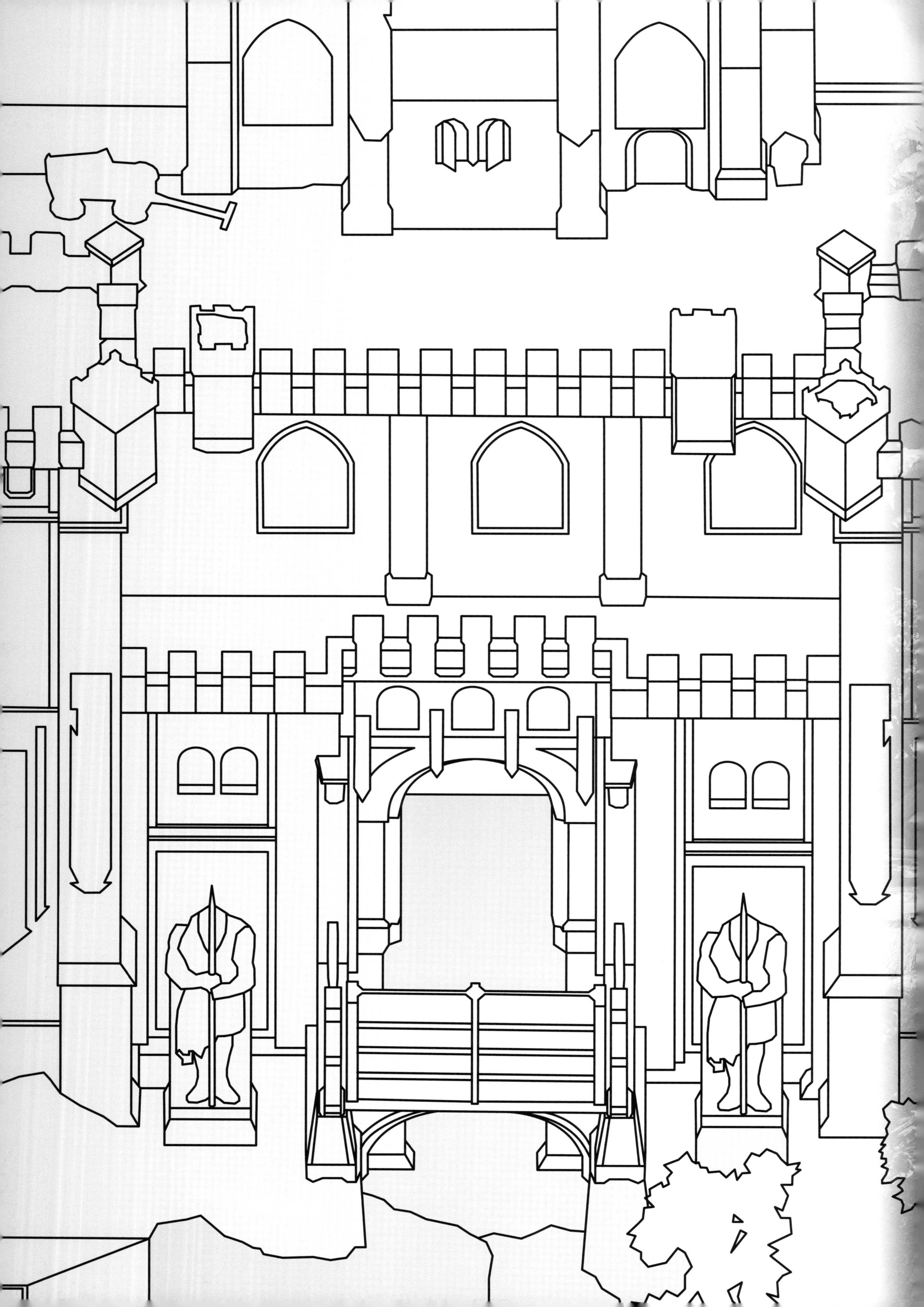

CHAPTER 01

BALDUR'S GATE 3

DEVELOPER
PUBLISHER

LARIAN STUDIOS

Platforms	PlayStation 5, Xbox Series X and Series S, GeForce Now, Windows, Mac
Year	2023

A MAP OF THE WILDERNESS IN ACT 1 OF THE GAME, SHOWING THE MAIN SETTLEMENTS CARVED INTO THE LANDSCAPE OR REPURPOSING EXISTING ARCHITECTURAL STRUCTURES.

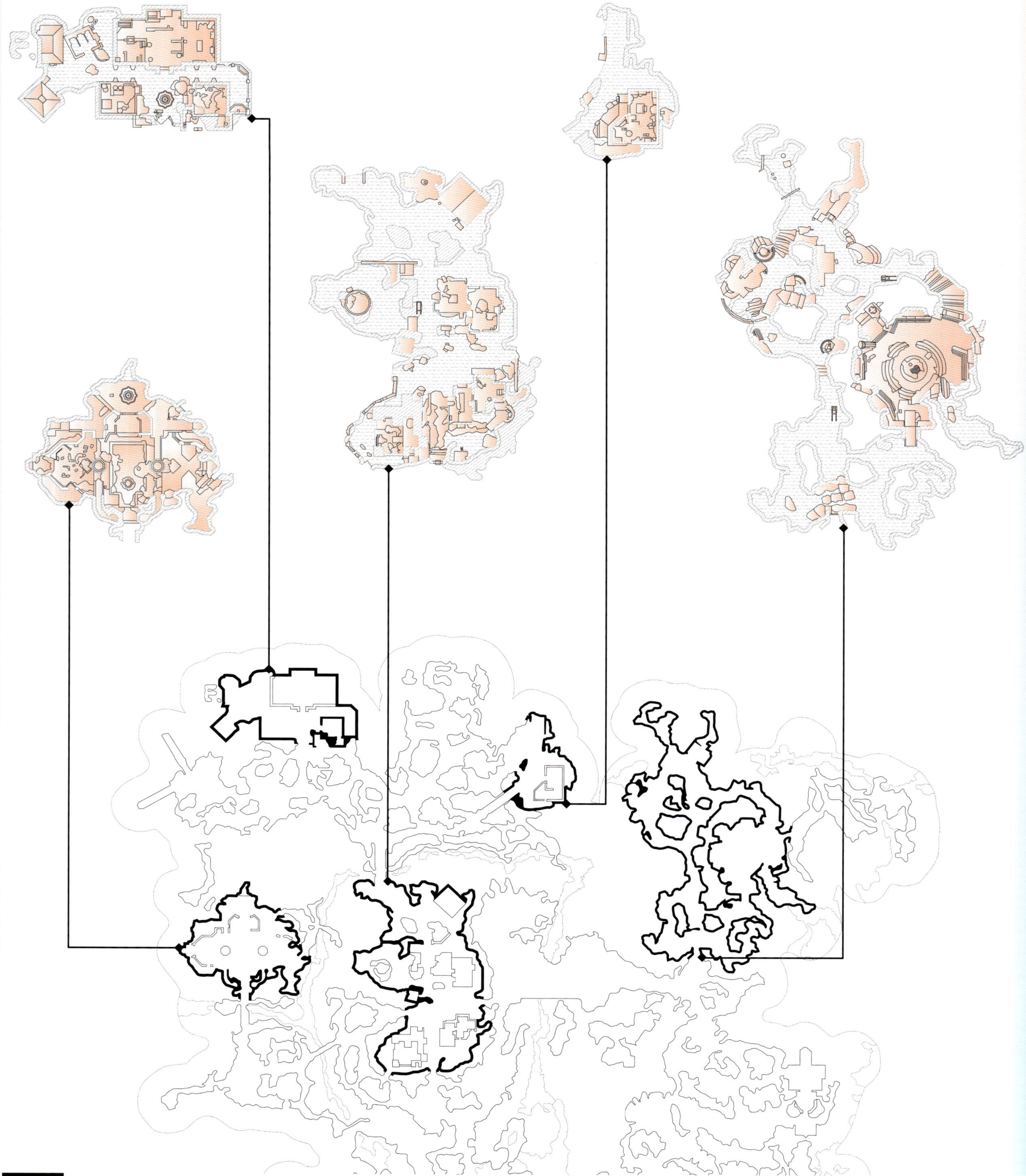

[Fig.01]

1.1 DUNGEON MASTERING

Realizing the world of *Baldur's Gate 3* posed a unique challenge to its creators: how to reimagine a place that has been thoroughly explored in the *Dungeons & Dragons* universe for almost 40 years (including 25 years of the game series). Key to this was the creative interpretation of source material – maps and descriptive texts found in D&D campaign guides such as *Murder in Baldur's Gate.*[1] Like any good *dungeon master*, the developers explain that 'we're bringing you one particular visualization of this world, but that doesn't mean that there cannot be others.'[2] Larian's version of Faerûn takes us on a journey that becomes progressively more urbanized – starting in the open Wilderness, moving on to the main town of the Shadow-Cursed Lands before arriving at Baldur's Gate itself, one of the largest cities in the region with a population of around 125,000 people.[3] In *Baldur's Gate 3,* the city and its surroundings are modelled on the Iberian peninsula, drawing from Portuguese and Spanish architecture and landscapes. While this may diverge from written descriptions of the 'area's near-constant rain,'[4] Larian has shaped a consistent realm founded on the close observation of real-world landscapes and architecture. It reinforces its emphasis on 'implicit storytelling' in environmental design,[5] while referencing key concepts from American urbanist Kevin Lynch.[6] By using camera mods (by *Otis_Inf*)[7] and Larian's own *Baldur's Gate 3 Toolkit* modding tool, we can learn more about what shapes these design principles and the world they produce.

During Act 1 of the game, when the city of Baldur's Gate is still far in the distance, players engage with a world where settlements occur in a more organic and haphazard fashion. By using the region map as a starting point for exploring these areas in more detail, we build a picture of how the occupants of this environment have carved out their own unique types of living space – either friendly or antagonistic [Fig.01]. The Goblin Camp to the west of the Wilderness is a former temple, retrofitted by the goblins into a living space using timber and bone scaffolds built into the existing stone structure. They have also forged out into the landscape beyond, ransacking and leaving ablaze the Waukeen's Rest inn, and camping out in the Blighted Village. The most notable sense of an organically developed settlement comes when we visit the Druids' Emerald Grove in the east of the Wilderness. Here, stone structures, tents and other quarters are built into and around the rocks and caverns that surround them. The Grove represents what we know as *vernacular architecture*, forms of localized and traditional building that are closely related to the communities that make them. Writing in *Architecture Without Architects*, architecture critic Bernard Rudofsky expresses that vernacular builders (like those of Emerald Grove) 'demonstrate an admirable talent for fitting their buildings into the natural surroundings. Instead of trying to "conquer" nature, as we do, they welcome the vagaries of climate and the challenge of topography'.[8] This seems a highly appropriate way of approaching the design of Emerald Grove, given that Druids are so implicitly connected to nature [Fig.02]. Despite being embedded into the natural landscape, Emerald Grove does have a clearly defined extent, guarded by a reinforced gate, emphasizing Rudofsky's argument that 'the tendency to build on sites of difficult access can be traced no doubt to a desire for security but perhaps even more so to the need of defining a community's borders.'[9]

[Fig.02]
PAGE 14

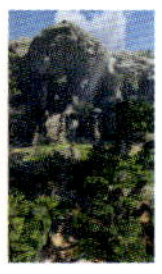

A view into Emerald Grove, showing the vernacular architecture of the Druids and how it is closely integrated into the surrounding landscape.

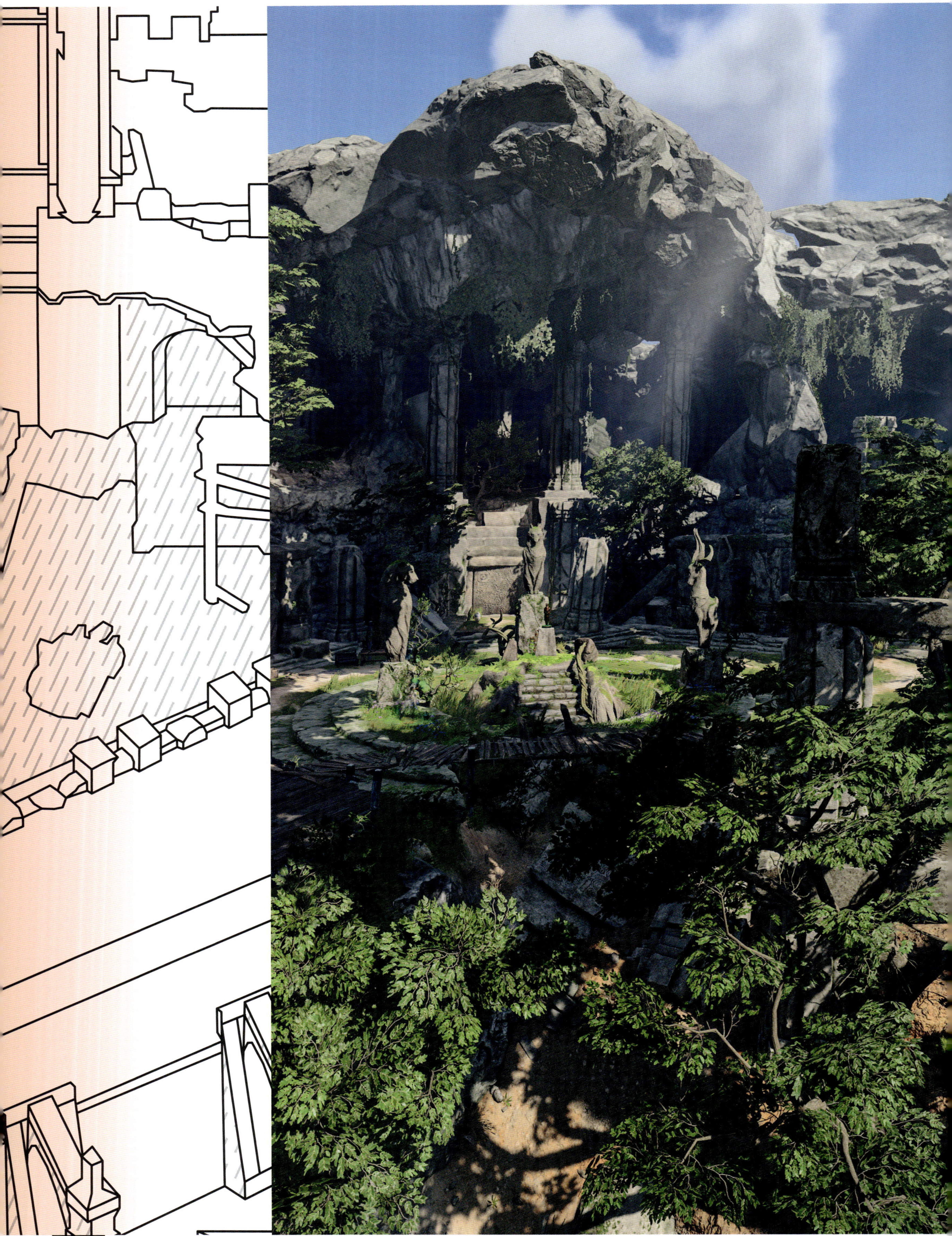

[Fig.02]

1.2 DARKNESS AND LIGHT

One of the key decisions that players can make at the end of Act 1, which will affect the parts of the world they experience – or at least their order – is deciding whether to travel to the Shadow-Cursed Lands via the Mountain Pass or Underdark. Mapping some of the key areas the player will explore demonstrates how different architectural languages are uncovered depending on the chosen path [Fig.03]. The Underdark is a realm where huge mushrooms proliferate, creating giant fungal structures, while other buildings show a progressively increasing mixture of architectural form and infrastructure. The Arcane Tower for example, has a façade penetrated by huge pipes and ducting, yet we can still broadly recognize its form as a building. But by the time we reach the giant Adamantine Forge, architecture and machine are completely combined. Taking the alternative route through the Mountain Pass, players encounter the Rosymorn Monastery, built into a cliffside with a waterfall to the rear. Here, a statue of the god Lathander cantilevers out on curving buttresses to emphasize the vertiginous setting of the landscape, inspired by Caminito del Rey in Spain.[10] The party finds their way through the ruined monastery down to the Githyanki base and the Crèche Y'llek within. Delving deeper, they find the Secret Chamber with a series of architectural traps to overcome, and obtain the Blood of Lathander, a powerful mace weapon. Upon retrieving the weapon, a (preventable) self-destruction of the monastery is initiated. While below ground we find a giant melding of building and machine, above ground it is building and bomb that are combined.

In Act 2 of the game, players journey through the Shadow-Cursed Lands, a realm where light and darkness form new territories that must be carefully navigated. The Shadow Curse will damage any character not exposed to light, and this gets stronger the closer the party moves towards their destination of Moonrise Towers. As such, players must find solutions that involve either sprinting between patches of light, using torches, or trapping a fairy within a special lantern (or freeing her to receive a curse-relieving item). The key areas for this part of the story are the Last Light Inn, a safe haven surrounded by a dome of light, Reithwin Town, a dilapidated former toll route settlement and Moonrise Towers, home of Ketheric Thorm, who the player is trying to find and defeat. Mapping these three main areas of the Shadow-Cursed Lands together as an oblique drawing shows how the architectural design of the world is predicated around the framing of light and darkness [Fig.04]. Using screenshots for reference, we trace the path of light shafts emanating from the sky and the patches of brightness they produce on the town below. The ruination of Reithwin, with buildings pulled apart by cursed tree roots (reminiscent of the effect seen at Angkor Wat in Cambodia) allows for this light to beam through holes in ceilings and walls. The developers describe this principle as 'dividing' space using light.[11] Almost like the Japanese concept of *ma* – a gap or 'negative space' between things[12] – these light rays can penetrate the town because of holes in the ruined structures, meaning these columns of light become a key part of the area's architectural landscape, despite having no physical form.

[Fig.03] PAGE 16

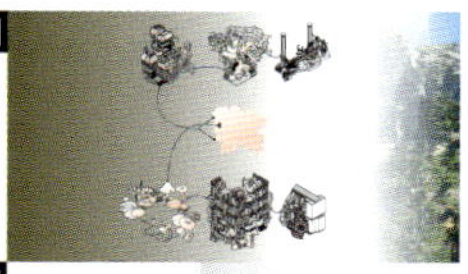

Isometric comparison between the architectural spaces encountered depending on whether players choose to journey through the Underdark or Rosymorn Monastery.

[Fig.04] PAGE 17

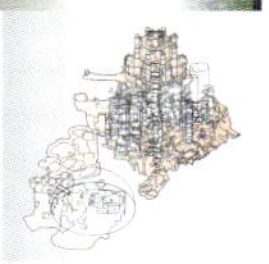

Drawing of Moonrise Tower, Reithwin Town and the Last Light Inn, showing how light and shadow become important architectural elements within the Shadow-Cursed Lands.

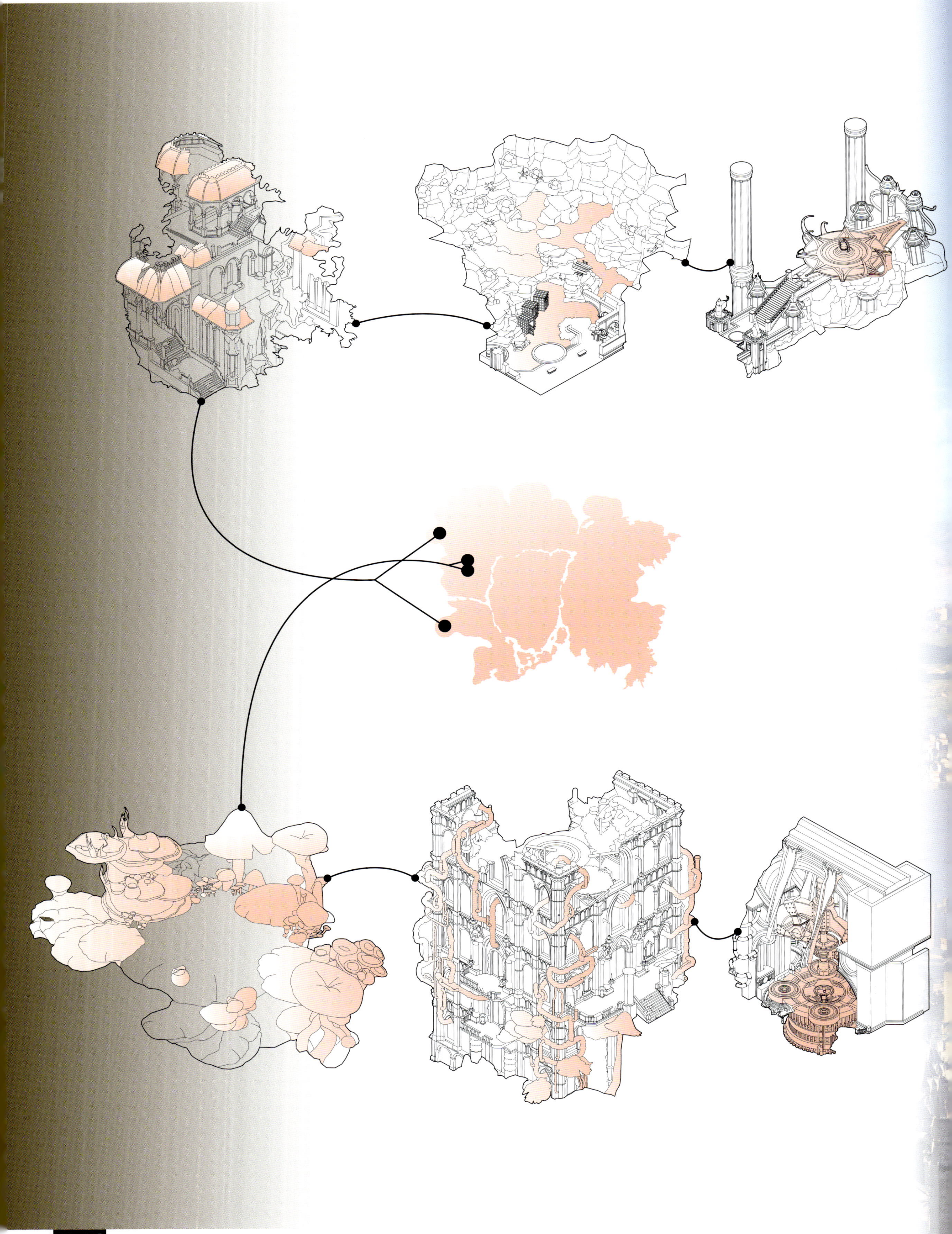

[Fig.03]

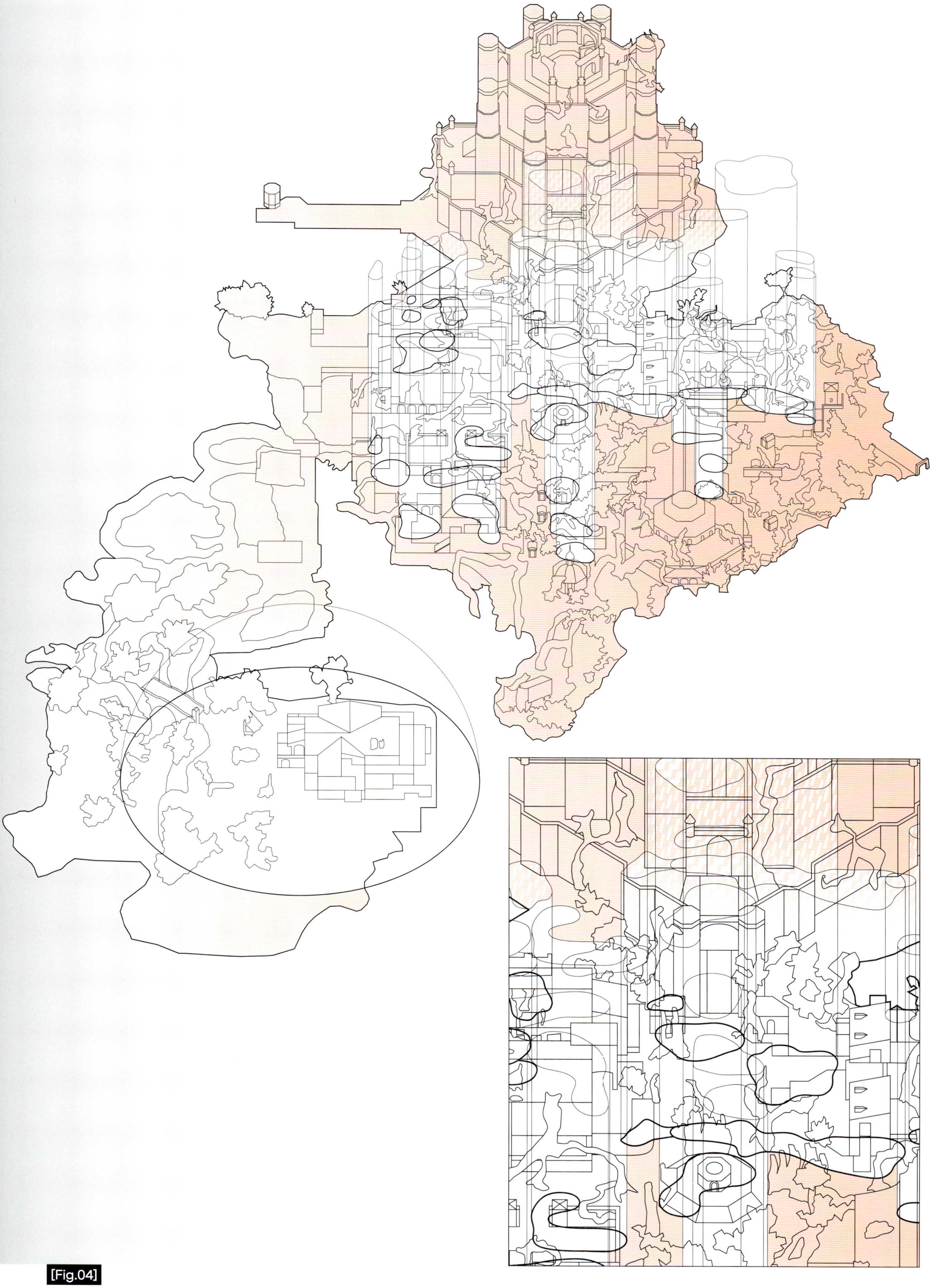

[Fig.04]

1.3 WELCOME TO THE GATE

Before arriving at Baldur's Gate, the player's party must navigate their way through Wyrm's Crossing, a large, occupied bridge that serves as a gateway to the city. Such structures have been built for hundreds of years and 'the inhabited bridge is the most representative of the hybridization between engineering and architecture.'[13] We also find this hybridization in the game. While we can walk the central pathway to try and gain entrance to Baldur's Gate, by means of persuasion or bargaining with local guards, Wyrm's Crossing also contains a warren of connected buildings on its edges for us to explore. By using the camera mod to create an oblique aerial view of the bridge, we start to align this with notional cross-sections of each part of the structure [Fig.05]. While the central boulevard of the crossing remains consistent, in each section we can see how the combination of buildings on the edges is constantly changing. As a result, the structures projecting out over the gorge beneath feel organically assembled, as if they have been built, and rebuilt, on top of one another. The combination of commercial and domestic architecture on Wyrm's Crossing particularly recalls Old London Bridge (1209–1831), then the longest inhabited bridge in Europe, where houses were built on top of a strip of trading posts at the ground floor level.[14] As our mapping shows, Wyrm's Crossing broadly follows a similar pattern, feeling historically and contextually appropriate as a result.

Arriving at the city of Baldur's Gate is a key part of the game's story, and one that represents a significant milestone for most players (only around 40% of Steam players have achieved this as of summer 2025). Yet it is a city that we have already seen plenty of times, as the background view whenever the game's title screen loads [Fig.06]. It is also a city that may be familiar to us from the real world, as Larian describes that players will 'see hints of Portugal throughout the city of Baldur's Gate: from its coastlines and romantic gardens to its villas and stone abbeys, all designed in a neo-Gothic style common to the region.'[15] Once we arrive at 'The Gate,' players may wonder whether the actual city is as sprawling as the one depicted at the start of the game. Using camera mods allows us to compare these two versions of the city to understand the discrepancy between portraying a metropolis that goes on forever and realizing it as a place the player can visit. As the game renders the start screen over an actual in-game scene containing geometry, we can obtain plan views of both versions of the city and overlay them for comparison [Fig.07]. By taking measurements in the modding Toolkit, we calculate that the city as seen from the main menu viewpoint is around one square kilometre (0.38 mi^2) in area, translating to 100 hectares contained within the city walls. While the in-game map only offers us the chance to explore the Lower City, using a camera mod reveals how the Upper City walls are depicted, and this playable version of Baldur's Gate is 0.46 square kilometres (46 hectares). Even in this smaller version of the map, players cannot walk everywhere, and the city as we experience it is much tighter at only 0.07 square kilometres, or 7.2 hectares.

[Fig.06] PAGES 20–1
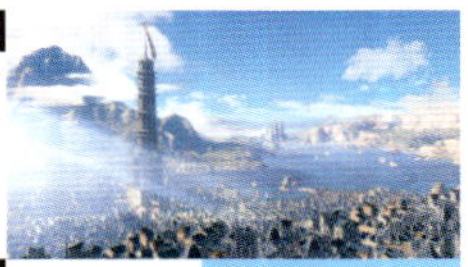
View across Baldur's Gate showing the level of complexity seen from the game's title screen, including the Upper City that players cannot explore in the main adventure.

[Fig.07] PAGE 22
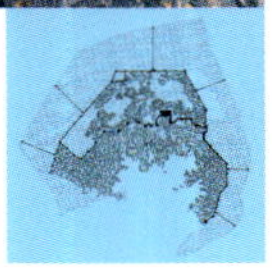
Map comparison between the city of Baldur's Gate as depicted in the game's title screen and the city as experienced once players arrive in Act 3 of the game.

OBLIQUE STUDY OF WYRM'S CROSSING WITH INDICATIVE CROSS SECTIONS SHOWING HOW THE INHABITED BRIDGE TYPOLOGY CREATES INTERESTING PATHWAYS FOR PLAYERS TO EXPLORE.

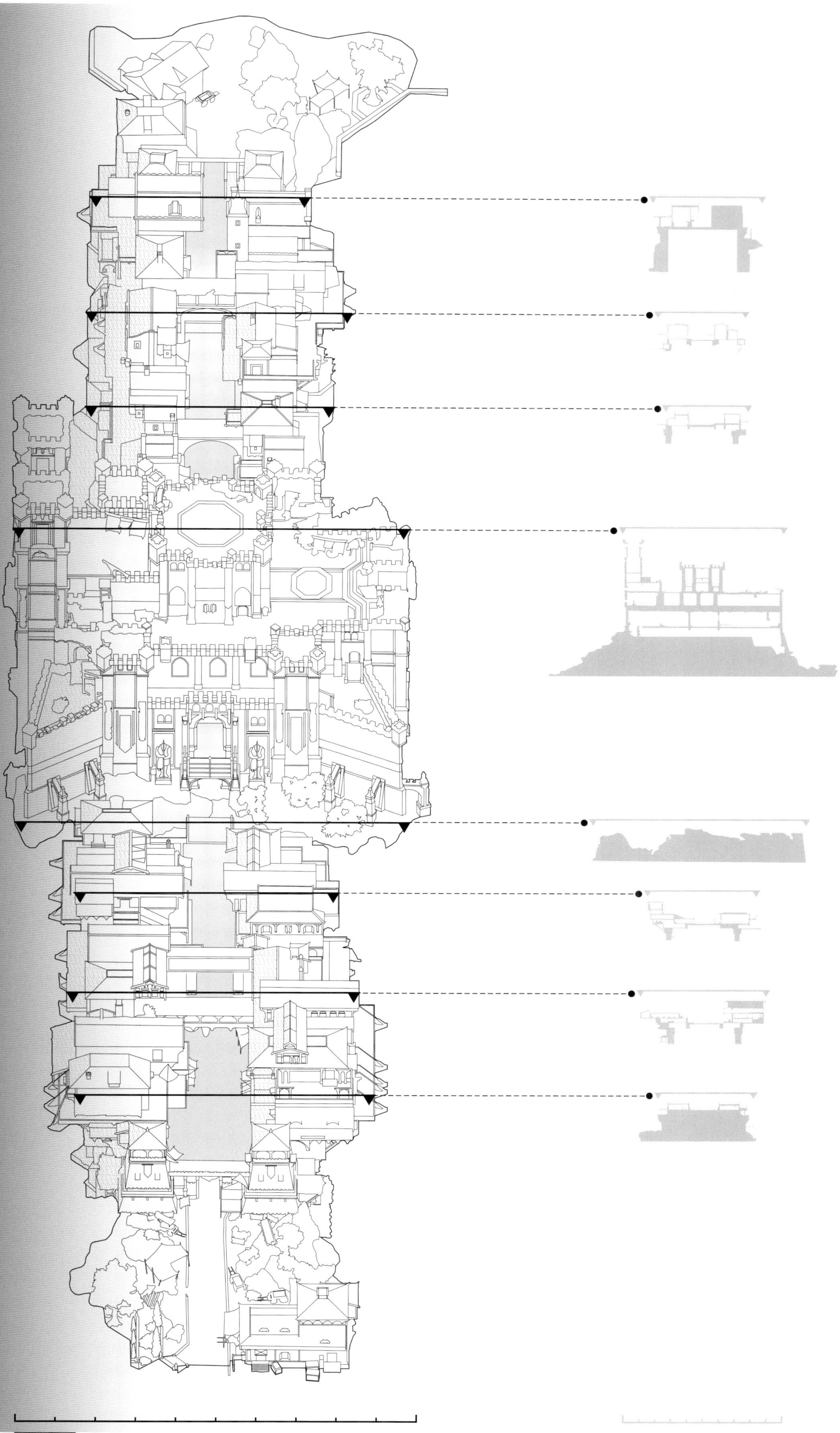

[Fig.05]

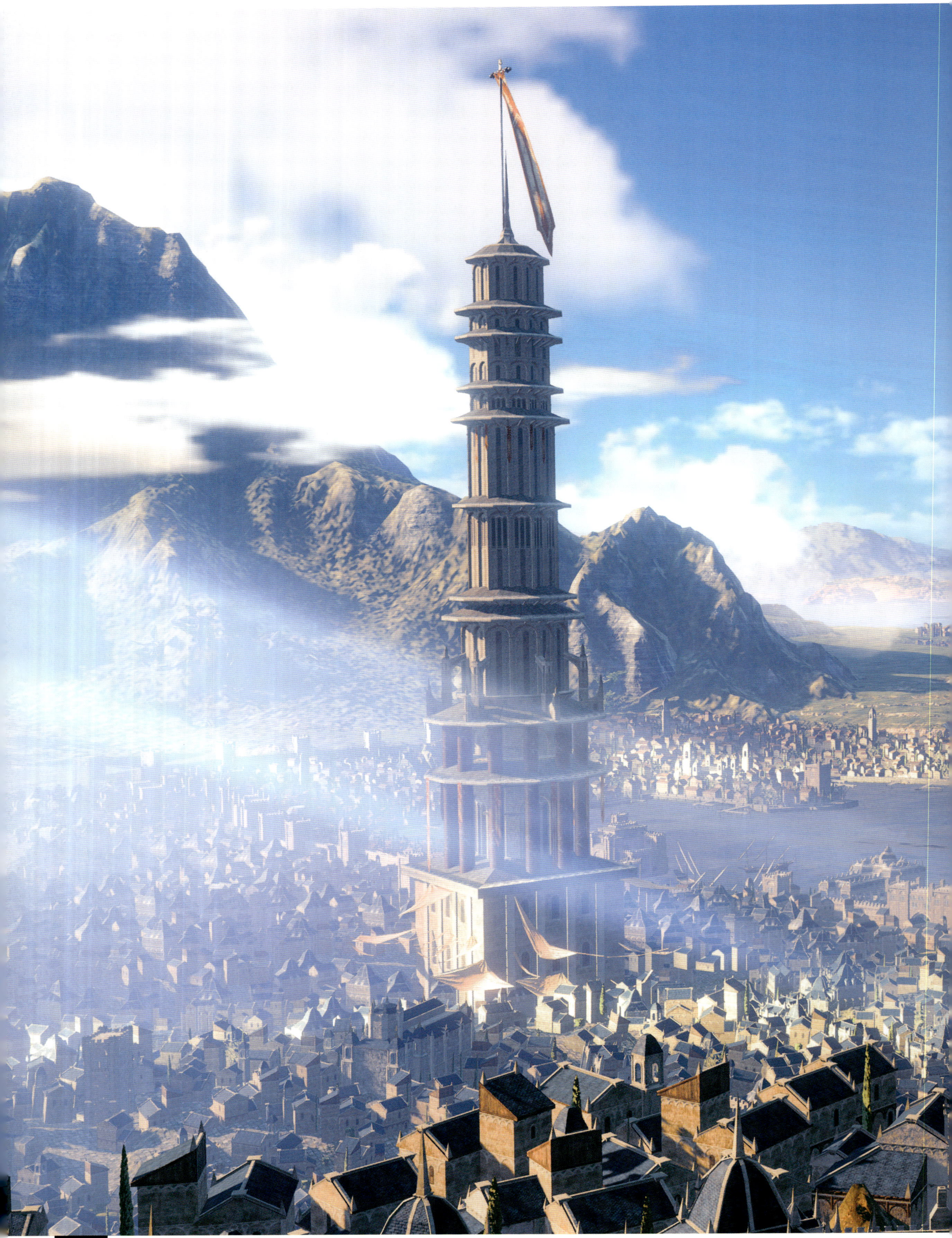

[Fig.06]

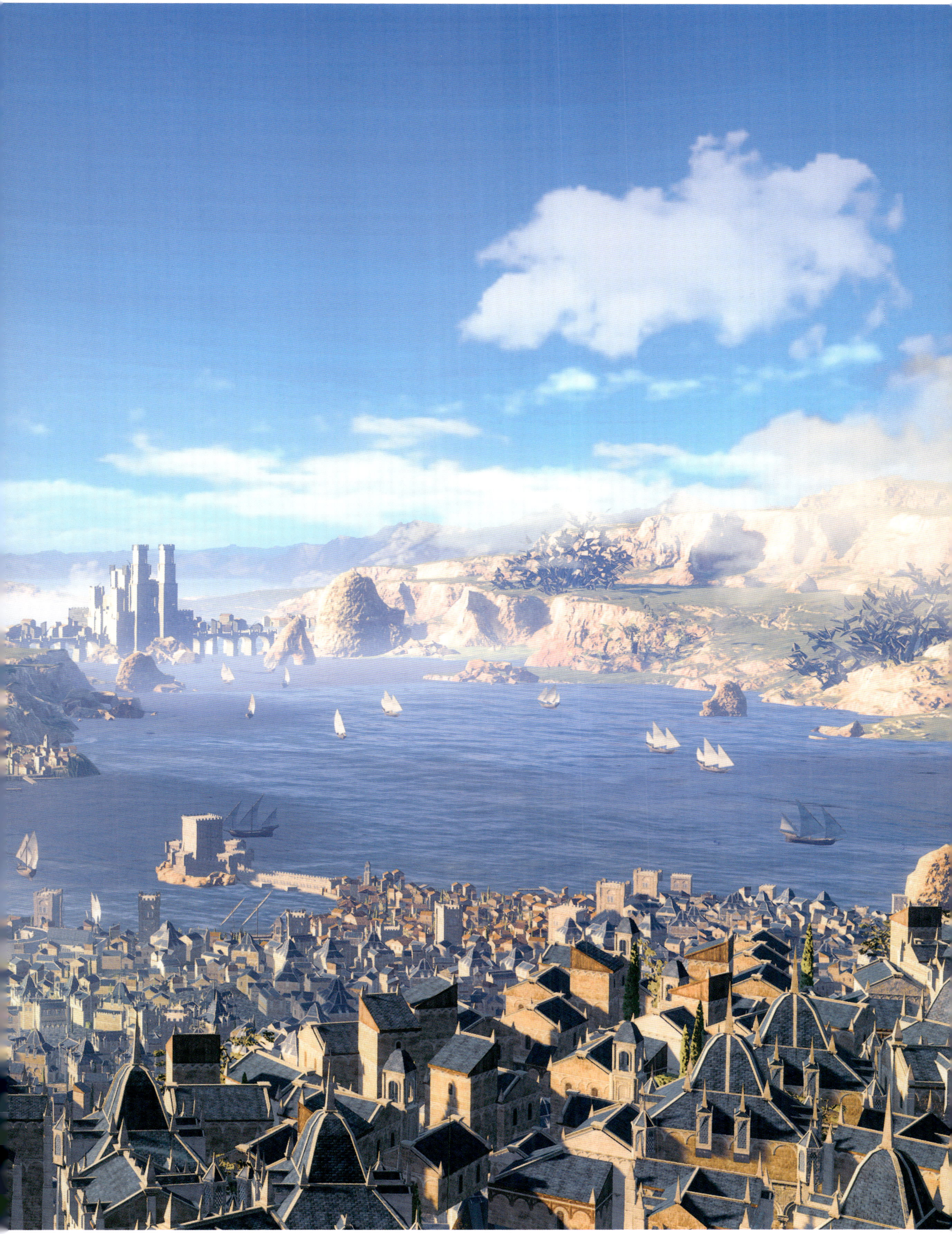

As such, the Baldur's Gate we experience is 7.2% of what we originally see depicted. It is a testament to the quality of the city's design, and particularly its use of different levels and unique contextual building forms, that Baldur's Gate feels sprawling yet organic, full of depth and lived-in, despite the comparatively small area we actually experience.

This sense of depth and complexity is also supported more literally. Baldur's Gate sits atop a vast network of basements, caves, sewers and other underground infrastructure that is even larger than the city above ground, leading players to question how it even stands up.[16] By using the in-game maps and analysing the connection points between underground spaces and the city above, we were able to create an isometric map that shows the huge amount of underground spaces carved into the rock below the city [Fig.08]. This reveals how Larian uses spatial gestures, such as small domestic interiors that unexpectedly unfold into huge and cavernous spaces through access hatches or ladders. The spaces beneath the city are so large that they even dwarf the city itself. Calculating the map areas both above and below ground demonstrates that the combined subterranean environments are nearly twice as large as the city above ground. Given the inspirations the developers found in the Portuguese region of Sintra, this underground landscape may have been developed with an eye on Quinta da Regaleira, a stately home surrounded by idiosyncratic gardens with a network of tunnels and secret passages including Knight's Templar iconography.[17]

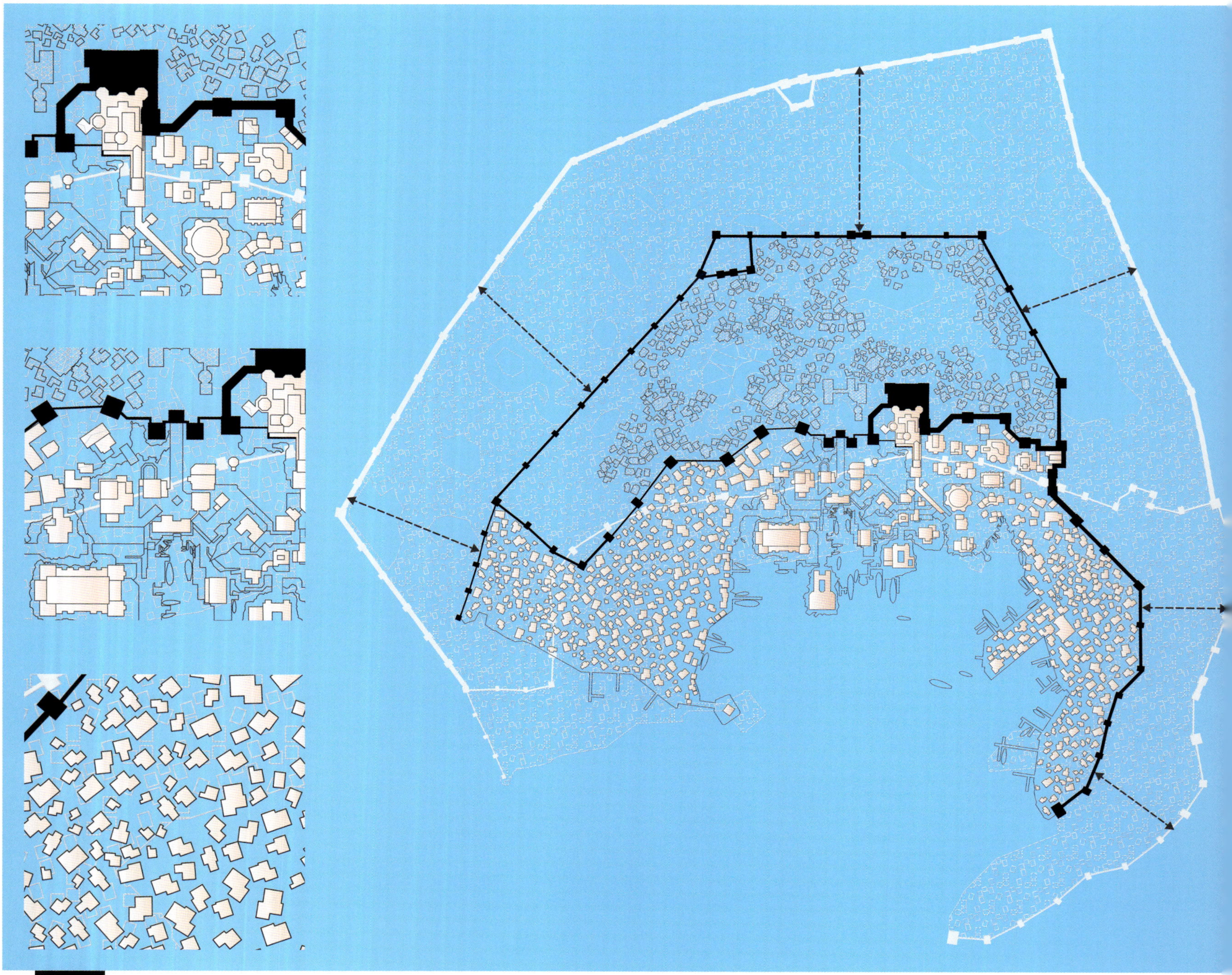

[Fig.07]

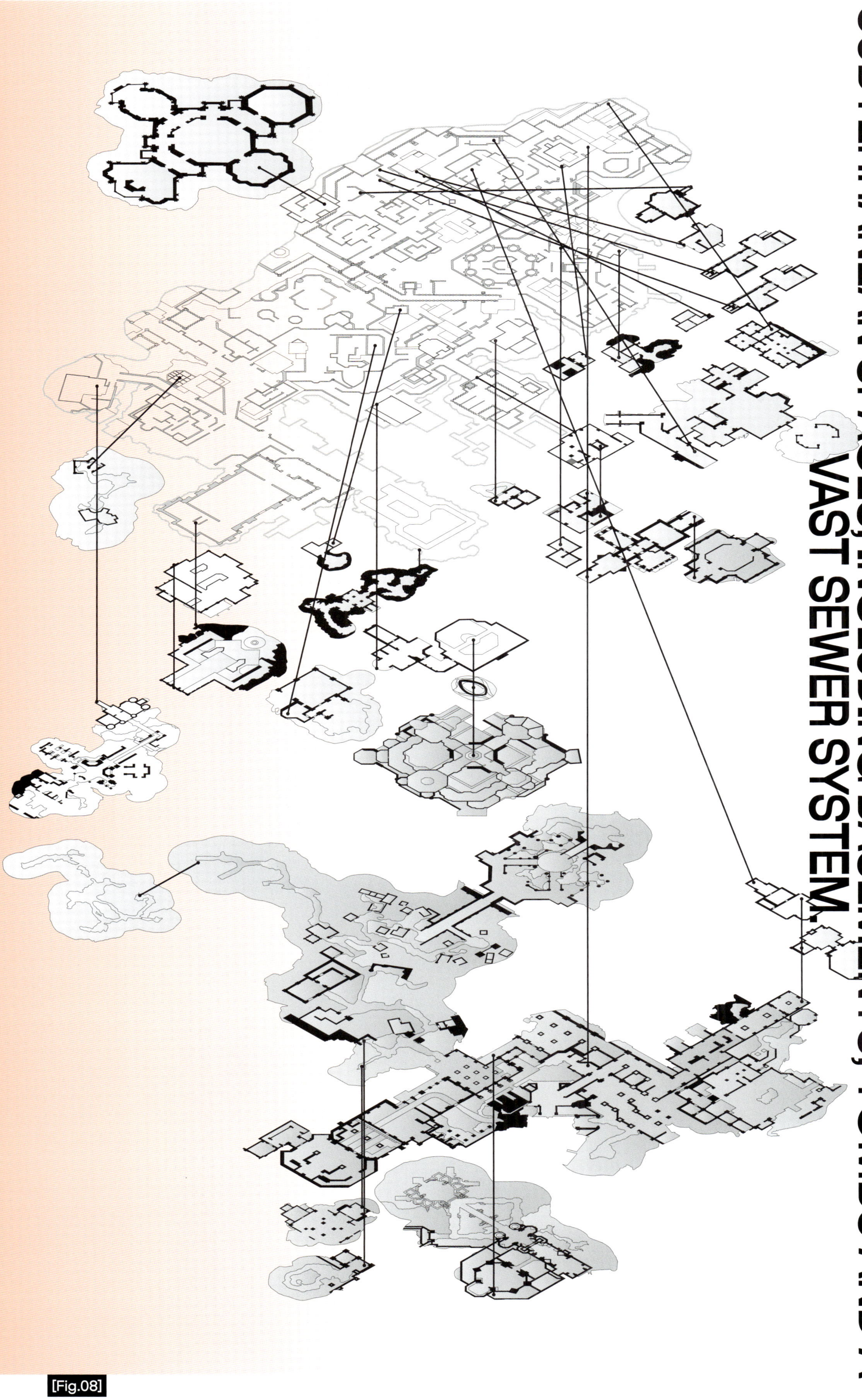

EXPLODED ISOMETRIC MAP OF BALDUR'S GATE, DEMONSTRATING THE LARGE NUMBER OF CONNECTIONS BETWEEN SUBTERRANEAN SPACES, INCLUDING BASEMENTS, TOMBS AND A VAST SEWER SYSTEM.

[Fig.08]

1.4
TIME SENSITIVE

While the city's architecture explicitly draws from these Portuguese inspirations, during their journey though Faerûn, players will see numerous architectural styles, all of which contribute to a general feeling of anachronism – a thing or space out of place with its time period. This creates interesting spatial juxtapositions. Visualizing some of the key architectural styles through elevational drawings shows that players will encounter spaces that appear to be inspired by very different points in real-world history [Fig.09]. Alongside architectural styles that date back to the 12th century, such as in Baldur's Gate or the smaller homesteads of the Wilderness, we find spaces that feel more inspired by 20th-century Art Deco designs, as in Cazador's Dungeon or The Gauntlet of Shar. The steampunk aesthetic of the Steel Watch Foundry and its semicircular roof recalls the Victorian-era architecture of The Crystal Palace and London's Great Exhibition of 1862, while Raphael's House of Hope in Avernus, seen from outside using camera mods, has a fully modelled exterior in a Gothic style. Given that Baldur's Gate generally defaults to a language that provides 'allusions to classical medieval stonework, Spanish cliffsides, and pastoral art,'[18] spaces from outside of this context gain an inherently mysterious quality in the same way that magic and machinery pervade the world and its society.

Time and timeliness are also an essential part of the game's mechanics. By using a turn-based combat system, architecture becomes a willing accomplice in achieving the player's aims, with designs typically offering numerous windows or holes for pushing enemies through, cunning traps to spring or places to take shelter and regroup. Linear distance becomes a key metric in Baldur's Gate, with higher-level characters offered numerous ways to subvert the building's floorplan through dashing, climbing, warping or even turning into a cloud of gas. Amongst all these spaces, the closest connection between turn-based mechanics and architectural space arguably takes place during the party's assault on the Iron Throne, a submerged facility that is put into a self-destruct cycle as soon as players arrive. As players only have a limited number of turns to free prisoners and escape, many players in the community have derived strategies to carry this out while looting everything available. By mapping the Iron Throne, along with one of these strategies,[19] we demonstrate how this architectural space becomes broken down into a series of carefully planned steps [Fig.10]. Luckily, turn-based combat gives us enough time to appreciate the careful design of the space before committing to our next move, lest we treat its bulkheads, prison doors and machinery as simply markers within a clockwork system.

[Fig.10] PAGE 26

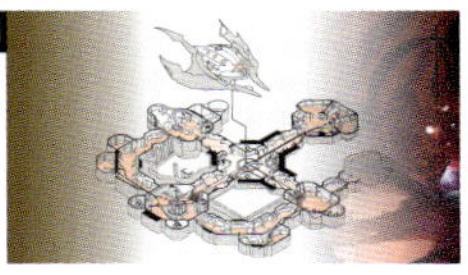

Turn-by-turn breakdown of how the underwater Iron Throne becomes a point of spatial tension for players due to its imminent and time-limited self-destruction.

ELEVATIONAL STUDIES OF THE DIFFERENT ARCHITECTURAL STYLES ENCOUNTERED WITHIN THE GAME, INCLUDING ART DECO-INSPIRED DUNGEONS, PORTUGUESE FARMHOUSES AND STEAMPUNK FACTORIES.

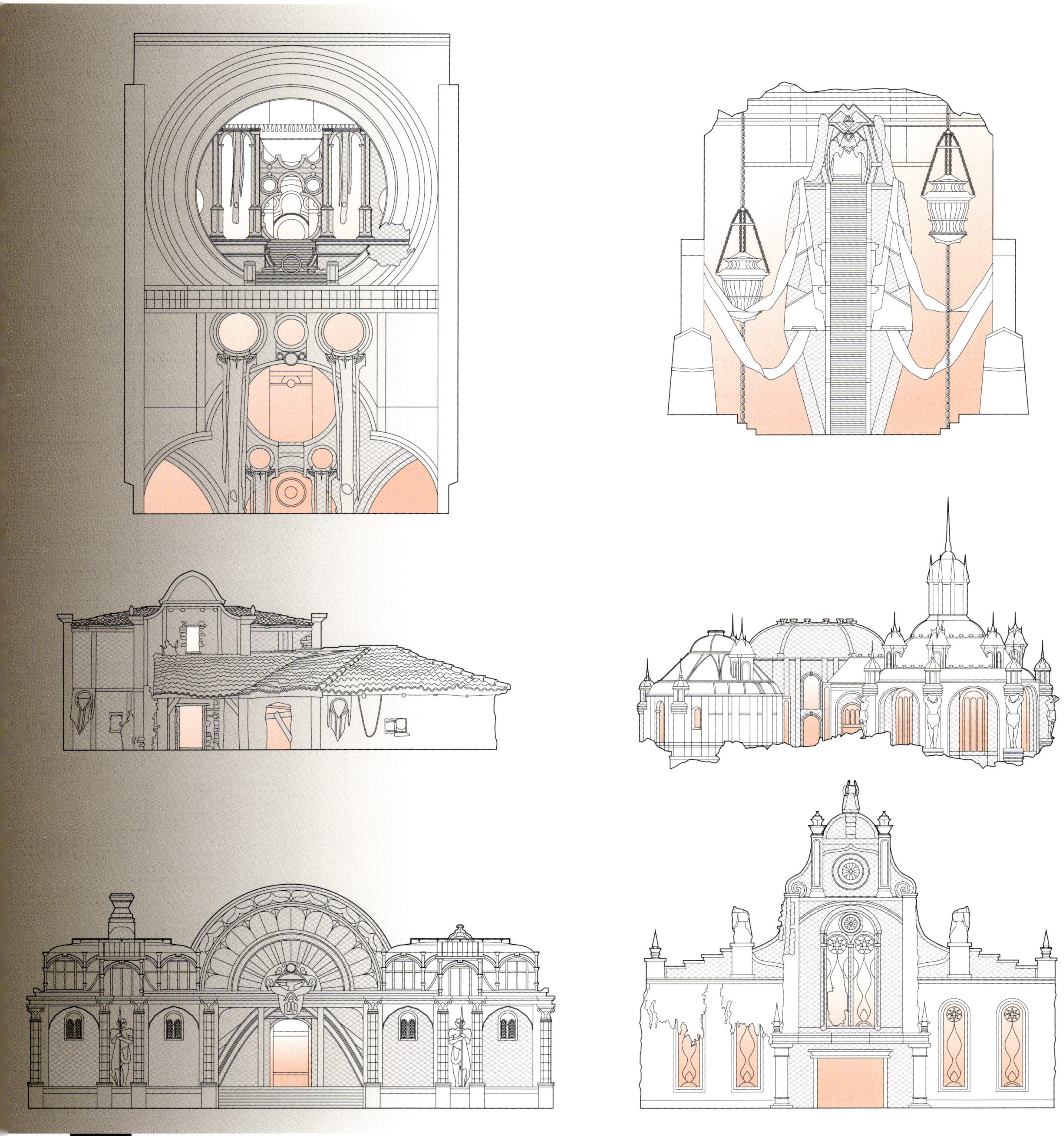

[Fig.09]

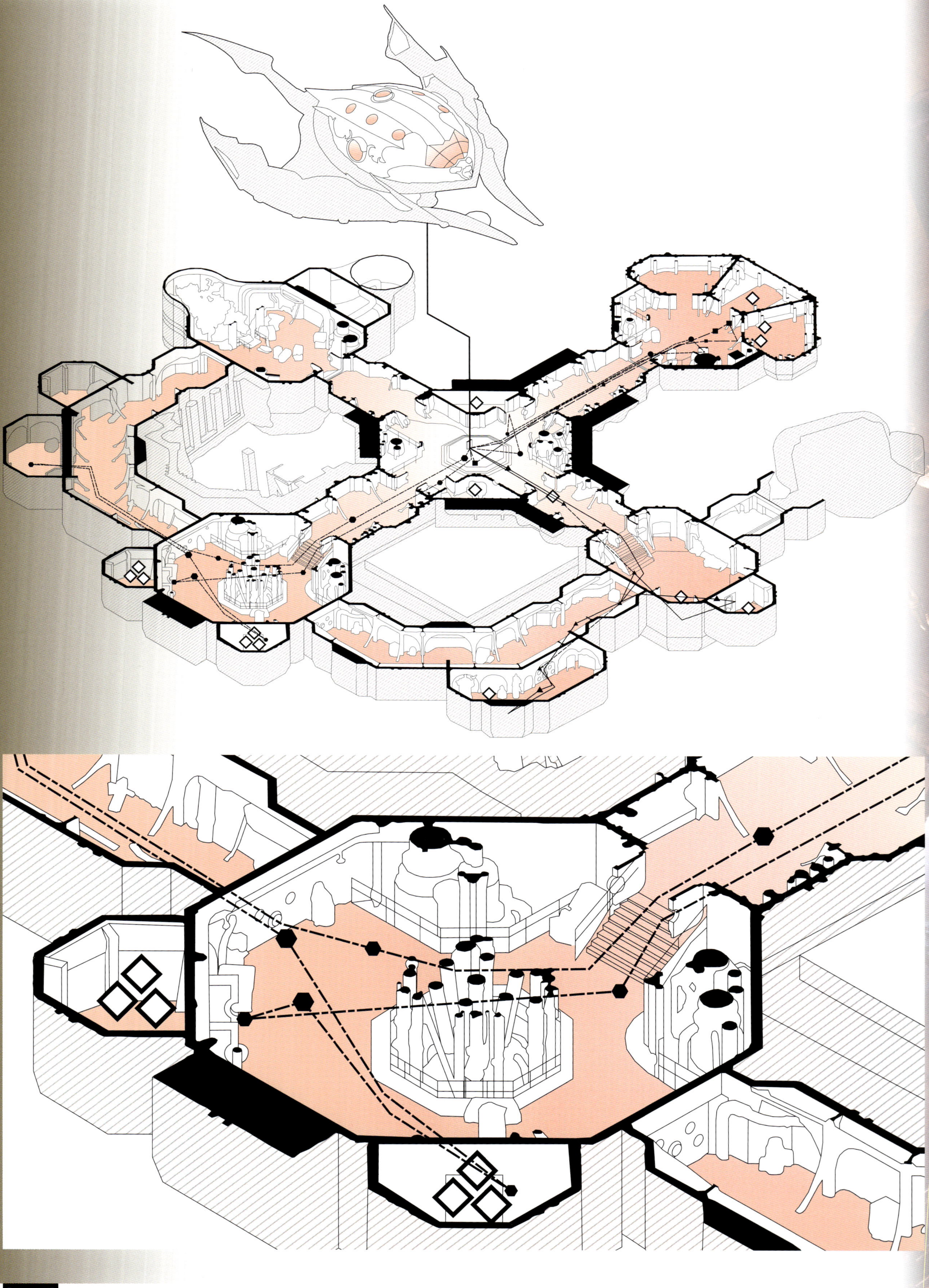

[Fig.10]

1.5 ARCHITECTURE AND FLESH

From the start of the game to its end, players experience the uneasy synthesis of architecture and flesh, a language that continues up until the climactic battle that finishes the story. Awaking in a Mind Flayer 'Nautiloid', a huge flying vehicle covered in tentacles and protrusions, the player must escape a space where fleshy growths contain abductees, bone formations serve as structural elements and doorways are literally called 'sphincters.' The Nautiloid itself is named after a shell-dwelling mollusc. While marine biology has inspired plenty of architectural designs such as Ojo del Sol by Eugene Tsui or the work of Bruce Goff, none of them lean into the body-horror of the Nautiloid's interior [Fig.11]. This also recalls the work of artists such as Atelier Van Lieshout, who have used various body parts and orifices as inspiration for architectural structures that, although not built from flesh, evoke the quality and morphology of the bodylike in their design.[20] Similarly, the fleshy 'corridors', protrusions and bumps evoke work such as Brazilian artist Ernesto Neto's strange woven bowel-like interiors in galleries, or architect Rachel Armstrong's research into spatial forms that grow and metabolize. This fleshscape at architectural scale sets up the Mind Flayers as cruel and strange antagonists, making the uneasy alliances the player forms later in the game a constant source of tension.

This relationship reaches its peak at the very end of the game, where the player's Tav and their party need to fight their way across the top of the Netherbrain, a giant mind-controlling creature that is the shape of a brain and the size of a church. As the Netherbrain flies over Baldur's Gate, the game treats its fleshy bobbles and crevices the same way it would any other architectural space, as a surface for turn-based combat. Viewed isometrically, the brain scene represents the combination of architectural themes that run throughout the game: flesh-like structures that must be navigated turn-by-turn, with Baldur's Gate sprawling beneath us, showing the human cost of failure [Fig.12]. Following this battle, the game offers us choices as to how we want the world to be resolved, and whether we will be kind or malevolent with the power we have been afforded.

Combining the rich lore of D&D with site-specific architectural studies, Larian has built a world that is convincing and consistent, even when the narrative creates strange ruptures between the physical and magical realms. In the devil Raphael's House of Hope we meet the Infernal Mason, a skeletal figure who has signed away his soul. The Mason tells us 'I was an architect in life, a builder of tombs and temples, but most of towers. My proudest work reached for the stars and sought to dry Selune's tears.'[21] In the game, we encounter many tombs, temples and towers, but our path ultimately brings us to stand atop the Netherbrain, hovering over the metropolis below. As with so many societies across history, the gravitational pull of the city is irresistible, literally so when you have a tadpole in your brain. Despite the developers offering us but one possible version of many Faerûns to play with, all roads lead to Baldur's Gate.

[Fig.11] PAGE 28

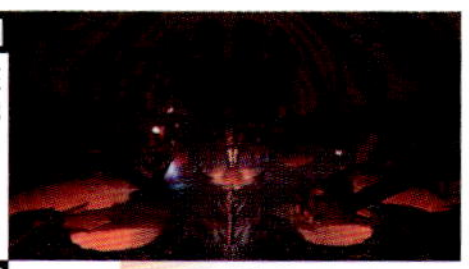

View from inside a Nautiloid, illustrating how the space represents a meeting point of architecture and flesh, structured like a twisted body at the scale of a building.

[Fig.12] PAGE 29

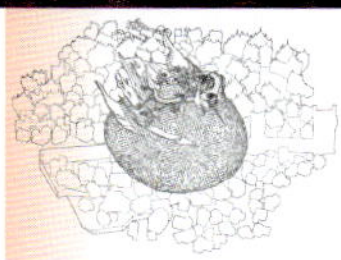

Isometric view of the game's final battle atop the giant Netherbrain, where the relationship between flesh and building is pushed to its furthest point.

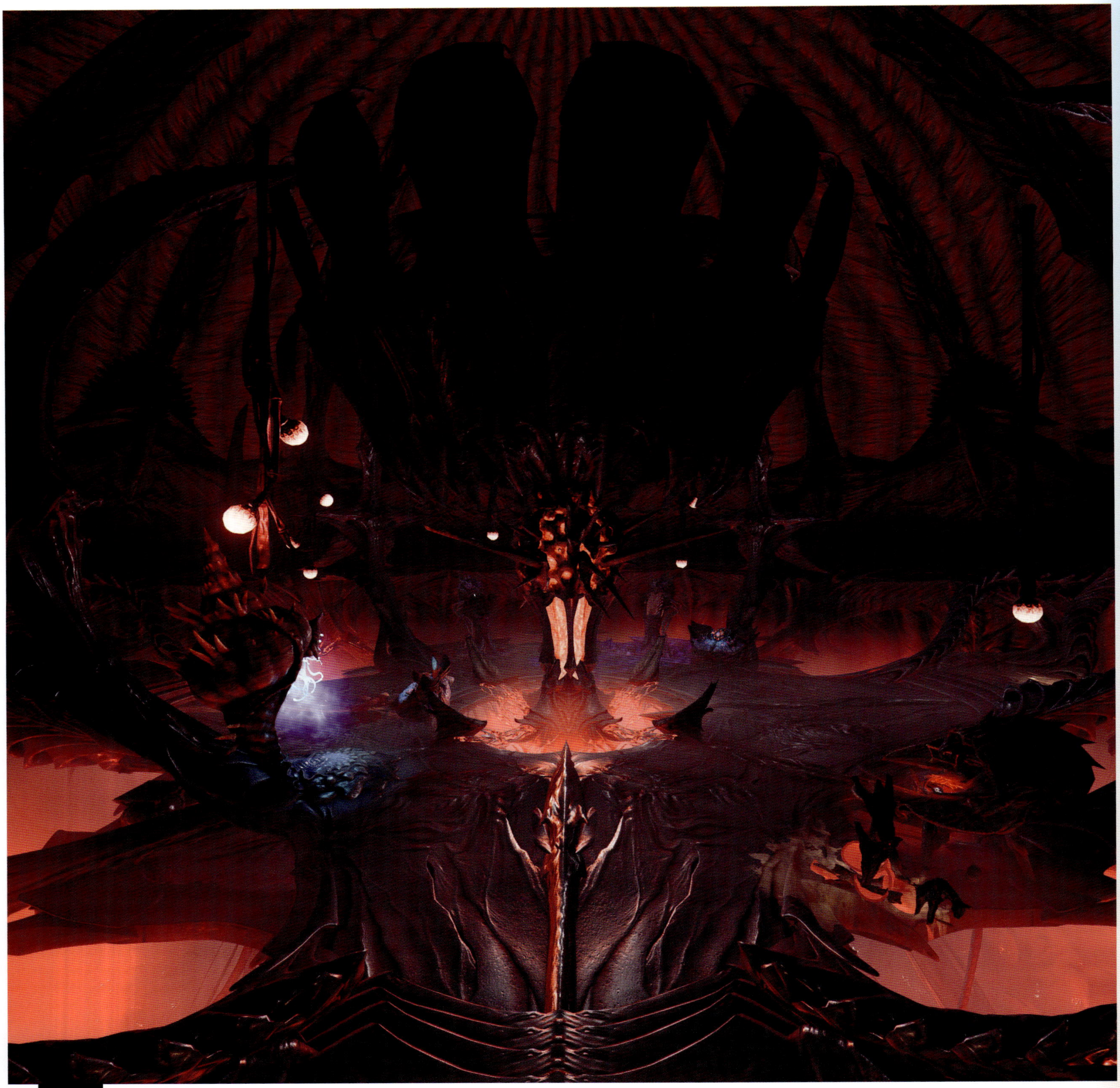

[Fig.11]

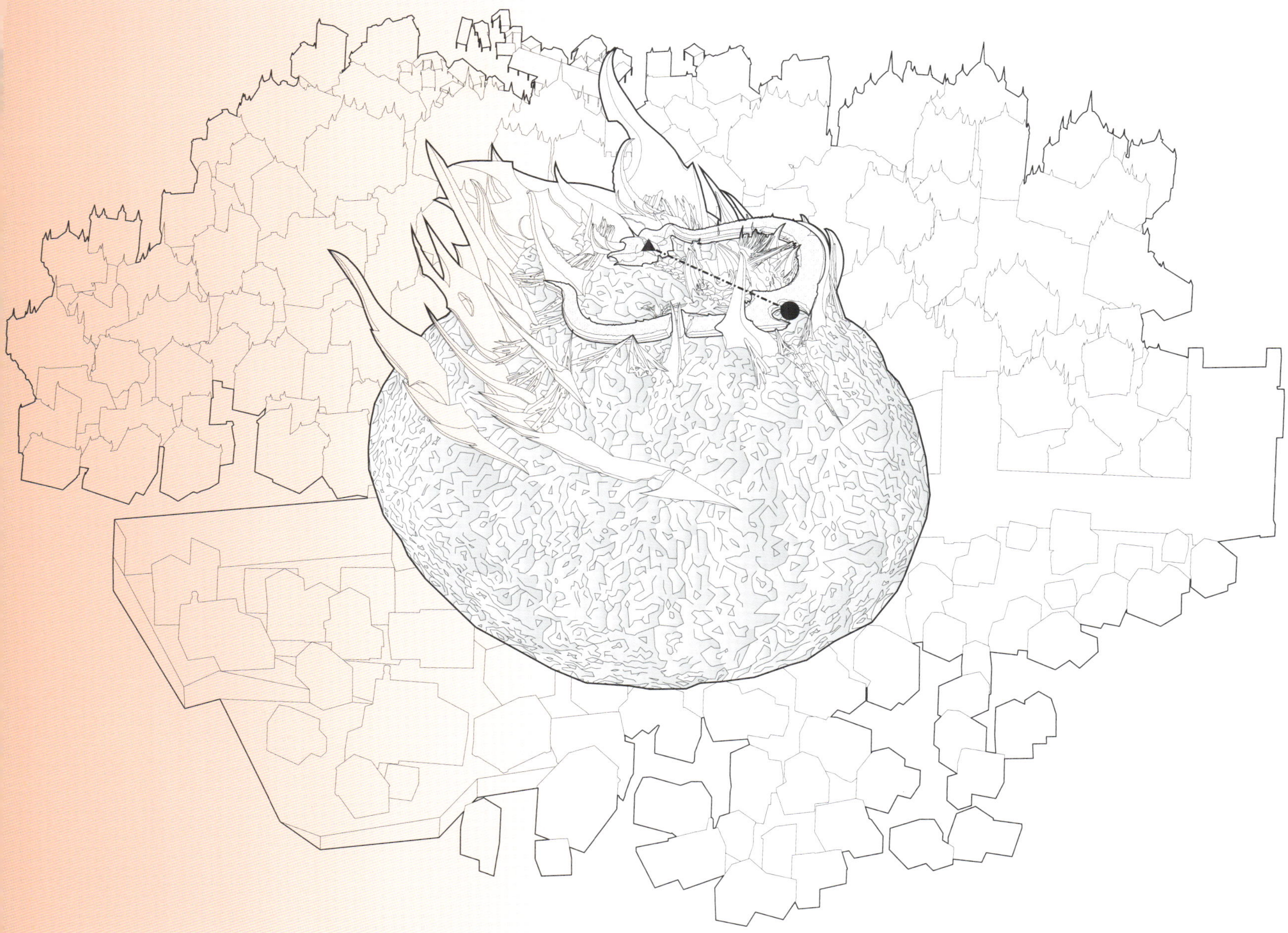

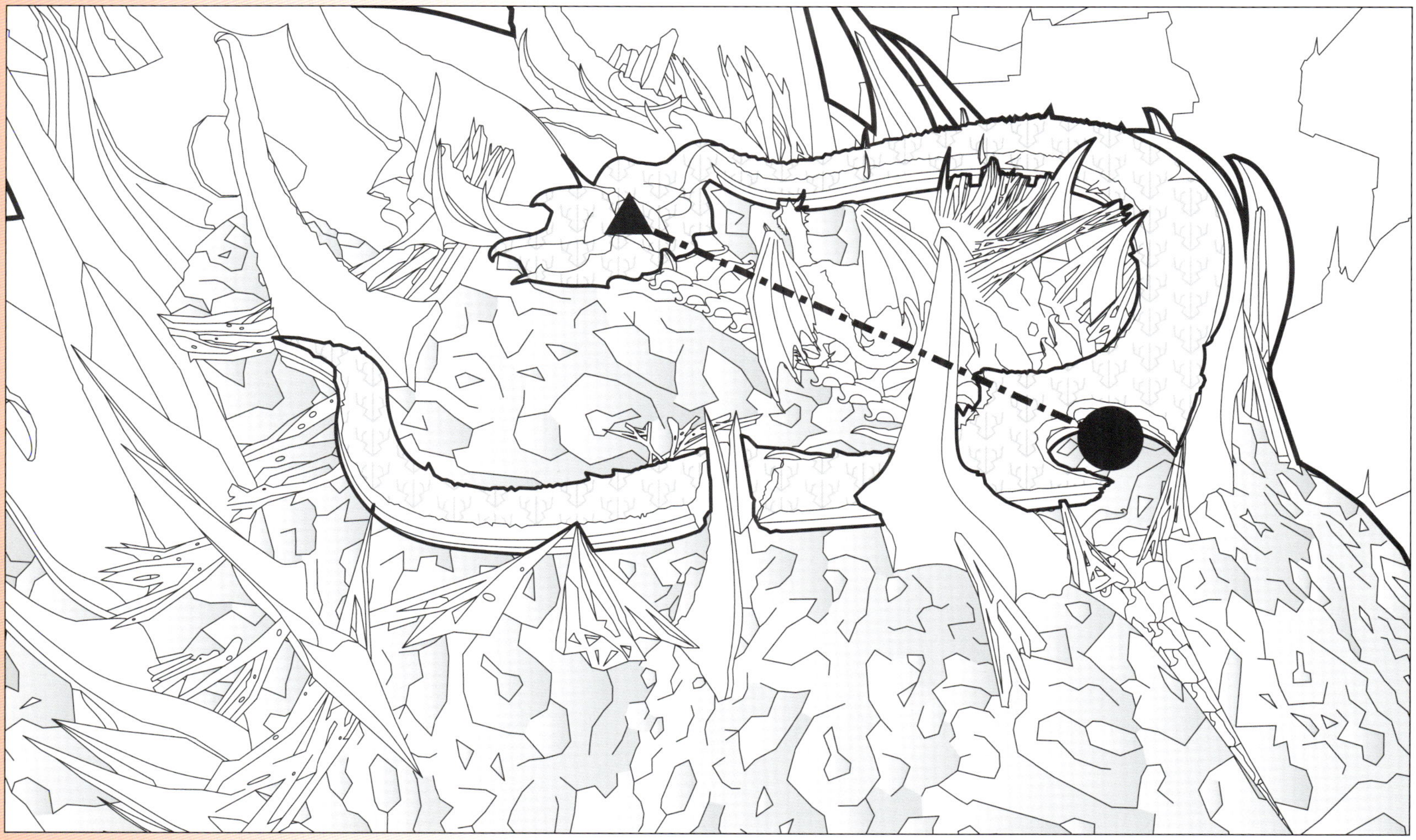

[Fig.12]

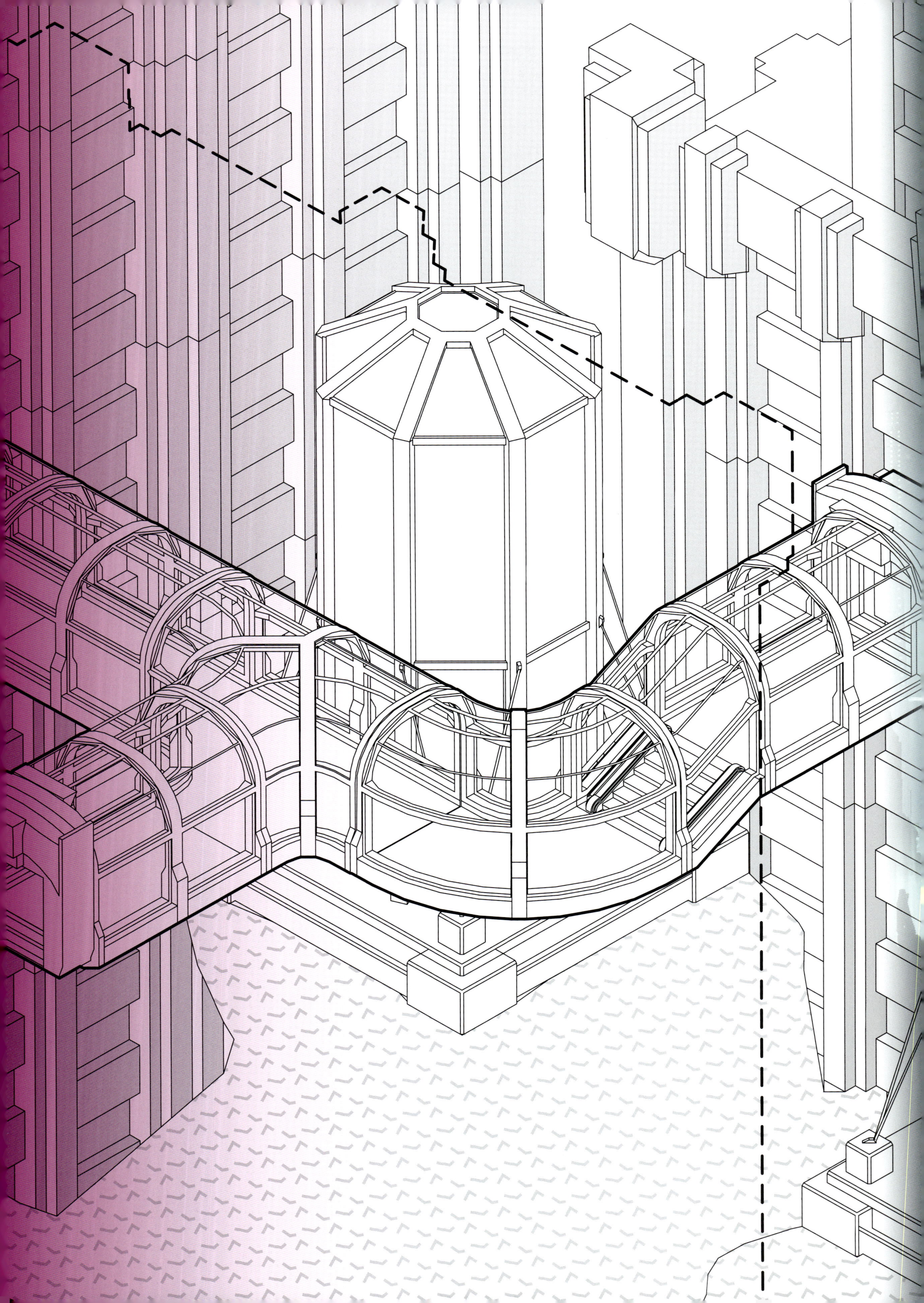

CHAPTER 02

BIOSHOCK

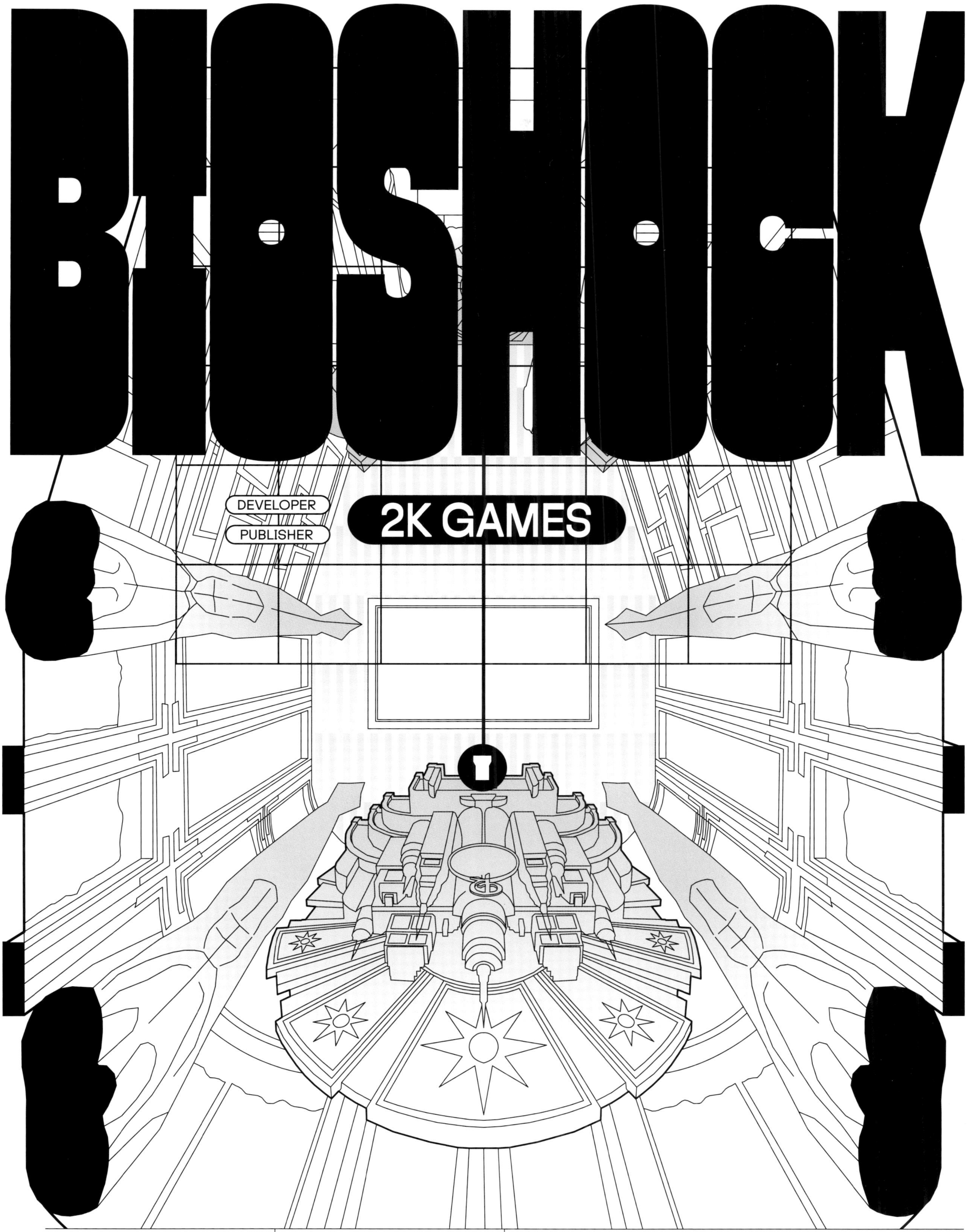

DEVELOPER
PUBLISHER
2K GAMES

Platforms	Windows, Xbox 360, PlayStation 3, Mac, iOS
Year	2007

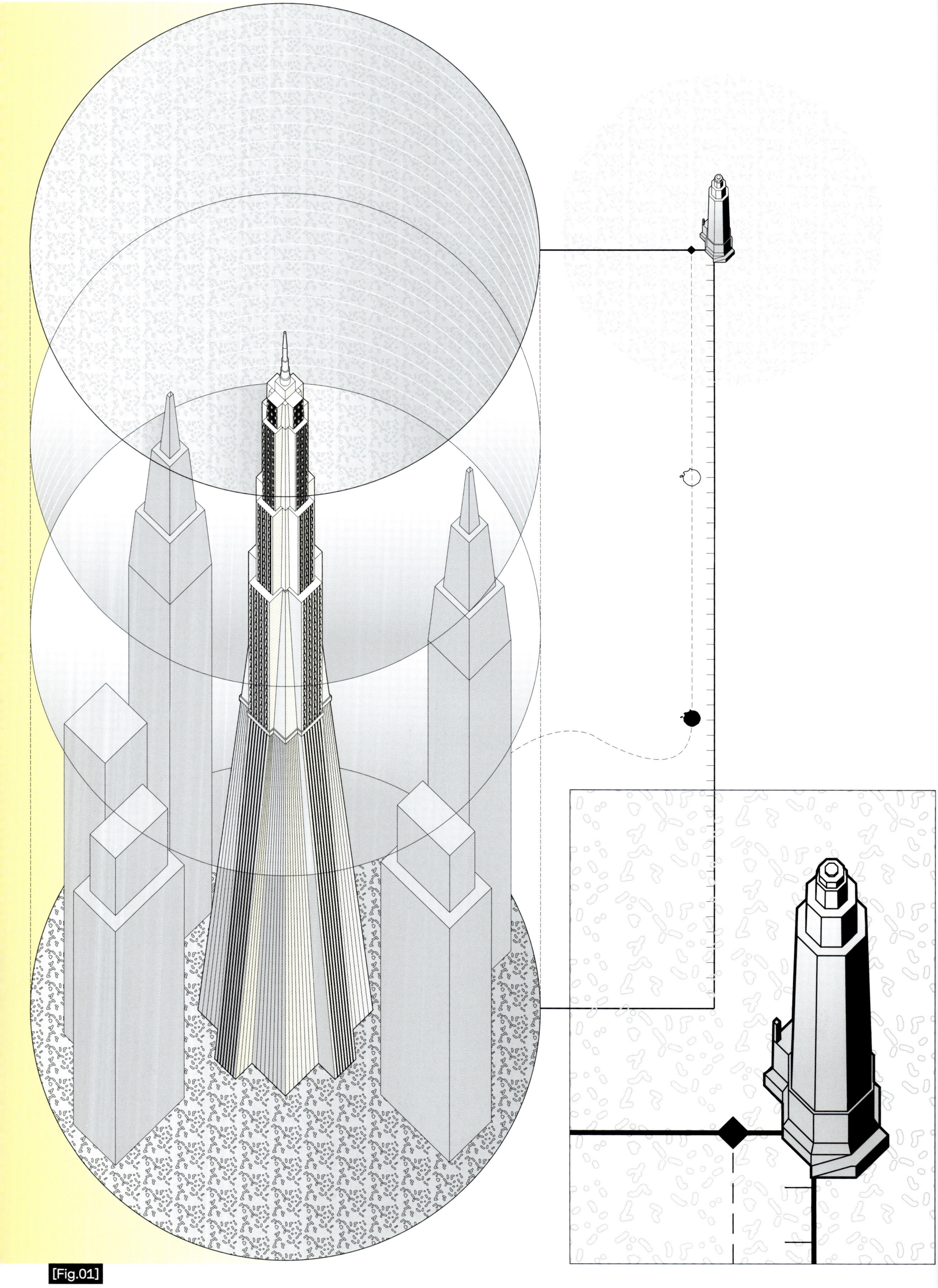

[Fig.01]

2.1

DEPTH CHARGE

When we think of the most iconic cities in videogames, Rapture is likely to be one of the first names that comes to mind. The underwater metropolis of *BioShock* has several key features that make it so compelling as a location. Rapture appears as if a real-world city with distinctive architecture has been transported to the sea floor, placing it in an entirely new context. Recalling the 1957 book *Atlas Shrugged*,[1] this Ayn Rand-inspired setting was established by a great captain of industry, Andrew Ryan, overseeing the construction of a utopian society beneath the waves, only for the project to fall into ruin in the most spectacular way. Rapture is a city where some of the most striking views come while riding public transport, and where the agency of the player themselves is questioned as they journey through the spaces of high and low society. One of Rapture's strengths is that by resonating so strongly with the architecture of our real world, it makes us question how this place came to be. Where is it? Who lives in such a place?

We clearly know that Rapture is located beneath the sea, but how deep? There are several ways to estimate the depth of Rapture, and the likely forces placed upon the city as a result. During a sequence of the game that recalls why the plane carrying Jack crashes into the sea and introduces him to Rapture, we see a pair of mysterious numbers scribbled onto a note, which turn out to be the longitude and latitude positions of an area on the Mid-Atlantic Ridge near Iceland[2]. Examining GEOTiff files, containing depth data obtained from the GEBCO Gridded Bathymetry Data archive[3], shows that the depth of this area varies between 1,400–2,430 metres (4,600–8,000 ft). This order of depth, in the 'midnight zone' of the ocean, is one that many community studies and YouTube channels such as ShoddyCast have used to examine the design of Rapture.[4] Yet the sea around Rapture is not pitch black, even accounting for the artificial light of the city.

We could use the game's introduction as a more direct indicator of depth. In the first level of *BioShock*, we encounter a strange lighthouse in the middle of the ocean as Jack swims away from the wreckage of the plane. Inside we take a bathysphere – Rapture's form of underwater transport – down into the depths, before the city is revealed to us in one of the game's great set pieces. By tracking this descent over time, we map out an understanding of the ocean depth implied by the game and compare this to the size of Rapture's buildings to estimate the actual depth of the city [Fig.01]. As Jack descends in the bathysphere, Art Deco fathom markers show that we dive 10 fathoms in the first 10 seconds, and to 18 fathoms by 15 seconds. Players then witness a short introductory film explaining the origins of Rapture and, one minute after we enter the ocean, the projection screen pulls back to reveal the city in front of us. Although the imposition of the projection screen means anything could have happened outside the bathysphere (unless we escape it with a console command), the blue haze of the city suggests that we are not in the midnight zone of the ocean, but perhaps the 'twilight zone' depth, somewhere between 200–1,000 metres (650–3,300 ft) down. The initial acceleration of the bathysphere reinforces this. As one fathom is 1.83m, the bathysphere is initially travelling at 1.83m/s before accelerating to around 2.92m/s. If we took this acceleration to be linear, the bathysphere is travelling $0.22 m/s^2$ faster as it goes,[5] meaning that over the 60 seconds we descend, it has dropped around 393 metres (1,300 ft). When we emerge into Rapture, it is at a mid-city level, with buildings still rising high around us. By using console commands, we capture views in order to count the number of storeys in building façades by their glowing windows. From this we estimate that the mid-city point appears to be some 170 metres (560 ft) up from the base of the buildings, putting the foundations of Rapture at around 560–570 metres (1,830–1,870 ft) deep. While this method doesn't account for subjectivities of level design, it does suggest that Rapture might be located on a ridge at a shallower depth than the surrounding ocean, especially considering the city's reliance on volcanic geothermal energy.

[Fig.01] AXONOMETRIC DRAWING SHOWING THE POTENTIAL DEPTH OF RAPTURE AS CALCULATED FROM THE INITIAL BATHYSPHERE DESCENT INTO THE CITY.

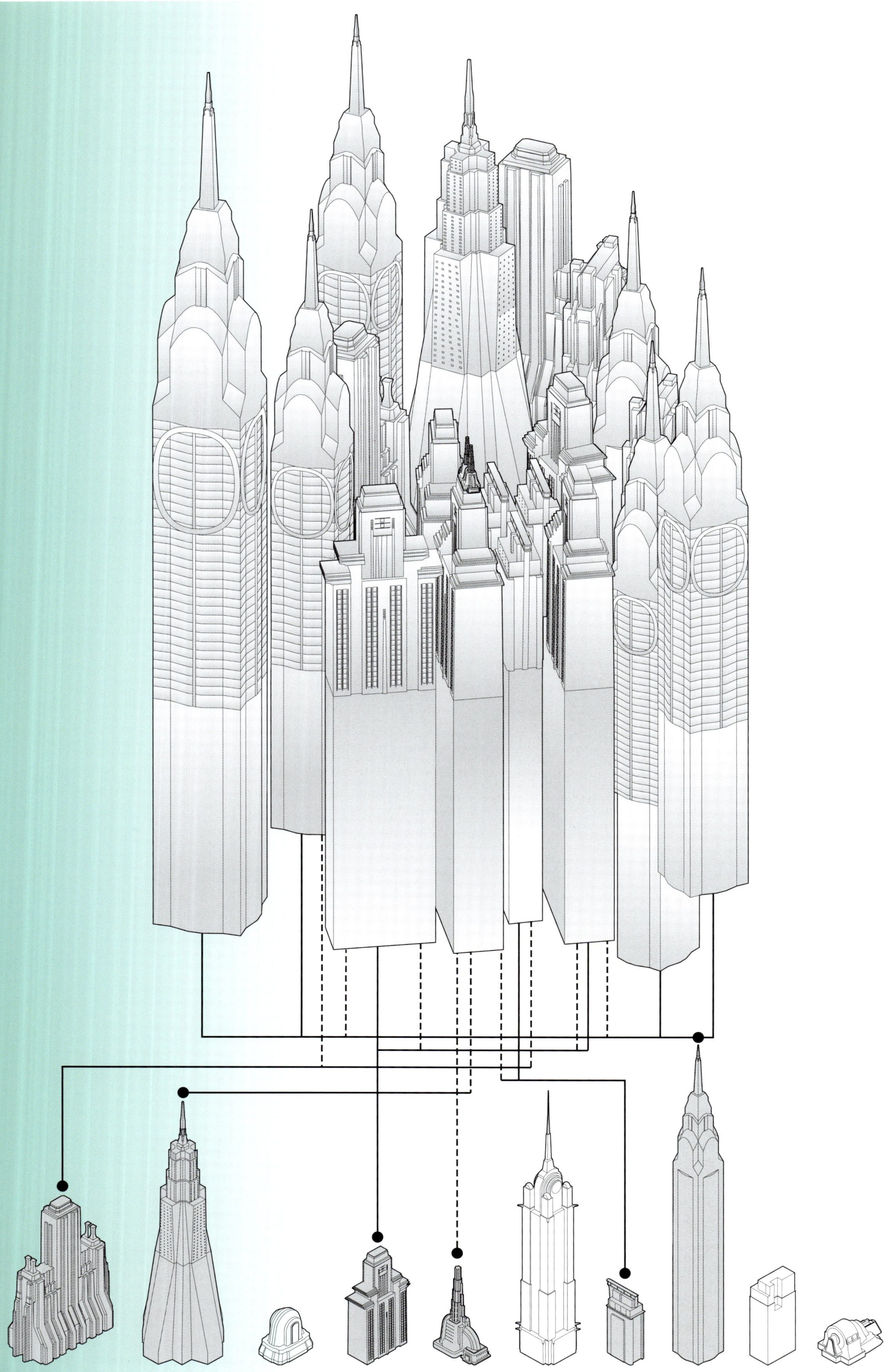

[Fig.03]

2.2

ORNAMENT AND CRIME

This introduction to the city gives us by far the best overview of its architectural form and scale, with its Art Deco 'seascrapers' clearly evoking the language of real-world Manhattan [Fig.02]. Emerging from the murk of the sea, Rapture is reminiscent of the architectural fantasies of draftsman Hugh Ferriss, whose chiaroscuro charcoal renderings of New York tower blocks were responsible for shaping the city. Ferriss dedicated much of his working life to imagining new and speculative visions of urban forms, such as his famous *The Metropolis of Tomorrow* project.[6] Many of Ferriss' drawings show an imaginary city immersed in a charcoal murk, a 'Ferrissian Void,'[7] that could easily be read as a piece of *BioShock* concept art. Similarly, there are clear references to the projects of other architects working in New York, such as Raymond Hood and William Van Alen, designers of the Rockefeller Center and Chrysler Building respectively. Hood's building is specifically referenced in an interview with game director Ken Levine.[8] Art Deco designs underpin the power of both imagined and real American cities, making it an ideal style for Ryan's submerged utopia. However, the form of Manhattan's skyline is defined by a 1916 zoning law concerning a building's right to light, visualized by Ferriss. Sitting in the diffuse twilight zone of the ocean, this would not be a concern for Rapture.

Using the community tool *UE Viewer*,[9] we explored the game's files to find and view all the different building models that are used to represent the city's external form. As such, we can chart how the different outdoor areas of Rapture that the player sees are made through repeated building types [Fig.03]. The opening sequence, for example, uses several building models and a repurposed façade model to portray Rapture through the repetition, scaling and combining of geometry. While this repetitive depiction of Art Deco skyscrapers might evoke the style's proliferation around the world, many of the real-world buildings that inspired Rapture were often commissioned and designed with the precise aim of standing out. The original Chrysler Building possessed 'enormous metallic gargoyles resembling the 1929 Chrysler car hood ornaments' alongside 'large replicas of the company's hubcaps and winged radiator caps at its lower levels.'[10] The building's famous stainless-steel spire was unfolded at the last minute in a grand constructional gesture that made it the world's tallest building. Likewise, Hood's American Radiator Building, also in New York, traded heavily on the symbolism of its industrial patron, using 'playful, classically styled corbel figures at the third-storey cornice, including a pipe fitter with a wrench, refer[ring] to great moments in the history of steam heat.'[11]

[Fig.02] PAGES 36–7

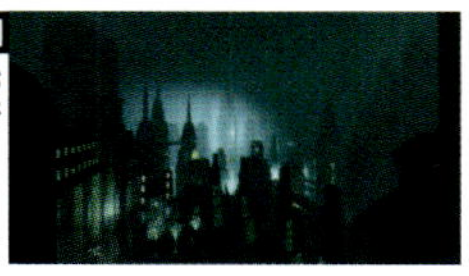

A view across Rapture as seen from the first bathysphere descent, showing the repeated use of Manhattan-inspired architectural forms.

[Fig.03]

ISOMETRIC STUDY OF THE BUILDING TYPOLOGIES USED TO DEPICT RAPTURE'S EXTERIOR FORM AND HOW THEY ARE ASSEMBLED INTO DISTRICTS OF THE CITY.

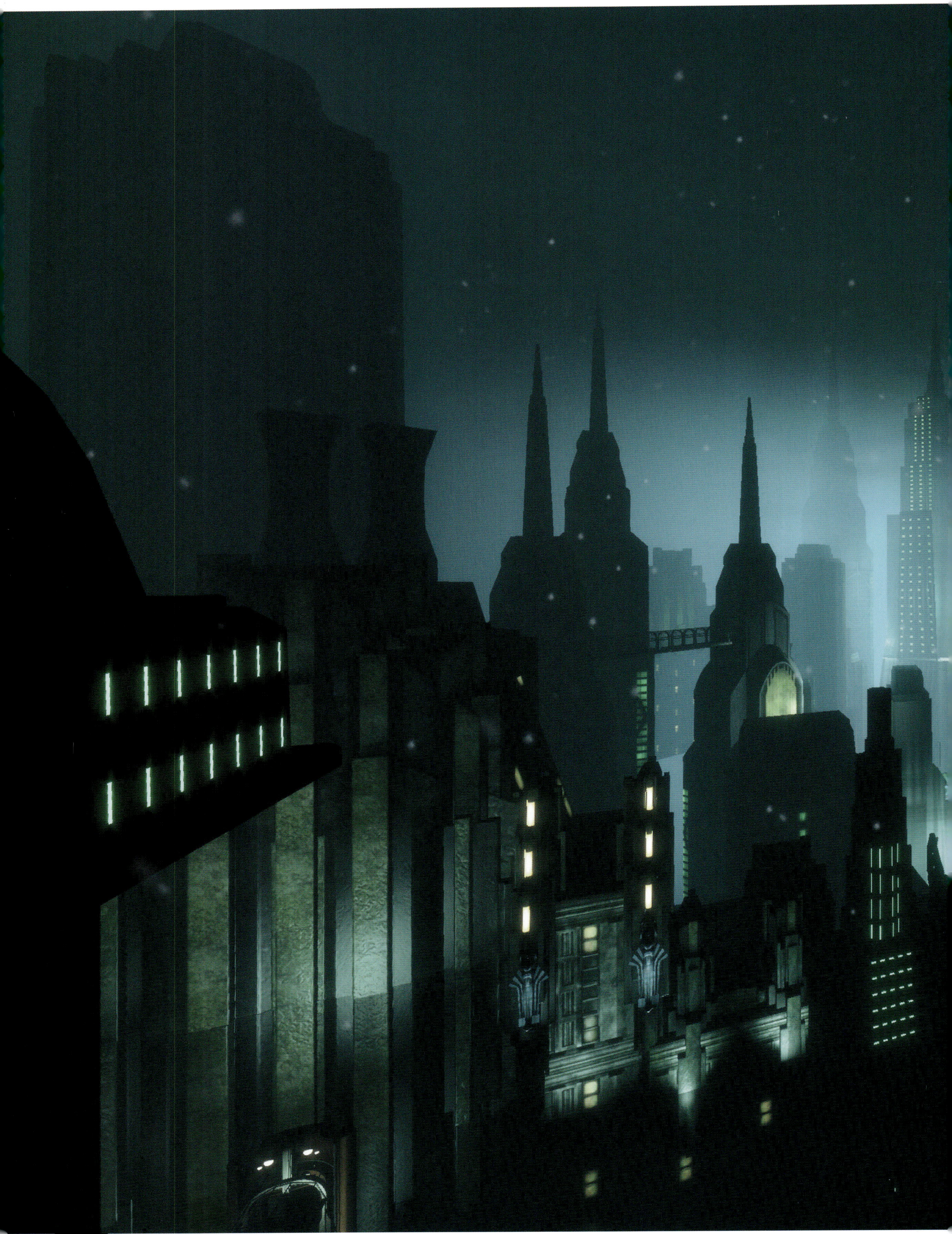

[Fig.02]

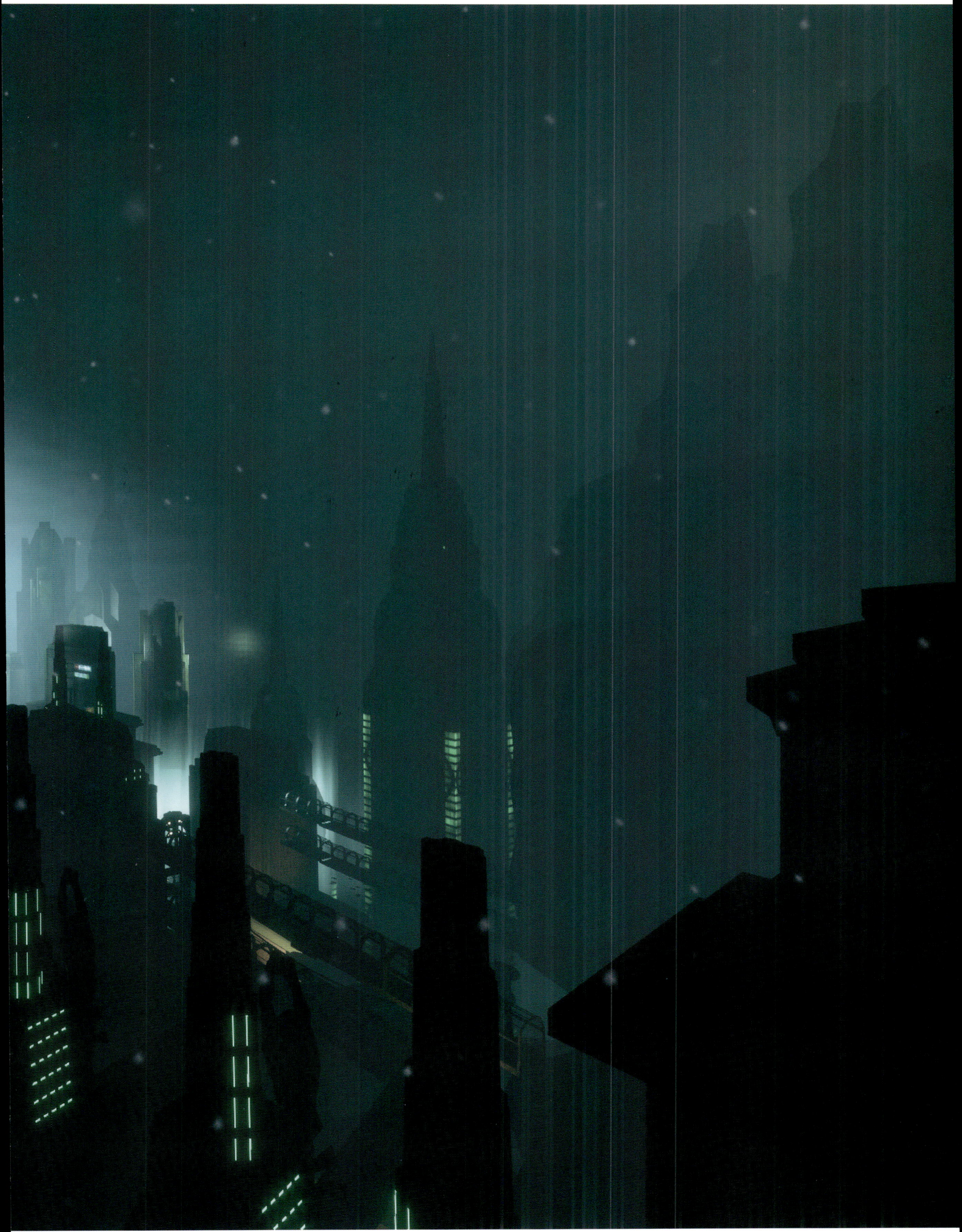

Rapture also employs a heavy dosage of figural and symbolic Art Deco imagery. UE Viewer allows us to search through the 3D models of the game to identify Art Deco design elements in Rapture and their different scales. By drawing these in elevation we establish typologies of how these are applied [Fig.04]. There is a repeated use of statues with their arms reaching towards the heavens, and ornamental clocks and doorways. What might be less expected is the Art Deco influence on industrial pipework or heavy machinery found in places such as the Hephaestus power station, where even generator wheels and heating systems have the same level of ornamental flourish as pieces of furniture in a restaurant or bar. Such details are reminiscent of the stranger Art Deco objects found in the real world, like the ornate slot machines of Mills Mechanical or the 1933 Robbins and Myers oscillating fan.

The variety of Art Deco objects in Rapture speaks to the style's greedy appetite for subsuming 'motifs and forms drawn from nature and machines as well as different regions, cultures and historical periods' from 'sleek locomotives' to 'Mesoamerican ziggurats.'[12] The appropriation of global references and their integration into a new style matches Ryan's desire to control and synthesize a new world beneath the waves.

ELEVATIONAL STUDIES SHOWING EXAMPLES OF HOW ART DECO DESIGN AND ICONOGRAPHY IS USED AT DIFFERENT SCALES THROUGHOUT RAPTURE.

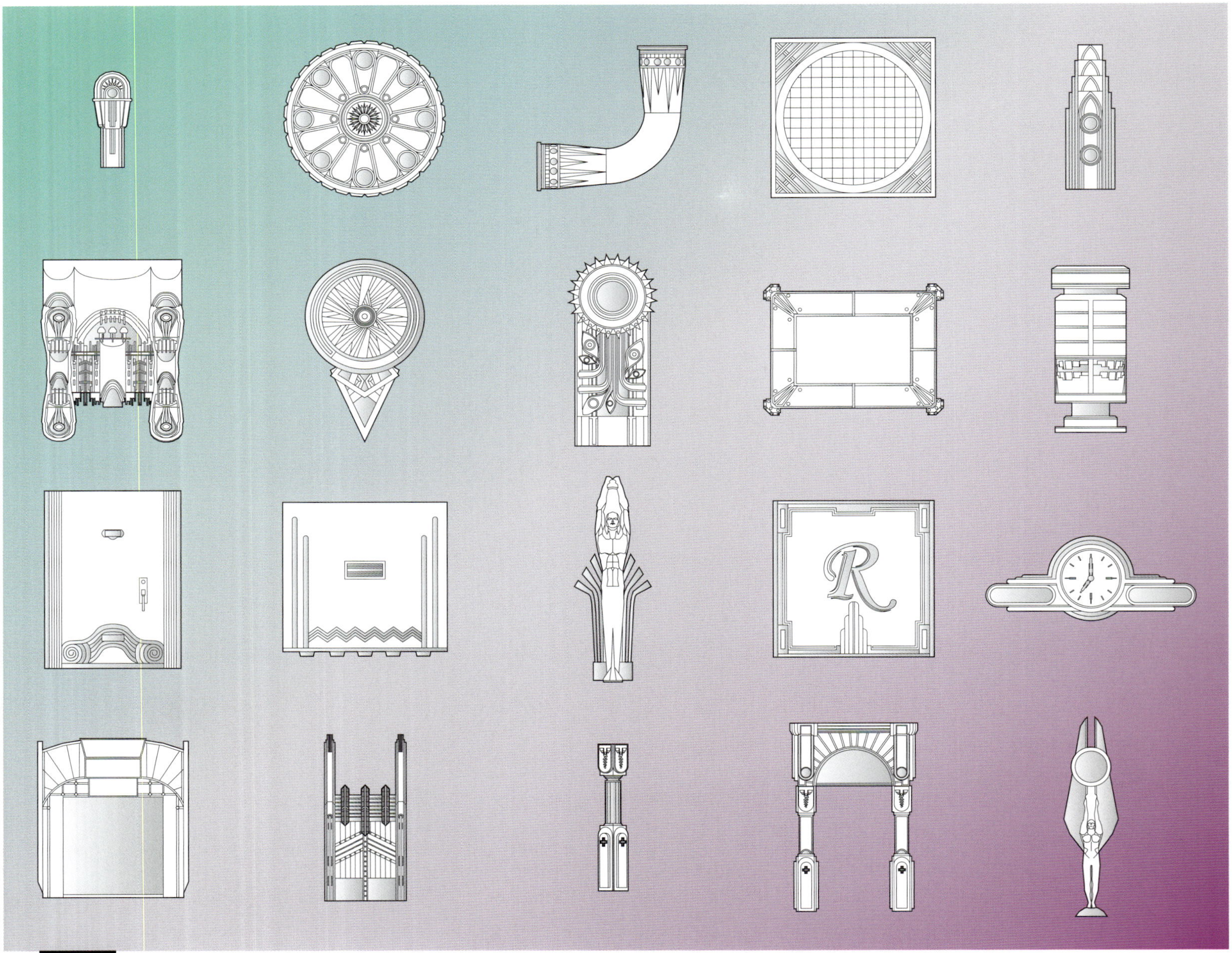

[Fig.04]

2.3

UNDERWATER URBANISM

Beyond the proliferation of symbolic elements in Art Deco, architects such as Raymond Hood established that 'architects would deal with the arrangement of large masses as solids set against the void of the sky.'[13] In *BioShock*, the hulking extents of Rapture are often framed as backlit forms in the distance, emerging from the underwater murk. Analysis at the level of the entire city allows us to examine how these urban clusters could work at a larger scale. We used UE Viewer to view *skybox* textures – the sphere-mapped surroundings the player sees while looking out of the windows at any point in Rapture. By cross-referencing these locations with the in-game Rapture Metro map, we build up a sense of the topography of the city [Fig.05]. In areas such as the Welcome Center or Neptune's Bounty the view from windows shows the player's eyeline deep within the city at a mid-level. By the time we reach Arcadia to the south, we start to see buildings tower over us and huge tendrils of seaweed growing upwards. Further south at the Hephaestus power plant, players look out across a volcanic landscape at the very bottom of the city where it meets rocky outcrops. Yet the final boss battle takes place at the far north of the city, at the top of the Memorial Museum, a point that suggests both a supertall building and elevated geography.

Combining this map with the building types used to create Rapture, we developed this into a larger scale massing study of the city. In-game maps were stitched and scaled based on known elements such as underwater connections between buildings. Levels that are separated in-game but connected through airlocks were rearranged as one contiguous plan. From this we could create potential urban forms of Rapture by arranging buildings to accommodate these floorplans. Each of these represents a cluster of the city based on the locations the game takes us to [Fig.06]. By distributing these according to the key locations shown on the Rapture Metro map, we produced a notional diagram of the city's density. Although questionably canon, the novel *BioShock Rapture* describes the city as 'a small city, three miles to a side so far, rising from the depths to tower over the deep seabed,'[14] and by aligning the map of Rapture to that size, we build a picture of the overall city form. Given real-world Manhattan is 3.7 kilometres (2.3 mi) wide at its widest, this demonstrates that Rapture has a broadly similar order of scale to reality.

[Fig.05] PAGE 40

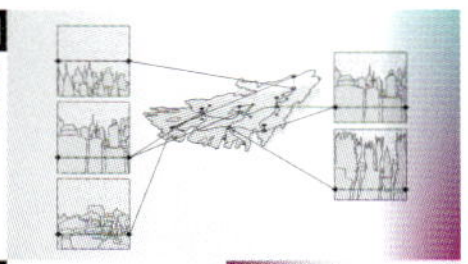

The skyboxes of *BioShock* are used to analyse the relative heights of different in-game locations and combined with the in-game bathysphere metro map.

[Fig.06] PAGE 41

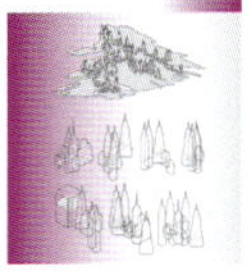

Study exploring how different areas of Rapture might be constructed from building units based on the scale and layout of their in-game mini-maps, and how this shapes the city form.

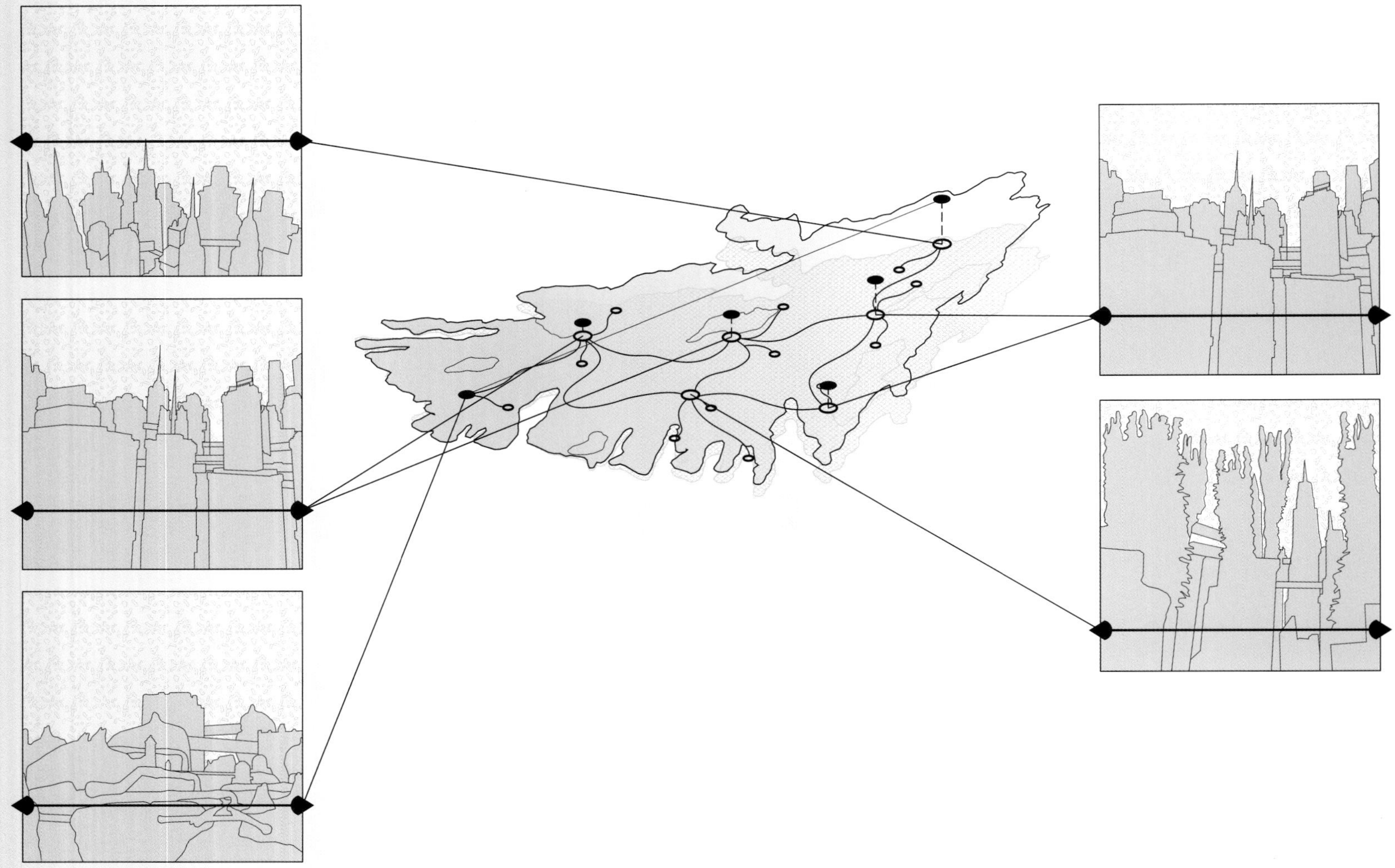

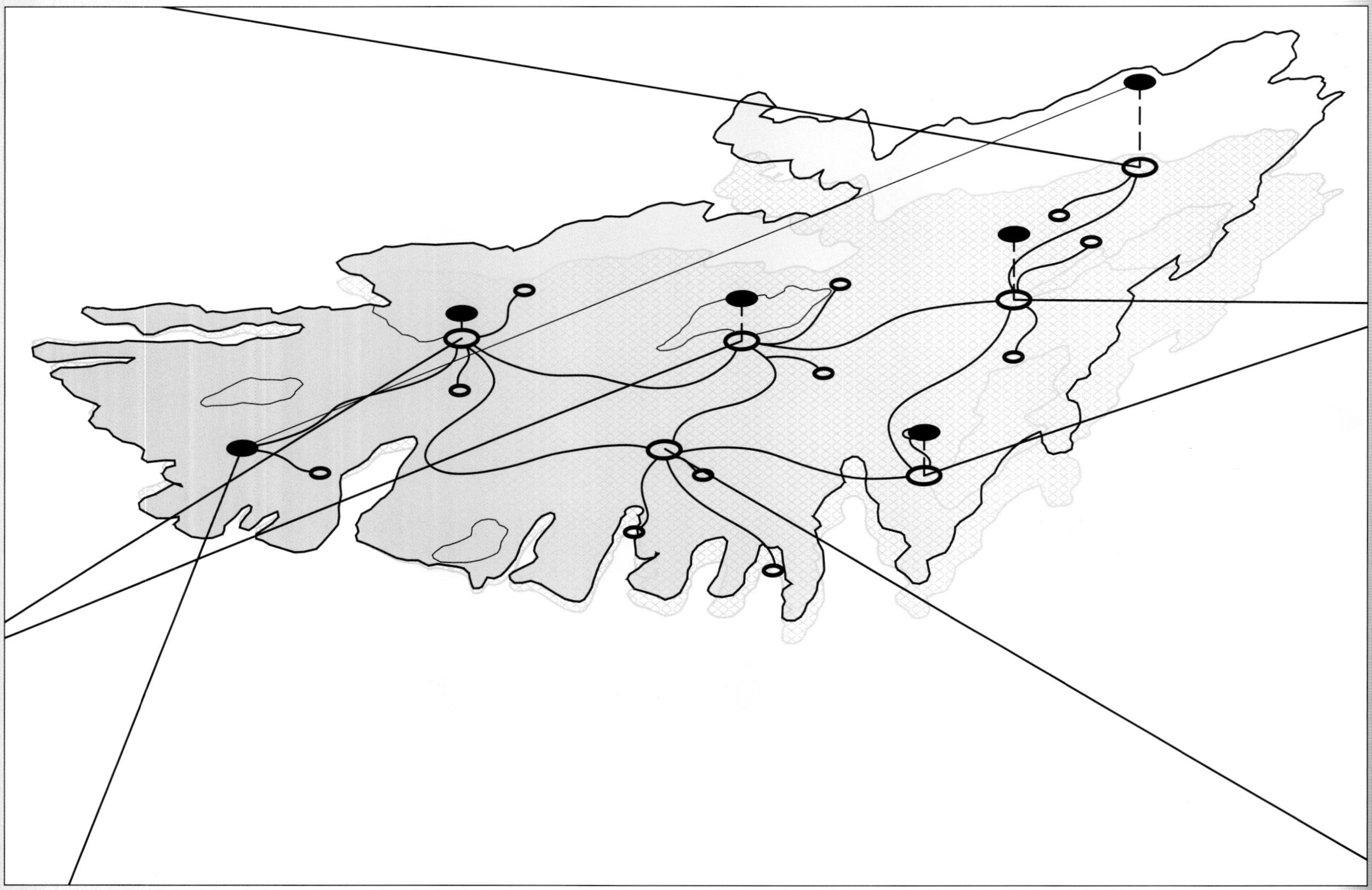

[Fig.05]

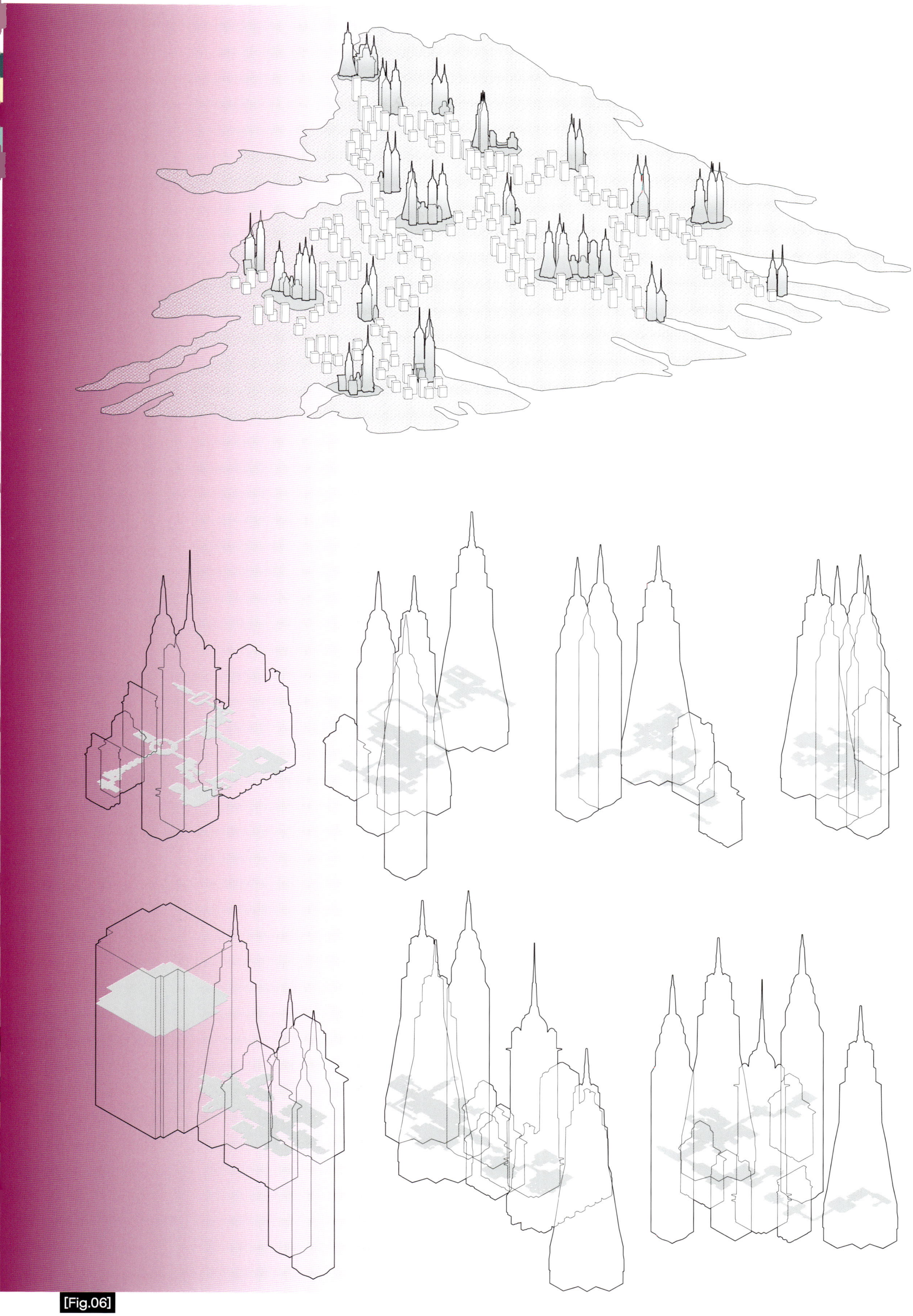

[Fig.06]

2.4

SUBMERSIBLE CITY

Bathyspheres are key to the experience of Rapture, not only because their network provides a helpful basis for examining the city's form and infrastructure, but because of the way they frame our encounters with the space. From the very beginning of the game, the bathysphere's window is used to control our view of the city. Similarly, as our mapping shows, the first view from an arriving bathysphere is used to set a context to each area we visit [Fig.07]. In a place like Fort Frolic, players can see their final goal directly opposite the bathysphere but must take a (literally) tortuous route to finally get there. The dingy and leaking spaces of the Emergency Access stations show us the decrepit infrastructure that underpins the city, while the 'regular' bathysphere stations we visit all show different contextual details that hint at the world beyond, whether that is bodies strung up, or overgrown plants taking over the architecture. The stations themselves represent moments when we look up and see the city rising above our heads, with their improbably large semicircular rooflights evoking the type of structure that might cover a train station, such as Grand Central in New York or the glazed roof of St. Pancras in London [Fig.08].

The other main way in which Rapture is tied together is through underwater connections between buildings. UE Viewer analysis reveals that there are nine main component pieces that are used to connect the various buildings of Rapture. These glazed walkways offer routes between buildings, as well as moments to gaze out into the city beyond. Components are assembled into different forms throughout the game, emerging from and entering different building façades which are themselves repeatable components [Fig.09]. Such connections between skyscrapers are reminiscent of pedestrian transit systems, such as the Chicago Pedway, where a series of tunnels and high-level bridges allow for the movement between buildings at several different heights. As spatial devices they work well to break levels into manageable chunks while also reinforcing the exterior context of Rapture.

[Fig.07] **VIEWS OUT FROM THE BATHYSPHERE AS IT ARRIVES AT DIFFERENT LOCATIONS WITHIN RAPTURE, DEMONSTRATING HOW THE LEVEL IS VISUALLY FRAMED BEFORE IT CAN BE EXPLORED.**

[Fig.08] PAGES 44–5

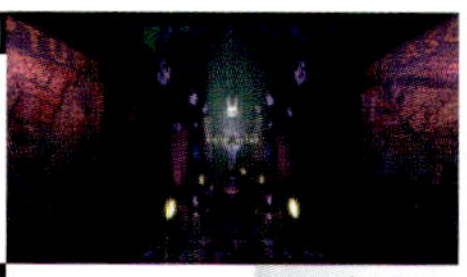

A view of a bathysphere station in Fort Frolic, showing how the design of these spaces reinforces the importance of the transit system in the game's story.

[Fig.09] PAGES 46–7

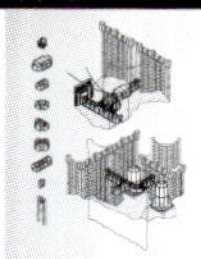

Isometric drawing illustrating examples of the different underwater connections between buildings and the component system used to engineer them.

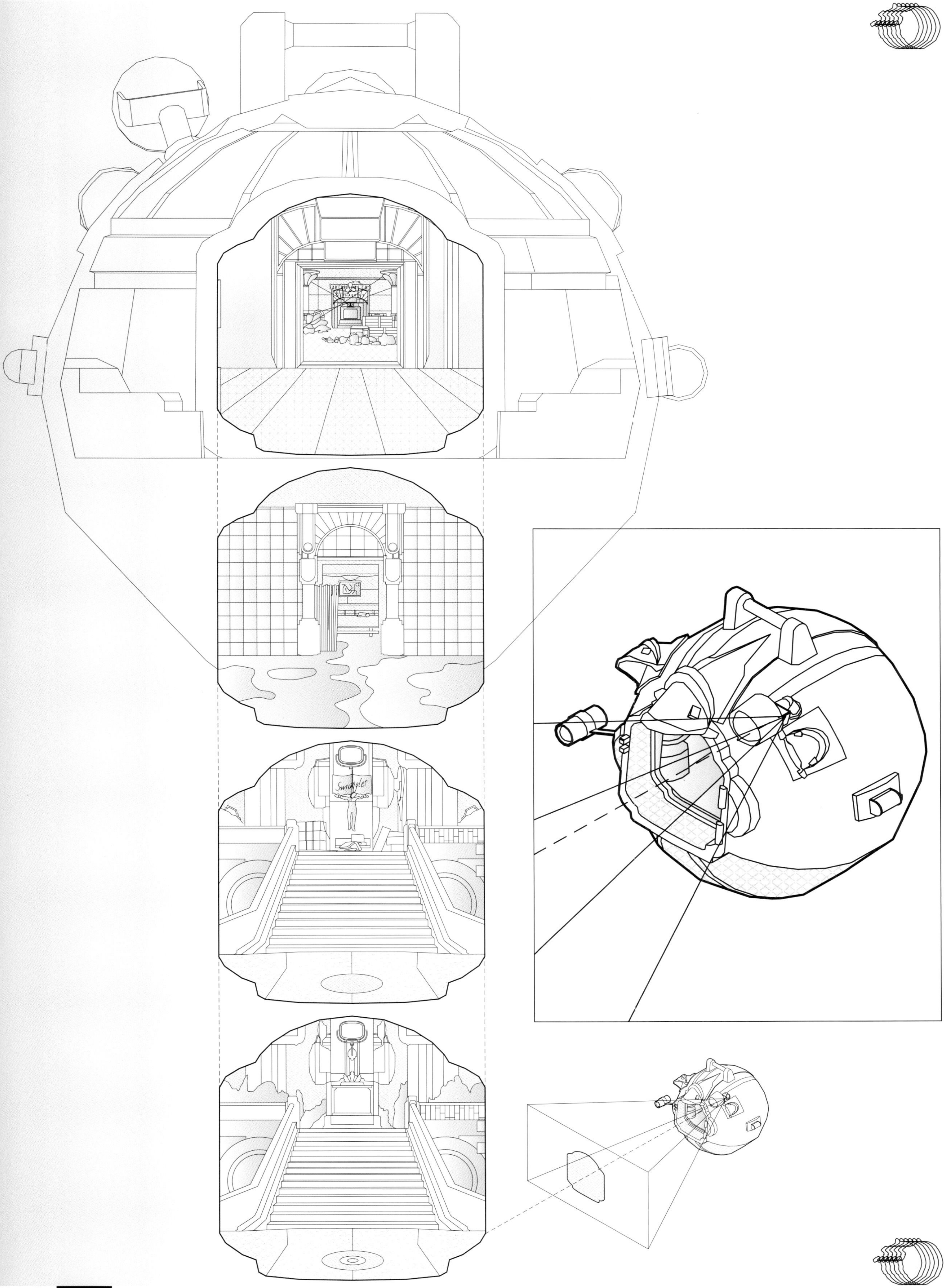

[Fig.07]

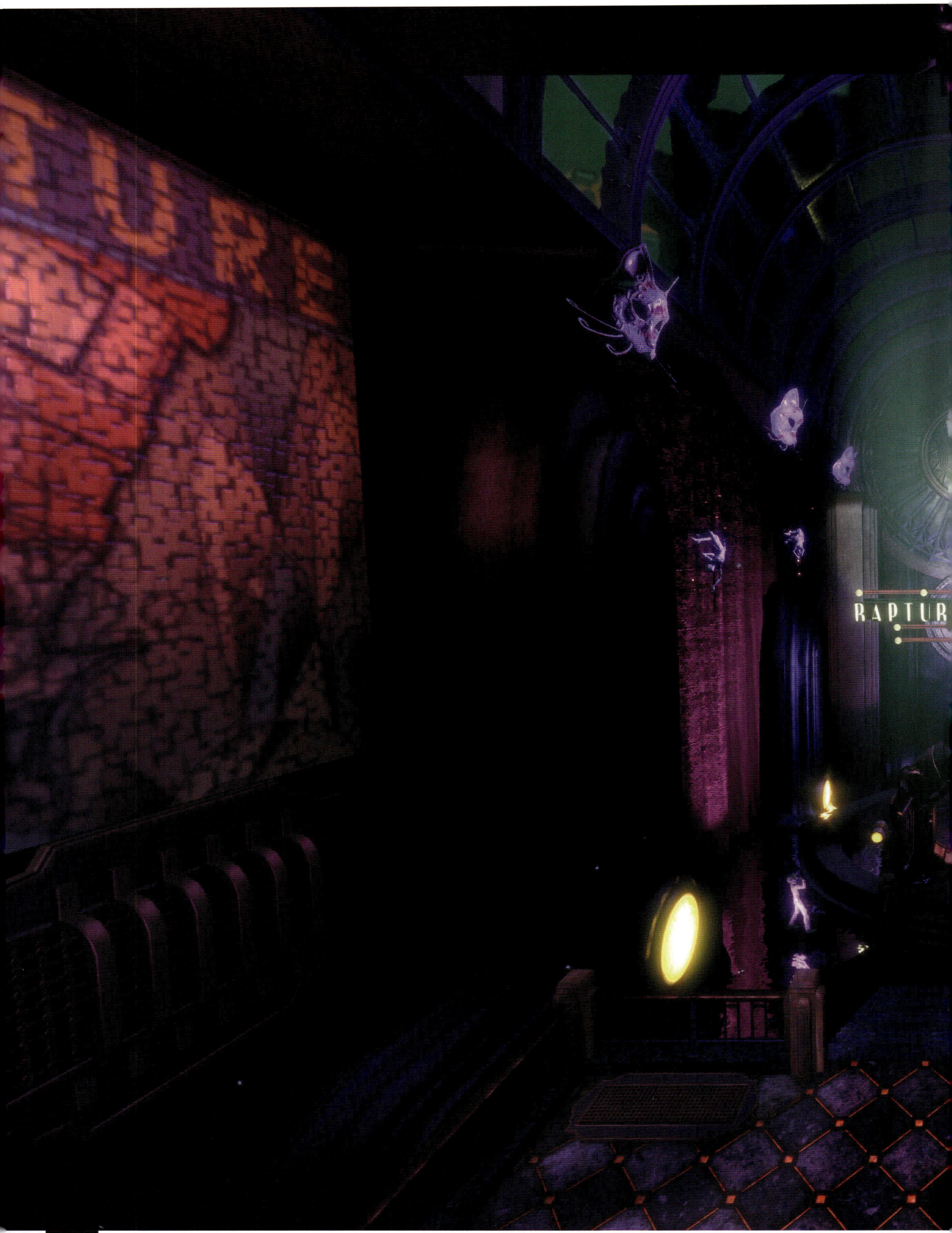

[Fig.08]

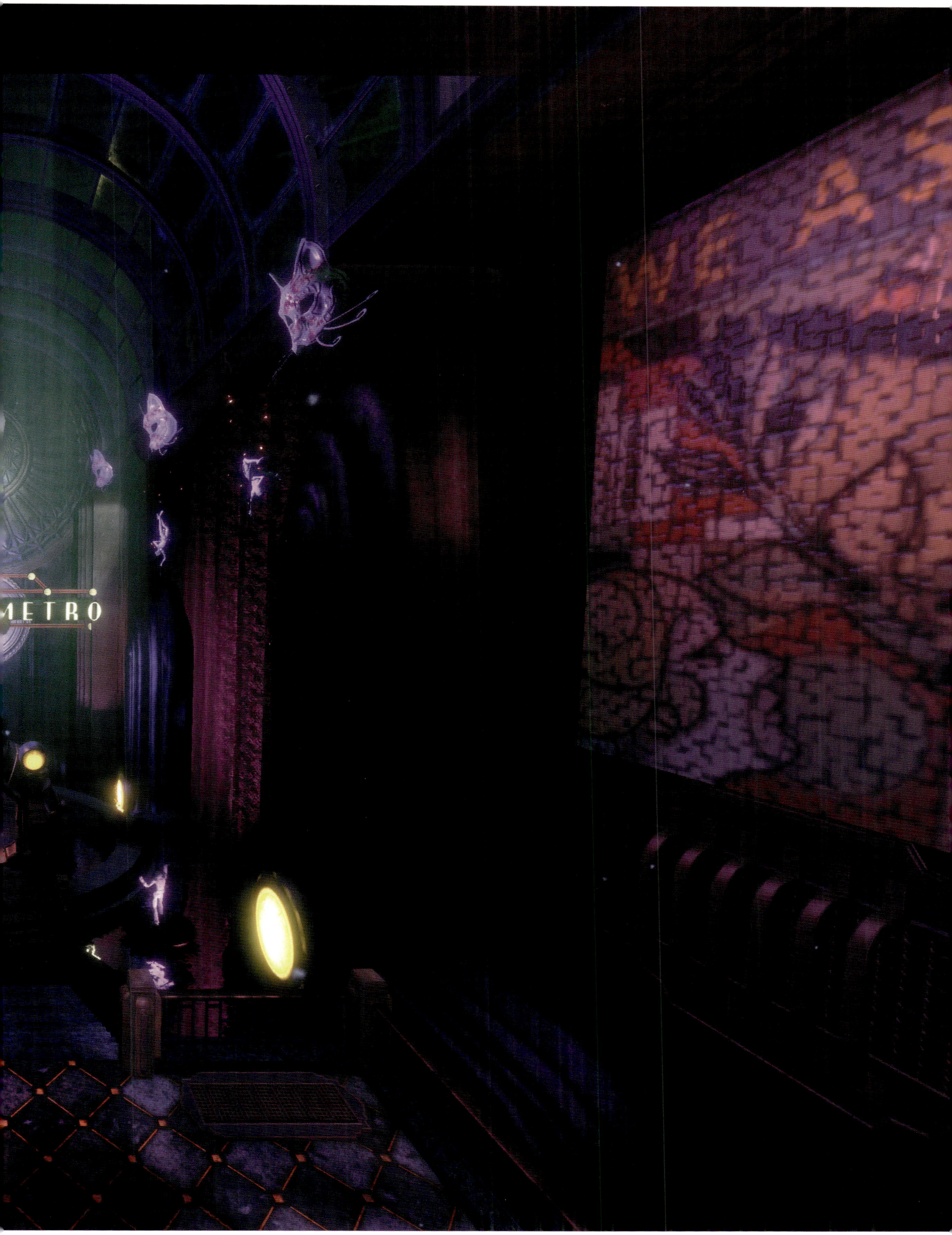
METRO

Perhaps more than anywhere in Rapture, these walkways lead us to question whether there is any way this city could be possible. Constructed from a metal framework holding thin sheets of glass, these structures would likely be too small even above ground, where they would only have gravity and not water pressure to contend with. Several YouTube videos have attempted to discuss the impact of water pressure on Rapture, although they typically assume an ocean floor depth of thousands of meters as a reference point, which increases pressure by many magnitudes.[15] By viewing models from the game and cutting cross-sections through them, we make more direct comparisons to the composition of other structures designed to contain, or exist within, bodies of water [Fig.10].

The vast curved windows of the Rapture Metro are comparable in size to a Russian Project 667 Yankee-class nuclear submarine, rated to a depth of around 400 metres (1,312 ft) like our earlier Rapture calculation, yet there is clearly a vast difference in thickness between the two structures. Comparing an Art Deco window detail to the 500 metre-rated (1,640 ft) U-Boat Worx leisure model Cruise Sub shows how the material thickness and ultra-strong spherical form are completely disregarded in Rapture's detailing. While the walkways and even the giant windows in the end-game boss battle may be at a similar order of magnitude to the largest contemporary aquarium designs, such as China's Chimelong Ocean Kingdom, those structures are resisting a miniscule mass and pressure of water in comparison.[16] The *Rapture* novel describes Andrew Ryan explaining that Rapture uses 'a new method for constantly equalizing air pressure at any depth with no special gasses.'[17] It also suggests that a proprietary material combining glass and metal called 'Ryanium' was used in the construction of the city, along with 'steel and glass and copper.'[18] Whatever the properties of this fictional super-material, it is combined with existing and well-known materials so we are able to understand it in the context of real worldbuilding performance. Even beyond pressure, phenomena like 'thermal bridging', where the sea would transfer cold straight into the metallic structure of the city, would render it unliveable.[19]

[Fig.09] Detail

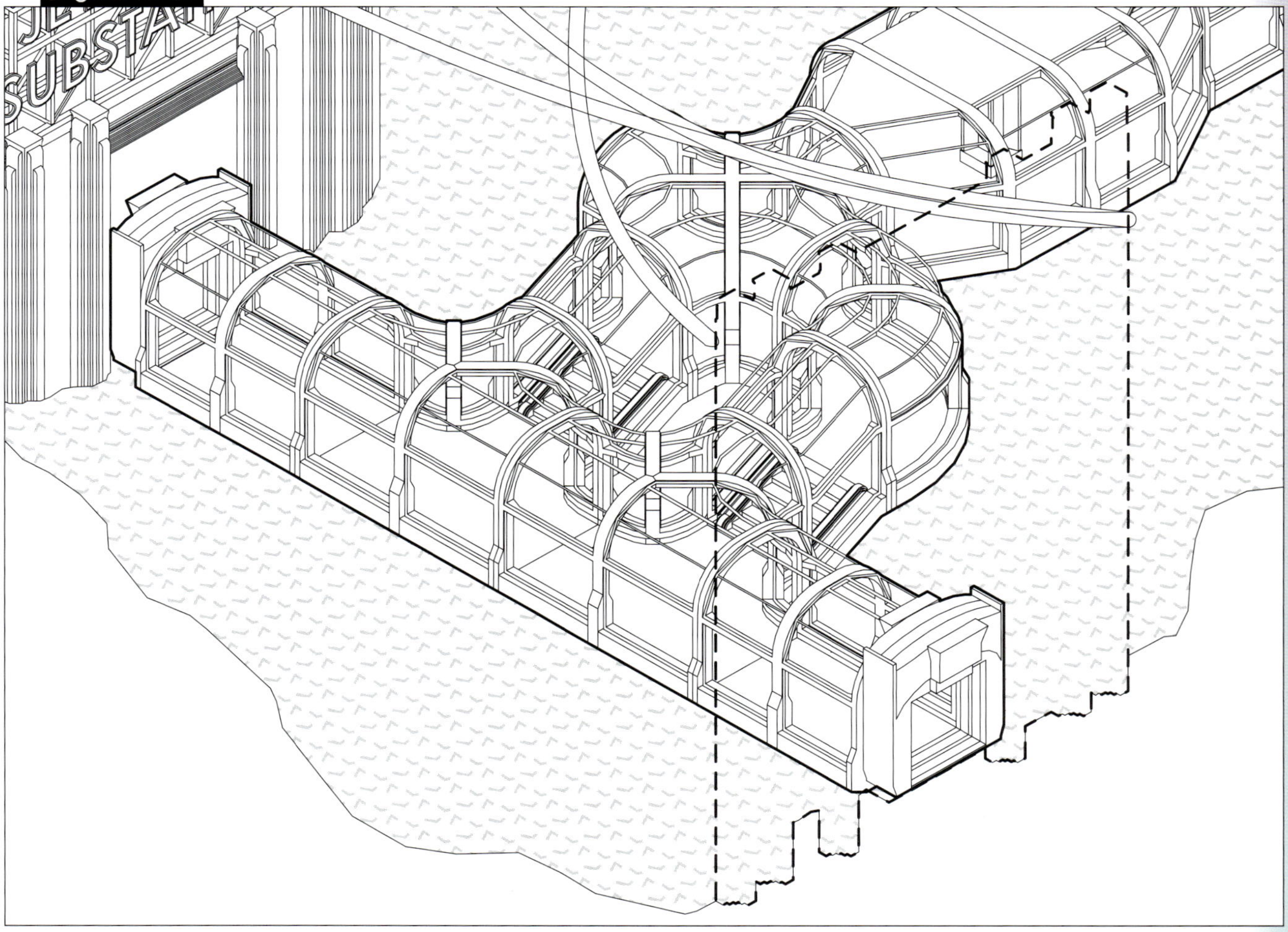

[Fig.10] PAGE 48

Cross-sectional drawings through different architectural details in Rapture, comparing their design to real-world vehicles and structures designed for deep sea exploration.

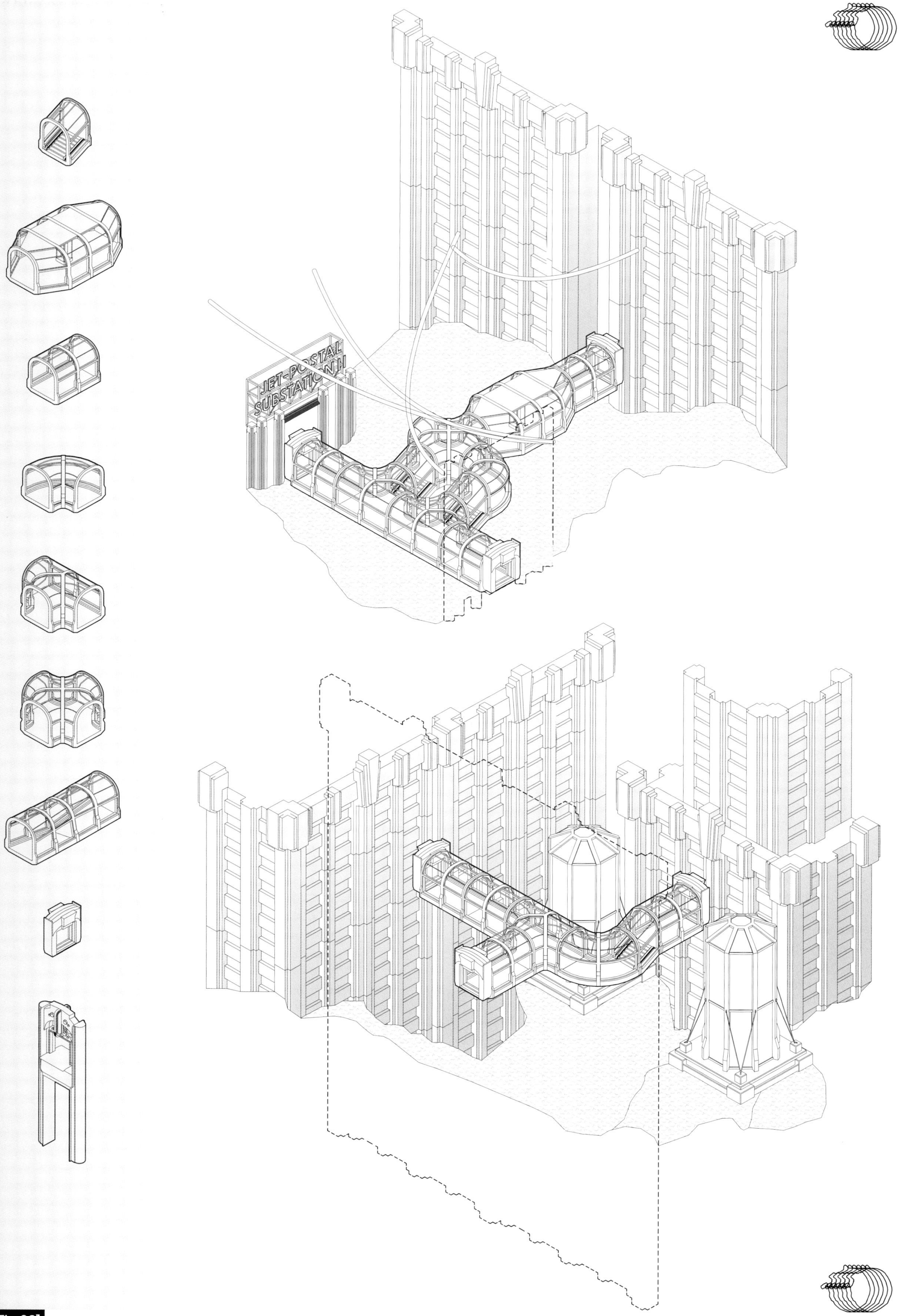

[Fig.09]

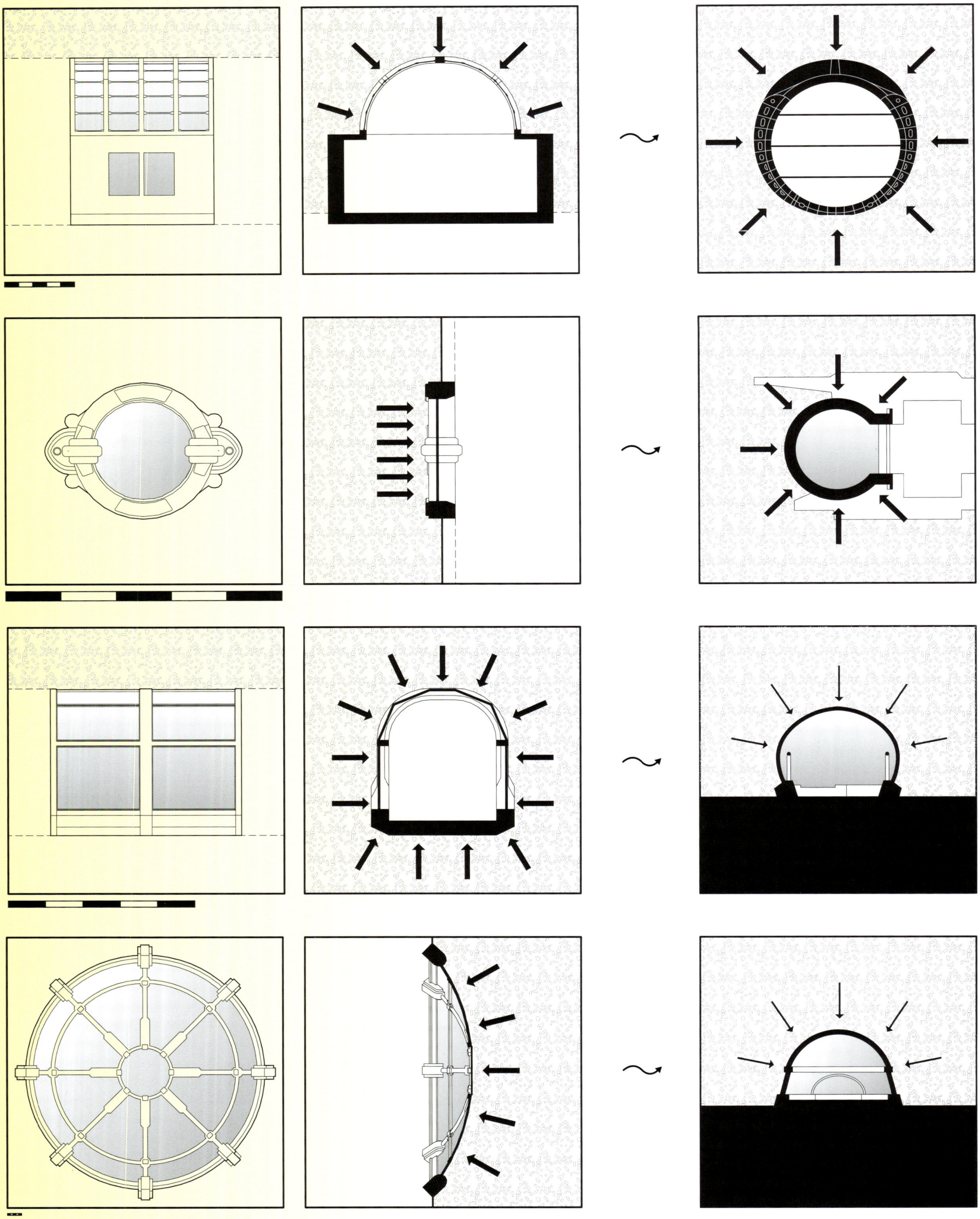

[Fig.10]

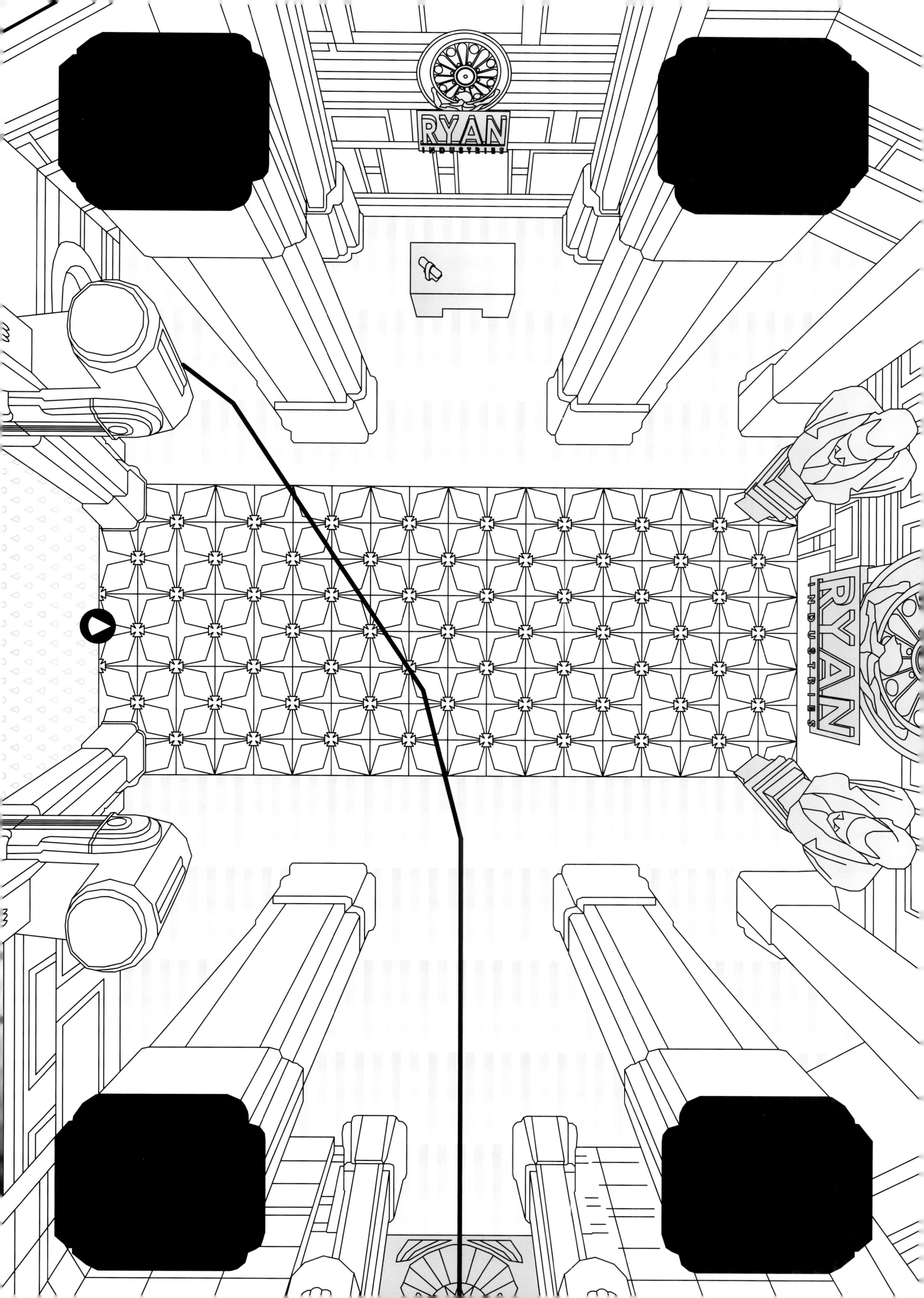
RYAN
INDUSTRIES
RYAN
INDUSTRIES

2.5

WOULD YOU KINDLY?

Of course, we know that Rapture is unliveable, because we experience it and realize that there are very few 'normal' humans left in a city where everything is out to get us. This is often made clear through the spatial experiences Jack has while trying to engage with the populous of Rapture, 'where characters that have not yet turned completely crazy can mostly only be heard over the radio or be seen through windows.'[20] Throughout the first half of the game, Jack is guided by the voice of Atlas, who is eventually revealed to be Frank Fontaine. By the time the player meets and battles Fontaine, it becomes clear that he is no longer truly human, and the space he has occupied reflects this. Taking the elevator up to the top of the Memorial Museum tower, we find Fontaine has installed a vast infrastructure to juice him up on ADAM [Fig.11]. Rather than the private social clubs or tourist viewing platforms of Manhattan's towers, Fontaine has taken the highest point of the city as the place to transcend and subjugate his humanity.

The one time that we are able to go beyond the threshold and actually speak with one of these people directly is when Andrew Ryan emerges from his office and orders Jack to kill him with an instruction he cannot help but obey. Although Ryan's office is encountered at the midpoint of the game, spatially and symbolically it represents a climax of the story. Mapping Ryan's office as a perspectival plan shows how it brings together the symbolic iconography of Rapture, closes the implicit distance between Jack and other human characters, and provides one of the key tests of agency within the game's structure and narrative [Fig.12]. This is a test that Jack fails, revealing a lack of self-determination which is reinforced by the mechanics of the story itself. We arrive as Ryan has triggered a self-destruct sequence, but it will never actually finish, as the game does not move on until it is cancelled by the player. If we don't abort the sequence, it will go on forever, Rapture will never actually self-destruct and 'that choice has been exposed as meaningless within the basic fabric of the game's mechanics.'[21]

As a city founded on Andrew Ryan's myth of self, what we come to learn about Rapture shows it was destined to fail, socially and technologically. French philosopher Paul Virilio argues that we should not be blind to the negative possibilities of such innovation, citing the '*invention of the shipwreck* in the invention of the ship.'[22] The wrecked and ruined Rapture we find is a product of the political and technological frameworks that created it. Even its Art Deco stylings portend failure, given the style's 'association with the Depression, and a time when nationalism and fascism fomented war and showed the ugliest side of human nature.'[23] But failure can be seductive. As we see from the design of Rapture and the esteem with which this dystopic city is held by players and critics alike, if you are going to fail, you should at least fail beautifully.

[Fig.12] PERSPECTIVE PLANS OF ANDREW RYAN'S OFFICE, WHERE JACK FINALLY MEETS THE MOST SIGNIFICANT HUMAN OCCUPANT OF RAPTURE FACE-TO-FACE, OUTLINING THE STRICT SPATIAL CHOREOGRAPHY OF THE LEVEL.

[Fig.11] PAGES 52–3

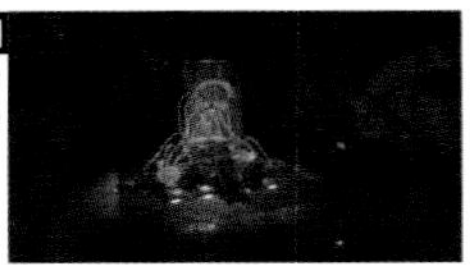

A view of Frank Fontaine in his lair, pumping ADAM into his body at what appears to be the tallest point of the city, in the tower of the Memorial Museum.

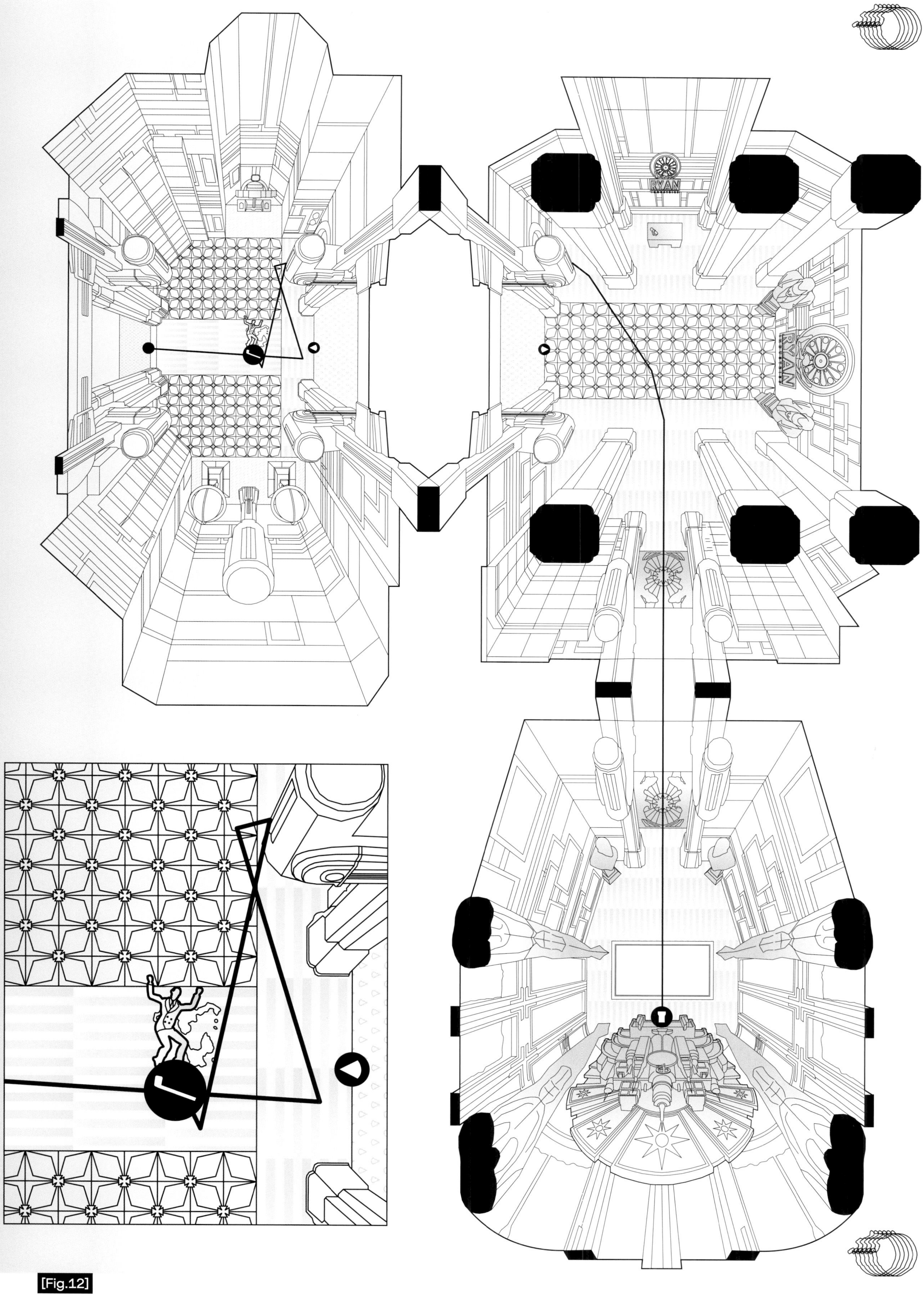

[Fig.12]

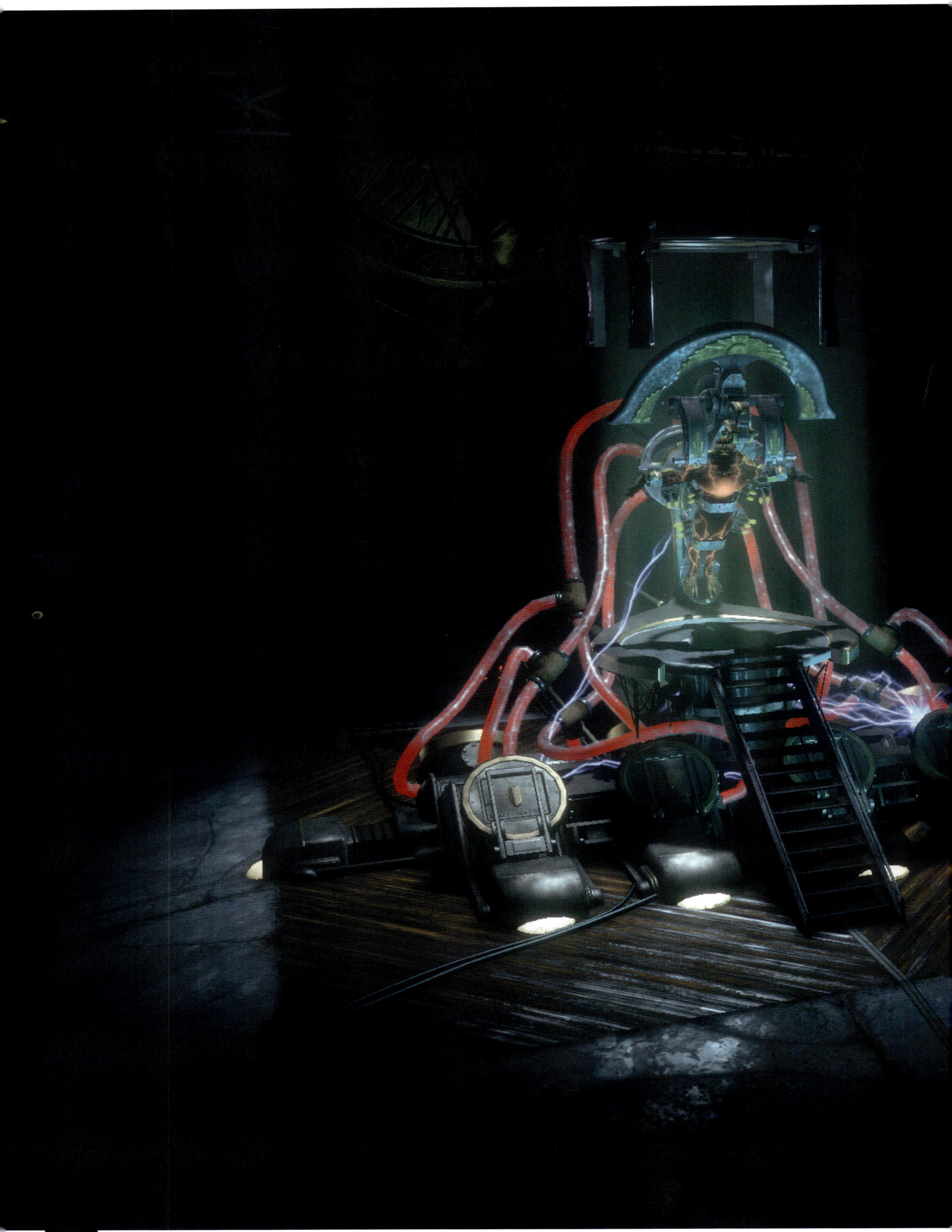

[Fig.11]

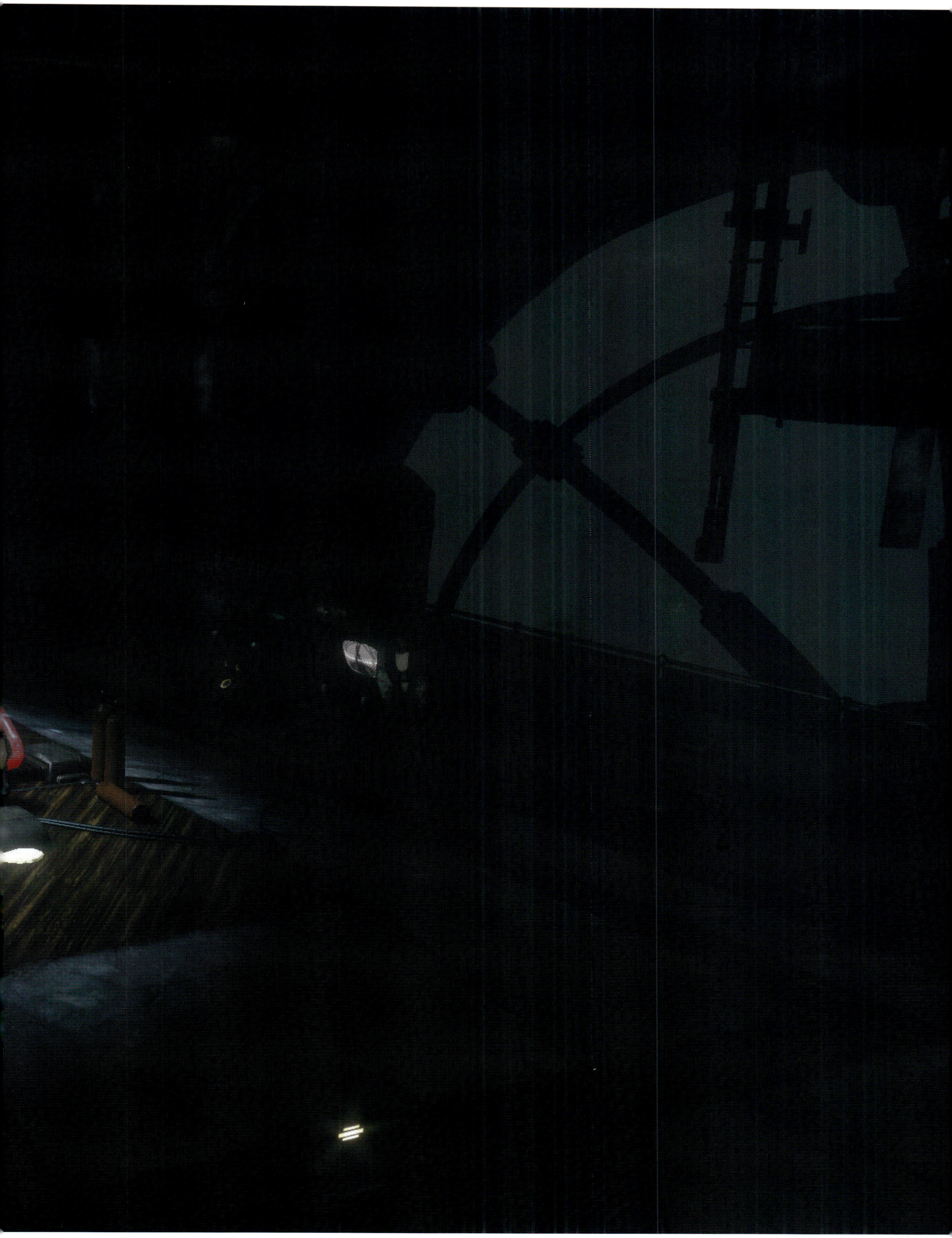

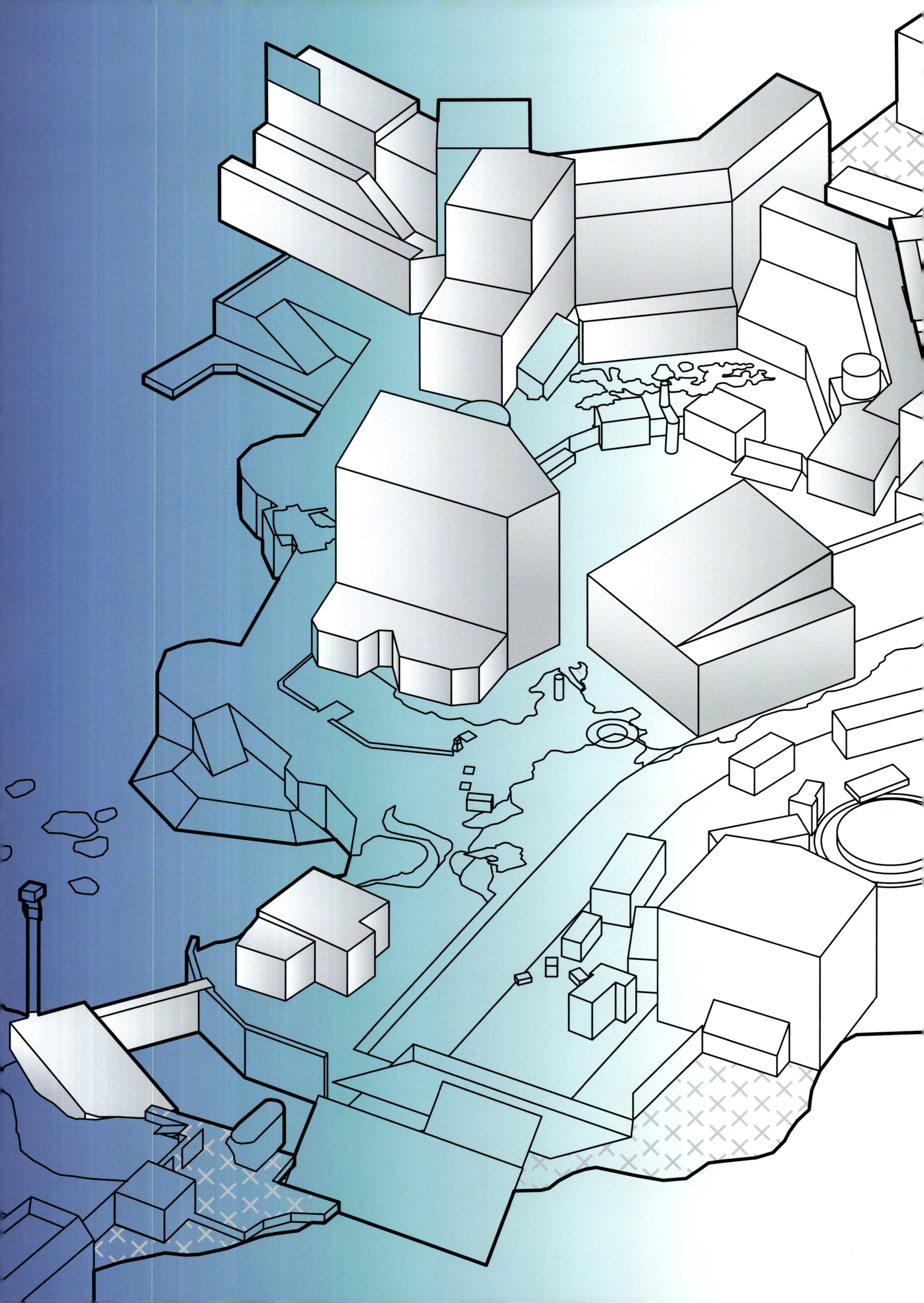

CHAPTER 03

DISCO ELYSIUM

DEVELOPER / PUBLISHER: ZA/UM

Platforms	Windows, Mac, PlayStation 4, PlayStation 5, Stadia, Nintendo Switch, Xbox One, Xbox Series X/S, Android
Year	2019

THE MAP OF MARTINAISE BASED ON A 2D RECONSTRUCTION FROM THE ISOMETRIC VIEWPOINT OF THE GAME, SHOWING THE EXTENTS OF THE NAVIGABLE WORLD.

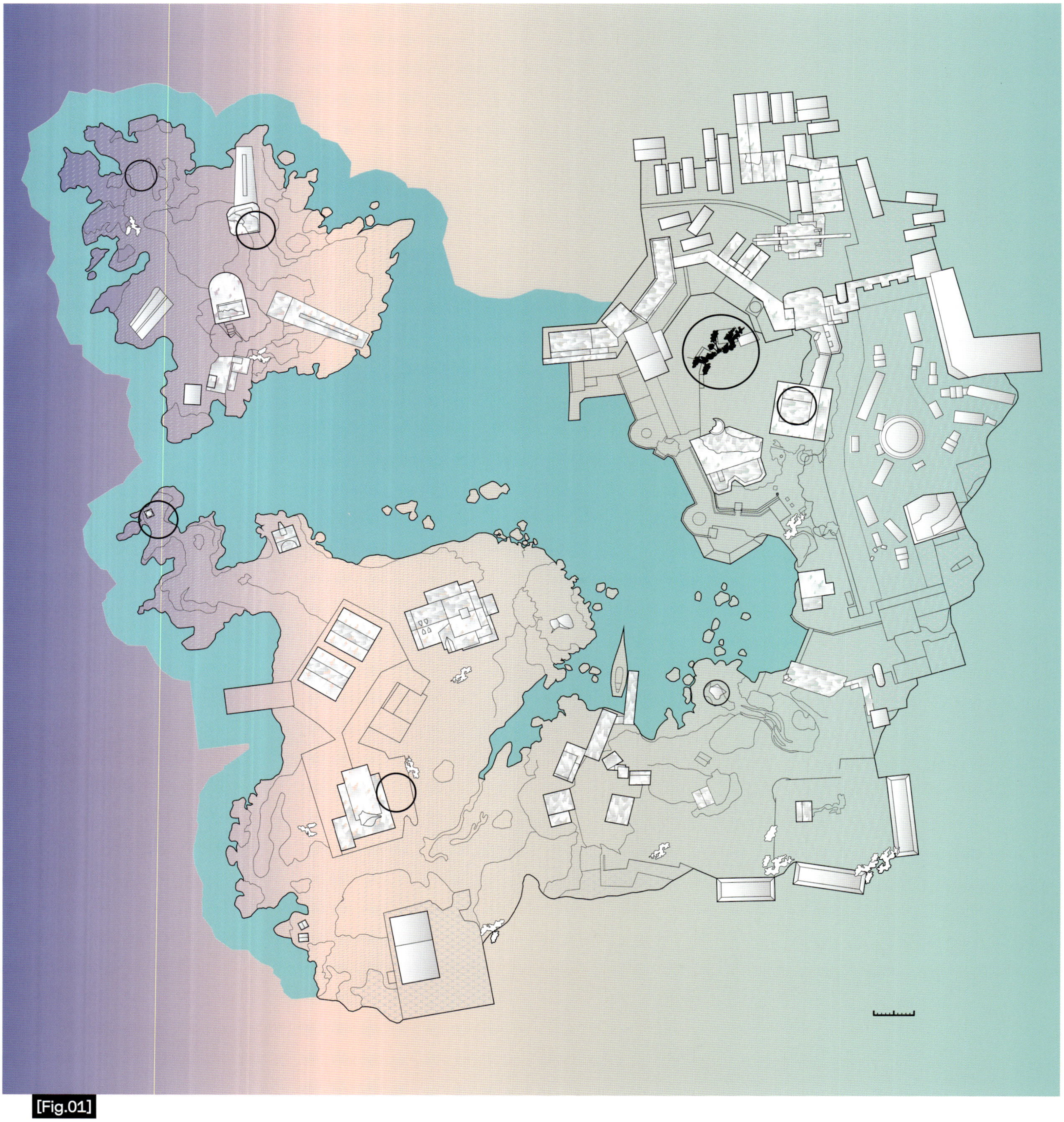

[Fig.01]

For a relatively compact urban neighbourhood, few game worlds are as ambitious as *Disco Elysium*'s Martinaise. As a district in the city of Revachol, Martinaise is a rich and singular place that also fits into a much larger conceptual and narrative context developed by ZA/UM's Robert Kurvitz – Elysium, a world outlined in his novel *Sacred and Terrible Air*.[1] Martinaise is where detective Harrier (Harry) du Bois awakens to find he has lost his memory and must overcome amnesia and other impositions in order to solve the murder of a man hanging from a tree behind his hotel. As players investigate the area, they find that the district is a juxtaposition of different architectural styles and time periods, providing a strong sense of the multiple forces that have shaped it. Through the game's unique use of pre-rendered backgrounds and the application of 'overpainting' with real time lighting and weather, the world feels textural and lived-in, a place produced by history and speaking to us – often literally – in a way that many other game worlds cannot.

Key to this is ZA/UM's decision to use a fixed isometric perspective. As Helen Hindpere explains, this viewpoint informs the compositional decisions the developers made when designing the world, making Martinaise a 'chaotic mix that looks hideous in real life, but great in isometric 3D.'[2] This chaos contradicts traditional understandings of isometric projection. In *Engineering Drawing*, Murali and Parthasarathy describe isometric views as having 'the convenience of observing the dimensions without any ambiguity and projecting the shape with all its three faces,' producing 'an inherent visual appeal.'[3] While *Disco Elysium* certainly fits the criteria of visual appeal, it uses an isometric perspective to make a more complicated and indeterminate architectural landscape, rather than the informational style of an engineering or architectural drawing. But there are parallels in drawing practice. The American architect John Hejduk was noted for explorations using isometric and axonometric techniques, where, as Ray Lucas argues, 'the observer is largely responsible for constructing the space from the data provided by the drawing.'[4] Hejduk calls this a 'memory condition', where viewers interpret the isometric view back into 3D themselves.[5] As Hindpere suggests, in *Disco Elysium* this means that players comprehend a seductive, layered version of an architectural space through the isometric camera, that may not seem so appealing in reality.

The *Disco Elysium* artbook offers many illustrations and designer testimonies, but never truly lets us look behind the isometric curtain of the three-dimensional world. However, isometric projection affords us the opportunity to rebuild Martinaise ourselves, detaching it from the camera to explore its urban form. By using a screenshot composite depicting the entire world and projecting it to match an isometric camera in 3D modelling software, we trace the image, drawing 'through' it onto the ground plane below. This method enables the rebuilding of a reasonably accurate 'massing study' of Martinaise which we use to further analyse the world. Massing is an architectural technique where the abstracted overall form of a building is portrayed, to assess the relationship to a site and other buildings. This allows us to understand the compositional qualities of Martinaise and explore several questions that the game's story poses. Because vertical lines in isometric projection retain their relative real-world dimensions (0.816 times their true length), elevation and scale can be approximated using Harry's height, stated as around 180 cm (5'9") in the game. This process was used to reconstruct a scaled map of Martinaise, showing that the walkable environments encompass an area of around 2.7 hectares, stretching roughly 240 by 240 metres (787×787 ft) from edge to edge [Fig.01]. Given that Martinaise could fit nearly forty times into Tallinn's Vanalinn Old Town area (as defined by Google Maps), it represents a spatially compact yet atmospherically powerful world.

The extents of Martinaise unlock (and re-lock) over the course of the investigation, based on specific days in the week or milestones in the case. As our isometric mapping of the city shows, this creates a territory that changes around the player, opening or closing routes to us [Fig.02]. This is a well-used trope of game city design, from mysteriously closed bridges to the innumerable unopenable doors in games throughout history. But the world registers this more deeply in *Disco Elysium*, given that Harry can speak not only with people but with objects and *the city itself* (through the Shivers skill for example). Because game time only proceeds through the investigation and interactions, this means that, as Michał Kłosiński argues: 'time in *Disco Elysium* has been reduced to the tension between objects and Harry's intentionality.'[6] Given that certain parts of the map are locked either by specific days or particular insights – that may come from people, spaces or inanimate objects – the more Harry interacts with the fabric of the city, the more it changes around him.

[Fig.02] PAGE 58
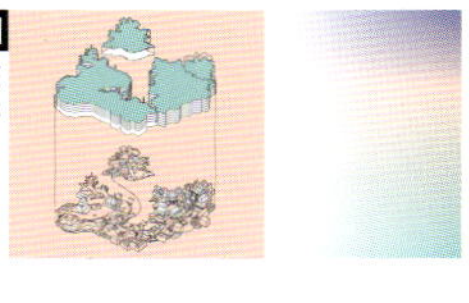
Map demonstrating the different areas of Martinaise that become accessible or closed off over the course of the week.

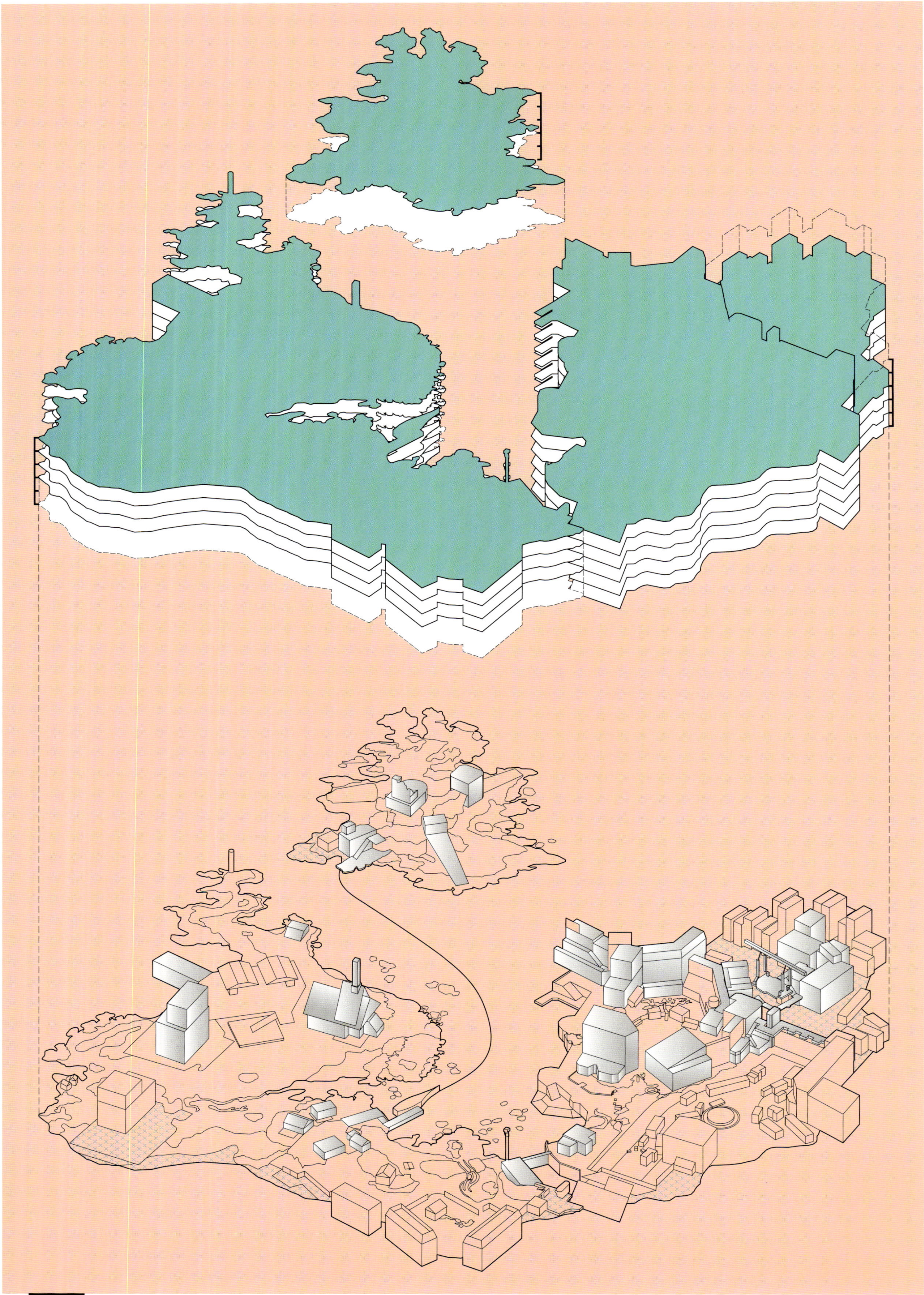

[Fig.02]

While the extents of Martinaise are defined by the progressing investigation, it does have a distinct border. Yet the way these edges are designed changes based on their context. As Aleksander Rostov explains, his overpainting techniques emphasized 'edge hierarchy', working with an 'understanding of which edges need to be sharp and which need to be soft or lost entirely.'[7] Creating a screenshot matrix of edges within Martinaise allows us to identify different approaches that are used [Fig.03]. Certain borders to the world use a classic 'fog of war' fade, while other edges are more integrated into the architectural form being depicted. The kitchen of Whirling in Rags has an irregular edge that does not match to the implied floorplan [Fig.02]. Buildings and details in Greater Revachol Industrial Harbour or near the Horseback Monument fade into chiaroscuro brushwork. Edges are used to play with the sense of scale and keep the world constrained. For example, the Capeside Apartments are described as a formerly twelve-storey block, levelled down to four floors by artillery, but while the western side of the building juts out into the ocean, presenting a defined boundary, the top of the building fades to black, leaving the full form of the architecture to our imagination.

This use of different visual techniques is combined with a diverse set of architectural styles that emphasizes a city that has undergone rapid change and subsequently disintegrated. Helen Hindpere relates this design approach to the post-Soviet Eastern Europe, calling Martinaise 'a mix of two 70s: the 1870s and the 1970s.'[8] Our elevational drawings of notable structures in the game show how the district's design encompasses numerous architectural styles [Fig.04]. These aesthetic clashes are representative of 1990s Eastern Europe, not least Estonia, where ZA/UM was founded. Maris Mändel discusses how the introduction of the capitalist market took Estonian design away from the Soviet language of 'plastered and painted walls, exposed brick walls, prefabricated gravel-coated concrete panels or limestone cladding.'[9] The modernist steel and glass structure of Whirling in Rags, with its corrugated metal roof emphasizes 'the expanded use of metals'[10] previously designated for military or infrastructure purposes. In the Harbour, by contrast, we see shipping containers for transporting goods providing accommodation to the union boss Evrart Claire. Shipping containers have become a trendy design object, used in projects as varied as housing, football stadiums, hotels and coffee shops. Evrart explains that his container can be moved around by the harbour cranes, which makes the architectural landscape more like British architect Cedric Price's *Fun Palace*, where containerized building units could be moved and plugged in to make architecture that was 'a short-term plaything'.[11] By contrast, the Dolorian Church is a 320-year-old structure reminiscent of timber churches built around Europe. A notable real-world Estonian example of this is the wooden Saint Magdalene Church in Ruhnu, which was constructed nearly 400 years ago. With its cascading rooftops it also bears a resemblance to the Stave Churches that proliferated around Scandinavia from the 12th century onwards. While the use of specific materials puts buildings into a historical context, when Harry speaks to the raver Noid about the Dolorian church, Noid argues that the building is 'folk Dolorianism' but that 'everything between an ancient concrete cathedral and a glass cube is Dolorianism.' Noid describes how Dolorians 'liked to show off large and intricate structures, arches, spires', but these are not features that particularly define Martinaise's architecture.

Beyond the buildings of Revachol, the street furniture also provides a contextual design lineage. Compiling a lexicon of street furniture allows us to outline the technological and social cues offered by the game's world at a more human scale [Fig.05]. Details such as the moulded tubular trashcan in which the Hanged Man's clothing is found, or the public payphones with their plexiglass domes recall the language of Soviet-era design. A classic example of this is the K67 kiosk designed by Slovenian architect Saša J. Mächtig, using similarly moulded and shaped space-age forms, that has become a design icon.[12] Different types of streetlamps each hint at the forces that may have shaped their immediate context. In Martinaise West they consist of lights on slender stems that are lashed to poles, much like the Soviet-era RKU-03 streetlamps, while at the southerly end of the Martinaise Waterfront they are a much more elaborate design with three lighting elements encased in large glass housings, in keeping with their proximity to the Horseback Monument.

[Fig.03] PAGES 60–1
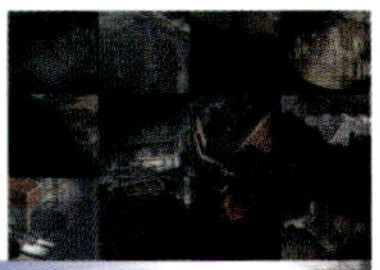
Screenshot composition demonstrating the different types of 'edge hierarchies' used across the world, from defined edges to abstract zones and fades.

[Fig.04] PAGE 62
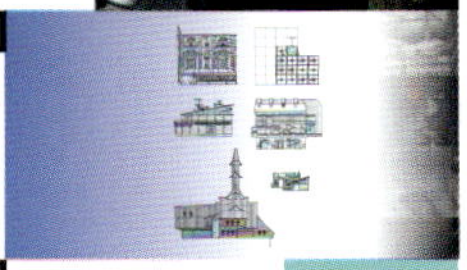
Elevational studies showing the different architectural styles of notable buildings in Martinaise.

[Fig.05] PAGE 63
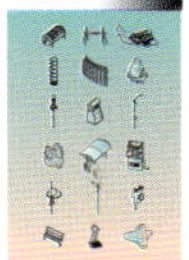
Street furniture details across Martinaise, offering clues to the geographical and cultural inspiration behind the world's design.

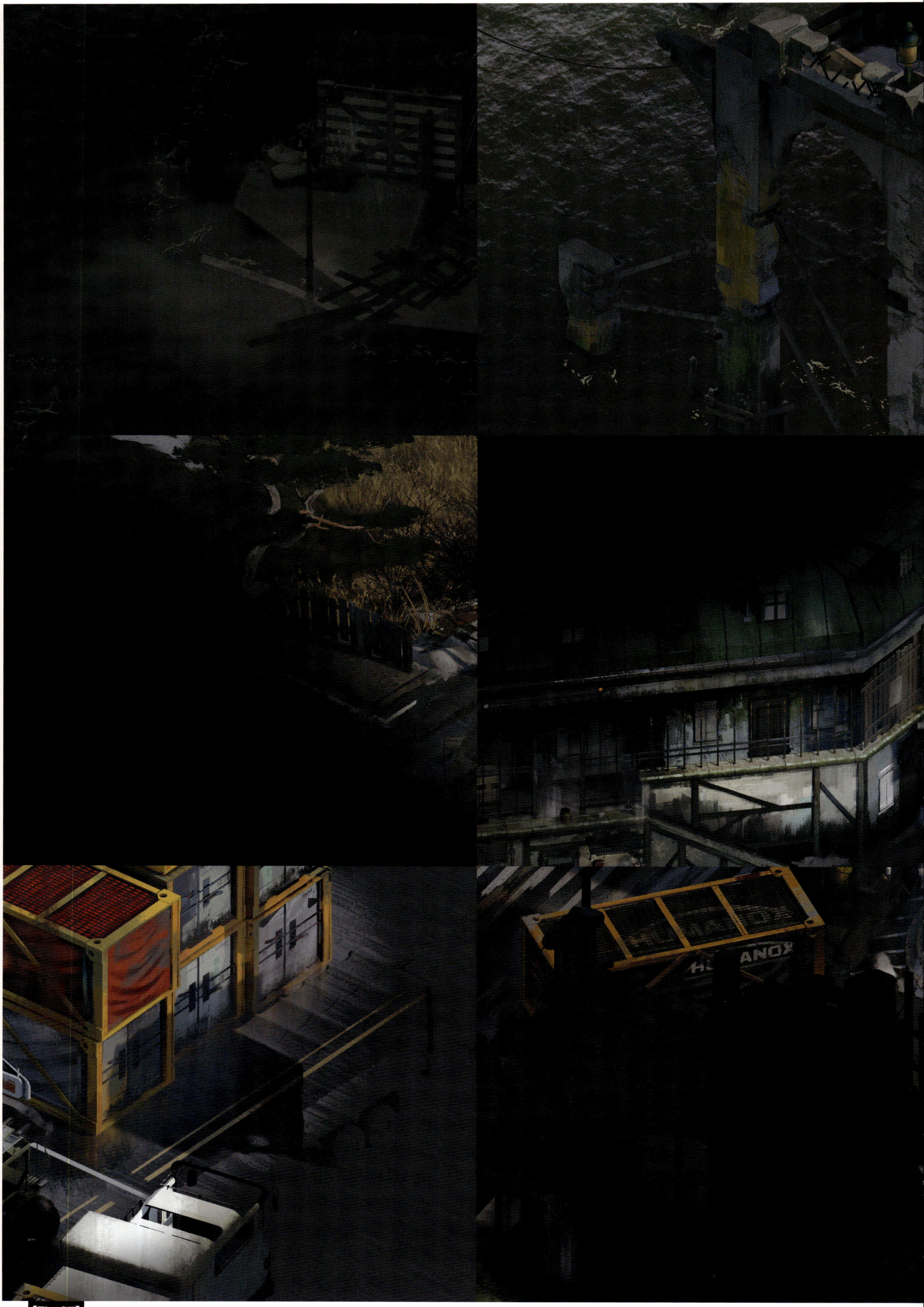

[Fig.03]

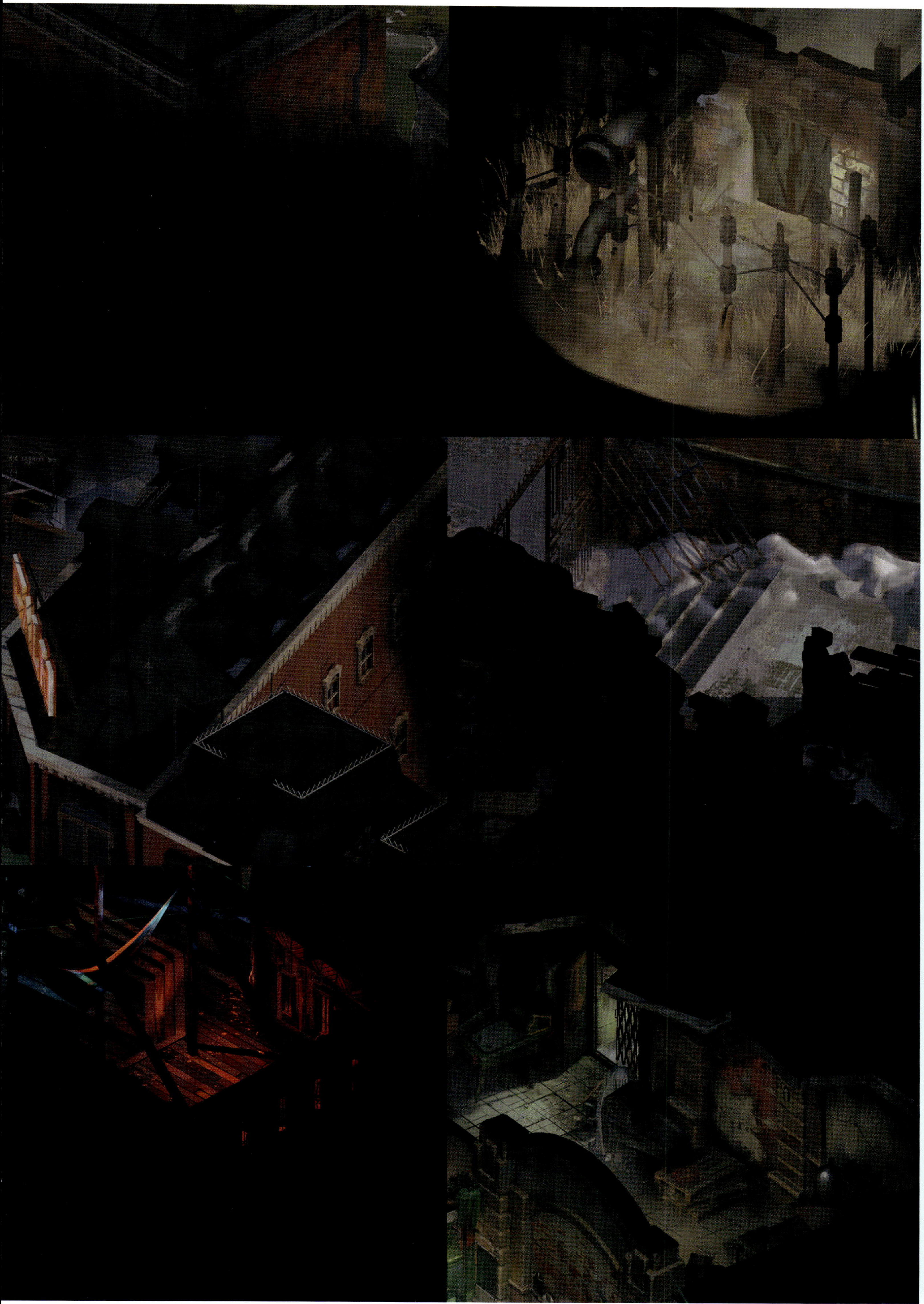

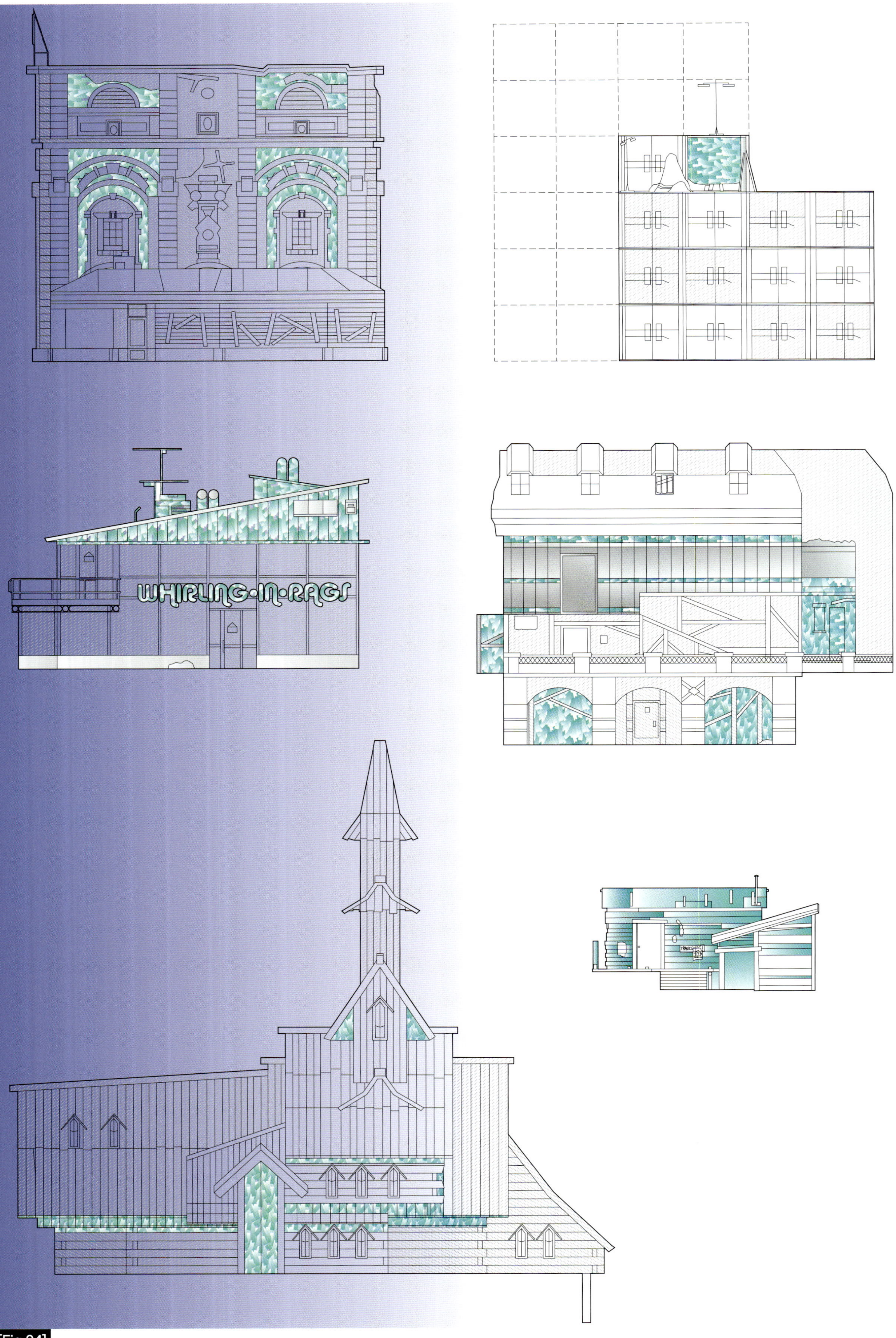

[Fig.04]

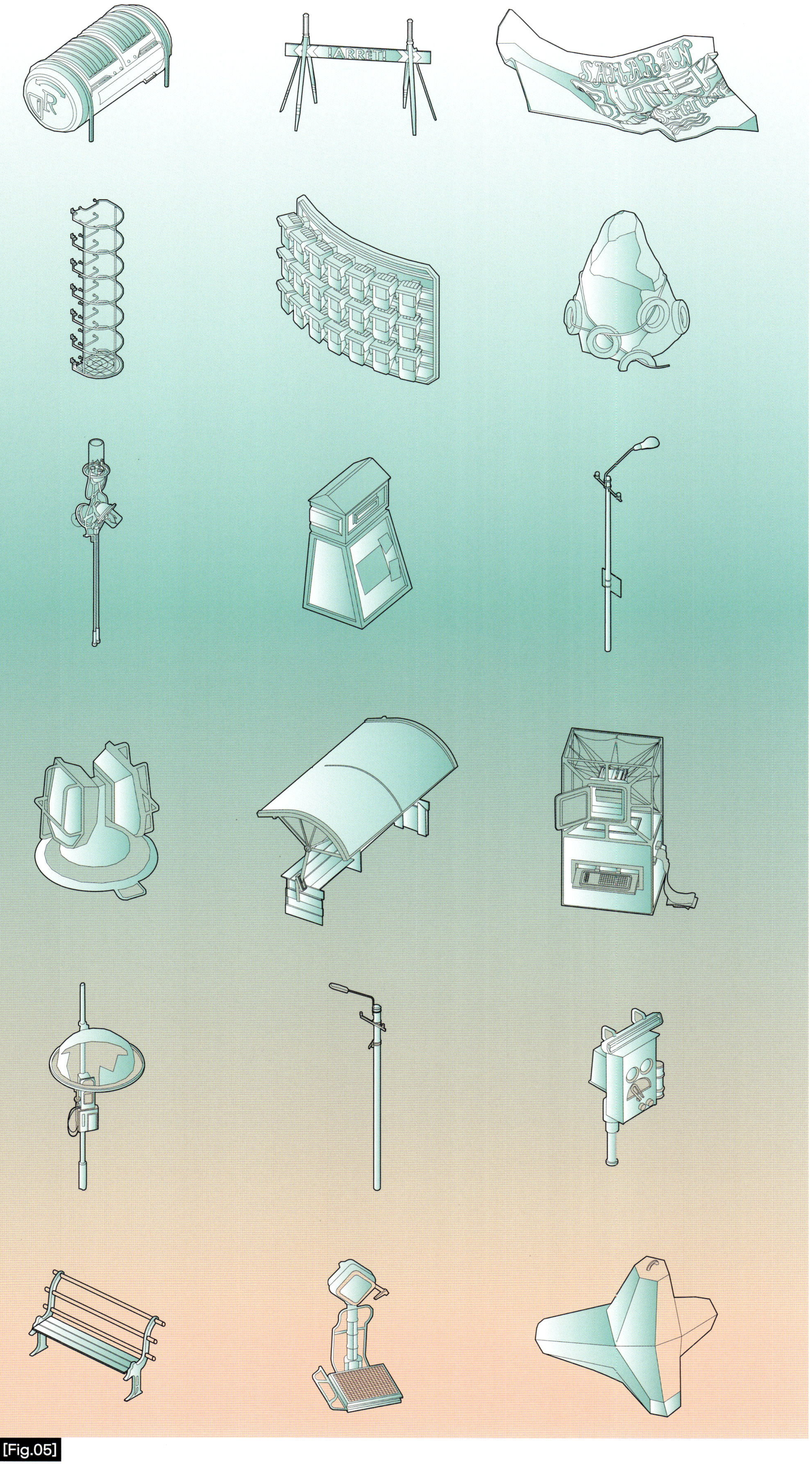

[Fig.05]

Patternation is also a key signifier in the architectural landscape. Many surfaces within the game's architecture are adorned with expressive tiles, wallpaper or paving. By compiling these into tiled 'swatches' we demonstrate how common motifs are repeated throughout the city [Fig.06]. In an interview with *The Face*, Aleksander Rostov explains that because isometric makes large expanses of floor and wall visible, patterns create surfaces that are 'interesting, inviting and full.'[13] Notably the game uses the Hicks' Hexagon pattern featured in Stanley Kubrick's *The Shining*. This pattern has become symbolic of spaces that are not what they seem, tied to horror or the supernatural, lending the world of *Disco Elysium* a dreamy and contingent atmosphere. Pattern also has an inextricable link to history and politics. Reddit users connected Martinaise tile designs to those found in pre-Soviet buildings in their own countries, putting them into the context of political rises and falls.[14] In the 20th century, pattern and ornamentation were often shunned by revolutionary modernist designers. As Annete Tietenberg argues, 'pattern...stood for the uncivilized, the unrestrained and sensuous' contrasting against 'the uniformly grey world of the bourgeois, against the functionalism of the Establishment.'[15] Whirling in Rags symbolizes this nicely. The interior spaces, covered in patterns, are where we first meet Harry and his hedonistic tendencies, in stark comparison to the functional glazed exterior the building presents to the world.

As Rostov explains, Martinaise's design embraces an implicit visual gradient between pattern in urban areas and textural, painterly qualities in open areas.[16] By creating another screenshot matrix we show that this overpainting technique emphasizes two things – firstly, the weathering and battering that Martinaise has taken from both natural and political forces and secondly, the city *as an image* in and of itself [Fig.07]. In the 20th century, many architects used the painterly as a way of expressing space, from the conceptual towers of Russian constructivist architect Ivan Leonidov to the dreamlike watercolours of Italian architect Lauretta Vinciarelli or the energetic geometric landscapes of the Iraqi-British architect Zaha Hadid. Perhaps the architect who most exemplifies this approach is the American designer Lebbeus Woods, whose *Radical Reconstruction* projects used highly textural drawings and an expressive language of forms (such as 'injection', 'scab' or 'scar') to reconstruct cities destroyed by wars or economic forces. Woods describes an approach 'based on the principle of building on the existential remnants of war as a way to transform and transcend violent change' that relies on 'leaving behind the principle of hierarchy and using in its place that of heterarchy.'[17] Overpainting onto Martinaise allows the designers to portray a city that has undergone similar changes, depicting a scarred and lived-in place whose hierarchy is being renegotiated. The viewpoint is still important for this, as the developers explain: 'isometric is where the finer techniques of classical painting can take the lead and pre-rendering the scenery is how we can make the actual painting come alive.'[18]

The isometric depiction of Martinaise places the city in a dual position – co-existing as an expressive and painterly realm, while also employing a viewpoint that allows for the quantifiable analysis of the world. Our three-dimensional reconstruction of Martinaise allows us to explore one of the key questions facing Harry and Kim during their investigation, namely their task to 'determine where the shot came from.' This requires solving the game's central murder through the calculation of bullet trajectories and visiting possible shooting locations. By comparing the in-game isometric viewpoint to our 3D reconstruction we can assess whether the assassin's firing point suggested on the Sea Fortress island is actually viable [Fig.08]. The game proposes it is, through a narrow channel between two buildings on Rue de Saint Ghislaine. Our reconstructed architectural massing, based on the comparative heights of the buildings – even accounting for the holes and gaps of partially collapsed structures – suggests this is impossible. Such reconstructions are inspired by designers like Forensic Architecture, a research group built around a field that 'refers to the production and presentation of spatial evidence within legal, political and cultural contexts.'[19] While Harry relies on his Visual Calculus skills to determine where the shooter could have been located, the isometric viewpoint combined with fixed datums such as the sea level, allow us to reassess these hypotheses.

[Fig.07] PAGE 66
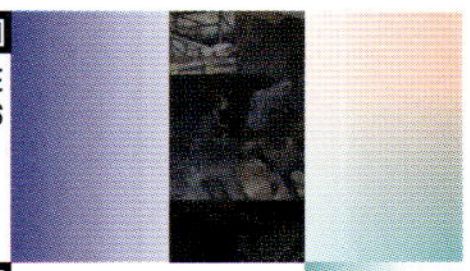
Screenshot composition showing moments of 'painterly architecture' where Aleksander Rostov's overpainting style starts to blend with architectural form.

[Fig.08] PAGE 67
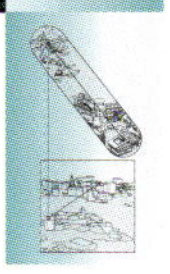
Using a 3D reconstruction of the isometric game world to explore the possibility of the sniper's shot coming from the Sea Fortress island.

STUDIES OF THE PATTERNS FOUND ON VARIOUS SURFACES ACROSS THE TOWN, INCLUDING DESIGNS THAT APPEAR TO REFERENCE SPECIFIC GEOGRAPHIC LOCATIONS AND EVEN OTHER MEDIA SUCH AS FILMS.

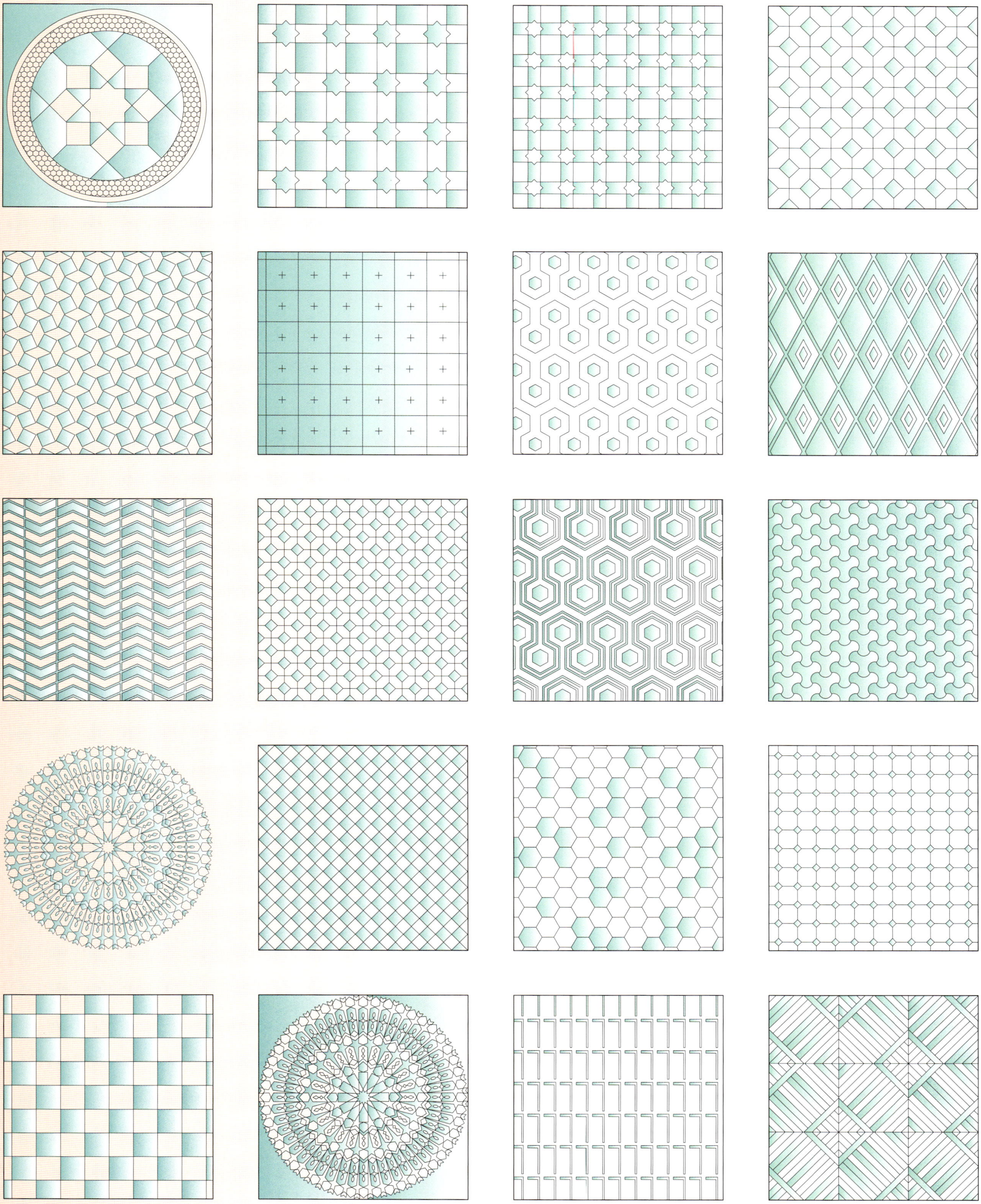

[Fig.06]

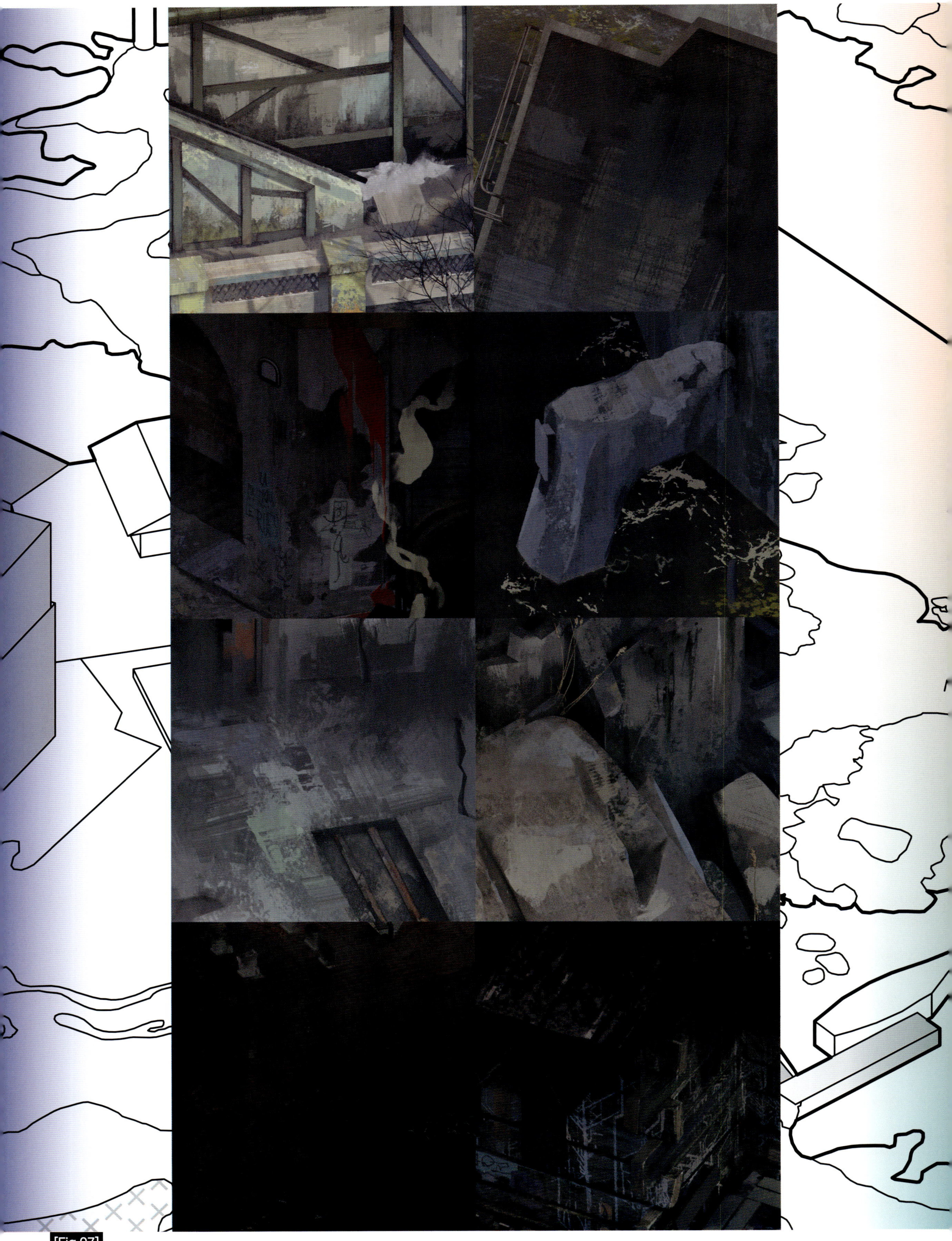

[Fig.07]

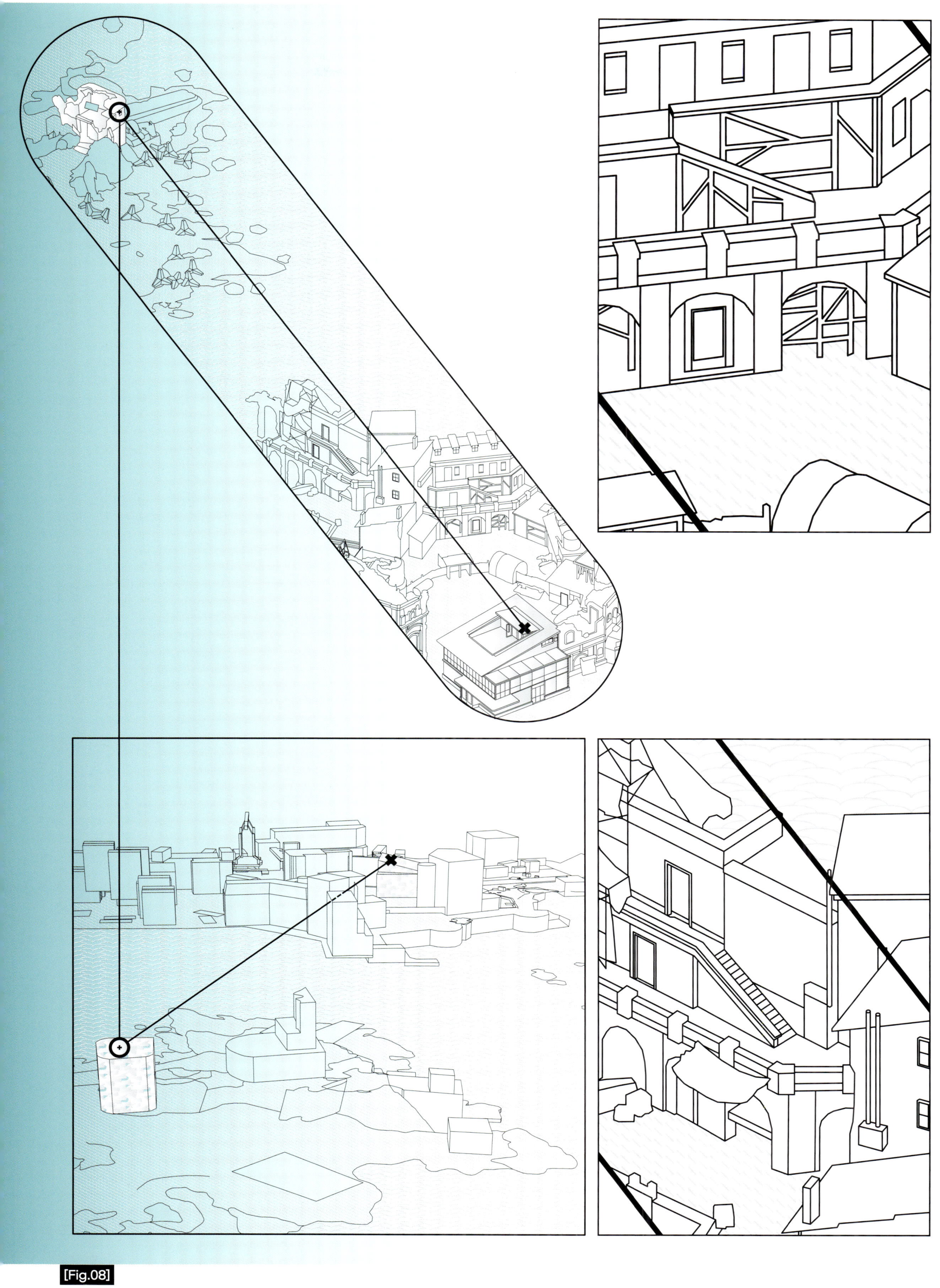

[Fig.08]

We used our reconstruction to evaluate the two other positions that Harry calculates the shot could have come from, the northerly edge of the mainland at Land's End, and under the boardwalk of the Feld R&D Building. In addition, in-game descriptions were analysed to recreate Harry's drunken car crash that leaves his Coupris 40 car embedded in the sea ice in Western Martinaise [Fig.09]. Each of these scenarios is somewhat questionable based on our recreations, requiring the subversion of optics or physics to have taken place. The design of the Whirling in Rags roof terrace questions the viability of *any* of the shooting locations. Likewise, Harry's motor carriage is described as an older and more utilitarian model, yet by reconstructing its journey we see it vaulting through the air like a stunt vehicle. Perhaps the indeterminacy of these mysteries is emblematic of Harry and the game's world itself – we cannot be truly sure what is real and what is in our mind. When Harry receives the book *A Brief Look at Infra-Materialism* we see a passage that describes a similar situation, describing 'the potential for an "extra-physical architecture" that disregards the laws of "bourgeois physics" and instead relies on the revolutionary faith of the people for structural integrity.'

The isometric viewpoint also encourages a detachment between interior and exterior space. Comparing the inside and outside of buildings, using Harry for scale, demonstrates how far some of the spaces diverge from one another [Fig.10]. In some cases, this is clearly the product of an emergent design process – ZA/UM describe how 'half the stuff inside the Capeside Apartments is there simply because Kasparov wanted to make a cool indoor area,'[20] and 'play around with "interesting shapes"', subsequently getting 'carried away with adding rooms.'[21] The interior layout of the apartments is rather more haphazard than the building's exterior suggests. This interior hovers within a black background, the 'poché' thickness of the walls blending with the black background, recalling the 'worm's-eye' axonometric drawings made famous by designers like the British architect James Stirling. Both the Sea Fortress and the Raver's Tent are also substantially larger inside than they appear on their exterior. The largest discrepancy comes in the Dolorian Church, the interior of which appears significantly more grandiose and modern than the exterior timber structure. Of course, many buildings are different between inside and out. For American architect Robert Venturi, 'since the inside is different from the outside, the wall – the point of change – becomes an architectural event' creating 'its drama.'[22] The scale-shifts between inside and out in Martinaise also show the developers using spatial transition as a theatrical device.

Exploring this distinction between external and internal space was predicated on the human scale of the characters, and what feels 'correct' in the context of outdoor or indoor environments. By using the game's (somewhat maligned) Collage mode, we can assemble all the characters from the game within the plaza in front of Whirling in Rags, site of one of the game's key narrative moments [Fig.11]. This reinforces that these characters, through both their physical scale and their stories, are equally responsible for portraying the architectural qualities of the world. Rather than the blank figures or 'render ghosts' that might be found in many architectural visualizations, the characters steer the granular experience of Martinaise. Some characters, such as 'Mega Rich Light-Bending Guy', even erode the distinction between personality and architecture, able to distort Harry's perception of space through sheer wealth.

[Fig.10]
PAGE 70

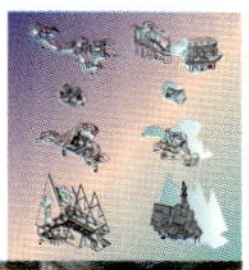

Isometric comparison between the external forms of buildings and their interior spaces, demonstrating how their scale diverges from one another.

[Fig.11]
PAGE 71

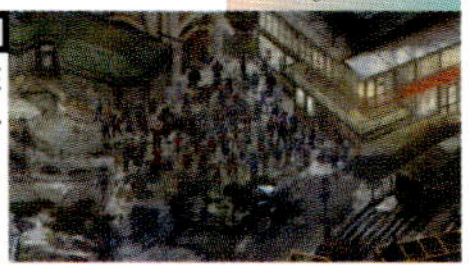

Screenshot composition showing every character in the game gathered outside Whirling in Rags for contextual scale.

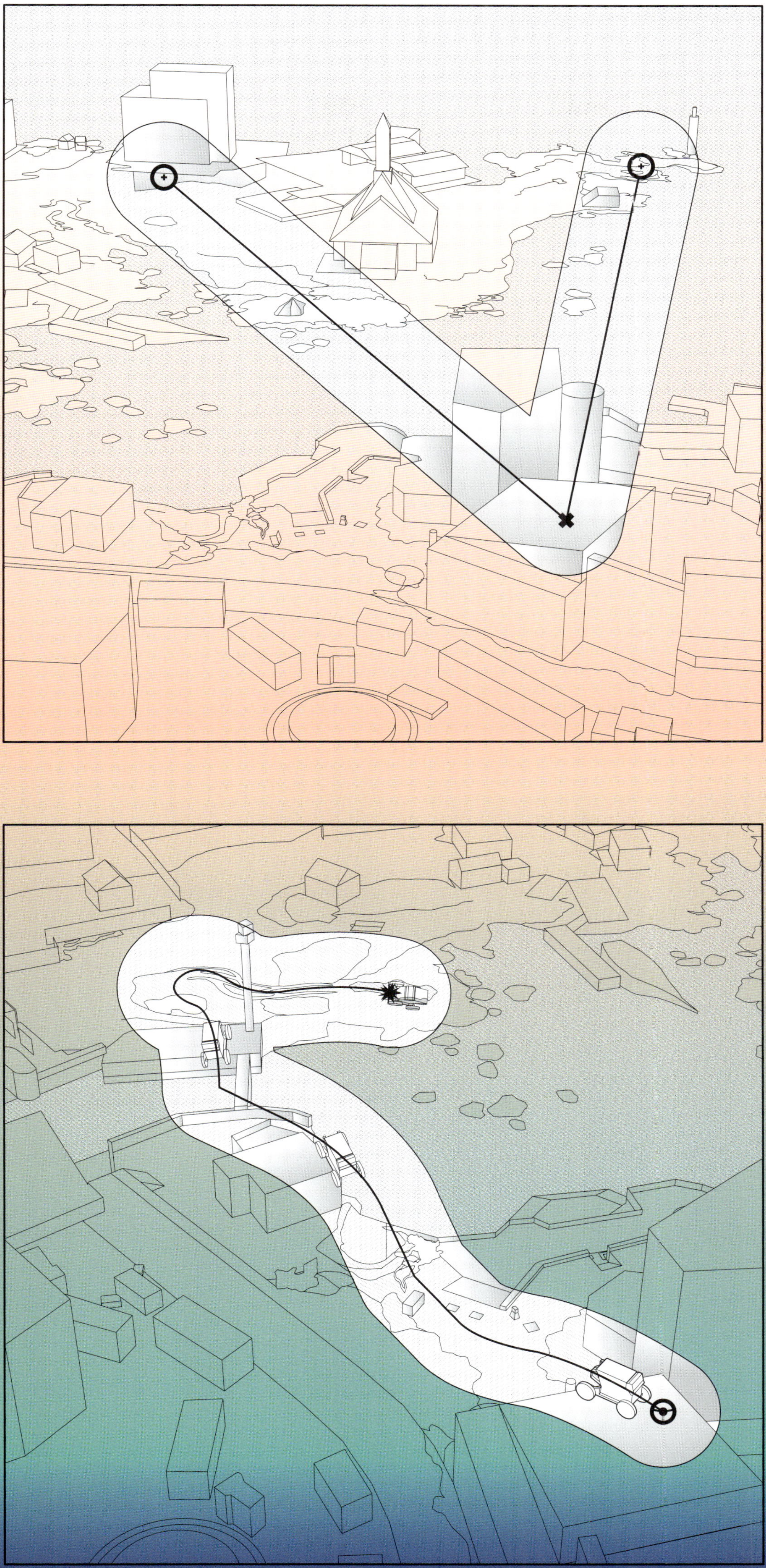

[Fig.09]

THE 3D RECONSTRUCTION USED TO EXAMINE THE TWO FIRST SHOT LOCATIONS AND THE PATH TAKEN DURING HARRY DU BOIS' FATEFUL CAR CRASH.

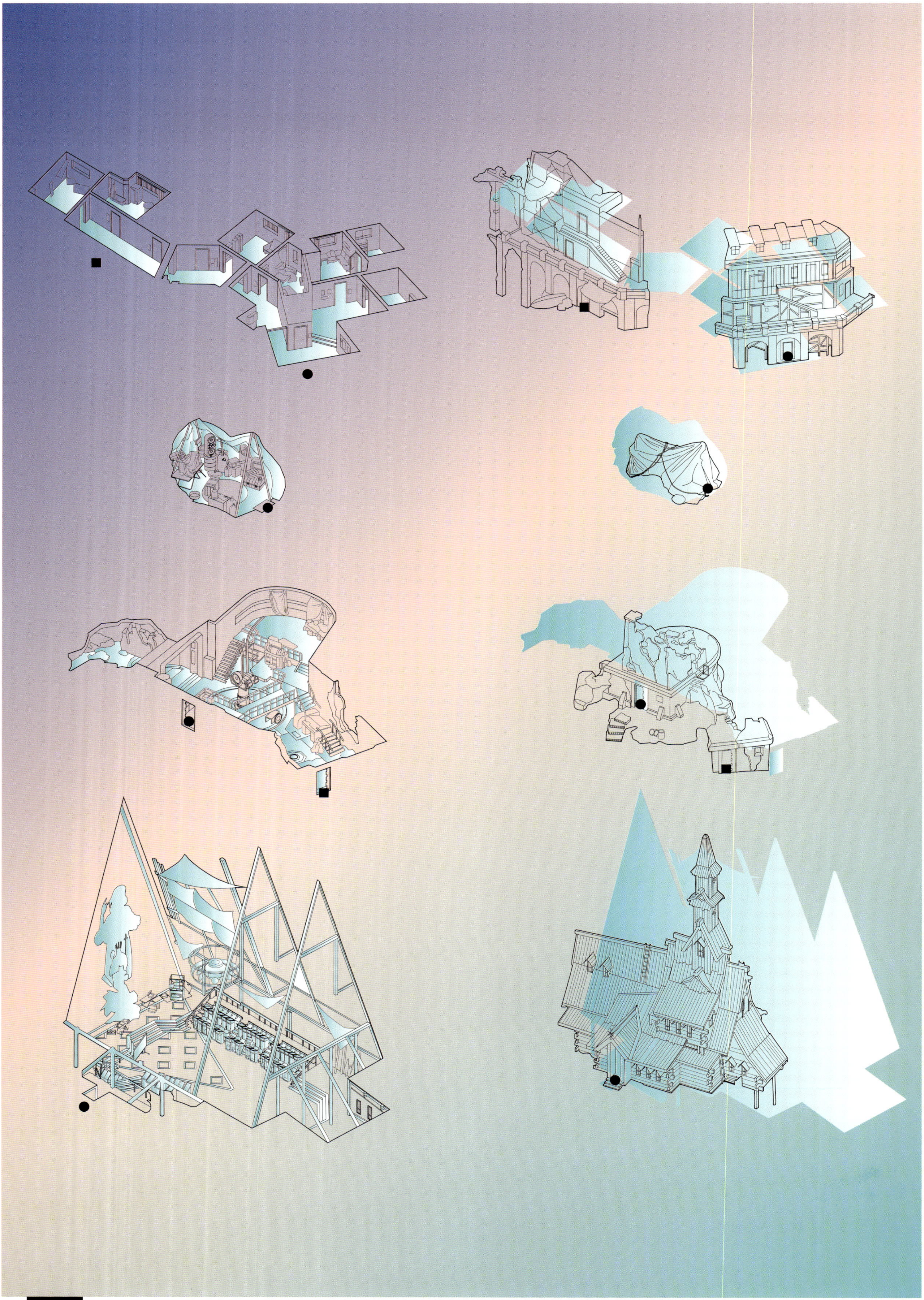

[Fig.10]

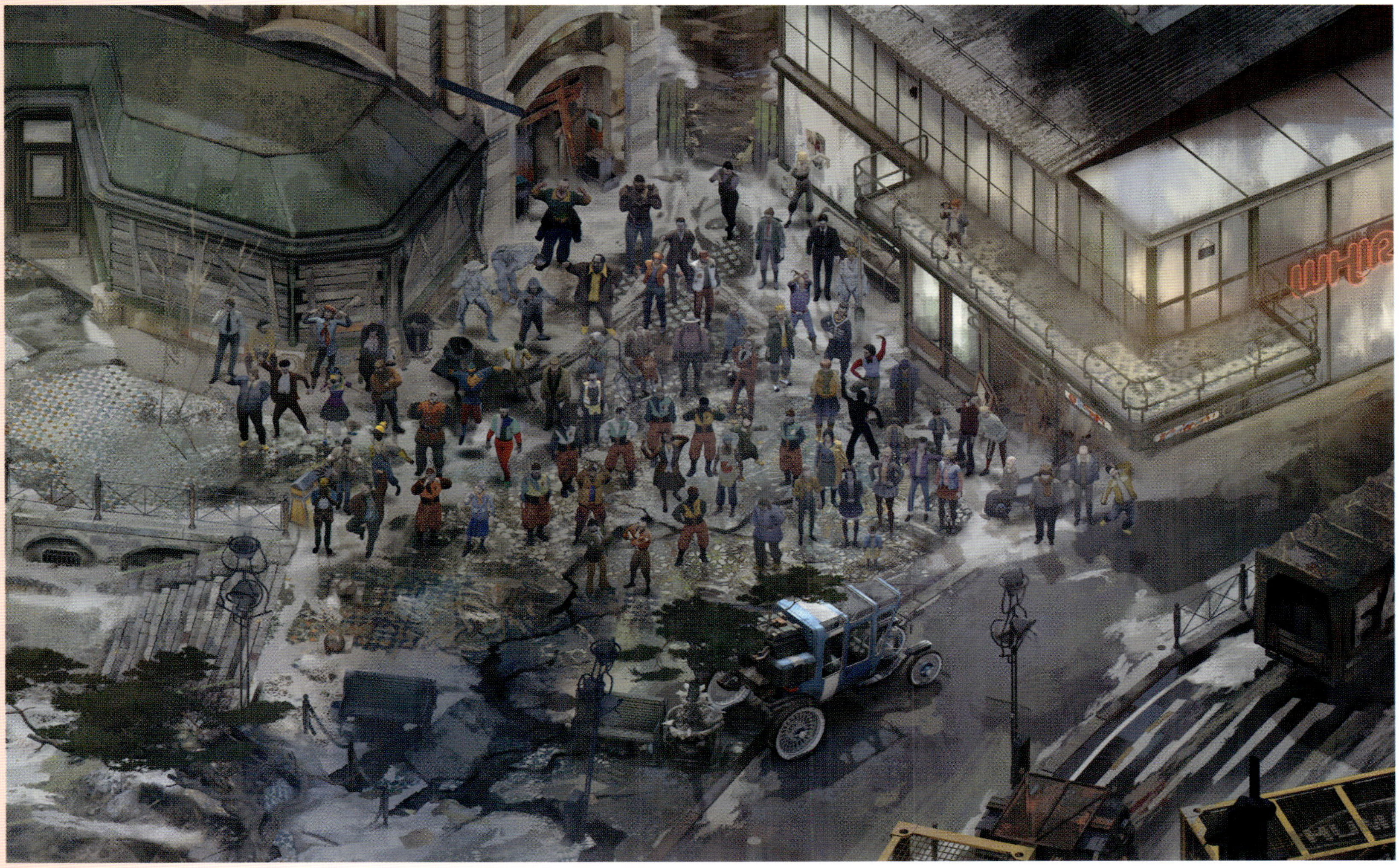

[Fig.11]

These spatial distortions are best exemplified by the late-game dream sequence where Harry meets his former fiancée, Dora Ingerlund, personified as the 'Innocence' Dolores Dei. Falling asleep in the Sea Fortress, Harry awakens and is beckoned to walk out into the ocean. As our mapping of this brief journey shows, a new part of the world appears where Dolores Dei's footsteps in the water guide us to a dream-space that emerges out of the murk [Fig.12]. Once more we experience this idea of 'extra-physical architecture' described in the game, where Harry's delusions take architectural form and are overlaid onto reality.

Disco Elysium pokes fun at architecture, with Harry's Conceptualization skill dismissing it as 'autism', 'box-drawing' and 'masturbation with a ruler.' But as we have seen, ZA/UM have created a poetic and often dreamlike world by exploiting a geometrically and mathematically defined isometric viewpoint connected to the discipline.

By leaning into the conceptual space produced by a specific camera projection, *Disco Elysium* creates an architectural environment that speaks to the complex histories of real-world cities, but also knowingly fits into a lineage of virtual videogame cities. ZA/UM assert that 'isometric isn't nostalgia for us, it is continuity...made with an eye towards [the] history'[23] of gaming. As such, Martinaise is a place that looks backwards, forwards and in on itself at the same time, collapsing multiple readings of the city into the seductive 30-degree angles of an isometric world.

ISOMETRIC MAPPING OF HARRY'S DOLORES DEI DREAM, EXPLORING HOW THE DREAM WORLD CONNECTS TO THE PHYSICAL WORLD ACROSS THE OCEAN.

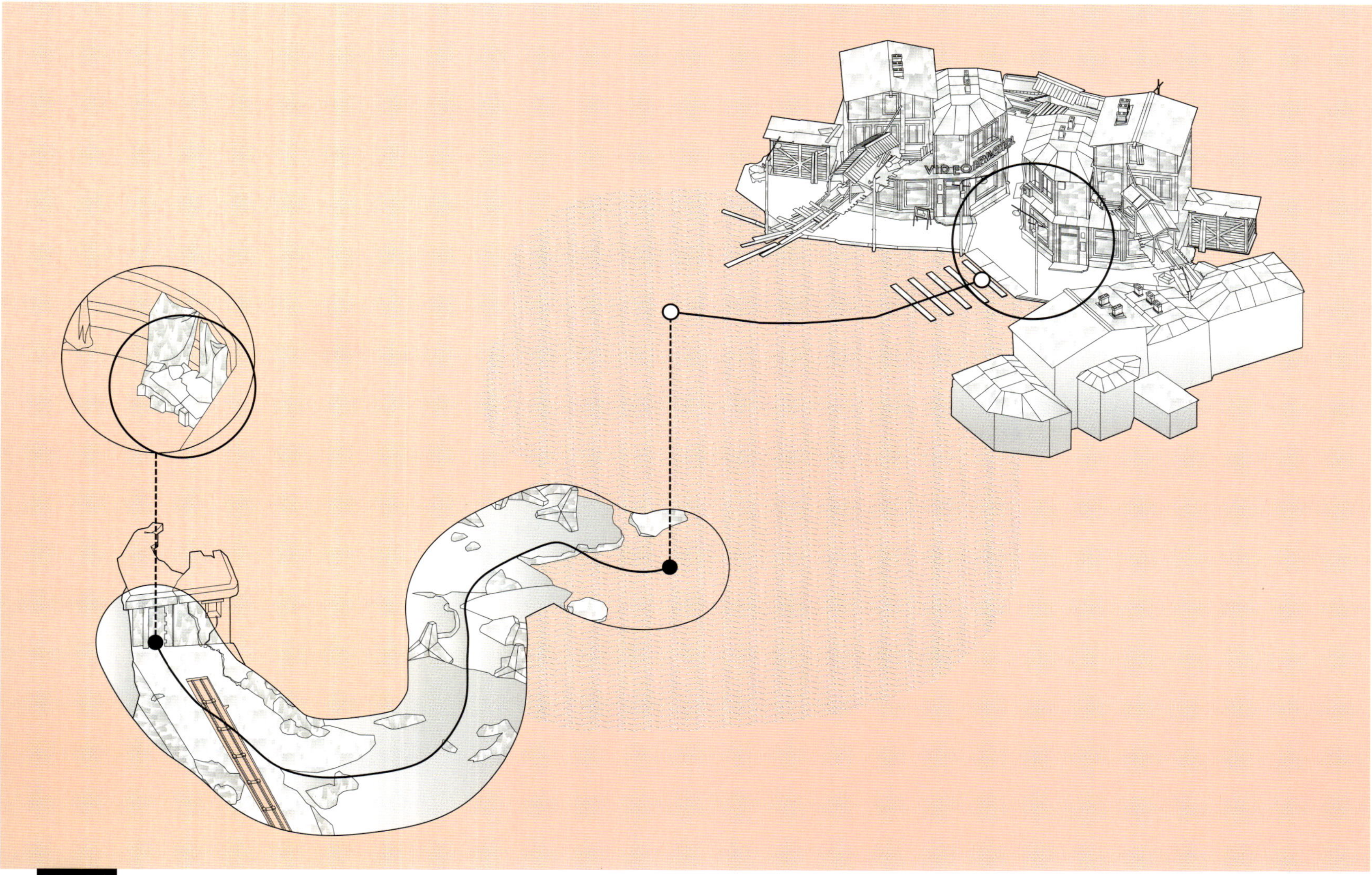

[Fig.12]

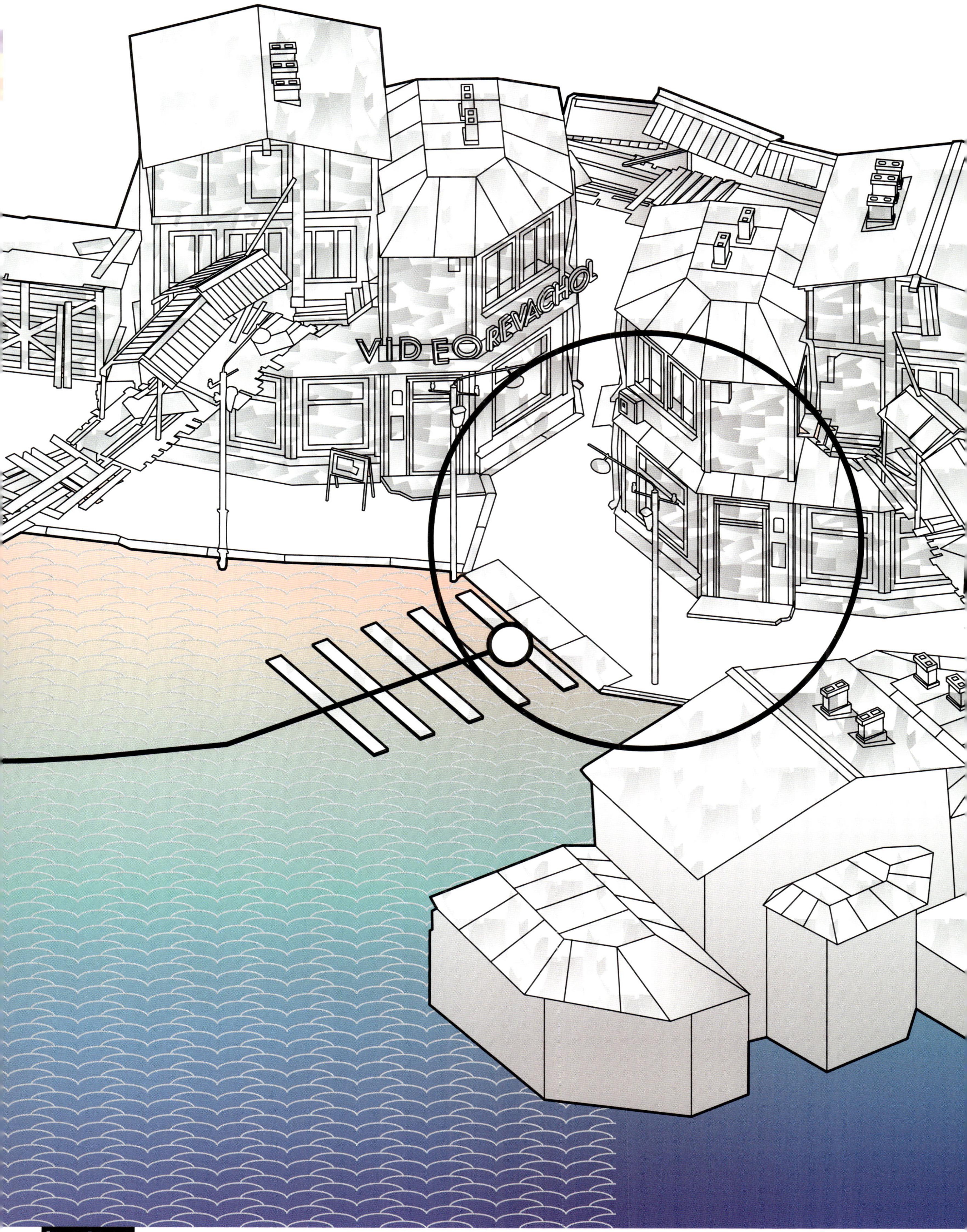

[Fig.12] Detail

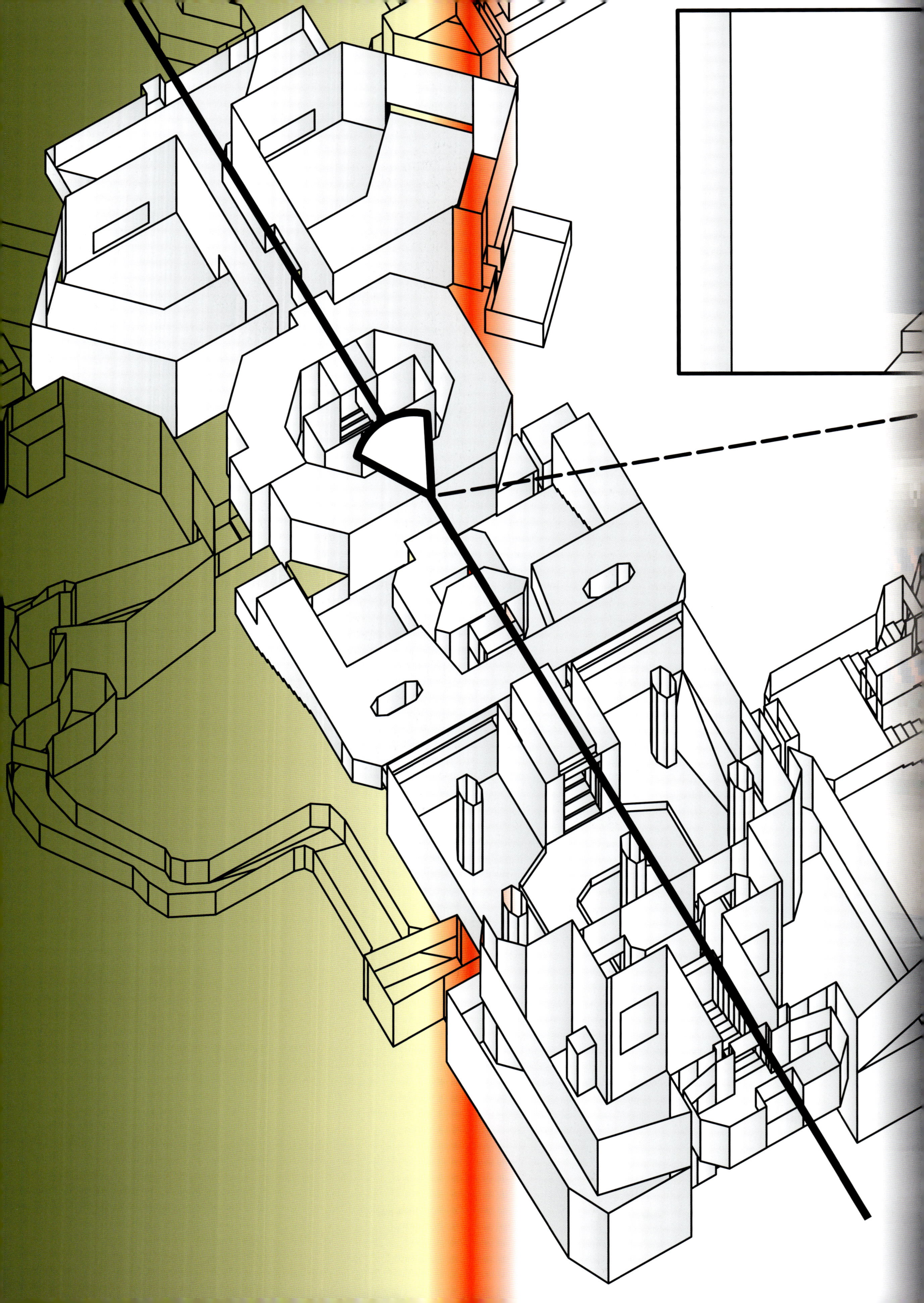

CHAPTER 04

DOOM

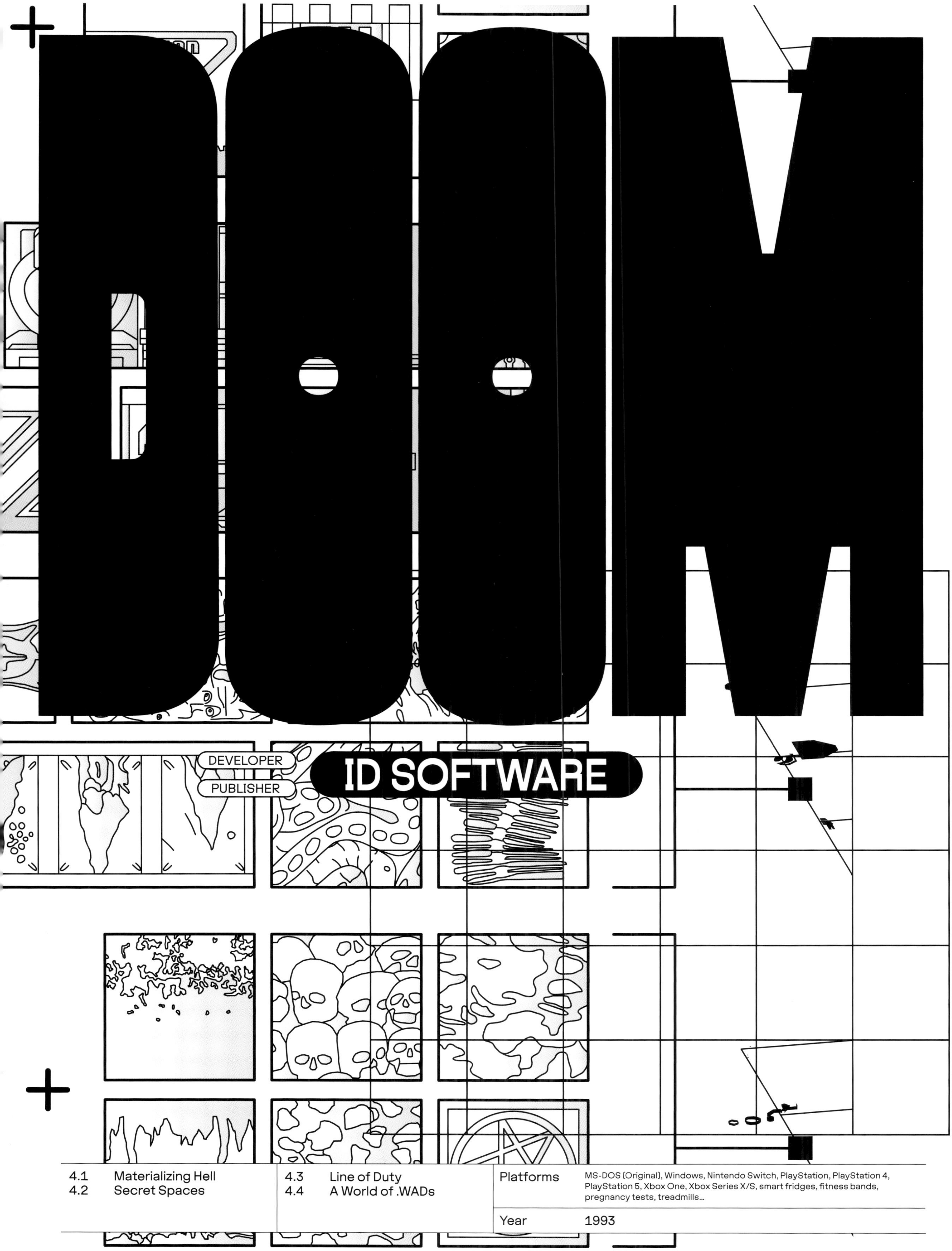

DEVELOPER
PUBLISHER
ID SOFTWARE

Platforms	MS-DOS (Original), Windows, Nintendo Switch, PlayStation, PlayStation 4, PlayStation 5, Xbox One, Xbox Series X/S, smart fridges, fitness bands, pregnancy tests, treadmills...
Year	1993

ISOMETRIC DETAILS SHOWING HOW JOHN ROMERO'S DESIGN RULES SHAPE VARIOUS ASPECTS OF *DOOM*'S LEVELS, FROM THEIR STRATEGIC PLANNING TO SPECIFIC ARCHITECTURAL DETAILS AND JUNCTIONS.

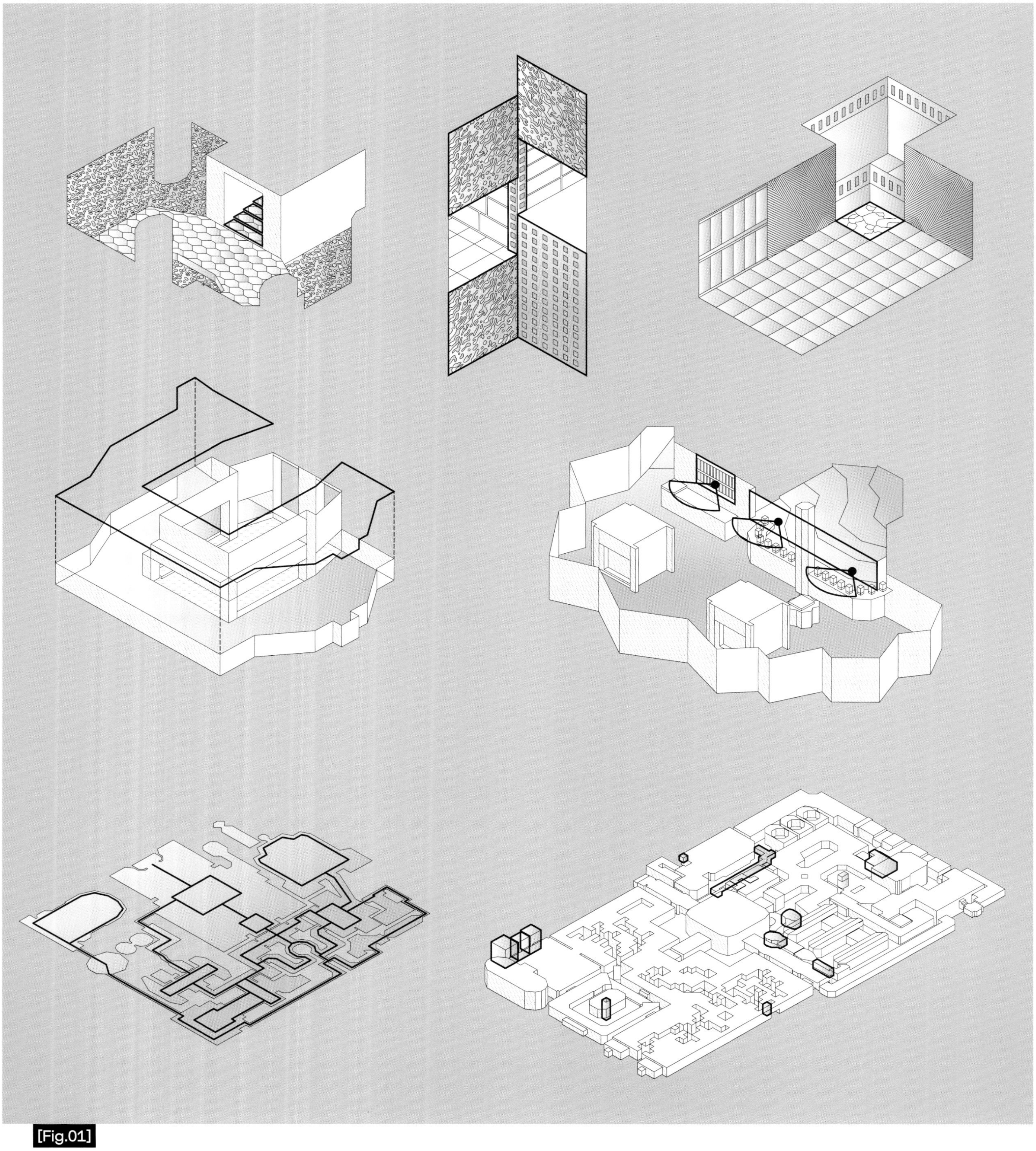

[Fig.01]

4.1

MATERIALIZING HELL

DOOM is undoubtedly the most influential game in this book. It not only defined the modern First-Person Shooter but also established the game engine as a software tool, with new titles built on its technology for decades afterwards. The game's shareware release broke the early '90s internet and made instant stars of its designers. *DOOM* has been blamed for school shootings and became a symbol for the pernicious influence of gaming. The meme 'Will it run *DOOM*?' has seen the game ported to all manner of unlikely devices, including a smart toothbrush and a McDonalds kiosk. Amidst this legacy, it is easy to forget that the game's success rested on two key factors: the speed and feel of the game's traversal and shooting, and the architectural quality of its level design. *DOOM*'s story is simple, with players assuming the role of a soldier (aka 'DOOMguy') who is sent to investigate an incident – the unfortunate opening of portals to Hell – at a corporate facility on Phobos, one of the moons of Mars. Everyone else is dead and he must venture into the facility alone, ultimately journeying into Hell itself. The game's world supports this minimalist story through intimidation, fiendish layouts and inventive designs promoting high-speed gameplay rather than a slower, narrative-driven exploration of space.

DOOM's world was initially guided by two main principles – John Carmack's id Tech 1 engine and the level design philosophy of John Romero. While the engine would revolutionize 3D gaming, establishing id as perennial innovators, Romero's ideas produced iconic spatial designs. Speaking in 2003, Romero details his design guidelines like 'always changing floor height when I wanted to change floor textures'; the 'conscious use of contrast everywhere in a level between light and dark areas'; emphasizing 'cramped and open areas'; the repeated use of both recognizable landmarks and secret spaces and 'making my levels flow so the player will revisit areas' to aid in understanding the space.[1]

We interviewed John Romero to gain further insight into the process behind *DOOM*'s level design. As he explains, the creation of rules was important because id was 'in a design space with the new technology that we'd never been in before.'[2] Studying books on military building construction and replicating its real-world scale made early versions of *DOOM* 'really horrible' and 'no fun,'[3] so the team abandoned this approach and developed their own design style that emphasized the possibilities of the engine. This meant exploring, as Romero says, 'what will that data let me do visually? What can I do with this data that's interesting?', producing new architectural approaches where 'it's slightly believable to be military, but is more geared towards fun gameplay.'[4] Interviewed in Devs Play, Romero notes how often the 'classic horseshoe' is used in the first map of every id Software game where space is 'a U, so you're not in a straight line and boring,' with the design employed regularly: 'map one in *Doom II* is like that, *Heretic* is just like that, *Quake* is just like that.'[5] There is a signature to id's spatial design, and by finding and mapping examples of these rules appearing in the context of *DOOM*'s levels, we frame these as architectural typologies applied consistently across the game [Fig.01].

DOOM's different level designers brought specific idiosyncrasies to their designs, aided by the geometric possibilities the game afforded. *DOOM*, as Romero puts it, 'brought people out of the 90-degree world of any game that was in 3D'[6] that preceded it, allowing for new shapes and angles. While Romero authored the E1 levels, E2 and E3 were finished by Sandy Petersen, whose environments were considered more 'cerebral and strategic' yet architecturally 'not nearly as pleasing as Romero's' and even 'downright ugly'.[7] From these first maps, to the eclectic architectural styles of *The Ultimate DOOM*'s E4 and through to the countless community-made maps, what remains consistent is the playful relationship between the architectural plan and the space experienced by the player. As architectural theorist Robin Evans argues 'if anything is described by an architectural plan, it is the nature of human relationships, since the elements whose trace it records...are employed first to divide and then selectively to reunite inhabited space.'[8] By making axonometric drawings of several *DOOM* levels, we reveal how the designers intentionally confuse players and hide symbolic meanings within the plans of levels for them to discover [Fig.02].

[Fig.02] PAGES 78–9
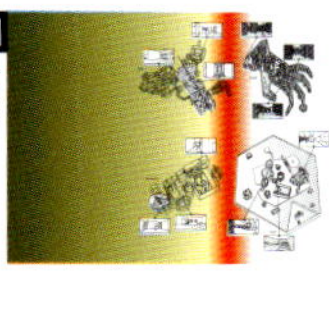

Axonometric studies of four maps that establish a playful relationship between the symbolic qualities of the plan and the player's experience on the ground.

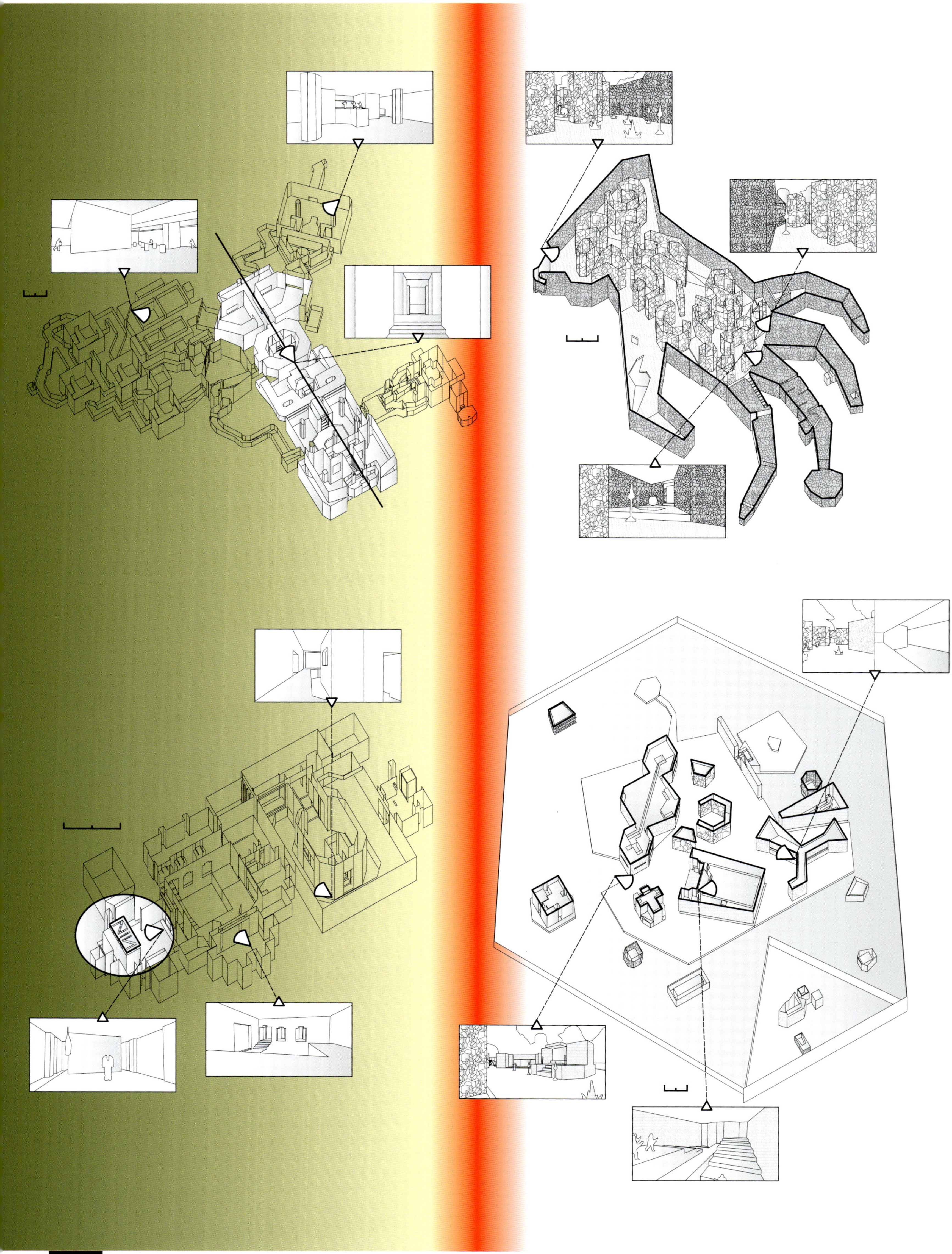

[Fig.02]

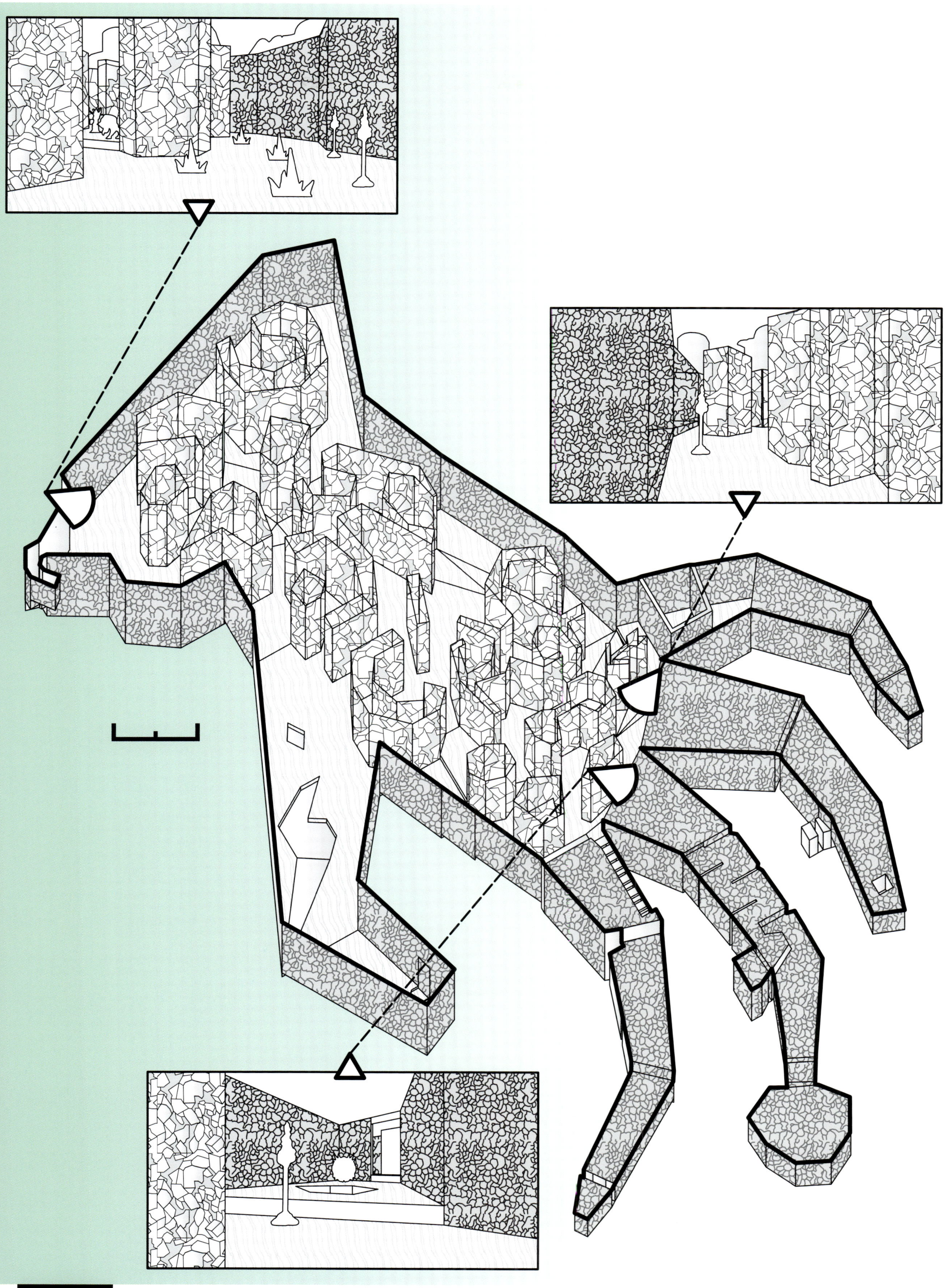

[Fig.02] Detail

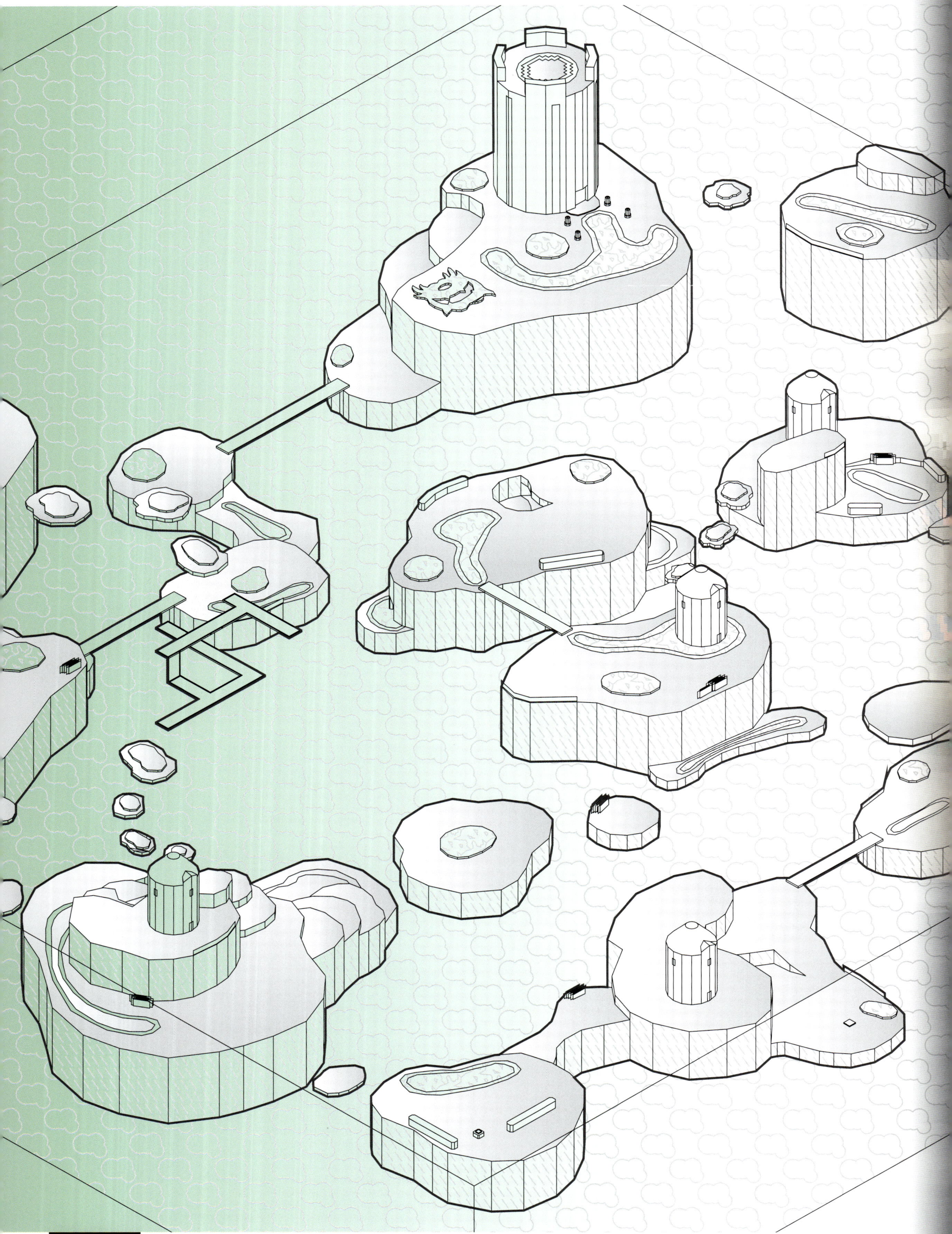

[Fig.12] Detail

Romero describes how 'if the player opens their automap, for example, they're going to see something very suggestive,'[9] requiring further exploration to completely uncover. In Central Processing (E1M6), the map is built around a symmetrical central 'spine' which quickly devolves into asymmetrical floorplans on either side, providing a challenging layout for the player. Slough of Despair (E3M2), presents a semi-natural landscape of rocky caves, but is shaped like a giant hand in plan, as if the player is walking across its palm. Mt. Erebus (E3M6) is an open level with various buildings and geometries scattered across a blank island. Finally, in Hell Beneath (E4M1), the logo of the band Nine Inch Nails is embedded into a room, reflecting the developer's musical tastes. *DOOM*'s playful relationship between plan and space echoes fascinations of architects and designers throughout history. American architect Stanley Tigerman's Daisy House (1976) embraced a similar controversial spirit to Romero's designs through a floorplan that resembles male genitalia. Petersen's scattering of objects in Mt. Erebus is resemblant to the types of floorplans seen in the work of the Japanese architects Kazuyo Sejima or Junya Ishigami. The sudden transitions between architectural styles defined by Romero's rules echo the approaches of American architect Andrew Kovac's Floor Plans project which are 'a set of new plans made from old plans.'[10]

The limitations of *DOOM*'s geometric possibilities means that the architecture of the game's levels is particularly defined by their materials. *DOOM* uses a total of 346 different material tiles that are projected and repeated over the geometry like a wallpaper. Romero and the level designers would request materials from the artists, whether that was 'the 'Star Wars' lived-in universe look' of military bases or 'guys hanging from the ceiling...guys cut in half'[11] for Hell. Materials communicate DOOMguy's voyage from the human world to Hell itself. By exporting the game's levels to 3D modelling software, we analyse how material usage changes over the course of this journey. Sorting these materials into architectural classifications and scaling the levels to the 'real world' approximations defined by the *DOOM* wiki[12] allows us to examine the amount and composition of each material. By separating each material into a different layer of an isometric drawing, material trends become clearly defined [Fig.03]. Concrete finishes, processed stone materials and unrefined rock account for nearly half of all the materials used in *DOOM*'s world, appearing throughout the game. Other materials appear more sporadically or frame specific moments of progress. 'Demonic' materials and lava barely appear in E1 but become key parts of the material language in E2 and E3. Similarly, what we classify as 'fleshy' materials, such as orifice-like doorways, walls of torn skin (from photos of a knee wound) and clumped-together faces, barely appear before E3, but subsequently signify that the player has entered the realms of Hell. While the fleshy material represents a mere 2.7% of the total used, it is often applied in smaller-scale spaces, generating uneasy, grotesque environments. Approximately 1% of the material landscape comprises what we term 'ornaments', such as satanic wall carvings, gargoyle heads and 'decorations' like strung-up corpses. While many materials were drawn from stock image CDs, including sky textures – taken from photos of various landscapes including Guilin in China[13] – the gargoyles of *DOOM* are sourced from the photographic book *Nightmares in the Sky: Gargoyles and Grotesques*[14], which details building elements from across America. 'Computer' materials were developed from scans of circuit boards.[15] id's material depiction of Mars and Hell draws from a broad set of locations, appropriately making it a place-between-places, where we can make out fleeting resemblances to reality amongst the blood and gore.

[Fig.03] PAGE 82

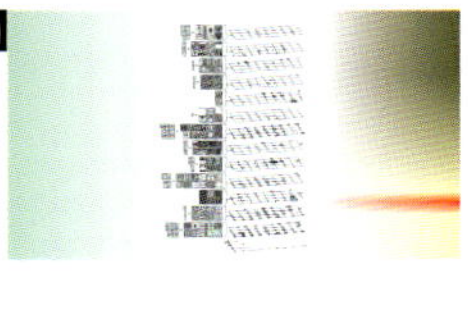

Analysis of the architectural materials used across *DOOM*'s four episodes, showing how the materiality changes over the course of the game and where certain materials are emphasized.

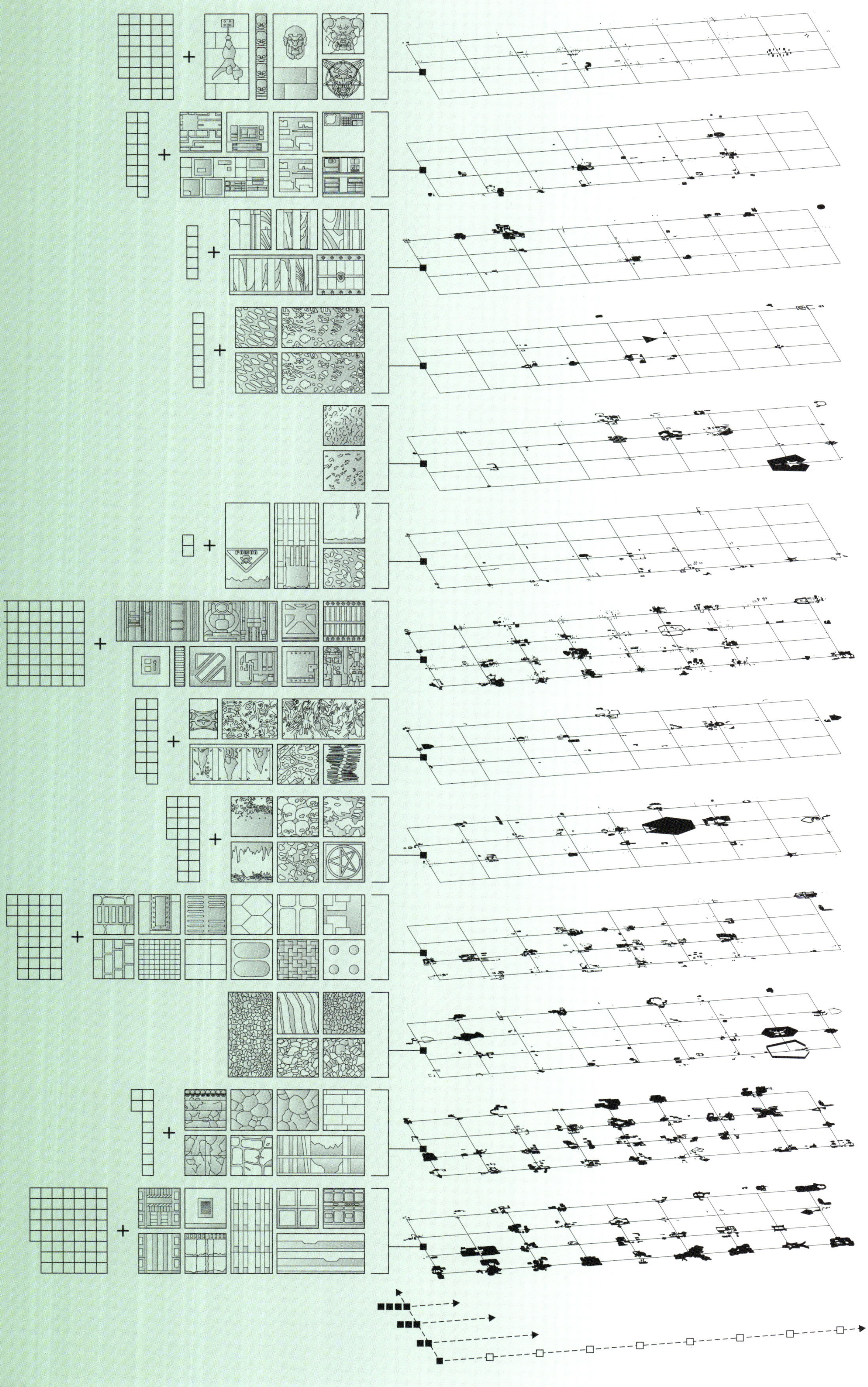

[Fig.03]

4.2
SECRET SPACES

Romero advises at least four secret spaces per level, working with the rule that 'everything you see, you can get'[16] and this is borne out by the prevalence of hidden chambers, moving walls and mysterious switches across *DOOM's* maps. In total there are 165 secret areas found in *DOOM*'s four episodes and thirty-six maps (including *The Ultimate DOOM*). Following Romero's argument that the start of the game should draw the player in through its architecture, we analysed the Hangar (E1M1) map – which contains three secret spaces – to gain an understanding of the design tactics used in the early stages of the game [Fig.04]. These hidden areas each use different methods to reveal themselves to players. The first unlockable space is found after moving through a room with a zigzag walkway, marked by a discolouration of the wall material, which hides a secret door. In the zigzag room, players will notice an imp standing at an inaccessible level. As players reach the end of the level, the platform containing the imp will drop down, revealing a new space, while leaving a shadow in the shape of the room's original form. To access the final secret, players must retreat further, behind a line of shadow that cuts across the room, before sprinting to an elevator that has dropped in the space previously revealed behind the imp. Moving through a corridor, picking up items, players arrive at a one-way textured hole, which is open when looking from the secret space but appears as a concrete edifice from the main area. As our drawing shows, even in this early stage of the game, *DOOM* creates complex architectural games, where players must hold back, retrace their steps and peer carefully into the darkness to uncover the full complexity of the environment. By taking screenshots, we also build a record of how these tactics are applied repeatedly across the game's levels – an invisible wall here or an out-of-place material there, where 'because people pattern match, just by nature, they might notice the pattern has changed on that wall'[17] [Fig.05].

The design of secret spaces does encounter limitations in *DOOM's* technology – it is impossible to have one space on top of another. Each space is defined by a floor and ceiling height, and in the base version of the game this cannot be broken. To demonstrate how this shapes the internal landscape of a level, we took ten cross-sections through the level Deimos Lab (E2M4) and placed these together to show a slice-by-slice reading of the space [Fig.06]. Although the level is complex in plan, it is volumetrically simple when cut through. Even where the shape of the level is complicated, it remains one-storey in height. This is despite Romero's design rules *prioritizing level changes*, so he employed tricks like 'making bridges by having a gap that was 64 units'[18] where the player could pass across, effectively rendering a *DOOM* level more like an internalized landscape than how we would see a multistorey building in section. But this design approach still resonates with ideas from architecture and the cross-sectional view of space, particularly the notion of *raumplan*, a theory developed by the Austrian architect Adolf Loos. Raumplan was an organizational approach that emphasized small and numerous level changes, a 'differentiated play with leaps of level' producing 'more complex spatial structures and a multitude of new perspectives between individual rooms.'[19] Without the ability to create multi-levelled structures, Romero's approach echoes that of Loos, by using elevational changes and playing with scale to draw the player through space – methods similar to those employed in the house designs of architect Frank Lloyd Wright or the strange undulating interior landscapes of Japanese/American architect duo Shusaku Arakawa and Madeline Gins.

[Fig.04] PAGE 84

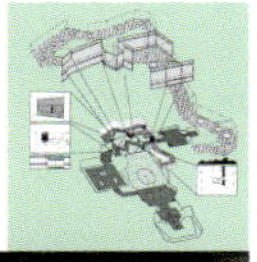

A study of the secret spaces in the Hangar (E1M1) level, indicating the architectural hints that are offered and the moves that players need to enact to reveal the secrets.

[Fig.05] PAGE 84

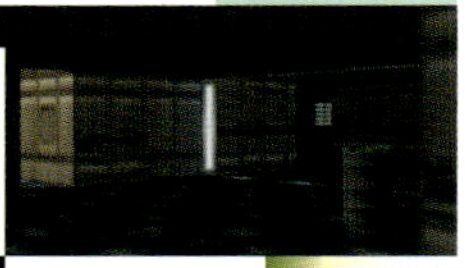

A view through the level Nuclear Plant (E1M2), showing an example of how subtle material changes are used to communicate the presence of secret doors to players.

[Fig.06] PAGE 85

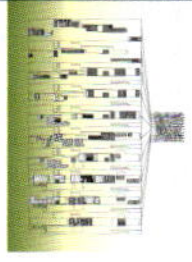

Cross-sections cut through Deimos Lab (E2M4) demonstrating how the space remains strictly one-storey despite its complicated layout, due to the engine not accommodating stacked spaces.

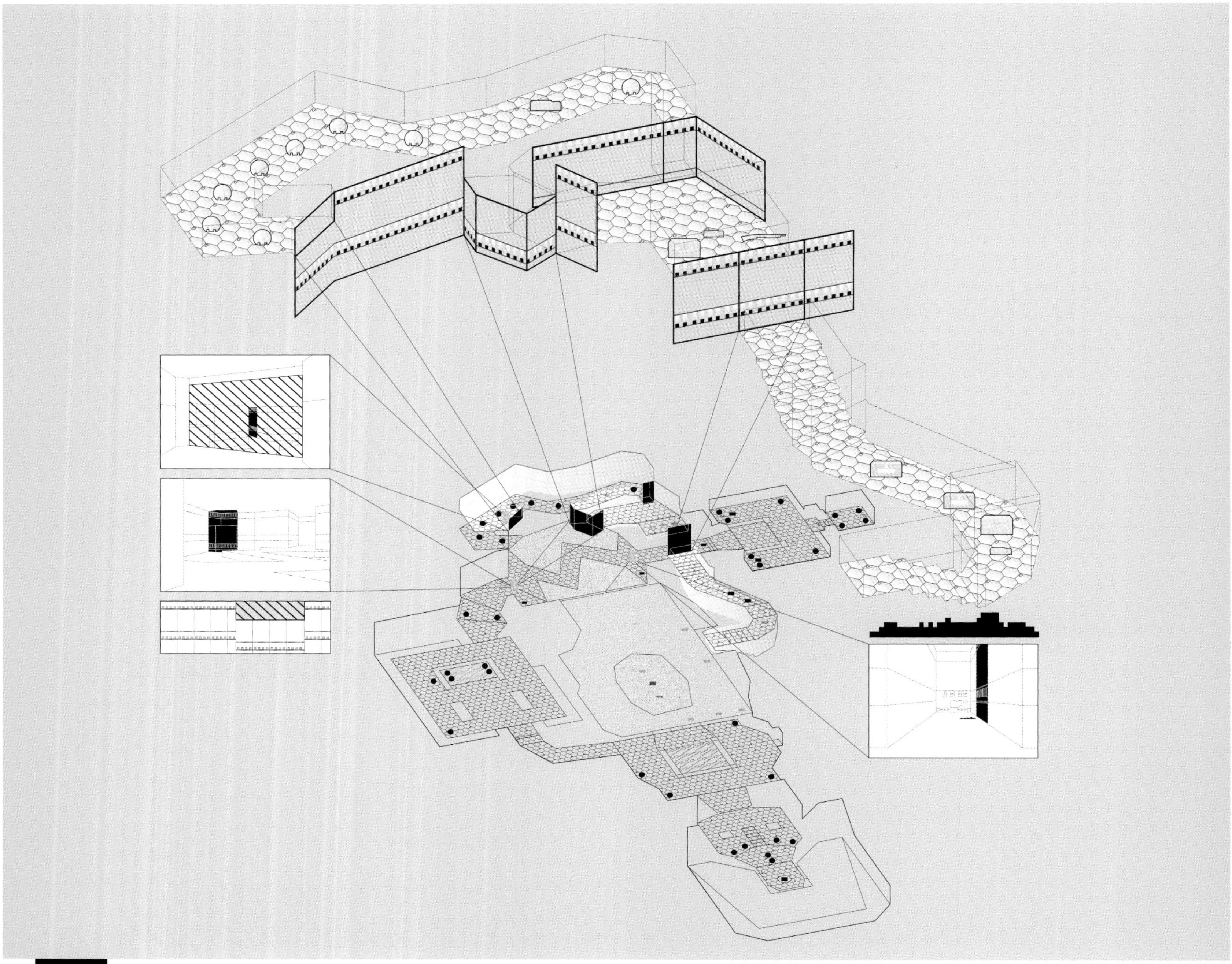

[Fig.04]

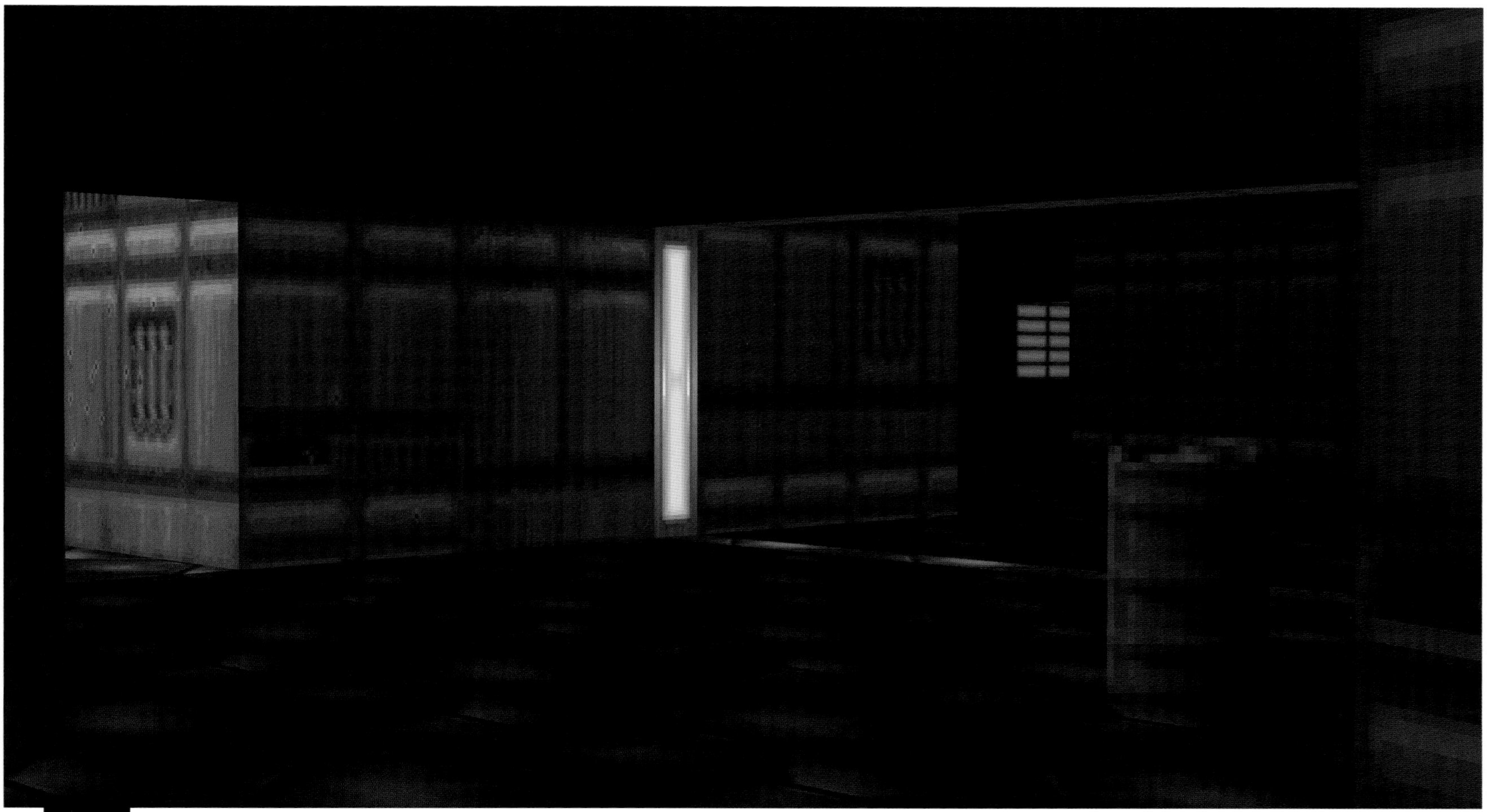

[Fig.05]

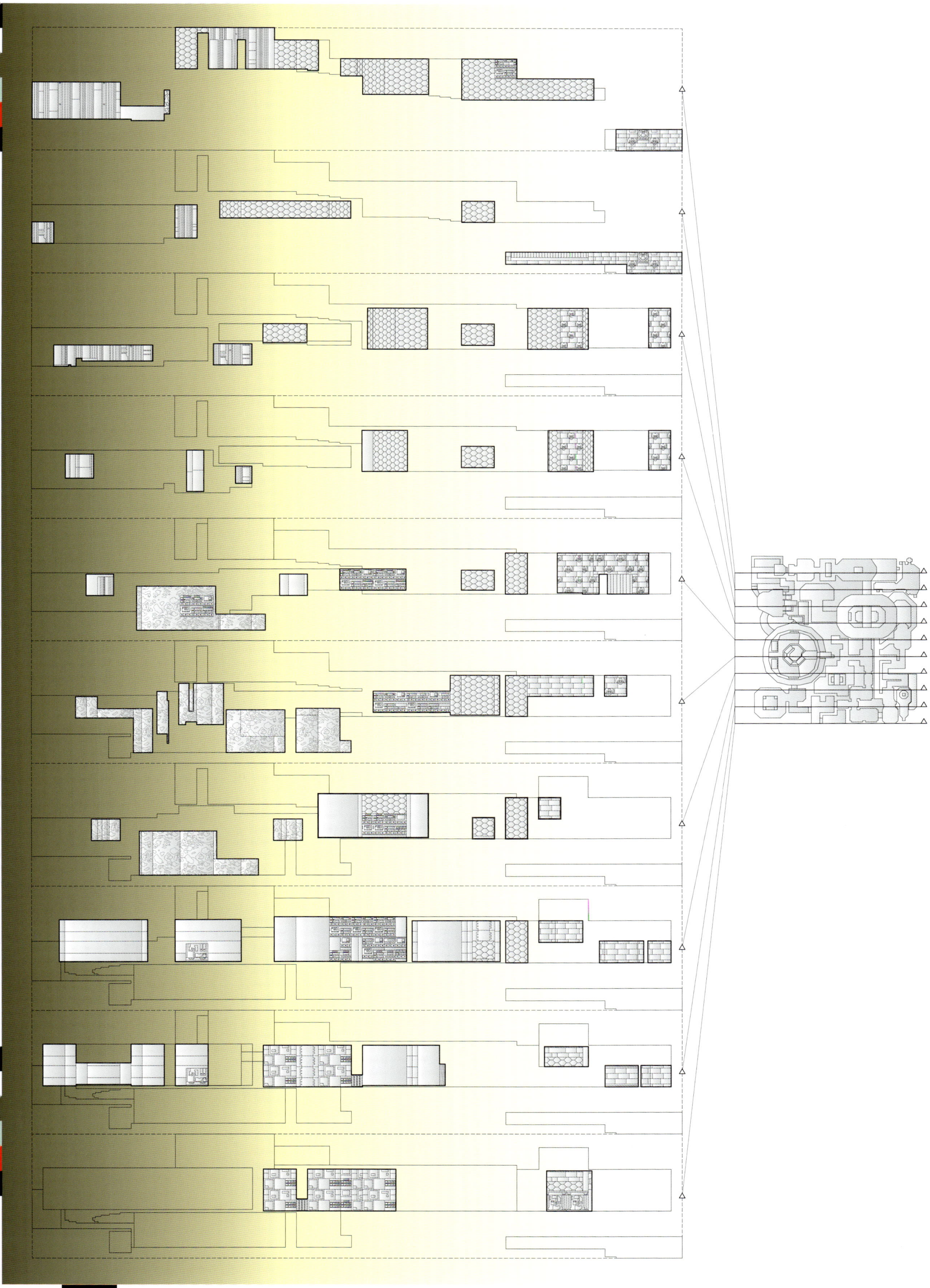

[Fig.06]

4.3

LINE OF DUTY

When creating a *DOOM* level using community level design software like *Ultimate DOOM Builder*, it is hard to miss the resemblance to architectural design. The game's worlds are built like an architectural drawing, through the composing of lines – called *linedefs* – that combine together into *sectors* – the surfaces that the player can navigate. While in architectural CAD programmes different line styles denote a range of symbolic meanings, in *DOOM* the linedef can be assigned different *behaviours*. Lines are not only geometric notations that can then be given *sidedef* materials to become a wall, they can also assume other functions such as becoming triggers or secret exits. To demonstrate the varying utility of linedefs within a *DOOM* level, we mapped Command Center (E2M5), visualizing the relationship between lines that denote architectural features such as room boundaries or level changes and those linedefs that contain interactive logic [Fig.07]. As can be seen through the drawing, there is a complicated network of relationships overlaid onto the geometric form of the level, yet shaped by the same system of lines. This system emerged organically during *DOOM*'s development because Romero was building the level design tools at the same time as the levels themselves. As John explains, 'if I had an idea for something, like it'd be really cool if these stairs came out of the ground,' he added the functionality himself, meaning 'I'm doing the tool, the engine programming and the level design all at the same time and creating brand new functionality.'[20]

The sectors defined by linedefs can similarly be assigned functions, and other properties such as brightness levels. This means that they can be used to literally draw light into a space and suggest the fall of shadows, allowing designers to apply Romero's fourth rule – the emphasis on providing contrast. By altering *DOOM*'s camera, allowing us to take close-up screenshots, we identify moments where different linedef and sector types converge, showing how the system defines both the 'concrete' and atmospheric aspects of the world's design. A detail from a junction in the map Computer Station (E1M7) shows a border of light and shadow meeting the recessed frame of a door, operated by means of an action 'DR Door (Yellow) Open Wait Close,' all of which are controlled by linedefs [Fig.08]. As architectural theorist Catherine Ingraham argues, 'in architecture the line is never acting purely geometrically'[21] – it always carries other meanings. In this tiny detail we can see how *DOOM*'s system of lines regulates not only architectural geometry, but also atmosphere and user agency.

The effects of linedefs run from simple and repeatable interactions, such as opening a door, through to semi-automated and game state-specific actions. The original *DOOM* provided around 100 different linedef types, which have subsequently been extended through new versions of the engine made by the community using the original *DOOM* source code. Alongside the basic linedef types, there are many 'special' and more unusual types of behaviour that produce specific spatial effects, developed alongside the level design process, as documented by the YouTuber decino.[22] By drawing a series of these linedef typologies, we show not only how their spatial logic operates, but also how this is communicated through the 2D plans in the editor and extrapolated into a three-dimensional environment [Fig.09]. In the case of the semi-automated 'stair builder,' the orientation of linedef faces must be precise to produce a staircase rising out of the ground, step-by-step. As previously discussed in relation to the cross-sectional appearance of *DOOM*'s levels – these are not 'new' steps as such, instead the level of the *floor itself* within that sector is being raised. State-specific actions can be used to affect the world, such as when defeating a particular monster sends a message to every object with the (thematically appropriate) tag of 666, causing them to disappear into the floor.

[Fig.09]
PAGE 88

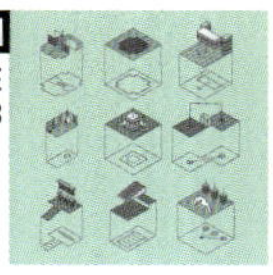

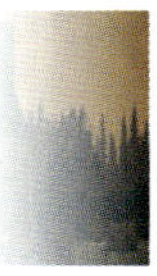

Isometric drawing of special linedef types, ranging from simple doors to automatic 'stair builders', texture scrollers, teleporters and triggers that activate every 'sector' possessing the demonic tag 666.

[Fig.07] A PLAN OF THE COMMAND CENTER (E2M5) LEVEL REVEALING THE 'LINEDEFS' USED TO CONTAIN THE LOGIC FOR THE GAME'S SYSTEMS AND SECRETS, ALONGSIDE THOSE WHICH SHAPE ITS ARCHITECTURAL GEOMETRY.

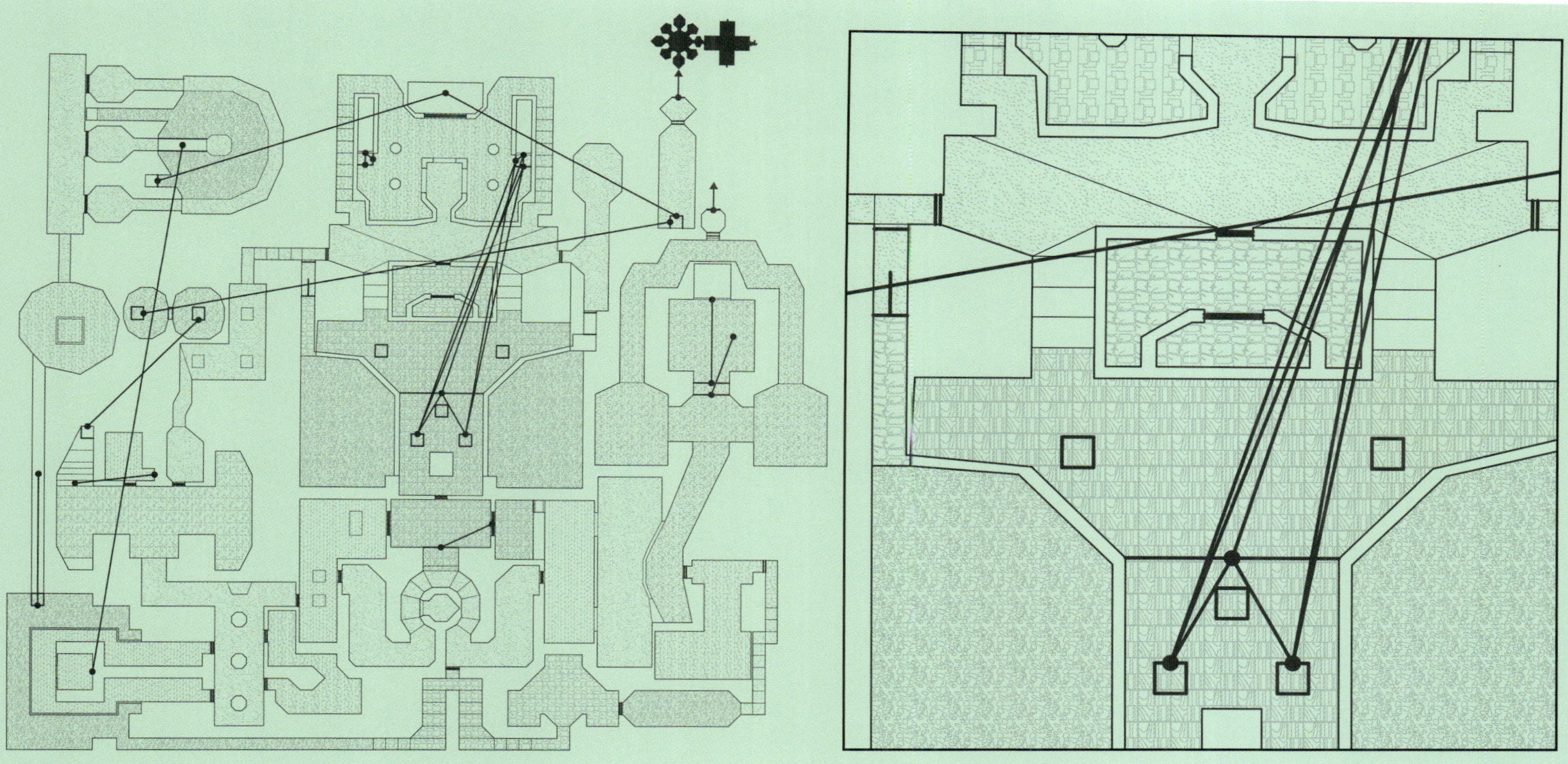

[Fig.07]

[Fig.08] A CLOSE-UP VIEW OF AN ARCHITECTURAL JUNCTION IN THE MAP COMPUTER STATION (E1M7) SHOWING LINEDEFS CONTROLLING ARCHITECTURAL FORM, THE FALL OF LIGHT AND SHADOW AND THE LOGIC OF A KEY-LOCKED DOOR.

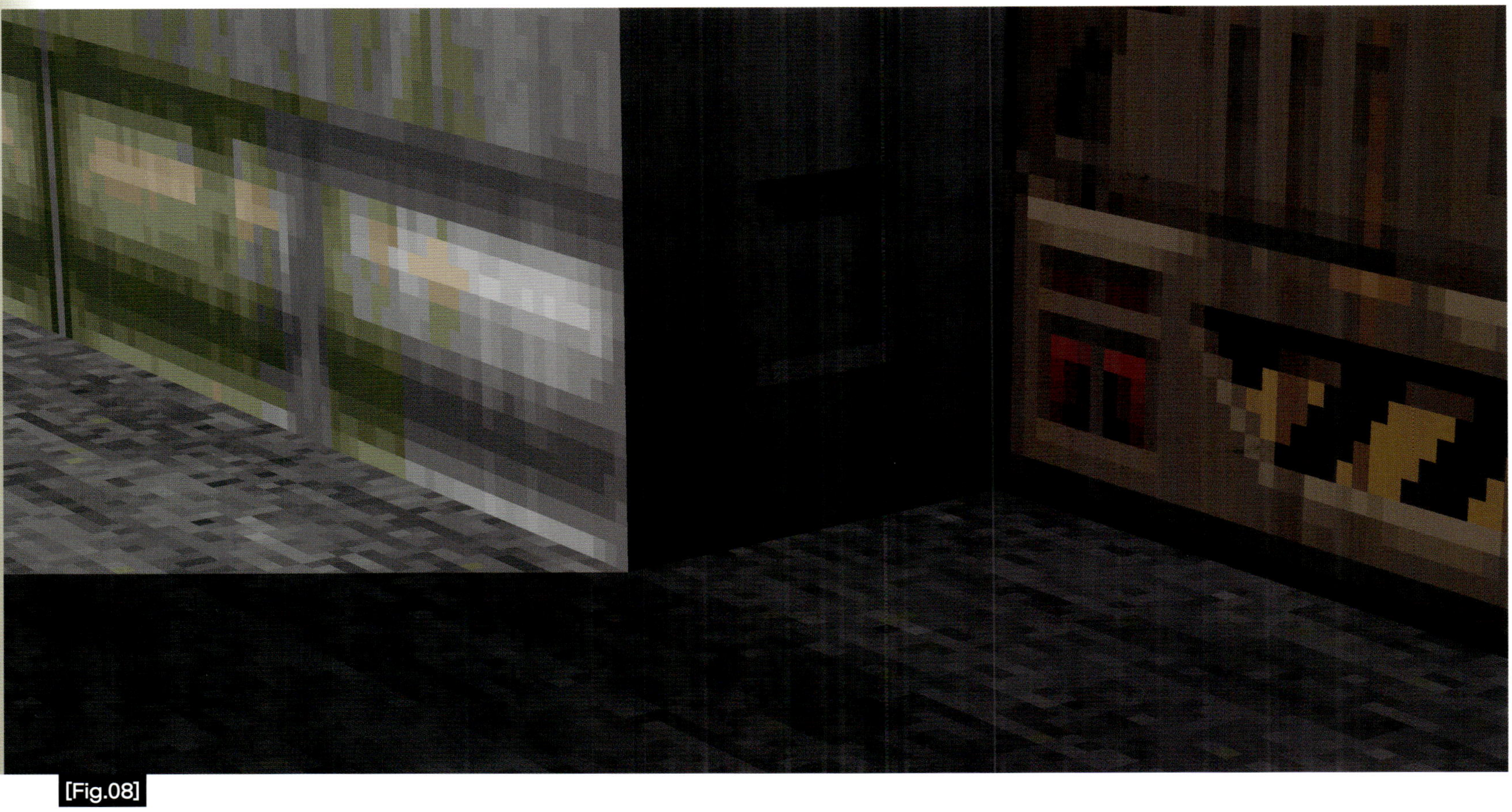

[Fig.08]

Linedefs are also key to how the AI of enemies works within the game. *DOOM*'s monsters all possess 180-degree vision and can ostensibly see infinite distances, though this is of course blocked by linedef-defined walls, doors and other obstacles. This can be controlled with the use of elements like invisible 'untextured' floors raised to just below the height of the ceiling, but vision is generally defined per-monster. In contrast, sound propagation is mediated by linedefs and their associated sectors, with sound bleeding across maps for often considerable and perhaps unrealistic distances. While enclosed spaces will not propagate sounds outside themselves, to achieve elements such as windows – in order to embrace Romero's idea of being able to get everywhere you can see – players must activate the 'Block Sound' property of a linedef, ensuring sound cannot pass through this opening. As such, the capabilities of the line are extended even further, being able to create perceptual boundaries for the enemy characters that are imperceptible to the player. Mapping these together allows us to see the sensorial landscape that exists within a level, defining how monsters will react to the player's presence and actions. Our exploded map of Pandemonium (E3M3) demonstrates both the 'cones of vision' and sound propagation sectors that define the level through the eyes and ears of the enemy [Fig.10].

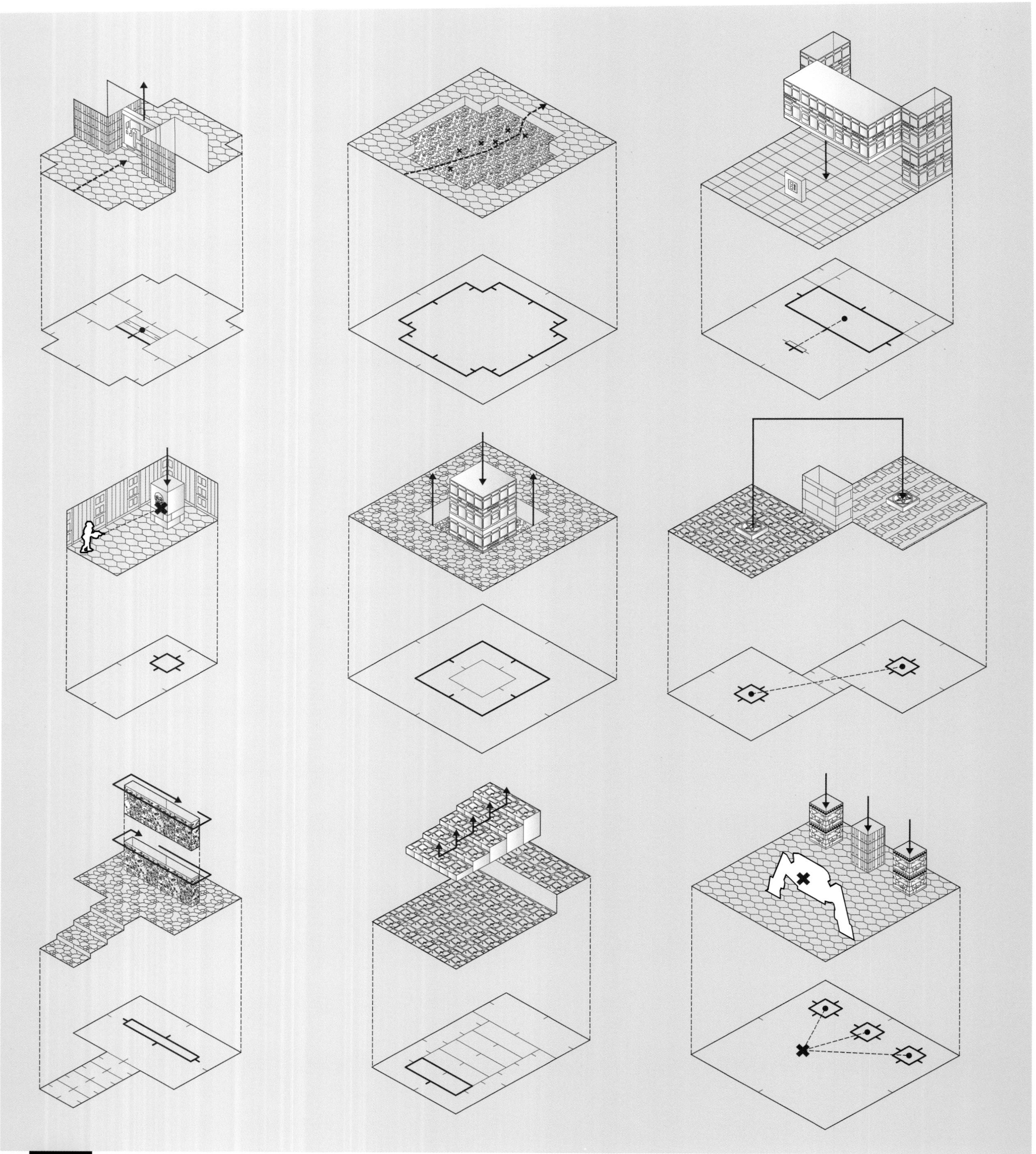

[Fig.09]

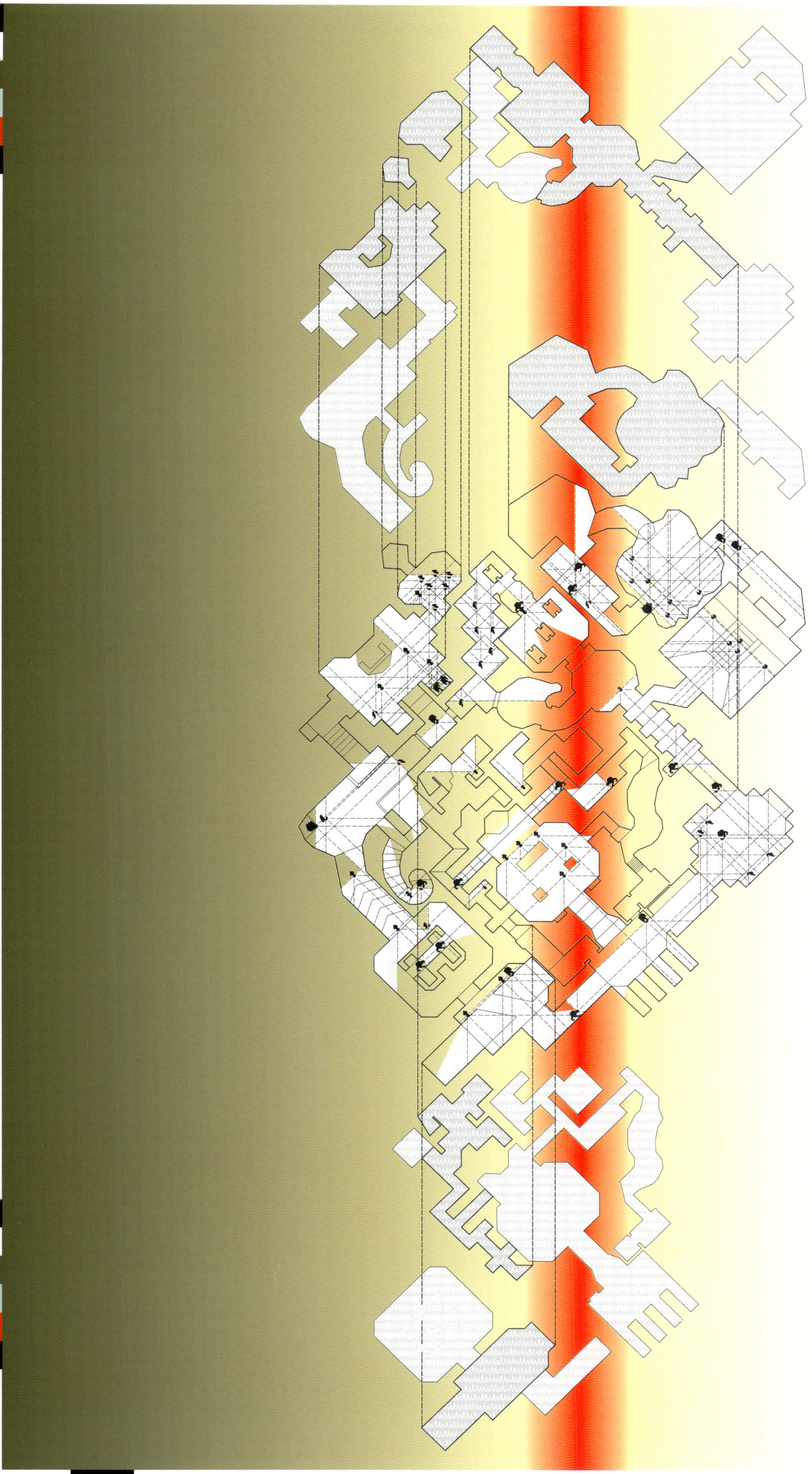

AXONOMETRIC PLAN SHOWING THE SIGHT LINES OF MONSTERS AT THE START OF THE LEVEL PANDEMONIUM [E3M3] ALONG WITH MAPS OF HOW SOUND PROPAGATES ACROSS THE SPACE DEPENDING ON WHERE THE NOISE IS MADE.

[Fig.10]

4.4

A WORLD OF .WADS

DOOM's engine has led a storied life, achieved 'through a genealogy of the engine's organizational structure designed by Carmack to be separate from game assets,'[23] meaning that it could be used to make many different games. The original engine has been evolved by the community into more contemporary 'source ports' such as GZDoom (2008), based on ZDoom (1998), itself a port of earlier community versions of the 1993 original. GZDoom adds functionality to the original game such as full mouse look and graphical options and has even been used in modern commercial shooter games such as *Selaco* (Altered Orbit, 2024). The creative energy keeping the game alive comes through the *DOOM* community's sharing of designs. As Romero describes: 'They've done so much, even back in the very beginning, as soon as we released *DOOM*.'[24] These run from map packs contained in WAD files, to what is known as *Total Conversions*, where most aspects of the *DOOM* experience have been replaced with new assets. These modifications can completely change the game and its spatial possibilities. *Brutal Doom* (Sergeant_Mark_IV, 2012) ramps up the violence of the game and even offers the ability to drive vehicles like tanks and helicopters. As our screenshot of the horror mod *CountryCide* (Trenchwork, 2022) shows, the technology can even be pushed to create an open world of bucolic, haunted villages [Fig.11] that look a world away from the original game. *DOOM* has also been extended into an artistic tool, such as the 1995 project *ArsDoom* (Orhan Kipcak, 1995) that recreated a real-world gallery of artistic exhibits, with players able to shoot the floating heads of contributing artists using a paintbrush.

We have contextualized the spatial ambitions of total conversion modifications by taking two maps from popular mods and composing them alongside the game's original starting point at Hangar (E1M1) [Fig.12]. In the mod *Doom: The Golden Souls 3* (Batandy, 2019), the original game's hellscapes become a bright and cheerful world of colour, with the player collecting gold coins by climbing, wall-running and long-jumping through the world. The game presents a series of floating islands using a specific innovation called '3D Floor Mode', made possible in the modern GZDoom engine. Many developers use 'dummy sectors' to achieve more complicated geometry, by building reference points outside the level that then utilize linedef logic to control geometry within the level itself. This allows for the creation of complex shapes, but also produces strange, crystalline reference structures on the fringes of the game world. In the *Ashes 2063* mod (Ashes Dev Group, 2021), players traverse a post-apocalyptic open-world and can ride a chopper motorbike to navigate the large distances between settlements. Far away from the original plans of E1M1, *Ashes 2063* creates an environment that resonates with reality, a landscape of dilapidated highways, gas stations and fortified towns complete with all the dumpsters, air conditioning units and vehicles we would expect to find.

The ambition of these total conversion mod worlds and the fact that they are still being made today using decades-old technology, is testament to the enduring influence of *DOOM* and its innovations. Romero himself has recently revisited the game with his *SIGIL WADs*, asking 'what can I do that people have not seen in 25 years, with the data that's already in the game?'.[25] The game's levels are rich in architectural secrets, and their complex floorplans challenge the tendencies towards linear level design that underpin many FPS games nowadays. In this context it is no wonder that a new genre of 'boomer-shooters' has emerged, trying to recreate the nostalgic energy of *DOOM*'s world. This is a place that people have spent millions of hours in over the last decades, which is ironic, when the EXIT is so clearly marked.

[Fig.11]
PAGES 92–3

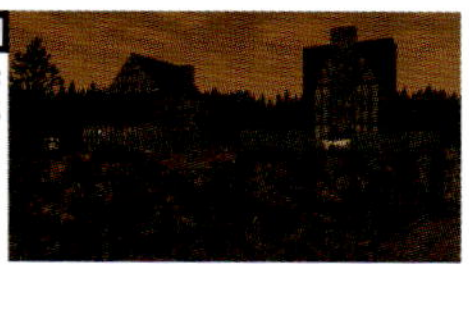

A village within the Forests of Slakartvia in the total conversion mod *CountryCide* by TrenchWork, demonstrating the *DOOM* engine applied to the design of a naturalistic open-world level.

COMPARING THE SCALE OF *DOOM*'S HANGAR LEVEL (E1M1) TO TOTAL CONVERSION LEVELS FROM *DOOM 3: THE GOLDEN SOULS* BY BATANDY AND *ASHES 2063* BY ASHES DEV GROUP, SHOWING HOW FAR THE ENGINE CAN BE PUSHED BEYOND ITS ORIGINAL CAPABILITIES.

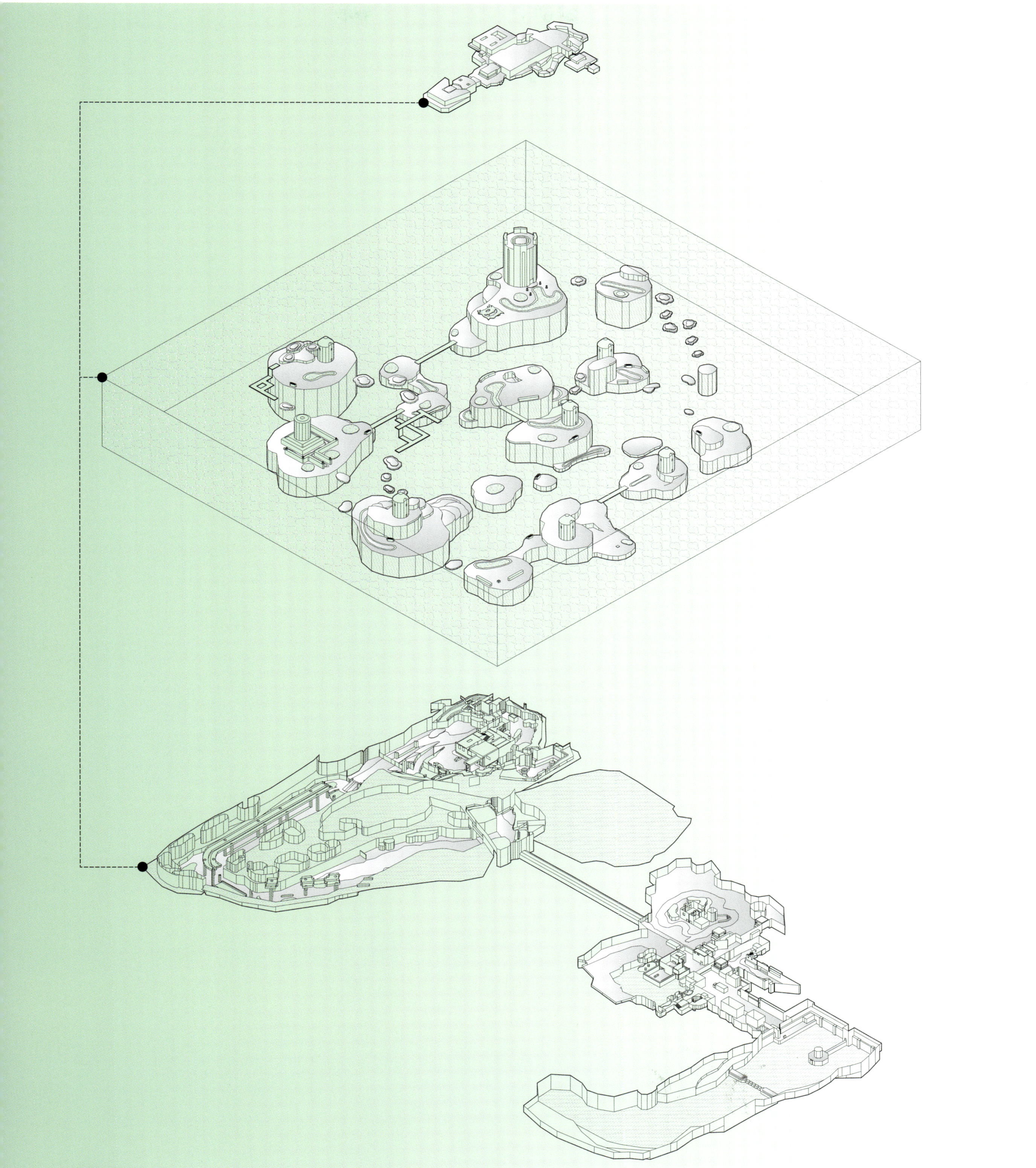

[Fig.12]

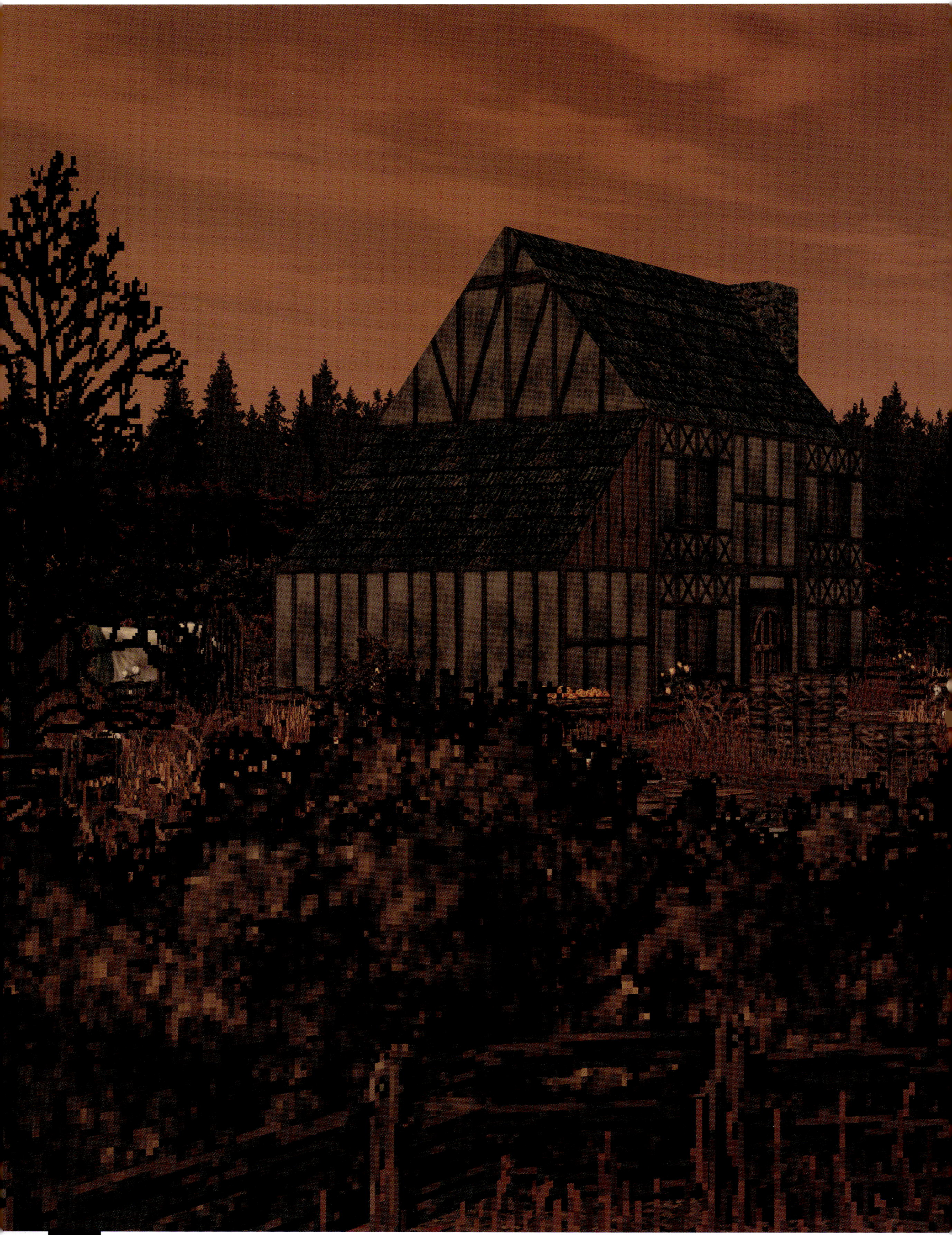

[Fig.11]

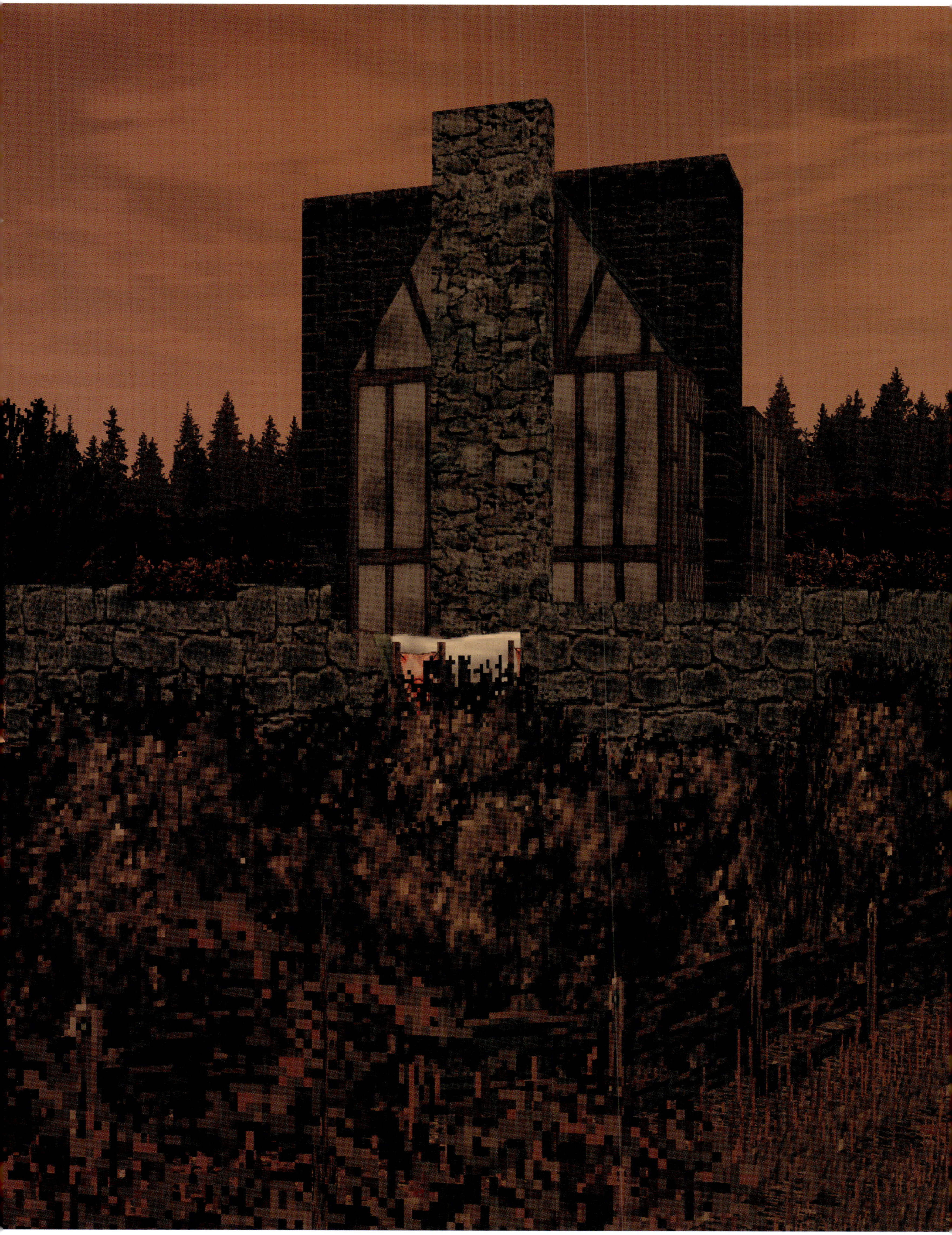

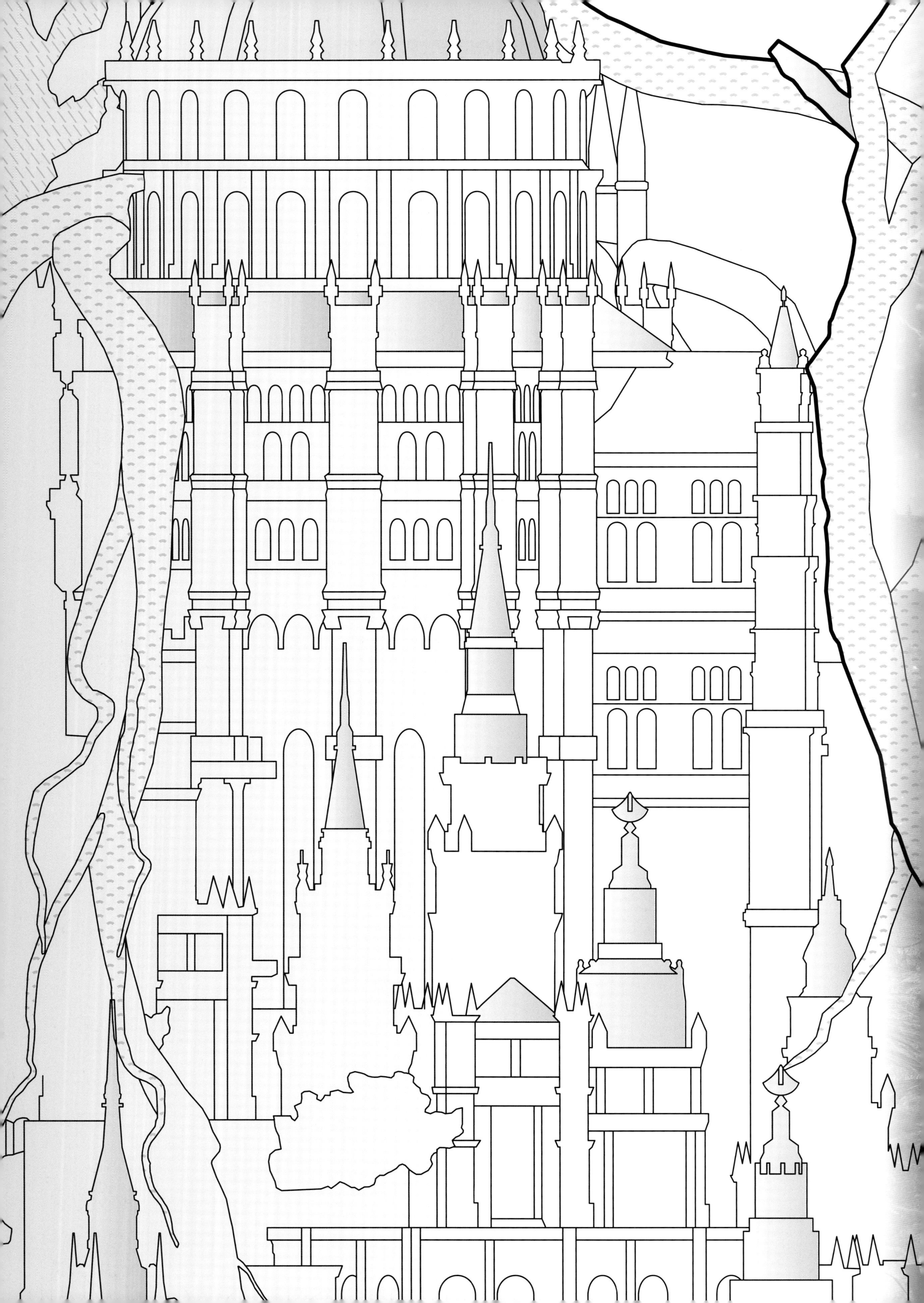

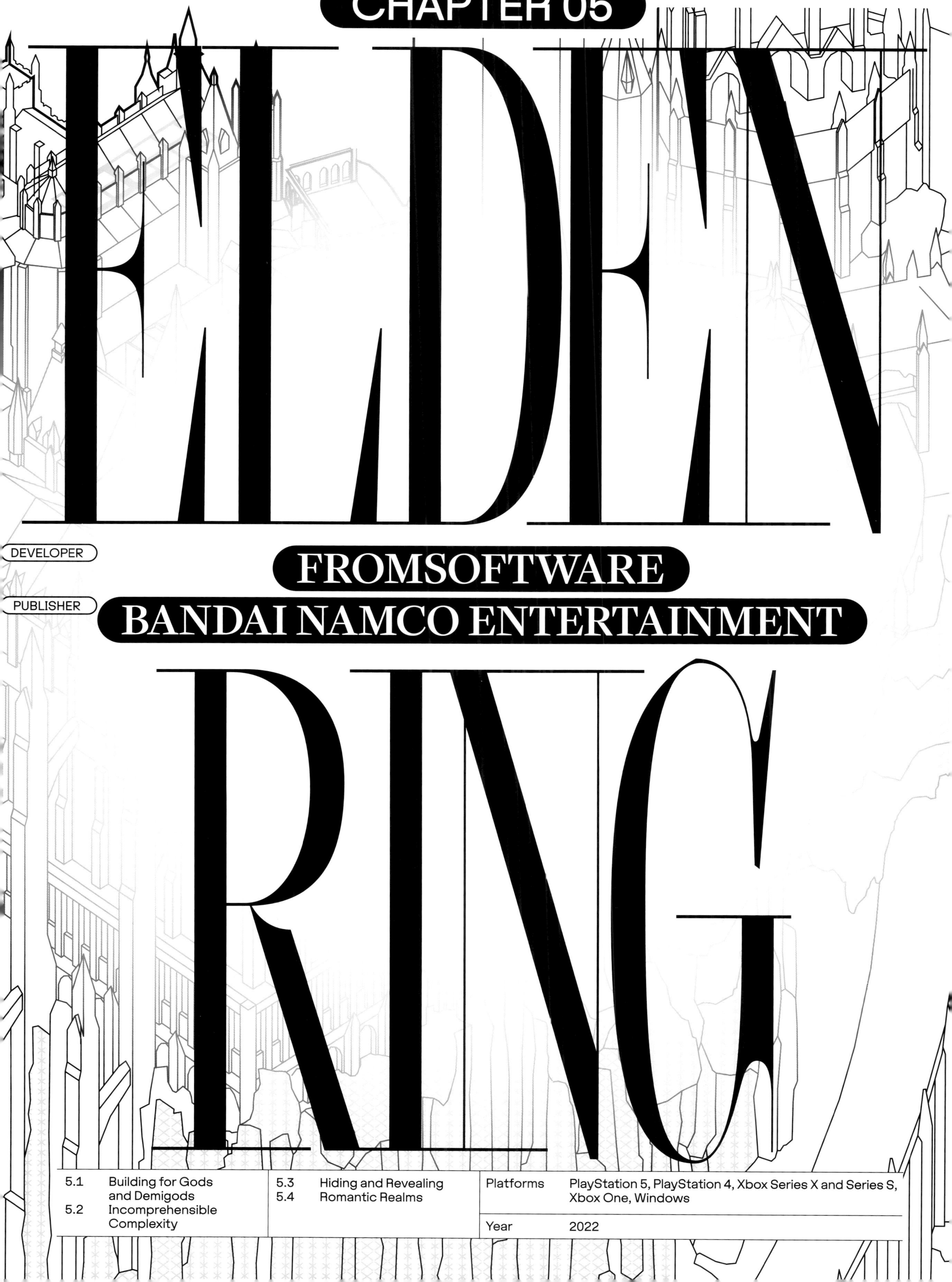

CHAPTER 05

ELDEN RING

DEVELOPER FROMSOFTWARE

PUBLISHER BANDAI NAMCO ENTERTAINMENT

Platforms	PlayStation 5, PlayStation 4, Xbox Series X and Series S, Xbox One, Windows
Year	2022

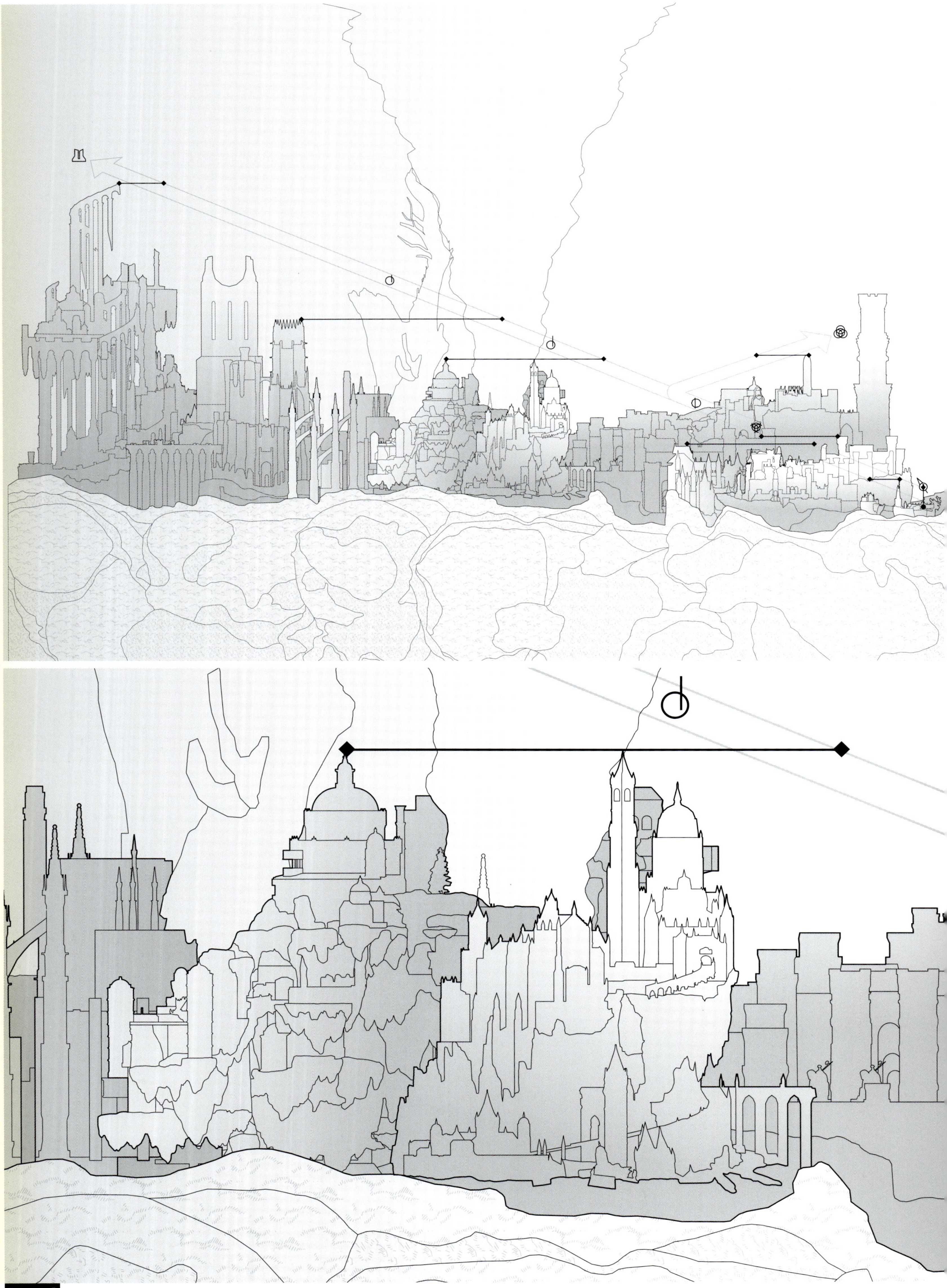

[Fig.01]

5.1

BUILDING FOR GODS AND DEMIGODS

Elden Ring represents FromSoftware's most ambitious and extravagant worldbuilding achievement to date, building on the studio's deep expertise in environmental storytelling. The game and its DLC, set in the Lands Between and Shadow Realm, is also the developer's first attempt at combining a traditional open-world game with its much-praised dungeon design. Assuming the role of a 'Tarnished,' returning from exile following the shattering of the Elden Ring by Queen Marika the Eternal, players must journey through the Lands Between to gather the Great Runes from Marika's offspring, a cabal of warring demigods, and ultimately ascend towards the towering Erdtree, assuming the throne as Elden Lord. Underpinning this typically complex and arcane story was director Hidetaka Miyazaki's aim 'to give the world a mythological, fantastical, painting-like look, with a feeling of romanticism in solitude.'[1]

As the ambition of FromSoftware's worldbuilding has grown, architecture assumes the role as a symbolic marker of the player's progression. While the world offers innumerable possible directions to explore, the huge architectural structures that punctuate the landscape provide natural destination points, demarcating significant challenges that the player will encounter. Along with the glowing Erdtree at the world's centre, these buildings provide a landscape that encourages, rather than directs, the player towards goals. This approach recalls long-established visual principles, such as Walt Disney's idea of the 'weenie': a building designed to attract people towards it from a distance.[2] These larger structures in *Elden Ring* are known as 'legacy dungeons', complex levels designed to test the player's abilities as they move onwards through the world, representing ascendancy towards the Elden Throne. These are buildings that host gods and demigods, architecture that evokes divine power. As architectural critic Deyan Sudjic argues 'architecture has its roots in the creation of shelter in a physical sense, but it has become an attempt to construct a particular view of the world.'[3] Players see this transition as they progress from the small shacks of Limgrave to the glistening city of Leyndell, where the architecture clearly communicates the gods and their vision.

Ascension is key not only to the design of *Elden Ring*'s landscape but also the architectural design of these significant buildings. Ascendancy is mirrored by the ever-expanding scale of the architecture that players encounter. As YouTube commentators such as Addypalooza have shown,[4] the scale of architecture in *Elden Ring* is many times greater than we find in the real world, especially considering the architectural style, materials and building techniques implied in the game. By using community-made modding tools such as Smithbox,[5] which allow users to load and mod *Elden Ring* maps, we can reasonably accurately calculate the relative height of these legacy dungeon buildings. Compiling these buildings into one elevational drawing [Fig.01] shows how architectural scale tends to grow along with the difficulty scale of the game, and path through the story. This way of analysing distributed spaces through a single representation was a mapping technique developed in the 19th century to visualize complex and disparate landscape features comparatively, such as rivers and mountains.[6] *Elden Ring*'s architecture is challenging to compare, given that many buildings protrude from giant cliffs (Raya Lucaria), straddle deep valleys (Shadow Keep) or defy gravity and physics (Enir-Ilim or Farum Azula).

[Fig.01] **A COMPARATIVE MAPPING OF THE HEIGHTS OF ELDEN RING 'LEGACY DUNGEONS' SHOWING HOW ARCHITECTURAL SCALE OFTEN MIRRORS THE PLAYER'S PROGRESSION THROUGH THE LANDS BETWEEN AND SHADOW REALM.**

Despite this, many of the game's notable buildings do present a 'front door' of sorts, allowing us to establish a common ground-level datum from which their size and elevation can be estimated. Early legacy dungeons such as Stormveil Castle already rise to significant heights (around 152 metres [500 ft] from the front gate to the tallest rampart), but as the player moves closer to the sites of godhood, so the architecture grows in scale. By the end of the *Shadow of the Erdtree* expansion, players will have reached the top of Enir-Ilim, an improbable structure hovering on slender and fragmented columns rising some 768 metres (2,520 ft) into the air. Although these structures are still dwarfed by contemporary real-world skyscrapers such as the Burj Khalifa in Dubai (828 metres or 2,722 ft), the use of historical building styles such as Romanesque or Gothic architecture and implied materials shown by techniques such as stonemasonry play with our expectations of impossible scale, going beyond what we know to be achievable in the physical world. This ascension is marked from the start of the game, where if players look carefully, the Flame Peak and the Forge of the Giants can be seen from 'The First Step' Site of Grace, where the players first emerge into the Limgrave landscape [Fig.02]. Flame Peak, as per the game's map description, is the highest point of the entire world and host to a key moment in the game's story, yet is visible from our very first moments in the journey.

In the main story, the player's ascension ends at the Erdtree, entered through a gigantic gate at the top of the city of Leyndell. This city represents one of FromSoftware's most complex architectural creations, a warren of fortifications, churches, houses and other remnants of the society that once resided there. As with much of *Elden Ring*'s architecture, the world is articulated not only through the bigger design moves, such as the fossilized Ancient Dragonlord Gransax that straddles half of the city, but also through all the small details the player encounters as they tread furtively through its streets. To explore Leyndell's multi-scalar architecture, we use a beaux-arts[7] era drawing technique called the *analytique*, combining different types of architectural drawing, such as plans, elevations and small details into one composition. Such drawings are made with the express purpose of 'emphasizing the relationship of parts to the whole, and of details to overall proportions.'[8] By compiling Leyndell's forms, we can see how the city's design works at multiple scales [Fig.03]. Here, Leyndell's symbolic use of gold produces a shimmering roofscape while the city's layout cascades out from grand boulevards into the twists and turns of alleyways. This back and forth between palatial and tight spaces and use of compression as an 'architectural gesture' that 'induces us to follow a dynamic impulse',[9] is a hallmark of FromSoftware's spatial design. This brings us into close contact with Leyndell's strange details, such as the waxy material emerging from doors (that lore-hunters consider to be a corpse-preserving substance,[10] hinting at the fate of Leyndell's citizens) and a key, but easily missed, statue of Radagon that changes to reveal its true form of Queen Marika. The analytique drawing demonstrates the recursive logic to Leyndell's design, with symbols and design moves repeated at different scales.

[Fig.02]
PAGES 100–1
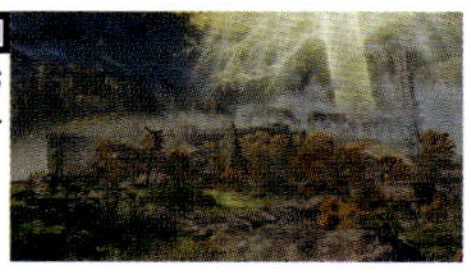
A view from 'The First Step' Site of Grace at the start of the game showing the world's highest point, Forge of the Giants, in the far distance.

[Fig.03]

AN 'ANALYTIQUE' DRAWING SHOWING THE COMPLEXITY OF LEYNDELL'S ARCHITECTURE AT MANY SCALES, FROM URBAN PLANNING DECISIONS TO SMALL SYMBOLIC DETAILS AND MYSTERIOUS MATERIALS.

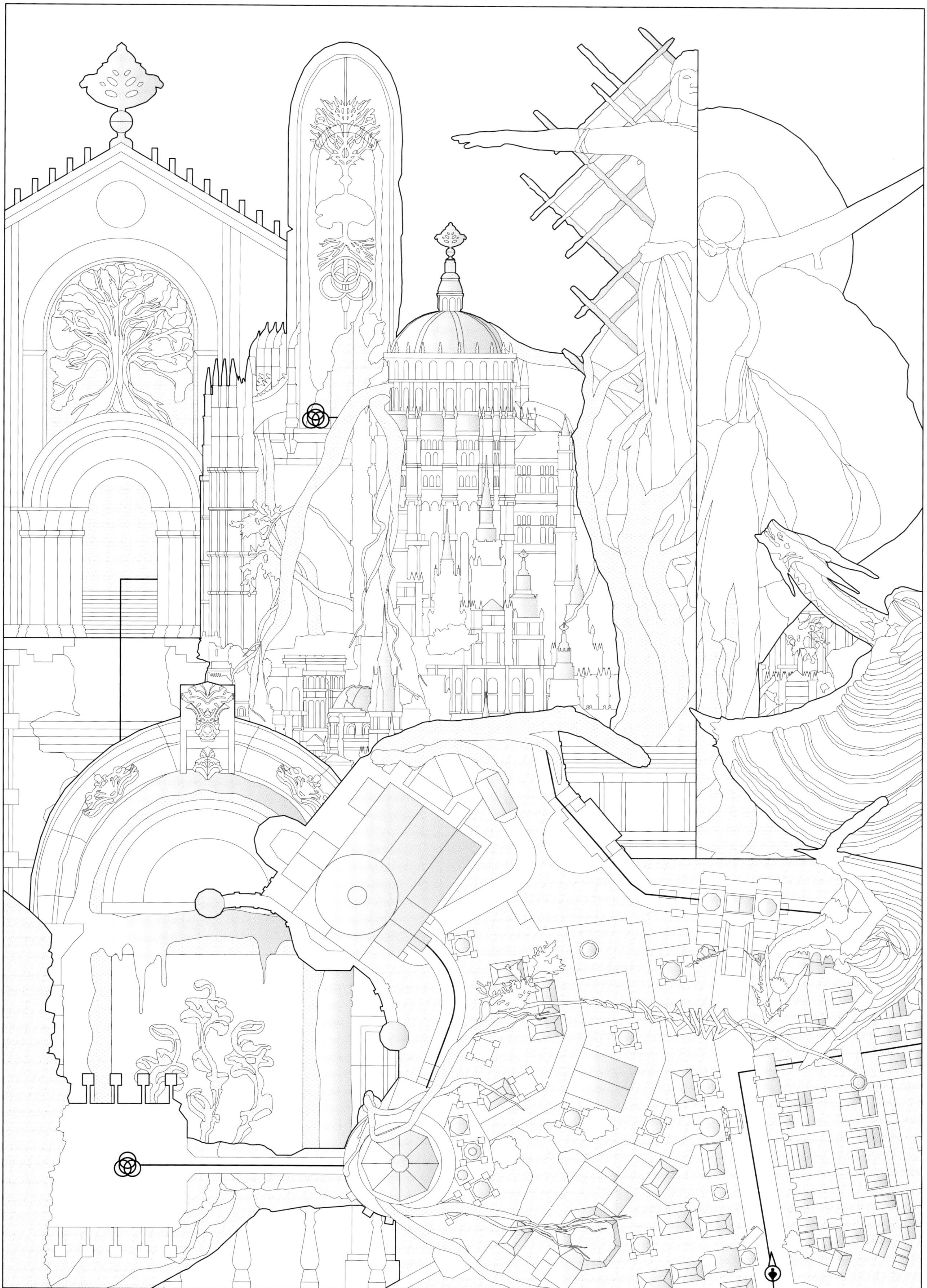

[Fig.03]

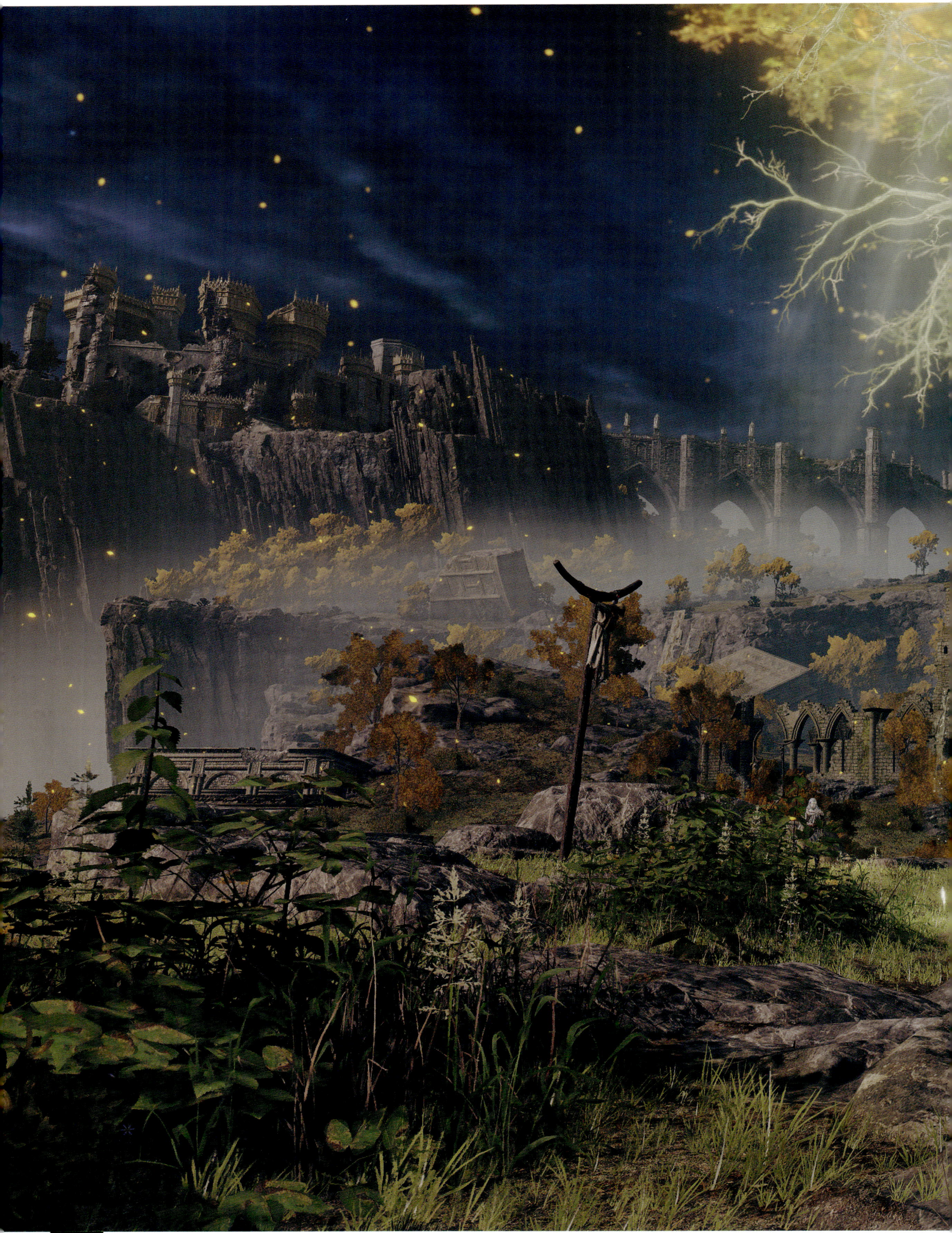

[Fig.02]

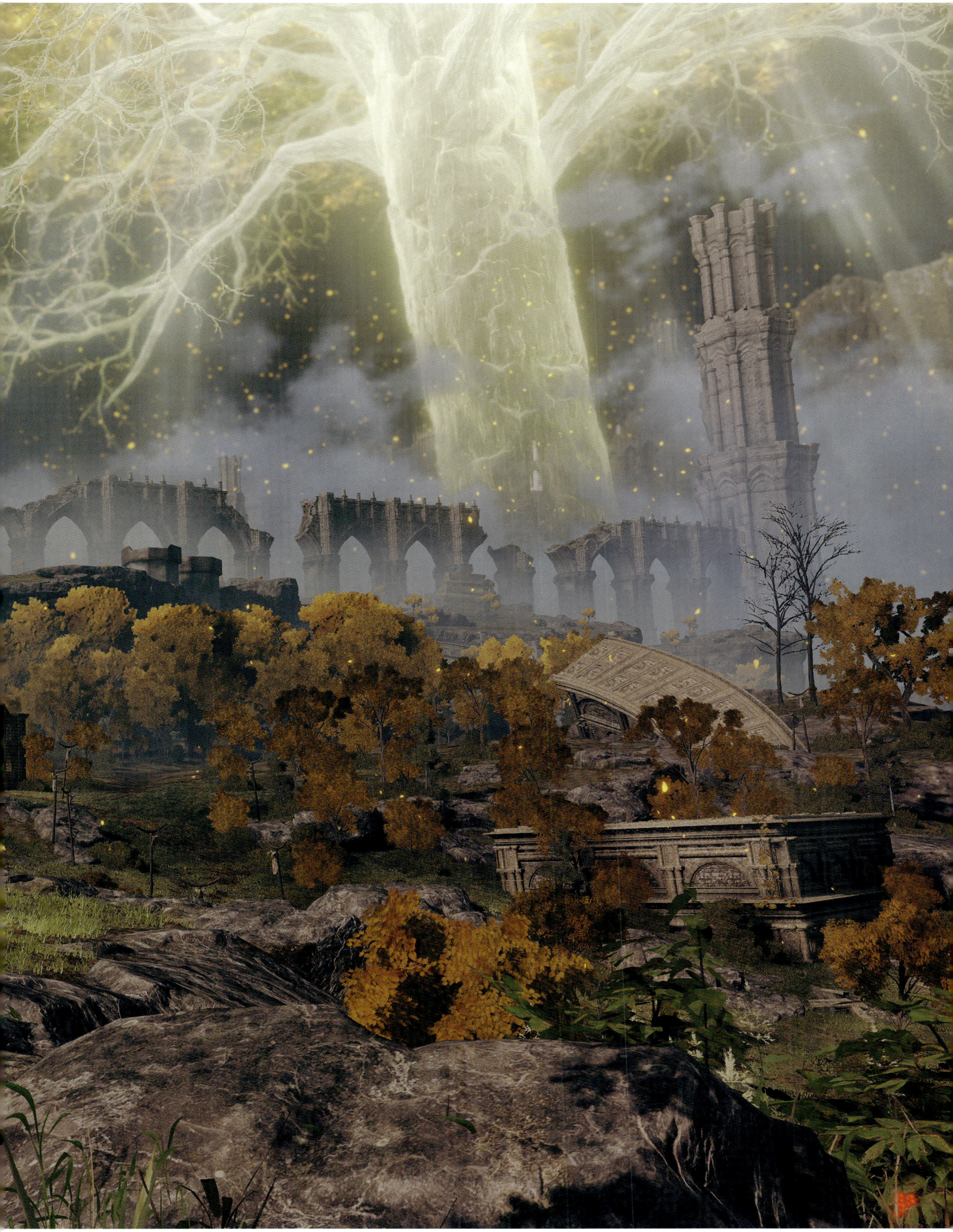

5.2 INCOMPREHENSIBLE COMPLEXITY

Leyndell shows that the relationship to *Elden Ring*'s gods is communicated through architectural scale, symbolism and complexity. We can recognize details similar to real-world architecture, yet the sheer amount of implied labour behind the buildings takes them beyond human comprehension. Continuing our research using modding tools like Smithbox, we can understand that this is achieved by carefully balancing the navigable boundaries of a level and the architectural elements making up the building beyond it. Smithbox shows us that *Elden Ring* levels are constructed from two types of geometry: 'map' pieces that players can walk through and 'asset' pieces that are used to decorate the rest of the building. In a large legacy dungeon such as The Academy of Raya Lucaria, we can see how far these two might diverge [Fig.04]. By extracting all the walkable surfaces from the map and overlaying them onto its overall built form we can see that while the level is complex and full of intertwining paths, it is a small section of the overall architectural form. The building is constructed from over 190 'map' models, containing walkable surfaces – floors, certain rooftops and various balconies and gantries. Together these establish the territory that the player can explore, yet the building's full form remains incomplete.

Raya Lucaria is finished by more than 510 individual 'asset' models, which typically represent architectural elements including buttresses, gargoyles and pinnacles, as well as interior furniture such as desks, lanterns and bookshelves. Many of these assets are reused multiple times over, and so the total number of elements is likely in the thousands. In reality, complex buildings such as churches often took tens, if not hundreds of years to build, such as the six centuries spent completing Milan's Duomo (itself an earlier FromSoftware inspiration) and its stone carvings, including over 3400 statues.[11] Yet repeated assets allow the developers to evoke building forms at a scale that seems almost impossible for humans to accomplish in a realistic timescale, suggesting the hand of a god.

[Fig.04] Detail

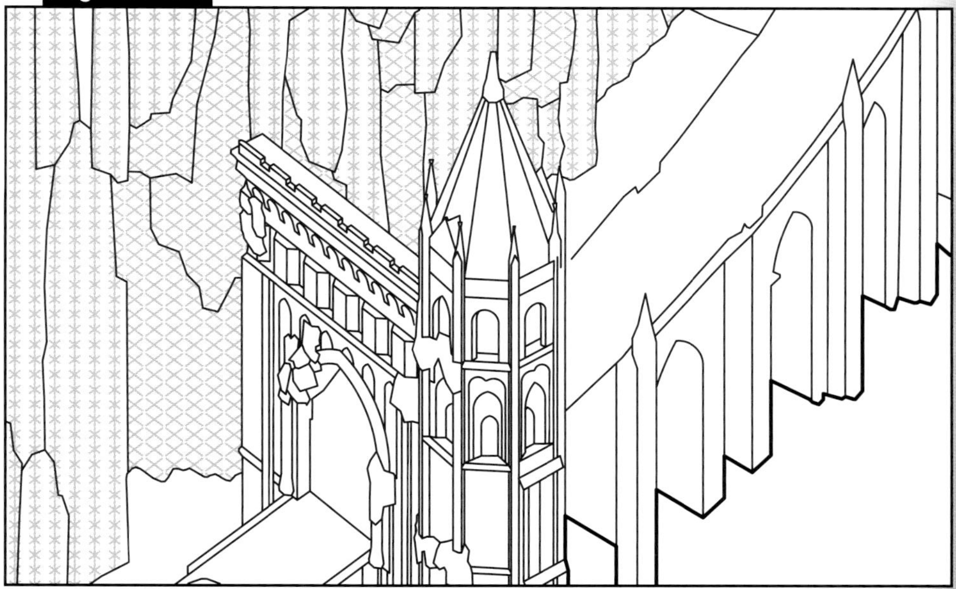

[Fig.04] MAPPING THE WALKABLE 'MAP' SPACES ONTO THE FULL ARCHITECTURAL EXTENTS OF THE ACADEMY OF RAYA LUCARIA, DEMONSTRATING THE SCALE AND COMPLEXITY OF THE BUILDING'S DESIGN BEYOND THE AREAS THE PLAYER CAN TRAVERSE.

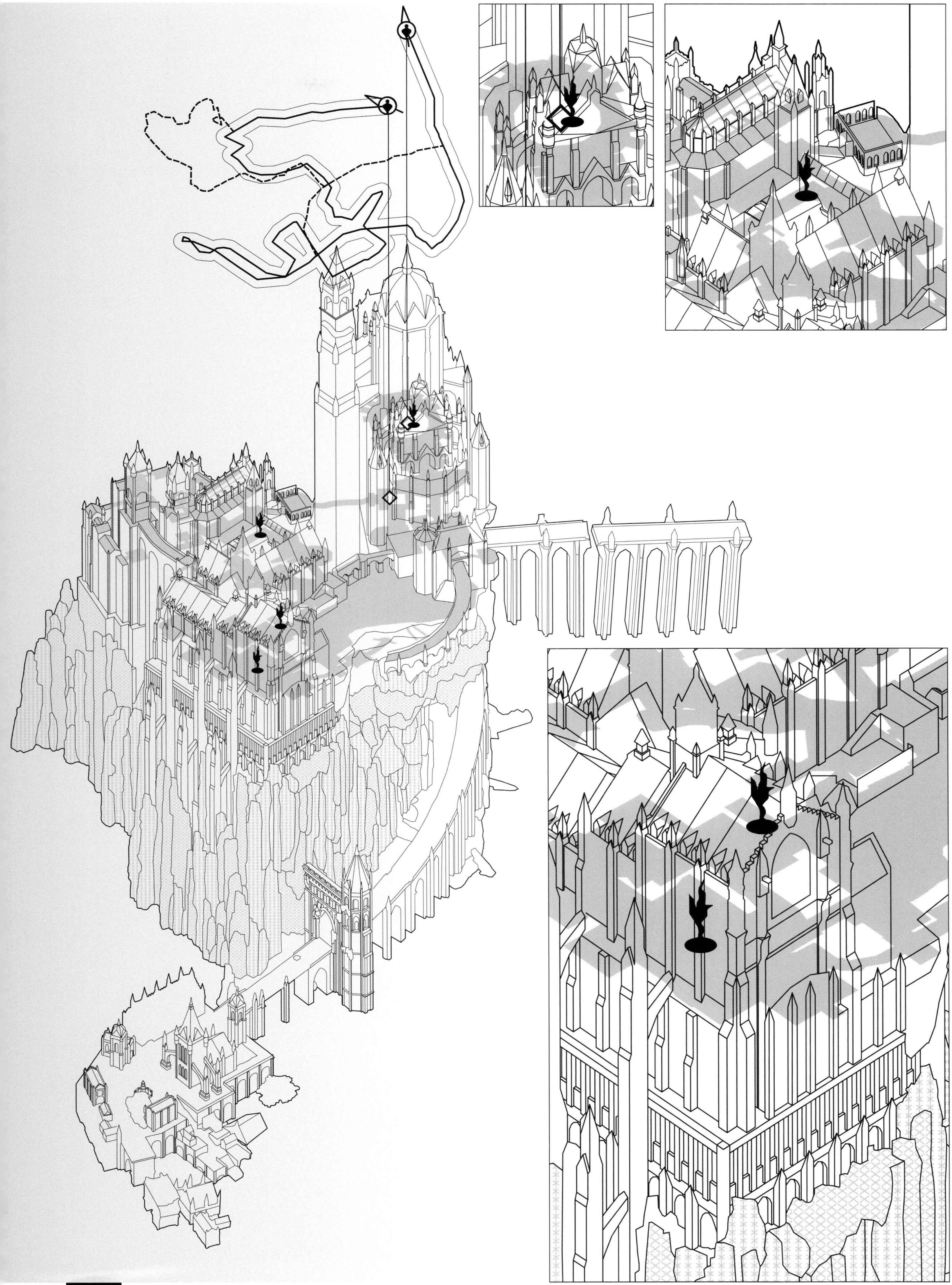

[Fig.04]

This is even more striking in the design of Stormveil Castle and its intricate layout. Stormveil's Romanesque architecture contains an elaborate web of pathways that, in typical FromSoftware fashion, might preclude a straightforward journey to the destination (although this direct route is also offered to players) [Fig.05]. Stormveil's design is marked by the addition of complex filigree on its ramparts, comprising thousands of small golden spires which appear to be 'retrofitted' and attached after its initial construction.[12] It is also even more complex than Raya Lucaria, comprising more than 260 map pieces and 540 reusable asset models. To understand Stormveil further we use a drawing technique called 'oblique', which presents the building face-on while also showing its depth. Oblique drawings were commonly used to depict castles and other fortifications, such as in the 16th-century work of Giacomo Castriotto (France's chief fortress designer) and Girolamo Maggi, which they termed 'soldierly perspective.'[13] Drawing in this way was meant to give an overview of a complete structure while also offering an understanding of its layout. By similarly overlaying the walkable map onto Stormveil's full form we can see that they are deeply intertwined, but as with nearly all game maps, we cannot explore every room, producing a gap between the implied complexity of the building and its reality. Taking screenshots with Otis_Inf's camera tools[14] we can photograph the castle to see how the player's journey forward is always framed by an imposing architecture of complexity [Fig.06].

Stormveil Castle is also being torn apart by roots penetrating its structure, leaving it pockmarked and decrepit. Ruination is a common theme in *Elden Ring*, drawing on aesthetics found in art and architecture where the ruin 'acknowledged the effects of time and place' and demonstrated 'the creative influence of natural as well as cultural forces.'[15] This touches on the work of 'archaeogaming,' where researchers analyse games by 'treating videogames as archaeological sites.'[16] In this case, the battles of demigods are the forces that have ruined the architecture, rotting out from the corpse of Godwyn the Golden, which is found in the castle's depths.

[Fig.05] Detail

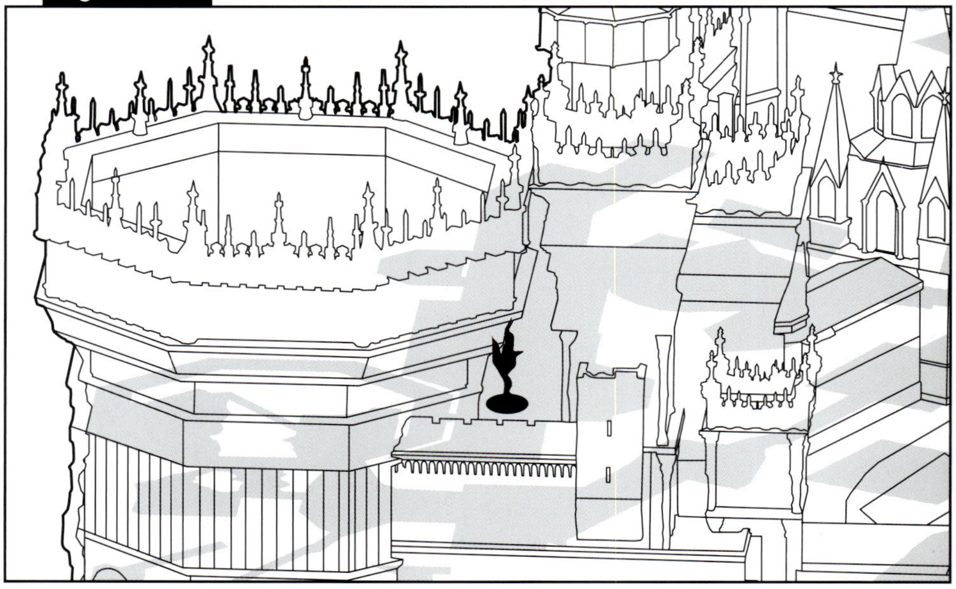

[Fig.05] **OVERLAYING THE NAVIGABLE MAP OF STORMVEIL CASTLE ONTO THE FULL STRUCTURE, SHOWING HOW THE BUILDING COMPRISES A SET OF INTERWEAVING PATHWAYS WHERE THE SCALE AND COMPLEXITY OF THE CASTLE'S ARCHITECTURE OVERWHELMS THE PLAYER.**

[Fig.06] PAGES 106–7

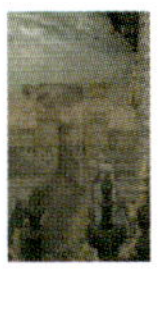

A view through Stormveil Castle, contrasting the player's route with the visual language created by thousands of golden spires and filigree retrofitted onto the building.

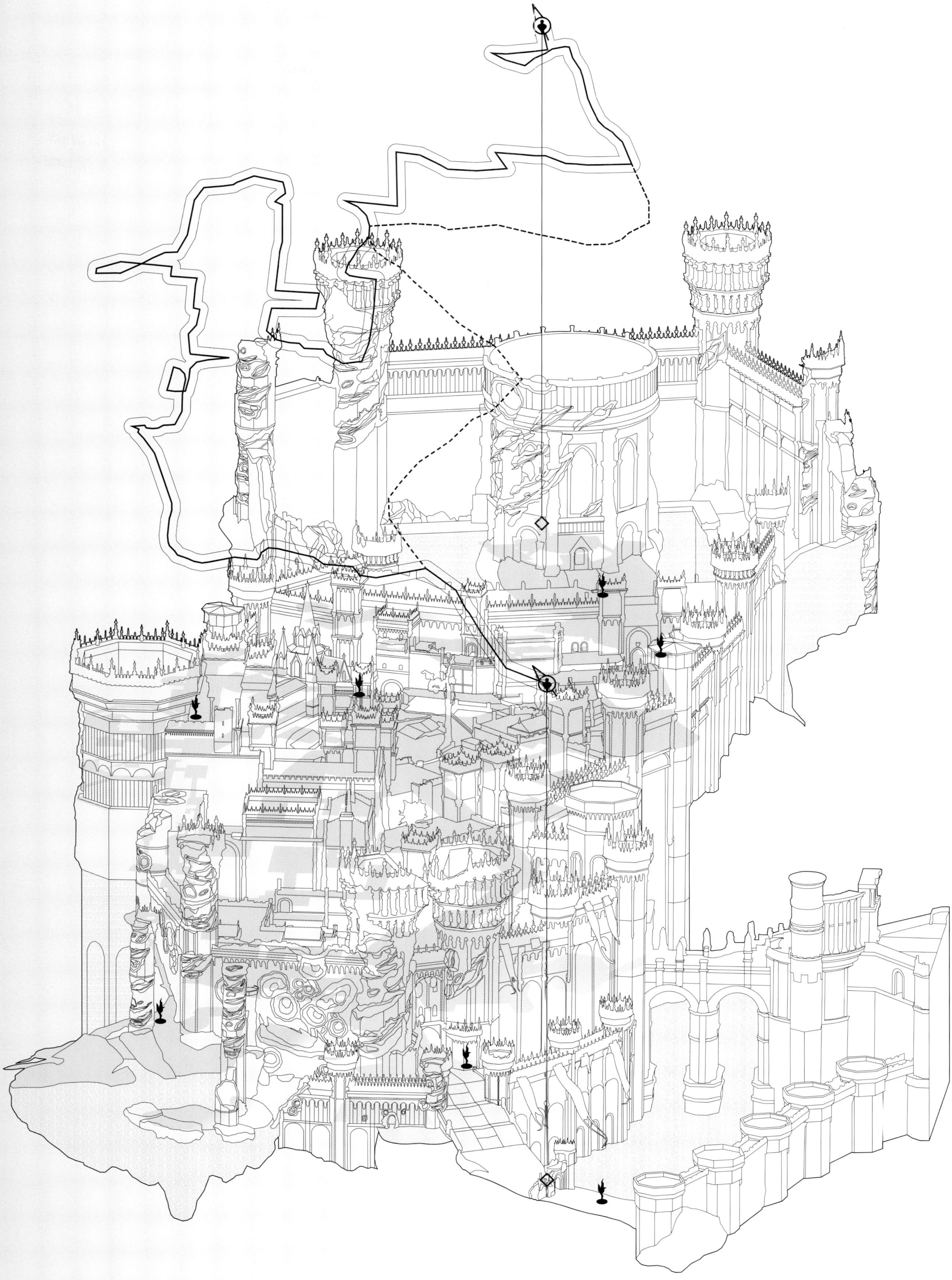

[Fig.05]

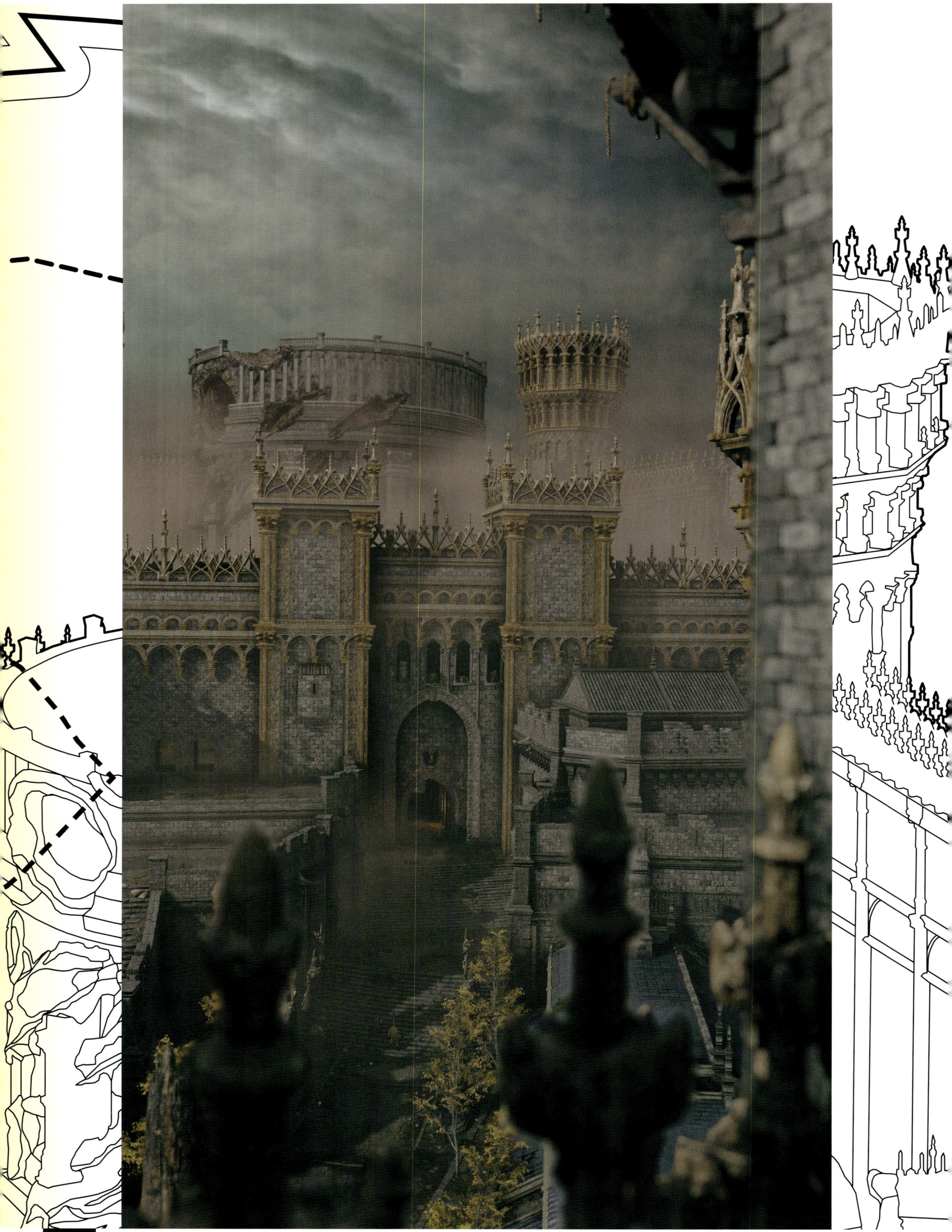

[Fig.06]

This evocation of the godly through scale and complexity is something that we can find in many real-world buildings, yet *Elden Ring* takes it to steroidal levels. This is most clearly seen when we compare some of the buildings in the game that seemingly make direct architectural references to reality [Fig.07]. By using Google Earth mapping and analysis of game levels in Smithbox, we can compare notable structures in *Elden Ring* to the real-world counterparts that inspired them. In some cases, referential buildings are part of a much larger construction, such as Leyndell's Cathedral. Here the structure is approximate in size to the building that appears to have inspired it, Istanbul's Hagia Sofia,[17] with a cubic volume roughly twice that of the real-world building. Yet in other parts of the Lands Between, the difference between real-world reference points becomes more pronounced. The Mohgwyn Palace takes the rough form of Athens' Parthenon but nearly doubles its dimensions, producing a volume approximately 3.4 times the size of the original structure. In Farum Azula, we can see the Baptistery at Pisa inflated to radical proportions (a 66-times volumetric increase) and given many more additional floors. Going further, Raya Lucaria appears to take architectural inspiration from Aachen Cathedral, combining Romanesque and Gothic architecture but significantly increasing its size and complexity, with a volume some 120 times larger than the German church.

This maximalist approach to architectural scale has also affected a spatial typology typical to FromSoftware games: the boss arena [Fig.08]. As with the developer's previous games, *Elden Ring* continues to use a set of defined forms for these areas, from the traditional round designs in Farum Azula, and the rectangular halls we find in Leyndell. However, with the advent of horse-mounted battle, the scale of the 'environmental' arenas has grown beyond all previous comprehension to incorporate more spatial and mechanical gimmicks such as the Radahn Festival where the player becomes part of a larger army fighting the boss across sand dunes. In general, the huge architectural scale of the boss arenas has allowed for a greater focus on the bosses themselves, rather than some of the smaller and more punishing battlegrounds of previous FromSoftware games. Yet as with all 'Soulsborne' style games, the arenas can still pose environmental threats themselves, such as the chasms in Stormveil Castle or the chandeliers that fall from the ceiling as we fight Rennala, Queen of the Full Moon. They can also provide 'cheesing' opportunities, such as firing poison arrows through a tiny gap in the ramparts of Castle Sol to gradually wear down Commander Niall.

[Fig.07]
PAGE 108

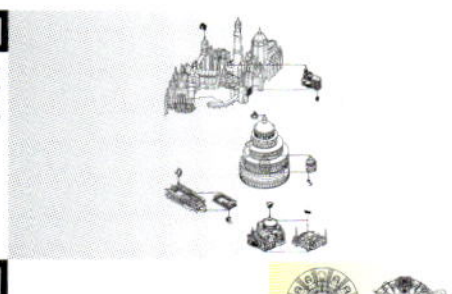

A comparison between notable buildings in *Elden Ring* and the real-world structures they appear to be inspired by, demonstrating how scale is warped and changed in the design of the in-game architecture.

[Fig.08]
PAGE 109

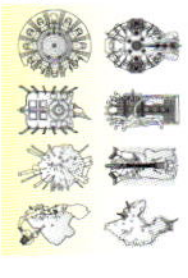

Floorplans of different boss arena typologies, showing how the developers use a catalogue of architectural and spatial tropes in their design.

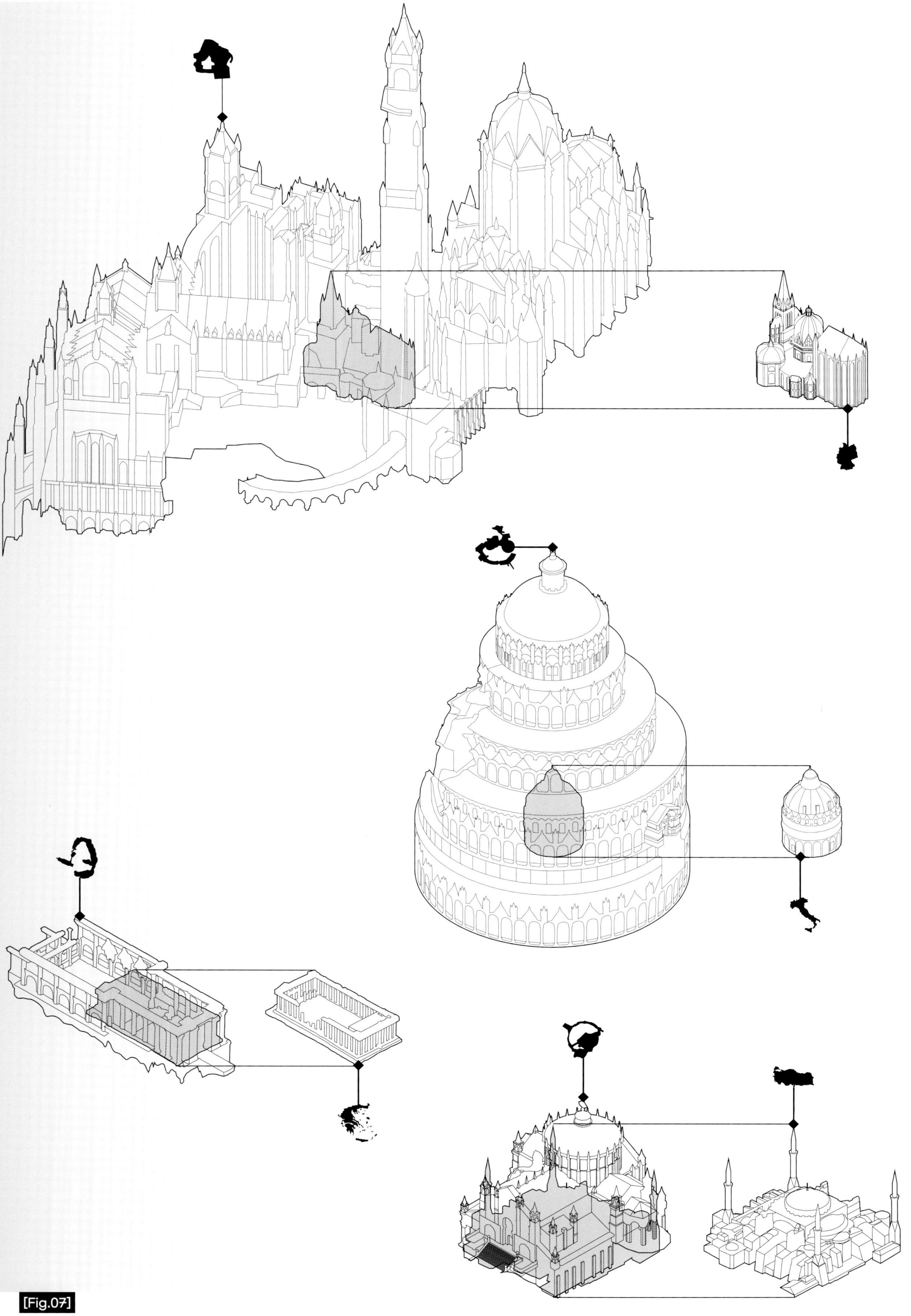

[Fig.07]

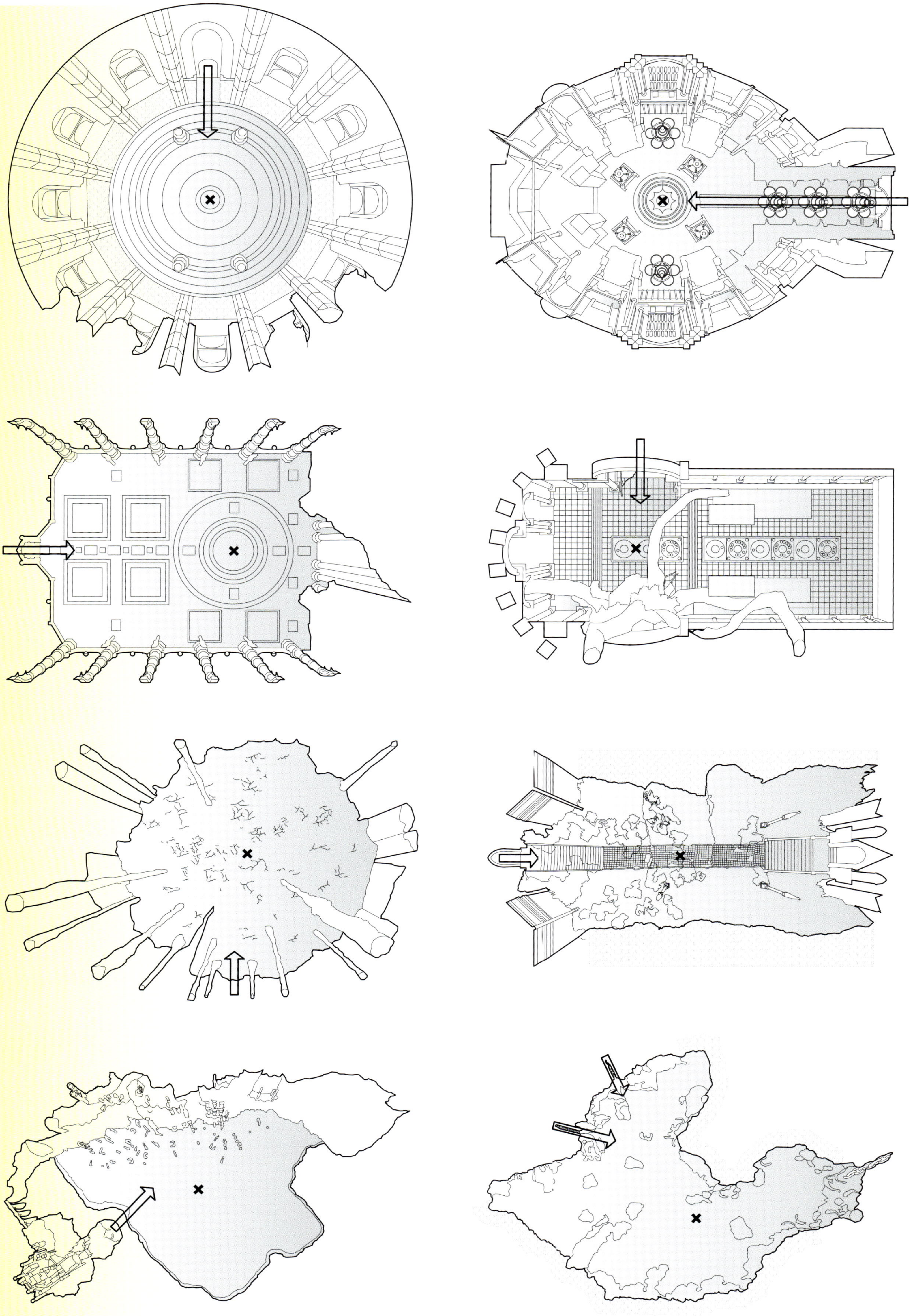

[Fig.08]

5.3

HIDING AND REVEALING

Along with hidden cheesing possibilities, the huge scale of *Elden Ring* allows for an unprecedented number of secret spaces to be included in the game, including entire areas that can be easily missed by players. FromSoftware themselves 'are always surprised and delighted by how much the players do discover, and how much these communities work to uncover these secrets.'[18] By mapping different typologies of these secrets we can see how these also represent a set of common spatial tropes [Fig.09]. Illusory walls, typical in FromSoftware games, have been joined by illusory floors, typically found in ruins strewn across the Lands Between. Bookcases and altars slide back to reveal new areas and items, while the designers also make good use of invisible platforms, exploiting how visibility and material form can be detached from one another in game worlds, in ways not possible in reality. A particularly mean secret door in Volcano Manor requires a good few minutes of bashing to disappear, testing the patience of the game's players who enthusiastically hunt down every one of these secrets. The use of secret spaces in architecture, particularly in the design periods referenced in *Elden Ring*, has a long history. Priest holes, for example, were hiding places built into buildings in Great Britain, during periods in which Catholic worship was outlawed. These were reached through fake fireplaces or wall panels and even included secret rooms accessed through removable stairs and hidden within the thickness of the walls.[19] *Elden Ring* uses similarly inventive mechanisms that challenge the player to creatively interpret space in search of hidden treasure.

The sheer scope of the Lands Between has allowed for the hiding and revealing of architectural spaces on a scale never possible before. As both critics and players noted, one of the most transformative moments of the game arises from unwittingly encountering a small building in Limgrave, where a floating lift takes us over 500 metres (1,640 ft) into the depths of an entirely new world: the Siofra River and the Eternal City of Nokron. By mapping this vertical journey, we can see how this spatial transition is carefully designed to maximize the sublime and picturesque aesthetics of the experience [Fig.10]. For the first 170 metres (558 ft) of the descent, players are closely surrounded by repetitious building elements, before quickly passing a single set of open windows that offer a fleeting view into Nokron city. Further down, the landscape of Siofra River Well opens up, framed by rock faces, before the player lands at the bottom of the well. Here, players find a remarkably preserved city living 'under a false night sky.'[20] This notion of a world within a world, and architecture with its own sky is reminiscent of the speculative work of 18th-century French architect Etienne-Louis Boullée, whose seminal project Cenotaph for Isaac Newton employed a giant spherical form with tiny holes in the building's surface that created a night sky during daylight.[21] Through screenshot photography we are able to see Nokron's design in a similar lineage, as an impossible, but highly symbolic architectural landscape [Fig.11].

[Fig.09] **DOCUMENTING DIFFERENT TYPOLOGIES OF COMMON SECRET SPACES, SUCH AS ILLUSORY WALLS AND FLOORS, FURNITURE AND FITTINGS THAT MOVE AND INVISIBLE PLATFORMS.**

[Fig.10] PAGES 112–13

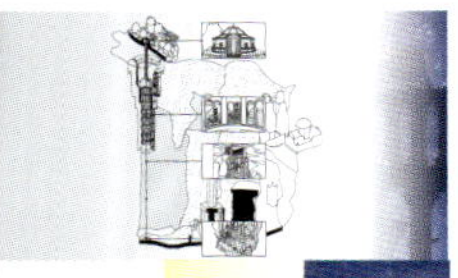

Mapping the vertical journey from Siofra River Well to the Eternal City of Nokron, showing how snippets of architectural views and careful visual reveals are used to surprise the player.

[Fig.11] PAGE 114

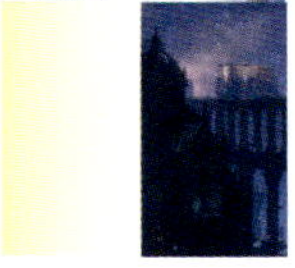

View across Nokron and the Siofra River area, showing the rich architecture and underground skyscape of the Nox people.

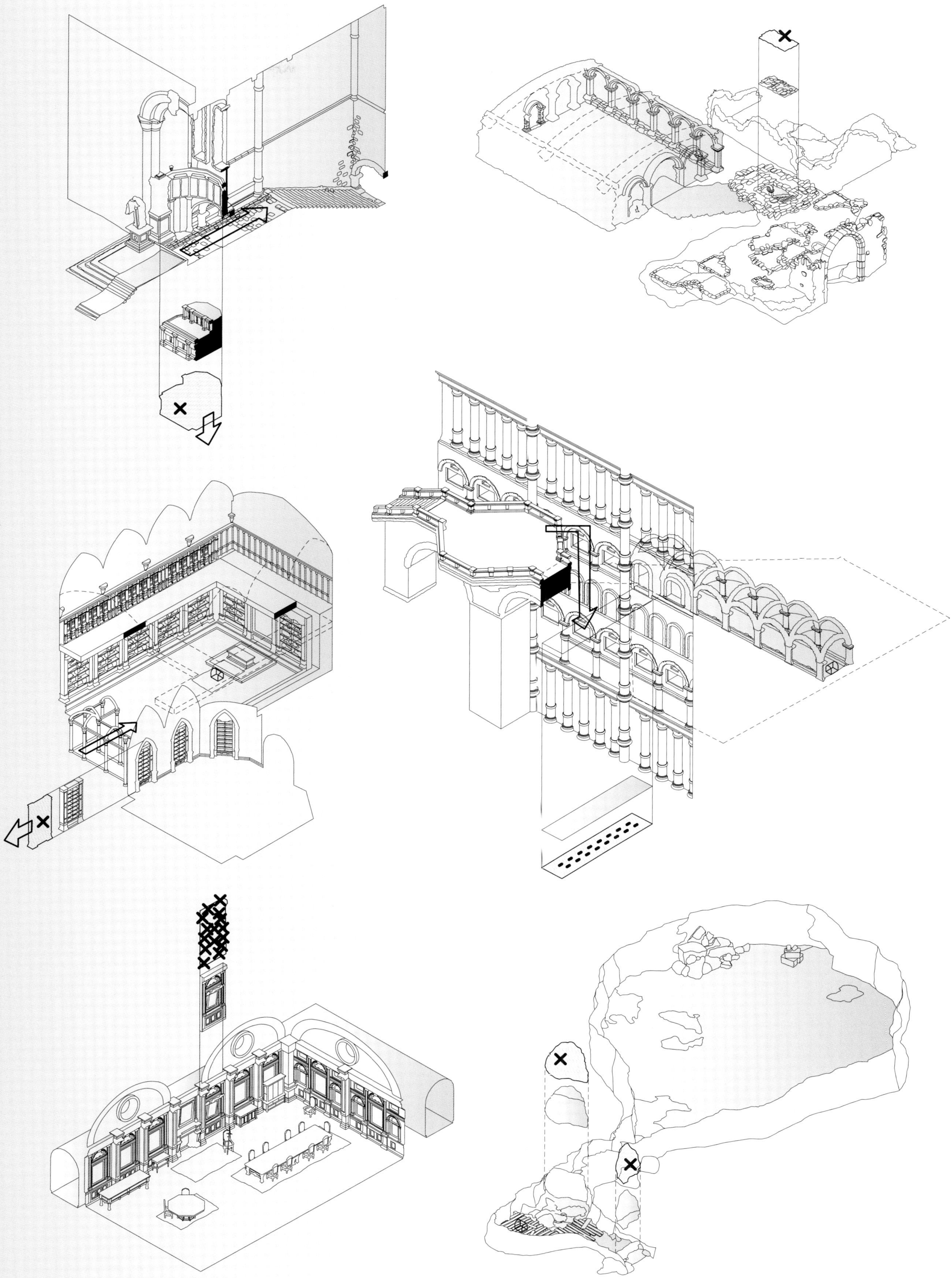

[Fig.09]

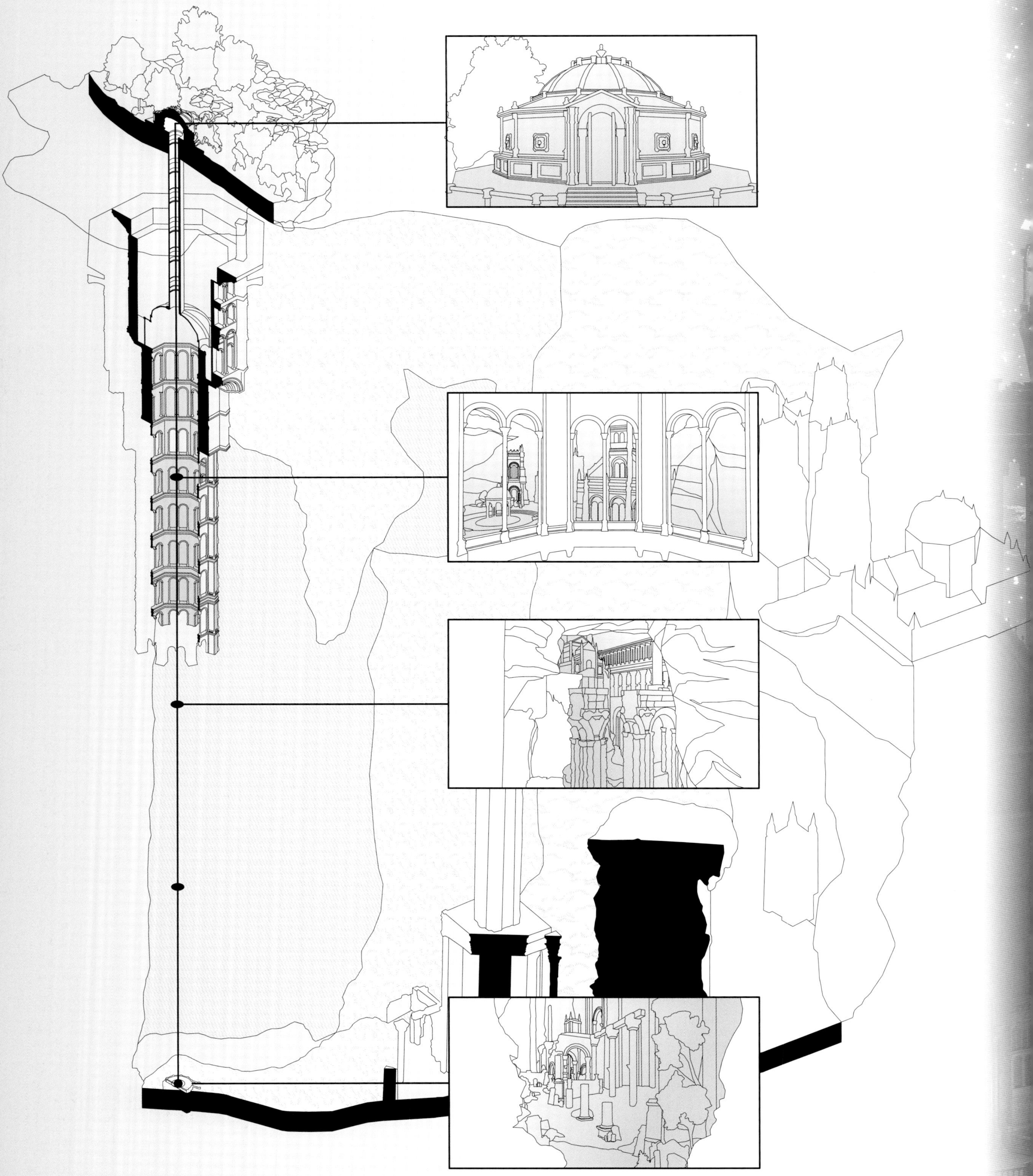

[Fig.10]

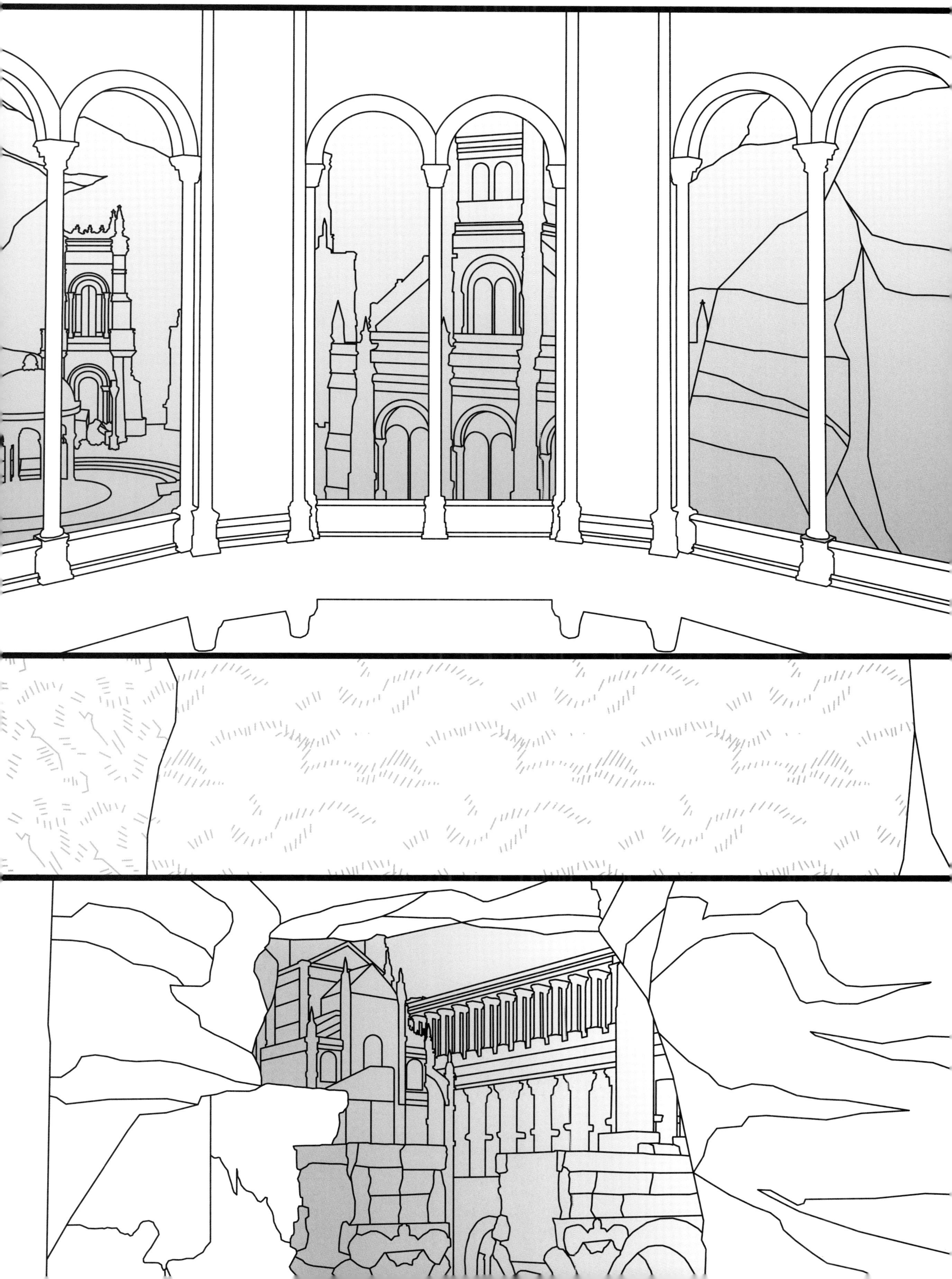

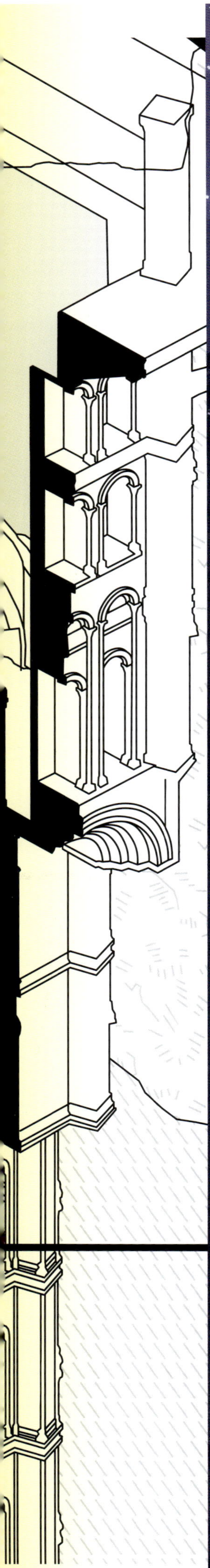

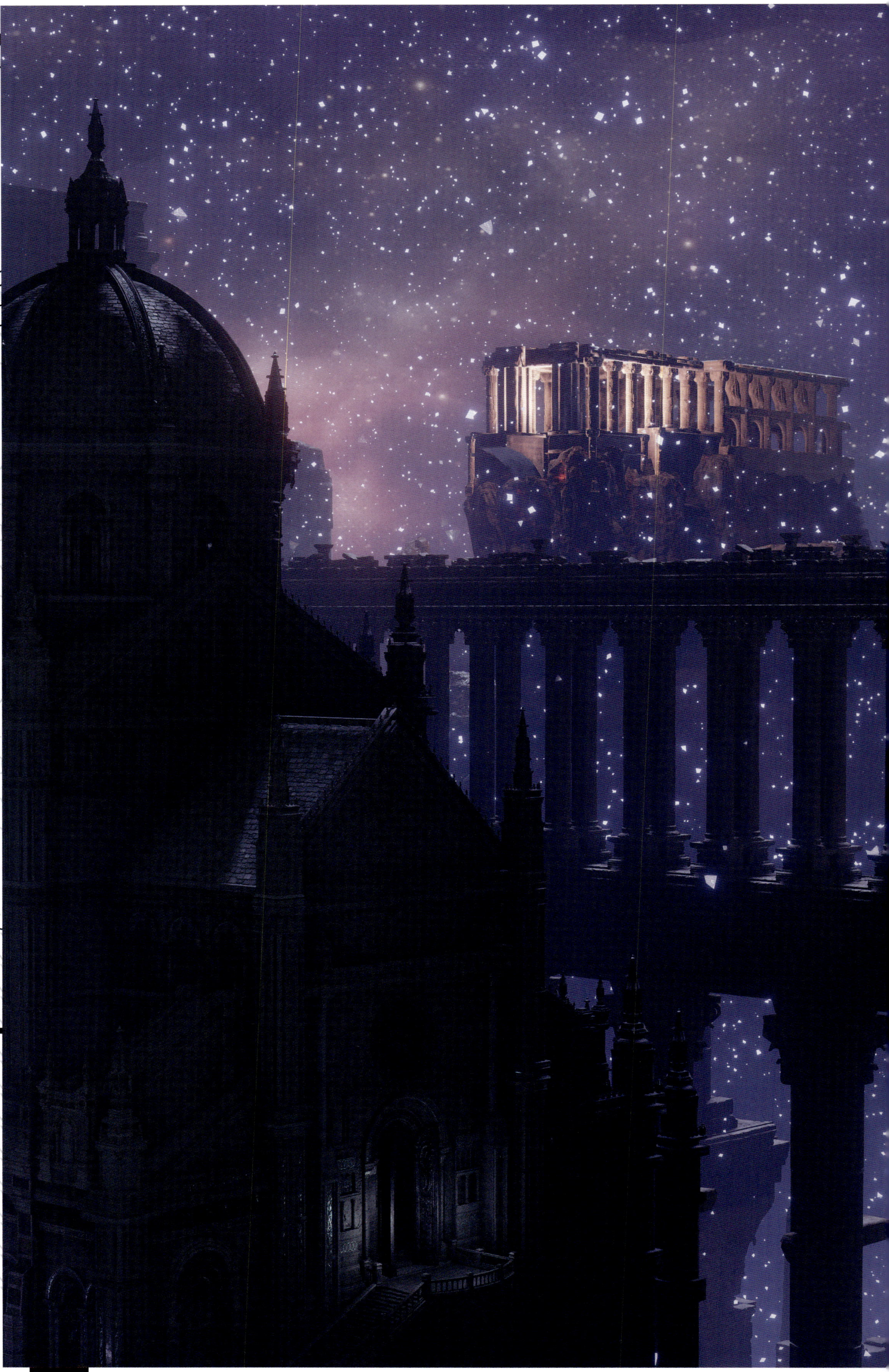

[Fig.11]

5.4

ROMANTIC REALMS

Perhaps more than any other FromSoftware game, *Elden Ring* manifests a sense of architectural and spatial sublime through its picturesque landscape design, emphasizing the old adage of William Shenstone that 'the foot should never travel' to an object 'by the same path, which the eye has travelled over before.'[22] This relationship to art aesthetics as described by Miyazaki is quite literally established through the paintings that can be found across the world. By locating the picturesque viewpoint depicted in the painting, players can find rare items, but this requires the type of winding journey Shenstone's ideas call for. Having found *The Sacred Tower* [Fig.12] painting in a cave in the Gravesite Plain region of the DLC, one such journey traces a circuitous path to locate a viewpoint of the towering structure of Enir-Ilim. Even the most direct route to this overlook requires looping around on oneself, passing multiple Sites of Grace and unlocking secret Spirit Springs. The reward, as well as the item, is to see the architecture of Enir-Ilim in its perfect, most picturesque setting, where the space of the world and the space of the painting combine into a single vista.

All ten paintings (across the base game and DLC) romantically depict an architectural structure in the world, recalling the work of artists such as John Martin (1789–1854) and Caspar David Friedrich (1774–1840) whose bombastic romantic landscapes that captivated the public were arguably the media equivalent of *Elden Ring* in their own time. These paintings emphasize how important the world's buildings are for communicating scale, context and lore. The paintings in *Elden Ring* underpin a relatively simple 'treasure hunt', yet these journeys take us away from seeing the game's landscapes and buildings as pure spaces of danger and aggression, and allow us to appreciate them as aesthetic experiences: sublime, and godly. We might wonder if these are the moments where FromSoftware's spatial vision is most poetically manifest, not only through the trials of combat and adversity, but in the simple pleasure of standing atop a hill and gazing over a wondrous landscape, beholding all the spectacular architectural fantasies it contains.

[Fig.12]
PAGE 116

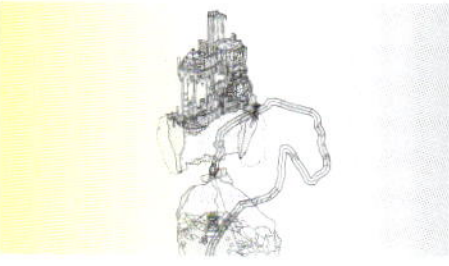

A map showing a player's route to find the picturesque view of Inir-Elim, as depicted in the in-game painting, *The Sacred Tower*.

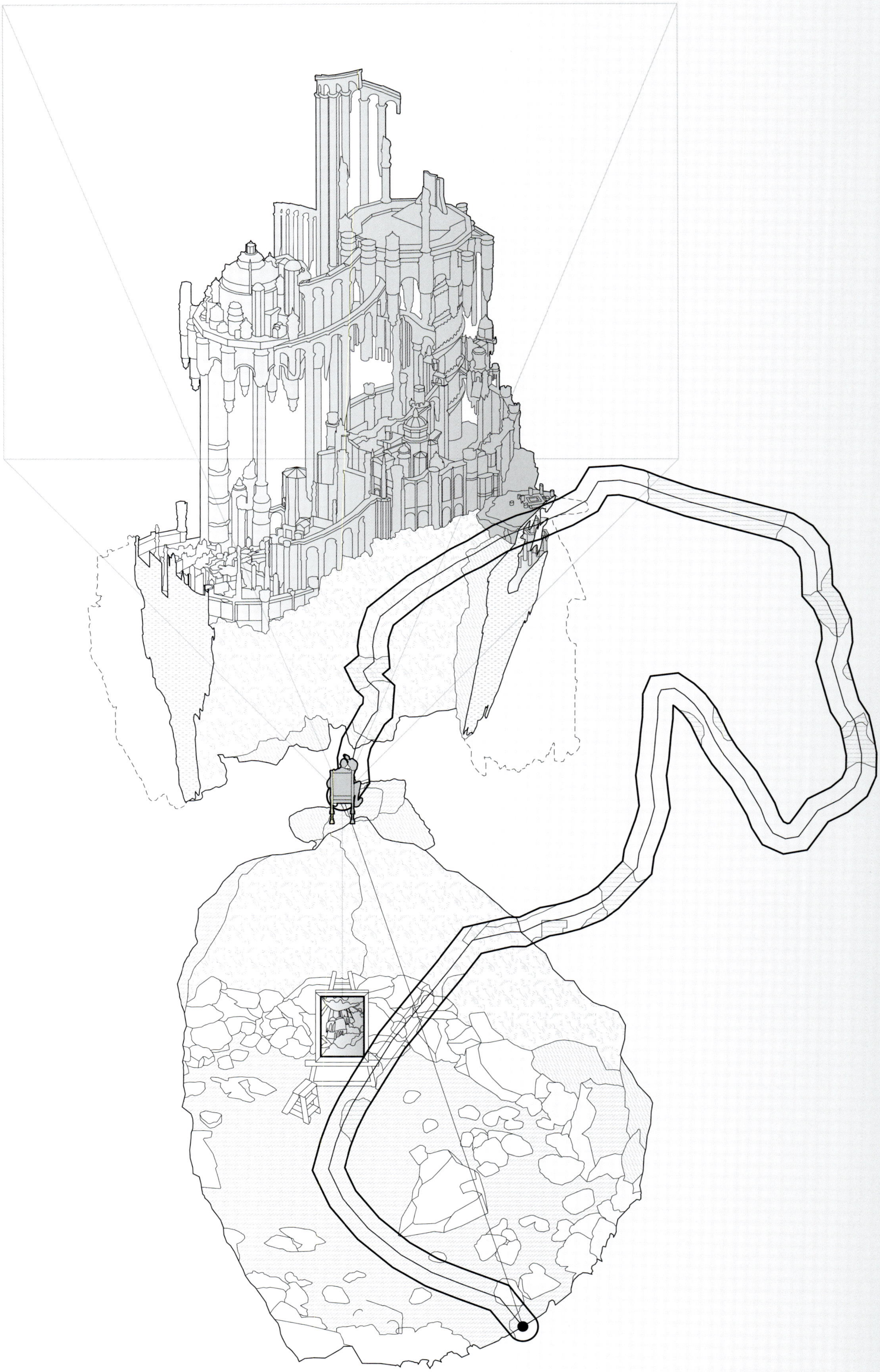

[Fig.12]

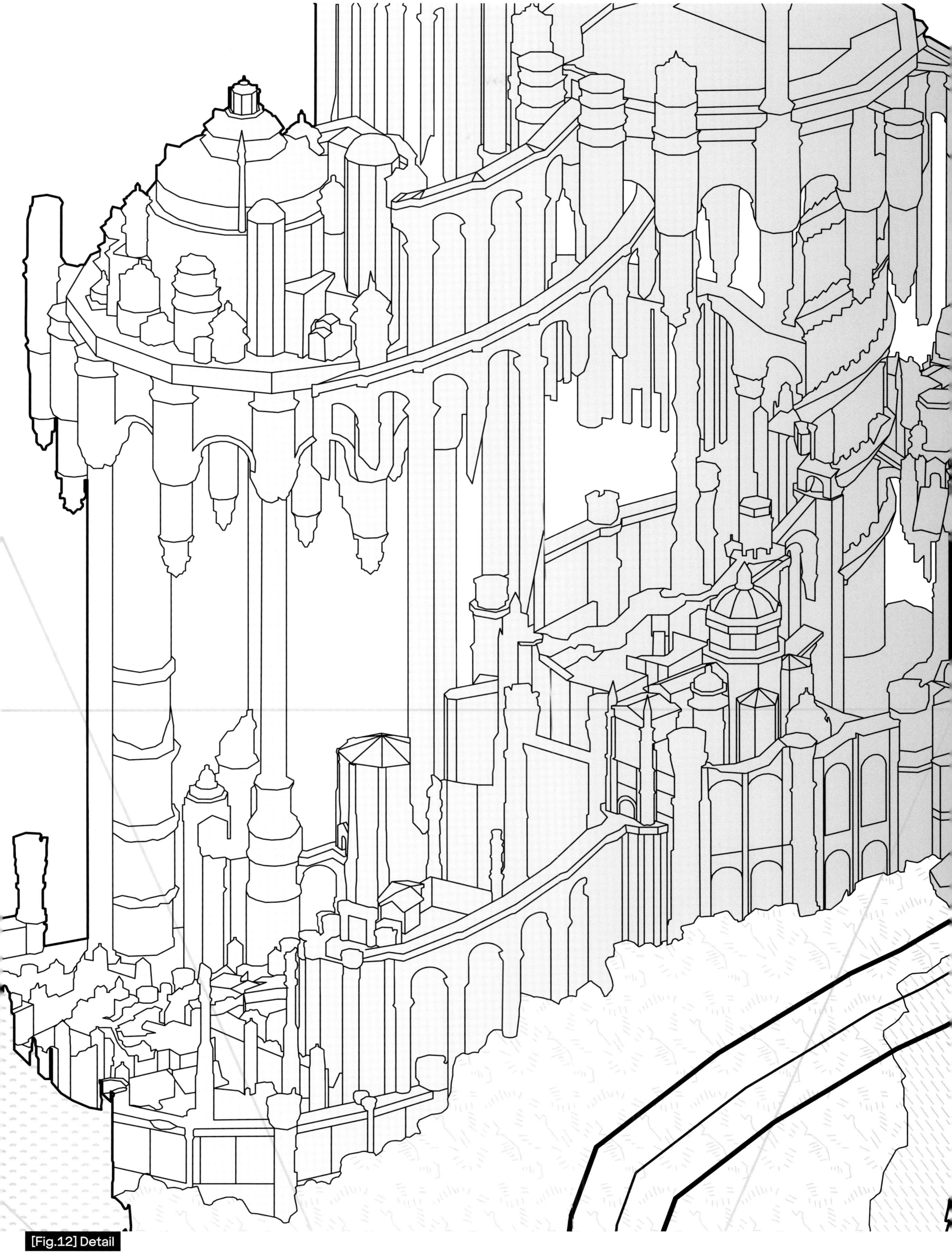

[Fig.12] Detail

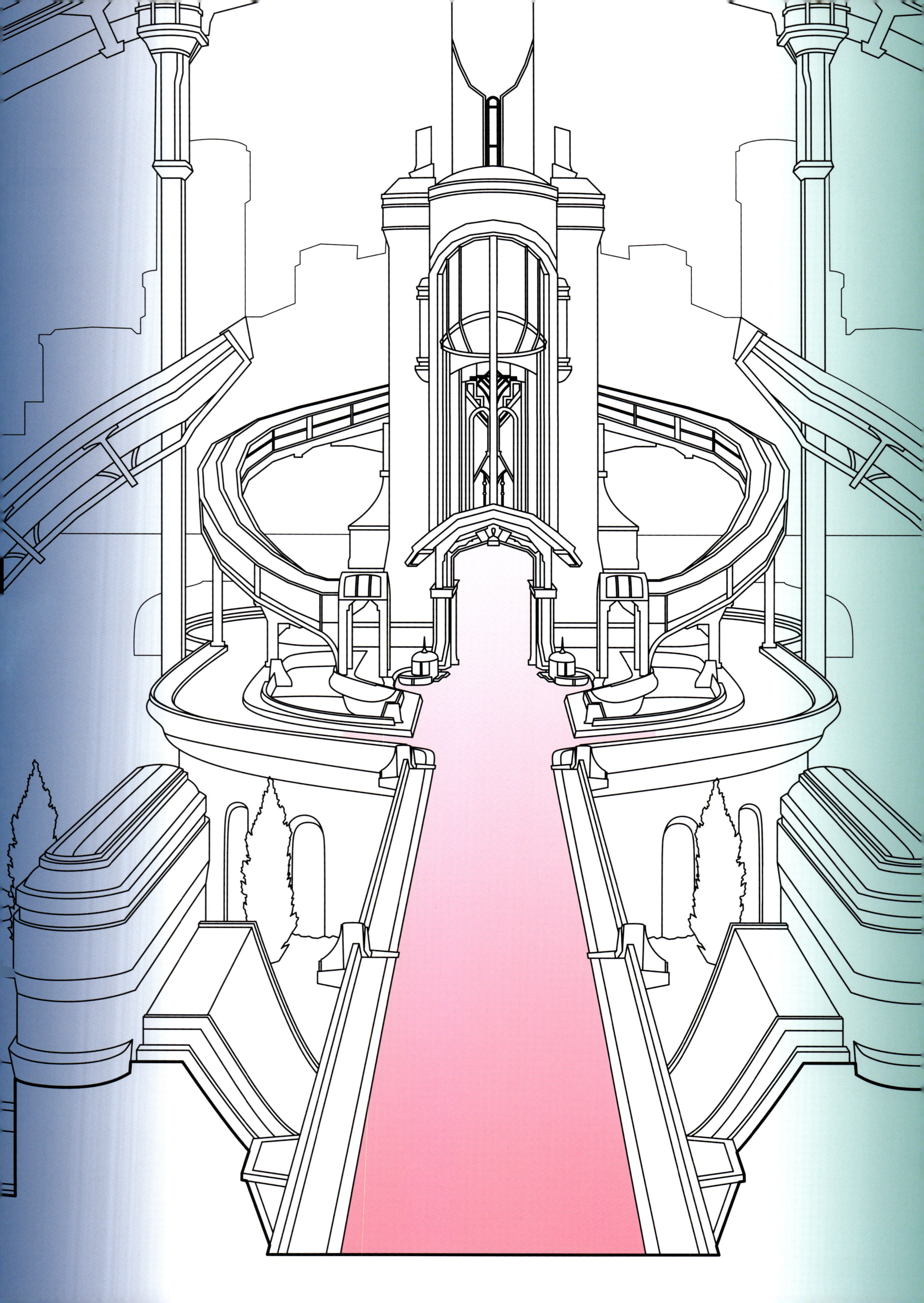

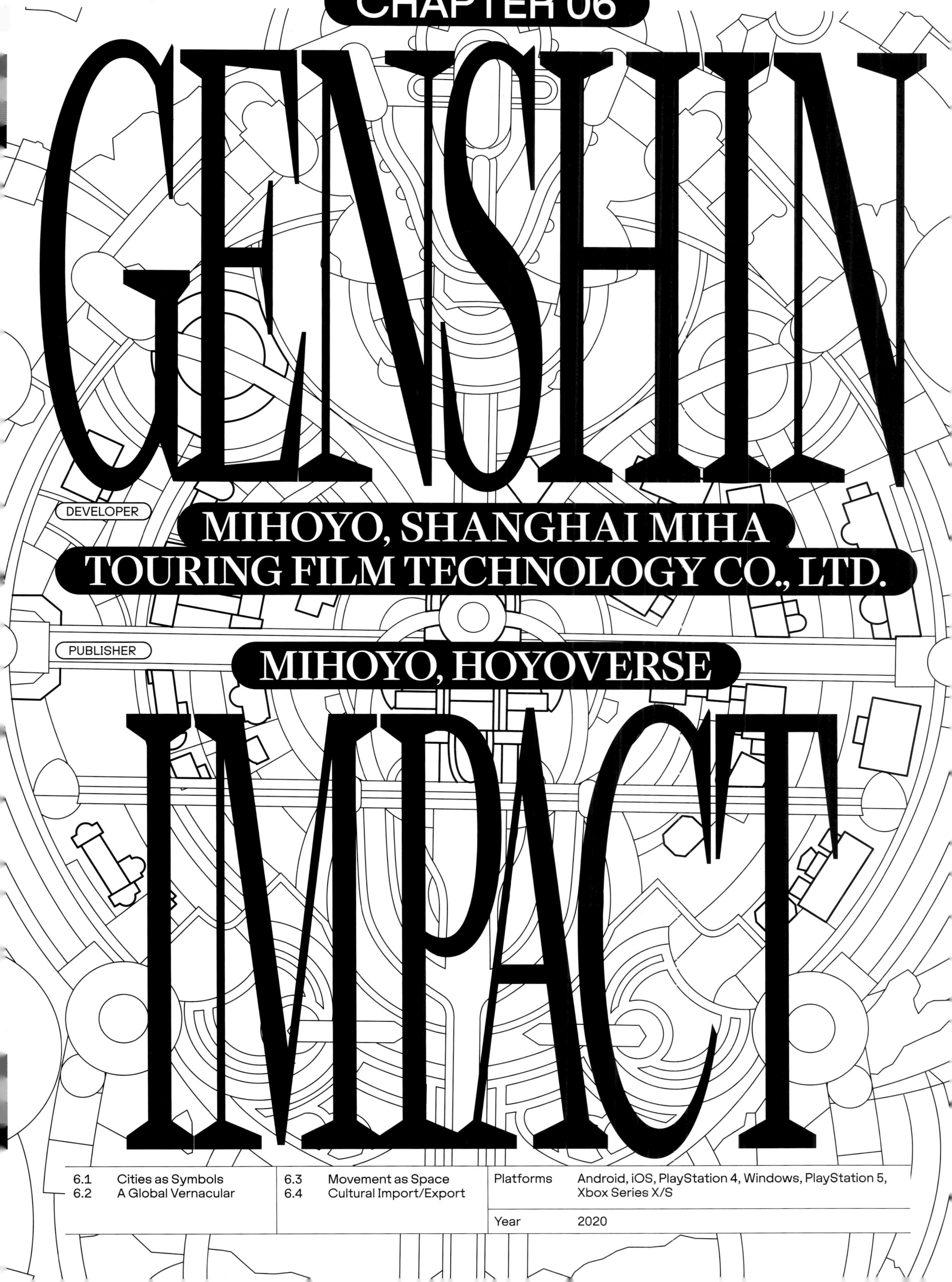

CHAPTER 06

GENSHIN IMPACT

DEVELOPER

MIHOYO, SHANGHAI MIHA TOURING FILM TECHNOLOGY CO., LTD.

PUBLISHER

MIHOYO, HOYOVERSE

Platforms	Android, iOS, PlayStation 4, Windows, PlayStation 5, Xbox Series X/S
Year	2020

STATUES OF SEVEN ARE WAYPOINTS THAT CORRESPOND TO DIFFERENT GEOGRAPHICAL TERRITORIES, WHICH ARE UNLOCKED BY THE PLAYER AS THEY EXPLORE NEW AREAS IN THE GAME.

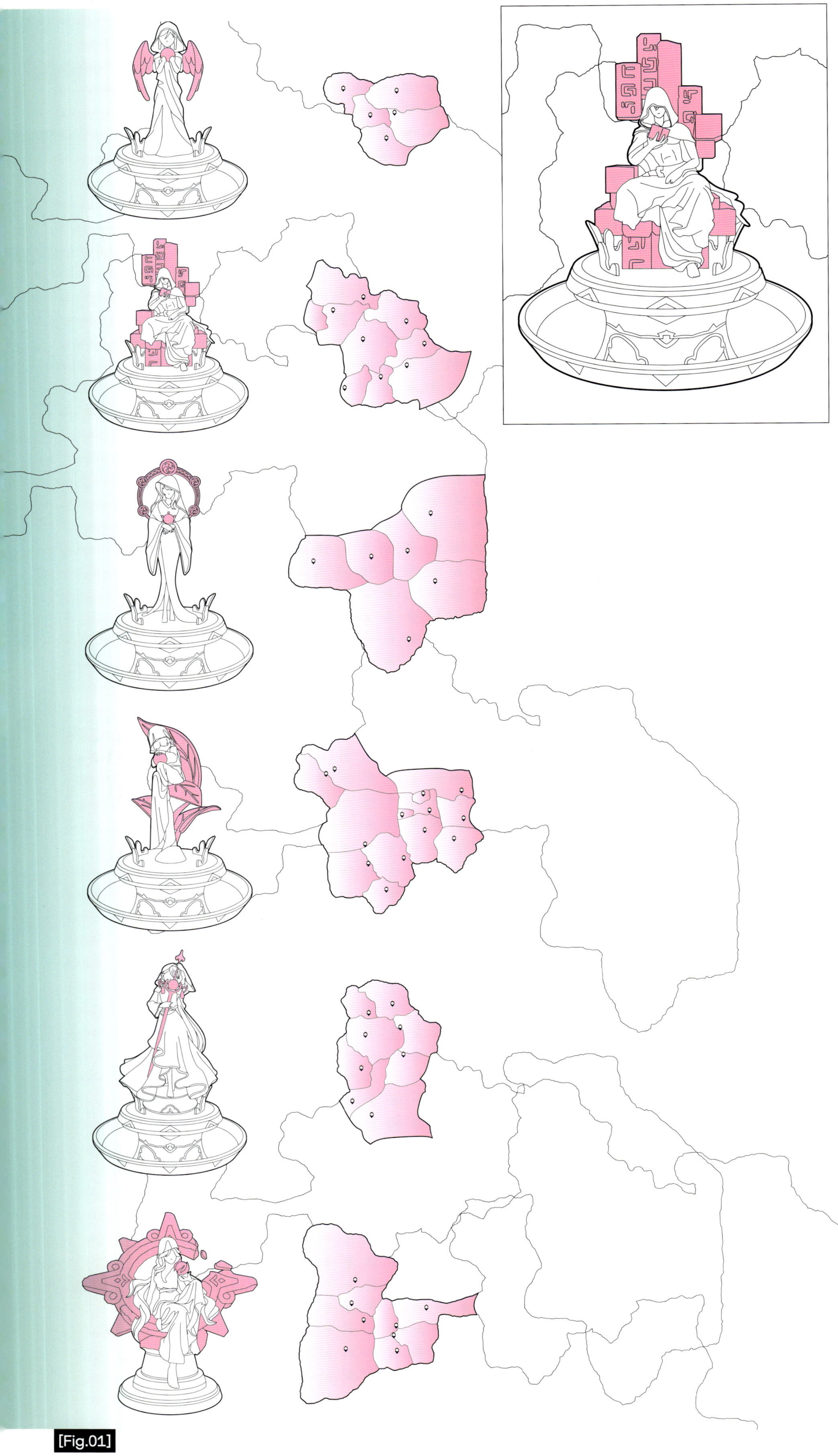

[Fig.01]

6.1

CITIES AS SYMBOLS

Genshin Impact's expansive, fantastical open-world is one of the biggest videogame exports to come out of the Chinese market, achieving worldwide success since its initial release in 2020, with translations in fifteen languages and cross-platform availability. *Genshin Impact* and its sister game, *Honkai: Star Rail*, have put young Chinese developer miHoYo on the global map, drawing hundreds of millions of players into its dynamic universe (aptly named the 'HoYoverse'). While it frequently draws comparisons to Nintendo's *The Legend of Zelda: Breath of the Wild*, the game carves a distinct identity through its gacha-style gameplay, elemental combat systems and ambitious worldbuilding that incorporates diverse cultural regions. An intricate storyline ties all these facets together.

Playing as The Traveller, a character that explores the seven nations of Teyvat to find their lost sibling, the game utilizes RPG mechanics and a vibrant, anime aesthetic within an extensive open-world environment. The exploration of Teyvat is incremental – while players can be guided in a more linear fashion through quest storylines that direct them to specific locations, it is also possible to walk between regions, seeking out ornate Statues of Seven that open new parts of the map and provide quick travel locations. Beyond their practical function as teleport waypoints and healing stations, the Statues of Seven represent the Seven Archons (gods) of each region, and their associated element, standing as visual statements of cultural and elemental sovereignty. Identified by a vertical beam of red light that turns blue once activated, they can be seen from a distance in the landscape, often positioned at peaks, edges or entrances to significant points of interest. Reaching a Statue symbolizes an act of conquest for the player, making them a marker of progress and success. The Statues vary in appearance, posture and material, with these differences tied to the identity of each Archon they represent, and the values of the surrounding region – for example, Mondstadt's Anemo statue shows a winged figure, evoking the region's spirit as 'the city of wind'. Through their function and design, they blend navigational logic with architectural curiosity, embedding game systems within distinct spatial monuments. Mapping these statues against the territory they are associated with allows players to position themselves in relation to the changing form of these symbolic structures [Fig.01]. While these boundaries are clear from above, the visual coding of the Statues of Seven enables players to broadly orient themselves within the world without the need for a map. *Genshin Impact*'s waypoints have also become a way to promote particular locations that inspired the game. The Chinese government commissioned real-life versions of the Statues to be built, one of which can be found in Zhangjiajie National Park, Hunan, China, which is a visual inspiration for the region of Liyue.[1]

Within each of the game's six current nations, we find cities that share common points of interest, including restaurants, blacksmiths, general goods and souvenir stores, alongside more localized specialities like teahouses and taverns. While these cities appear dense, with a rich variety of buildings and structures, most buildings within them remain decorative and inaccessible, acting as compelling yet non-functioning spatial backdrops to the player's journey through the city. This mirrors real-world architectural settings such as 18th-century Potemkin villages, designed to evoke an illusion of grandeur, or modern-day Parisian *fausses façades* (fake façades), which mimic the city's traditional Haussmann buildings but are used to hide engineering infrastructure within them.[2] As our comparative mapping of each city shows [Fig.02], the extent of accessible buildings are small in comparison, peppered between the dummy streetscapes. These act as open-world barriers, objects to climb on top of or navigate around rather than through.[3] Their artificial nature is further emphasized by the lack of doors and windows that look into empty or disjointed rooms – as YouTube user Beerevity observes, for the city and the image it projects, 'impression is more important than functionality.'[4] Many of the façades imply inhabitation rather than facilitate it – incorporating signifiers such as balconies, staircases and illuminated windows to give the buildings a sense of authenticity. Yet ultimately the player's agency to explore these spaces is limited, subjecting much of *Genshin Impact*'s inhabitable architecture to structured, more discrete moments rather than continuous urban environments.

[Fig.02]
PAGE 123
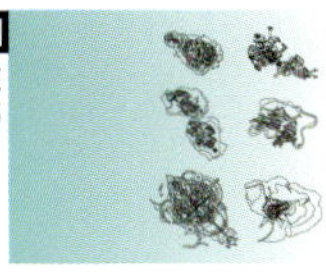

Each world's urban centre, highlighting buildings with inhabitable interiors in the game, and how the environment is designed as an elaborate yet largely inaccessible backdrop.

Looking beyond the volumetric plan and into the sectional layering of the city reveals deeper and more complex narratives about each region and their given histories. While most of *Genshin Impact*'s cities are most legibly experienced from a top-down perspective, their vertical arrangements both conceal and expose key historical developments. The city of Fontaine demonstrates this through its stacked nature – penetrating deep below the surface of the water and onto the seabed [Fig.03]. While the city above the water, in its high-rise and progressive Belle Époque style, signifies prosperity and innovation, beneath the water the player encounters ancient ruins from a prior civilization. This reveals how the city's elegance is ironically supported by a forgotten and failing foundation, drawing inspiration from real architectural history – from modern-day Rome, built on top of its own ancient ruins, to Kaifeng in central China's Henan, where excavations unveiled six 'layered cities' from different Chinese dynasties piled on top of one another.[5] This sectional logic echoes Fontaine's lore – a nation above ground that is consumed with image, order and justice, yet underpinned by fractures that are concealed by the water.

The image of each city is first understood by the player through its edges and boundary conditions when they reach the city, which range in varying degrees of porosity. Comparing the key entry points to each city [Fig.04] demonstrates how it presents itself to visitors, with openness or hostility, reinforcing Juhani Pallasmaa's concept on thresholds, writing 'The door is a mediating element between...invitation and refusal.'[6] Mondstadt City and Inazuma City adopted heavy, walled, fortress-like forms, tied to their Germanic and Japanese design influences. The scale of the openings relative to the surrounding structures is small, evoking a defensive nature that reinforces their lore. In contrast, Natlan's Stadium of the Sacred Flame showcases a more expansive and triumphant thoroughfare, supported by monumental columns and plazas with low boundary walls that allow unrestricted sightlines into its civic core – a ceremonial space for gathering and collectivity. Liyue Harbour faces outwards onto the water, and is flanked by large, ceremonial *pailou* (gateways) that frame the player's approach into the city. In Sumeru City, the architecture is ecologically integrated into the surrounding rainforest landscape, blurring the transition between wilderness and man-made structures. This results in a more multi-faceted and permeable boundary, with smaller, more diffused entry points into the city. The boundary conditions of each city become architectural statements that project the city's values onto the outside, before the player crosses the threshold. As in many real-world cities, from the fortified gates of medieval Avila to the ceremonial grandeur of Babylon's Ishtar Gate, thresholds in *Genshin Impact* function as architectural declarations of identity and ideology. Their design facilitates both movement and meaning, shaping the player's psychological transition from nature into culture.

[Fig.03]
PAGES 124–5

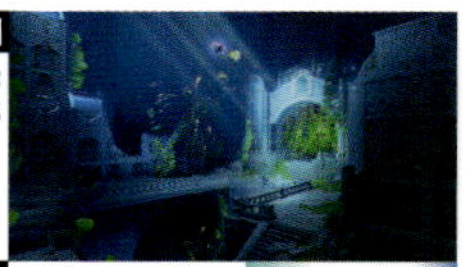

Encountering ancient ruins that reveal the hidden history of a city's past, emphasizing the importance of collapse and renewal within the game.

[Fig.04]
PAGE 126

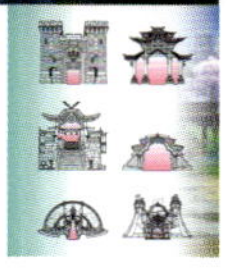

Thresholds that demarcate entry into the city through expressive, architectural gateways, communicating different levels of porosity.

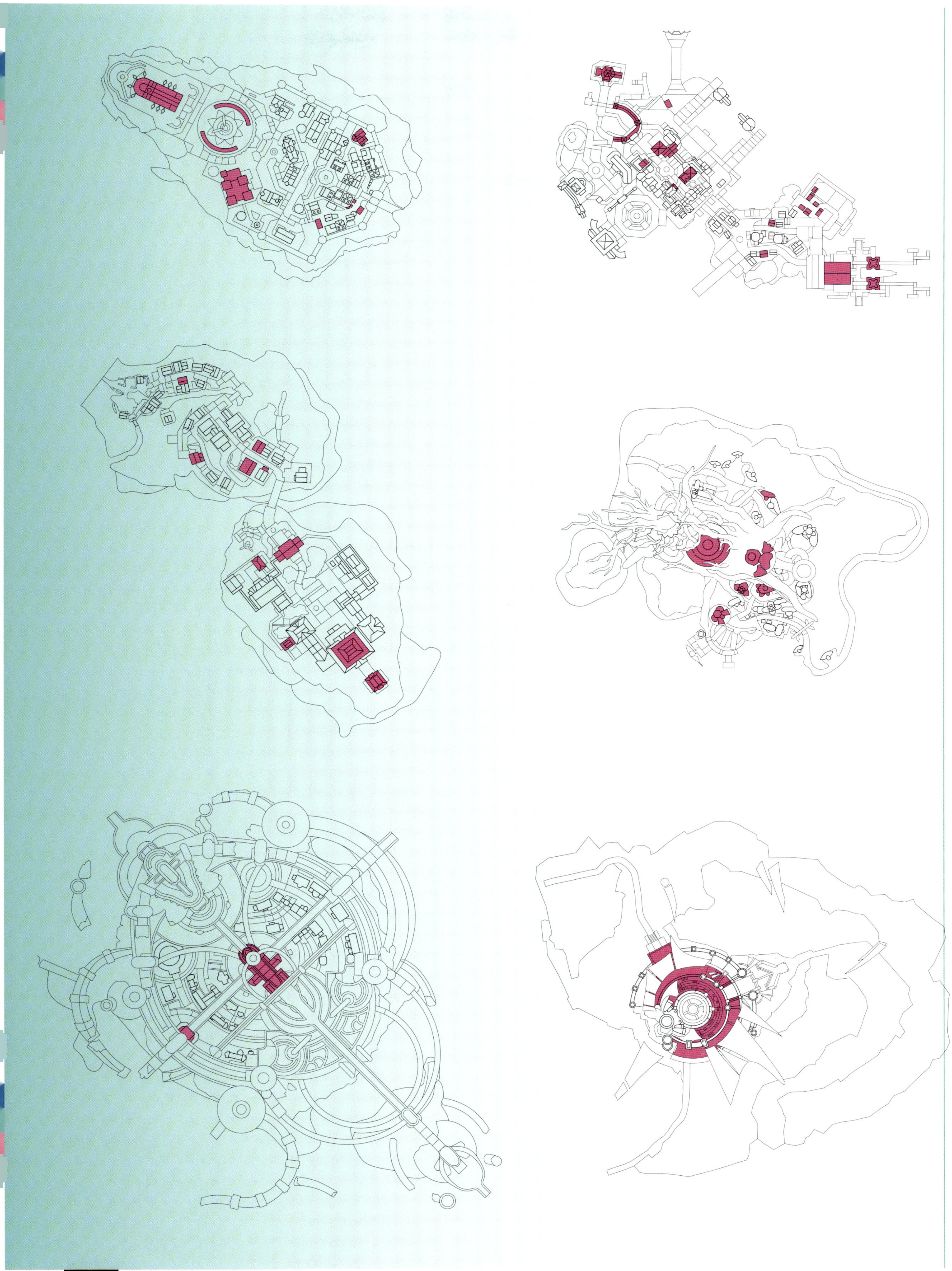

[Fig.02]

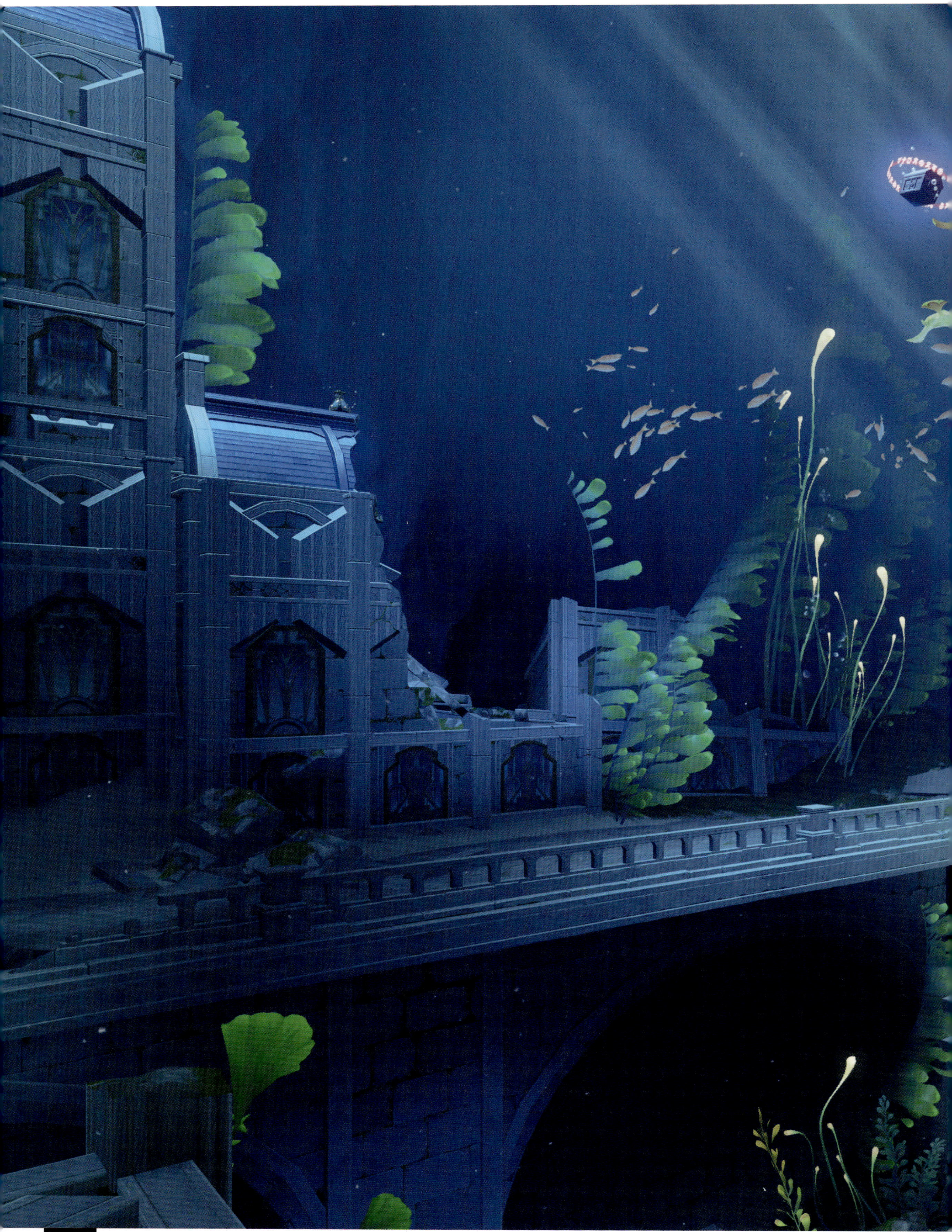

[Fig.03]

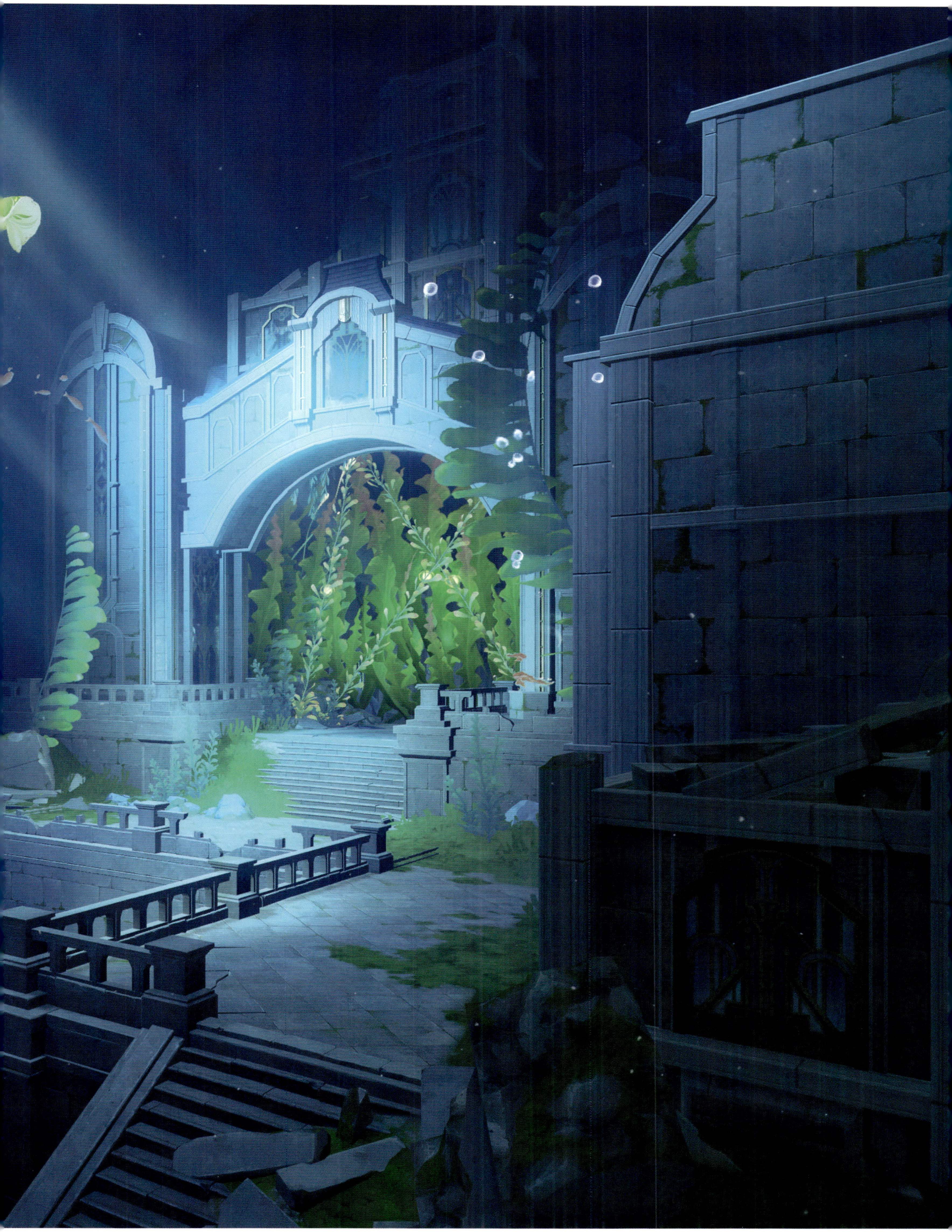

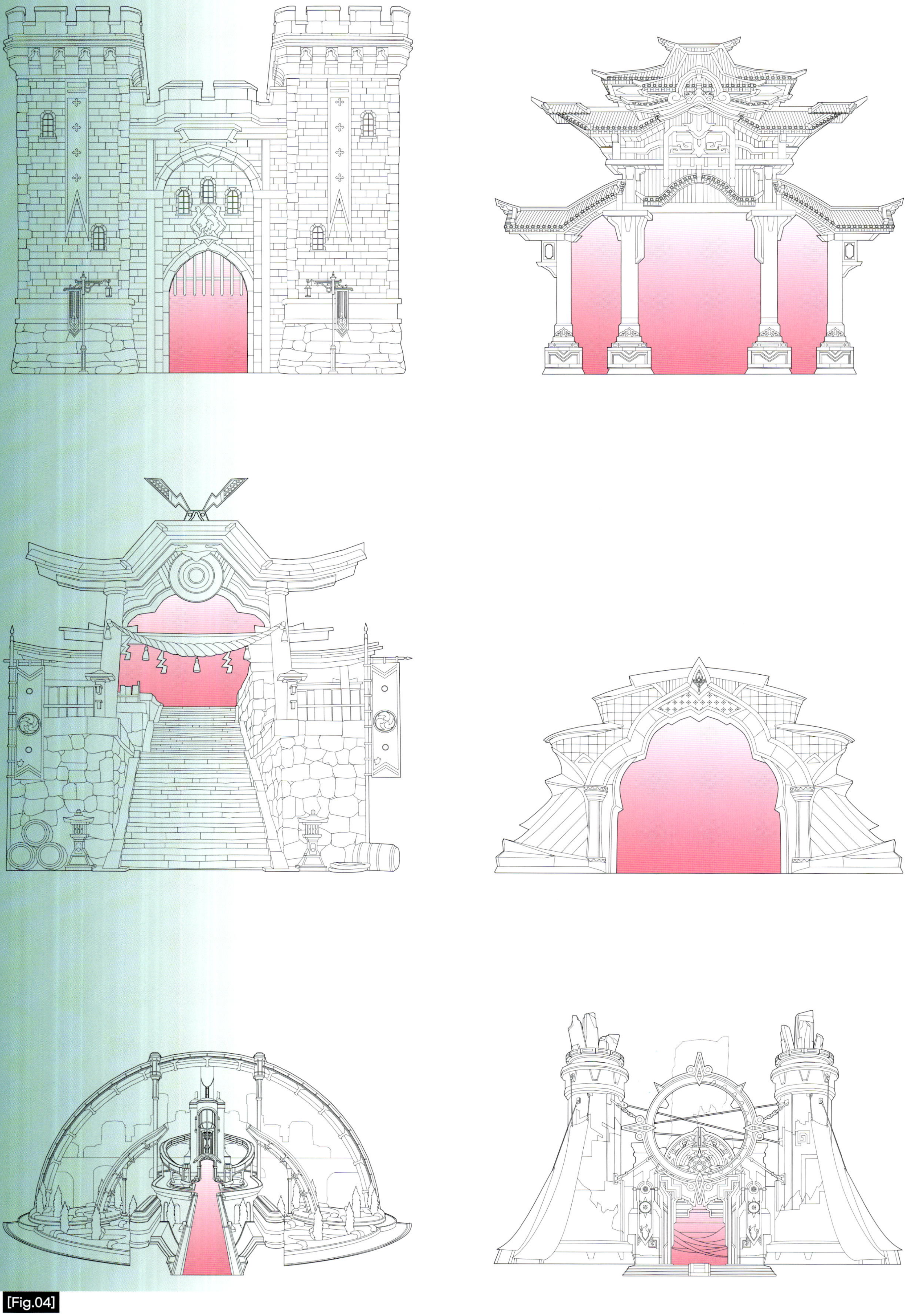

[Fig.04]

6.2 A GLOBAL VERNACULAR

Genshin Impact's architectural influences have long been discussed by both players and developers since the game's launch, and alongside the release of new nations over the years. Each nation adopts a stylistic template from the real world, often fusing various spatial and cultural influences. The game's original release introduced players to Liyue and Mondstadt, two vastly different nations in which the developers focused on bringing together eastern and western approaches within the same overall world. Cai Haoyu, the Producer of *Genshin Impact* and CEO of miHoYo describes this as a way of increasing the game's global appeal, making it more relatable to a wider audience, while through the Liyue region, offering fresh perspectives on Chinese culture.[7] The game is also influenced by a number of real-world settings – landscapes such as Tianzishan Nature Reserve and Huanglong National Park in China, and Ha Long Bay in Vietnam, create dynamic backdrops for the game's more natural settings. Architecturally, iconic buildings such as Osaka Castle in Japan, and Freiburg Minster in Germany are used as reference points for some of the cities' more flagship buildings, in which their function is informed by the region's lore, rather than reality. While these are more straightforward comparisons, the region of Sumeru blends various architectural influences together, like the Moorish architecture in Spain, such as the Alhambra Palace, and Persian influences from palaces in Iran. Throughout the game, these references are incorporated to encourage associations with the real world, reshaping global architecture into a playable and symbolic landscape [Fig.05]. Tying these vastly different global styles together within one game relies heavily on the visual style – an anime world that compliments rather than contradicts the appearance of the characters that inhabit it. This was done through multi-layered terrains, painted textures, dynamic lighting and careful shadow play to achieve a 'flattened' anime effect.[8] In this way, *Genshin Impact* synthesizes a diverse range of global architectural and landscape references with its characters to create a unified visual language. This reinforces the game's narrative worldbuilding objectives through an overall stylistic framework.

Genshin Impact also provides space for player-led creativity through the Serenitea Pot creation system, allowing players to generate their own designs within a series of parallel realms, which can be accessed via a teapot gadget. As they unlock Remarkable Chests, players gain access to a total of 316 Furnishing Blueprints, which are located within every region in Teyvat. These Blueprints can be used in combination with regional materials to create different furnishings, which fall into Exterior and Interior subcategories, encompassing landscape features, entire buildings and decorative objects. Within the Building subcategory, the Blueprints obtained are based on in-game buildings from each region, allowing players to create designs based on the multi-faceted nature of the architecture experienced within the game. By showcasing the diversity of architecture across regions, as well as within them [Fig.06], the game brings together styles that communicate private and public; urban and suburban; formal and informal languages to frame the architecture as a narrative device, at the disposal of the player within this system. Placing them in this way showcases the local vernacular within each region, and the many different architectural languages of Teyvat that we encounter within the game.

[Fig.05]
PAGE 128
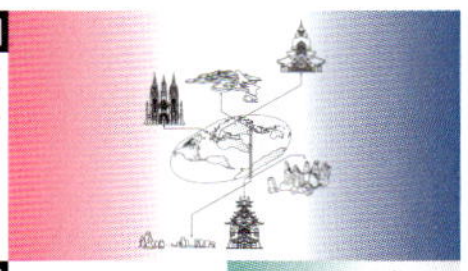
In-game locations inspired by real-world architecture, mapped on a global scale to demonstrate the diversity of cultural influences within the game.

[Fig.06]
PAGE 129
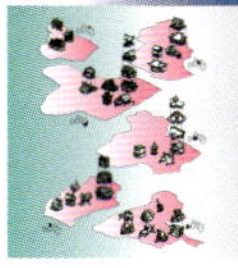
Architectural furnishings available to the player within the game's Serenitea Pot building system, mapped onto the game world to demonstrate each region's local vernacular.

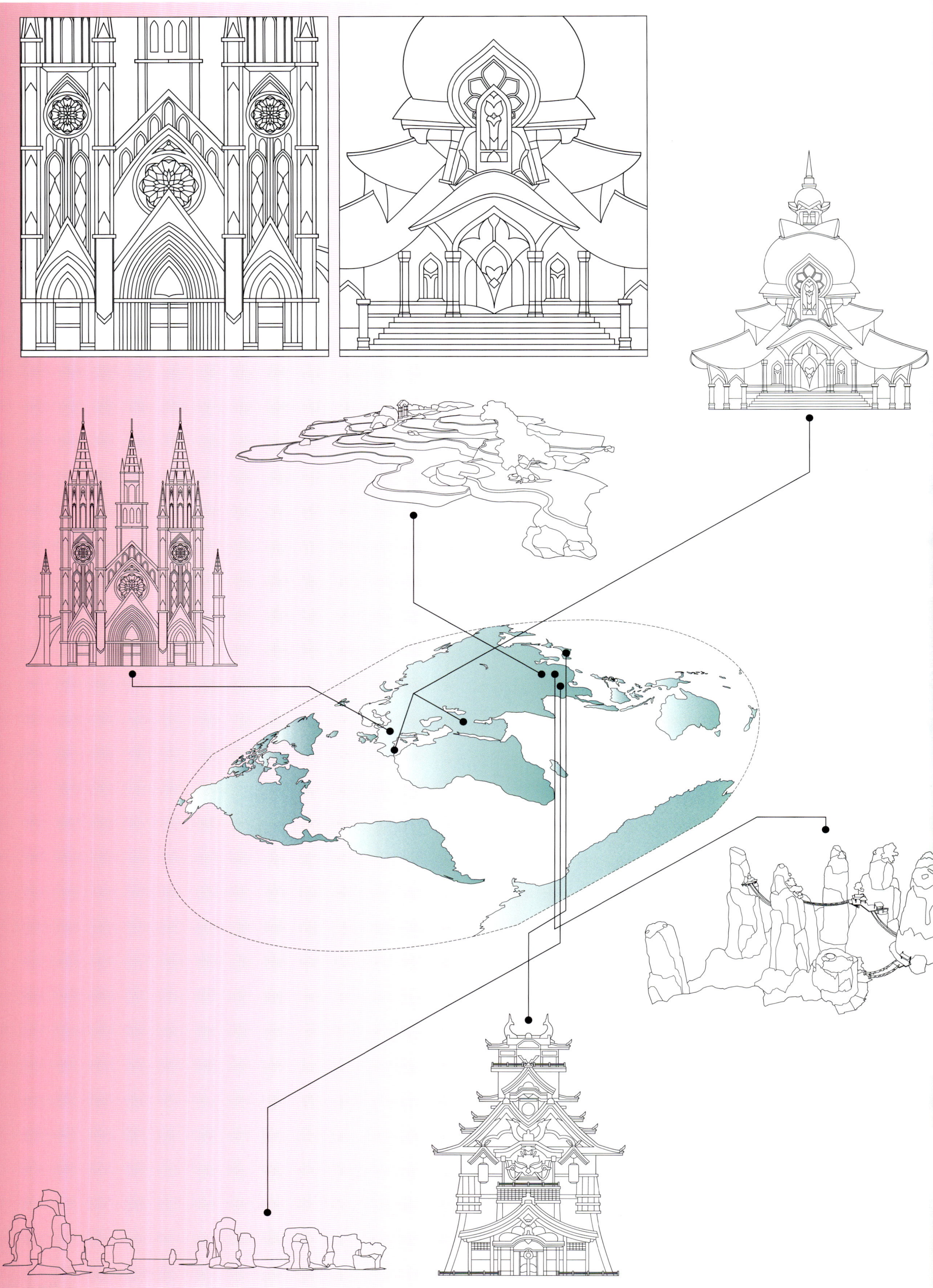

[Fig.05]

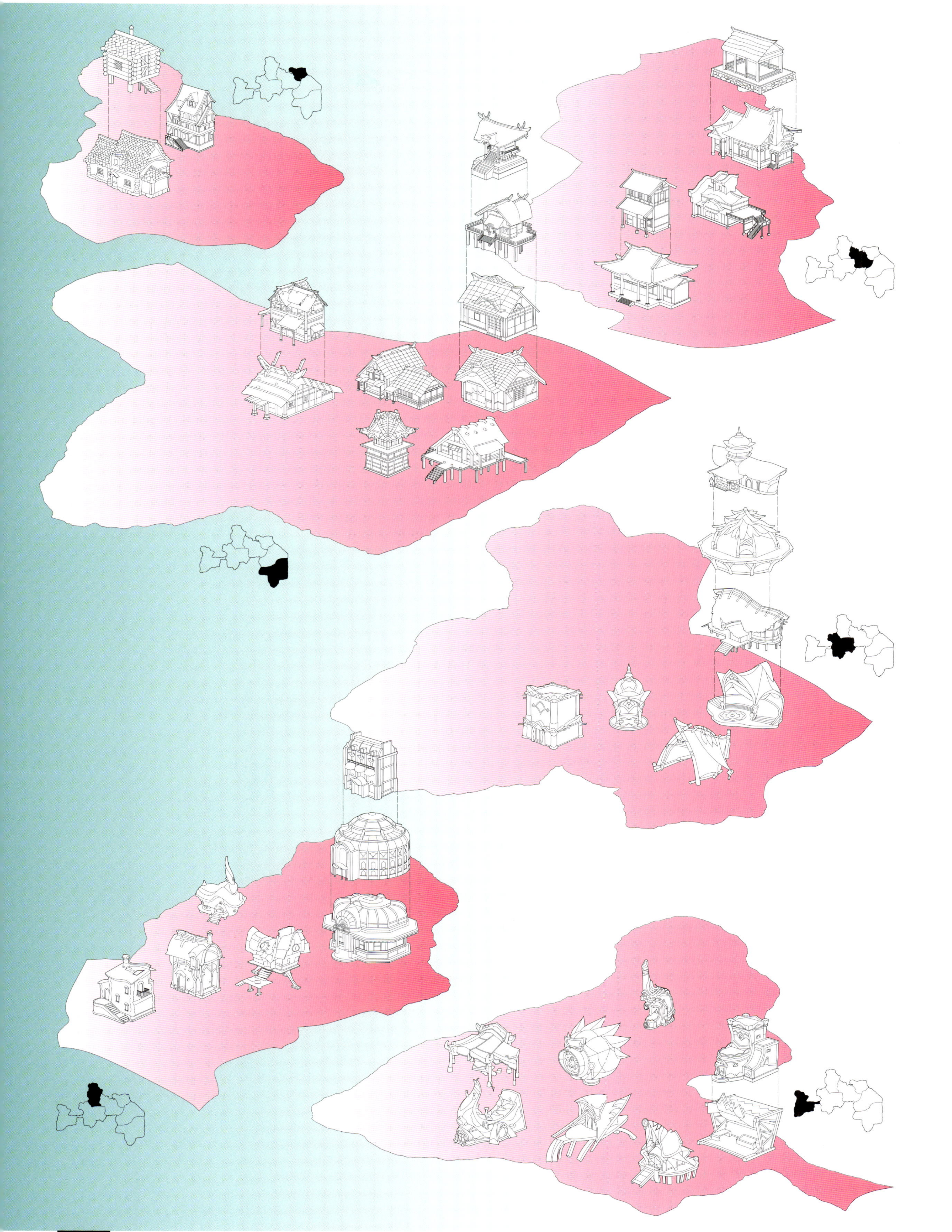

[Fig.06]

This vernacular is responsive to the landscape – once again reinforcing *Genshin Impact*'s sectional depth as a narrative device. Seats of power and buildings conveying social hierarchy are positioned further up in the terrain, on peaks or upper terraces, highlighting the association of knowledge and wealth as ascension. This is highly emblematic within Inazuma City, where Tenshukaku (a shogun residence) sits at the top of the hill, and can be viewed from the lowly agricultural outskirts of Hanamizaka [Fig.07]. This technique is mirrored in other regions – Liyue Harbour's snaking pathways and terraces echo this through the ascent from a more informal waterfront marketplace to elevated grand residences. This architectural symbolism echoes real-world instances, such as imperial pilgrimage routes up Mount Tai, the eastern mountain of the Sacred Mountains of China, where ascending through formal gates, terraces and inscriptions became both a spatial journey, as well as a political and ritual performance. Lifeng Han notes how these routes were carefully staged to translate imperial power into terrain, framing authority and spiritual legitimacy through elevation.[9]

Comparing some of Serenitea Pot's most popular player-created builds – a flowery bistro, an azure cottage and small swimming pool resort – shows us how they tend towards strictly reinforcing a particular style, establishing a clear regionalism to the designs and reusing the same elements many times [Fig.08]. Emphasizing thematic consistency rather than clashing experimentation seems to be a key approach for the most popular builders, creating designs that could be seamlessly transplanted into the game world. We could see this as a result of placing predefined modules on a building-by-building, object-by-object basis, rather than brick by brick – offering less flexibility to create truly custom designs. These in-built restrictions encourage players to think more creatively, scaling objects to use in different ways, or utilizing the top of a building as a footbridge, where thematic truth becomes more important than true scale.

[Fig.06] Detail

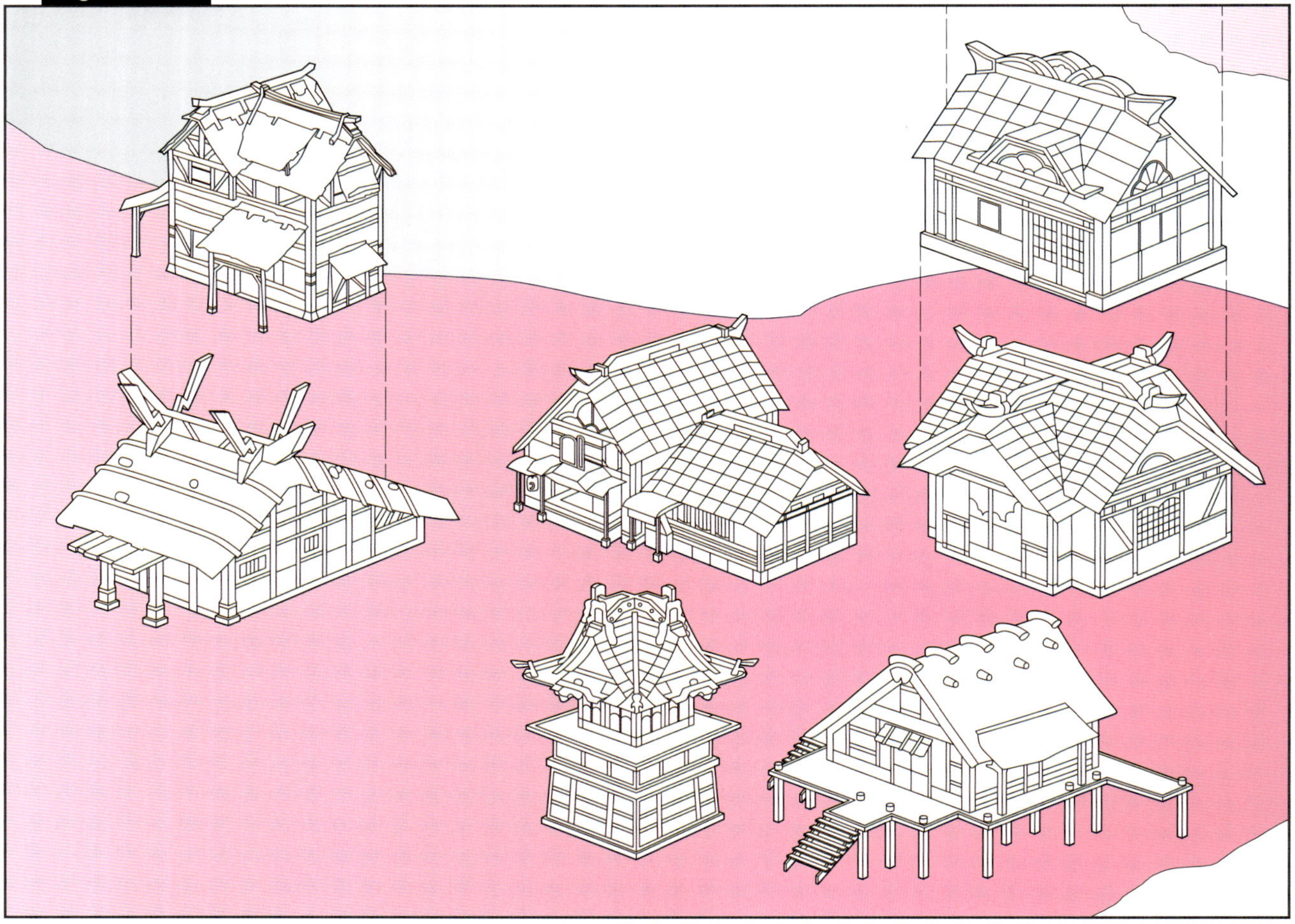

[Fig.08] PAGE 132

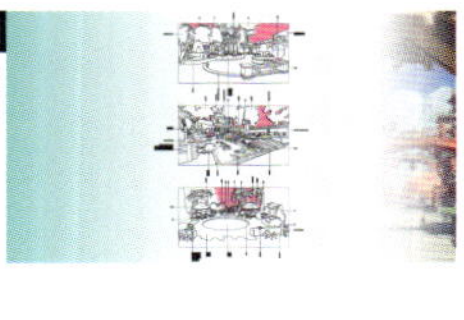

Stylized scenes created by players using the Serenitea Pot system, and the quantity of architectural furnishings required to construct each space.

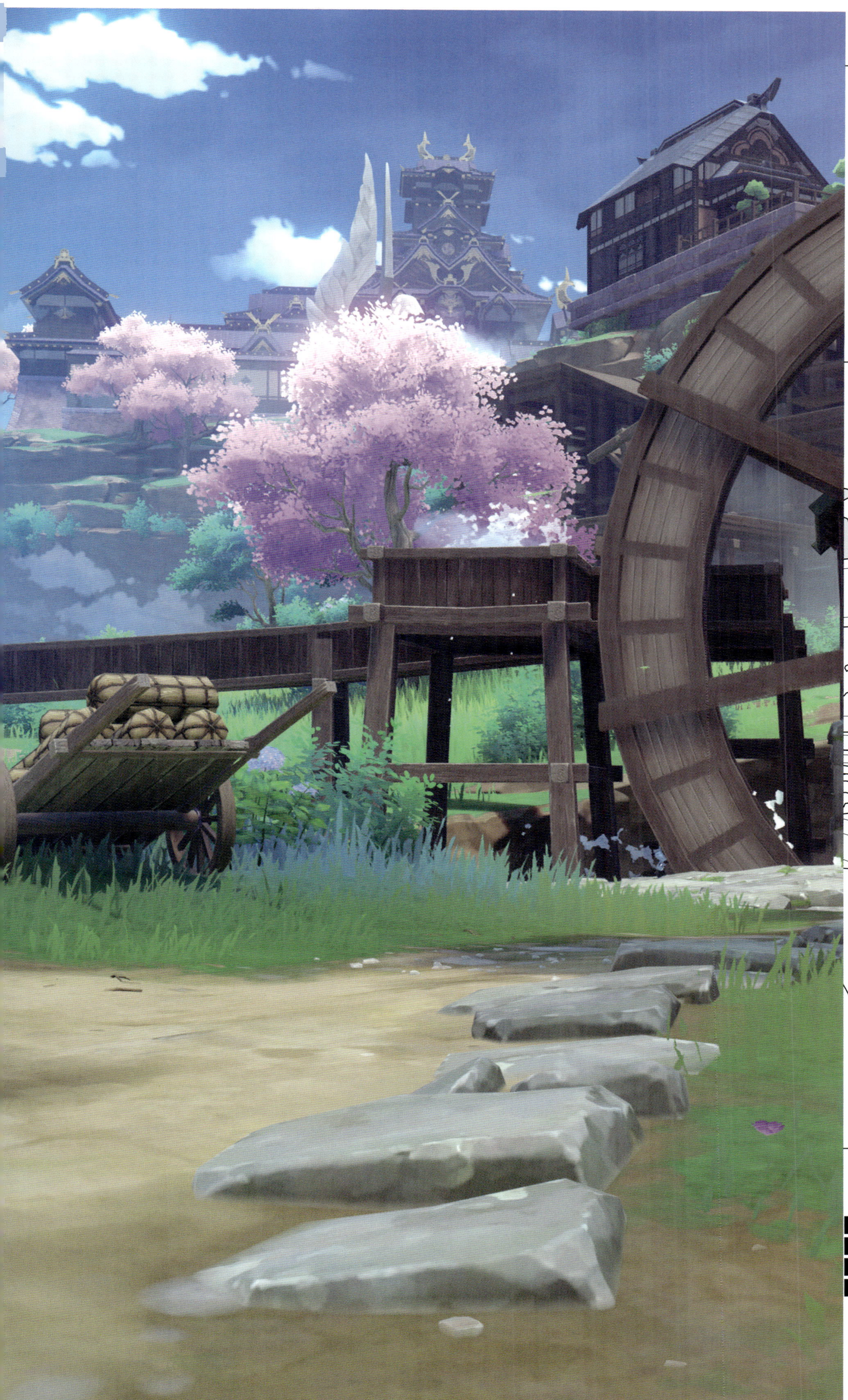

[Fig.07]

SOCIAL AND STYLISTIC LAYERING OF BUILDINGS IN INAZUMA, WHERE WEALTH AND POWER TOWER OVER MORE MODEST AGRICULTURAL SETTINGS.

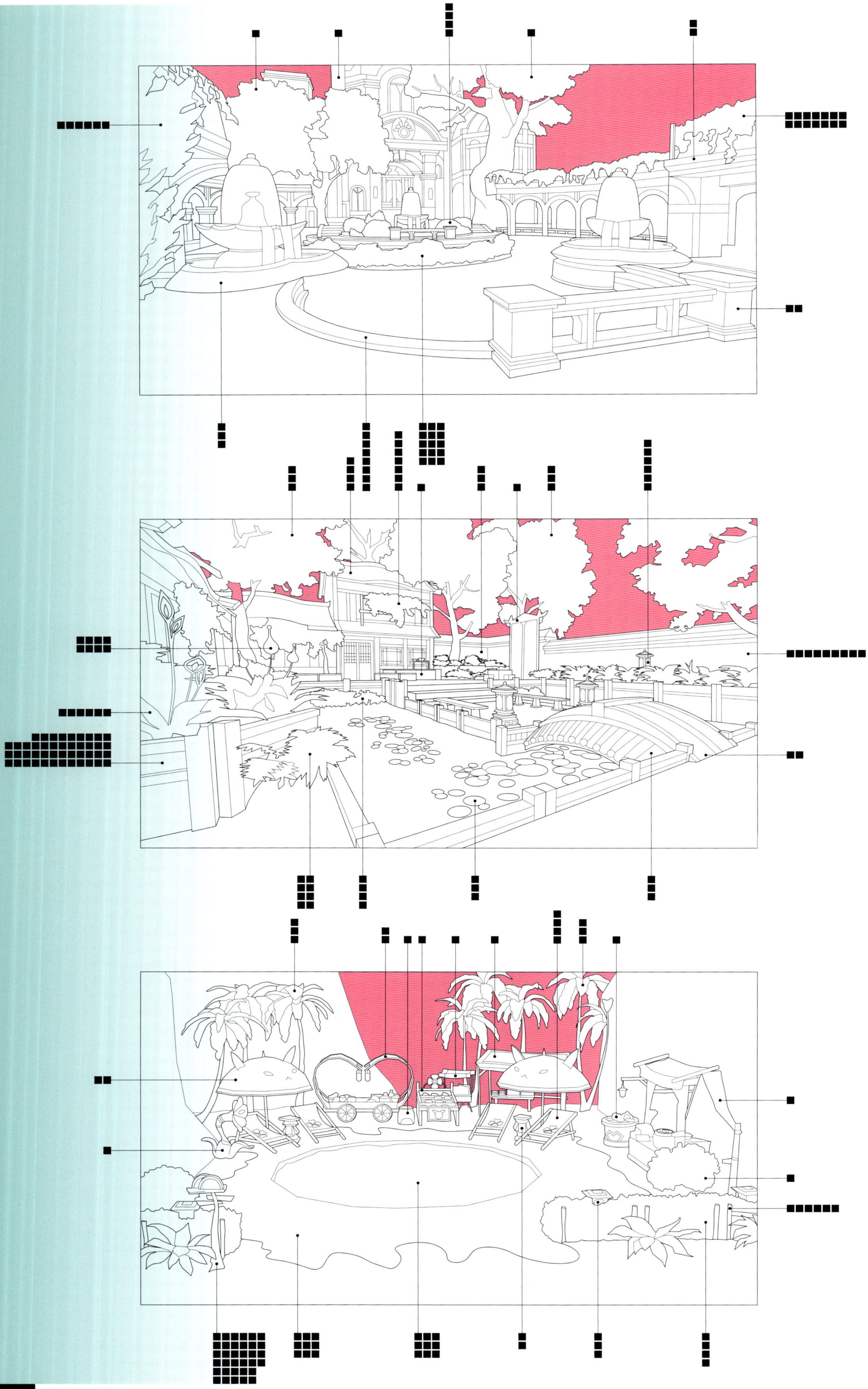

[Fig.08]

6.3

MOVEMENT AS SPACE

One of the most characteristic elements of *Genshin Impact*'s gameplay is the level of engagement with NPCs during quests, undertaken by the player to gain rewards, level up and advance the main story of the game. Reddit user displacedindavis counted more than three and a half days' worth of voiced content in the game[10] as of 2022, up to the game version 3.2, which has significantly increased following subsequent releases. These interactions are spatially embedded, requiring the player to navigate diverse architectural environments to complete the objectives. Taking three quests set in Liyue Harbor, we track the player's route as they explore the area and engage with various NPCs in search of information to complete the quests [Fig.09]. Demonstrating its layered spatial complexity, players navigate Liyue's bustling vertical harbour by traversing the main routes or taking shortcuts by flying, climbing or teleporting across the terraced waterfront, maximizing the changes in elevation that reinforce the area's spatial and economic symbolism. Divided into three points of interest, the architecture is reflective of its wealth and class: Chihu Rock is the lower-class district, containing modest, low-rise timber structures; Feiyun Slope is the prosperous mercantile district, stacked with shops and restaurants; and Yujin Terrace is the wealthy residential district, with larger-scale grand temples and high-rise structures. The architecture is also notable for its varied and purposeful colouration – red representing prosperity, and yellow representing power[11] in Chinese culture – to demarcate the different districts. As a civic space, players meander through tea houses, restaurants and kiosks – a combination of performative and practical uses that bring Liyue Harbour to life. Its non-linearity transforms it into a dynamic storytelling medium, allowing players to carve their own journeys into the landscape. Taking a view through one of the most frequented thoroughfares within the quests demonstrates how it is structured around a framed threshold, echoing the Chinese garden design concept of *jie jing* (borrowed scenery) where architecture acts as a visual filter, choreographing how the landscape in the distance is perceived [Fig.10].

Traversal in *Genshin Impact* establishes a unique mode of spatial interaction that defines the ways players navigate the different regions of Teyvat, informed by unique landscape conditions. Each method is deeply tied to the regional geography, encouraging players to adapt their approach in response to the terrain and its associated environmental hazards. In the high cliffs and open plains of Mondstadt, the player takes advantage of wind to navigate the terrain. In Liyue, they negotiate the region's geological extremities by climbing – from mountainous peaks that reach the clouds to waterfront terraces. Sumeru's ecological contradictions, incorporating both desert and rainforest biomes, require the player to negotiate dense and sparse landscapes by using mid-air grappling systems. Traversal in Inazuma relies heavily on navigating an archipelago hindered by extreme weather, in contrast to Fontaine's waters that open a subterranean world for exploration through swimming. In Natlan, the region's vertical dynamism and extreme volcanic landscape can be tamed by embodying animals with unique abilities, such as flying or jumping, that transcend the player's human capacity. Combining these modes of traversal into one sectional drawing [Fig.11] allows us to view the world of Teyvat as a vertically layered and fully navigable space, where air, land and water go beyond acting as mere environmental backdrops and become orchestrated terrains of movement. In doing so, *Genshin Impact* constructs a playable stage where these elements are both obstacles and opportunities. This extends into the architectural design, such as deep ledges and parapets that prevent the player from climbing any higher, or extensive façades that exceed the limits of the player's stamina.

[Fig.09] PAGES 134–5

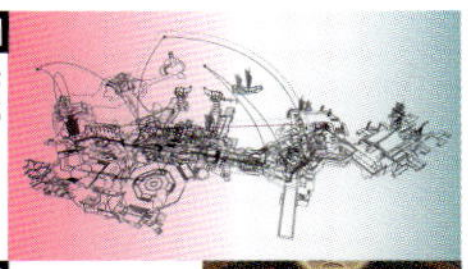

A trio of quest journeys overlayed to show how players engage with objects and NPCs that often require venturing back, forth and further afield, as can be seen through these winding routes within Liyue Harbour.

[Fig.10] PAGE 136

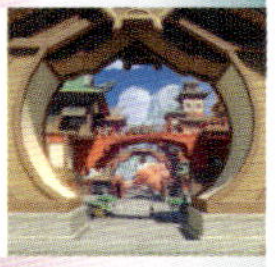

View through a common thoroughfare within Liyue Harbour, showing how the modes of circulation are supported through the framing of routes and intersections on different levels.

[Fig.11] PAGE 137

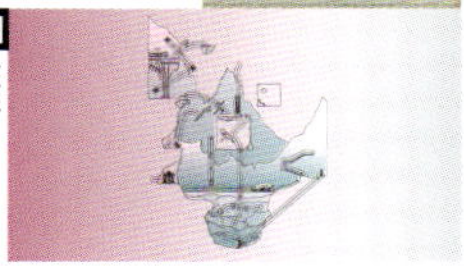

Methods of traversal within the game, demonstrating how players occupy land, water, and air to explore the vast open-world environment of Teyvat.

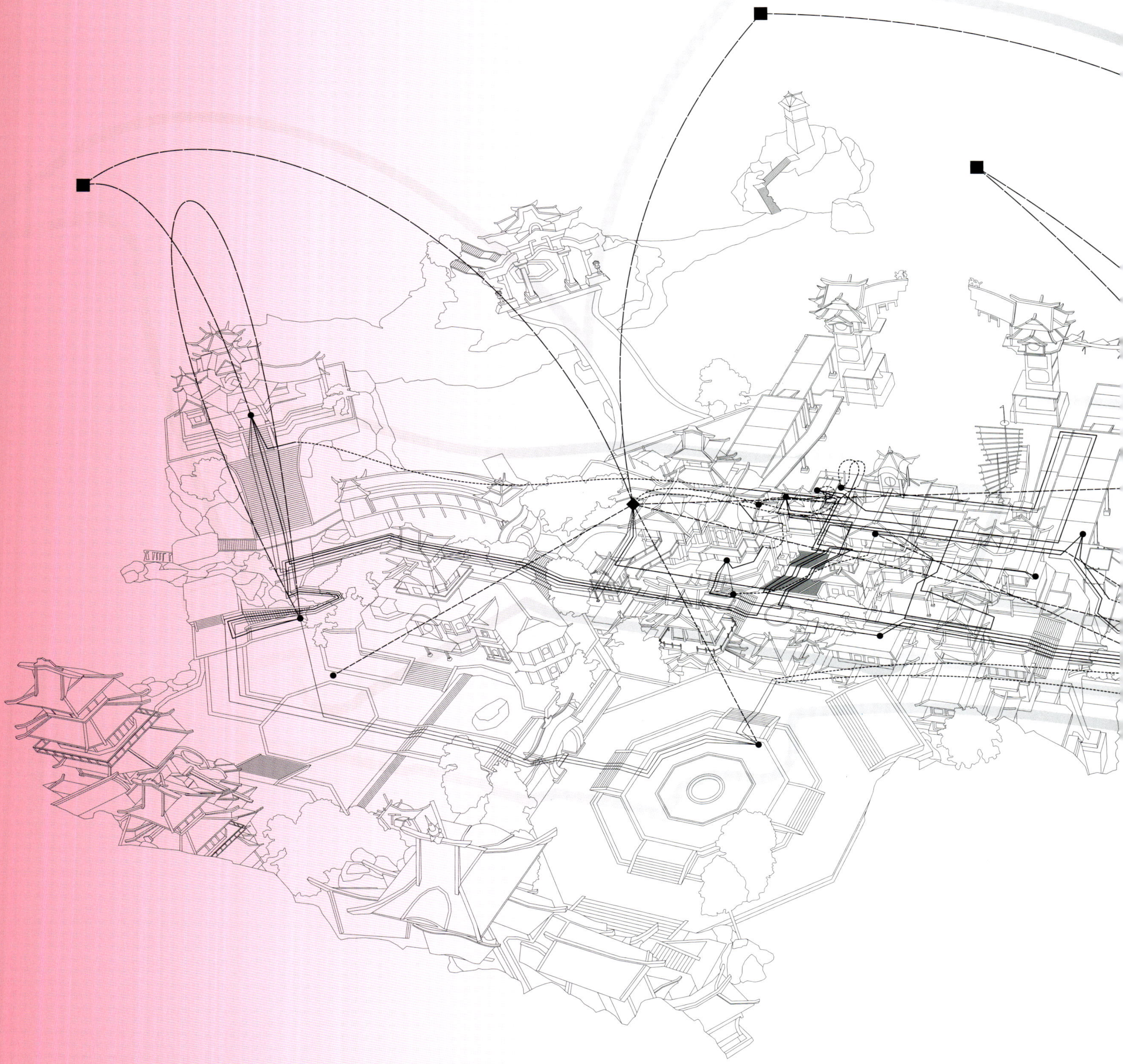

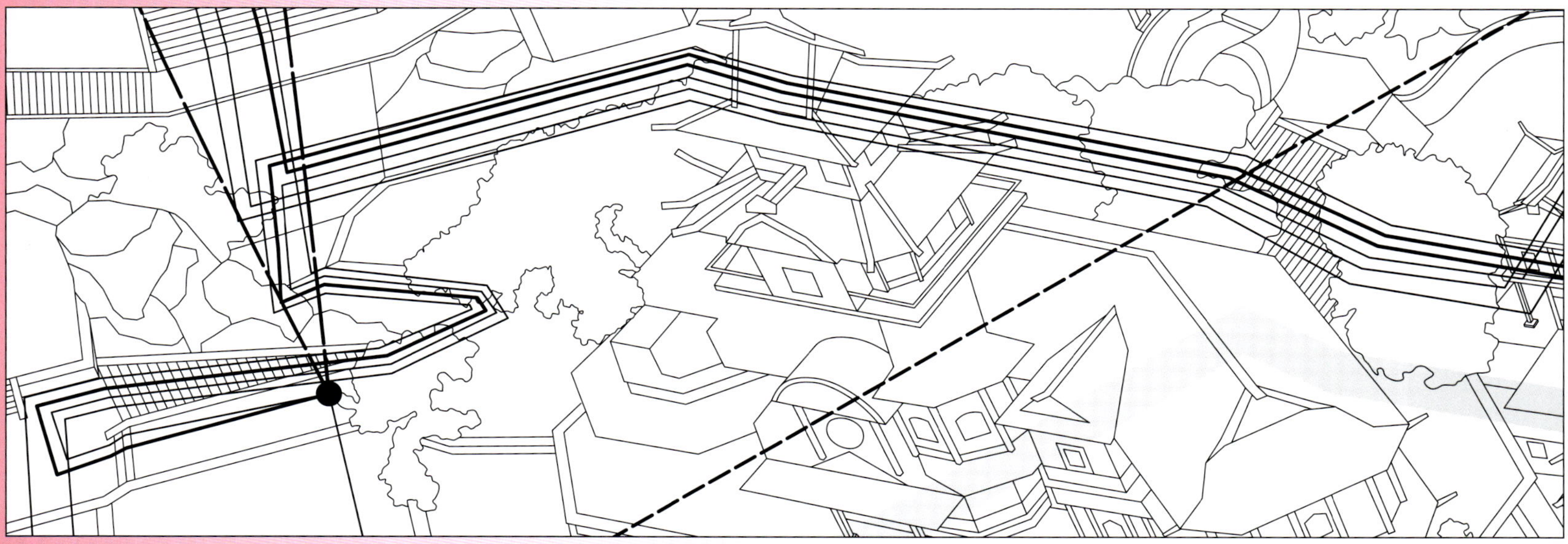

[Fig.09]

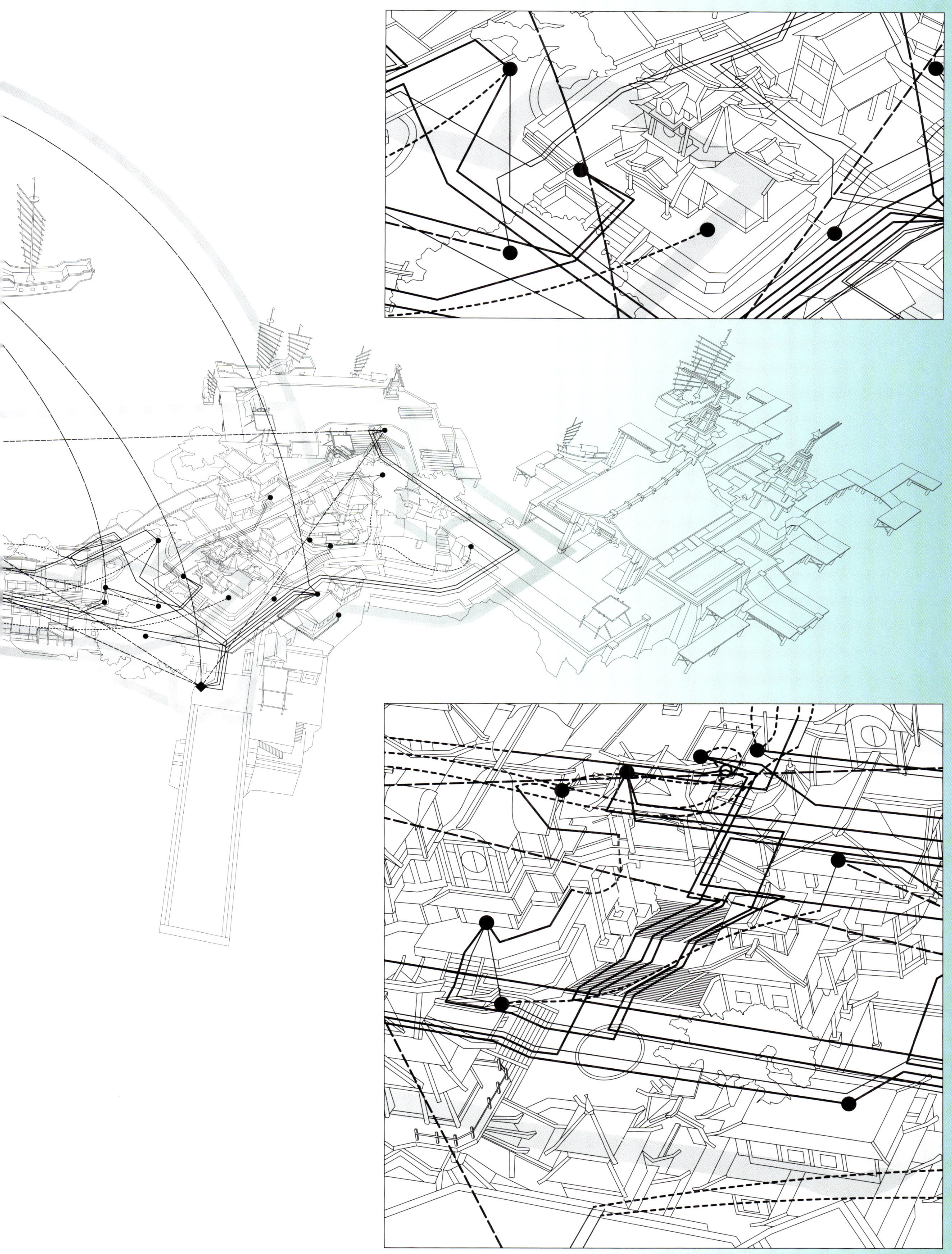

This interactivity extends into the playful design of spatial puzzles within the game, where the player engages with their environment as a problem-solving interface to unlock chests or gain resources. The puzzles embed themselves in a variety of settings – within ancient ruins, temple complexes, subterranean vaults or mountaintop shrines – elevating the environment beyond an aesthetic backdrop. The act of solving these puzzles is spatial rather than abstract; players need to explore a space with the intention of further understanding it [Fig.12]. This can involve gliding between platforms, climbing columns to activate switches or aligning structures that are only visible from certain viewpoints. Clues can be mapped onto the sky or learned through repeated action. Strategy also plays a role in the completion of puzzles, and the player must carefully select a character from their party with the correct element or skill to complete the puzzle, freezing or firing at structures to activate them. The architecture becomes a container for the puzzle's mechanics, reinforcing a core principle of *Genshin Impact*'s environmental design, where space itself acts as a medium of logic and reward. Such puzzles continue a long lineage of architectural and landscape designs using playful tricks of circulation and visual framing, from the islands of the Humble Administrator's Garden in Suzhou, to Borromini's forced perspective colonnade in the Palazzo Spada in Rome.

[Fig.12]
PAGES
138–9

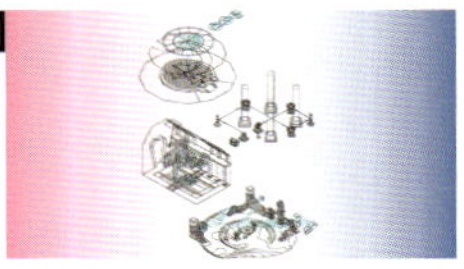

Spatial puzzles are a key component of the game, hosted within a variety of locations that act as architectural containers for play.

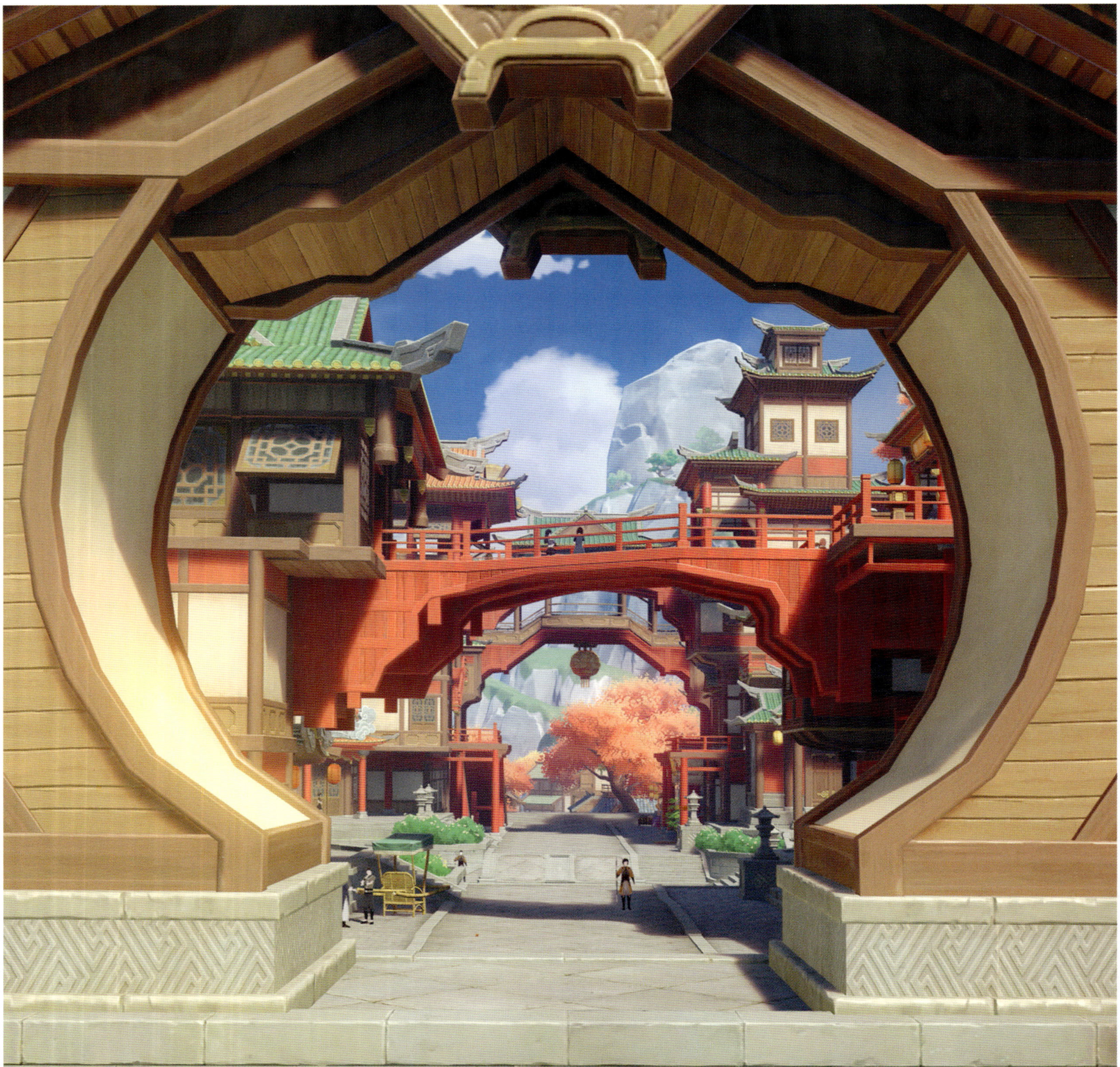

[Fig.10]

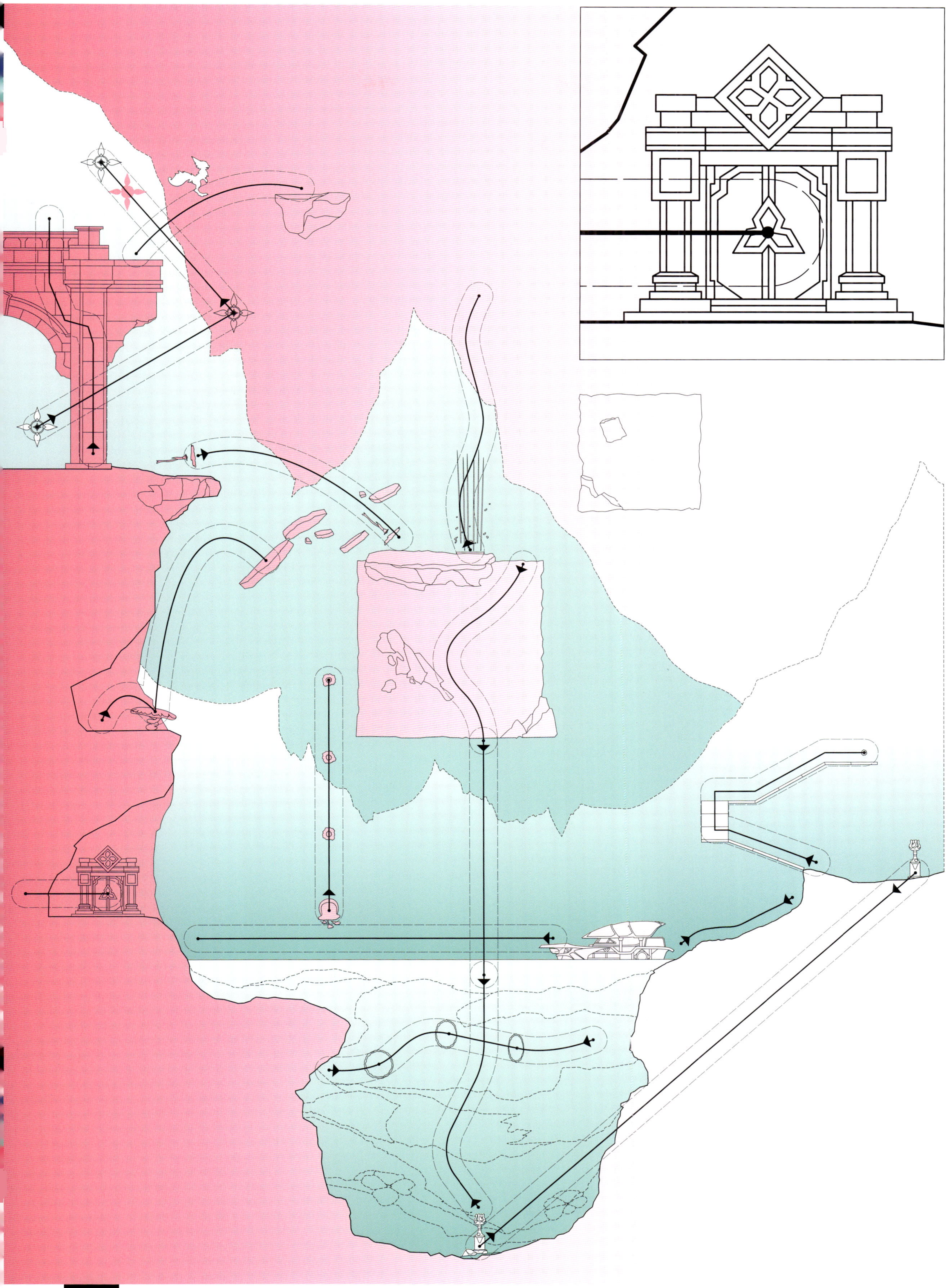

[Fig.11]

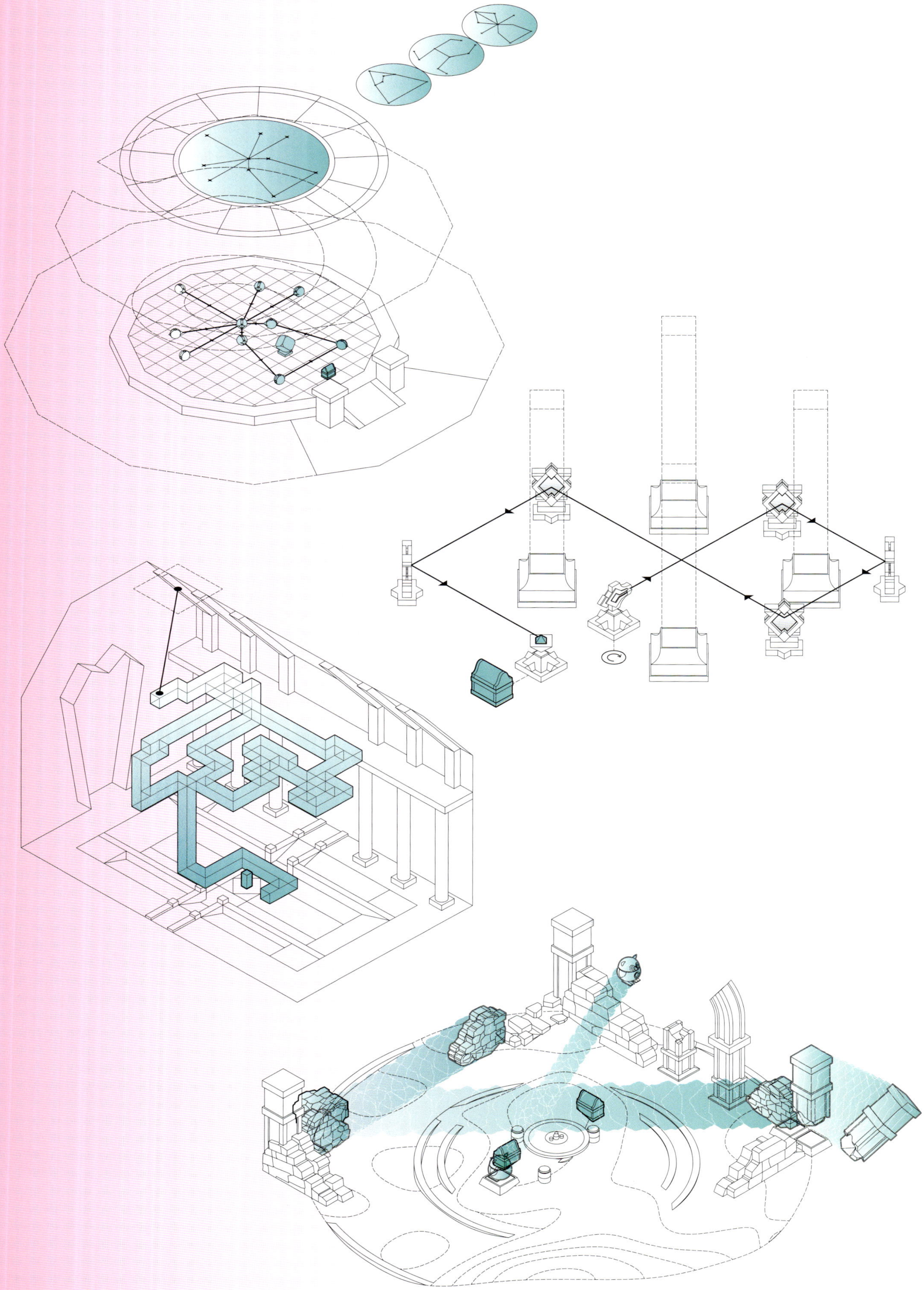

[Fig.12]

6.4 CULTURAL IMPORT / EXPORT

Genshin Impact's success lies in the depth of its world-building techniques and freedom to explore the world at the player's own pace. Despite the game's extensive list of playable characters, Teyvat stands out as a world that can enable all the many different kinds of gamers and behaviours that inhabit it – whether that be to pick flowers, raid chests or befriend the 3,817 NPCs.[12] There is some debate over whether miHoYo's slogan, *Tech otakus save the world*, refers to the notion of being whisked away to a fantasy world in order to save it and so live out a power fantasy, or to bona fide ambitions for this world.[13] While the multi-region nature of Teyvat has always been a core element of the game, it is hard not to let the compelling aura of Liyue dominate the discourse surrounding the game, acting as a transmission medium for exporting Chinese culture to a wider audience. It can be said that its 'soft power' also contributes to improving the impression of China's ability to produce a popular cultural product with global appeal.[14] With all eyes on the seventh and final release, an upcoming Russian-inspired nation called Snezhnaya, some have argued that the depictions of real-world locations and cultures are uneven.[15] Given the game has become one of the world's most popular RPGs, the enduring charm of Teyvat will surely persist.

[Fig.12] Detail

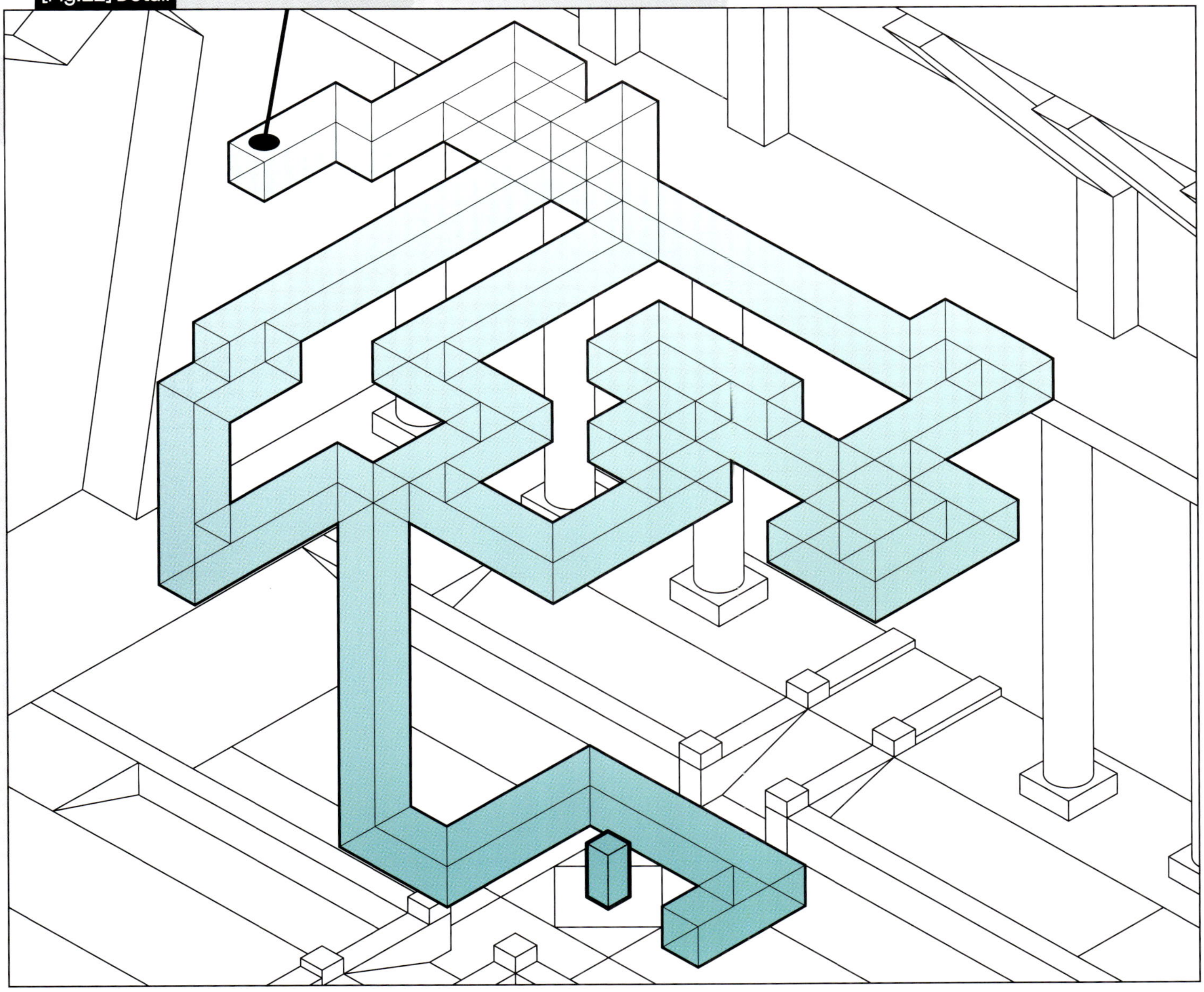

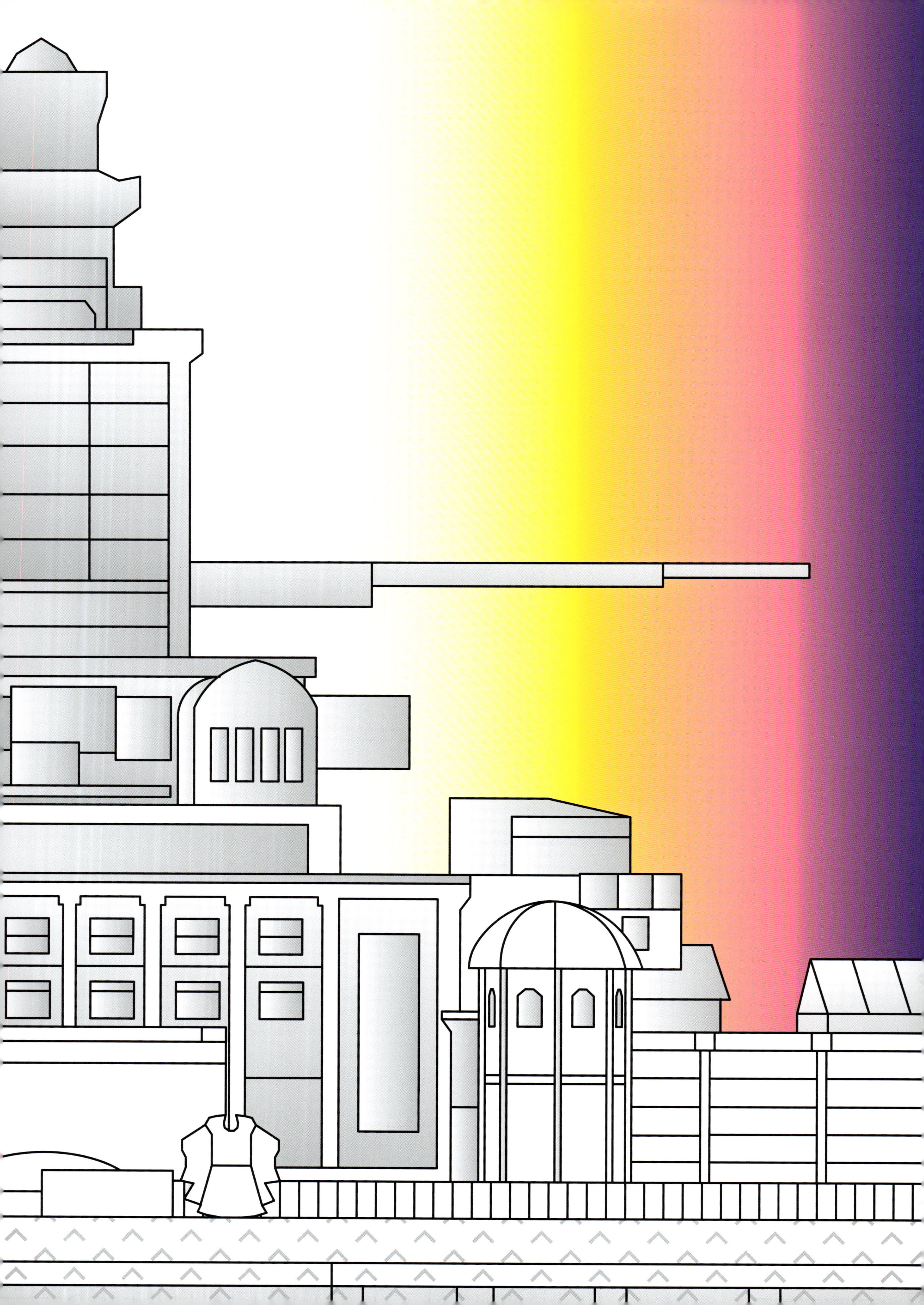

CHAPTER 07

GRAVITY RUSH 2

DEVELOPER
JAPAN STUDIO

PUBLISHER
SONY INTERACTIVE ENTERTAINMENT

Platforms	PlayStation 4
Year	2017

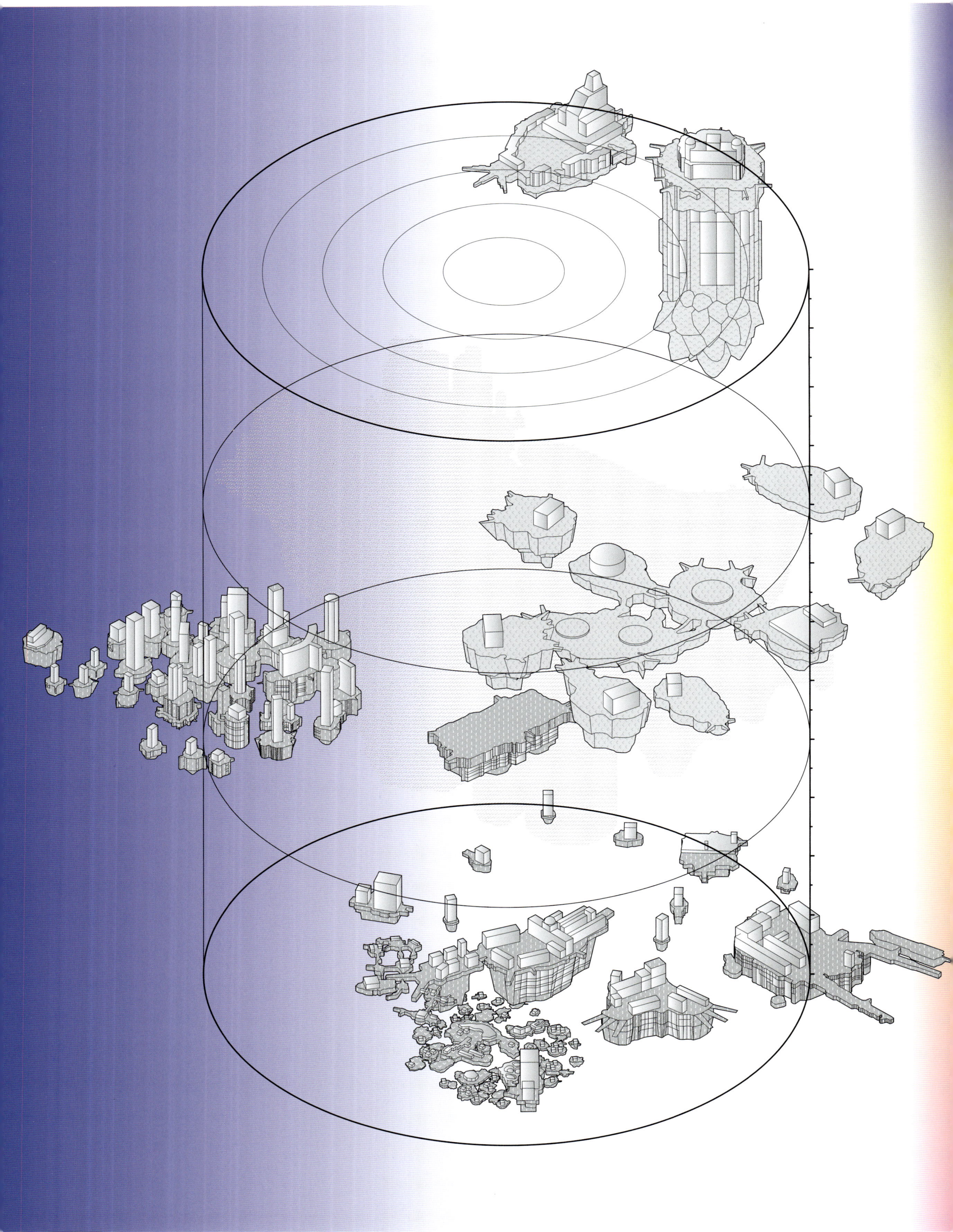

[Fig.01]

7.1

AERIAL ARCHIPELAGOS

In most game worlds, ground level is a given. Yet in *Gravity Rush 2*, the one thing we can always be sure of is that this datum is never certain. We play as Kat, known to some as the 'Gravity Queen', a *shifter* who can change gravity at will. In doing so, Kat can 'fall' in any direction across the world. *Gravity Rush 2* is a tale of three cities, with Kat first journeying to Jirga Para Lhao – a giant floating metropolis of islands – where she battles creatures called Nevi who emerge from 'gravity storms', eventually becoming involved in the revolutionary overthrowing of an oppressive governmental regime. Following an invasion by a giant monster 'Lost City' comprised of amalgamated buildings, Kat ends up back in Hekseville, the city that formed the backdrop for the first *Gravity Rush*, where she uncovers yet more political intrigue. By the end of the story, players will also briefly visit Eto, a city at the very top of the world, and engage with many complicated narratives including a scientist freezing time, kidnapped friends and Kat's own royal lineage. Through the highly intricate story and space experienced by gravity shifting, *Gravity Rush 2* presents a world that is always switching dynamically between different viewpoints.

It is well-documented that the design of the *Gravity Rush* world draws from the work of French cartoonist Moebius, such as *The Incal*.[1] Moebius' drawings illustrate a giant, vertiginous city, and the granularity of this drawn world is translated into the game, while the ability to fall anywhere means that the environment provides the potential for player exploration that most other titles cannot offer. Writing in *Killscreen*, Gareth Damian Martin argues that 'what [game director] Toyama understood so clearly, [is] that Moebius's iconic dense cities were not just a collection of richly layered stories, but a perspective too.'[2] In *Gravity Rush 2*, this perspective is made clear as soon as we reach the city of Jirga Para Lhao – a city clearly designed to complement Kat's unique abilities.

Although the in-game maps provide a basis for understanding the layout of Jirga Para Lhao, its vertical nature and fragmented urban form make it hard to grasp the city in its totality. However, it is possible to construct a reasonably accurate picture of the city's organization by using Kat as a form of measuring instrument. Selecting mission or fast travel markers on the main map indicates the linear distance in yards between Kat and that waypoint, allowing us to calculate the scale of the map both horizontally and vertically between city layers. By counting the floors of buildings around the city, we can estimate both the size of these structures and the scale of the floating platforms upon which they sit. This data was used to construct a 3D map of Jirga Para Lhao, which demonstrates the scale of the city to be around 1,600 yards (1,460 m) from the top of Avarash au Govena, the government island that overlooks the city, to the bottom of the Lei Elgona shanty town hovering at the bottom [Fig.01]. Our mapping shows that Jirga Para Lhao is made of over 125 separate islands spread throughout this area, and the archipelago's extents in plan are similar in scale to Murano near Venice, one of the real-world cities that is most famous for its island construction. By overlaying the outline of Hekseville onto this map, we showcase how much larger and yet fragmented this new city is compared to its predecessor in the series.

[Fig.01] **AN ISOMETRIC OVERVIEW OF JIRGA PARA LHAO, SHOWING HOW THE CITY IS DIVIDED INTO FOUR LAYERS OF CLUSTERED ISLANDS, EACH WITH THEIR OWN UNIQUE ARCHITECTURAL LANGUAGE AND SOCIAL STATUS.**

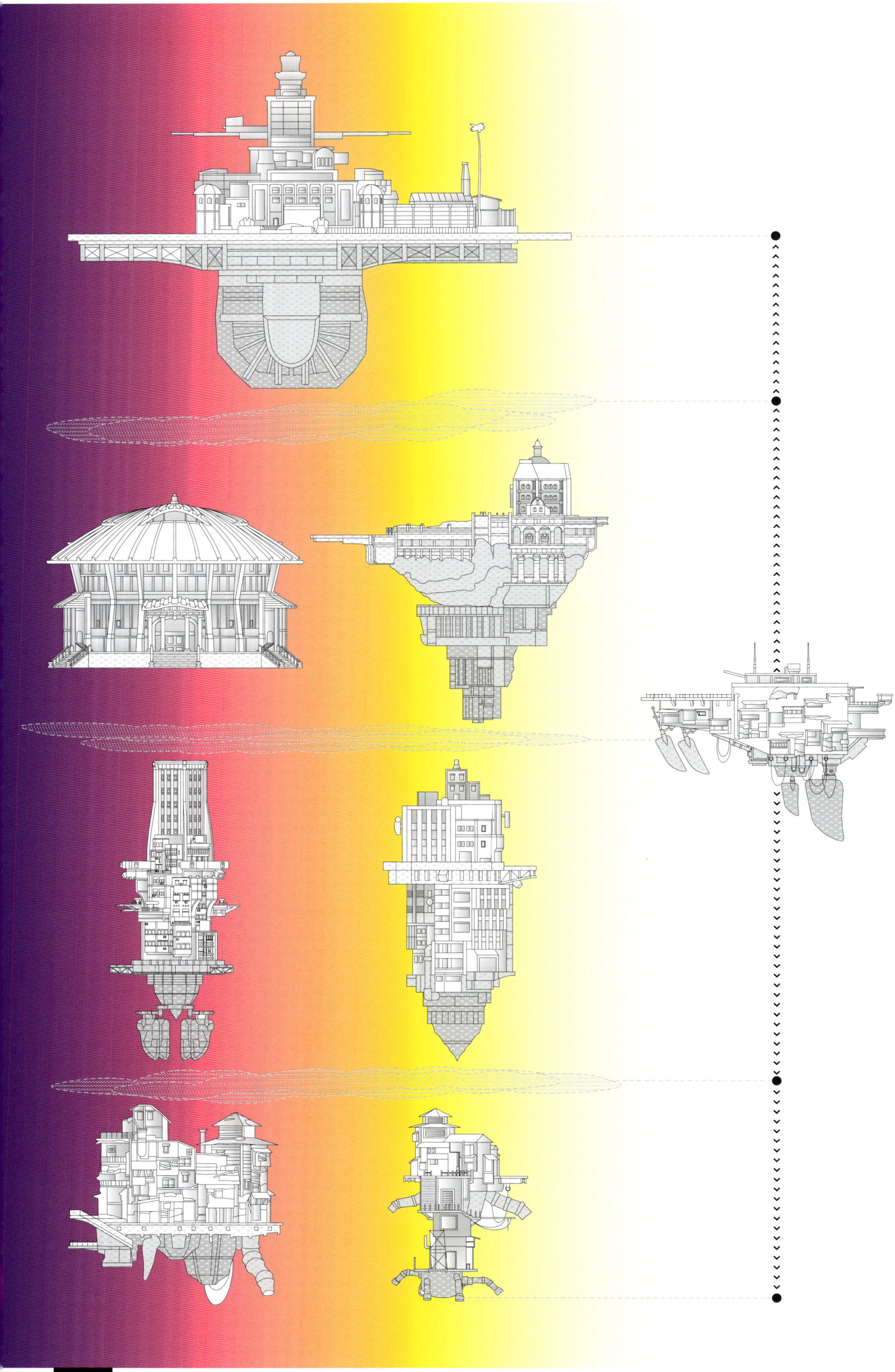

ELEVATIONAL STUDIES OF BUILDINGS IN EACH LAYER OF JIRGA PARA LHAO, DEMONSTRATING THAT THE ARCHITECTURAL FORMS RELATE TO BOTH TECHNOLOGIES FOR FLOATING AND THE CLASS BOUNDARIES OF THE CITY.

[Fig.02]

7.2

SOCIAL CLIMBING

The game's story makes it clear that Jirga Para Lhao is a very stratified city, with producer Nick Accordino explaining 'we have a city that has lower tiers, higher tiers and different classes of society in them.'[3] Class separation is reinforced through the layers of cloud that mask the levels from one another. This is also clearly communicated in the diverse architectural design of the city, reflecting that the developers 'did a lot of location research in places like Mexico and all across Asia.'[4] By using Kat's in-game camera to capture the topology of buildings and create elevational studies, it's possible to highlight how the building forms and the islands they sit upon change layer by layer. At the lowest part of the city, Lei Elgona, timber shacks are built on top of each other, with wooden platforms and walkways forming the substructure that keeps the buildings anchored to the metal anti-gravity hulls below. As we move to Lei Colmosna, the city's commercial district, the ratio between building and base completely changes, with vertiginous towers and clusters of small apartments perched atop tiny gravity stone pediments. Here the architectural symbolism is clear, as each island is occupied to its maximum commercial efficiency. Progressing upwards to Lei Havina, the style shifts dramatically, with large, detached mansions surrounded by immaculately maintained gardens sitting on expansive islands, denoting the type of low density, residential developments found in country estates or suburban 'McMansions'. At the top of the city we find the two sites of power, with Avarash au Govena representing governmental control and Fort Bismalia asserting an architectural language of military control, halfway between a city block and a battleship. As our drawing shows, the materiality of the world is closely tied to these architectural styles, moving from nailed timber to precast concrete, and further upwards to crafted masonry and high-tech military materials [Fig.02].

The game does not explain exactly how the buildings of Jirga Para Lhao are constructed, but flying Kat close to the façades allows us to examine the architecture in more detail to understand the design decisions. By making an exploded isometric drawing of a typical smaller-sized island found in Lei Colmosna, the different parts that constitute the structure become clear [Fig.03]. This type of island consists of three structural layers, with five-storey buildings above a masonry platform and another storey of buildings below, which contain a variety of designs indicating domestic occupation mashed together. The lowest structural level is the metal hull and rudder system that presumably controls the island's ability to float and move. Unlike the larger structures of Lei Colmosna, which have an exposed gravity stone at their base, we must conclude that a smaller gravity stone is encased within the hull to provide flotation. Yet the familiarities of the design language are very far from ideas for floating cities made by actual architects – speculative projects such as Buckminster Fuller's 'Cloud Nine' proposal of floating city spheres where 'city air is both limitless and contained'[5] or the atomic powered skyborne pods of Soviet architect Georgii Krutikov.[6] In contrast, gravity stones allow for 'everyday' architecture to be suspended in the sky and take on new forms through their aerial context.

[Fig.03]
PAGE 146

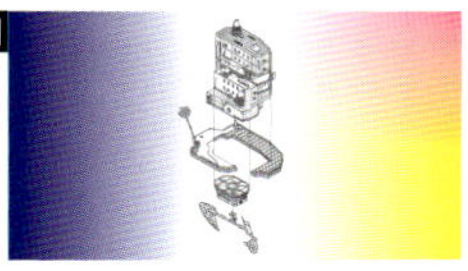

Exploded isometric view of a typical building in the Lei Colmosna district, outlining how the structure is supported on a gravity stone with the rudder apparatus typical of the area.

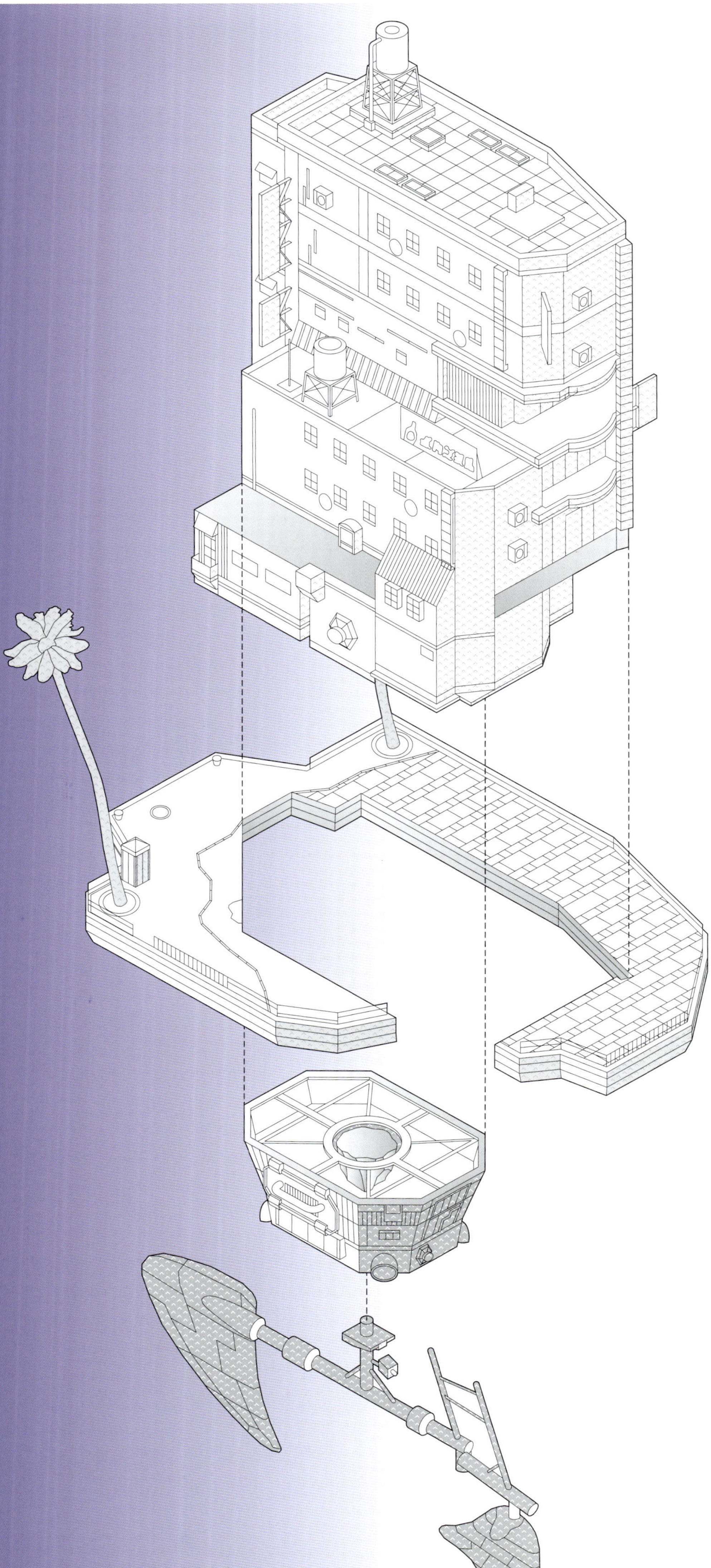

[Fig.03]

7.3

DENSELY PACKED

While a small individual island is still densely packed with architectural elements, flying Kat below the 'ground line' of larger islands reveals the huge density of buildings that make up their structure [Fig.04]. At this level, the city most resembles the architectural façades of Hong Kong, such as the 'Monster Building', or even the infamous Kowloon Walled City, once the densest urban space in the world. The sheer amount of façade that confronts Kat is reminiscent of Michael Wolf's *Architecture of Density* photographs of that city, where buildings are presented as a wallpaper of repeated windows, balconies and air conditioning units.[7] The design of façades in *Gravity Rush 2* also applies 'greebling' techniques often used in science fiction production, adding many small details to break up surfaces and give them visual interest. In this case, the 'greebles' are architectural elements: each 'greeble' symbolizes an occupied space behind the surface. Window and floor heights are often mismatched between adjoining buildings, suggesting that these islands have been gradually occupied by different structures over time. This reinforces the resemblance to Kowloon Walled City, which grew as an '"organic megastructure"...continually responsive to the changing requirements of its users.'[8] This approach also connects to South American architectural projects such as Quinta Monroy in Chile by Elemental, where inhabitants build their own personal designs into a concrete superstructure, producing a frontage that incorporates many different visual languages.

The visual cacophony of intense façades in *Gravity Rush 2* also suits the game's central mechanic of gravity shifting. Any building within the city can be seen and then explored from many possible alignments based on the direction Kat lands on it while falling. As the game's Art Director, Yoshiaki Yamaguchi, says: 'since you're able to stand on any location in the environment it motivates you to view the terrain from any angle,' which is the antithesis of typical level design 'where everything is calculated and the player is left to follow the path.'[9] Moving in this way is encouraged. Kat can use gravity gems to improve her abilities, and these trinkets are often tucked away on every surface of a building, requiring shifting to reach them all. As such, buildings and islands no longer have floors, walls or foundations in the conventional sense – *everything* can be a floor. By mapping one of the larger central islands of Lei Colmosna, which houses the Radale Memorial Park, we can view this island as an unfolded net of six connected floor surfaces, each providing different opportunities for Kat to navigate depending on her gravity orientation [Fig.05]. In this context, the plans and elevations of the island are entirely interchangeable.

[Fig.04] PAGES 148–9

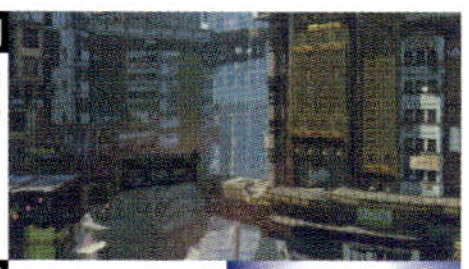

A view through Lei Colmosna indicating the high density of residential and commercial buildings nestled into the surfaces of island superstructures.

[Fig.05] PAGE 150

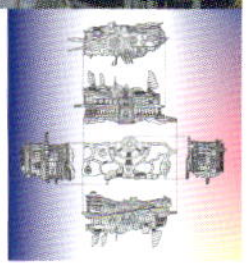

An unfolded elevation of an island in Lei Colmosna, revealing how each face of the building becomes a floorplan for Kat to move across depending on her gravity orientation.

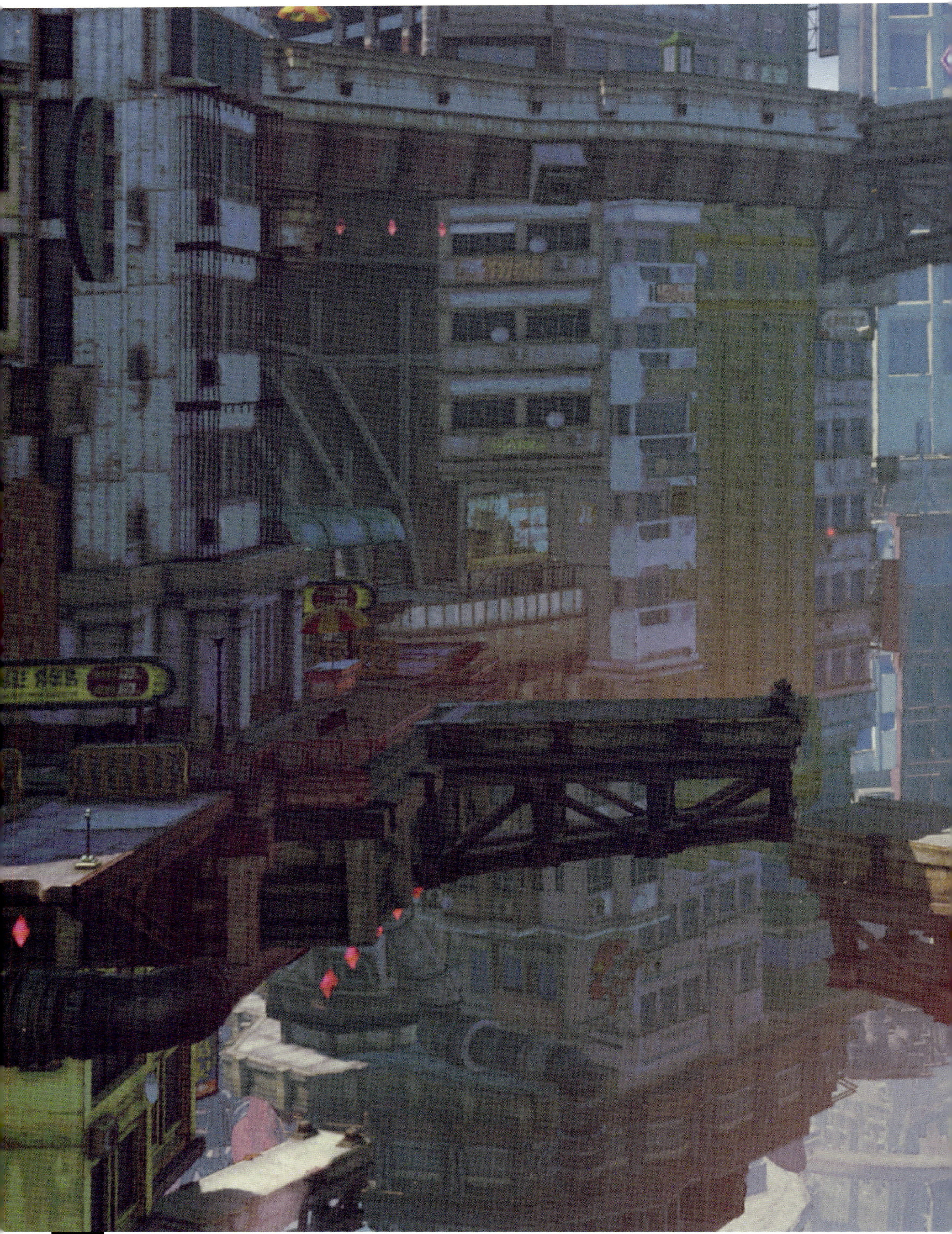

[Fig.04]

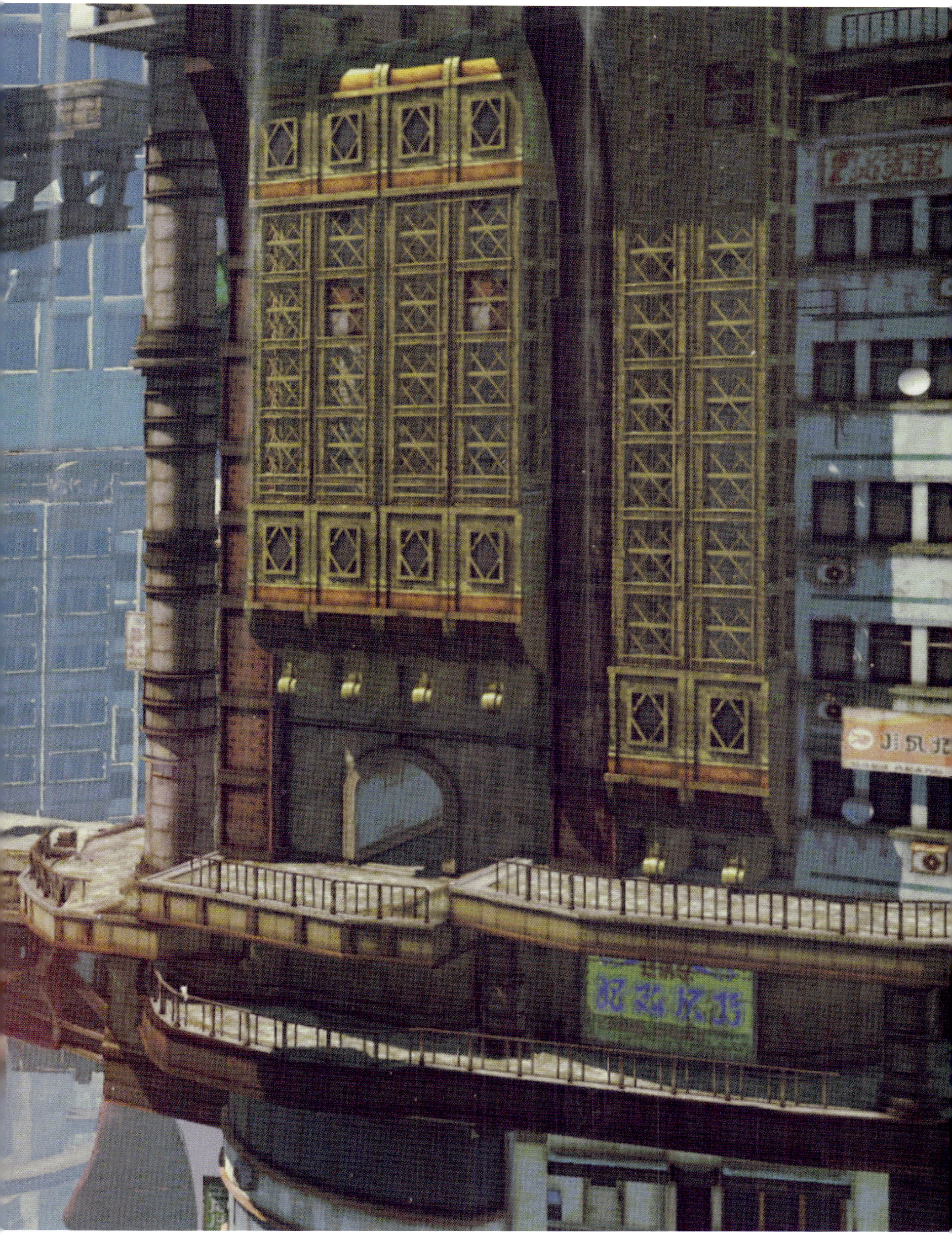

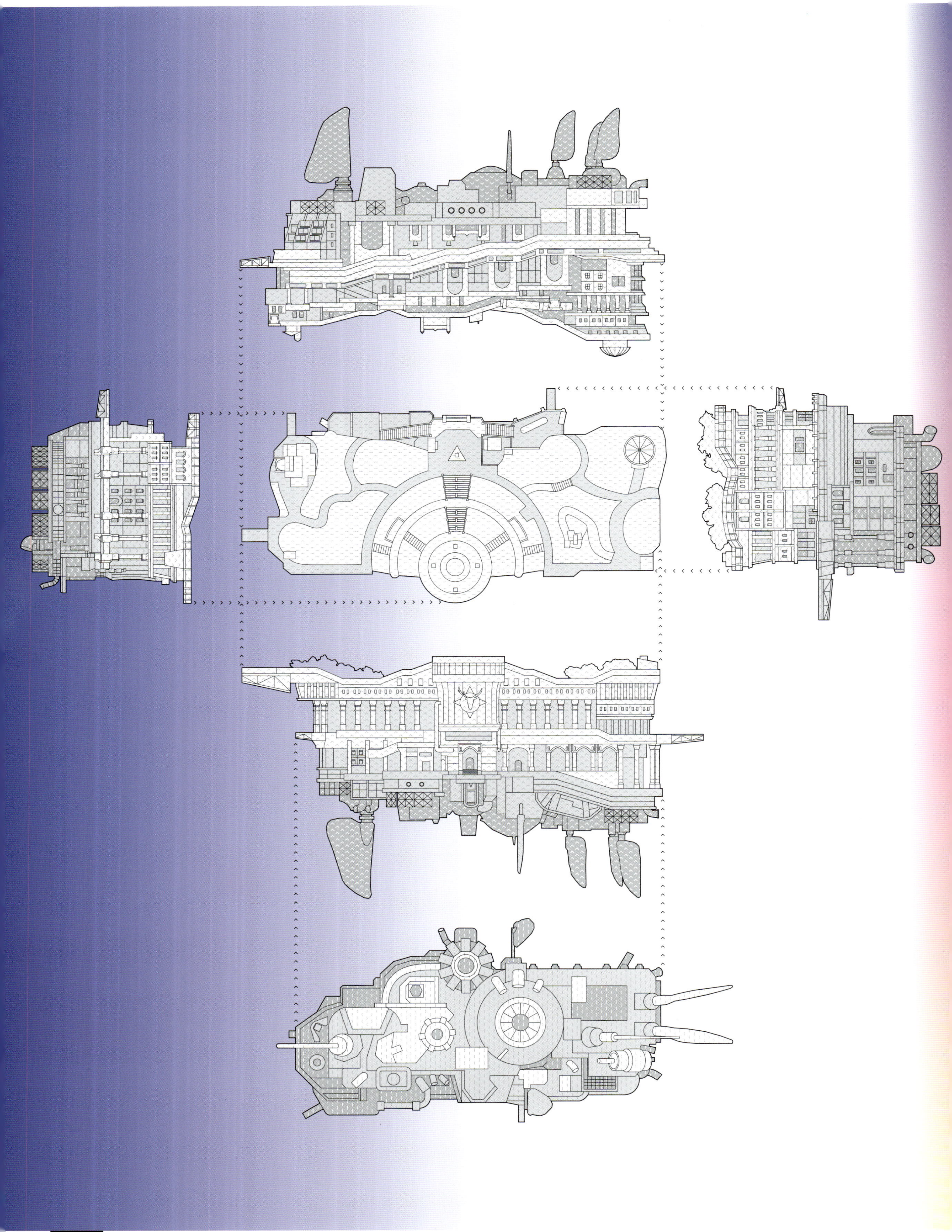

[Fig.05]

7.4

THE RADIANT CITY

In the second chapter of the game, Kat moves back to Hekseville, her home and the setting from the first game. By making an isometric massing study of the urban form of this city in relation to Jirga Para Lhao, we can compare the two to understand how their different shapes reflect different social and political structures within the world. By using the same method of dimensioning through objective markers, we demonstrate that the extents of Hekseville are much more compact than those of the other city. Constructed as a series of islands cantilevering out from the giant World Pillar, Hekseville is approximately 1,150 yards across, but compared to Jirga Para Lhao, it is much less vertically sprawling, with only around 500 yards of elevational difference across the city's extents. By overlaying Jirga's extents onto this drawing, the difference in scale becomes clear [Fig.06]. But in its more compact design, Hekseville also maintains elements that the other city lacks, such as a public transport system and large social gathering spaces that appear open to all. The city is also divided into strict boundaries between function, with the old town, business district, pleasure and industrial areas all clearly separated from one another.

As with Jirga Para Lhao, we created a series of elevational studies exploring the architectural language of Hekseville and how it varies depending on the district. The city is a little more unified than Jirga, clearly drawing influence from the architecture of cities like Paris and London, including the uneven roofscapes and rows of terraced buildings that are hallmarks of both places. Despite their clearly differentiated functions, the changes in language and density of buildings on each island are subtle, but, combined with localized shifts in atmospheric colour (and time of day), give each area a unique identity [Fig.07]. The narrow, gabled buildings of Pleajeune, and the glow of red lights from within, recall the canal-facing façades of Amsterdam and its red-light district, while on the fringes of that district, the hulking Arquebus Academy building references the 'Collegiate Gothic' language of school and university buildings seen the world over, from Cambridge to Yale or Tokyo. In Vendecentre, the architectural language of Paris is extended into a scale and density one might find in the Chicago works of architect Louis Sullivan, with a grand central building that looks like the Arc de Triomphe reinterpreted as a skyscraper. Endestria's architecture integrates heavy industry with historical styles, a similar approach to 19th-century buildings such as the Compressed Air Factory that is now Paris' National School of Architecture of Paris-Val de Seine. While Moebius is a well-cited influence on the worldbuilding, the architecture of Hekseville is also reminiscent of work in Belgian comic book artist François Schuiten's *Les Cités Obscures* series.

[Fig.06] PAGE 152

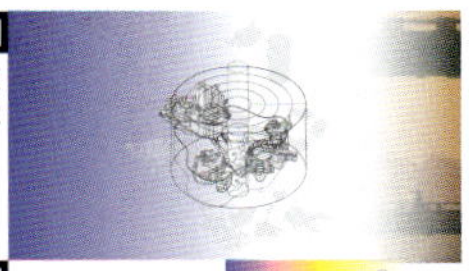

An isometric overview of Hekseville, where the city is comprised of four districts that cantilever out from the World Pillar, each with different urban forms and density.

[Fig.07] PAGE 153

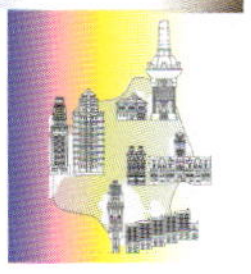

Elevational studies of buildings from each district of Hekseville, showing how the architectural form relates to the function and prestige of the area.

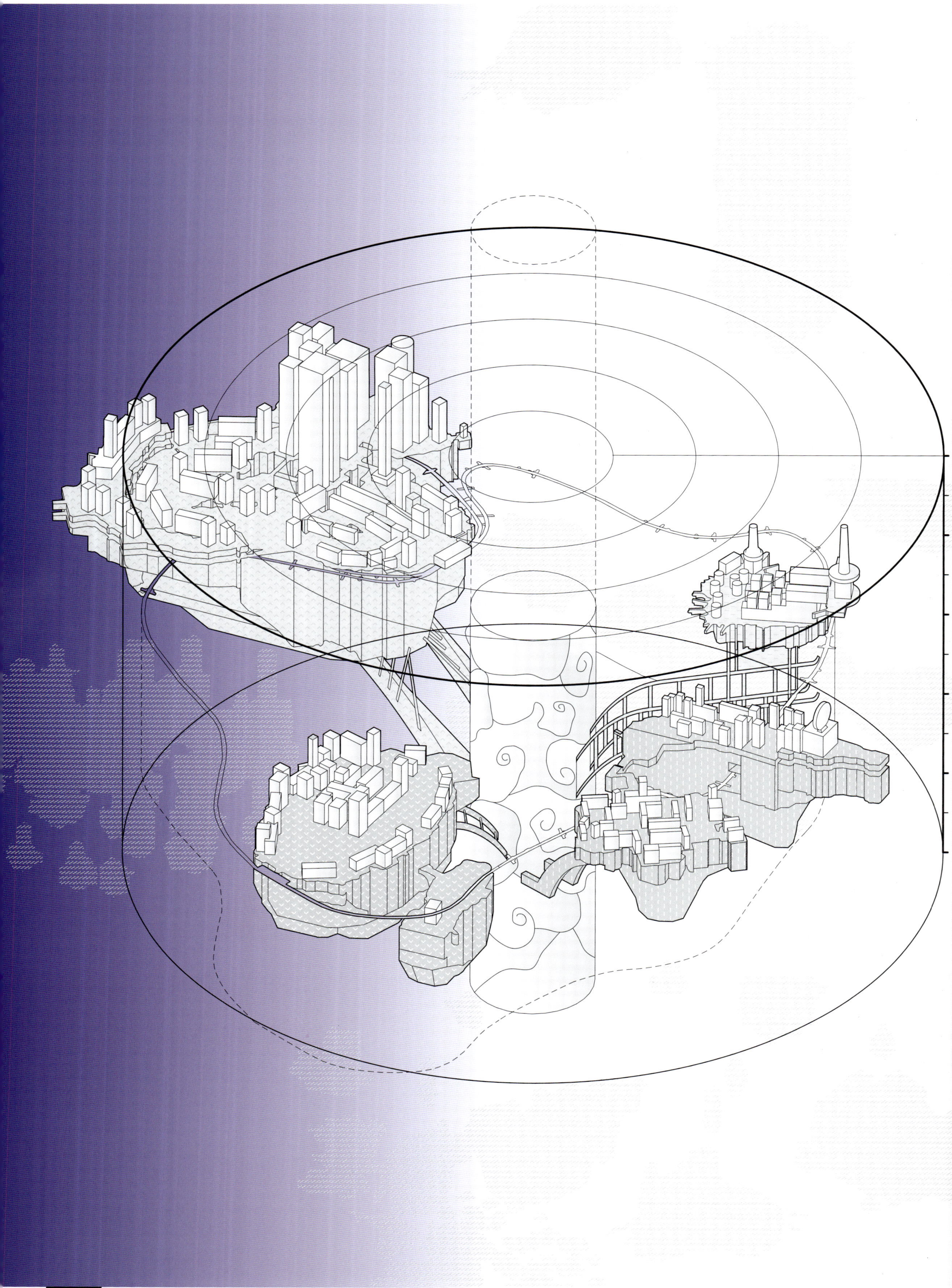

[Fig.06]

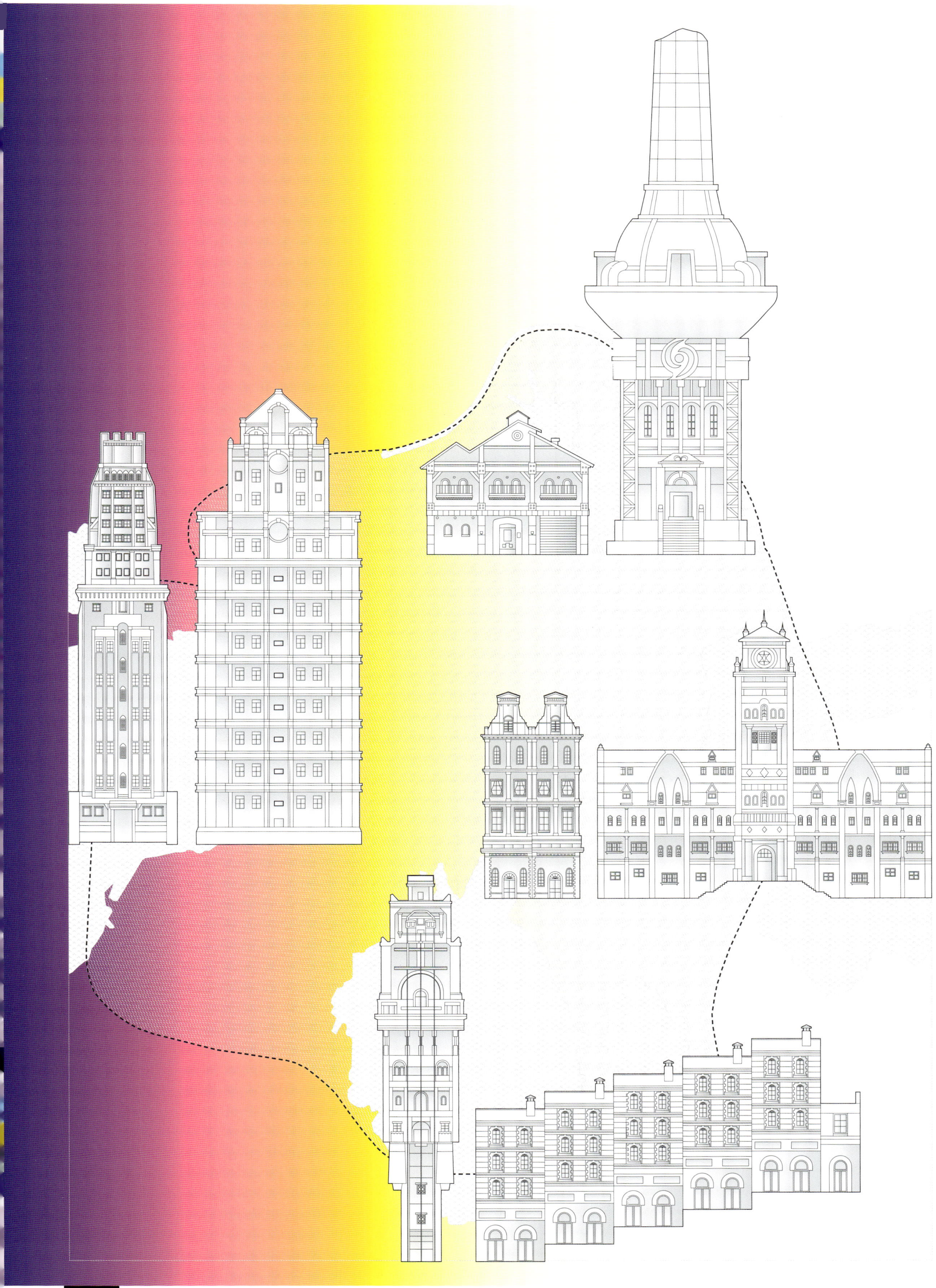

[Fig.07]

While Hekseville does not present as stratified a society as Jirga Para Lhao, we still get glimpses into the reality of life for its citizens. The picturesque buildings, town squares and boulevards above ground sit in contrast to the ultra-high-density residential units we see as we drop into the depths of the islands. Kat's home in Auldnoir is in an abandoned concrete pipe, and the lower levels in which she lives have a different material palette, featuring a liberal use of corrugated iron and timber, punctuated by the same air conditioning units we see in Jirga Para Lhao. Looking across these subterranean areas of the city, we see how the beautiful edifices above are surely maintained by the labour forces of those living below [Fig.08].

[Fig.01] Detail

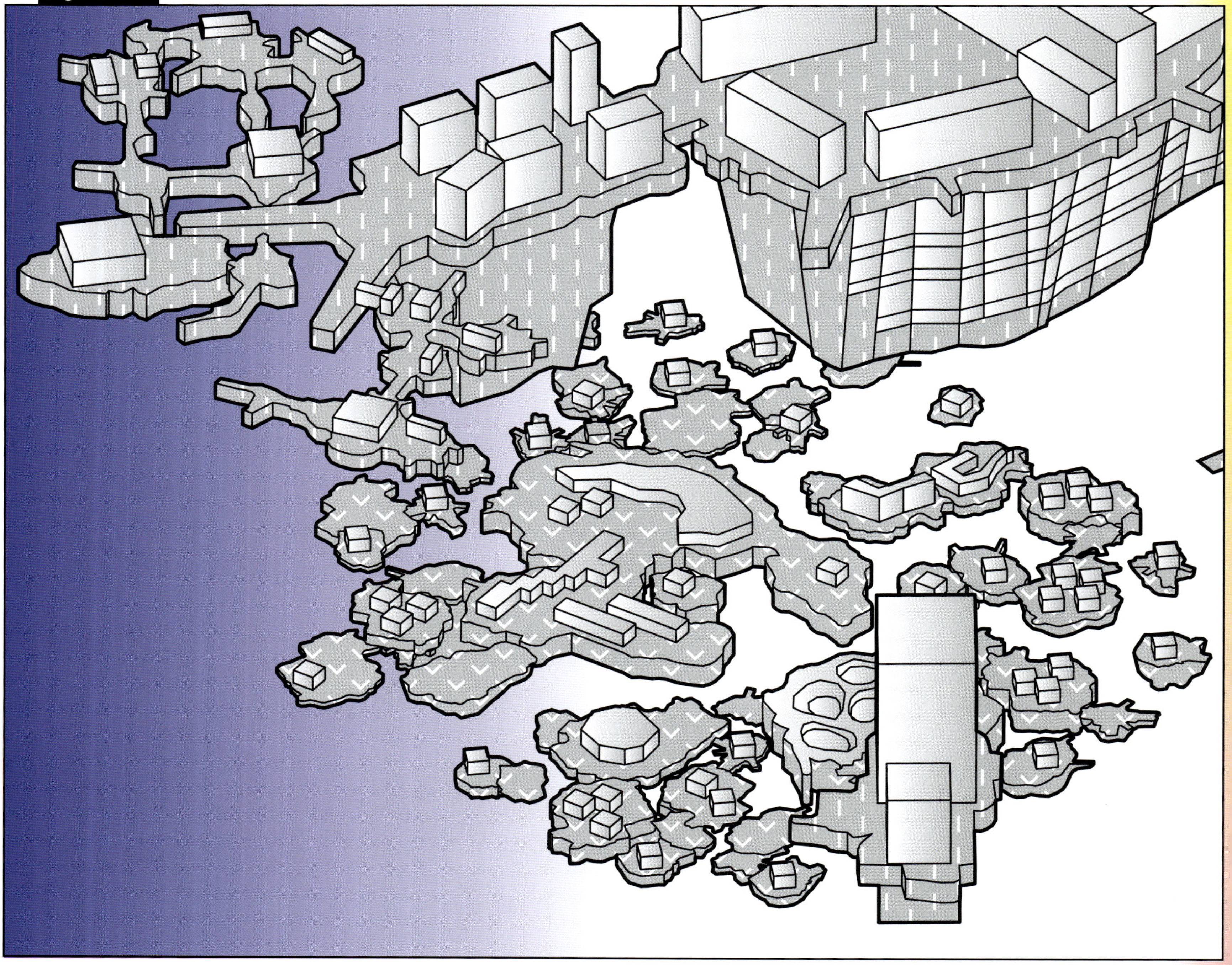

[Fig.08] A VIEW THROUGH THE LOWER AREAS OF KAT'S HOMETOWN OF HEKSEVILLE, WHERE HIGH-DENSITY RESIDENTIAL UNITS ARE CLUSTERED IN THE DARKNESS BELOW THE OLD TOWN OF THE CITY.

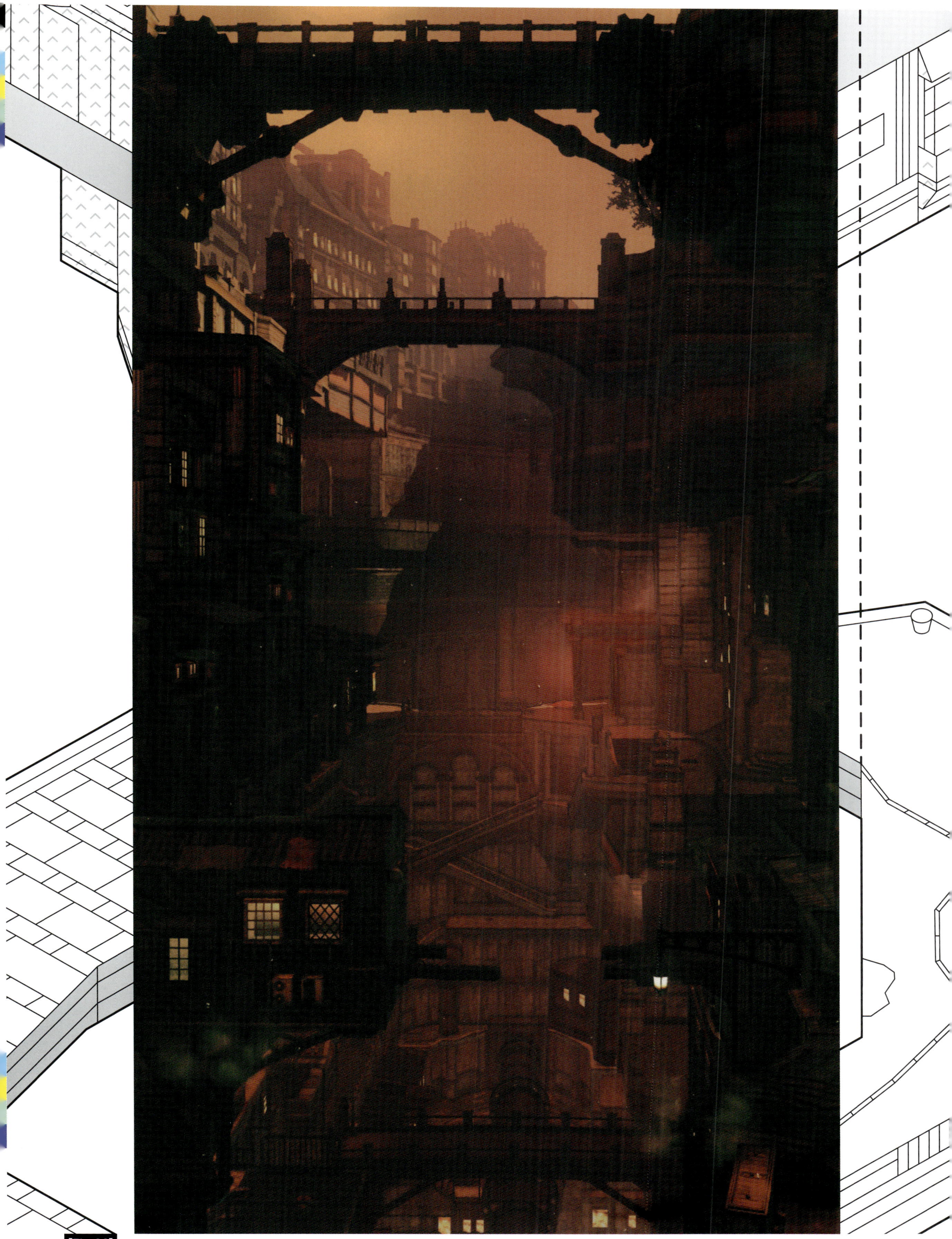

[Fig.08]

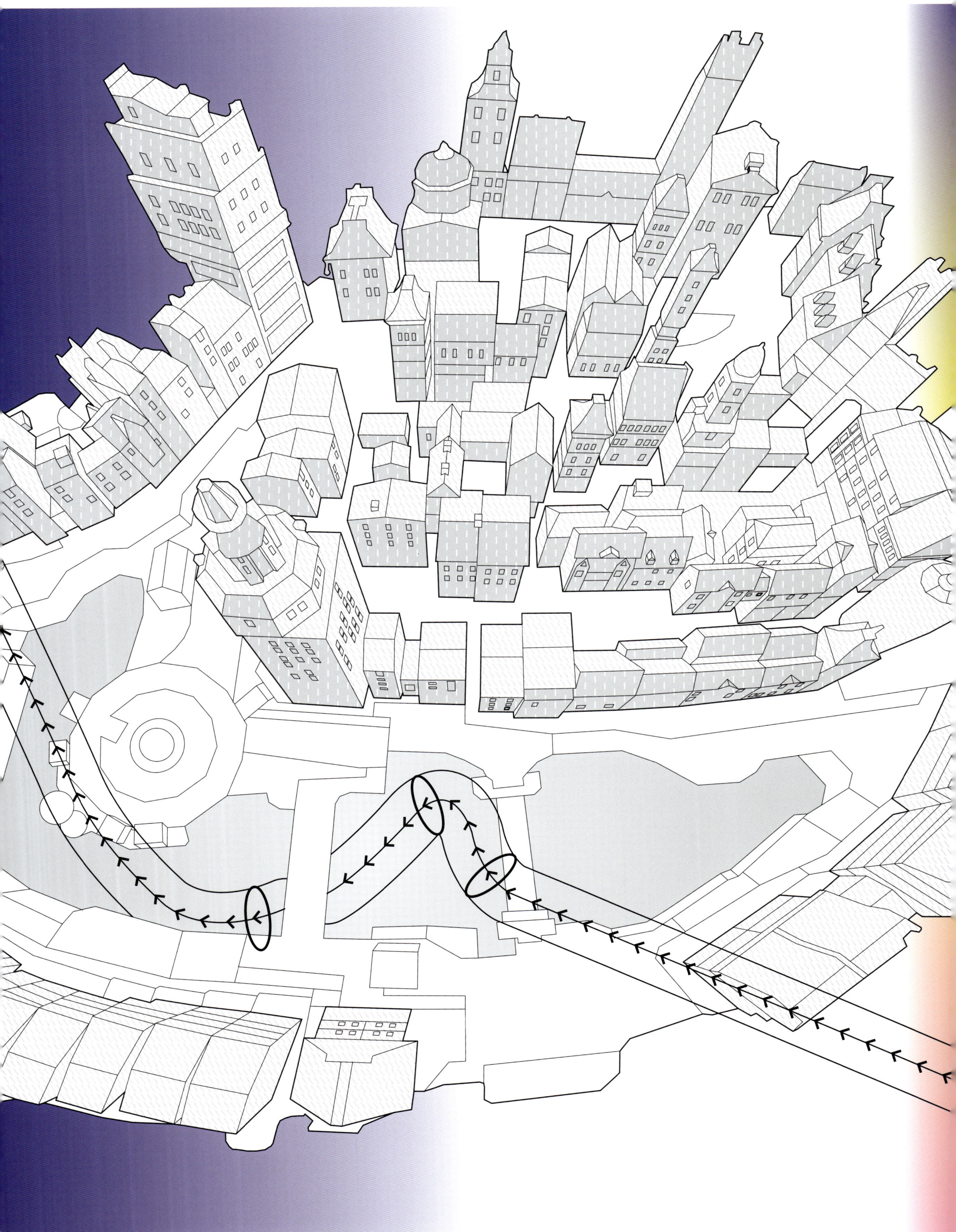

[Fig.12] Detail

7.5

ROLE PLAYING

The depth of both cities reveals how the society above can function through strict social hierarchy. But it is possible to dive even further to see where the material that the whole system relies upon comes from: the mining of gravity gems. By speaking with characters in both cities, Kat can venture out to various mines, where she is able to find gems and other resources. While mining is discussed in terms that relate to the real world – as the industrialized extraction of precious materials – the mines themselves have curious architectural forms, with gems found inside green pods that Kat must smash open [Fig.09]. Rather than representing the presence of industry, as we might find in photographs of marble quarries by Edward Burtynsky, the mines have an eclectic and surreal spatial language that doesn't fully align with their seemingly industrial nature.

Beyond her mining segues, Kat assumes various roles throughout the game that means she treats the city around her differently. Depending on the story and mission, she may become a freedom fighter, a gardener, a childminder or a private detective. Yet sometimes the metropolis itself can change role. During the 'Black Eagle' episode, a giant monster emerges that is itself a city – covered in protruding buildings and consuming the architecture of Lei Havina to add to itself. Here, the architectural and urban becomes monstrous [Fig.10]. Kat and fellow Gravity Shifter Raven must explore its interiors, where fragmented architectural surfaces close in around them, requiring precise and quick gravity shifting. This 'Lost City' is particularly notable when framed against Lei Havina's prominent architecture, such as the circular public forum, given that 'the monster runs against the idea of order usually discussed in architectural theory, namely that of...proportionality, subordination of parts to wholes and correct composition.'[10] Here the blissful detachment of the carefully maintained island paradises is disrupted by a pure mass of building *stuff*, forcing Kat back into the role of saviour by making her defeat this conglomeration from the inside out.

[Fig.09] PAGE 158

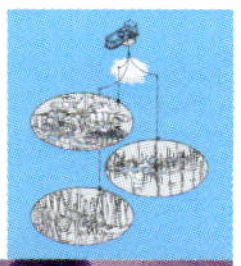

Drawing exploring some of the mining areas that Kat can visit, which all possess a unique architectural language and hint at the industrial underpinnings of the game world.

[Fig.10] PAGES 160–1

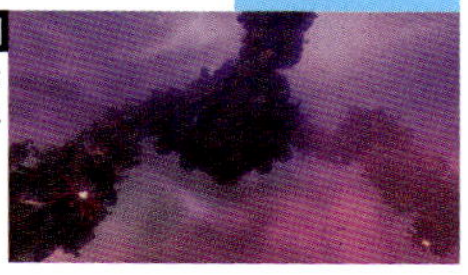

View of the giant 'Lost City' that attacks and eats the buildings of Jirga Para Lhao, subsuming them into its own body made of amalgamated architecture.

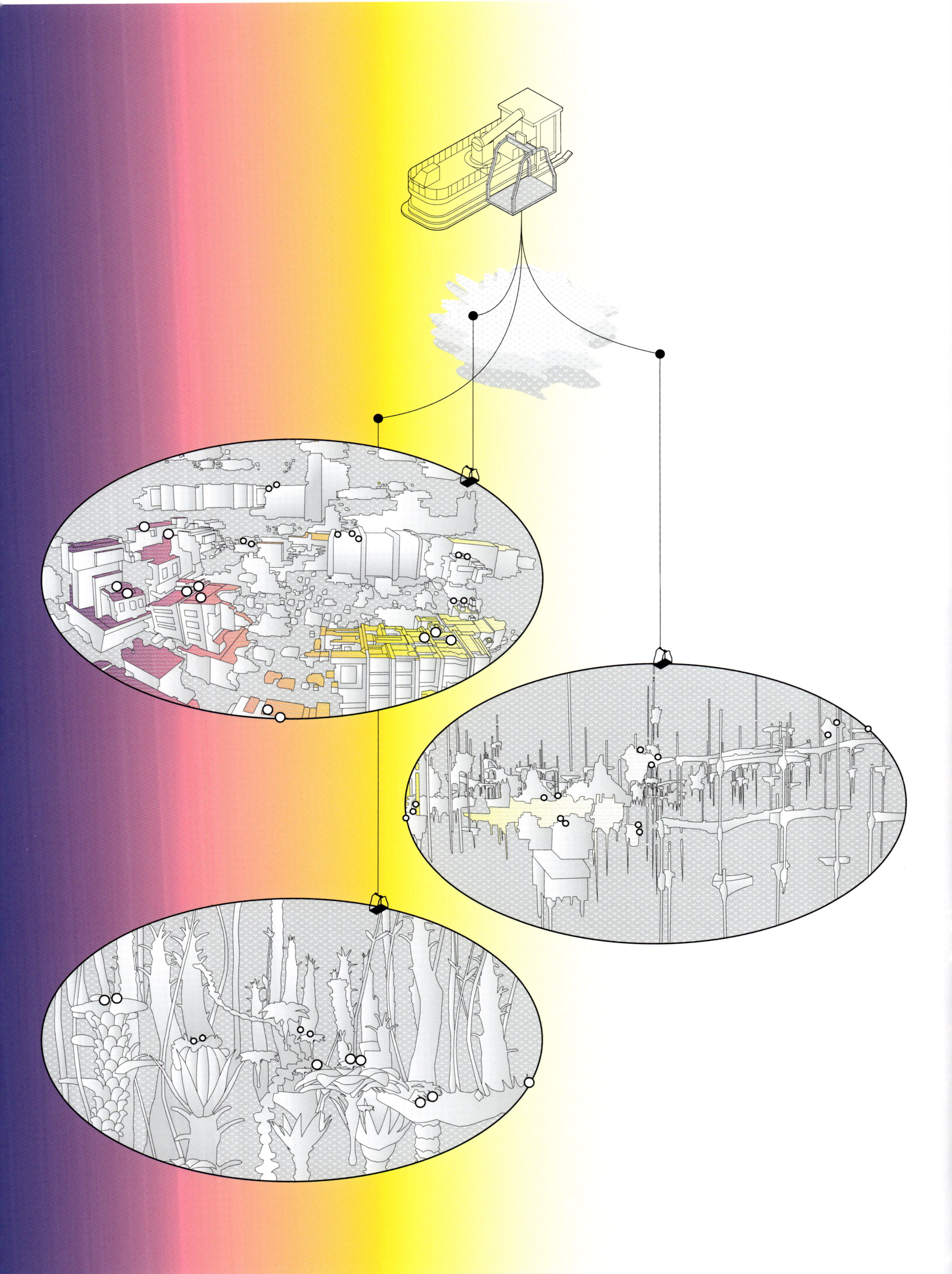

[Fig.09]

A more ambient role for Kat is that of the tourist. As an outsider in Jirga Para Lhao, Kat is given a camera by Syd, which she then uses to document the city. Certain achievements in the game are tied to visiting and recording the city just as a holidaymaker might. To receive the Tour Guide and Tour Conductor trophies, Kat must photograph twenty 'city sights' across Jirga Para Lhao and Hekseville using her camera. After finding all these viewpoints, we then draw them together as a landscape of touristic elements within the city [Fig.11]. Despite the political nature of the cities that we uncover during the story, the achievement stays on the superficial and touristic level, with Kat photographing numerous statues, large digital screens, notable building signs, a Ferris wheel and a floating tropical island. As Susan Sontag says in *On Photography*: 'taking photographs is a way of refusing [experience] – by limiting experience to a search for the photogenic, by converting experience into an image, a souvenir.'[11]

Only the view of the water tanks in Lei Elgona hints at the social situation of the city being viewed, showing infrastructure, which presumably provides the population drinking water, used by Kat to prevent Garrison soldiers from burning down the lower levels. Sontag also argues that 'using a camera appeases the anxiety which the work-driven feel about not working when they are on vacation,'[12] and Kat is evidence of that – when not saving the world or carrying out errands, she is collecting touristic images of the city. Through asynchronous multiplayer, Kat's camera can also be used to take pictures of secret stashes to guide other players, reinforcing the 'working' nature of her leisure photography.

[Fig.09] Detail

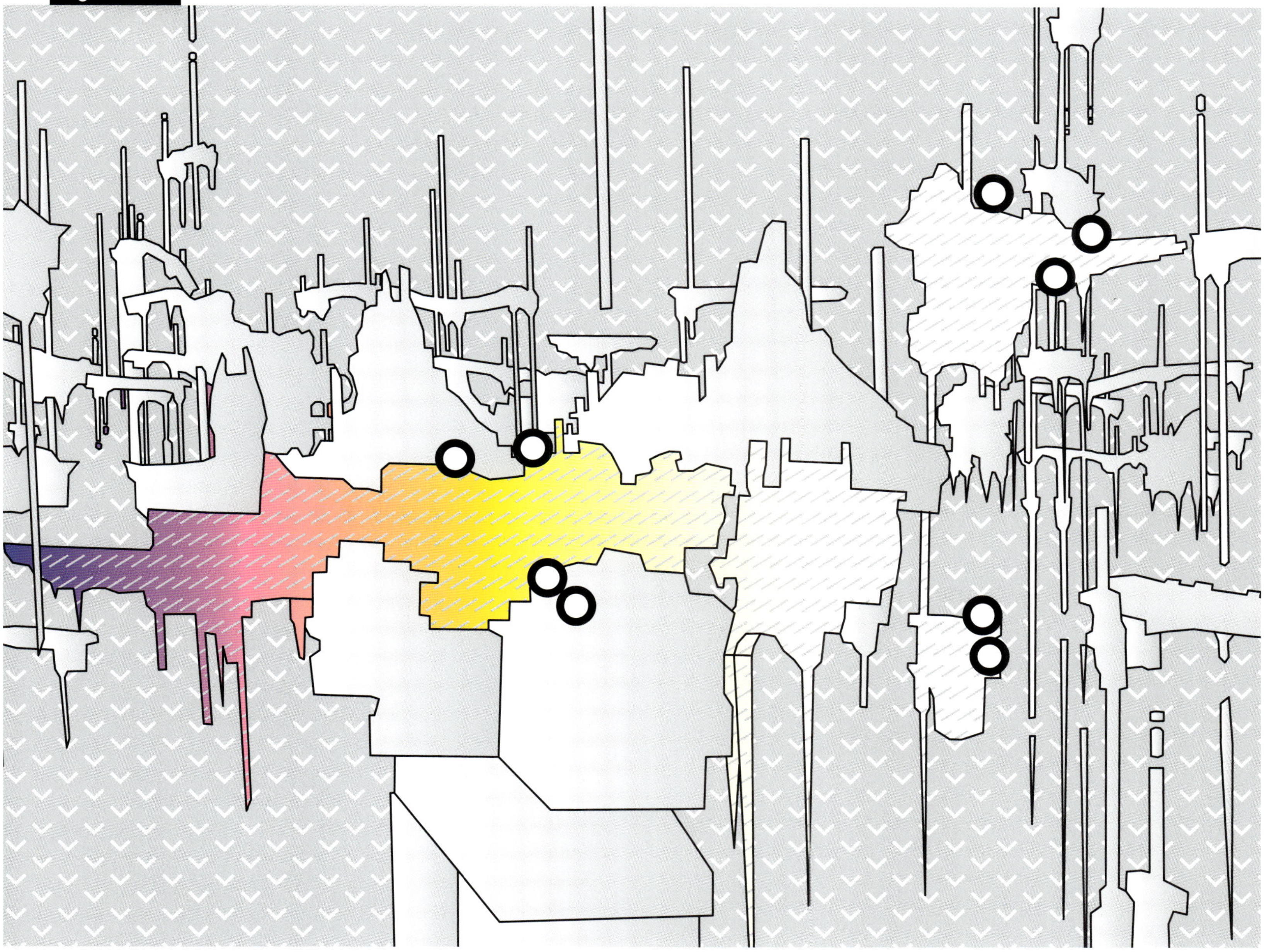

[Fig.11] PAGE 162

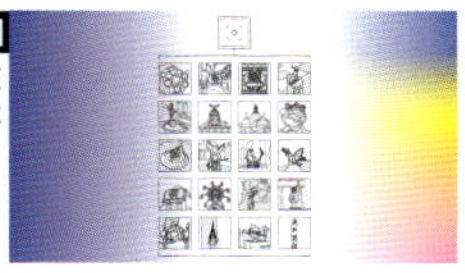

The twenty 'City Sights' that Kat captures with her camera during her touristic explorations of Jirga Para Lhao.

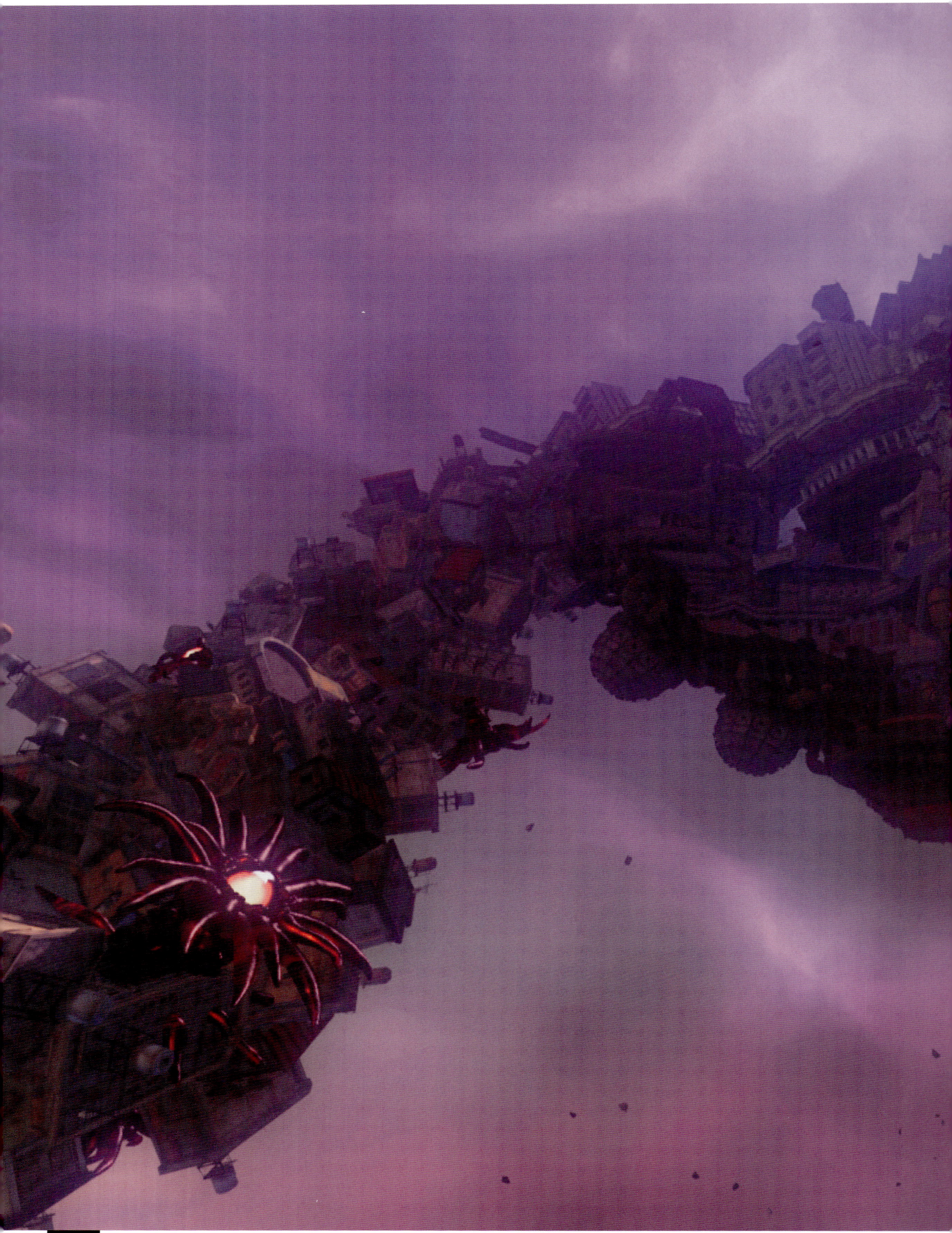

[Fig.10]

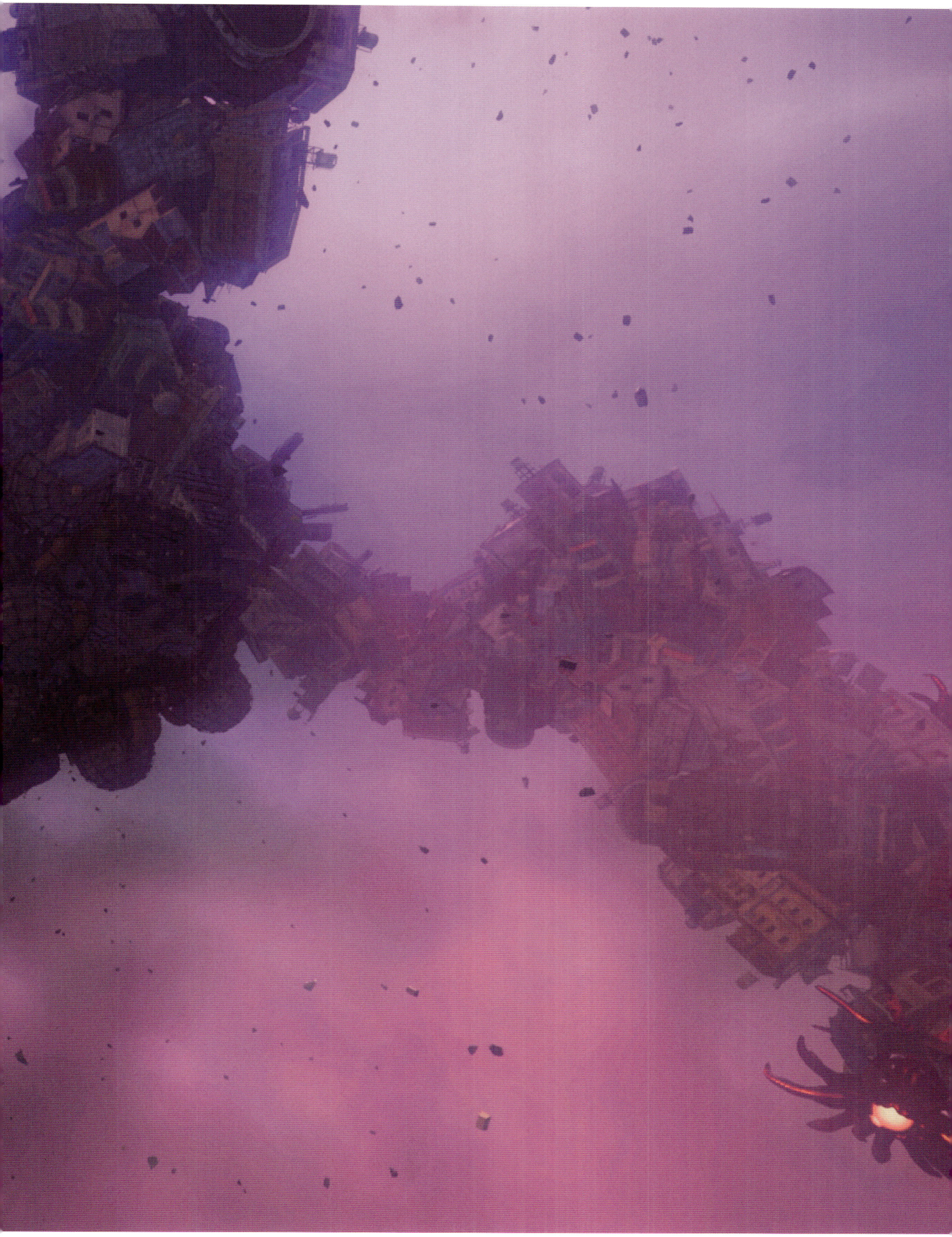

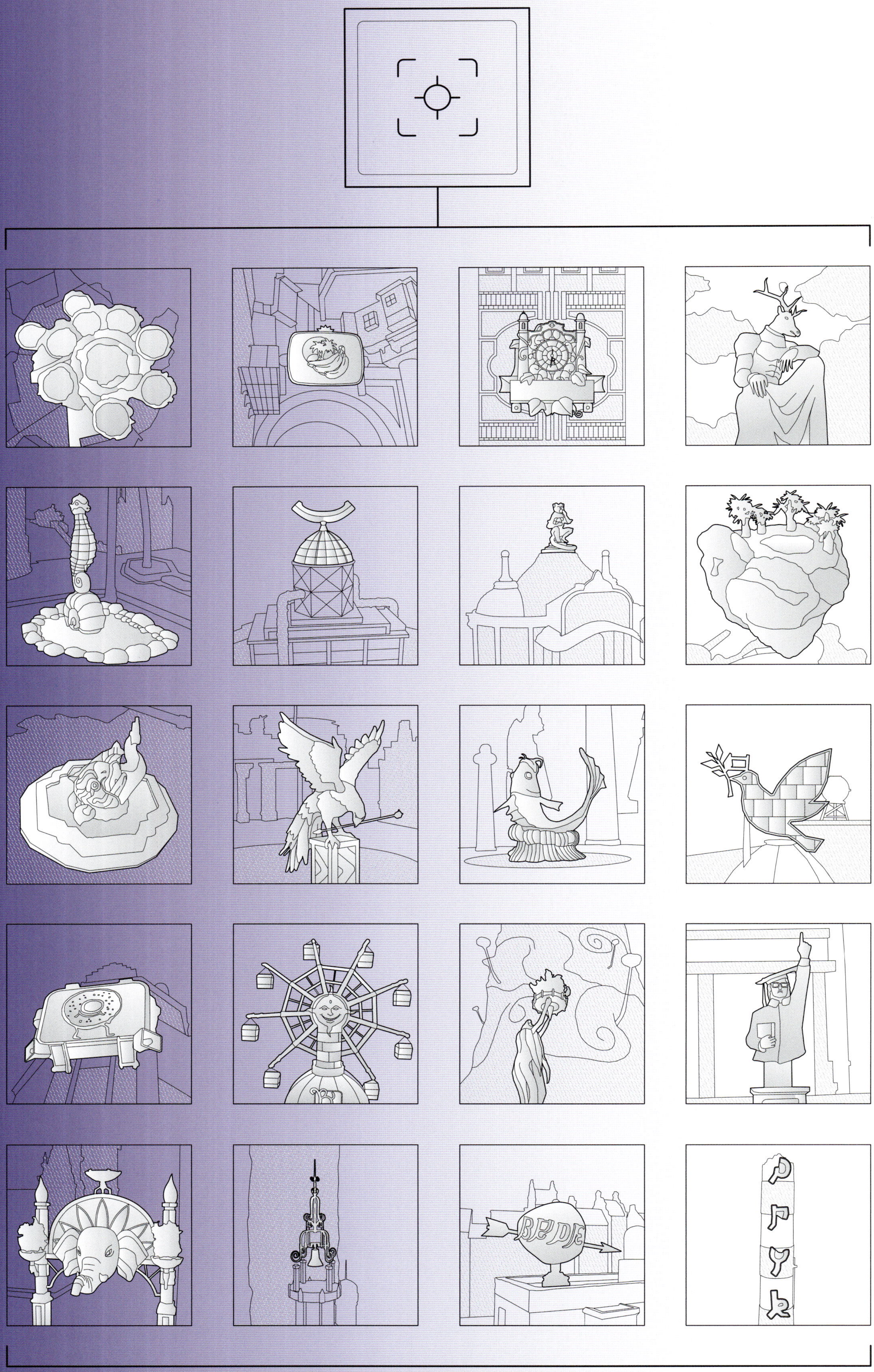

[Fig.11]

7.6

PANORAMIA

This traditional, touristic view of the world is at least a more gentle counterpoint to the experience of a city under perpetually shifting gravitational forces. We become used to seeing cities not from the ground as a normal citizen would, but from above and below, or at any of the other myriad angles Kat might approach from. This means that *Gravity Rush 2*'s world resists being represented by one single drawing type or flat image – it is more panoramic in nature, expanding in all directions. The 'panorama' is an 18th-century invention, originally meaning giant circular paintings typically installed in custom-made buildings, so that viewers 'must move around, choosing at will the direction of their gaze and the motion of their body…through 360 degrees'[13] to view the world. By using Kat's camera and stitching together multiple individual photos of the architectural landscape, we create panoramic viewpoints of Auldnoir from above and Lei Colmosna from below [Fig.12]. Through these panoramas we can better understand the way we, and Kat, experience the city not as specific singular viewpoints but as an urban landscape shifting in front of us where 'you can bisect the city, cutting through it at any angle…with new angles constantly revealing themselves.'[14] These views also demonstrate how Kat's aerial perspective mirrors those of other skybound explorers like pilots and balloonists where 'the aerial view completely changes the perception of large objects … objects that on the ground are of different scale, yet to the aerial observer look similar.'[15] As Kat dives all the way down (or up) through the city, it first appears flat, before becoming panoramic and finally a fully three-dimensional world that can be experienced at any angle.

Unlike other games that can leave the fringes of the world more abstract, every surface in *Gravity Rush 2* is designed to fascinate and draw us in because it can be approached from any angle. Architectural and structural forms we find in the real world are all dictated by a consistent force of gravity, yet the architecture of the game's world appeals to the specific viewpoint of a character for whom these rules can be upended and spun around. In doing so, Kat's voyage through the world exemplifies the stance of the famous Iraqi-British architect Zaha Hadid, whose work pushed at the geometric possibilities of architecture: 'there are 360 degrees, so why stick to one?'[16]

[Fig.12]
PAGES 164–5

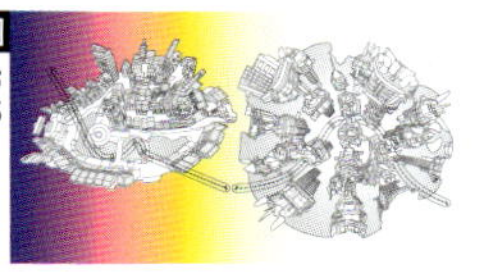

Panoramic drawings of Auldnoir in Hekseville and Lei Colmosna in Jirga Para Lhao, demonstrating how the city is typically viewed by Kat as she gravity-shifts around the world.

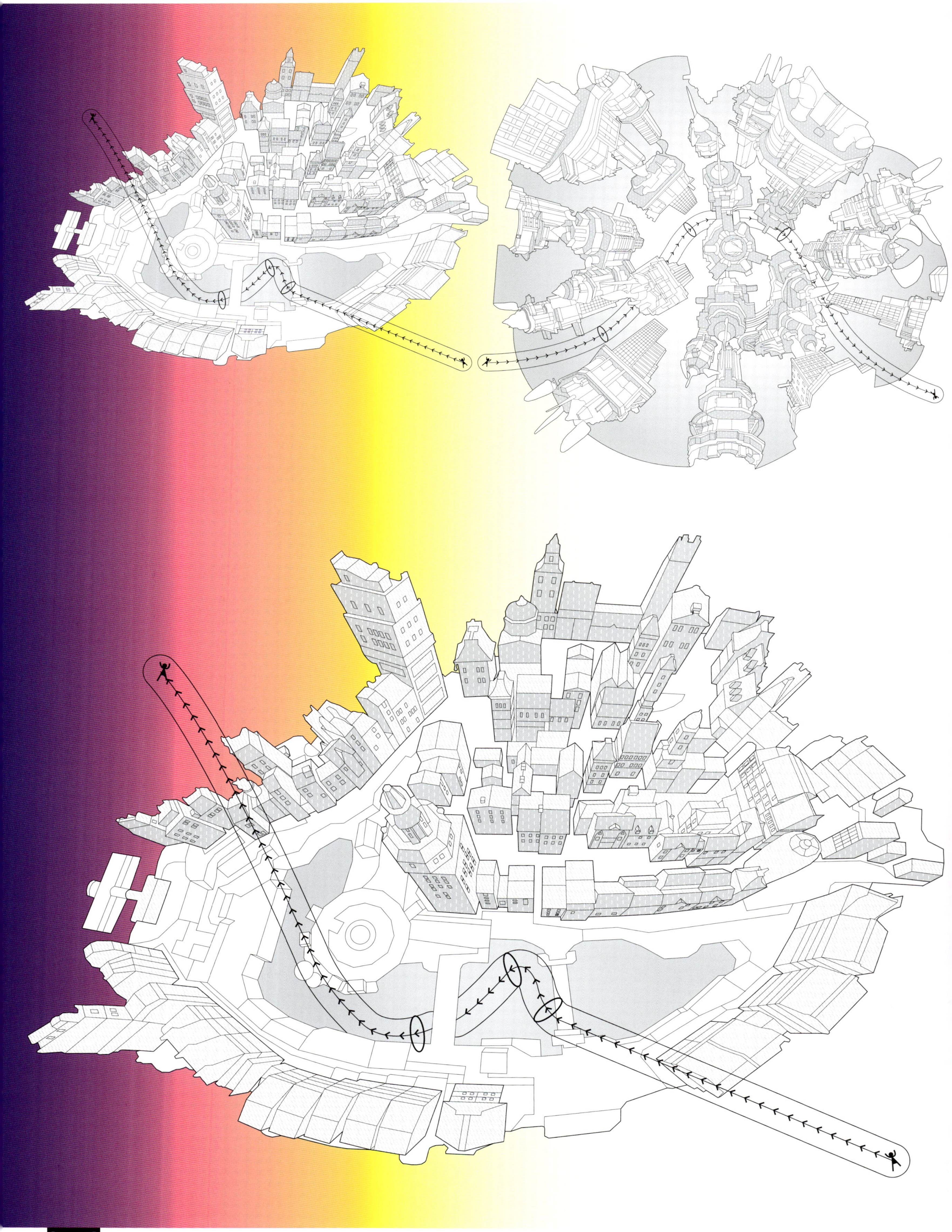

[Fig.12]

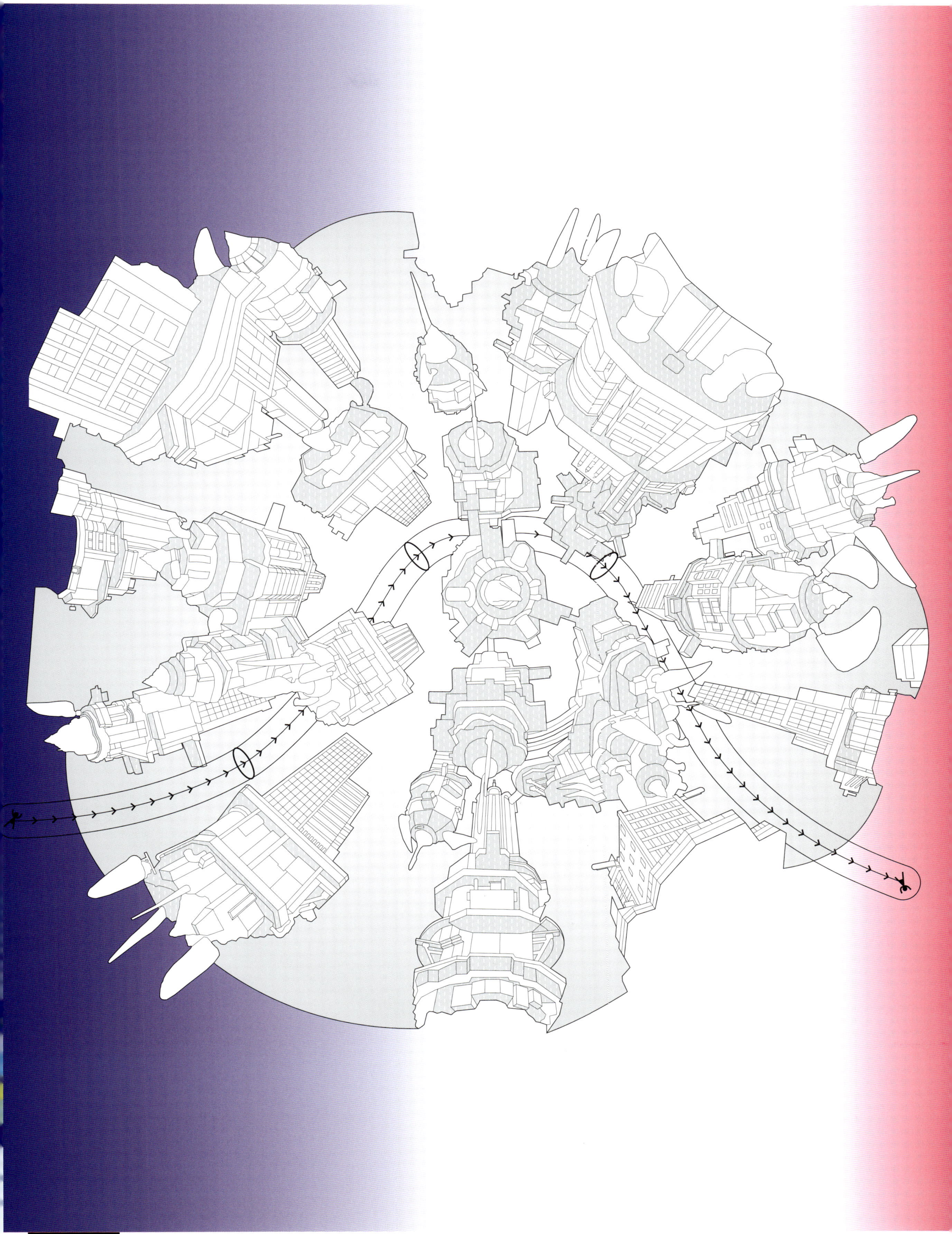

[Fig.12] Detail

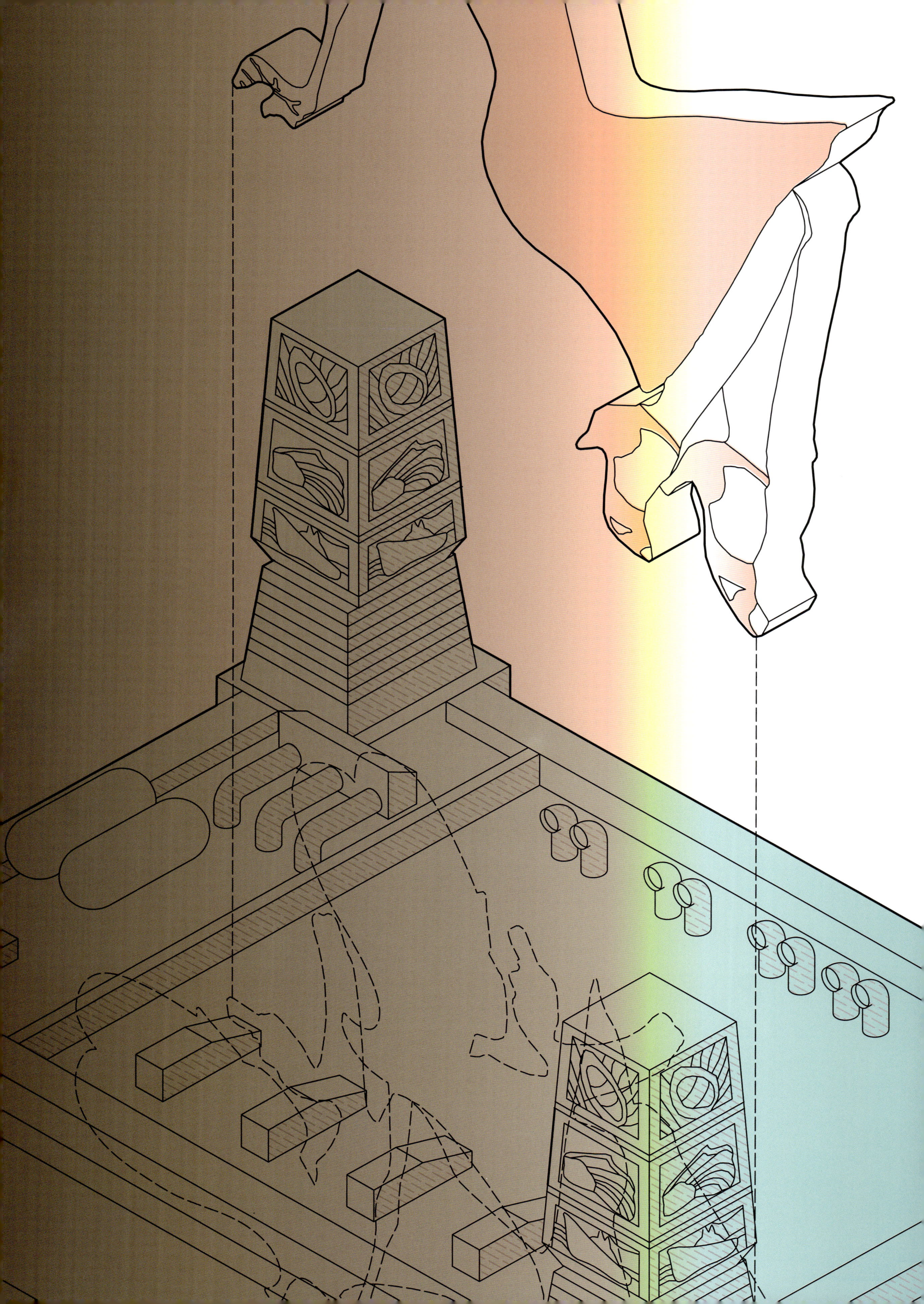

CHAPTER 08

GRIM FANDANGO REMASTERED

DEVELOPER
PUBLISHER
DOUBLE FINE PRODUCTIONS

Platforms	Windows, Linux, OS X, PlayStation 4, PlayStation Vita, Android, iOS, Nintendo Switch, Xbox One
Year	2015

MAP OF THE SPATIAL CONNECTIONS IN THE DEPARTMENT OF DEATH BASED ON THE PRE-RENDERED BACKGROUNDS DEPICTING THE BUILDING.

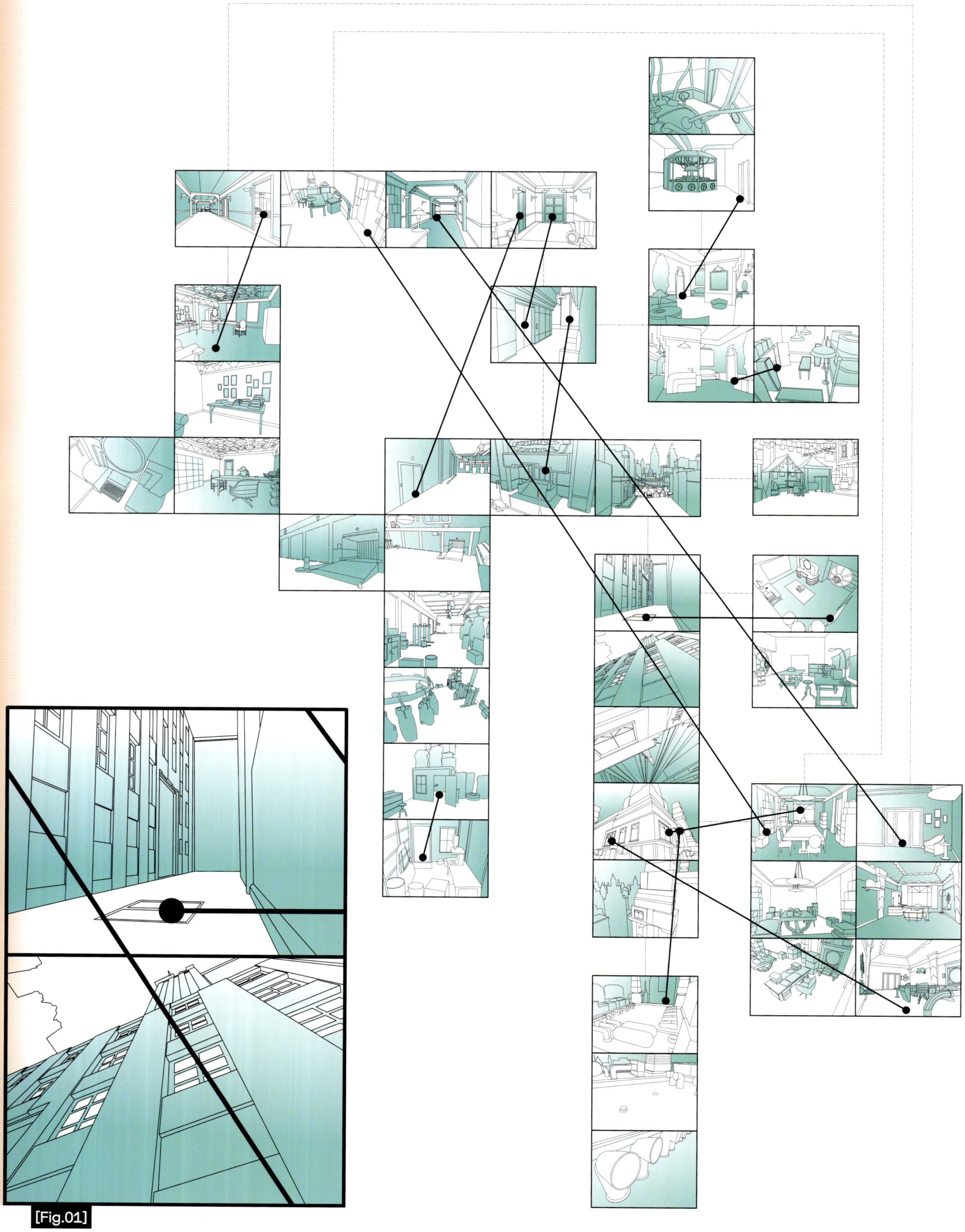

[Fig.01]

8.1 DECO NOIR

Grim Fandango is certainly one of the most stylish games ever made – so much so that Double Fine updated it for modern audiences and technologies in 2016 with the release of *Grim Fandango Remastered*. Its architectural landscape represents a creative visual collision between Mexican folk aesthetics, Art Deco design and the visual principles of Film Noir, producing a highly stylized world that frames the four-year journey of Manny Calavera though the Land of the Dead. Director Tim Schafer describes the original concept as 'cold crime and corruption in a wildly surreal and mythical world, combining elements of ancient Mexican folklore, classic film noir movies, and '60s-era custom hot rods.'[1] The Mexican folklore that underpins the game is *Mictlān*, an underworld of nine layers that souls travel through once they die, with the visual form of the characters inspired by the more contemporary Día de los Muertos festival.

The world of *Grim Fandango* strongly incorporates Art Deco-related styles including Mayan Revival and Mesoamerican design. One famous proponent of Mayan Revival architecture was the architect Frank Lloyd Wright, who used the style in projects such as the Ennis House and Hollyhock House during the 1920s. This style was most fully articulated by the Mexican architect Francisco Mujica, whose book *History of the Skyscraper* outlined a lineage from Mayan and Aztec architecture to the contemporary city of New York.[2] Mujica 'vindicated the indigenous architectures of America... as appropriate precedents for the skyscraper,'[3] suggesting that this would become a true *American* (the continent, not the nation) form of design. As we join Manny in the city of El Marrow at the start of the game, we see a whole metropolis designed around this idea. The city resembles New York but is saturated with Mesoamerican details and designs, including an Aztec temple. This contextual design immediately signifies a story about Mexican folklore seen through the lineage of hard-boiled American noir mysteries.

Grim Fandango is experienced through static viewpoints. Given the technologies of the time, the developers were unable to produce a fully navigable 3D world with the level of resolution and architectural complexity that the game's setting demanded. Instead, like other games of the period, the game employs a method of pre-rendered backdrops (made using the now-discontinued software SoftImage[4]) combined with invisible geometries that the developers called 'walk planes'[5] to dictate where Manny can move. In total, the game uses over 330 of these background renderings. This means that seemingly contiguous spaces, such as the Department of Death building, are broken into a series of spatial vignettes, where even single rooms can be represented through multiple views. By extracting these backgrounds using community tools such as ScummVM[6], we mapped the connections between each individual render and built a complete version of the building based on the information provided by the game [Fig.01].

The Year One version of the DoD building is comprised of thirty-six individual backgrounds, the majority of which depict the building's interior, with ten showing the building's external form in the context of El Marrow. Our map closely resembles the type of Location Layout diagrams included in the game's Puzzle Document, which appears as an alternative type of architectural drawing, focused on the story beats in each space rather than their design and form.[7] Despite being borne from technical limitations, this type of architectural approach is particularly suited to a film noir story, because as Renee Tobe argues, 'in film noir...we want to know what happens next because we can't "see" everything, the alley has a bend in it, the fog obscures the identity of the character scurrying away, the shadows evoke mystery and imagination.'[8] The static camera enables the designers to precisely control how Manny appears in a scene and what is revealed or hidden.

ISOMETRIC RECONSTRUCTION OF THE DEPARTMENT OF DEATH, MADE BY INTERPRETING PRE-RENDERED BACKGROUNDS USING SPECIALIZED PERSPECTIVE ANALYSIS AND 3D-MODELLING SOFTWARE.

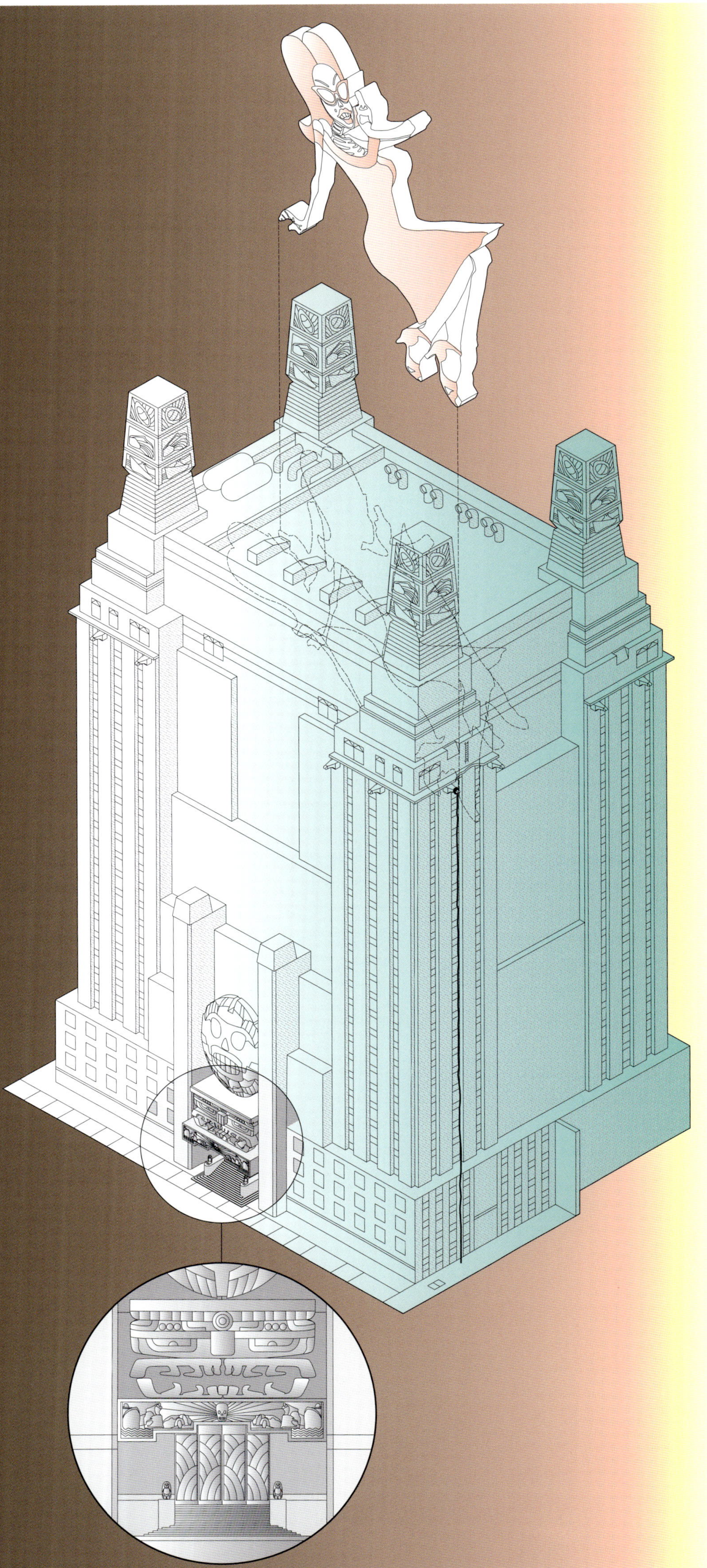

[Fig.02]

8.2 RECONSTRUCTIONS

Working with these viewpoints allows the developer to cut extraneous elements from the spatial experience. Long pathways and elevator rides are traversed instantaneously. In this context it is hard to establish what the Department of Death *actually* looks like as a building form because the ten static backdrops never depict it in its totality. In order to recreate the building's architecture, we employed a tool called fSpy,[9] which allowed us to set up the converging perspective lines from each background image and import this into the architectural 3D-modelling programme Rhino using a community-made script.[10]

We reconstructed the building based on the game's perspective viewpoints, alongside architectural interpretations such as estimating distances from the typical height of building floorplates and the number of windows depicted. The model was then tested and tweaked in relation to the next viewpoint, allowing us to arrive at what we can consider to be a reasonably accurate rendition of the building's geometry [Fig.02]. This interpretation is made challenging by some of the artistic decisions taken by the developers, such as employing wide-angle views, or the limited depiction of certain features. However, the building's architectural form relies on symmetry, a large podium level that contains our demon buddy Glottis' garage and the carpool, and the terracotta-coloured corner sections that house the offices in which Manny works.

Our interpretation diverges from the massing proposed in the old Prima's Official Strategy Guide,[11] but we can clearly see the extents of the building through the rooftop scenes where Manny tries to obtain pigeon eggs. Some of the more detailed elements, such as the building's entrance, are not completely depicted, so we examined Peter Chan's concept drawings for reference. This reconstruction shows that the Department of Death has the hulking form of Art Deco buildings such as those designed by Raymond Hood in New York (see Chapter 2: *BioShock* for reference). Director Tim Schafer has also spoken of a real-world inspiration for the architecture, the 450 Sutter Street building in San Francisco designed by Timothy L. Pflueger, which was referenced heavily in the design of the DoD and the broader city of El Marrow.[12] Marjorie Ingle uses 450 Sutter as a visual example in her book *The Mayan Revival Style*, explaining how similar designs were driven by an increasing scholarly and archeological interest in Mesoamerican architecture.[13]

Mayan Revival and Art Deco details proliferate throughout the world of *Grim Fandango*. Our elevational studies demonstrate how these details take many forms, from ornate doorways and furniture through to train tunnel entrances and even cadaver cabinets in a city morgue [Fig.03]. Many of these smaller contextual details use more 'typical' Art Deco tropes such as trains, boats, airships or cats, yet the strong influence of Mesoamerican design prevails throughout. One of the great manuals of architectural design in this style, which the developers may have referenced, is the 1926 book *Maya Architecture* by George Oakley Totten, which documents Mayan architectural details and decorations in a similar elevational style, with the aim of introducing them into the language of contemporary designers.[14] As Ingle explains, this type of work allowed Mesoamerican details to be used as 'elements or units' where designers would 'reshuffle them like playing cards into new architectural design in the Mayan Revival style.'[15] In *Grim Fandango* a similarly playful use and reuse of these design elements runs throughout the game.

[Fig.03]
PAGE 172

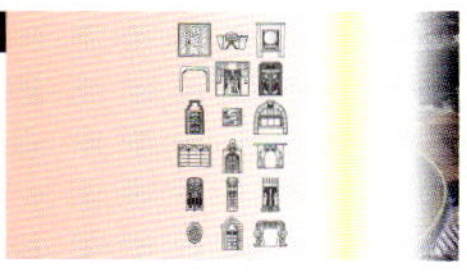

Elevational studies of Mesoamerican and Art Deco design details found on Manny's journey across the Land of the Dead.

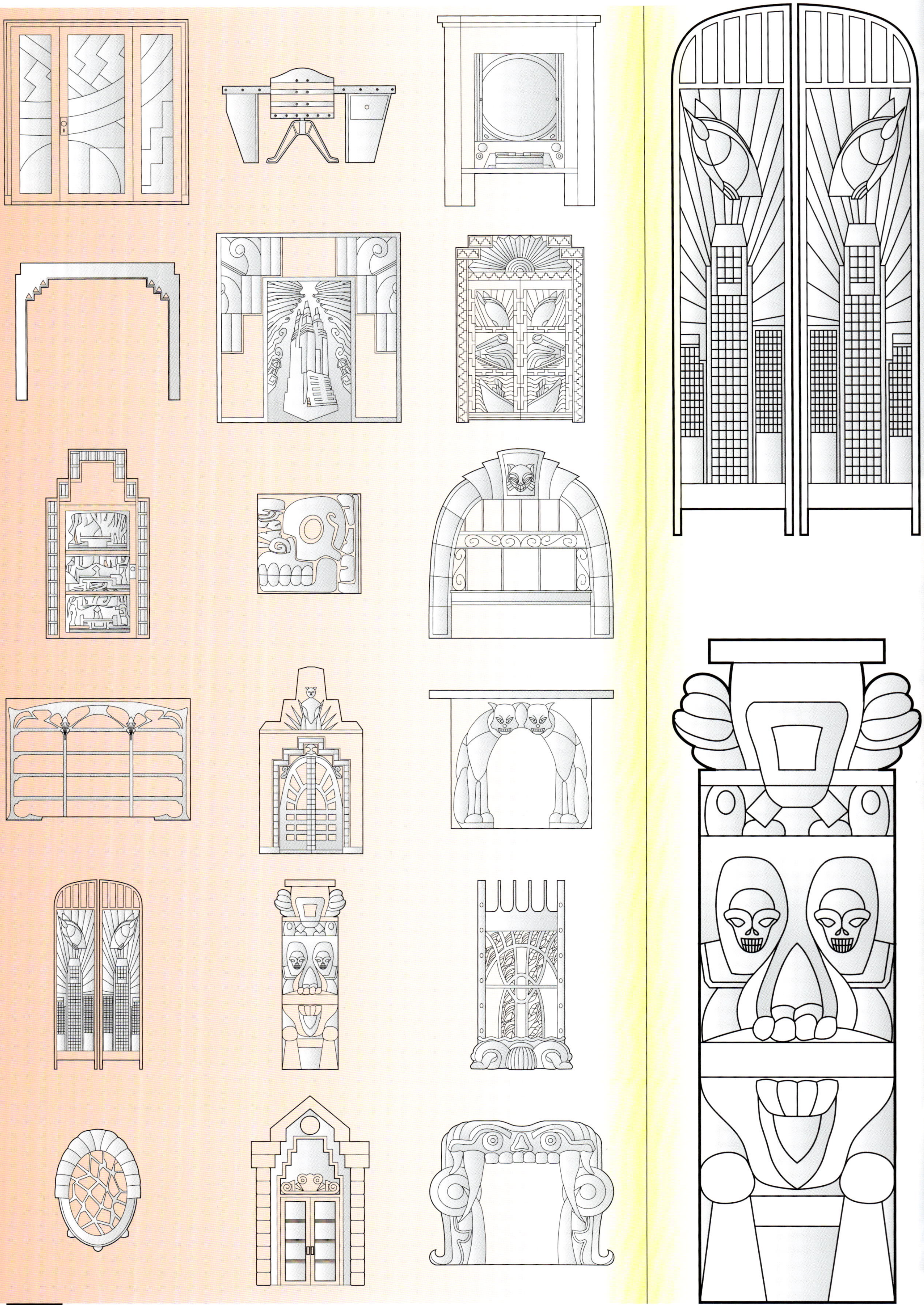

[Fig.03]

8.3

RECONSTRUCTING RUBACAVA

The end of Year One and start of Year Two brings us to the main port town of Rubacava on the journey through the Land of the Dead. Rubacava is represented as a warren of spaces straddling two ridges and centred on large bridge over a bay that connects both sides of the town. The town is experienced through eighty-four rendered views, of which twenty-eight show its external form. By using similar fSpy techniques as with the Department of Death, we reconstructed the city through these views to recreate the massing of the navigable world presented to Manny [Fig.04].

The use of creative camera angles and spatial jumps between rendered scenes make it even more challenging to achieve a true recreation of the city than with the DoD. However, by positioning Manny against buildings to dimension notable structures and help us estimate their size, we rebuilt the town from the original renders to better understand its layout. In this context the core area of Rubacava can be seen as quite compact – only around 200 metres (650 ft) from the cliffside Morgue to Feline Meadows, with the bridge looming some 50 metres (164 ft) above the water. In-game, the views roll off into the darkness of a starry night, making it impossible to estimate the town beyond, if it even exists. By fading the background to darkness, and emphasizing key buildings against the void, the design of Rubacava underlines Edward Dimendberg's idea that 'the universe of film noir, with its... seedy gambling joints, ramshackle urban neighborhoods, and threatening skyscrapers, seems akin to a modern vision of purgatory.'[16] Rubacava's 'purgatorial' design reinforces the story of *Mictlān* that the game draws from.

The most complete picture we get of the town is from a view high up on the cliff where Manny's club Calavera Café sits. Below us appear the docks and the hulking Feline Meadows cat racing track. This 'birds-eye' view of the town is not unlike other famous overhead cinematic shots, such as Bodega Bay from Alfred Hitchcock's *The Birds* (1965), foreshadowing the conspiracies that will unfold below. But from here the inconsistencies of the pre-rendered background are revealed – long walkways cross the bay, and the docks appear huge. Once Manny reaches the actual location, these distances disappear in the gap between rendered backdrops [Fig.05].

Tim Schafer described how the 3D world facilitates more cinematic spatial storytelling where 'you can do so much more thematically with the camera angles: you can show the ceiling, you can show the top-down views, you can have the characters lit very dark and walk into a light.'[17] The camera angles of Rubacava often create spaces that seem to contradict one another, but that make sense cinematically.

Rubacava's architecture is even more hybridized than we found in the Mayan Revival language of El Marrow. Our elevations of key buildings within the town showcase how its designers have started to blend other international influences into the architecture [Fig.06]. Rubacava starts to reflect Art Nouveau inspirations, as seen in the design of the Blue Casket and Calavera Café, with the former demonstrating a likeness to the work of Catalan architect Antoni Gaudí, particularly his Casa Batlló building in Barcelona. While the Rubacava Police Station and Morgue still bear Art Deco details, such as the statue of justice staring out over the city below, it also resembles the German expressionist architect Erich Mendelsohn's Einstein Tower.

[Fig.04] PAGE 174

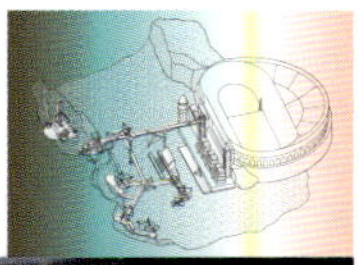

Recreation of Rubacava, indicating the pre-rendered perspectival viewpoints that were used to rebuild the space in 3D.

[Fig.05] PAGES 176–7

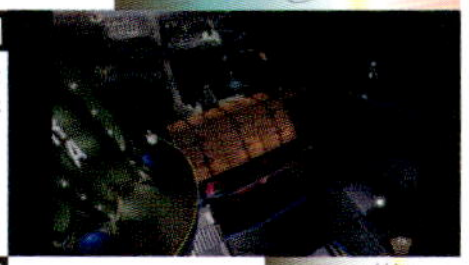

Screenshot of the view from the Calavera Café looking down across Rubacava, showing the overall scale of the town, which takes on a different form once we explore it.

[Fig.06] PAGE 178

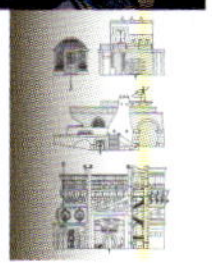

Elevations of notable buildings in Rubacava, demonstrating the influence of Mayan Revival, Art Deco, Art Nouveau and Expressionist architecture on the design of the town.

Snippets of views of the Feline Meadows racetrack show an undulating tiled or brick roofscape, that recalls the work of Uruguayan engineer Eladio Dieste or the Spanish-Mexican architect Félix Candela. The large ziggurat-like structures that protrude from its façade where it meets the docks represents a classic visual trope of Mesoamerica: 'the "zig-zagged" form'[18] that was a popular motif in Art Deco design.

Overlooking the town is the Calavera Café, renovated by Manny between the first and second year of the story as he becomes a self-made success. Here we see how the humdrum building of the Rub-A-Mat is converted into a Las Vegas-style casino and bar through the attachment of new architectural elements. Comparing the two structures, pre- and post-renovation, reveals how these details are not structural but instead reinvent the building through decoration that is concentrated on areas such as the entrance and ornate new window mouldings [Fig.07]. Such design approaches are common to casino architecture, such as the 'decorated sheds' of Las Vegas[19] observed by architects Denise Scott Brown and Robert Venturi. Simple building forms would be wrapped in thematic details, transforming them into symbolic representations of Roman Coliseums or Arabian Nights. Behind the façade, interiors of the café are remodelled in a Moorish style, a clear design reference to the film noir spaces of *Casablanca* (1942) such as Rick's Café Américain – along with Manny's Humphrey Bogart-inspired white tuxedo.

[Fig.07]
PAGES
179

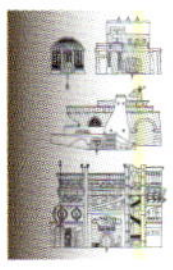

Drawing comparing the Calavera Café pre- and post-renovation, indicating the decorative architectural elements that are added to transform it into a stylized casino.

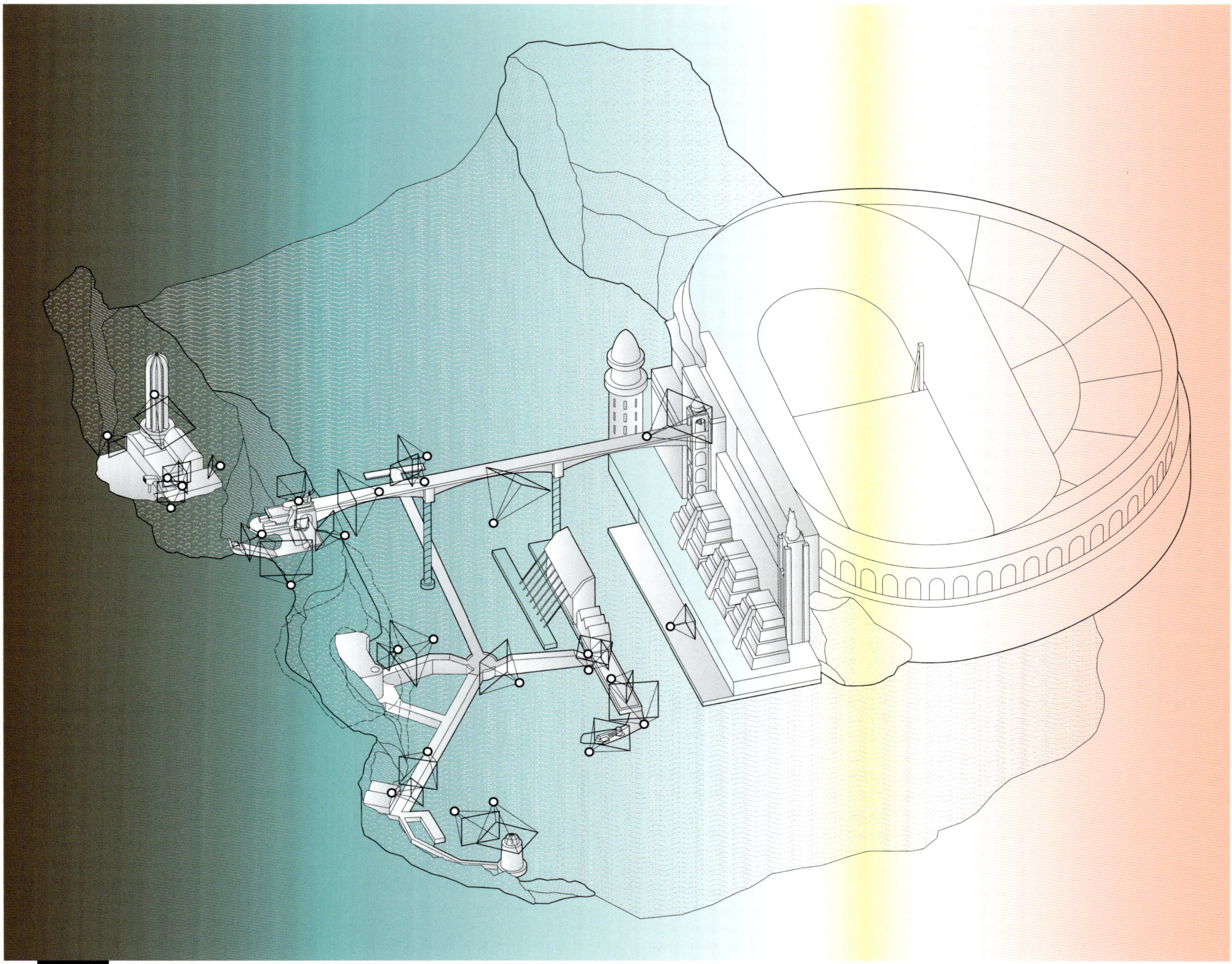

[Fig.04]

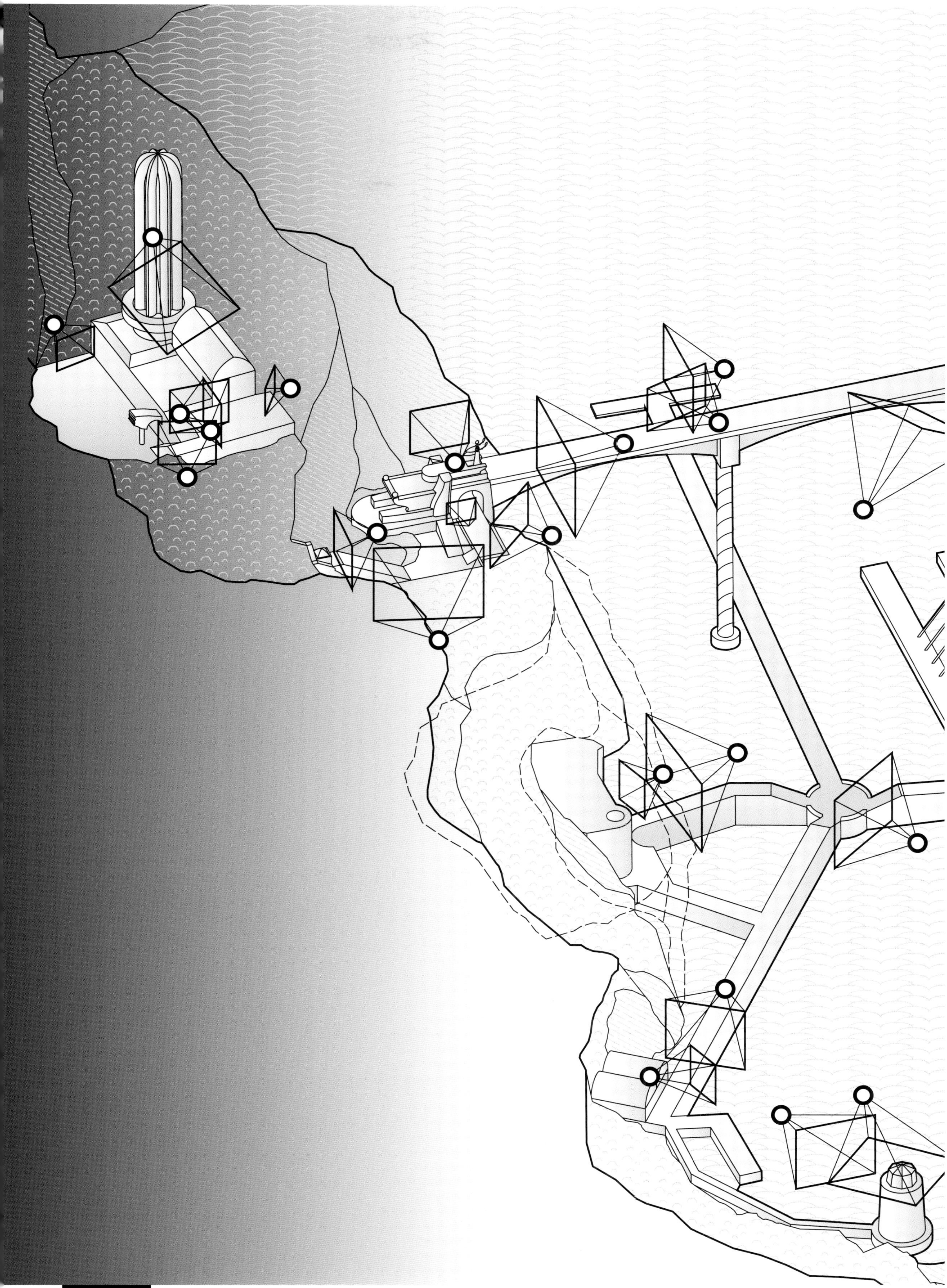

[Fig.04]Detail

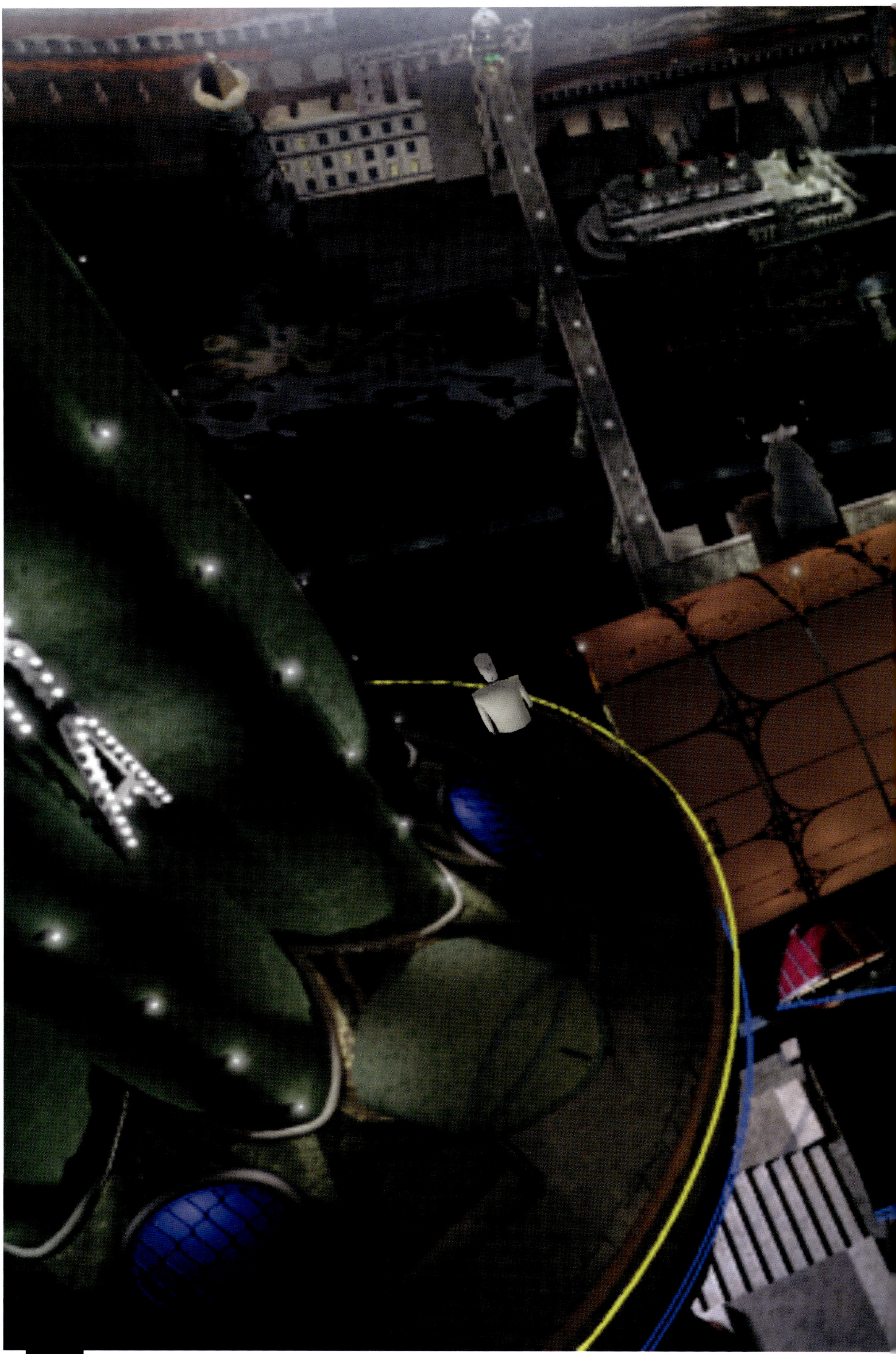

[Fig.05]

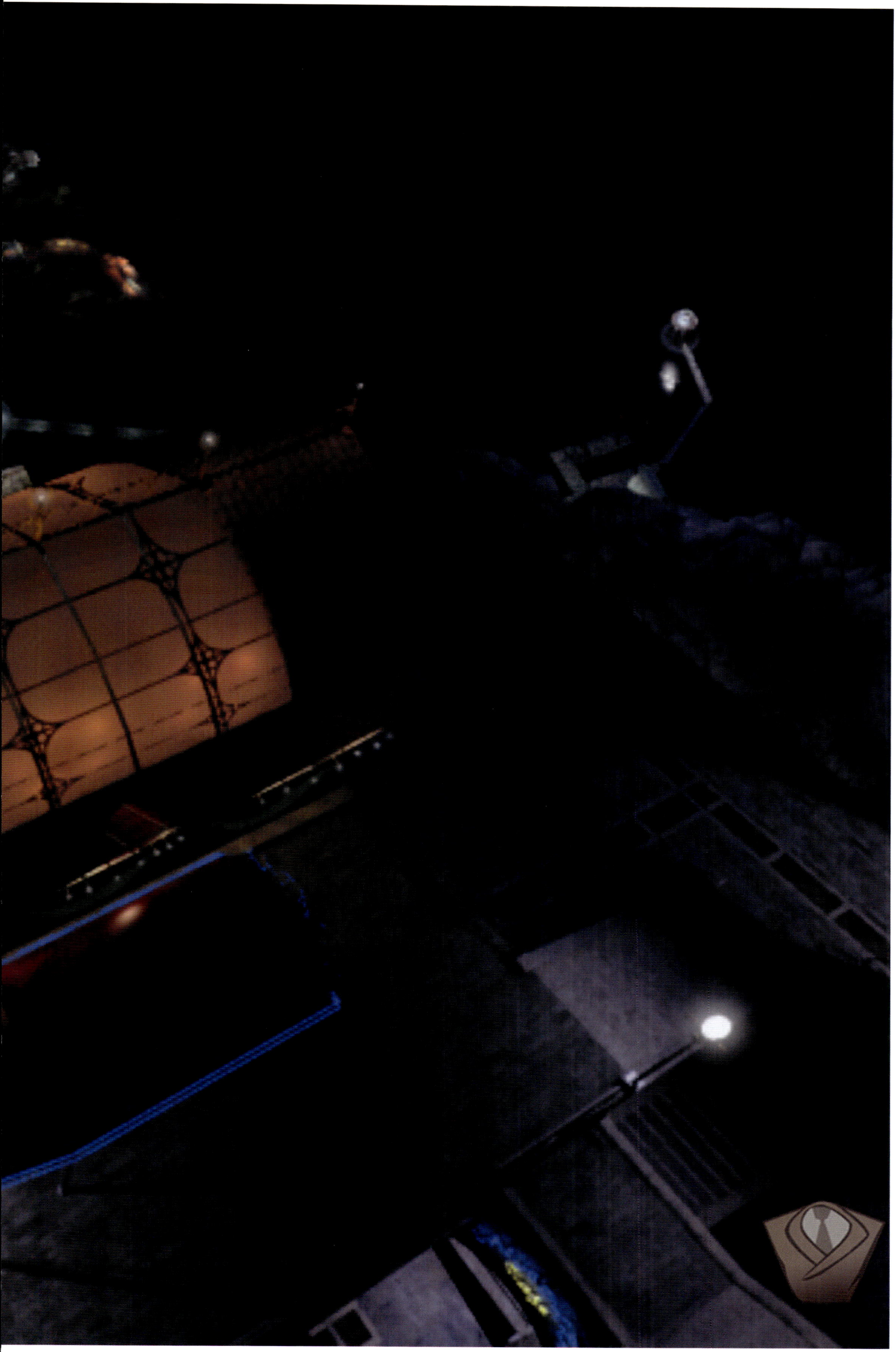

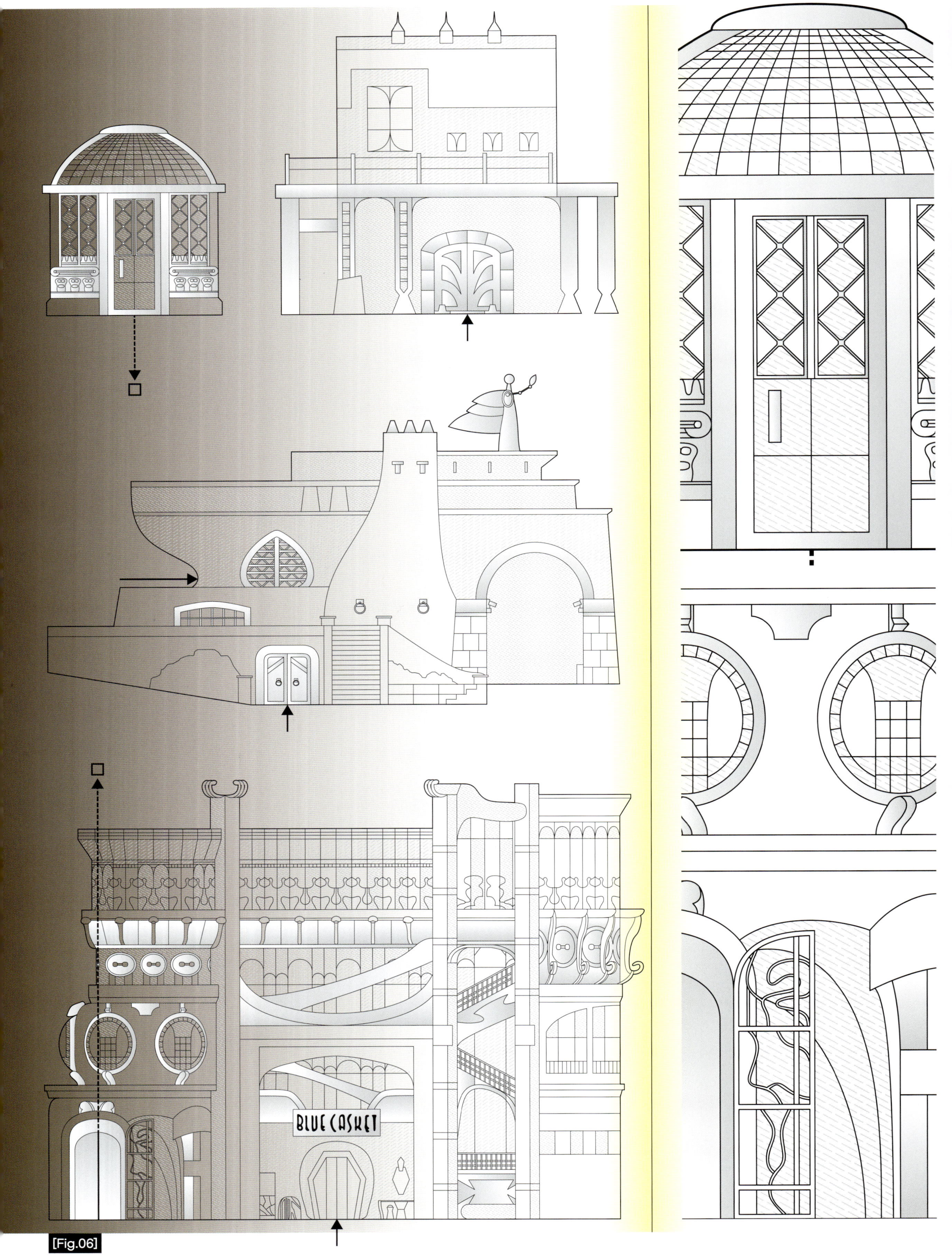

[Fig.06]

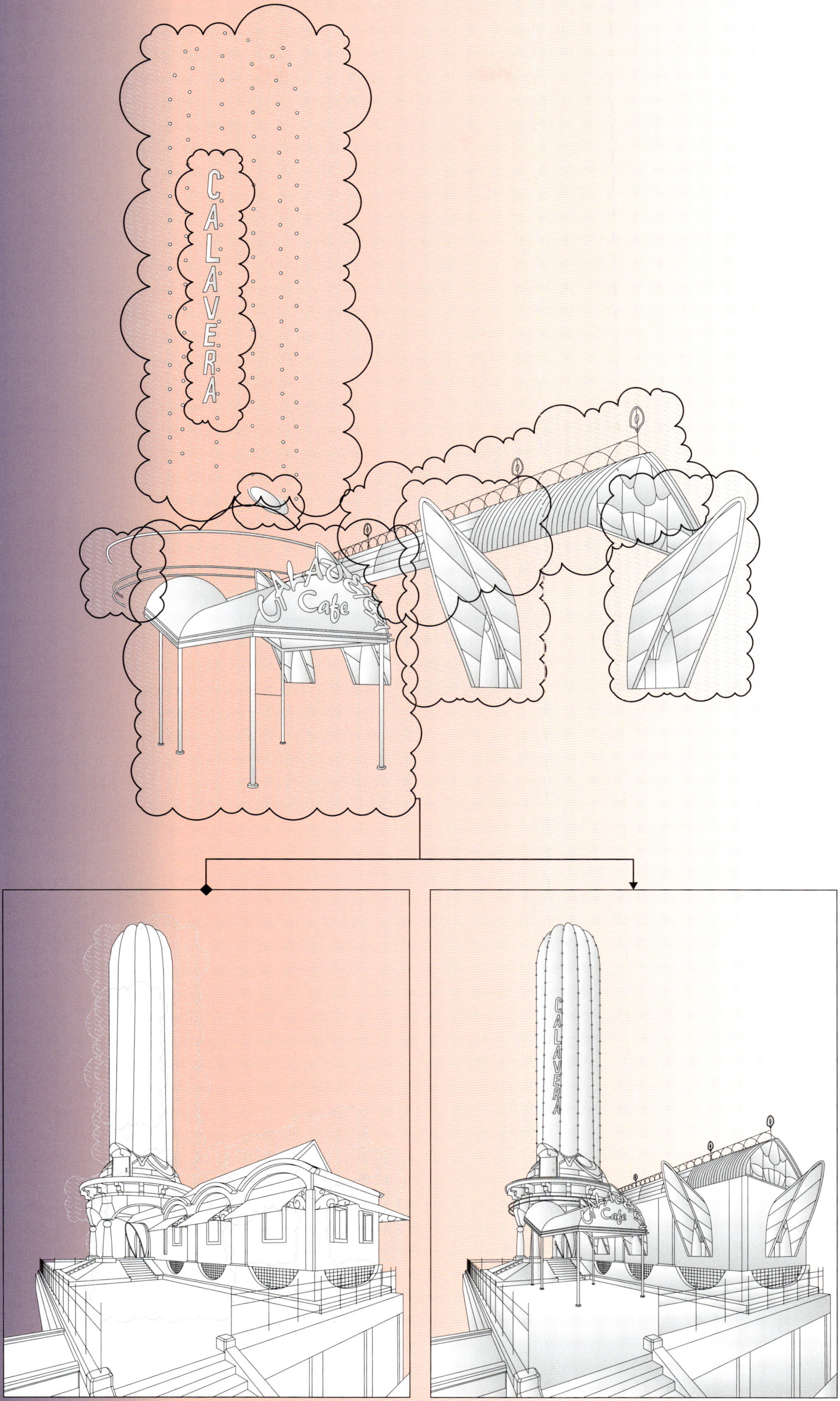

[Fig.07]

OBLIQUE DRAWING OF DOMINO HURLEY'S FACILITY AT THE EDGE OF THE WORLD, SHOWING AN ISLAND ARCHITECTURE CONFIGURED AROUND THE INDUSTRIAL EXTRACTION OF CORAL.

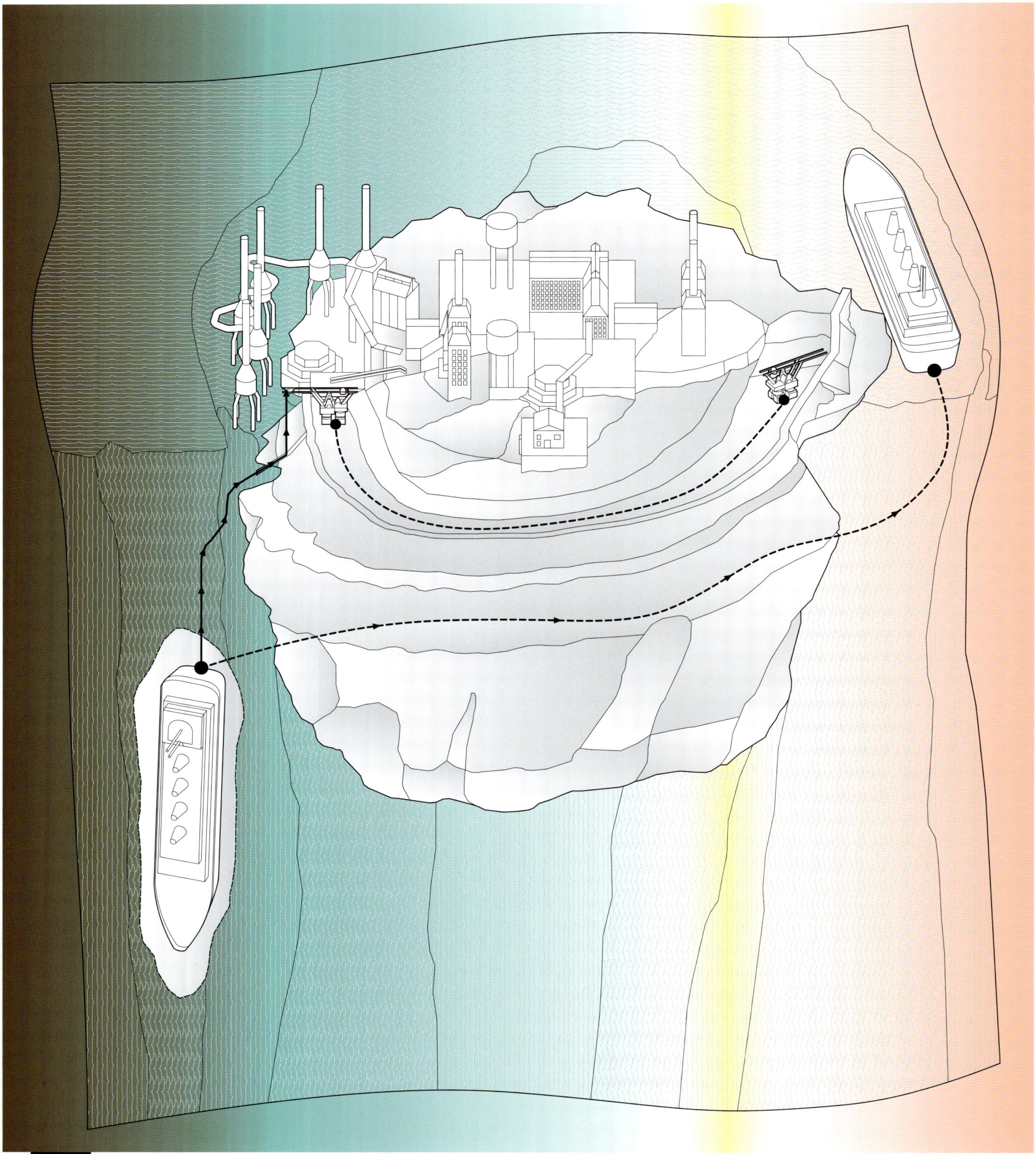

[Fig.09]

8.4

MODIFICATIONS AND MACHINE ARCHITECTURE

During the transition from Year Two to Year Three of the story, we see Manny once again rise to a position of influence, this time over the ship *SS Lola*. In a mirror to the architectural transformation of the Calavera Café, we see that Glottis has modified the ship into something unrecognizable, scaling his hot-rod tinkering to the building-like scale of the boat [Fig.08].

Around the same time that Las Vegas was decorating its sheds into themed gambling palaces, writers such as Tom Wolfe observed the burgeoning American trend for modifying vehicles in his book *The Kandy-Kolored Tangerine-Flake Streamline Baby* (1965). Wolfe describes how hot rod designers like George Barris and Ed Roth (whose Rat Fink character is a potential influence on the design of Glottis) created vehicles that 'developed out of a design concept that we can call Streamlined Modern,'[20] which was in fact a particular subset of Art Deco design focused on evoking speed through curving forms.

By the time we arrive at Domino Hurley's secret base at the Edge of the World, the Art Deco markers of architecture become more closely combined with the technology of mining coral, on an island half-circled by a giant crane which Manny must operate to escape. Using fSpy to reconstruct the island as an oblique drawing shows that while we experience some very gestural interior designs, such as Domino and Meche's offices, most of the island is industrial architecture created to facilitate the mining process [Fig.09]. The design is somewhat more constrained than Peter Chan's original 'Factory' concept art, which shows the island as an expressive combination of Escher-esque steps and bone-like structures. By estimating the scale of buildings through the lines of windows and floorplates, this island appears to be roughly 300–400 metres (980–1,300 ft) in both directions. This puts it at the same scale as similar industrial islands situated in the deep ocean, such as Gunkanjima, the coal mining island off the coast of Japan built in the late 19th century that features in the James Bond film *Skyfall*. Both islands have the uncanny appearance of architecture built where it shouldn't be. In the case of *Grim Fandango*, the island is precariously perched over the void of a disappearing ocean.

Edward Dimendberg argues that in film noir 'the movement of protagonists from the urban centre to periphery is a pervasive spatial trope,'[21] and we see this mirrored in Manny's journey from El Marrow to the Edge of the World and beyond.

This relationship between infrastructure and architecture at the periphery of the world is still present as we reach Year Four of Manny's journey, at the entrance to the Ninth Underworld. This giant structure is built around the railway tracks of the Number Nine express train, which disappears into the ether as it enters the Land of Eternal Rest. Through fSpy reconstructions using both the game backgrounds and views taken from the cinematics, the building becomes reminiscent of famous Mesoamerican pyramids, such as Santa Cecilia Acatitlan in Mexico or the older Tikal in Guatemala, bringing us back to the original forms of architecture that inspired the design language for the rest of the game's world [Fig.10].

These shapes have a contemporary twist, integrated with the infrastructure of the train tracks and playfully connecting back to folklore. When a train full of villains approaches the station, the gatekeeper passes judgment and reroutes the tracks into a fiery pit of damnation that opens in the structure below.

[Fig.08]
PAGES 182–3

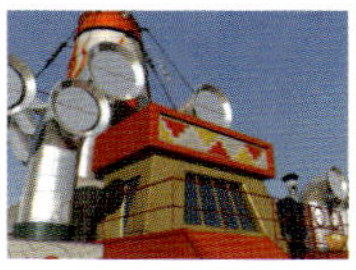

Screenshot of Manny on the modified *SS Lola* ship, demonstrating the hod-rod design influences of Glottis, which also draw from Art Deco styles.

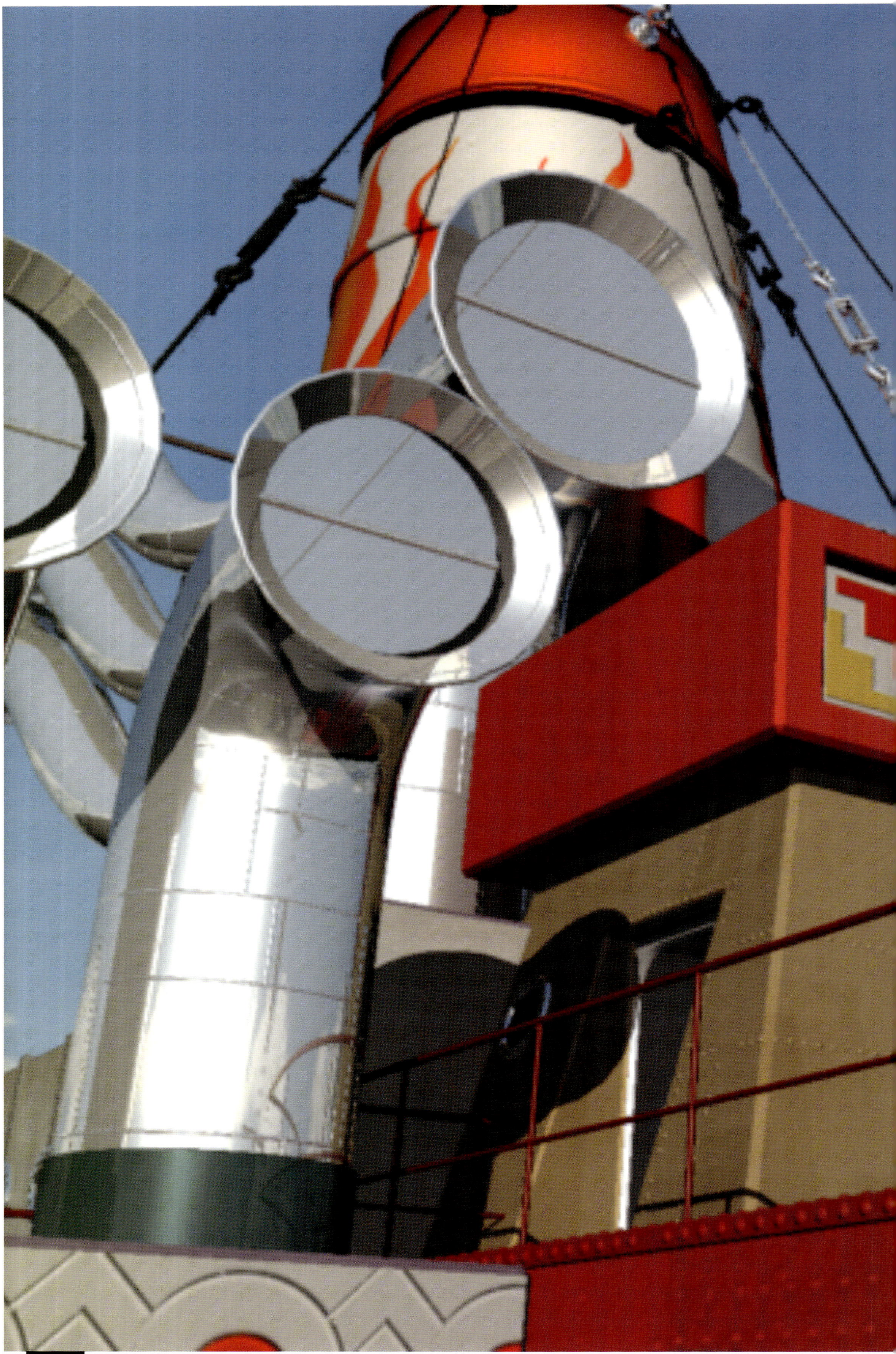

[Fig.08]

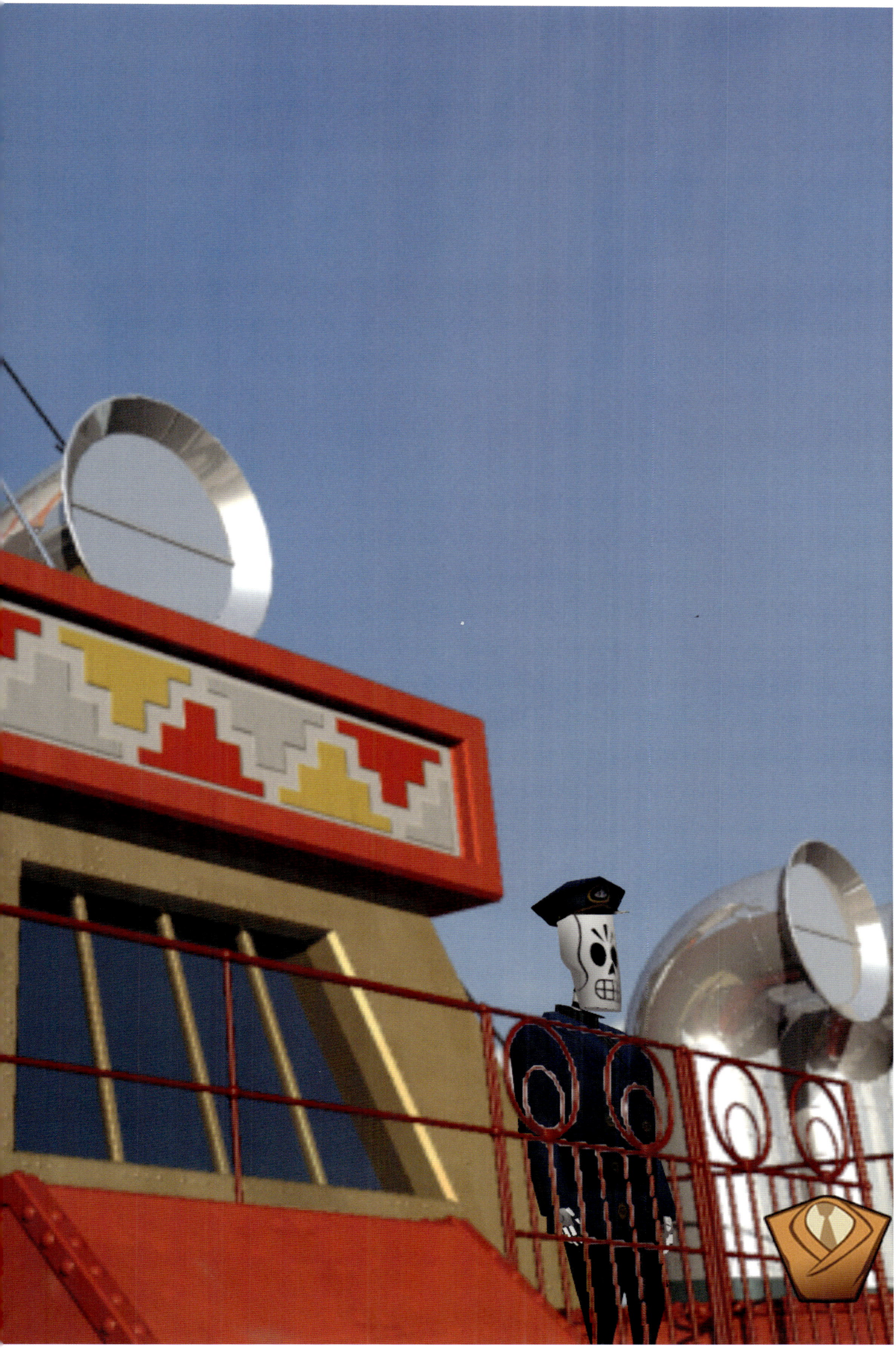

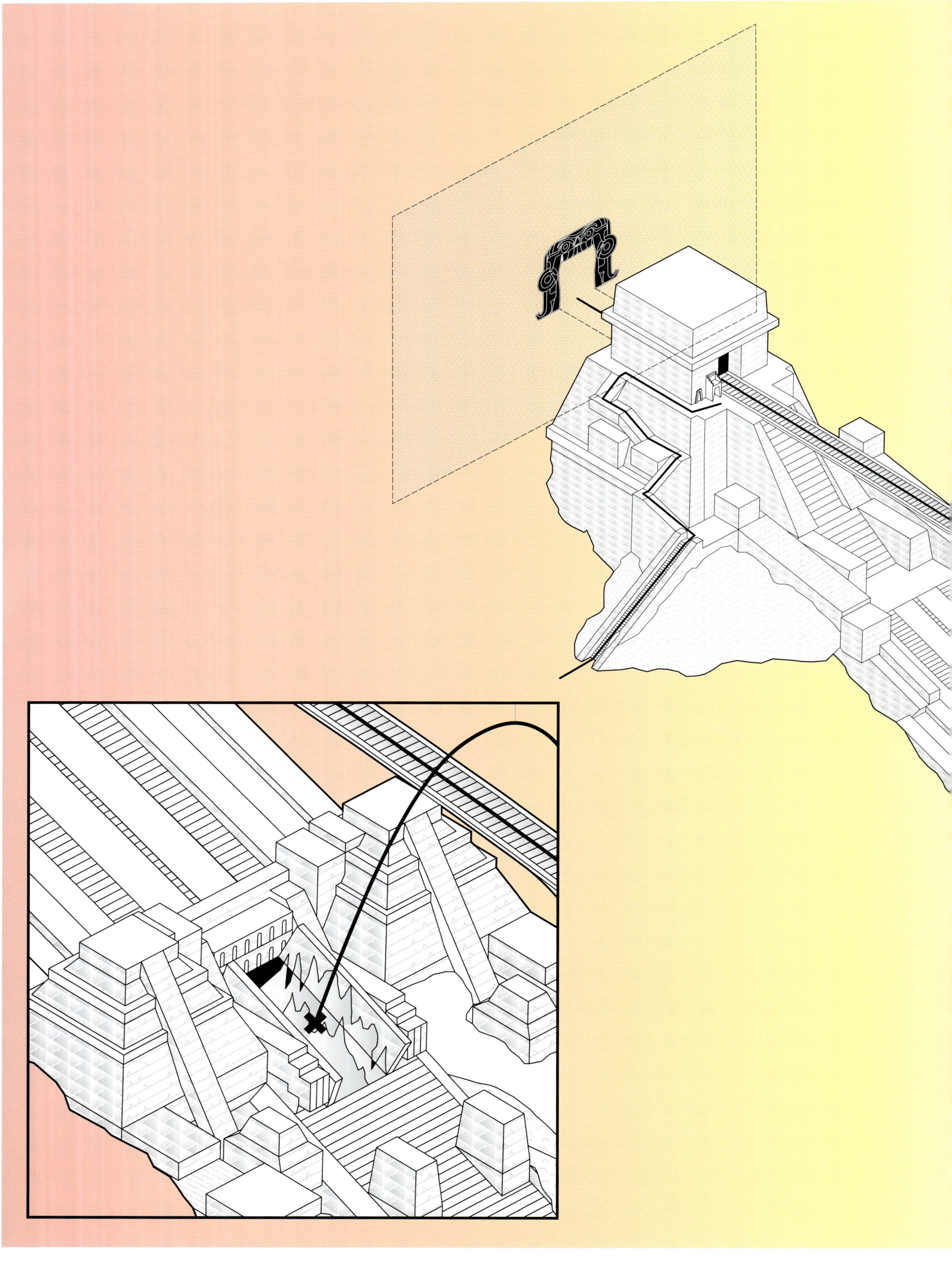

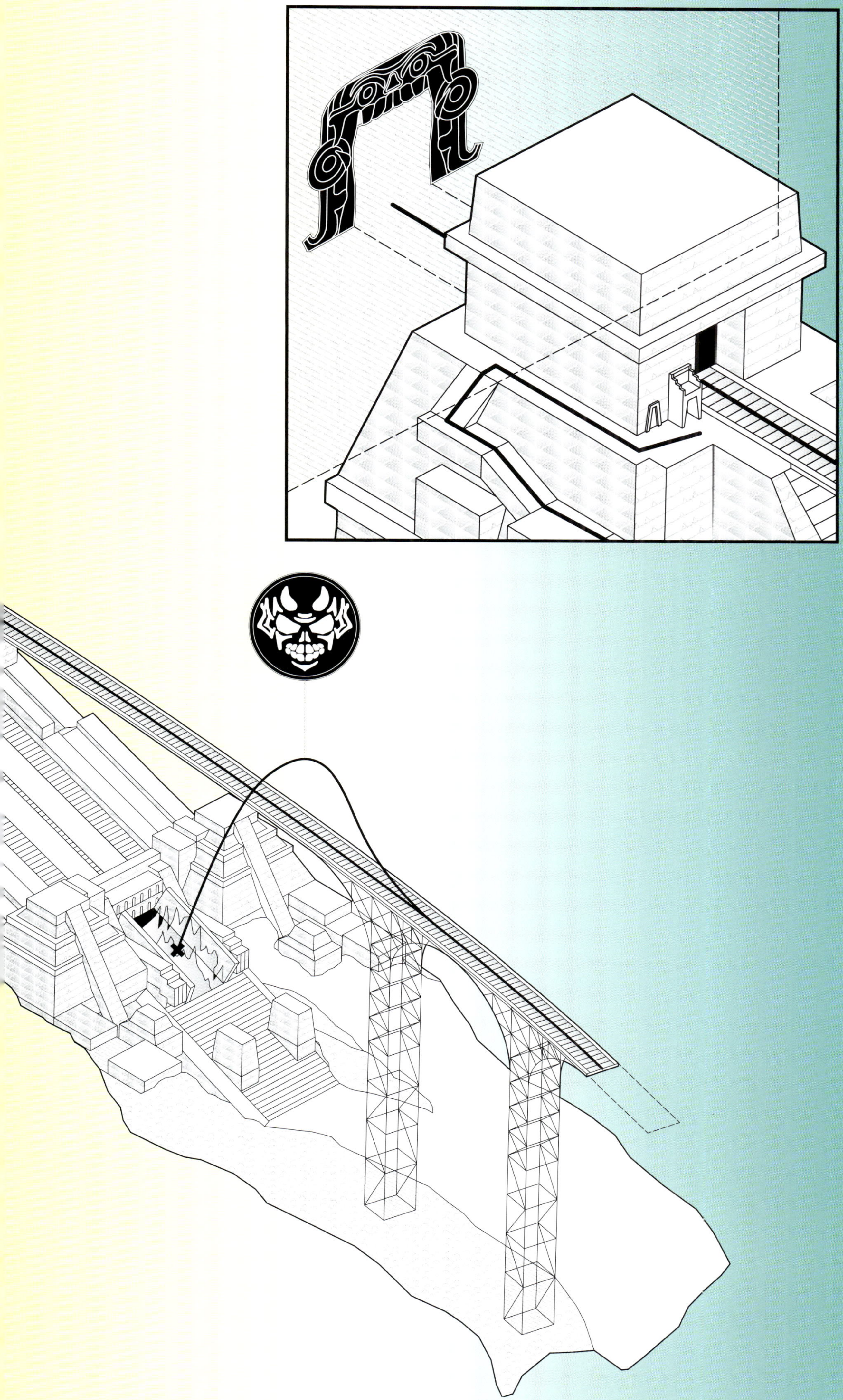

[Fig.10]

ISOMETRIC RECONSTRUCTION OF THE NINTH UNDERWORLD GATE, DEMONSTRATING A RETURN TO THE ORIGINAL FORMS OF MAYAN AND AZTEC ARCHITECTURE THAT INSPIRED THE WORLD'S MESOAMERICAN REVIVAL STYLES.

DRAWING RECREATING HECTOR LE MANS' GREENHOUSE, REPRESENTING HOW THE BUILDING ON A HILL FITS WITH THE DRAMATIC TROPES OF FILM NOIR, PROVIDING A CLIMAX TO THE GAME'S STORY.

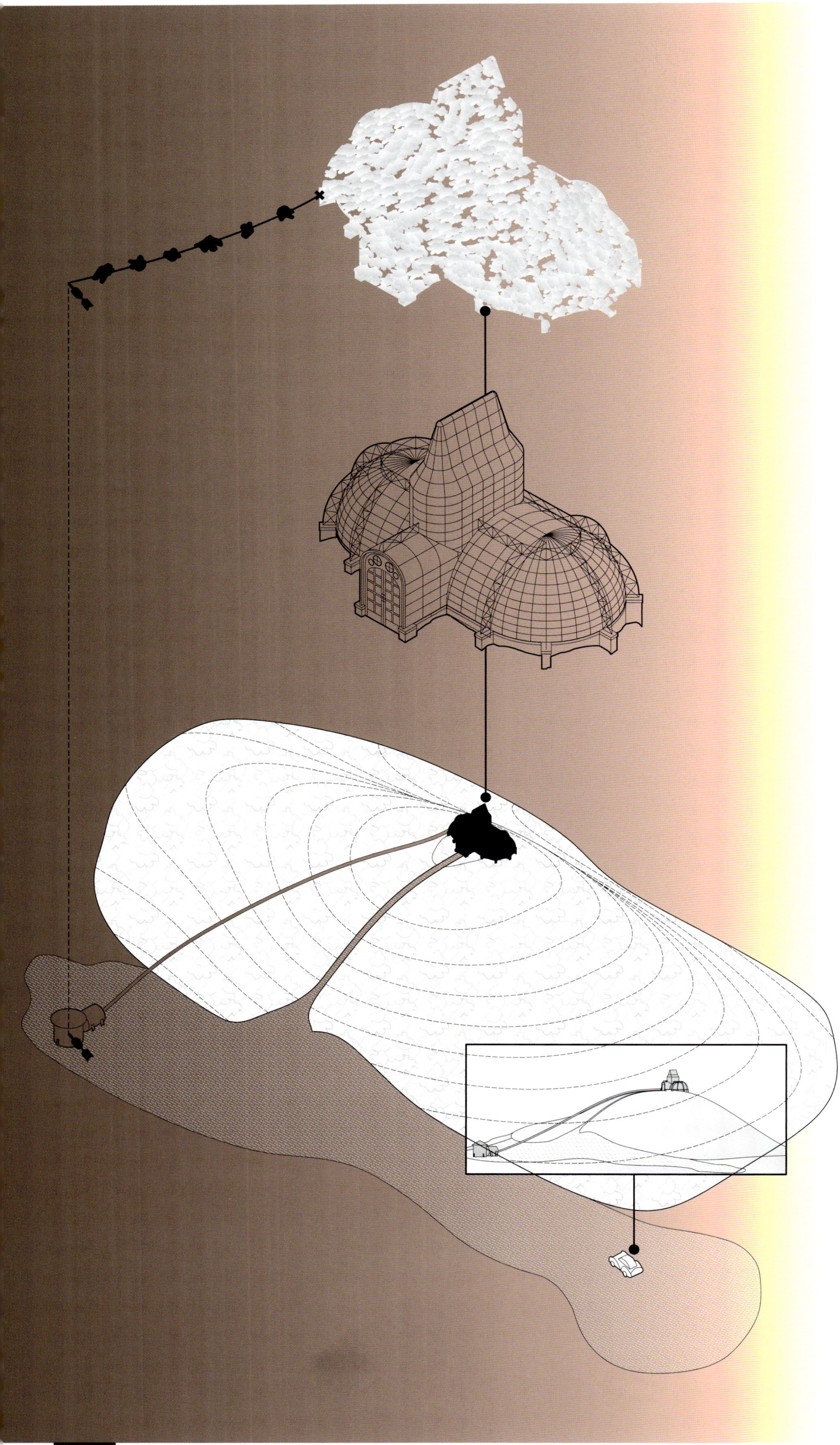

[Fig.12]

8.5

CINEMATIC RESOLUTION

Before Manny and Meche can escape to the Ninth Underworld, the film noir story demands a culmination, and this takes place back in El Marrow and its surrounding areas. Hector LeMans has turned the city into a Las Vegas- (or Atlantic City-) style gambling den, with buildings now covered in gaudy neon signs.

The Department of Death is seen topped by the reclining figure of a woman clearly inspired by the iconic 'Vegas Vickie' sign that adorned the Glitter Gulch casino in Las Vegas. Manny chases LeMans across the rooftop, using the sign to jump between buildings, illustrating how El Marrow has been transformed [Fig.11]. Giant, ziggurat-like skyscrapers covered in glowing lights have sprung up since the last time Manny was on the roof. Their form re-emphasizes the connection between Mayan and Aztec architecture and the 20th-century American city. As Francisco Mujica argued, the 'principle decorative elements' of skycrapers 'are brought out in in large surfaces' which 'strikingly recalls the Pre-Columbian architecture with its palaces and pyramids.'[22] Here, key historical and modern forms of American architecture are combined into a cinematic landscape: Mesoamerica meets New York meets Las Vegas.

Our final 3D reconstruction is of the game's climactic encounter [Fig.12], as Manny confronts Hector LeMans at his greenhouse, built on top of a hilly meadow covered with flowers that indicate all the souls that Hector has 'sprouted'. The building is represented through five background images, which all use wide-angle cinematic viewpoints to emphasize the drama. As this drawing shows, the game serves up a classic cinematic trope of the isolated, sinister building on a hill, before becoming a key protagonist in the downfall of Hector by allowing us to poison the irrigation supply and turn him into a mass of greenery. As the culmination of the conspiracy before the characters finally escape into the Land of Eternal Rest, the greenhouse evokes the compositional qualities seen in buildings such as *Citizen Kane*'s Xanadu, or Alfred Hitchcock's *Psycho* where Norman Bates' gothic house sits menacingly on top of a hill' framing the building as 'eerie and uncanny'.[23]

After the demise of LeMans, Manny and Meche can say goodbye to Glottis and pass through to their final resting place. *Grim Fandango* lives on, however, through its unique world design that uses the lens of Mayan Revival architecture to tell a classic American pulp noir story. The architectural design of the Land of the Dead reminds us of the productive frictions that can be produced by collaging together seemingly disparate influences. Yet as we have seen by delving into the architecture and design inspirations of *Grim Fandango*, these influences are deeply historically and culturally connected. This creates a world that is an aesthetic pleasure to explore, which is perfect, because as Manny says: 'nobody knows what's going to happen at the end of the line, so you might as well enjoy the trip'.

[Fig.11]
PAGES 188-9
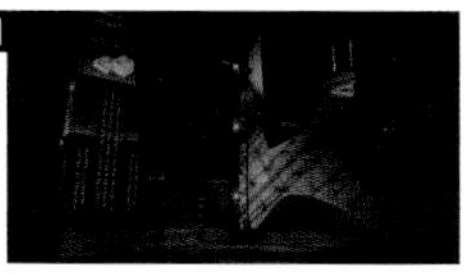
Screenshot showing El Marrow upon Manny's return, where Hector Le Mans has grown the city into a landscape of ziggurat-like skyscrapers, reinforcing the Mayan Revival style.

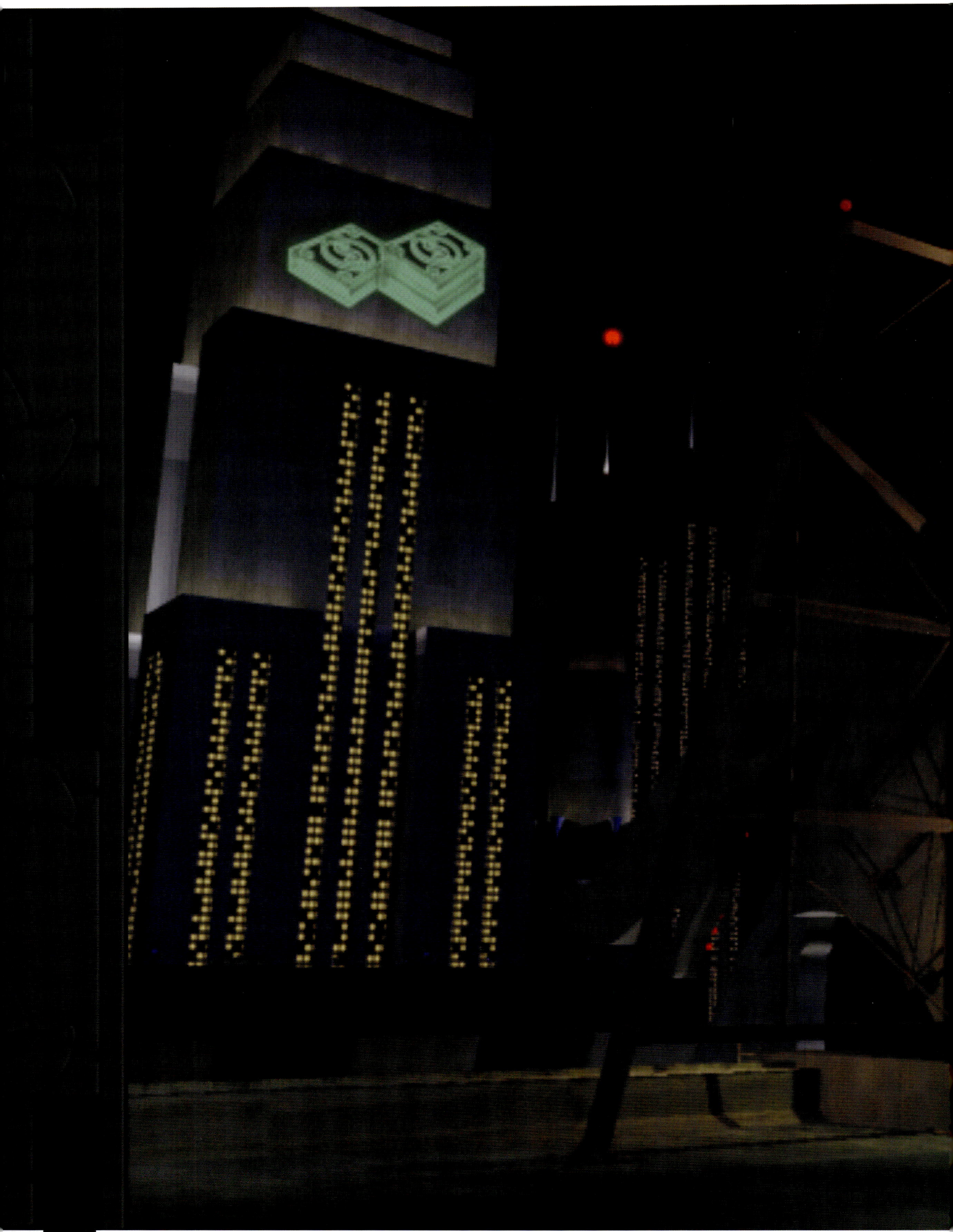

[Fig.11]

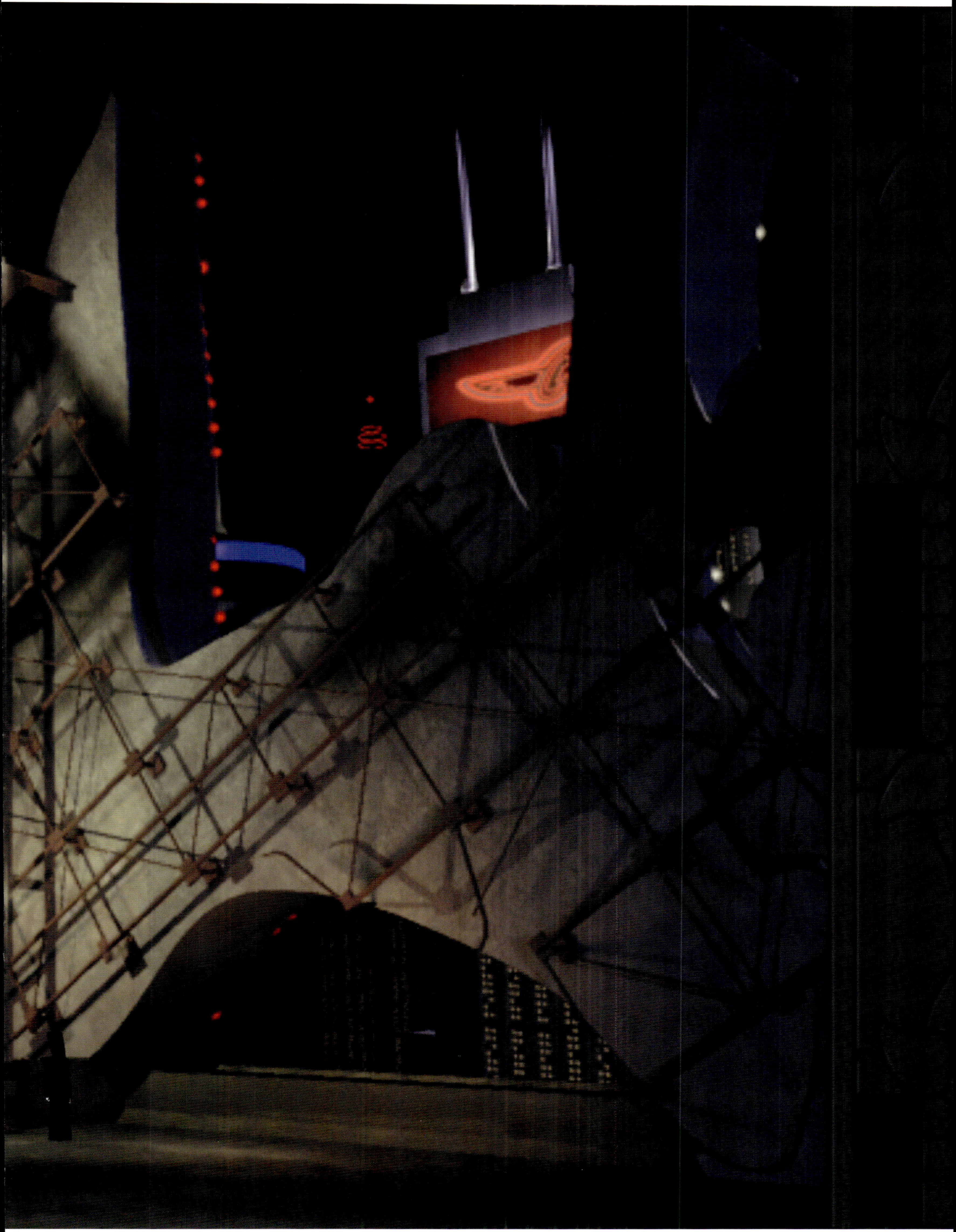

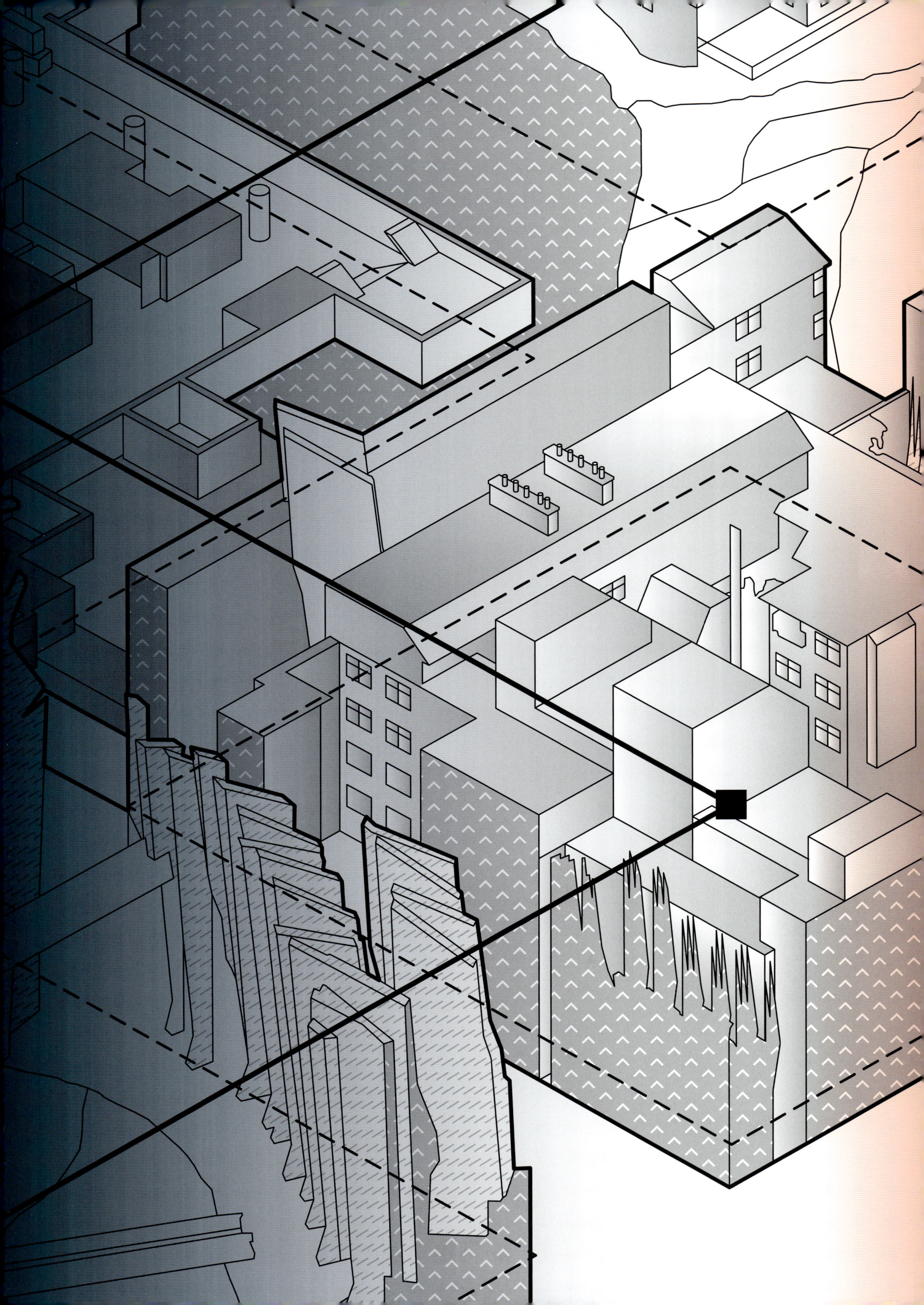

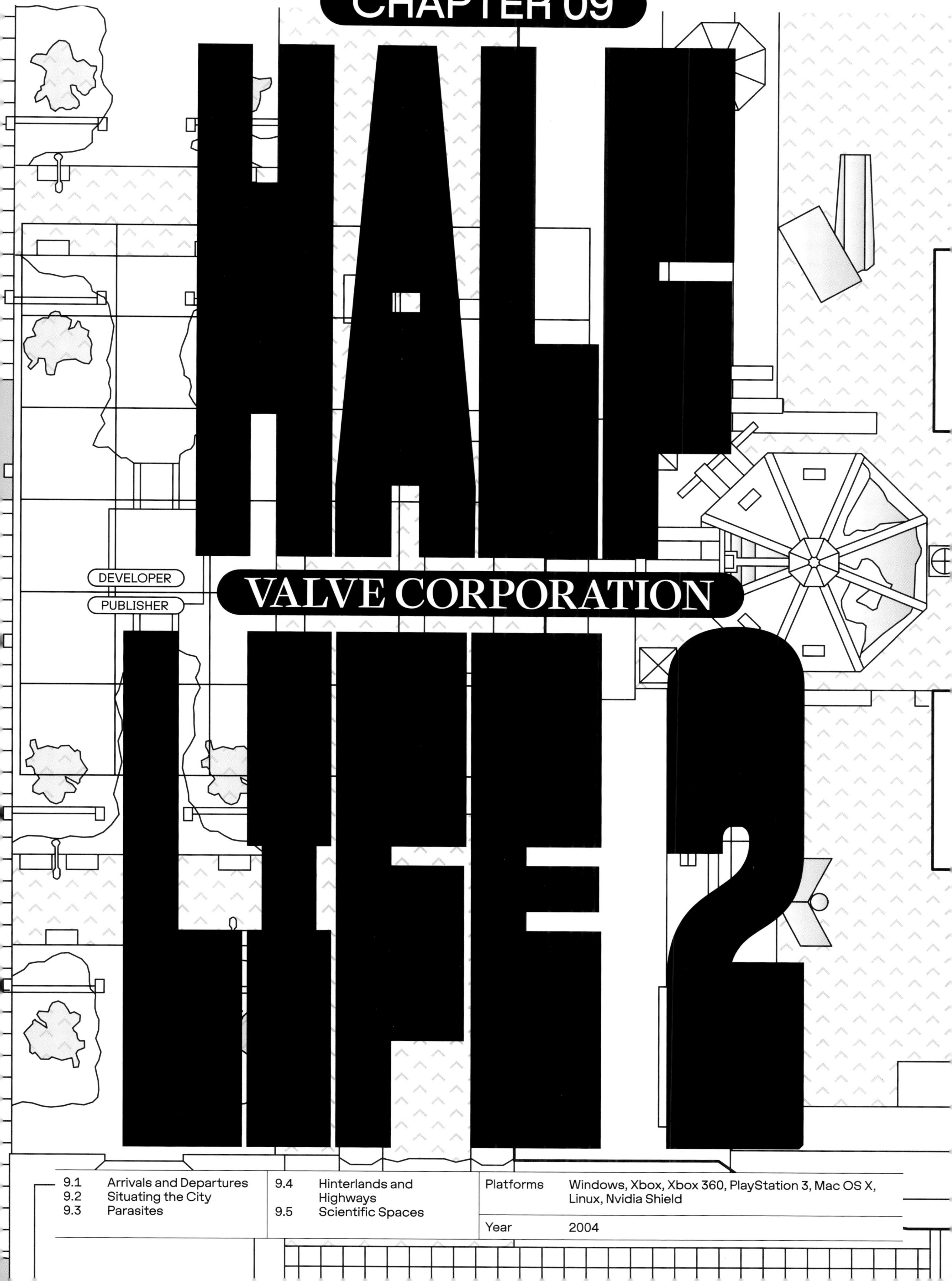

CHAPTER 09

HALF-LIFE 2

DEVELOPER
PUBLISHER
VALVE CORPORATION

Platforms	Windows, Xbox, Xbox 360, PlayStation 3, Mac OS X, Linux, Nvidia Shield
Year	2004

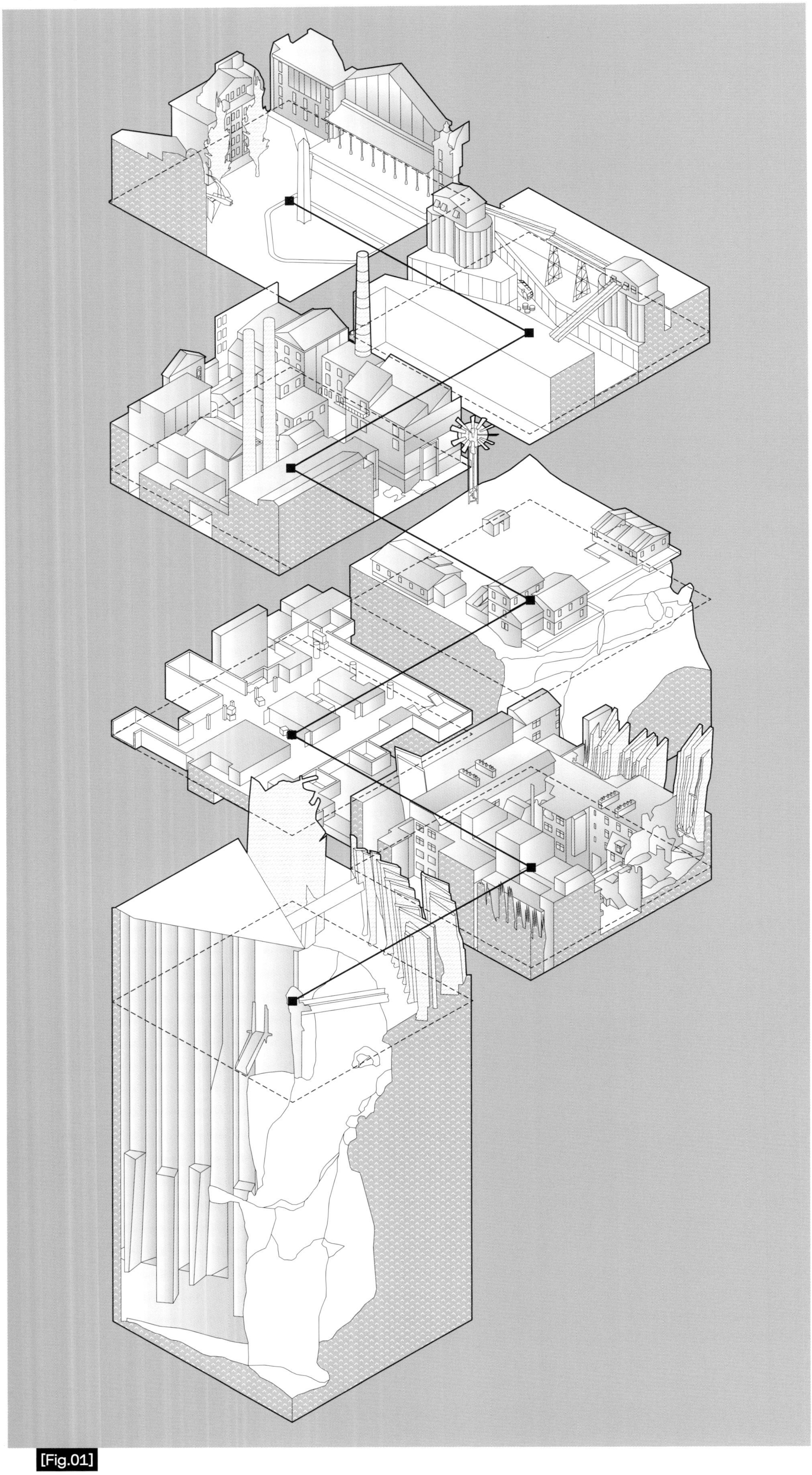

ISOMETRIC 'SAMPLES' TAKEN FROM HALF-LIFE 2'S WORLD, SHOWING THE COMPARATIVE ARCHITECTURAL DENSITY OF SPACES THAT GORDON FREEMAN VISITS DURING THE COURSE OF THE GAME.

[Fig.01]

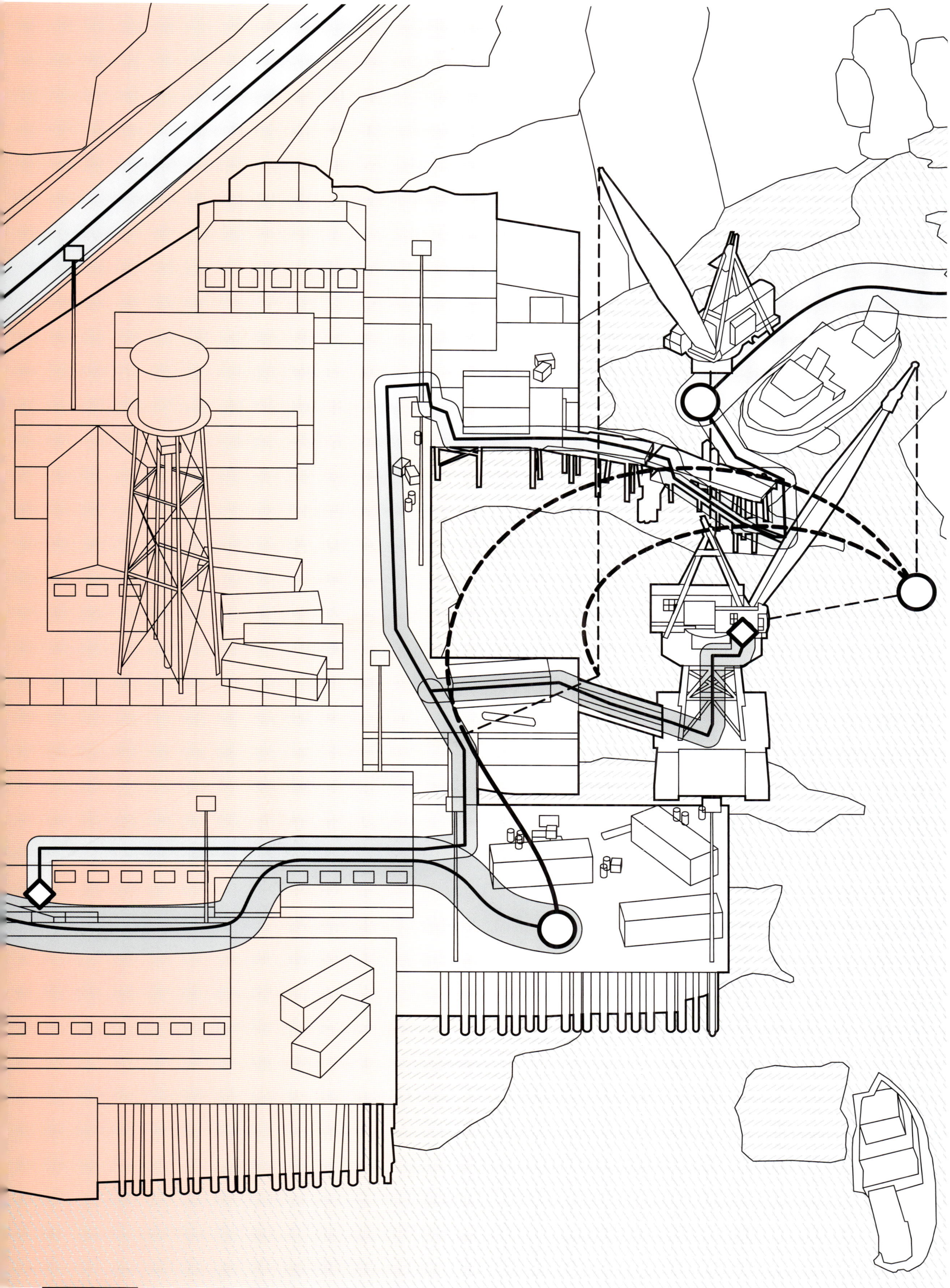

[Fig.10] Detail

9.5

SCIENTIFIC SPACES

Once Gordon reaches Nova Prospekt and journeys back to City 17 to ascend the Citadel, we reach the final moments of the game. These take place in the Citadel's Dark Fusion Reactor, as Gordon and Alyx try to prevent Dr. Breen escaping into another realm by destabilizing his teleporter. It is natural for the game to end in the space of a reactor, because laboratories and other scientific spaces are key to the story of *Half-Life 2*, and even more intrinsic to its 1998 predecessor (like the Anti-Mass Spectrometer that starts the whole Half-Life narrative universe). By mapping the laboratory spaces that Gordon visits, we observe how richly detailed they are in comparison to many other parts of the world [Fig.12]. Dr. Kleiner's laboratory in City 17 and Eli's in Black Mesa East are spaces used to drive the story forward, with many pieces of important information relayed through various interfaces. While labs are ultimately utilitarian spaces, there are many buildings that have also tried to recontextualize scientific spaces in a more designed and symbolic manner. Notable examples include San Diego's Salk Institute by the American architect Louis Kahn or in the Soviet context, Moscow's golden-topped Russian Academy of Sciences and the shimmering mirrored face of the Solntse Solarcomplex in Uzbekistan.[21] While the laboratories players encounter in *Half-Life 2* are hidden behind shuttered doors or buried deep underground, their importance, and that of science itself, is foregrounded in the game right up until the last moments.

As Freeman's journey comes full circle back at the heart of City 17, players have experienced a richly designed architectural world that feels strangely familiar, yet not. This uncanny feeling continues as time stops at the game's ending and the mysterious G-Man appears, beckoning Freeman onwards to his next destination. At the start of the game, this same strange, suited interloper tells Gordon that 'the right man in the wrong place can make all the difference in the world,' yet as becomes clear through the complex architectural journey that Valve has created, we were in the right place after all.

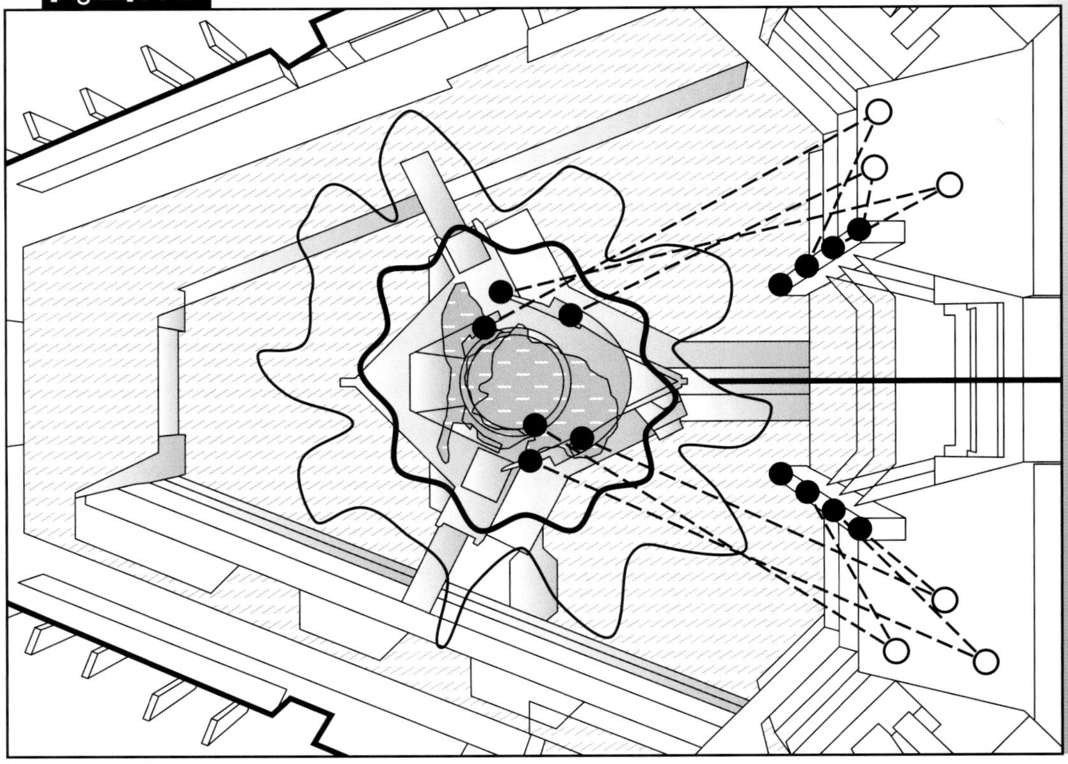

[Fig.12] Detail

PERSPECTIVE PLANS OF THE LABORATORY SPACES THAT FREEMAN VISITS DURING THE GAME. PLACES OF SCIENTIFIC RESEARCH PROVIDE THE SETTINGS FOR KEY STORY MOMENTS THROUGHOUT THE HALF-LIFE SERIES.

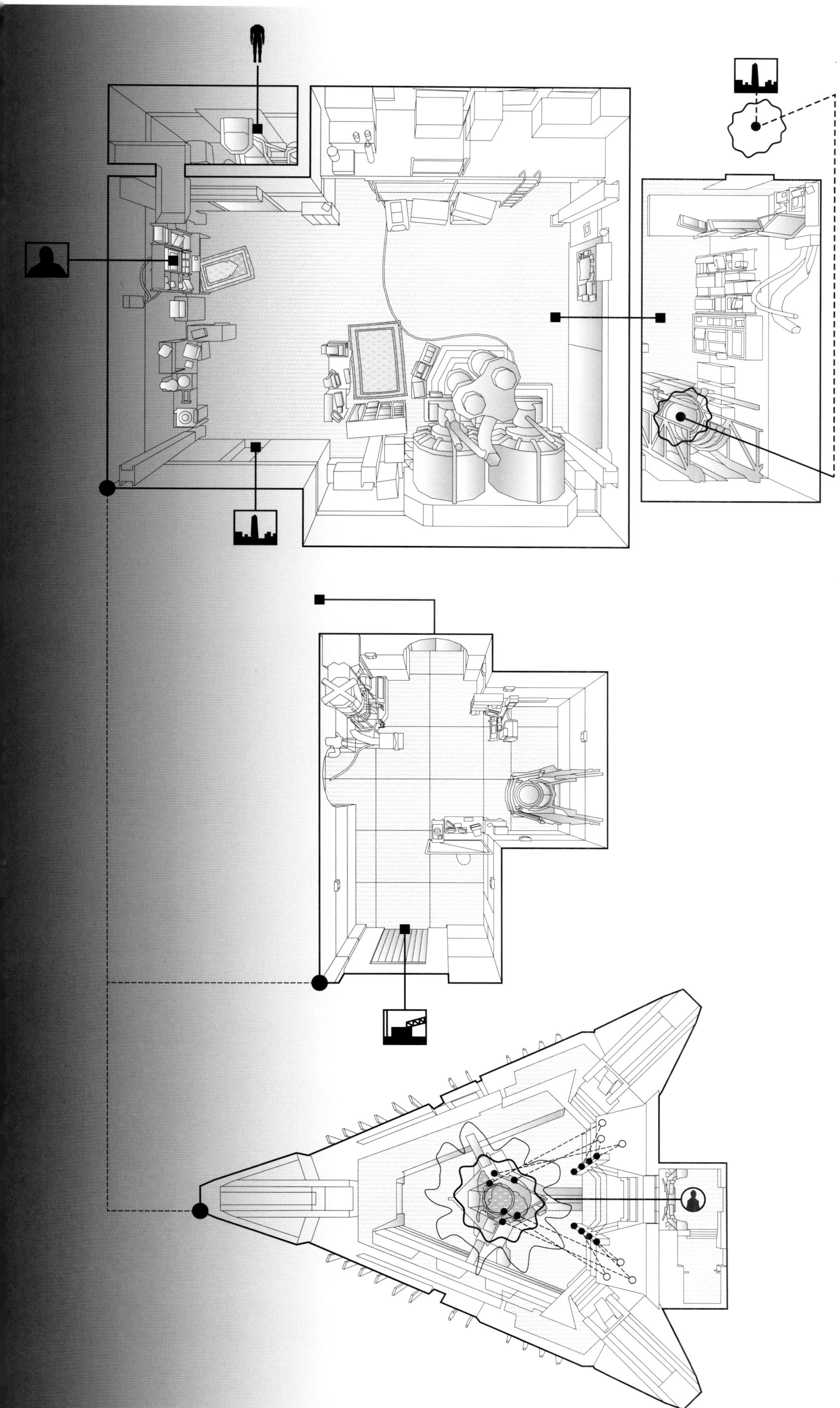

[Fig.12]

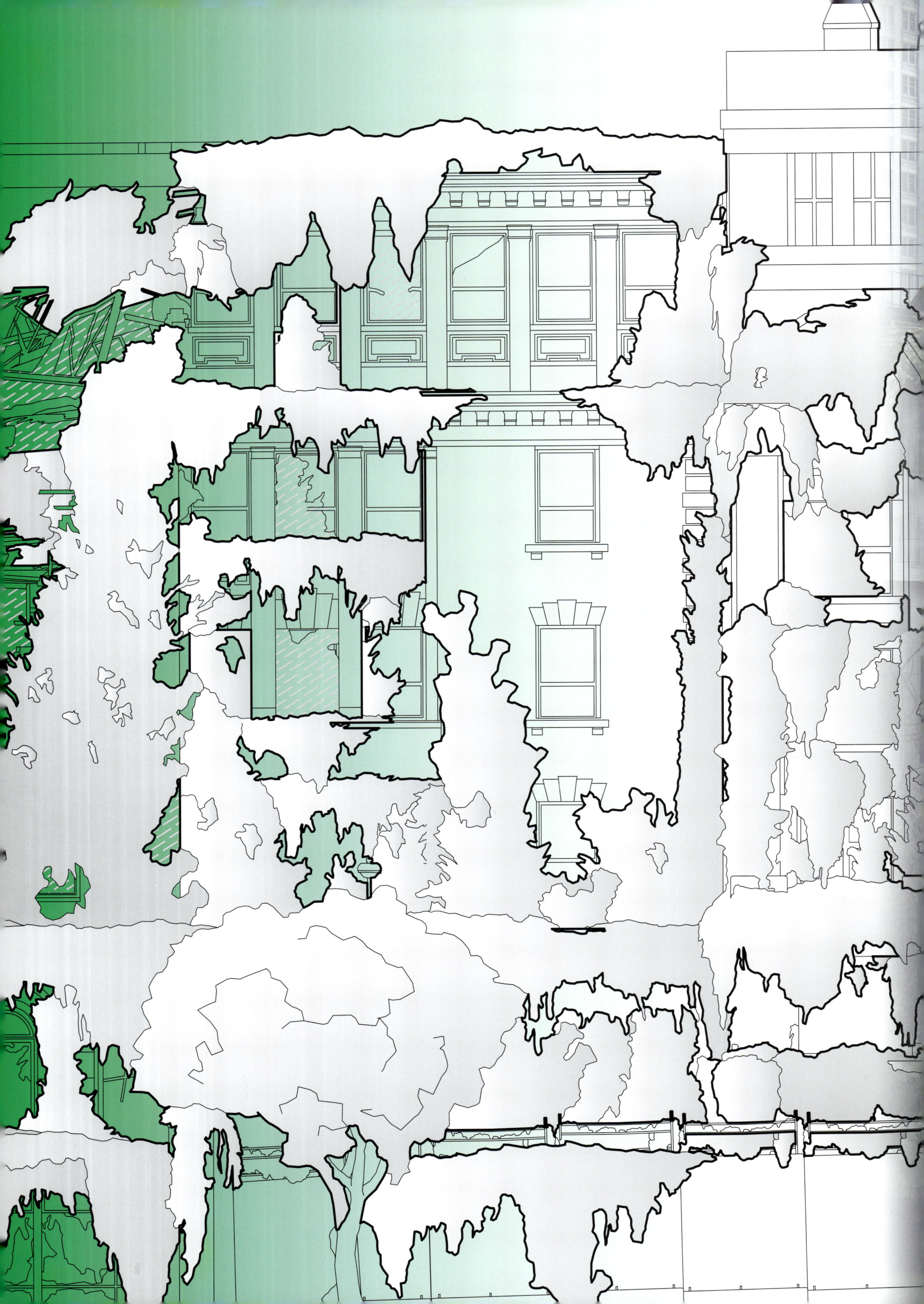

CHAPTER 10

THE LAST OF US PART 1

DEVELOPER NAUGHTY DOG

PUBLISHER SONY INTERACTIVE ENTERTAINMENT

Platforms	PlayStation 5, Windows
Year	2022

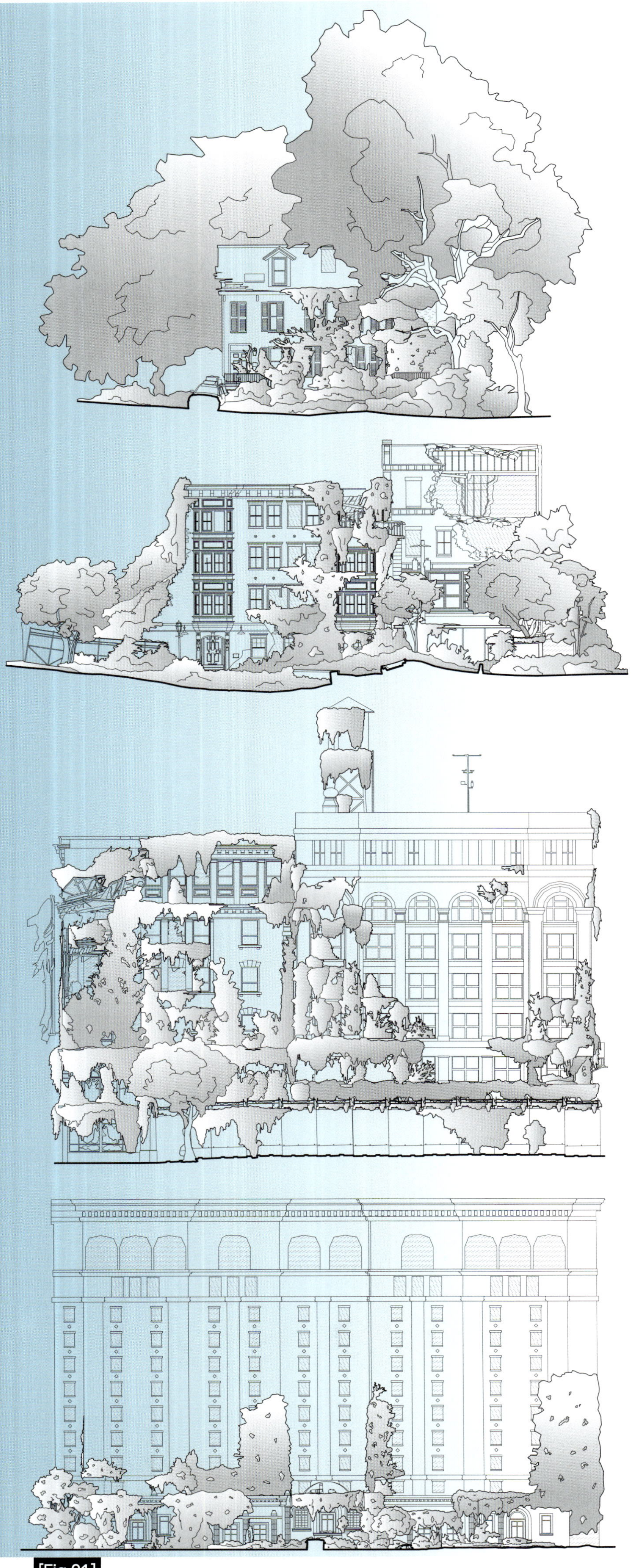

[Fig.01]

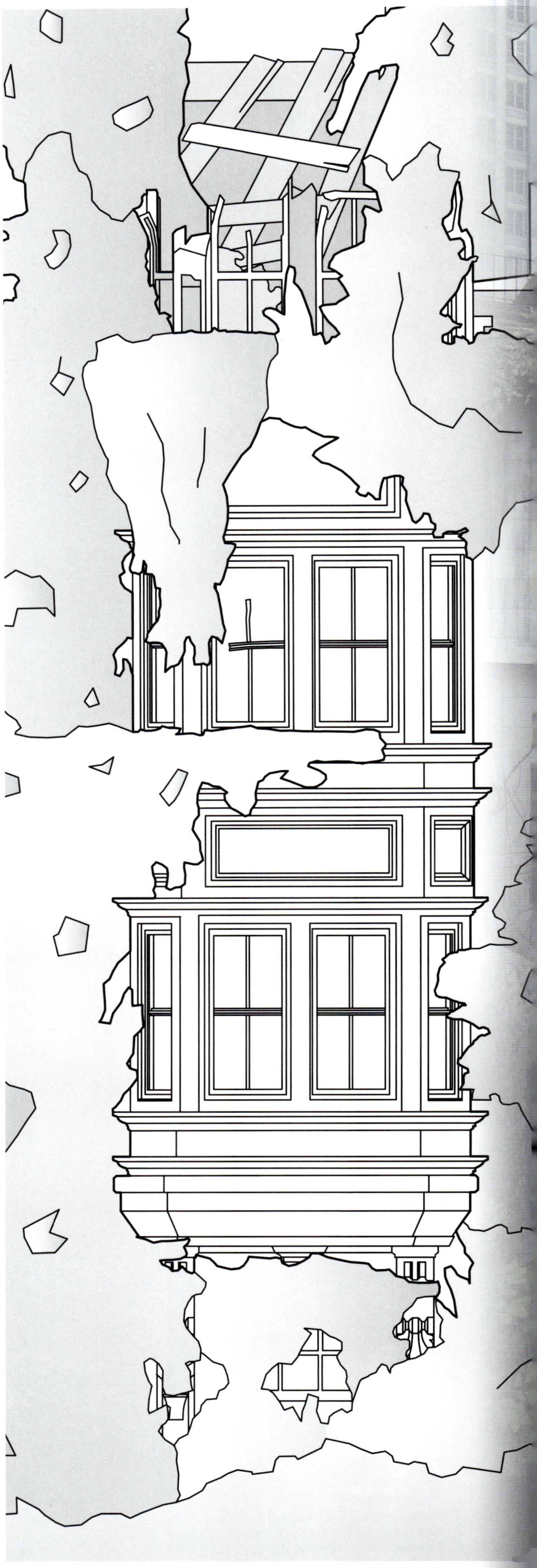

10.1

INTO RUINS

While the portrayal of violence in videogames is common, the brutality and harsh realism of the United States of America as depicted in *The Last of Us* remains shocking even today. Naughty Dog's post-apocalyptic tale of Joel and Ellie's journey through a society lost to a fungal plague is communicated through two central themes that run through the game. Players will regularly encounter characters and scenarios that illustrate the cruelty of human beings towards one another in the face of the unremitting threat from 'infected'. But more spatially, the game's central narrative takes us on a tour through cities and towns that have collapsed into ruin, questioning what urban and suburban environments might look like when humans retreat and nature returns.

While the game's story focuses on the harsh existence of life in a post-Cordyceps pandemic world, the environments that Joel and Ellie travel through communicate the complete breakdown of society. Great cities of America are shown dilapidated and overrun by the natural world, with buildings relegated to mute shells struggling to contain the proliferating flora. The world is presented to players *as-is*, with little exposition as to precisely how it came to be so overgrown other than the human retreat into quarantine zones. Yet as Sarah McCreedy argues '*The Last of Us* emphasizes environment such that it almost constructs it as a character in its own right.'[1] The status of buildings and cities as signifiers of decay within *The Last of Us* connects to a long cultural fascination with ruins and ruination. The treatment of nature also relates to a less well-known term, 'rus in urbe,' literally *country within the city*, a term first attributed to the Roman writer Martial,[2] which describes a fascination for bringing nature into an urban environment. The US as shown in *The Last of Us* is pure, distilled rus in urbe, with a design strategy of ruination allowing the developers to extend this aesthetic approach into a whole world view. As architect Jonathan Hill argues, 'a ruin's incomplete and broken forms expand architecture's allegorical and metaphorical potential' where 'a fragmented composition is a truer reflection of a contemporary society than a complete composition.'[3] This is particularly true for the environment we encounter, where the ruined architecture encompasses two of the great symbolic cultural spaces of America: the powerful city and the idyllic suburbia. By using camera mods to make a series of elevational studies of buildings encountered throughout the game, we can highlight how ruination through overgrowth is a repeated design motif that spares no built form. While smaller houses, such as those we mapped in the suburban areas of Waverly Township are easily subsumed by nature, our elevations show that even the larger buildings of Boston or Pittsburgh have large percentages of their surface area overcome by vegetation [Fig.01]. This has the effect of returning the American metropolis to a 'frontier' state, perfectly supporting the narrative of a 'Western'-style journey through the wilderness that just so happens to be within a city.

[Fig.01] **ELEVATIONS OF BUILDINGS FOUND ALONG JOEL AND ELLIE'S JOURNEY, SHOWING HOW NATURE HAS OVERTAKEN BOTH URBAN AND SUBURBAN ARCHITECTURE.**

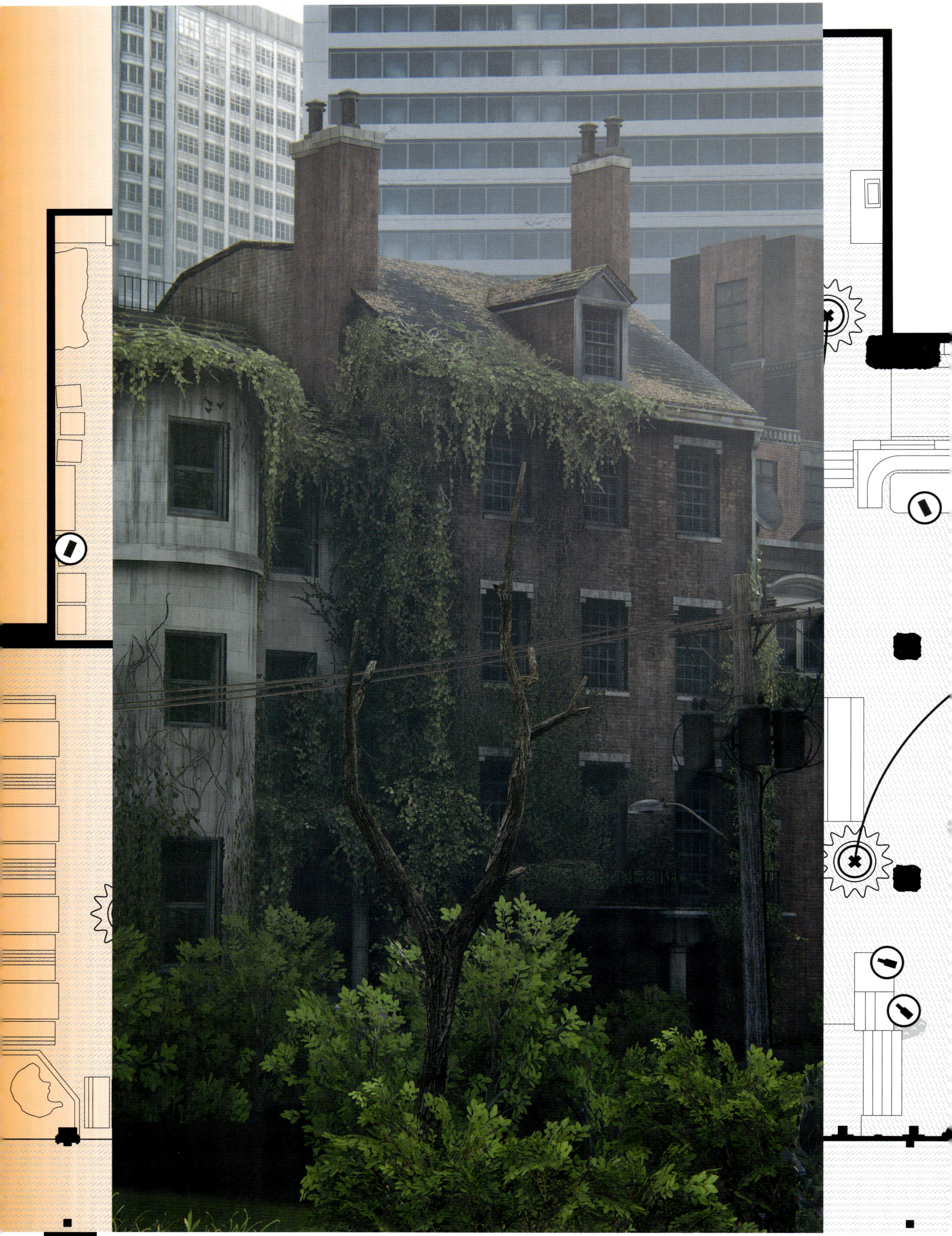

[Fig.02]

10.2

NATURAL SELECTION

This setting allows Naughty Dog to create a world that plays with meaning, which Melissa Kagen calls a 'postapocalyptic pastoral' where the developers 'juxtapose a failed modern civilization with nature's powerful, victorious reclamation of the places once controlled by human technology.'[4] A playful example of this in architectural design is the work of architect James Wines, whose studio SITE created a series of subversive designs for American store chain Best, one of which was called the Forest Building. This was a standard 'big box' store as found all over the US, but literally integrated with an existing forest, the brick structure of the building appearing to be torn apart by the trees growing outside of, and into, the building.[5] By using camera mods to detach ourselves from Joel, we look out across the landscape of Boston and find numerous other examples of how the developers explore where urbanism ends and nature starts in interesting ways. As we arrive at the Massachusetts State House, turning the camera round and flying off into the city reveals rows of buildings covered in vines, while wrecked cars, buckled trucks and twisted street furniture poke out of the lichen-green pools of floodwater [Fig.02]. Such images are not unlike photography studies of real-world Detroit where our 'fascination with images of first-world urban decline' intend to tell 'a history unsuited to the war memorials and equestrian statues that dot the national landscape.'[6]

If we move our camera even further beyond this, we encounter the 'hinterlands' of urban business districts, with huge skyscrapers looming over the city. While certain sections, such as the Downtown district found in The Outskirts chapter, allow us to venture into these structures, they typically remain in the distance, with derelict towers becoming ultimate signifiers of collapse. This is particularly emblematic of American urbanism, with the skyscrapers echoing the work of architects such as John Portman or SOM, masters of the huge, blank-faced buildings such as Atlanta's Peachtree Plaza and Chicago's Willis Tower, beloved by chain hotels and central business districts across the country. Using the camera mod to venture to the edge of the game's maps, we record examples of the skyscraper typologies that are used throughout the world and how they crack, crumble and fall in response to forces that are never made clear. Some of these structures are used repeatedly while others are designed to closely match real-world architecture such as the BNY Mellon Center in Pittsburgh. By drawing them together as a landscape of elevations that moves upwards as the story progresses, we can see how the broken skyscraper is a repeated motif that can both indicate a specific contextual location alongside a general atmosphere of social collapse [Fig.03].

[Fig.02] **A VIEW ACROSS BOSTON, SHOWING NATURE FLOURISHING IN THE CENTRAL BUSINESS DISTRICT OF THE CITY.**

[Fig.03] PAGE 218

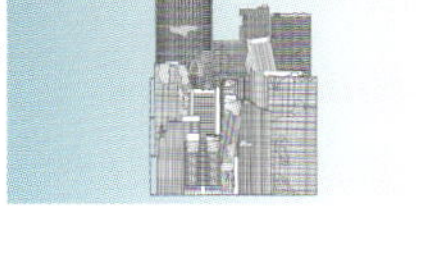

Elevational drawings of the various skyscrapers seen in the background skylines across America, which subtly reinforce the landscape of ruin and degradation found on the streets.

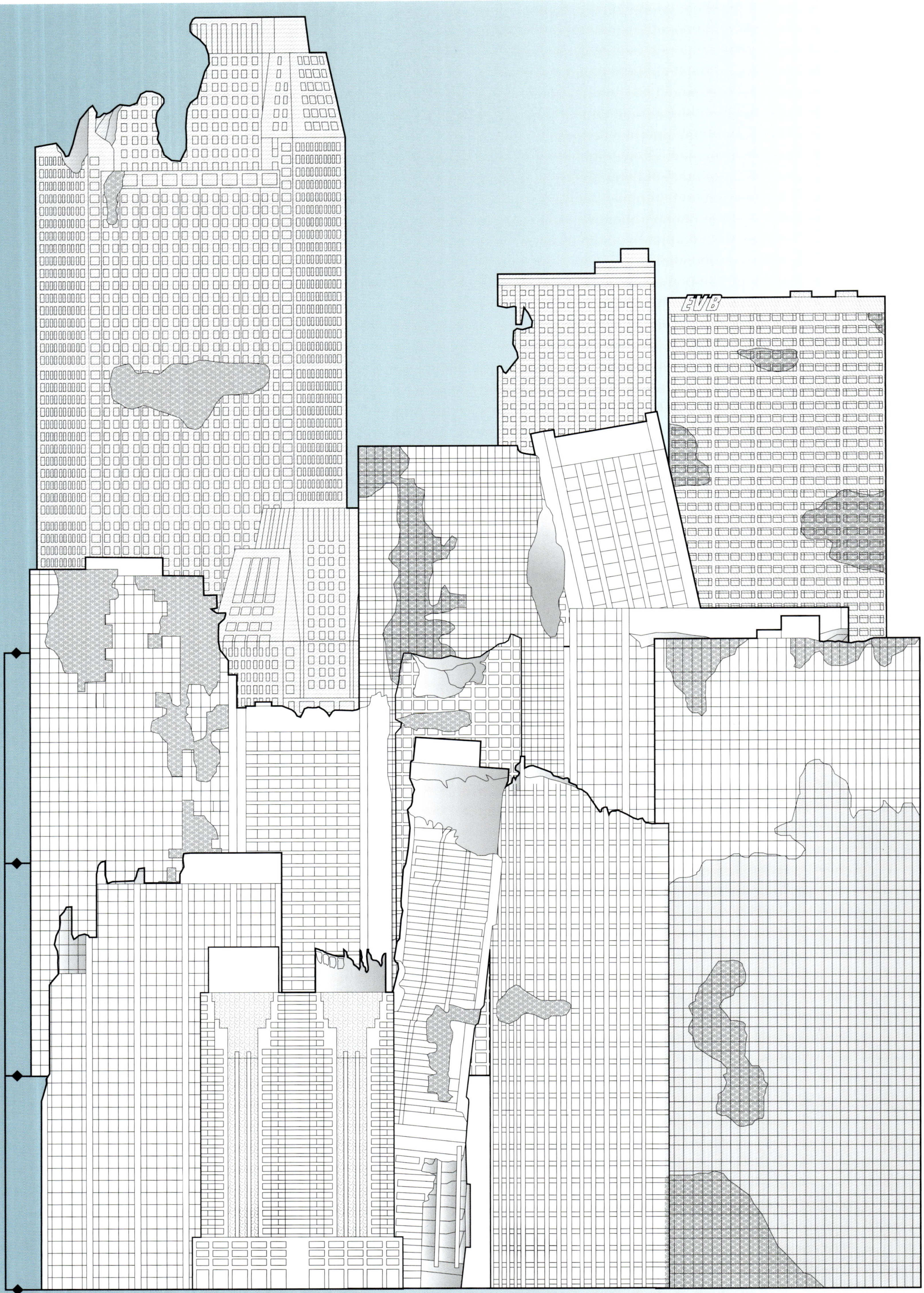

[Fig.03]

10.3 URBAN LANDMARKS

While some of the background buildings are well-known pieces of architecture that act as contextual symbols, *The Last of Us* makes strong use of landmarks as structural elements in both its gameplay and narrative. Most chapters of the story begin with a building seen from a distance, before the player carefully follows a path through a circuitous route to reach that destination. In Boston, we must reach the State House; in Pittsburgh it is the Fort Pitt Bridge; at the University of Eastern Colorado we are drawn towards the university's science building; and finally Saint Mary's Hospital in Salt Lake City. In his influential book on urbanism *The Image of the City*, Kevin Lynch discusses landmarks as 'point references external to the observer' and specifically references the Boston State House due to the power of its historical associations.[7] By using the camera mod to draw sectional elevations through the viewpoints at the opening of each of these levels, we reveal the spatial approaches used by the developers [Fig.04]. Elevated positions and long boulevards ensure the landmark can be seen properly, while shifting the relative scale of surrounding buildings provides visual emphasis that may not be present in the real world. This reinforces Lynch's notion that 'landmarks become more easily identifiable… if they have a clear form; if they contrast with their background.'[8] While the immediate level geometry will be loaded or unloaded depending on where the player is, these landmarks continuously hang in the void at the edge of the level, emphasizing their spatial significance.

This strategy of introducing landmarks through sweeping views and forcing the player through compact and indirect routes to reach them allows Naughty Dog to evoke the qualities of real-world cities without fully recreating them. While this is a common spatial tactic in game design, *The Last of Us* employs different levels of connection to reality during the course of our journey, which Emma Fraser says 'subverts a neat or knowable history by featuring ruins of real places, detached from their geographical origins'.[9] As the game gives us real-world reference points, by using 3D maps from Google Earth we can compare some of the key moments in the journey to their actual location in the US [Fig.05]. Early in the game, Joel and Ellie look across the city towards the State House in Boston from the roof of the (real-life) Bostonian Society Museum. By flying from their location to the State House using camera mods, we can estimate the distance is around 620 metres (2,000 ft) in game, which is broadly approximate to the 700m (2,300 ft) linear distance in reality. Yet this near 1-to-1 relationship does not persist. YouTubers such as Andrew Levitt have discussed how Naughty Dog rearranges the real world around iconic landmarks and as we progress through the game this becomes more obvious.[10] In Pittsburgh, Joel and Ellie emerge from a building that appears to be the Three Gateway Center, before sprinting towards the Fort Pitt Bridge. In reality, they would run nearly 500 metres (1,640 ft) past Point State Park and the Fort Pitt Museum, while in game they tumble straight out onto the bridge, pursued by an armoured vehicle. The final section of the game in Salt Lake City plays on views of the historic Salt Lake Temple, as Joel and Ellie trek towards Saint Mary's Hospital, yet the building that seems to most clearly inspire it is the Primary Children's Hospital over four kilometres (2.5 mi) away on the other side of the city, albeit connected by one long straight boulevard. In further acts of dislocation, entire real-world towns that appear to provide inspiration, such as Waverly Township and Silver Lake (containing Whitefish Lake) are moved tens or even hundreds of miles across America, morphing into new locations in the story.

[Fig.04] PAGE 220
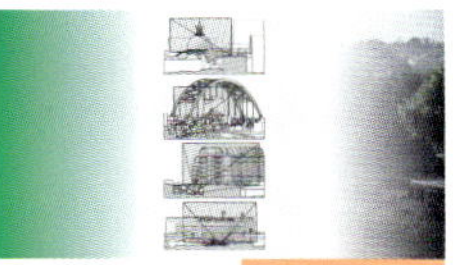
Sectional drawings showing the architectural landmarks that players are shown at the beginning of each story chapter, before navigating through the landscape to find them.

[Fig.05] PAGE 221
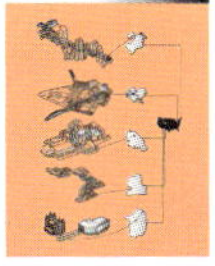
Studies of real-world areas encountered in the game, showing the architectural reference points that are compressed and distorted by the game's developers.

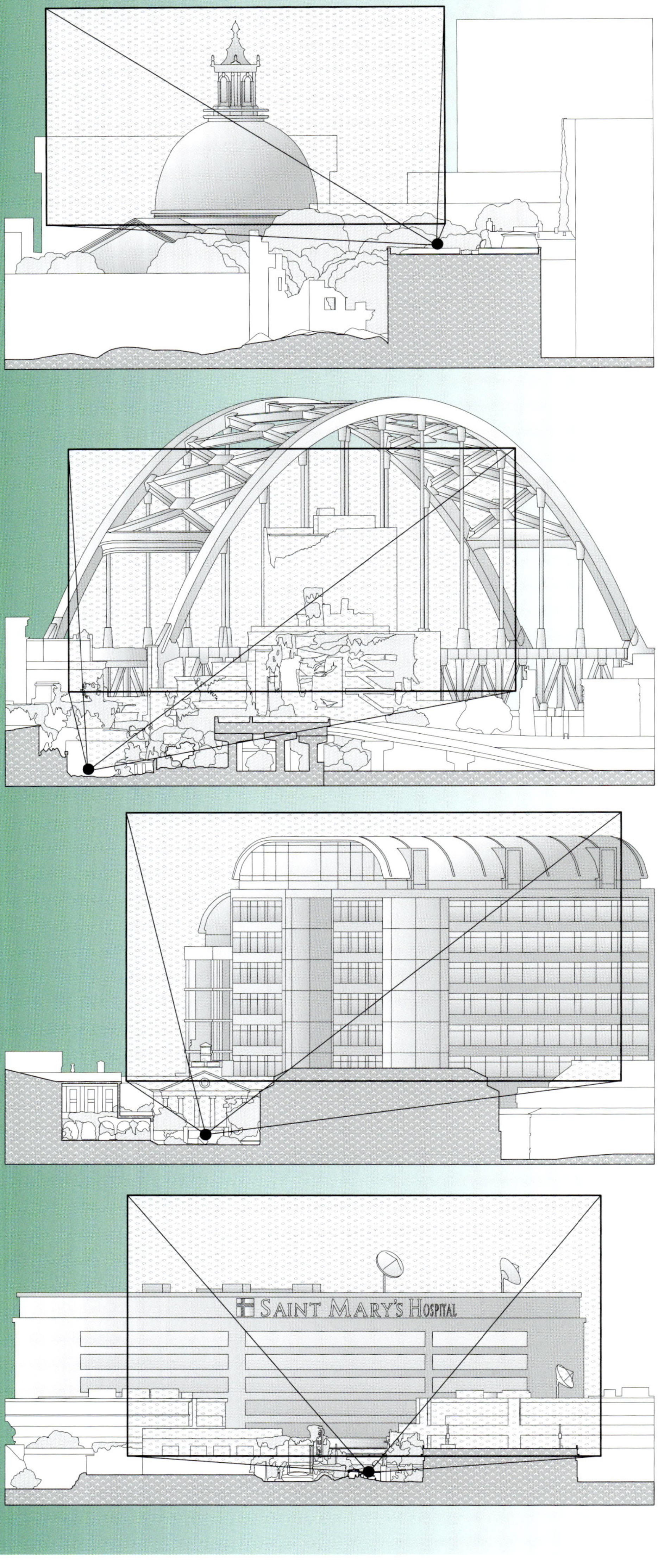

[Fig.04]

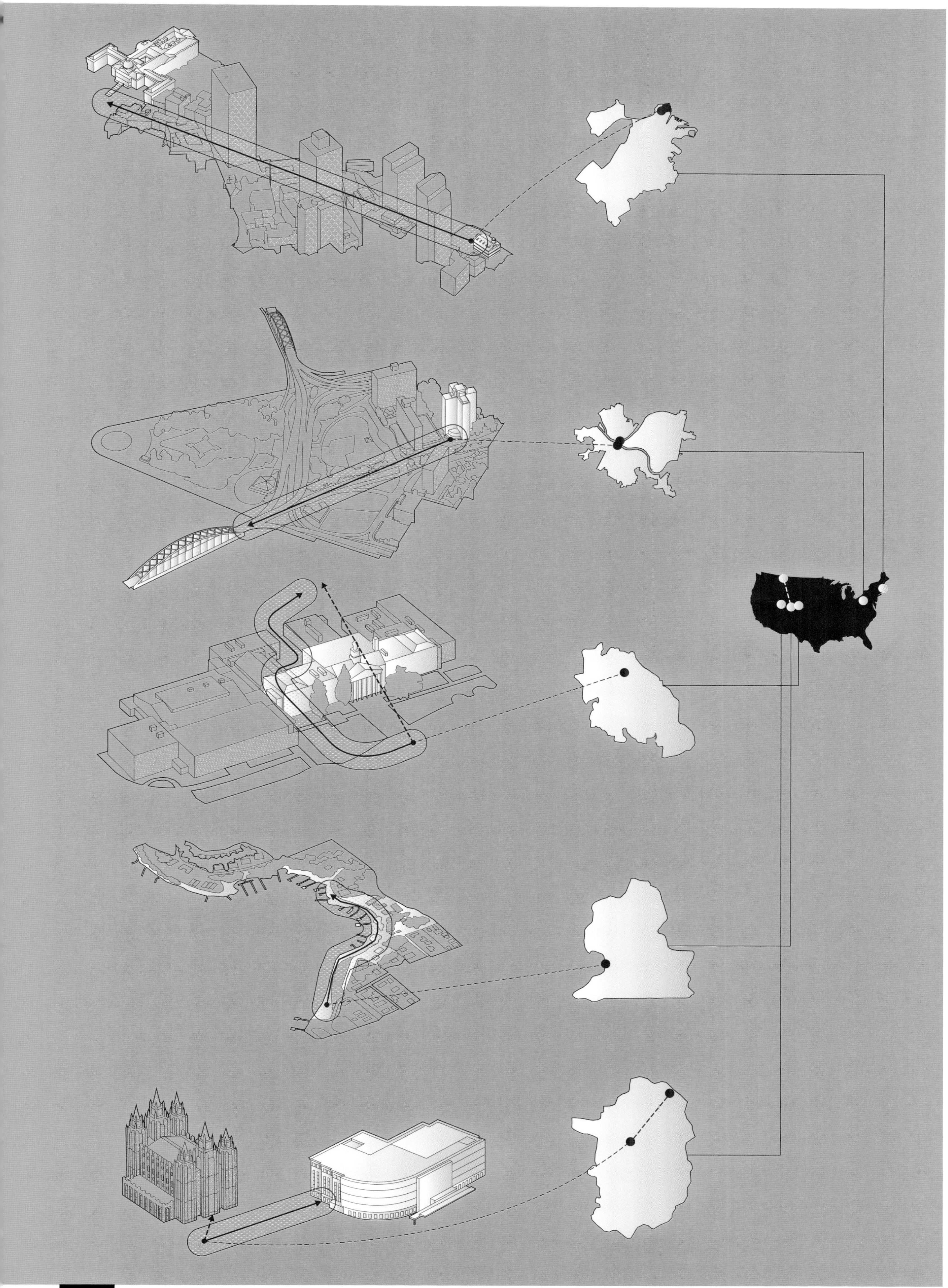

[Fig.05]

10.4

BROKEN BUCOLIA

Waverly Township is where we encounter the effects of the pandemic on suburban life, marking a shift in scale from the city centres. After being washed down a river and having navigated a tunnel system full of infected, Joel and Ellie find themselves picking their way through ransacked houses as they journey towards a radio tower. In a rare moment of downtime for the player, the walk through Waverly presents a romantic and almost bucolic atmosphere [Fig.06], with houses overgrown by plants, nestling into a lush green landscape. *The Last of Us* uses these environments as picturesque interludes, but at the same time, the destroyed cities we visit also connect to an underlying fascination in picturesque art and architecture, that of 'the ability of art to bring mean scenes – which in nature disgust – up to beauty.'[11] As John Macarthur explains, picturesque designers were fascinated by grotesque scenes such as butcher's shops or Rembrandt's paintings of animal carcasses.[12] Away from Waverly there is also the more monstrous beauty of buildings overgrown by Cordyceps itself, where nature, architecture and the human body become completely merged.

Of course, the quiet does not last long, and in one of the game's key encounters, a long suburban street must be traversed while under sniper fire. As Joel moves between cover, creeping room to room within houses, the type of domestic spaces we were just freely wandering around become ones of tension, scrabbling for crafting materials on worktops and using furniture to hide from hunters as we try to reach the sniper's nest. In this encounter, Joel will likely shield himself from view by means of family cars, fridges or upturned dinner tables. Brutal combat takes place in living rooms and kitchens. By using camera mods, we can move the camera to an aerial view to make an oblique mapping of this suburban terrain. From this, it becomes apparent that these domestic objects are strategically placed in a way that feels more naturalistic at ground level [Fig.07]. In this encounter, the abandoned objects of a previous life are carefully arranged to facilitate Joel's safe passage through the area. But, as the preceding moments of calm demonstrate, these domestic objects and the places they inhabit work throughout the game as a means of quietly communicating the magnitude of what has happened to society.

[Fig.06] A VIEW THROUGH THE SUBURBAN AREA OF WAVERLY TOWNSHIP, WHERE THE IDYLLIC LANDSCAPE STILL BEARS THE SUBTLE MARKS OF DECAY AND RUINATION WE FIND IN THE CITIES.

[Fig.07] PAGE 224

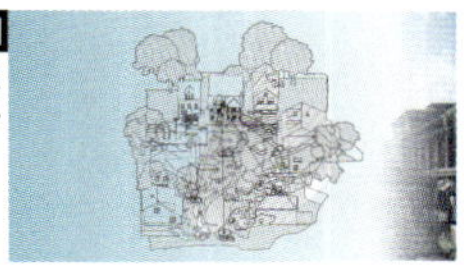

Looking over the street in Waverly Township where a sniper tracks Joel and Ellie, we see the landscape of objects and cover that allows players to find and flank the shooter.

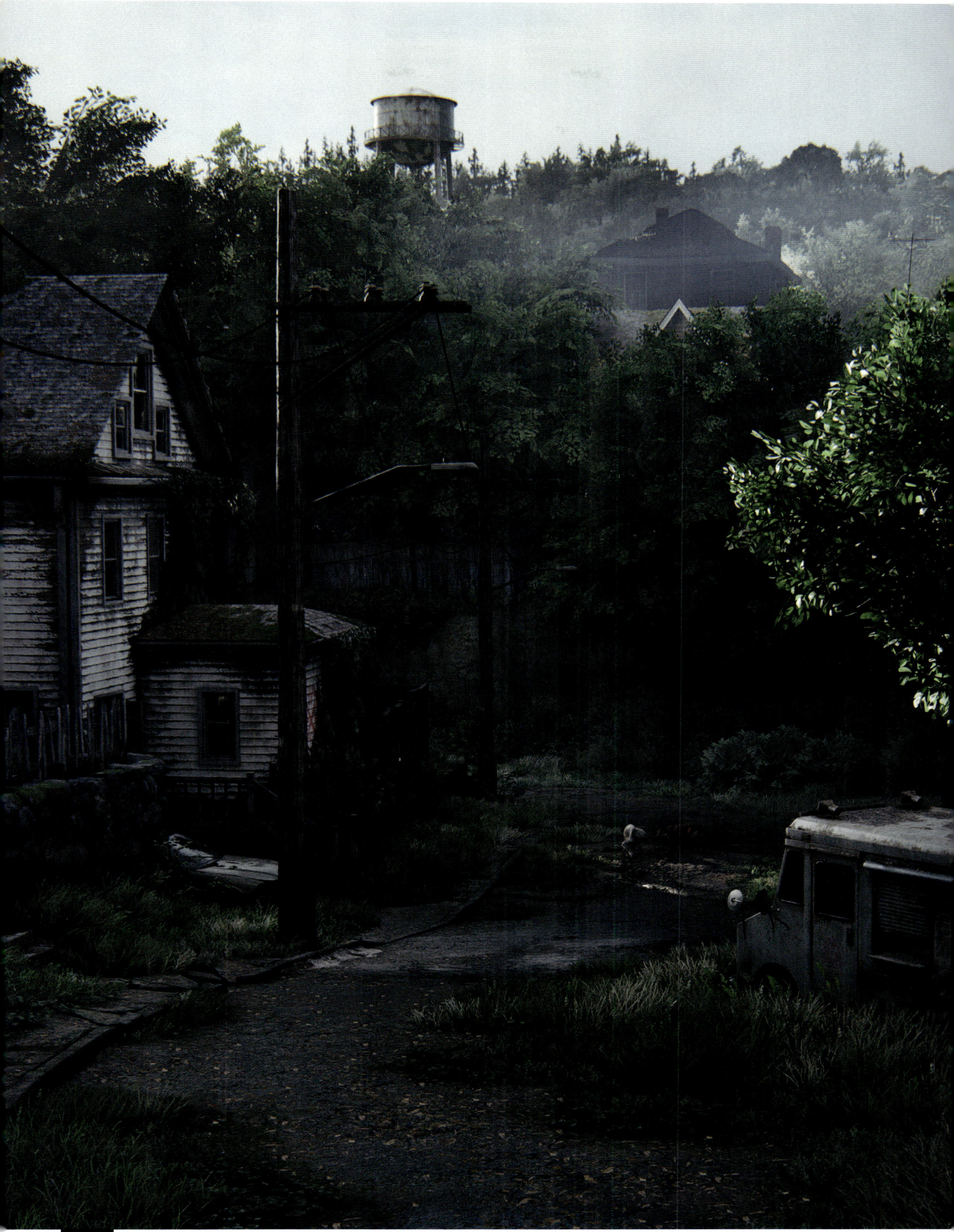

[Fig.06]

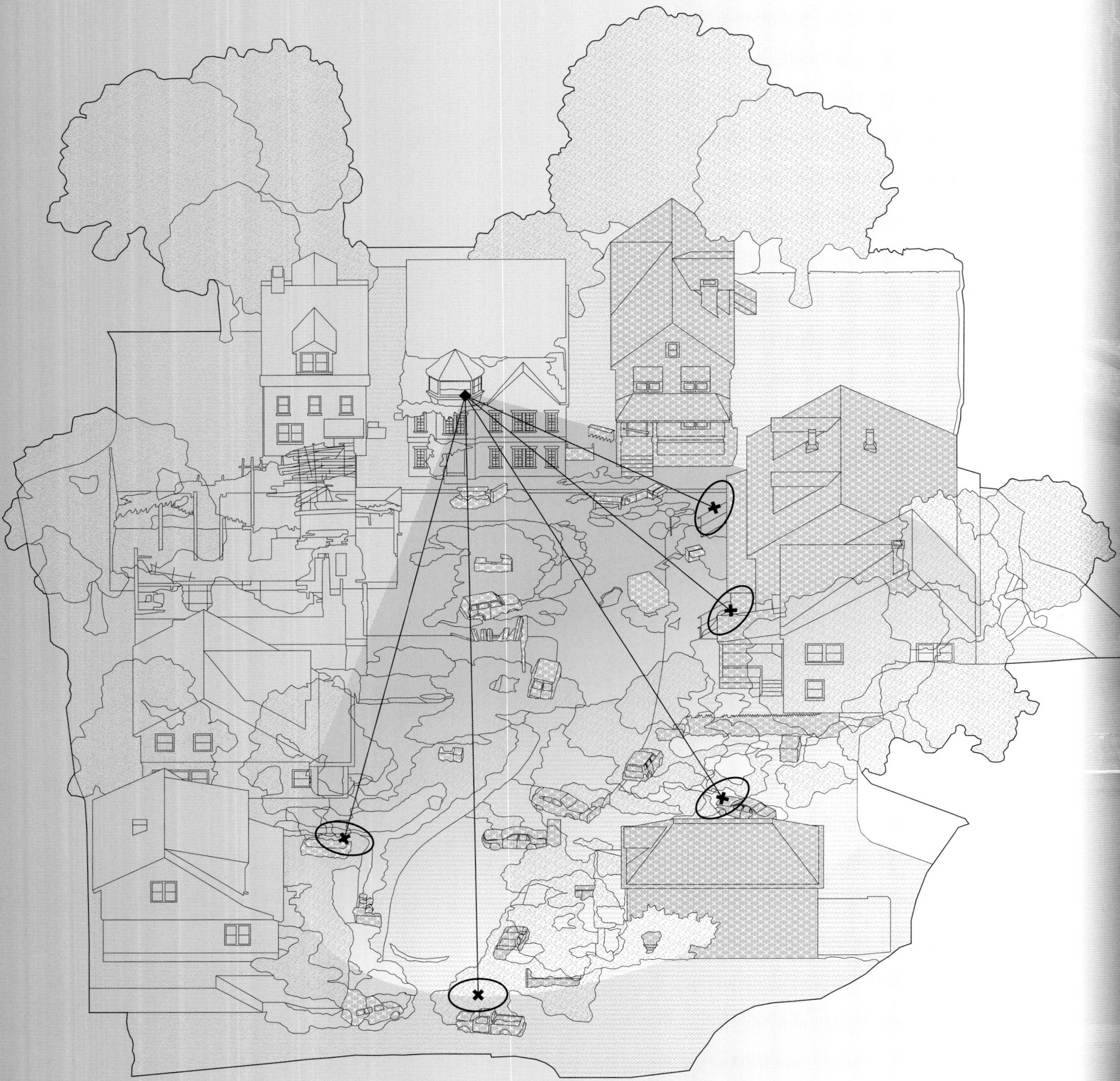

[Fig.07]

9.1

ARRIVALS AND DEPARTURES

Of all the introductions to game worlds, *Half-Life 2*'s is one of the most memorable. We awaken as Gordon Freeman, MIT-educated scientist and saviour of the world, on a train as it trundles into the main station of City 17. This city is the heart of a totalitarian state run by an alien society called the Combine, which has subjugated humanity, altered people's memories and prevented them from reproducing. At the heart of City 17 and the world is the Citadel, a huge tower that looms over human society, watching and controlling things below. *Half-Life 2* was influential through its employment of sophisticated physics simulations, companion characters and in-game narrative sections. But its singular quality also comes from the worldbuilding, led by the artist Viktor Antonov – an Eastern European-inspired landscape infused with aggressive and fragmentary alien architecture. In the story, Gordon Freeman will escape the city, using vehicles to explore the hinterlands beyond and connect with the human Resistance movement, before staging an attack on the Combine back in City 17 and ultimately conquering the towering Citadel.

Half-Life 2 was the first game to use Valve's Source engine, and many community tools have since been developed that can be used to research the game's world. Nem's Tools allows for the extraction of game models and textures, while *Garry's Mod* enables players to open *Half-Life 2* maps and experiment with them. By using a community-made plugin to import levels into the 3D modelling programme Blender and extracting 40×40-metre (131×131-ft) samples of the world, we examined the density of space Gordon encounters on his journey. Placing these together, we can see how the game creates a wave pattern oscillating between dense and desolate space [Fig.01]. City 17 exploits spatial compression by contrasting large plazas and boulevards to the backstreets and apartment blocks Gordon uses to avoid the Combine. The Canals on the city outskirts present sprawling civic engineering projects where Gordon is dwarfed by sheer concrete faces. Ravenholm is the densest and most intricate landscape Gordon explores, with closely packed buildings, lots of vertical circulation and a church, framing tense encounters with enemies. Heading out to the Coast by car, Gordon speeds between small villages and outposts dotted around the cliffs of the shoreline. The world's density then grows again, from the tight prison corridors of Nova Prospekt to Gordon's return to City 17, where Freeman picks his way through the demolished urban architecture towards the Citadel. The Citadel itself is a dense, internalized city containing a complex vertiginous layout. As our comparative mapping of these spaces reveals, spatial density is a key narrative device, where urban design mirrors the peaks and troughs of the story.

9.2

SITUATING THE CITY

City 17 itself is represented through twenty-seven individual maps, and by combining the sixteen maps comprising Gordon's return to the city on Day 3, we can examine the city's geography holistically. Density shifts are also at play within the city itself, with five key open spaces forming the backdrop for notable enemy encounters. The rest of the city is predominantly experienced through the winding backstreets, stairwells and alleyways that give us an insight into the urban form of the 'everyday' spaces that citizens occupy [Fig.02]. The 'negative space' of the city shown in our drawing is reminiscent of 'figure-ground plans' with buildings rendered as solid objects, which planner Michael Hebbert frames as a drawing type that 'focused attention on the lost space of the city.'[1] This fits with the designer's idea to 'go beyond the surface and the façades of the city' and instead 'construct[ing] it from its skeleton – the boulevards, the avenues and the hidden spaces.'[2] Together, these levels represent a chunk of the city that is roughly 820 by 643 metres (2,700 × 2,100 ft) in its bounding box, and while it is difficult to calculate precisely, Gordon travels a route of at least 1.75 kilometres (1.1 mi) from Dr. Kleiner's lab to the Citadel. Earlier, Gordon escapes the city through its infrastructural space, first sneaking and sprinting his way through rail yards and access tunnels, before eventually exiting through its systems of canals. Here we only see snippets of the city proper, with residential tower blocks peeking out into view, and Combine soldiers buzzing overhead as Gordon moves through subterranean channels, though the giant Citadel remains ever visible [Fig.03].

City 17's design combines architectural archetypes from across the Eastern European region and beyond, inspired by different periods of history. Our drawing showing the real-world locations of architectural inspirations demonstrates that the city is the product of artists who 'went on numerous research field trips' and 'took thousands of photographs' from 'around different Eastern European cities'[3] [Fig.04]. YouTubers such as NFKRZ have explored these real-world reference points and this helps us build a picture of the various cities and locations that find their way into the architectural language of City 17. Alongside the developer's stated references of 'Bulgaria, Russia and Romania,'[4] NFKRZ identifies urban signifiers from other Eastern European states such as the House of the National Assembly in Belgrade, which becomes the Combine Nexus building, or burned out cars littering the streets, which resemble models found in Serbia, the former USSR states and East Germany.[5] The architectural influence on City 17's train station is stated by Viktor Antonov as 'very close to a train station designed by Alexandre Gustave Eiffel, of Eiffel Tower fame' in Budapest,[6] though Antonov states it was subsequently inspired by a station in Paris, seemingly the Gare Saint-Lazare.

The station demonstrates that while most inspirations come from Eastern Europe, there are some moments of geographic dislocation. Throughout the game we encounter many classic 'Soviet-style' tower blocks, with similar designs used repeatedly, mirroring reality. This allows the developers to reuse assets and is nicely contextual – as historian Christine Varga-Harris explains, during rapid housing developments under Soviet leader Nikita Khrushchev, architects were 'expected to conform to the idea that Soviet housing be bright, clear and simple' and promote collective living where 'the modern socialist apartment...was supposed to reflect socialism as it was becoming and to make daily living socialist.'[7]

[Fig.03] PAGE 196

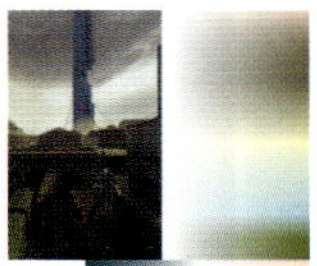

A view of City 17's train yards, where Gordon Freeman escapes the city, showing the ever-present Citadel looming in the background.

[Fig.04] PAGE 197

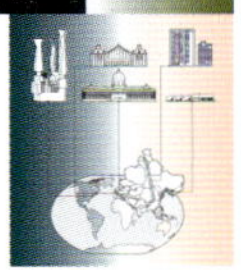

Elevational studies of in-game buildings and their real-world inspirations, demonstrating architectural designs drawn from Eastern European and former Soviet Union countries.

When Gordon enters such buildings, they are invariably collective spaces where citizens hide and gather away from the Combine. Rising high above the apartment blocks is the Citadel, and, when we reach its top, we can see a city stretching out beneath us, which is actually a digitally manipulated map of New York, placing the building in Brooklyn's Williamsburg district. While the later VR game *Half-Life: Alyx* shows City 17's map as a close proxy of Sofia in Bulgaria, this original version still has moments where it crosses the world for inspiration.

A PLAN OF CITY 17 MADE BY STITCHING TOGETHER IN-GAME LEVELS, SHOWING THE CONTIGUOUS URBAN TERRITORY OF THE CITY AND HOW KEY BATTLES ARE CENTRED AROUND PLAZAS AND PUBLIC SPACES.

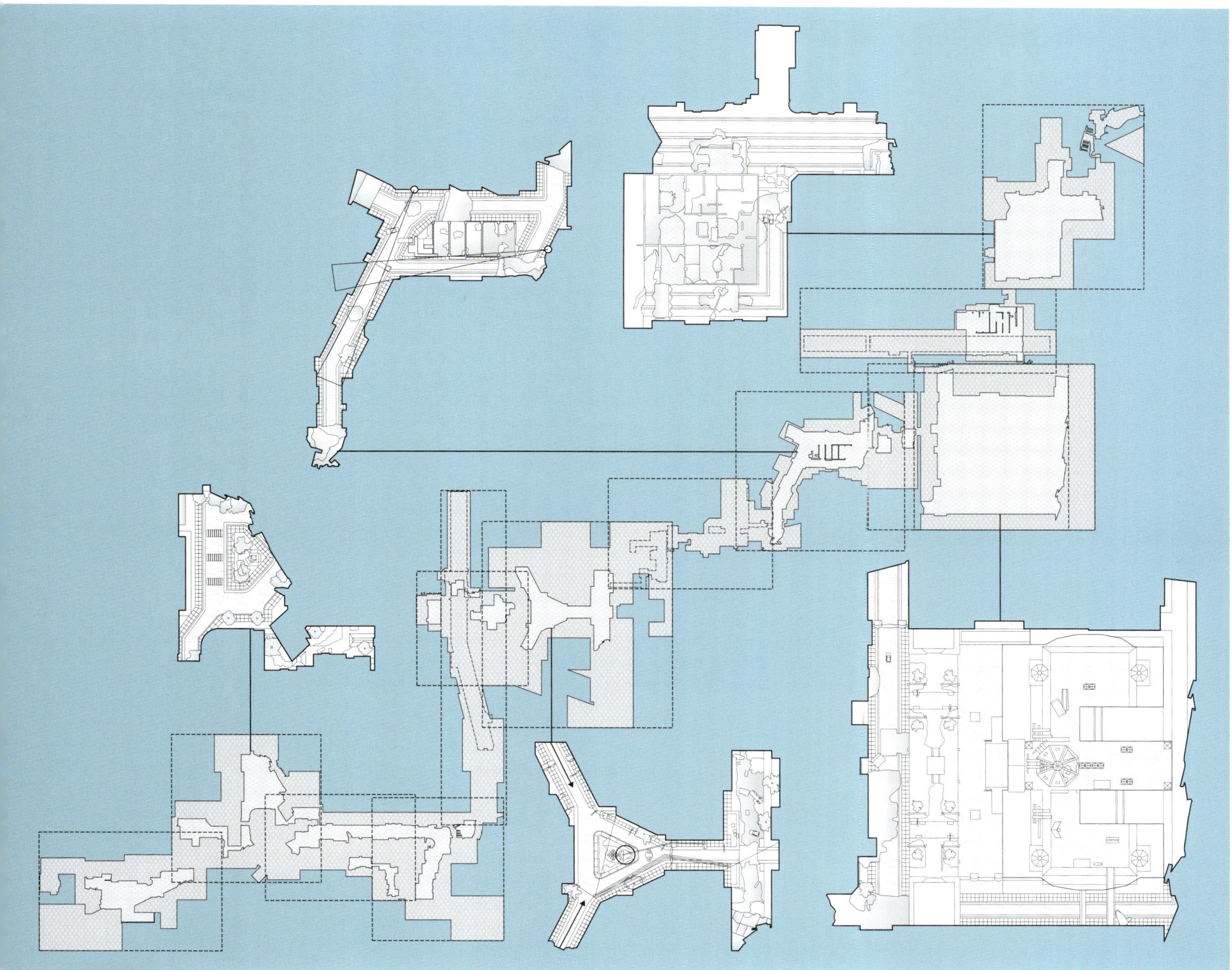

[Fig.02]

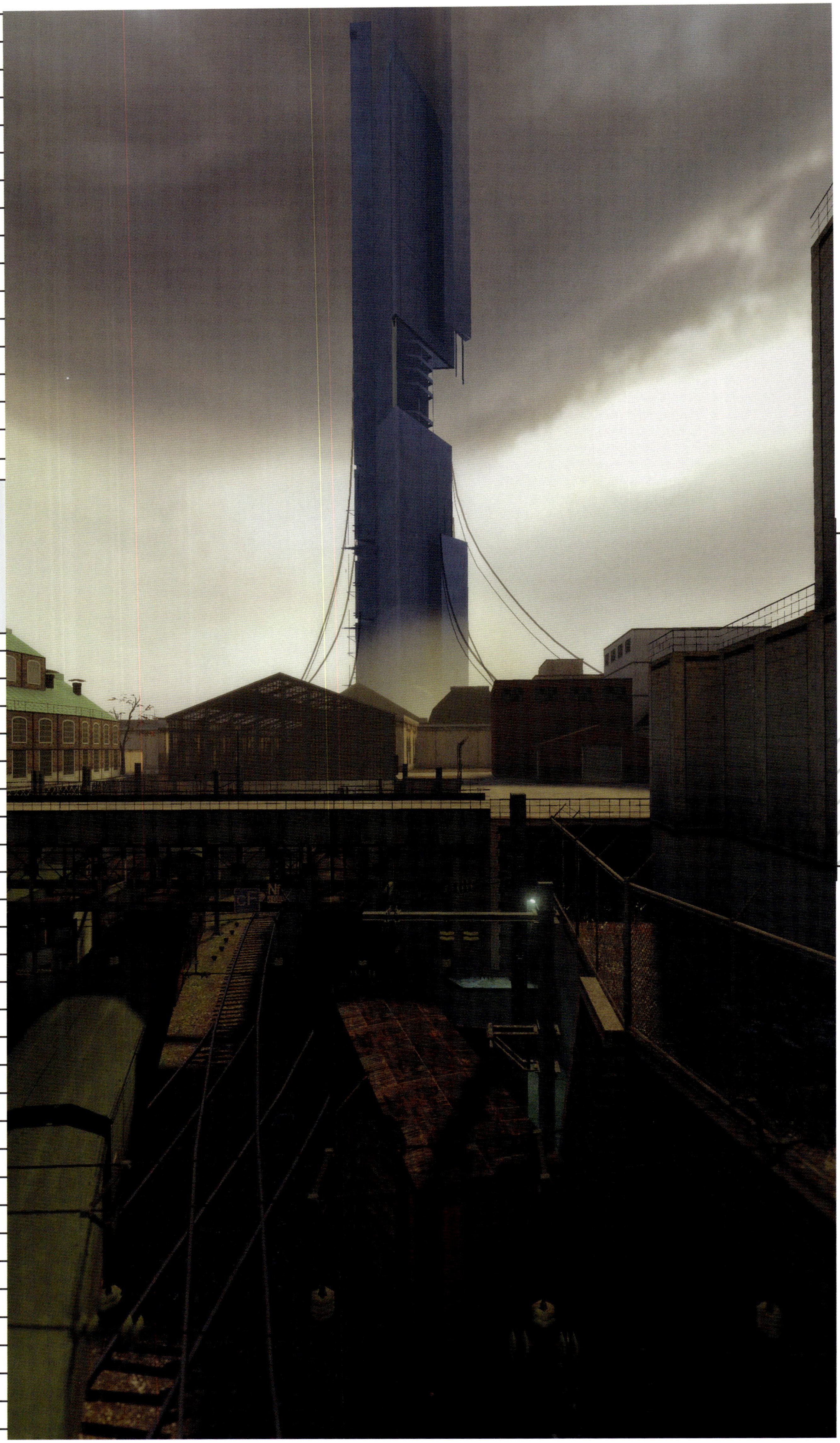

[Fig.03]

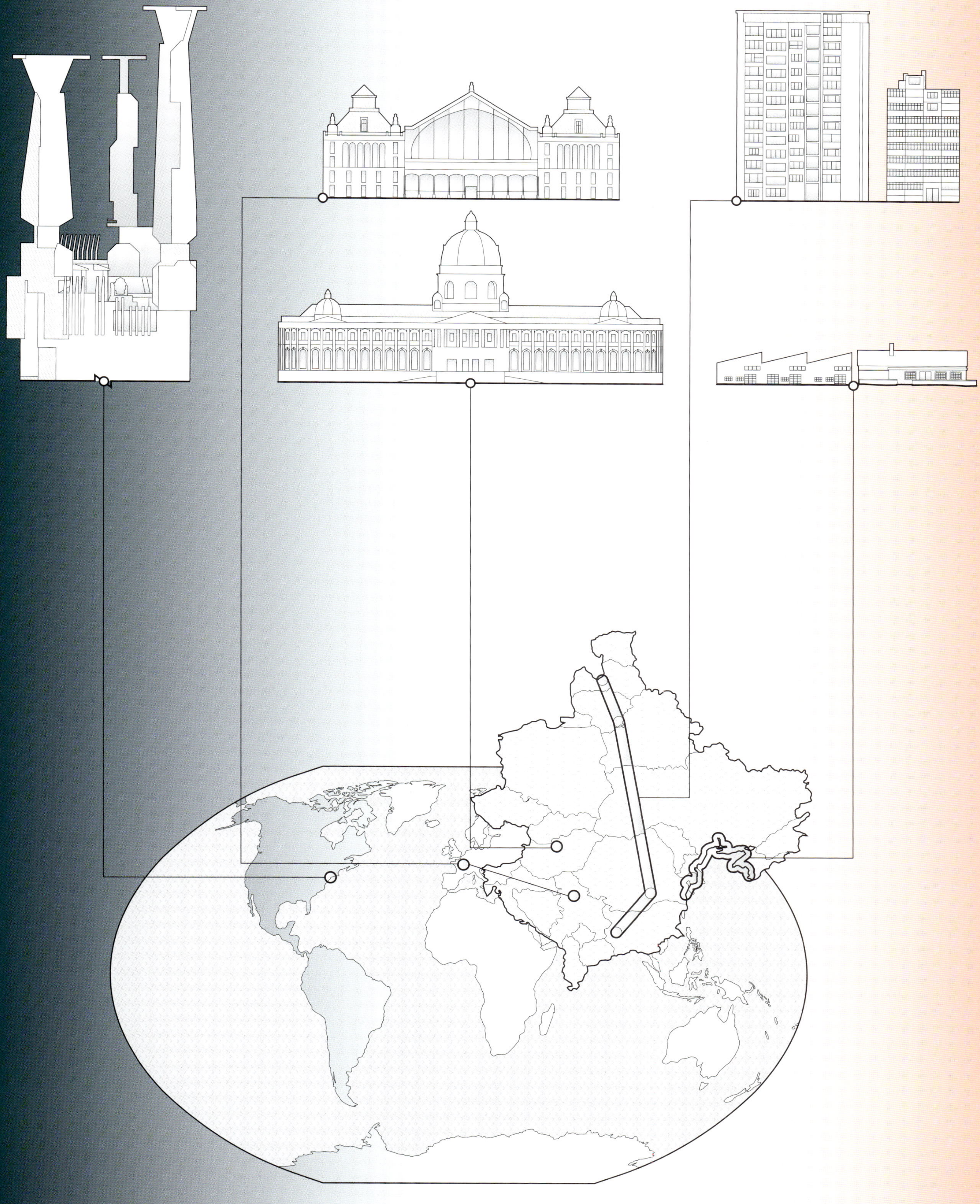

[Fig.04]

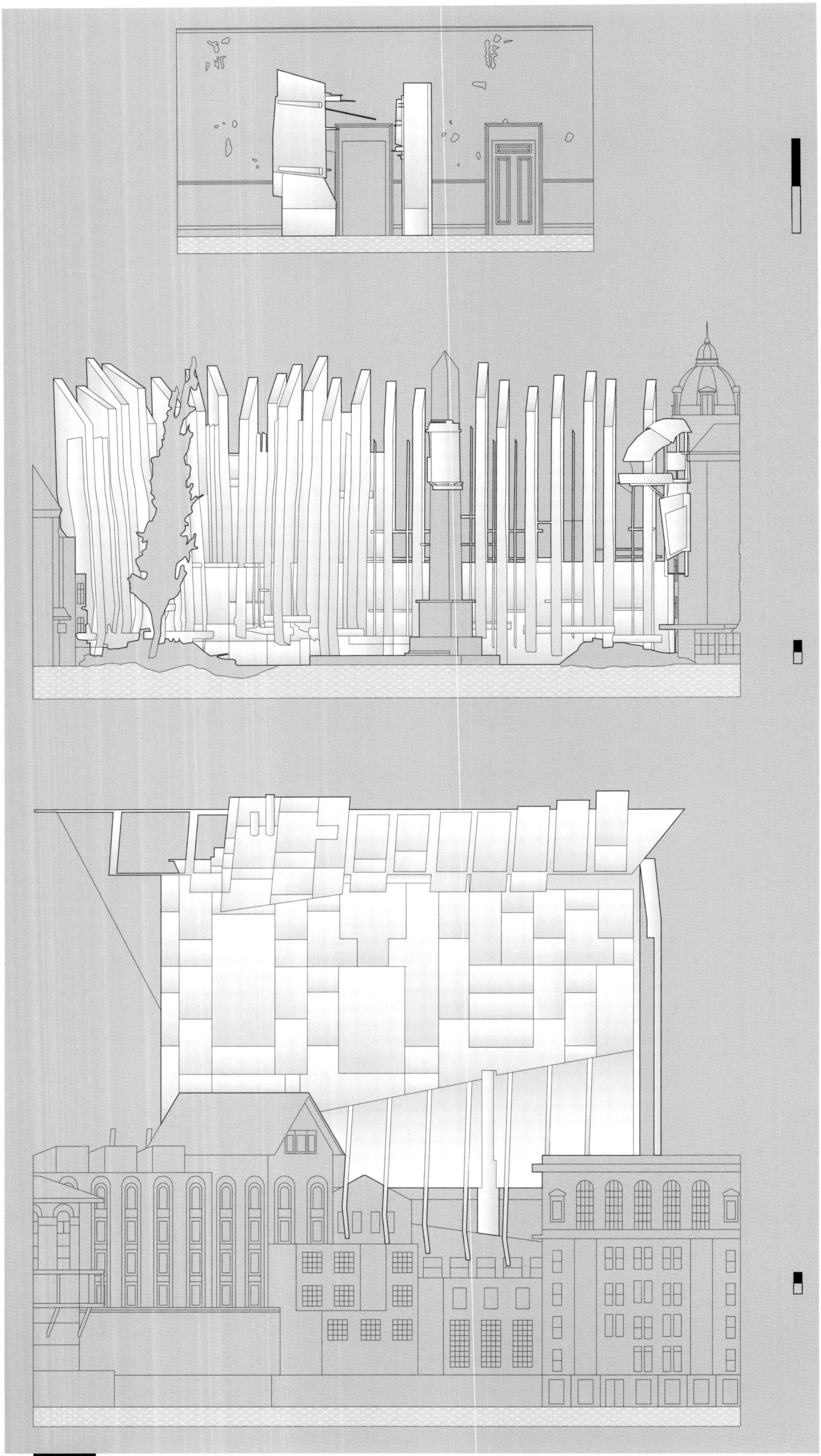

ELEVATIONS OF ‘PARASITIC’ ARCHITECTURE, SHOWING HOW THE COMBINE ATTACHES NEW ARCHITECTURAL ELEMENTS ONTO THE EXISTING CITY, FROM THE SCALE OF A DOOR TO A HULKING STRUCTURE OVERHANGING NOVA PROSPEKT.

[Fig.05]

9.3

PARASITES

The unique aesthetic of City 17 blends realistic architectural forms with the alien design of the Combine. This takes the form of 'parasitic architecture' where new buildings are built on top of the old. By collecting examples of these parasite structures, we show how Combine control over the world is asserted across architectural scales. The Overwatch Nexus is an existing public building retrofitted with security doors and force field generators. Giant walls puncture through City 17, reminiscent of a technological version of traditional palisade walls used in fortifications. Lookout posts and propaganda broadcasting screens hang from the sides of buildings. At Nova Prospekt this spatial control is even more aggressive – by 'noclipping' out of the level, we can clearly see a giant Combine architecture that sits atop the existing prison buildings, with large metal tendrils penetrating the smaller structures below [Fig.05]. Real-world examples of parasitic architecture are often experimental designs such as Makoto Sei Watanabe's Aoyama Technical College in Tokyo, which use the addition of building parts as a new form of design order 'through tolerance of chaos.'[8] The most influential exponent of parasitic architecture was American architect Lebbeus Woods (also discussed in the *Disco Elysium* chapter), who developed the idea though books like *War and Architecture* to present designs for reconstructing the city of Sarajevo that involved stitching together war-damaged buildings. Anecdotes suggest that Valve's art department were aware of Woods' work, although for Woods, parasitic architecture is one of liberation and restoration rather than hostility. Combine architecture is certainly reminiscent of Woods' drawings, such as *Studies for Broken Wall Houses* and *INJECTION Construction*, where he describes how 'in the spaces voided by destruction, new structures are injected. Complete in themselves, they do not make an exact fit, but exist as spaces within spaces, making no attempt to reconcile the gaps between what is new and old.'[9] For Woods, these structures would become fully integrated only by the passing of time, but luckily for the citizens of City 17, Gordon Freeman does not afford the Combine such time.

The Combine's biggest architectural insertion into the world is the Citadel, which appears at the centre of both City 17 and the game's story. By creating screenshots from each City 17 level and drawing their contextual building forms on top of each other, we demonstrate how the Citadel remains centrally framed as the context changes around it – every street we walk down will inevitably end with a view of the structure [Fig.06]. The ubiquity of the Citadel was a decision by the developers as 'from the first seconds of the game, we wanted the player to see where his journey would take him, so that when he finally got to the Citadel, he would have the strongest possible relationship with it.'[10] The Citadel becomes inevitable. In this regard it recalls both Walt Disney's design concept of the 'weenie'[11], a structure that beckons the viewer towards it, and the French philosopher Roland Barthes' discussion of the most iconic tower of all, the Eiffel Tower. Barthes writes 'wherever you are, whatever the landscape of roofs, domes, or branches separating you from it, *the Tower is there*...determined merely to persist, like a rock or the river.'[12]

[Fig.06]
PAGE 200

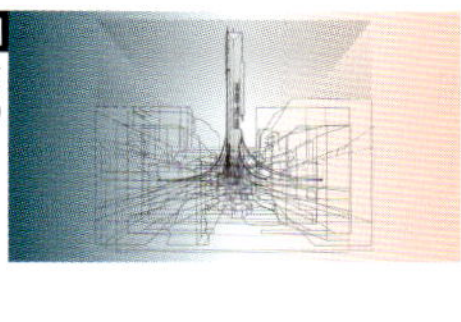

An overlay of multiple street view perspectives from City 17 demonstrating how the Citadel remains visually centred wherever the player moves within the city.

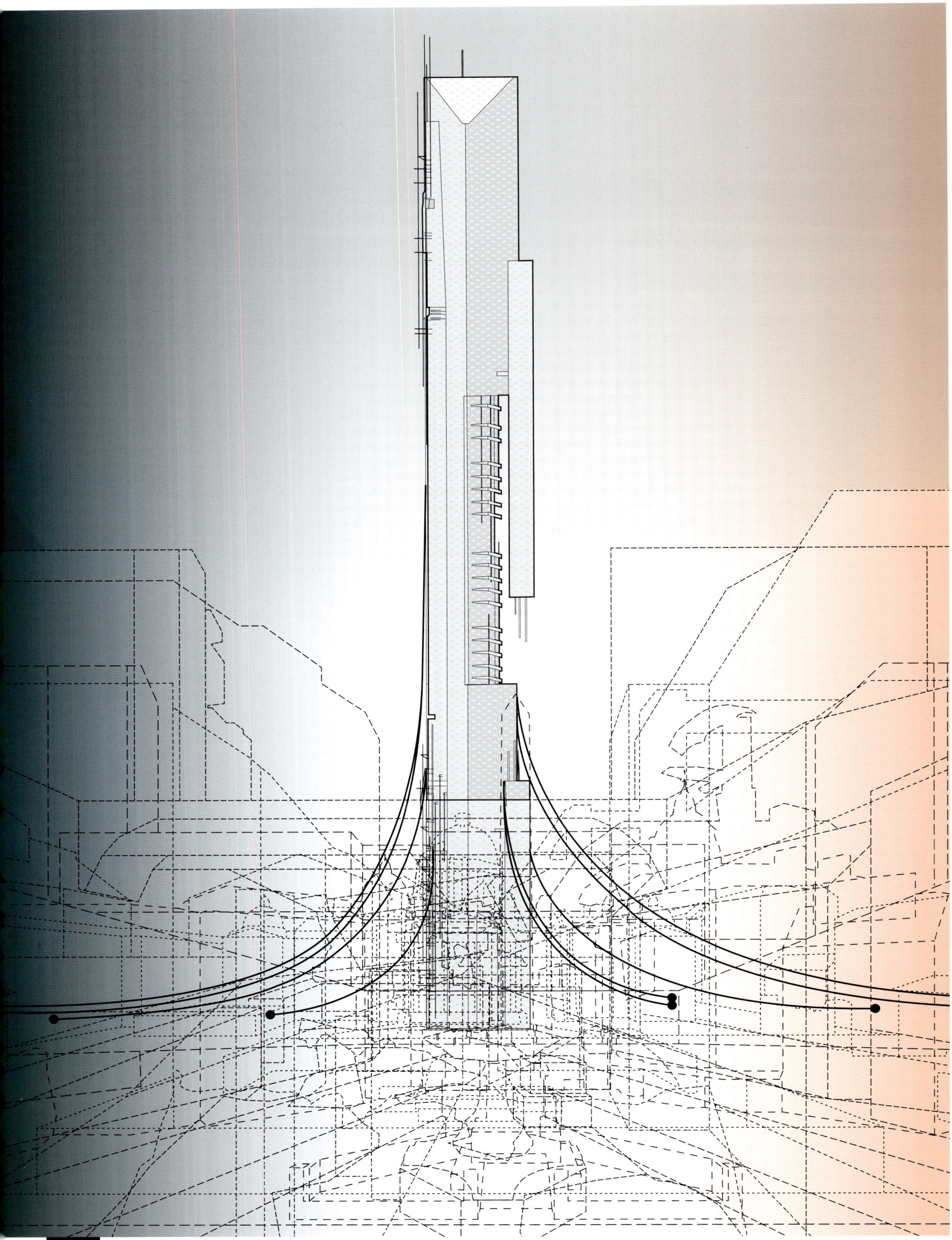

[Fig.06]

The only place to escape the view of the tower is from within it. In Barthes' writing about the Eiffel Tower, he discusses an inversion that takes place – when reaching the top of the tower, the city, rather than the tower, becomes an object 'simultaneously extended and collected beneath it.'[13] However, when Gordon finally enters the Citadel, views back out over the city are limited. Instead, the building is more like the mute brutalist form of the 33 Thomas Street building in New York, a former telephone exchange and a skyscraper built for machinery, entirely absent of windows. Inside the Citadel, Gordon and Alyx find vast halls of machines and hangars, crisscrossed by rails of pods carrying prisoners and workers [Fig.07]. Despite its iconic position in the city, it is clear this is not an architectural space made for humans.

The Citadel's iconic nature has led to many community attempts to establish its dimensions. This is tricky because the structure predominantly features as a 'skybox' geometry that is scaled in real-time around the player's position. A widely accepted height of the structure is 2,569 metres (1.6 mi), based on calculations derived from the game's *Hammer Editor* and the units it uses for such skybox geometry.[14] Other community mappers have questioned this scale due to the size of the building's interiors, using alternative calculation methods, such as analysing the previously mentioned satellite imagery of New York used to imply the height of the in-game building.[15] By the calculations of Redditor *Ascreamroad*, the Citadel is much larger, at around 8,406 metres (5.2 mi) in height. To interrogate this scale ourselves, we approached the building from inside and out, using new methods to assess the accuracy of these existing estimates [Fig.08]. To examine the building's exterior, we compared the main Citadel model to the fragment of building that players encounter in the level *d3_c17_13* where Gordon enters the structure after journeying through City 17. Here, we observe a ridge in the surface of the building that is clearly visible in the skybox model of the building. By scaling the skybox model to match this 'real world' scale, we find the structure to be 2,635 metres (1.6 mi) tall, aligning well with the 'official' estimate. Testing the contention that the interior of the building could not be contained by such dimensions, we combined level maps from *Half-Life 2: Episode One* in Blender, as these encompass the exterior edge of the building through to its central core and back out to the train station by which Gordon escapes the structure. Overlaying these interior maps onto the building's outline plan, we see that it must be at least 695 metres (2,280 ft) across to accommodate the internal spaces. By scaling the Citadel model to fit this, we arrive at a height of 8,330 metres (5.18 mi), surprisingly close to *Ascreamroad's* estimate. Even at the smaller calculation, the building still dwarfs real-world structures like the Burj Khalifa or Empire State Building. The larger estimate is improbable since the Citadel can be reached by the player – it is not being hidden in the far distance – and the building's floorplan would be bigger than the whole expanse of City 17 we experience in the game. Ultimately, the developers are playing with the time-honoured discrepancy between inside and outside space that we find in many videogame worlds.

[Fig.07] PAGES 202–3

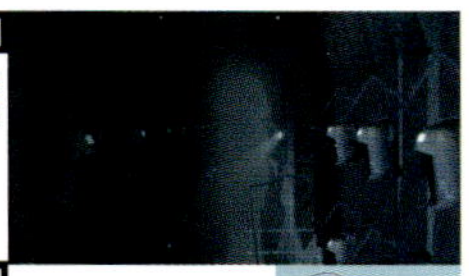

A view from within the Citadel, a 'non-human' architecture designed predominantly around maintaining control and providing infrastructure for the Combine.

[Fig.08] PAGE 204

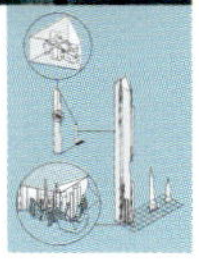

Comparing the potential size of the Citadel using community-created dimensioning methods as well as our own scale calculations made using the game's 3D models.

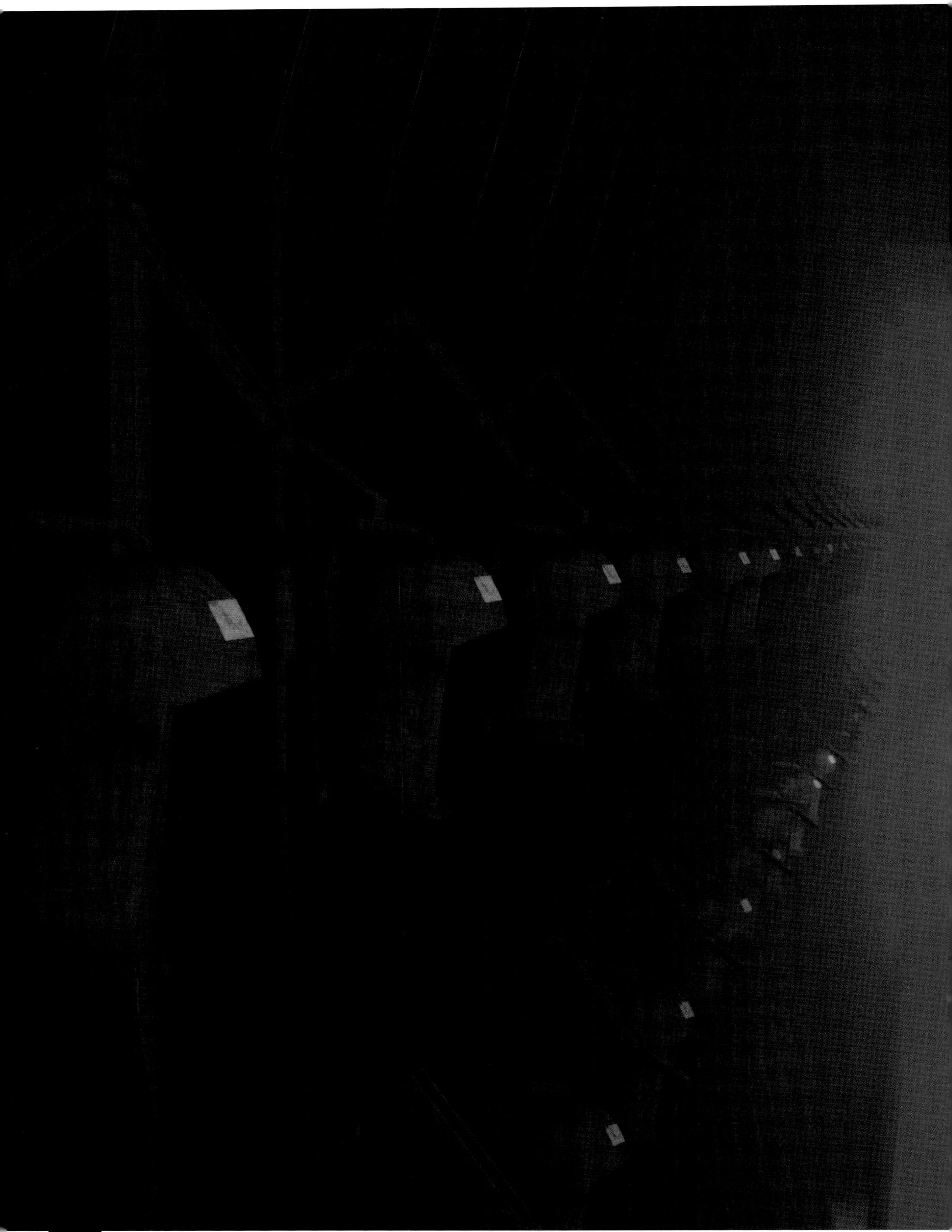

[Fig.07]

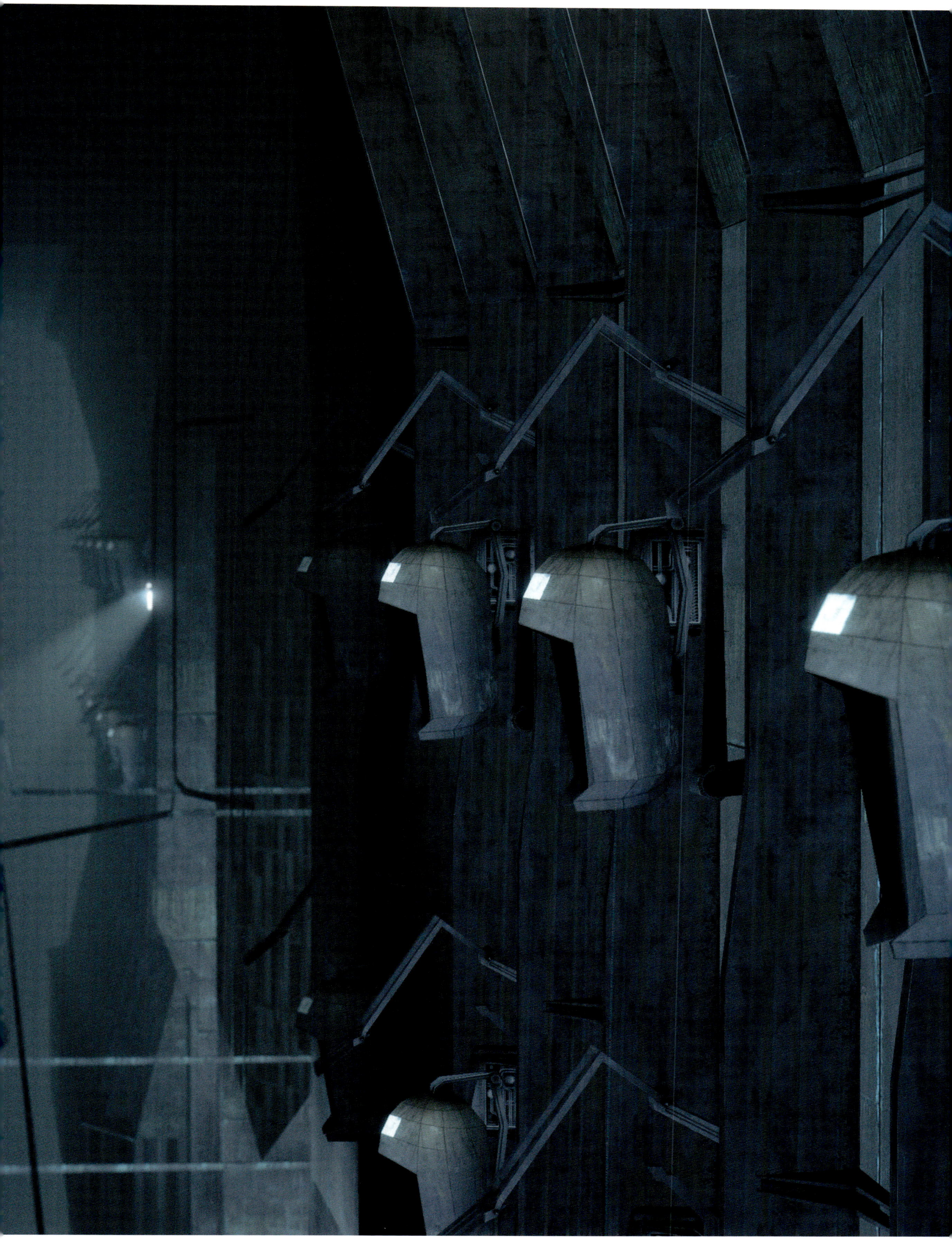

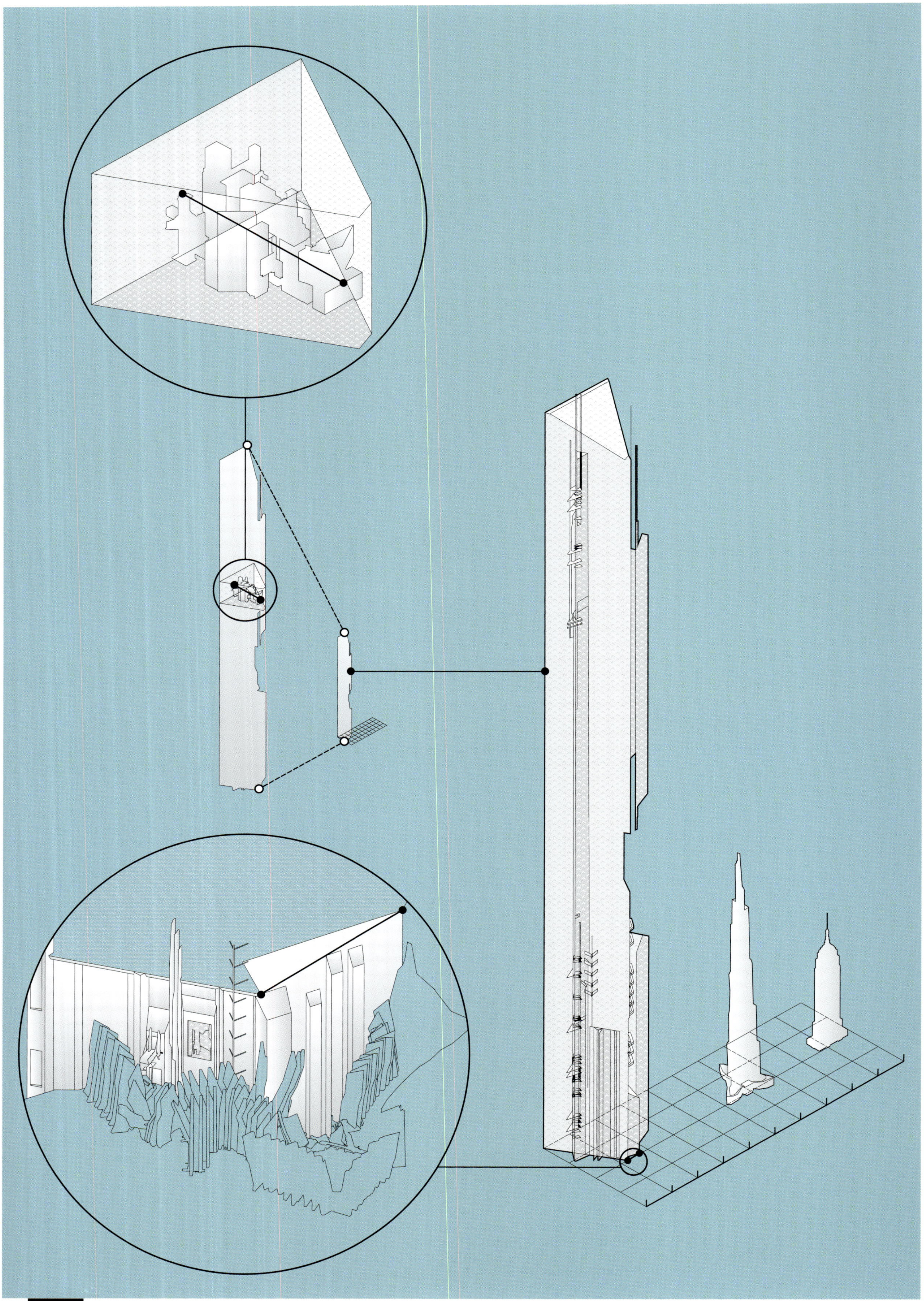

[Fig.08]

9.4

HINTERLANDS AND HIGHWAYS

While City 17 and the Citadel bookend Gordon's journey, other locations that he visits present their own specific logic that continues to demonstrate Valve's commitment to its 'formula of what makes a level look balanced', which is described as 'large, medium and tiny objects' from 'city blocks...and big architectural designs' followed by 'ornaments, antennas and trees' through to 'trash, posters and little decals.'[16] Gordon's journey takes him to Ravenholm, a former mining town now infested by zombies. Here, players meet Father Grigori, the town's priest, who helps guide Gordon through an environment that is even more winding and dense than the backstreets of City 17. Sketches from the game's production show how Ravenholm is designed around vertical circulation, including a dive into a water tank. By mapping two circuitous journeys through individual Ravenholm levels, we transcribe how the deserted industrial architecture is augmented through 'medium and tiny objects' like the homemade and 'jury-rigged' structures that enable Gordon to traverse the environment [Fig.09]. In both levels, Gordon's journey involves circling back on himself, using Grigori's systems of scaffolds, moving platforms and traps such as cars on winches that are used to crush enemies.

On the second day of his journey, Gordon drives towards Nova Prospekt, taking Highway 17 around the Coast to reach the prison where Eli is being held. Analysing the game maps shows this total journey is around six kilometres (3.7 mi) – a far more expansive terrain than the city. In an ironic twist, having escaped the totalitarian Eastern European city, Freeman takes to the open road in a nod to the American spirit of vehicular transport, where, as architectural historian Reyner Banham argues, highways become 'a single comprehensible place, a coherent state of mind, a complete way of life'[17] Gordon's 'Scout Car' provides freedom to explore the highway, alongside the industrial architecture and compact villages found along its path. Seen at speed, these structures contribute to the developer's desire to 'preserve the illusion of nonlinearity by sprinkling in rich, but optional, content – optional in that players could either miss it, or choose to move past it.'[18] These villages often house groups of Resistance fighters, repurposing domestic space as military outposts. This also contributes to the fleeting sense of freedom as 'although nature spaces in *Half-Life 2* do not provide complete safety...the countryside is where the resistance hideouts are located. Nature thus enables a space for Utopian enclaves.'[19] But as Dimitris Dalakoglou argues, in contexts like a totalitarian state 'automobility and high(er) speeds were so exclusive' that only 'the most powerful (e.g. the elite or the colonialist) could enjoy the symbolic and practical benefits of fast(er) and (more) private mobility.'[20] As the Combine ultimately control the roads, the game forces Gordon out of the car, requiring him to clear debris, power down force field barriers, or, in the specific level we map, operate a large dock crane to drag the Scout Car up to a higher level. Examining this journey through an oblique drawing, we can see how the whole dock area becomes a thoroughfare for the car [Fig.10]. Warehouses and buildings are curiously empty, save for a few barrels waiting for the buggy to pass through them. Finally, Gordon speeds up a wooden ramp, smashing through a set of windows and back onto the highway, free, if only for a moment.

[Fig.09] PAGE 206

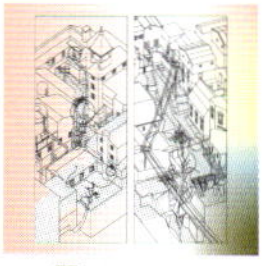

Street scenes from Ravenholm, where a network of jury-rigged traps and walkways enables Gordon to move through the town via circuitous and vertical routes.

[Fig.10] PAGE 207

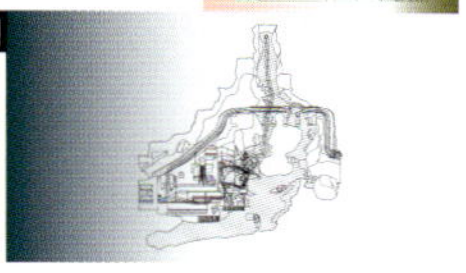

An oblique view of an area on the Coast, tracing Freeman's journey and showing how the level and architectural designs become calibrated to being driven through at speed.

Eventually we reach the end of the road, culminating in a rocket launcher battle with Combine forces atop a lighthouse in a Resistance settlement. Displacing the camera using the 'noclip' command, we look back at this point as an archetypal example of the architectural landscape of the Coast. This is a place of salt-eroded painted doors, broken children's swings, creaking timber fences and threadbare trees [Fig.11]. In original concept plans and leaked test levels, the lighthouse faced onto Nova Prospekt, creating a visual juxtaposition to the hulking mass of the prison. But in the final game it provides a hard stop, a last point of Utopian resistance before the cliffs give way to another section of coastline taking Freeman back towards the oppressive architecture of the Combine.

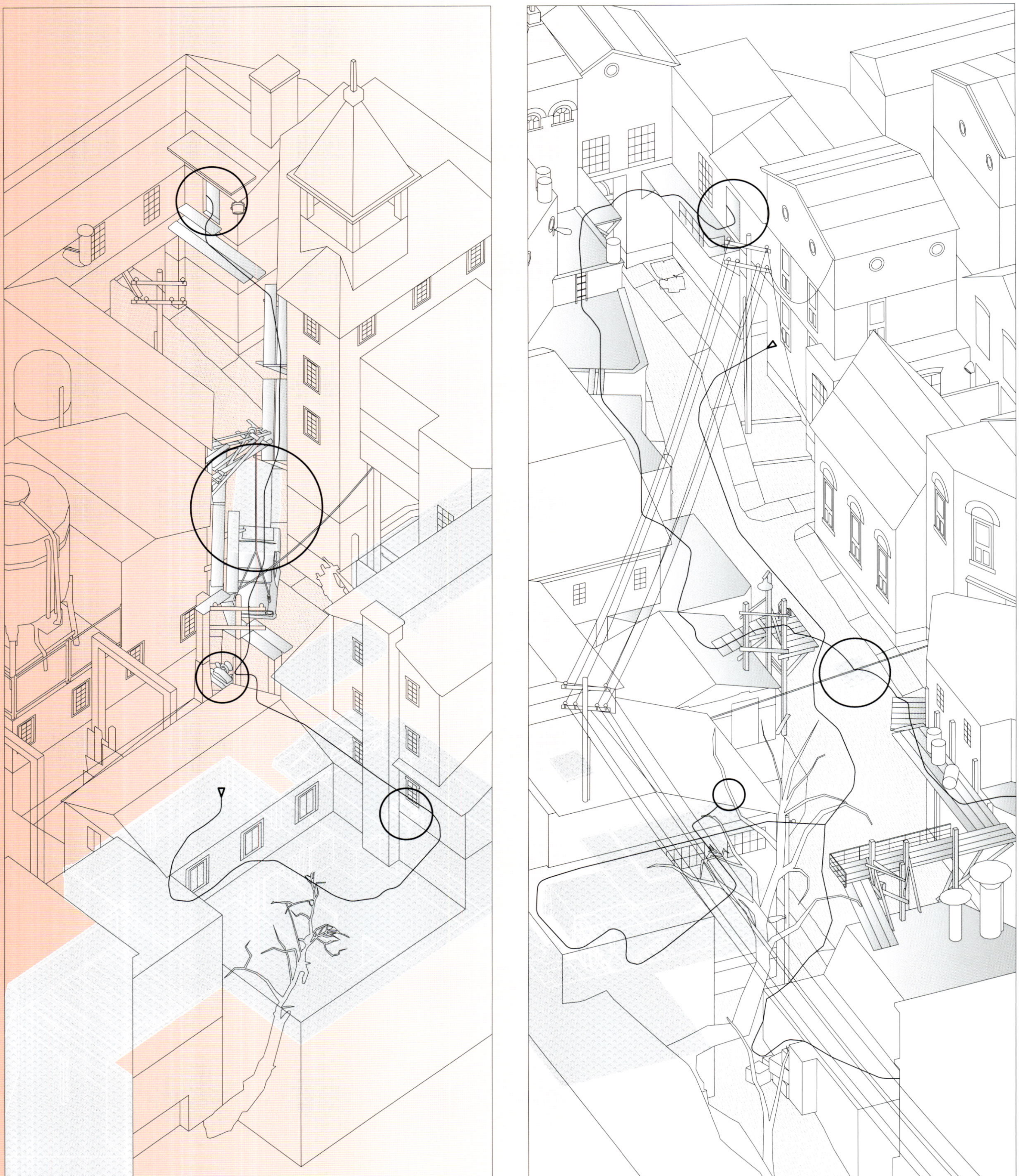

[Fig.09]

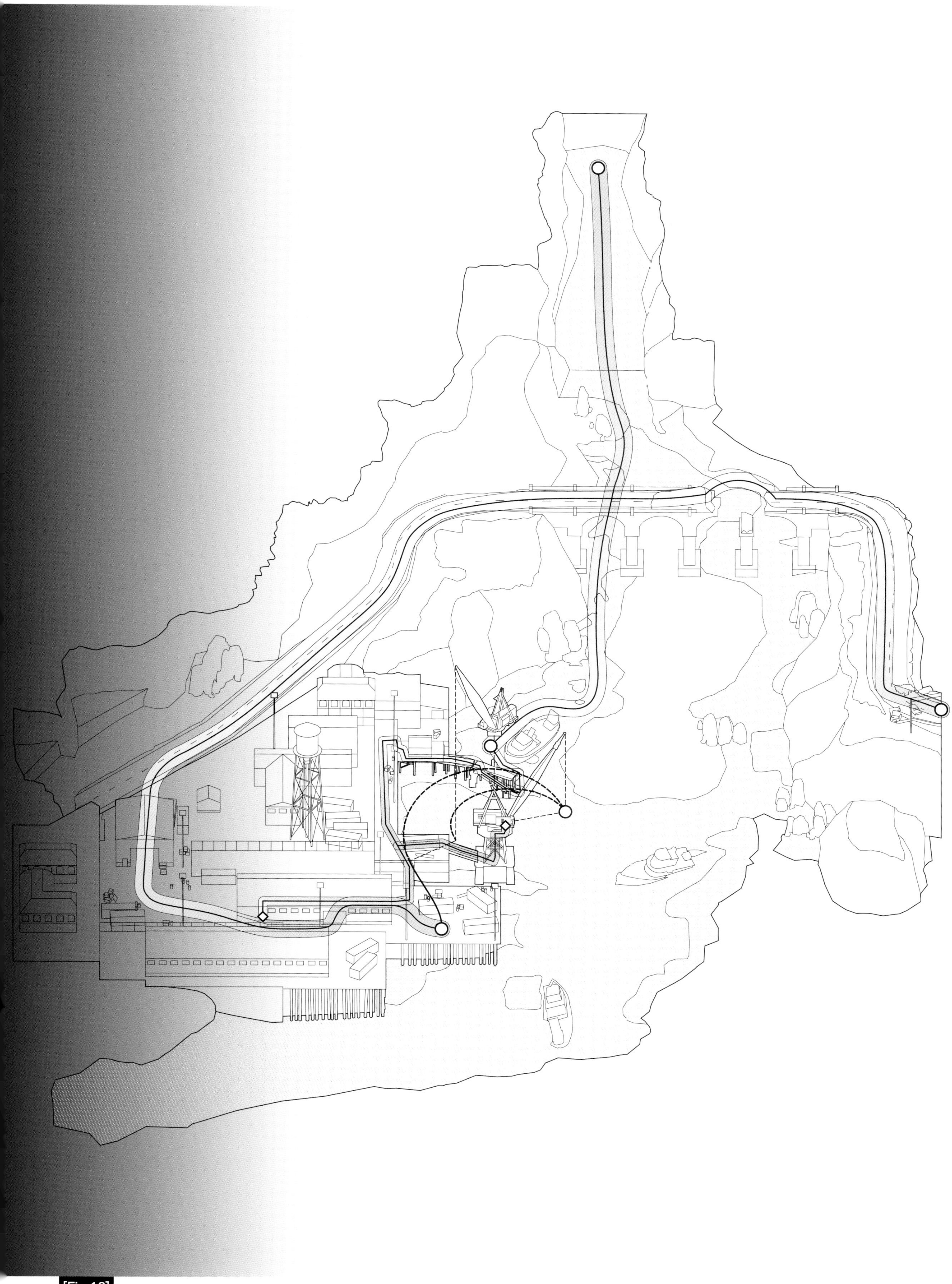

[Fig.10]

A VIEW AT THE END OF THE ROAD AT THE COAST, SHOWING THE TYPE OF SMALL VILLAGES AND RUN-DOWN HOUSES WHERE THE RESISTANCE PLAN THEIR COUNTER-ATTACK AGAINST THE COMBINE.

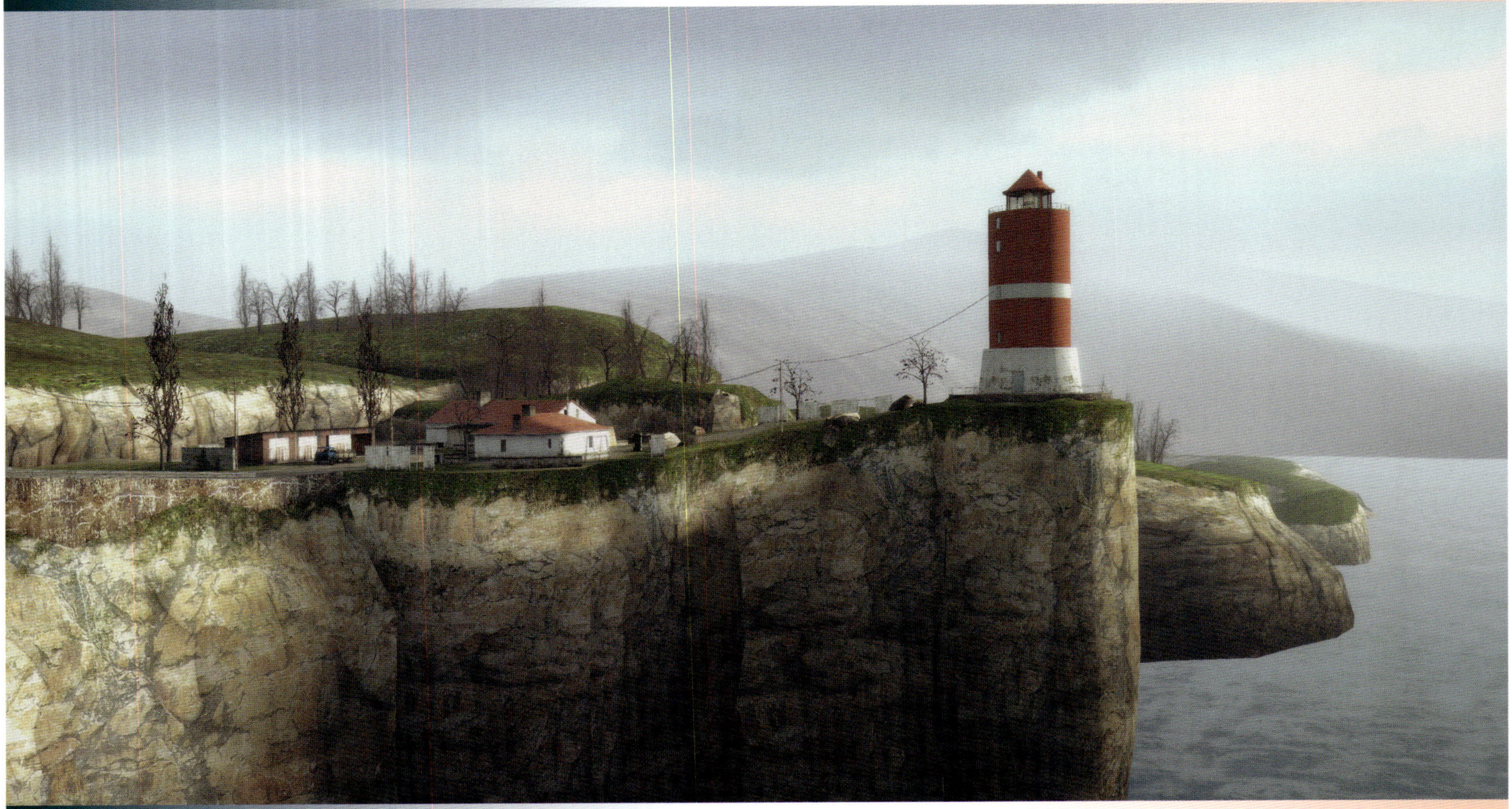

[Fig.11]

10.5

OBJECTIVITY

Because spaces in *The Last of Us* are very often at the scale of homes, offices or other everyday buildings, throughout the journey we find them littered with objects and detritus. For Enea Bianchi, these objects evoke Sigmund Freud's idea of the *uncanny* – they are both 'familiar and unfamiliar' spaces of 'desolate offices, non-operational computers and consoles, silent gyms, empty pools, vacant hotels, D&D games forever frozen on a table' where everyday objects become 'defamiliarized.'[13] Joel and Ellie even find themselves hiding out in an architect's office, surrounded by models of buildings that would have shaped the pre-pandemic city. By recording and collecting domestic objects found in various interiors throughout the course of the game, we start to build a picture of the lives left behind [Fig.08]. Removed from their original context and composed together as if in a Sears Catalogue,[14] each object communicates a small story to the player as they make their way through a suburban home, the rooms of the Hotel Grand or student dorms in Colorado. Some items clearly speak of the pandemic, like suitcases and duffle bags that indicate people on the move, while stacked tables, chairs and mattresses might have been barricades. Elsewhere, juicers, coffee machines, typewriters and architectural models suggest lives simply left behind in the rush.

Despite this emphasis on visual and spatial realism, certain players have jokingly questioned why elements like beds and doors are so oversized,[15] and beyond an amusing observation this touches on a second set of objects that are found within the game. The bed is big because in the mechanics of the game, Joel and Ellie may need to hide behind it. Likewise, there is a whole set of commercial objects such as dumpsters, ladders, pallets and even a grand piano that can be pushed and pulled around to allow Joel and Ellie to proceed through the world. Drawing examples of these as perspective plans allows us to identify common spatial characteristics that remain constant whatever the stylistic or narrative setting. The game repeatedly uses courtyard and cloister-like spaces that can only be exited by means of butting an object up against one of the edges, and gaps between buildings that cannot be jumped [Fig.09]. This establishes a new form of mobility particular to the architectural spaces of the game. As Melissa Kagen states, 'basic architectural conventions like elevators and stairs have disappeared, forcing you to think creatively about what leaps you can safely make from one decaying floor to another.'[16] When stairs disappear, a wheelie bin takes their place.

[Fig.08] PAGES 226–7

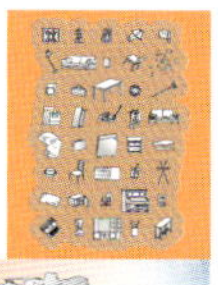

A visual archive of the domestic objects that can be found as players traverse houses, hotel rooms and makeshift living quarters, each communicating something about the lives left behind.

[Fig.09] PAGE 228

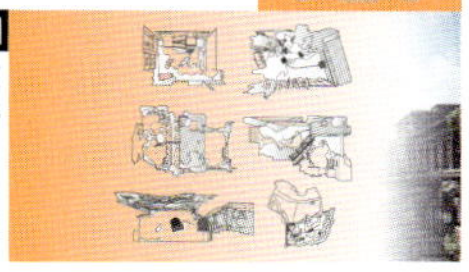

Perspectival plan drawings exploring how movement within the world is often predicated on the use of everyday objects such as large planks, dumpsters and even a piano.

The importance of objects within the world of *The Last of Us* peaks at the climactic fight between Ellie and the cannibal David in Todd's Steakhouse at Silver Lake. Ellie must sneak around the booths and tables to attack David from behind, while avoiding contextual hazards such as broken crockery on the floor, which will make a noise and alert him to her presence. By drawing a plan of this restaurant, we can show how the design of the space and the considered placement of detritus contribute to the mechanics of the fight [Fig.10]. There are multiple layers intrinsic to the restaurant's function as a battleground, with players needing to carefully consider sound as well as sight lines. The presence of broken plates and dishes means that while Ellie can technically creep anywhere, players are forced into taking circuitous routes to avoid alerting David. Here, one of the game's central mechanics of throwing bricks and bottles to distract enemies finds its logical conclusion at a restaurant where bottles naturally proliferate. Our map shows that while these objects tend to be a precious resource in the outside world, they are plentiful at Todd's.

[Fig.08] Detail

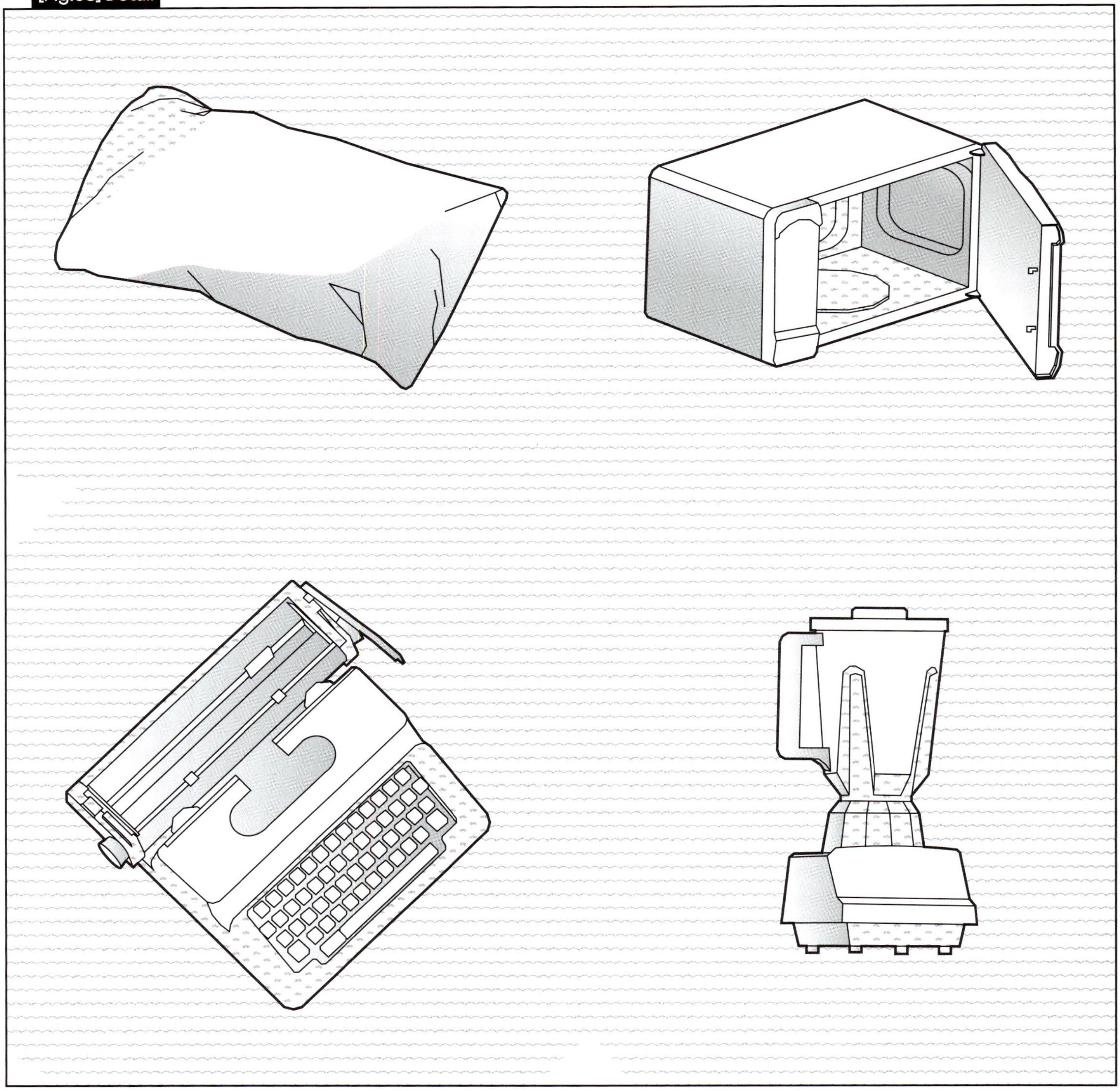

[Fig.10] PAGE 229

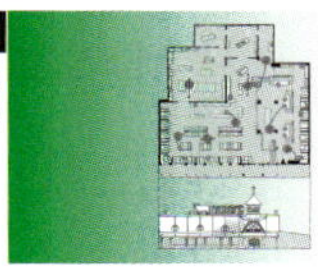

Plan of Todd's Steakhouse, site of one of the game's climactic battles, showing how the interior is a landscape of distraction through carefully placed bottles, bricks and broken crockery.

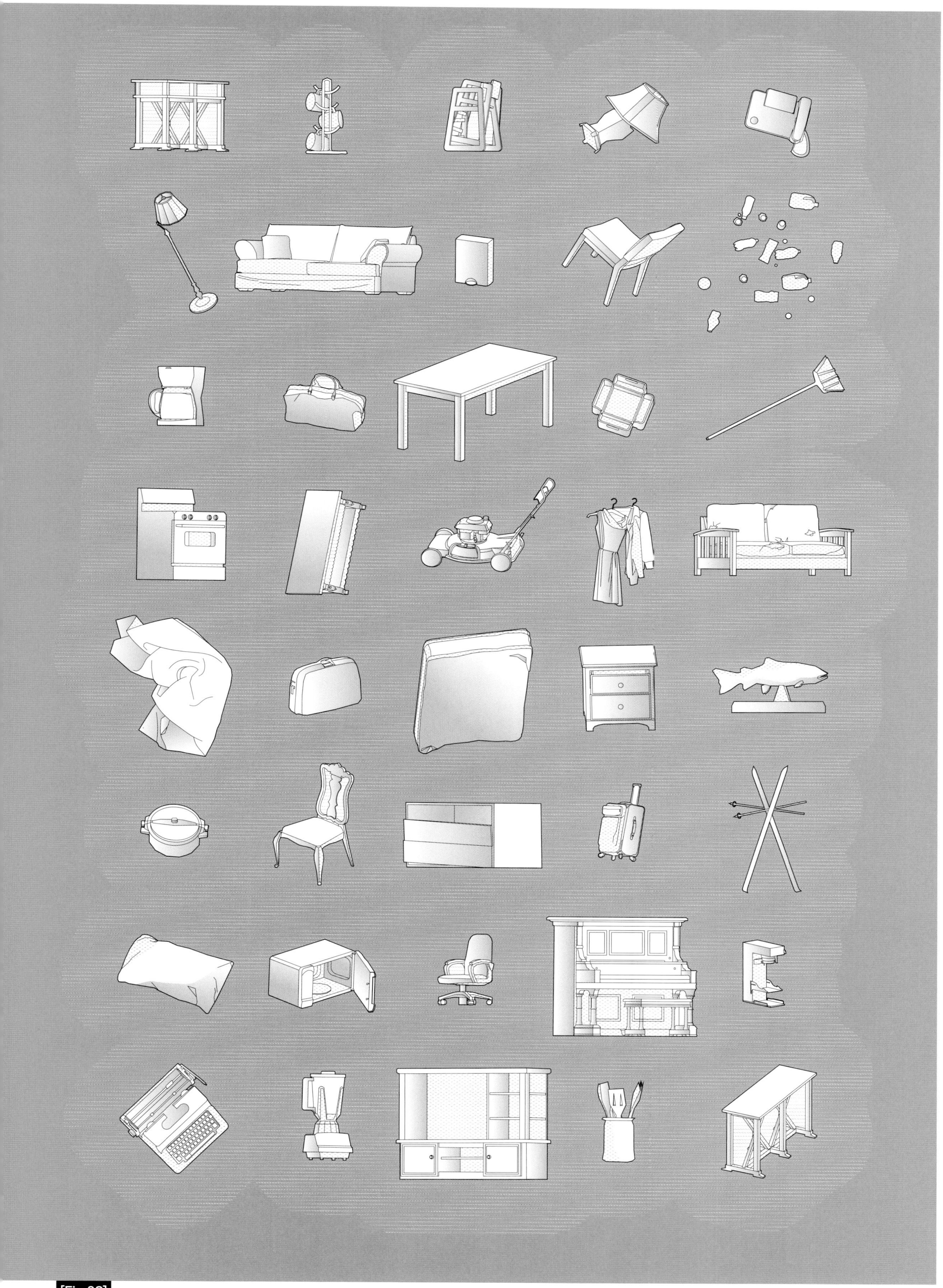

[Fig.08]

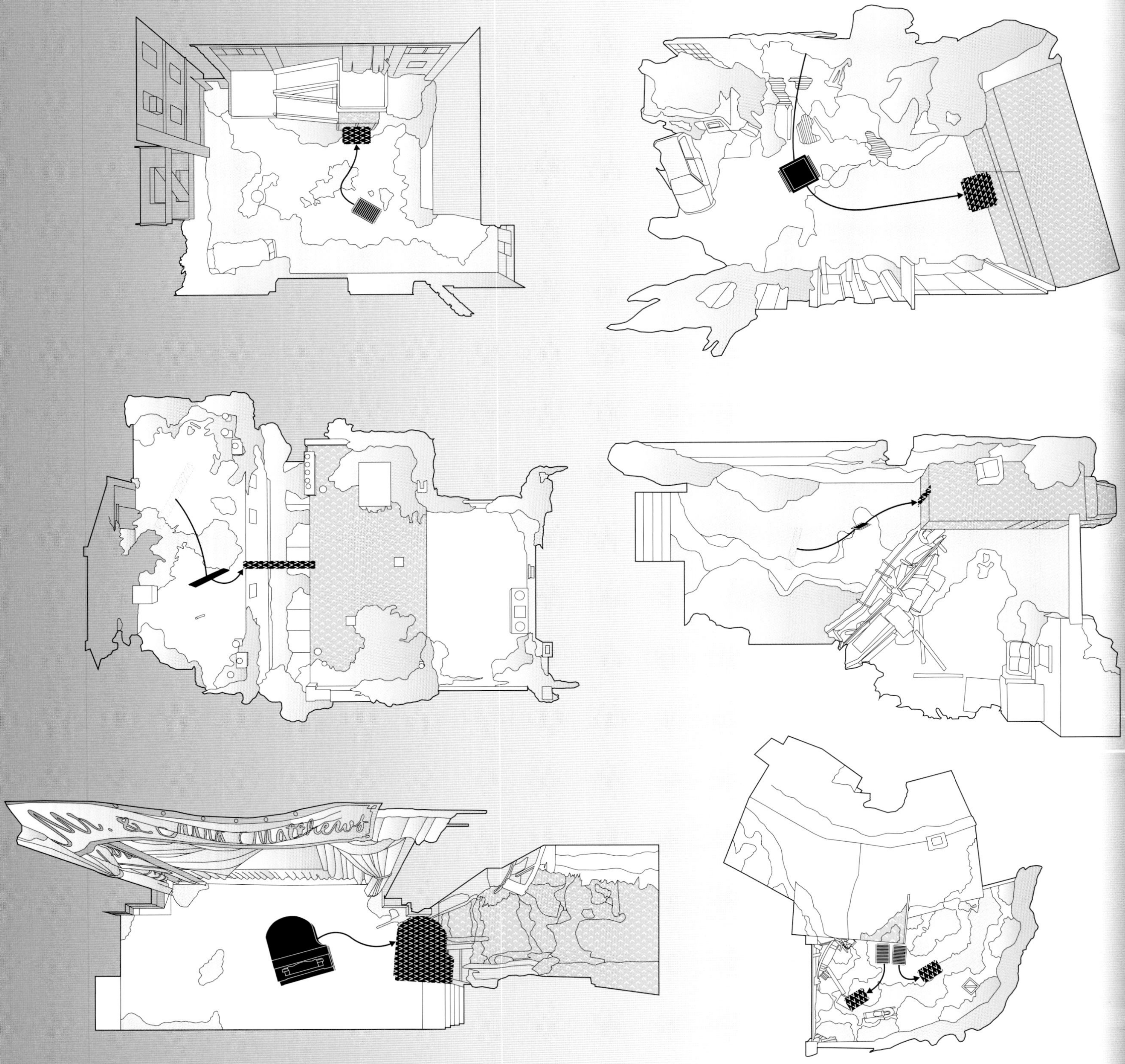

[Fig.09]

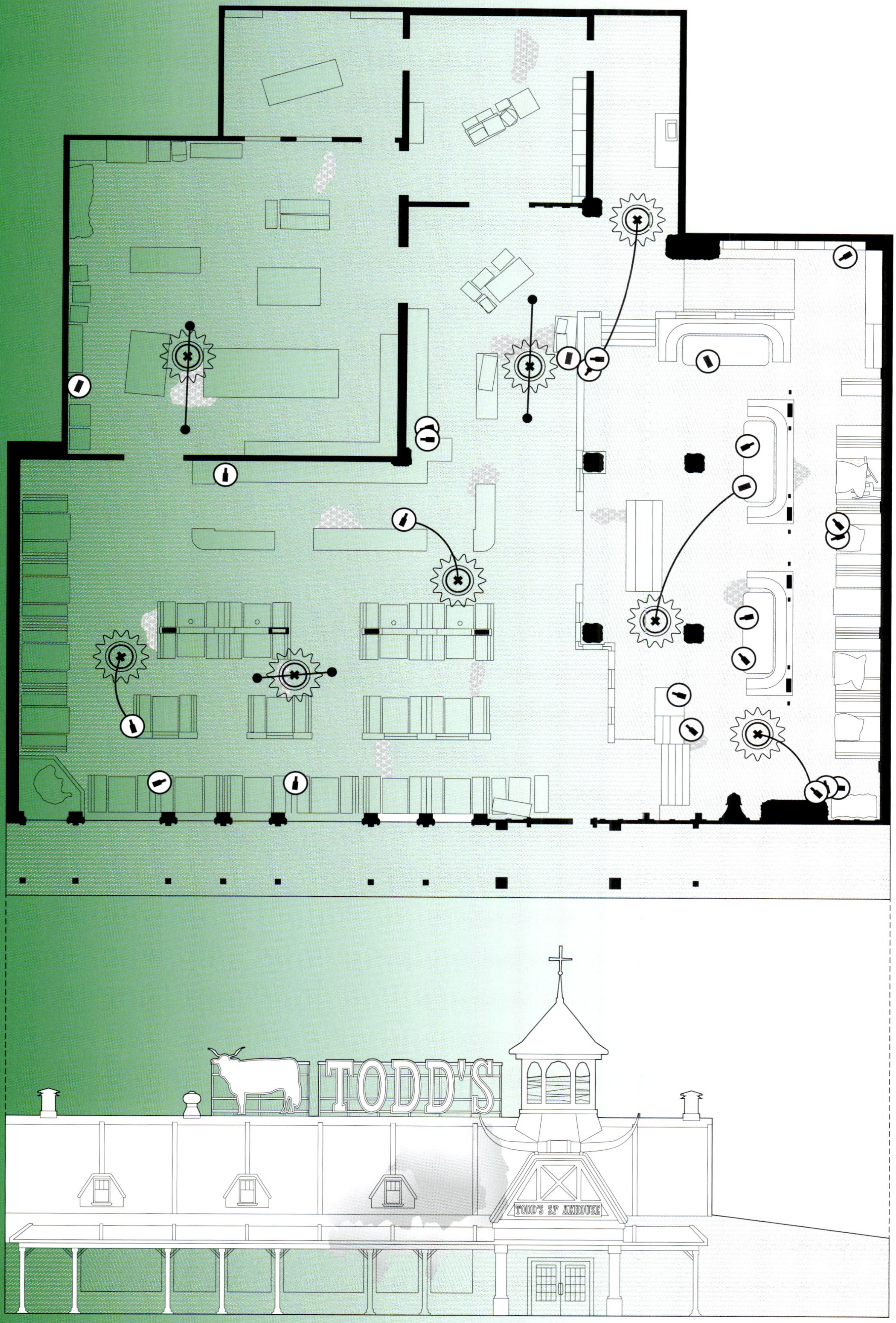

[Fig.10]

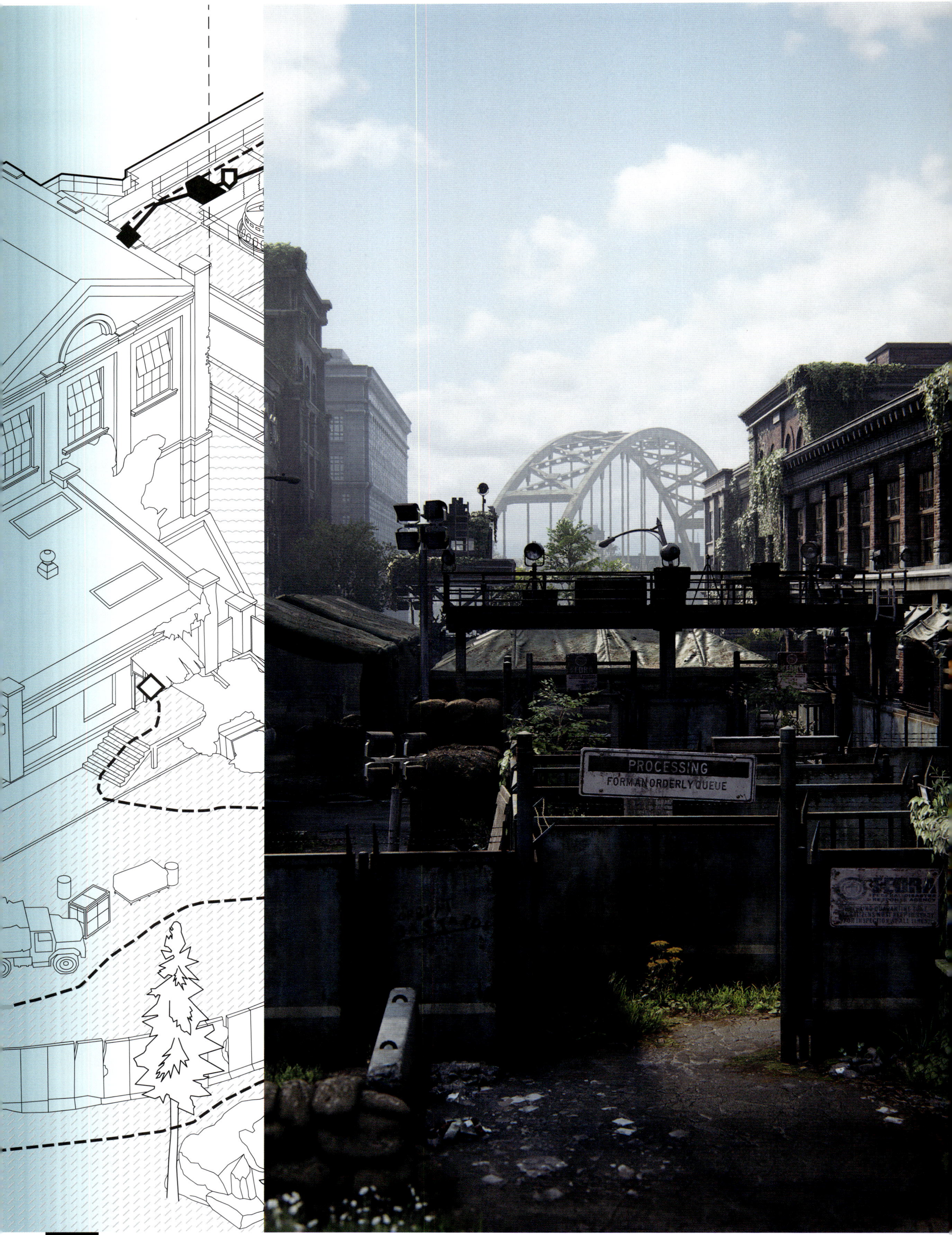

[Fig.11]

10.6

WALLED OFF

✚

The number of everyday objects and spaces that Joel and Ellie encounter allows us to engage with the minutiae of post-pandemic life and societal breakdown. However, there are several areas of the game where the restrictions imposed upon society are more obviously telegraphed. From the first moments of the game in Boston through to our creep towards the bridge in Pittsburgh, a spatial language of fortifications and temporary support structures proliferates, demonstrating lives lived under duress [Fig.11]. The language of Quarantine Zones and FEDRA facilities contrasts with both the natural world beyond and the parts of the city left to the infected.

While fortifications are common diegetic elements, in keeping with its naturalism, *The Last of Us* often attempts to mask its use of level design techniques such as 'chest-high walls'[17] through contextual details that maintain the gritty realism while still providing the necessary elements for gameplay. At the midway point of the game, Joel and Ellie visit Joel's brother Tommy at the hydroelectric dam he is working to reinstate. Tommy guides the visitors through the facility, taking Joel all the way through the generator building to a private room. Mapping this journey through the facility reveals all the props and objects that players will likely make a note of, given they hint at what is to come [Fig.12]. The brothers' discussion is interrupted by attacking hunters, and Joel must fight his way back across the dam, using these elements as cover. As with the bricks and bottles, and the everyday objects of Waverly Township, these built elements have a dual function within the space, as both diegetic props demonstrating the realism of the world, and as evidence of the 'gameness' of the environment. By taking the player on a journey to one end of a building and then back again under different narrative contexts, the dam becomes the emblematic example of the tension between the natural, the cinematic and the game-like in *The Last of Us*.

Joel's journey to the end of the dam and back again, and how the space is encountered differently both times, is a microcosm of *The Last of Us* story. While narratively the game presents an ultimately futile journey of two people across the new American wilderness and back again, nature and the post-pandemic wasteland is perhaps the true star of story. A world in ruins is 'an image of the future as well as the past, encouraging us to imagine not only what is lost, but also what is yet to occur.'[18] Tommy's hydroelectric dam represents a rare moment of hope and looking forward in the game, with the possibility of providing power for the town of Jackson. Rather than fighting nature, this is where people 'symbolically and literally make use of their natural environment by trying to work with it'.[19] At the end of the game, as Joel and Ellie crest a hill and look over Jackson, we return to the suburban idyll that so briefly exists at the start of the story. Gone, for a moment, are the cities and people torn apart by nature's antagonism. Yet we know they are never too far away.

[Fig.11] A VIEW ACROSS PITTSBURGH, WHERE URBAN SPACES ARE AUGMENTED BY THE PRESENCE OF FORTIFICATIONS, PROVIDING COVER AND STEALTH OPPORTUNITIES FOR PLAYERS.

[Fig.12]
PAGES 232–3
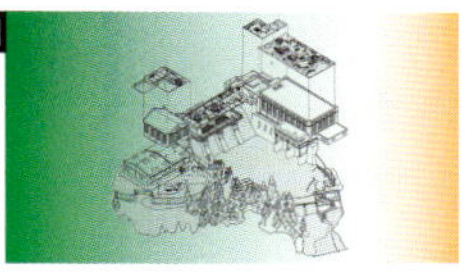
Isometric drawing of 'Tommy's Dam', showing how the architectural space is activated differently in combat, as crates and pieces of machinery suddenly become cover from attackers.

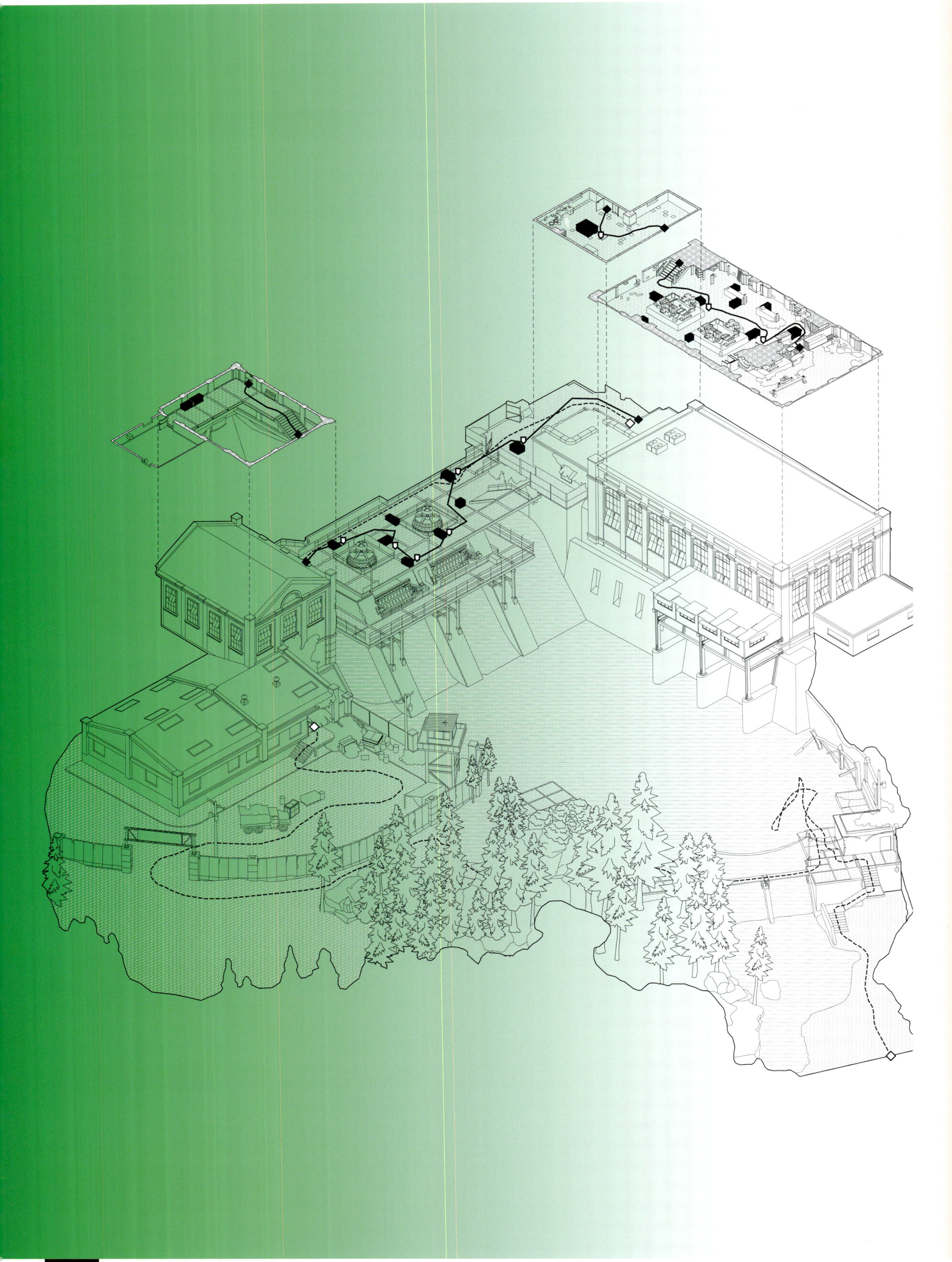

[Fig.12]

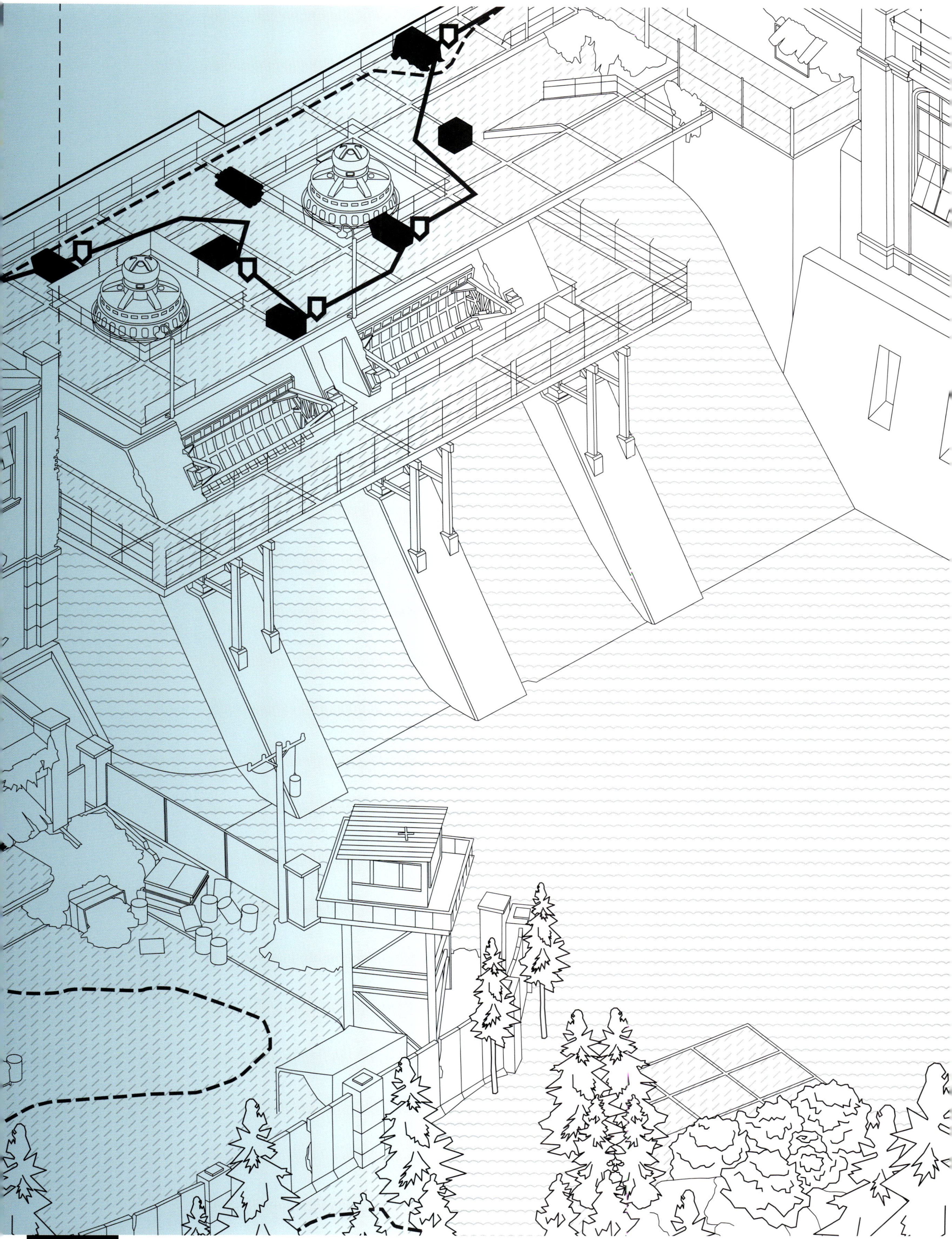

[Fig.12] Detail

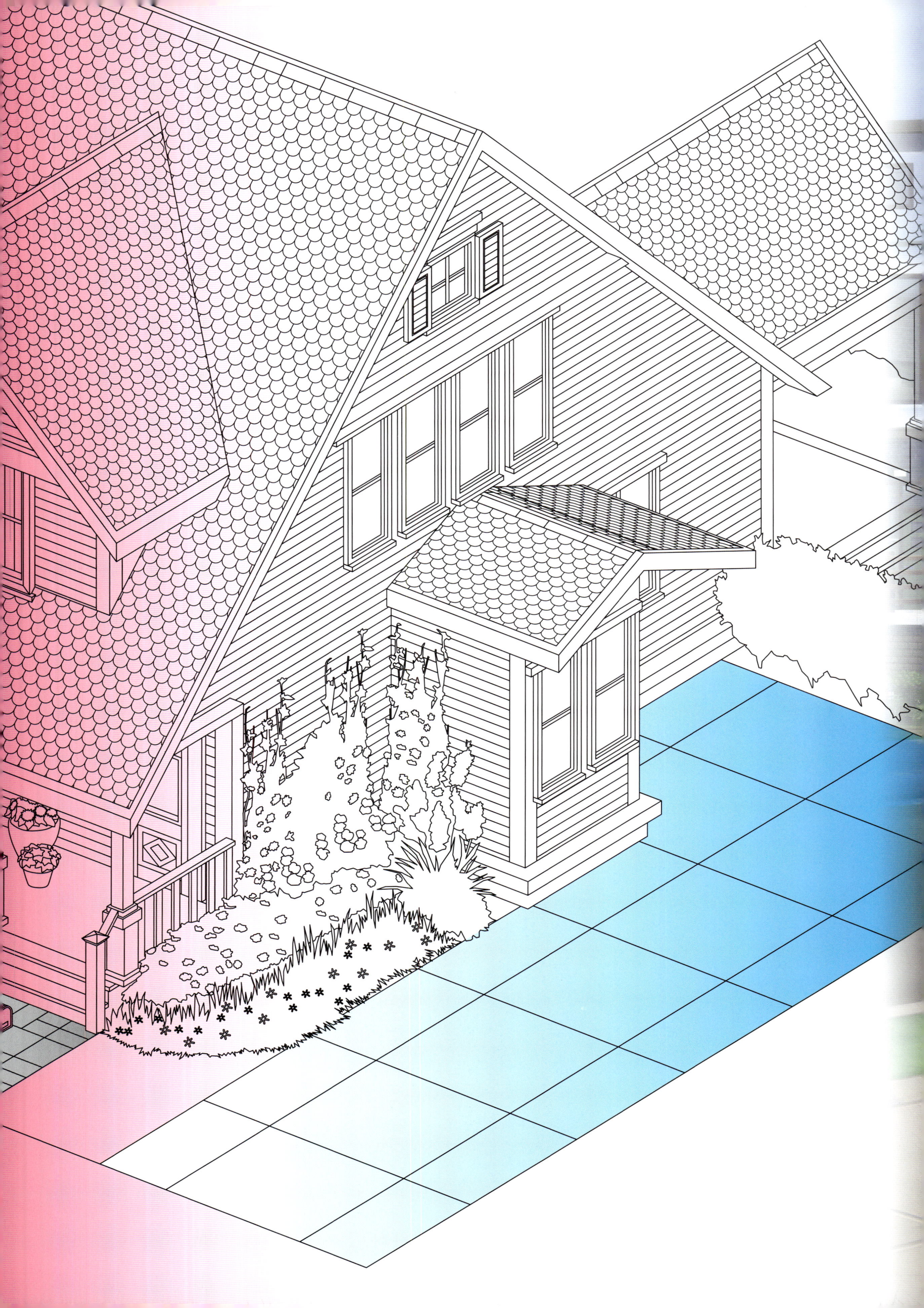

CHAPTER 11

THE SIMS 4

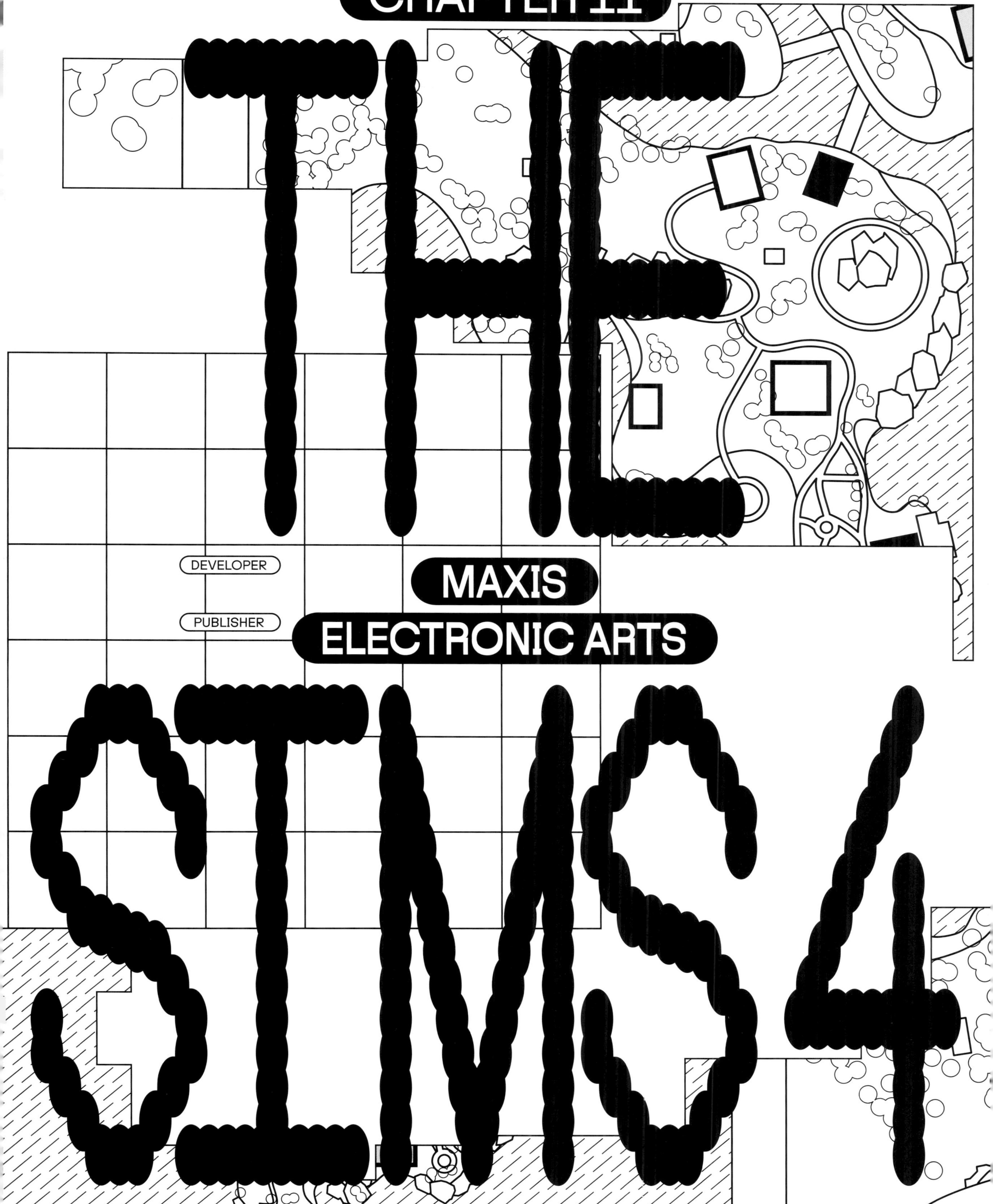

DEVELOPER **MAXIS**

PUBLISHER **ELECTRONIC ARTS**

Platforms: Windows, Mac, PlayStation 4, Xbox One

Year: 2014

ARCHITECTURAL CRITIQUE OF THE INFAMOUS 'GOTH HOUSE', OPHELIA VILLA, WHICH HAS BEEN THE SUBJECT OF NUMEROUS PLAYER RENOVATIONS DUE TO ITS UNDERWHELMING DESIGN.

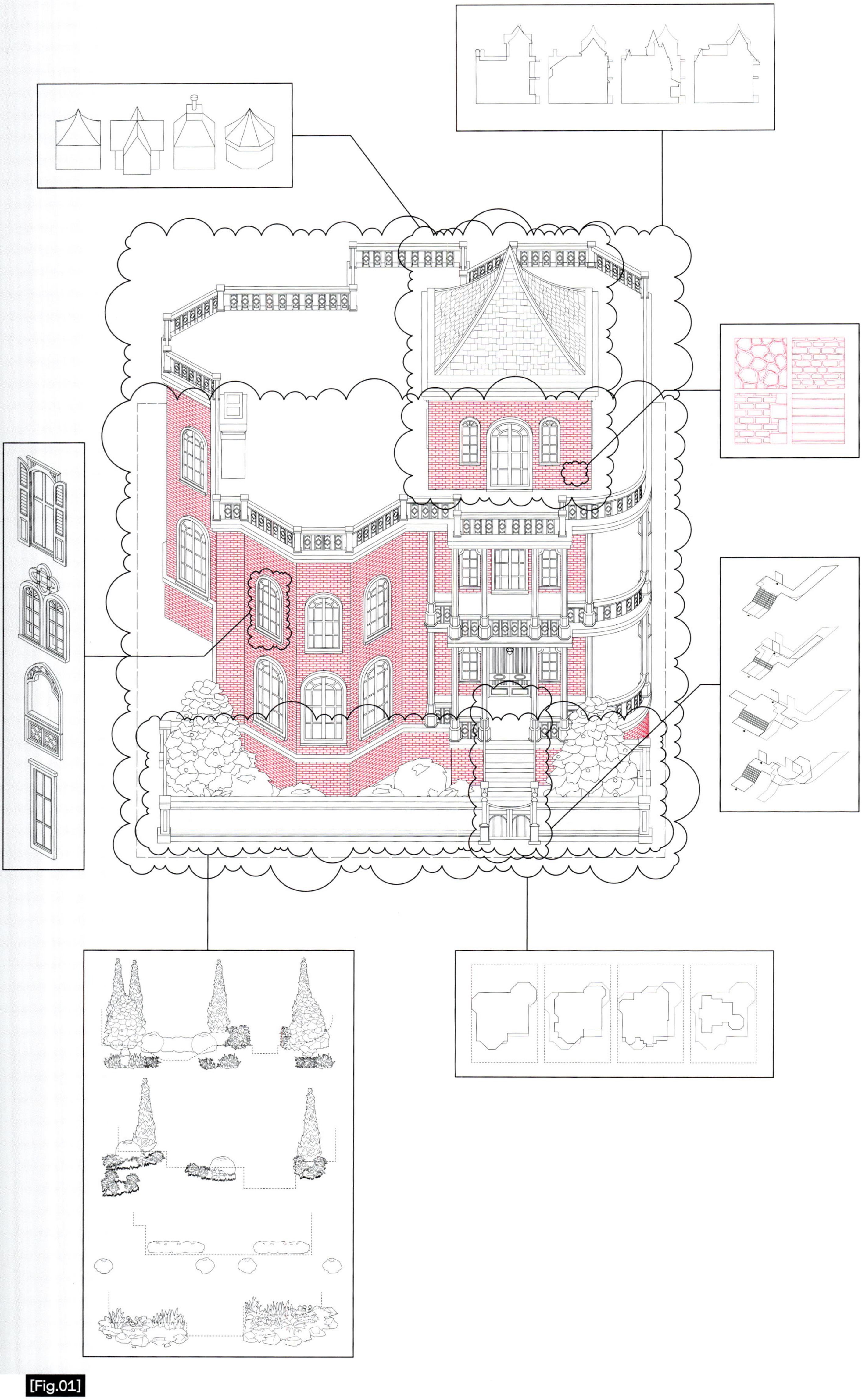

[Fig.01]

11.1

A COLLECTIVE SUBURBIA

The Sims series has been inviting players to explore their suburban, consumerist dreams for twenty-five years and counting, prompting and observing Sims in ways that have arguably mirrored the rise of reality TV and its aesthetics. The 'latest' title in the series, *The Sims 4*, has been thoroughly iterated and expanded upon since its release over a decade ago in 2014. During this time, the palette of possible Sims and their potential lifestyles, jobs and possessions has grown significantly through (at the time of writing) over seventy DLC additions including larger 'Expansion Packs', 'Game Packs' that add more gameplay features, pre-curated 'Kits' and 'Stuff Packs' containing new objects for Sims to purchase. The possible lives of Sims and the spaces they occupy are expanded further by the community structures that underpin the game, both through official tools such as the Gallery, which allows for the sharing of user-generated content, and in the large social media presence established by content-creators across platforms such as YouTube and TikTok.

We can see *The Sims 4* not only as a social simulation of the Sims we create and observe, but also as a social simulation of ourselves, and the desires that we project onto their worlds. This is most clearly defined in the design of Sims' living spaces, where the creativity of the game's player base challenges the assumptions and possibilities of the suburban architecture depicted in the game. Sometimes this might involve doubling down on the traditional and parochial view of what a house should be, but often this results in much more interesting and playful explorations of domestic space, as a game that exemplifies Jesper Juul's argument that 'something previously considered dull can actually be interesting.'[1] In an architectural context, this also mirrors work by Postmodern architects like Denise Scott Brown and Robert Venturi, whose joint project *Learning from Levittown* explored American suburbia and its architecture as a symbol of popular culture.[2]

The Sims player community has always been similarly analytical and outspoken about the developer-created architecture in the game, discussing how well these designs facilitate the needs of their inhabitants and blend into their surrounding neighbourhoods. No other building has received more critique than Ophelia Villa in Willow Creek, colloquially known as the 'Goth House', a residential lot that is home to long-standing Sims, the Goth family. In her video *The History & Evolution of Goth Manor in The Sims*,[3] YouTube user Savannah Goth analyses how the Goth family lore influences the changes to their residences across *The Sims 1, 2 and 3*, discussing how the style, layout and contents of the house relate to different events in the family's timeline. When it comes to *The Sims 4* iteration, many players are underwhelmed by its plain, blocky exterior, which seems pared down in contrast to its ornate Victorian appearance in earlier versions of the game. Just Nora Gaming expresses concern about the size of the house in relation to its lot, and internally, the oversized bathrooms, bland kids' bedrooms and off-theme furniture.[4]

Other players, such as Deligracy, revert to *The Sims 3* Goth House as inspiration,[5] while Devon Bumpkin alters the wall proportions to streamline the overall building volume, and more practically, fixes the dislocation between the internal and external chimney locations.[6] Other players opt for more ornate landscaping, wall textures and window types, to reintroduce the eerie grandeur to the house, befitting of its beloved residents. By drawing the Goth House's exterior and indicating these player alterations through 'revision clouds', we have presented the building as a marked-up architectural drawing that is typically produced to track the changes made to it during the design development [Fig.01]. This supports the observation that certain details of the building receive a particular focus from the player base. These codified drawing graphics communicate how the design has been changed over time, and in this context we can see how the Goth House has been constantly iterated upon by its players through a collaborative design process.

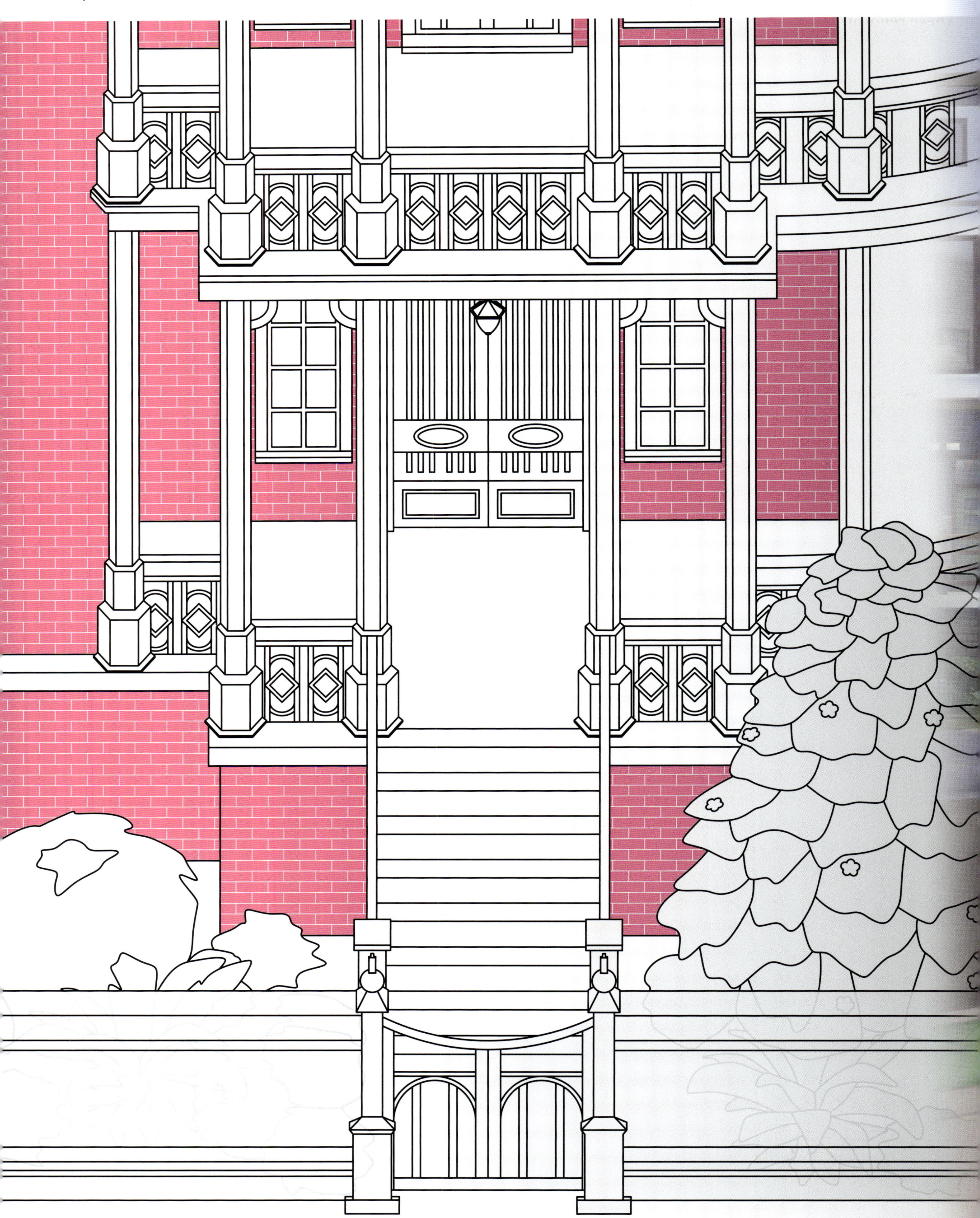

These renovations are showcased in *The Sims 4* Gallery, which is an in-built content-sharing resource that allows players to upload their designs and access those of others, for importing directly into their game. Organized into Households (Sim player characters), Lots (buildings), Rooms (interior spaces) and, most recently, Tattoos (for application onto Sims' bodies), players browse content and can organize it by downloads, favourites and newest uploads. For some time, the most downloaded house on the Gallery is Blue Moon noCC by Cayrees, which they describe as a 'modern house near a river' [Fig.02]. Uploaded in 2014, this two-bedroom, two-bathroom residential lot has amassed over 3.1 million downloads to date, yet it remains unclear whether this is due to the design itself, or the curiosity generated by the Gallery's ranking system. In a YouTube walk-through of the house by The Sims 4 Real Estates, they describe its strength as being 'very plausible... grand but not too grand,'[7] highlighting the readymade yet relatable nature of popular Sims builds.

Blue Moon noCC's boxy, interlocking volumes and permeable external walls are encircled by rainbow-lit fountains, BBQ and gardening areas and a Texas-shaped pool, catering to different lifestyle choices. These features are complimented by a series of functional, 'lived-in' interior spaces that occupy two floors, alluding to the realities of its inhabitants. Due to *The Sims 4*'s somewhat limited base-game palette, Blue Moon noCC feels at home slotted into most streetscapes, its polite and seemingly generic semi-modernist style working within many different contexts.

[Fig.01] Detail

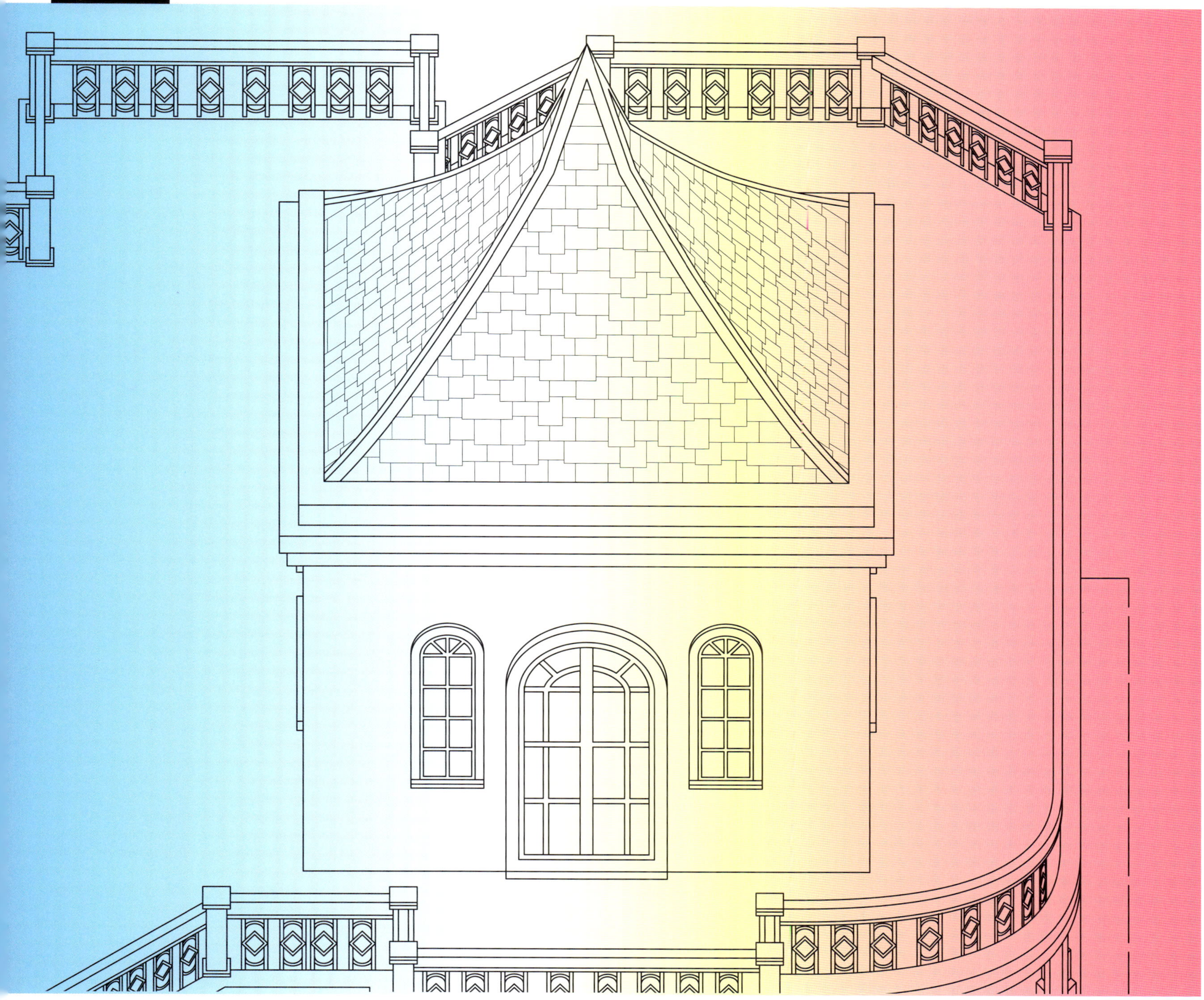

[Fig.02] PAGES 240–1

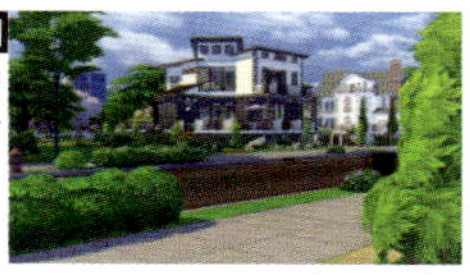

The most popular player-created lot on *The Sims 4* Gallery, with more than three-million downloads to date.

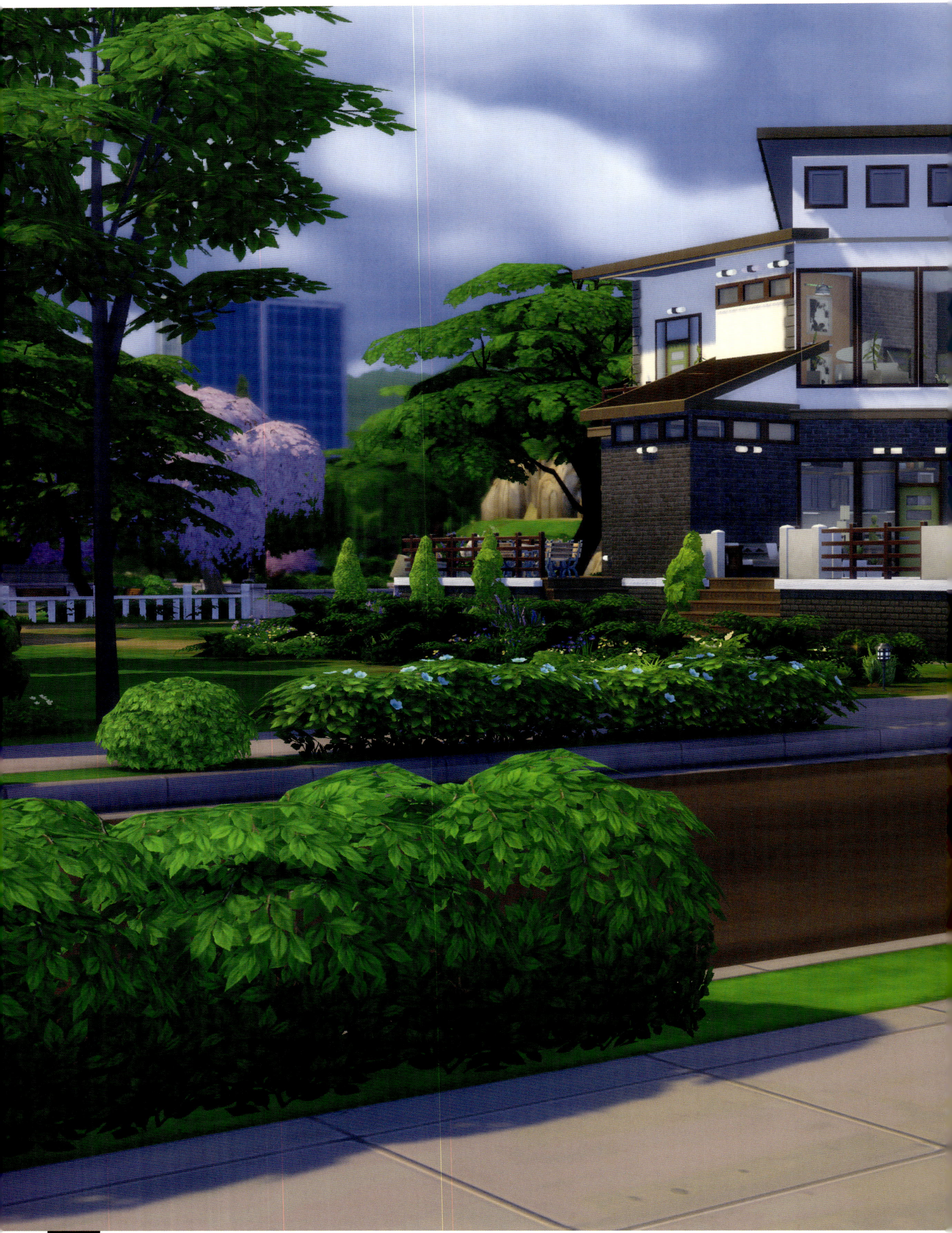

[Fig.02]

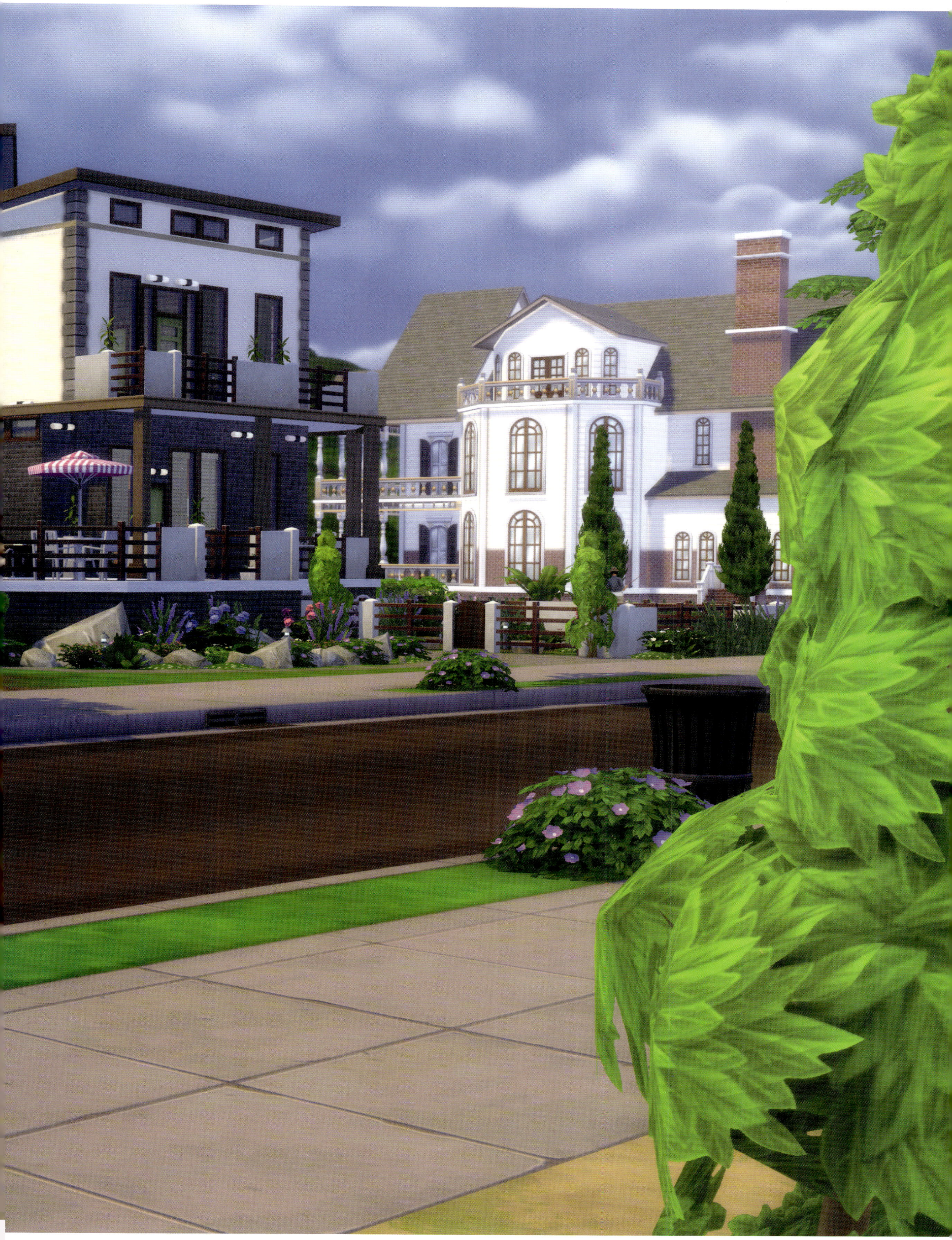

11.2

THE HACK HOUSE

The Sims' enduring popularity on TikTok can be attributed to its community-centric design, meme-worthy content through user-generated narratives and builds, and cosy nostalgia the game holds for both longtime and potential players. This isn't limited to the latest Sims instalment – Petrana Radulovic discusses a new cult following for *The Sims 2* content on 'SimsTok', as the older games become harder to play on modern consoles,[8] sparking curiosity despite their mechanical and aesthetic limitations. Exploiting the build system within *The Sims 4*, user mewbuilds' self-confessed 'chaotic' builds[9] showcase a number of gravity-defying postmodern fantasies that include houses shaped like stiletto shoes, AriZona Tea and a tall, narrow 'Homezempic' house trilogy constructed within a footprint that is two grid squares wide. Playing with the expectations of a suburban home is also something that architects have explored, such as Jennifer Bonner in her project *Domestic Hats*, where she creates new architectural forms by copying, pasting and deforming the shapes of suburban houses in Atlanta, subverting the typical domestic form into something new.[10] The work of social media designers resonates with the types of architectural research produced by Bonner and others, emphasizing a desire to challenge meaning and form in the design of homes.

Another example that supports this is the circulation of viral 'build hacks', ever-popular on the platform as a way to challenge the game's build system and create new design possibilities. One approach is to hide objects within other objects, forcing them to become interactive or incorporate new desired functionality [Fig.03]. For example, a kotatsu table is scaled down and placed underneath a low coffee table to allow a laptop to be placed on top, and a Sim to sit on the floor cross-legged and use it. In another scenario, a cushioned stool is scaled up to become a large, round bed, and a single bed is embedded within it to enable a Sim to lie down on the stool-bed. Another category of build hacks involves enabling cheats such as 'bb.moveobjects' and 'ALT-placing' to allow for greater flexibility in moving, scaling, rotating and positioning objects into their desired positions, free of the build system's grid constraints. For further precision in placing objects on the Y axis, sacrificial floors below or above the level of the object can be created to place and reposition the objects, which are then deleted. These act as digital scaffolding to support the required effect. This creates a new way of designing space that plays with the meaning of objects where, as A.M May writes, 'the videos thus serve as representations of literacies that can educate other players about game functions beneath the game's visible interface.'[11]

While build challenges proliferated in earlier versions of the game, prominent streamer lilsimsie popularized the 'shell challenge' – a build challenge set by creators who upload an empty 'shell' of a building that demarcates an overall envelope for other players to transform into a fully designed build. Shells can take different shapes and forms, appearing as animals or food items when viewed from above, or employing obscure geometry that seems impossible to transform into a plausible build [Fig.04]. While the architectural responses to each shell challenge abide by the same principles, strictly following the shell's exterior walls and footprint, they are often wildly diverse in their overall appearance, showcased through lilsimsie's recurring YouTube videos, 'Touring Your Incredible Builds in *The Sims 4* (Shell Challenge)'.[12] These design challenges inadvertently explore one of the great fascinations of architectural design – the relationship between the inside and outside of a building. While the large glass windows of Modernist design are intended to remove the boundary between inside and out, shell challenges fit into a longer historical lineage of architecture where, as Robert Venturi argues, a building 'can include things within things, as well as spaces within spaces' that ultimately mean 'its interior configurations can contrast with its container.'[13]

[Fig.04] PAGE 244

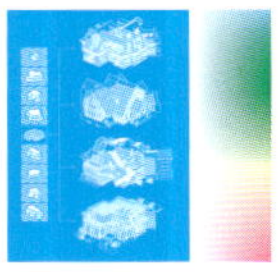

Players set each other 'shell challenges' to showcase different house designs that comply with a fixed overall envelope of walls, heights and floors.

VIRAL BUILD HACKS THAT SUBVERT THE CONVENTIONAL USE OF ITEMS AND BUILDING TECHNIQUES, EXTENDING THE ARCHITECTURAL POSSIBILITIES OF THE GAME.

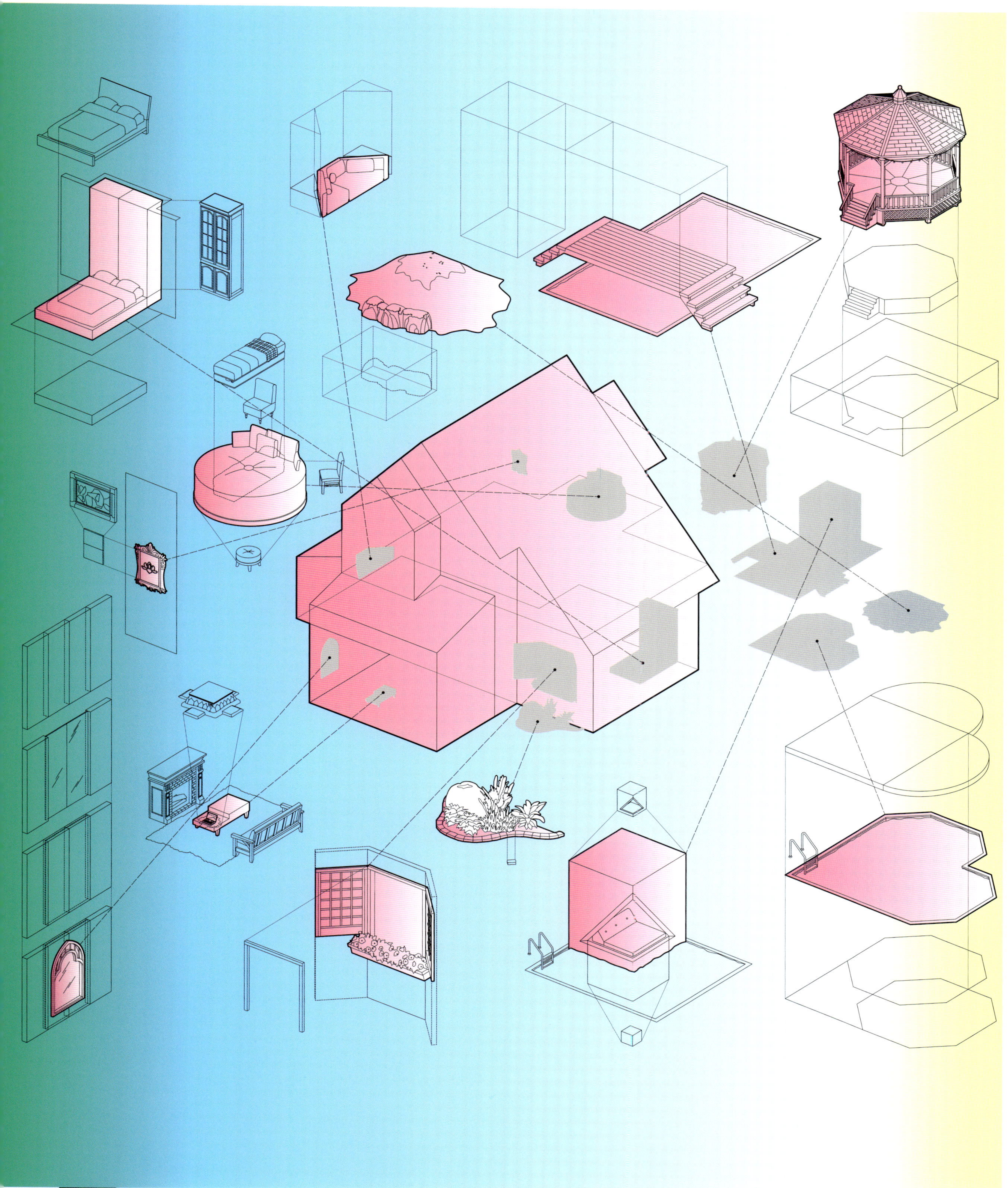

[Fig.03]

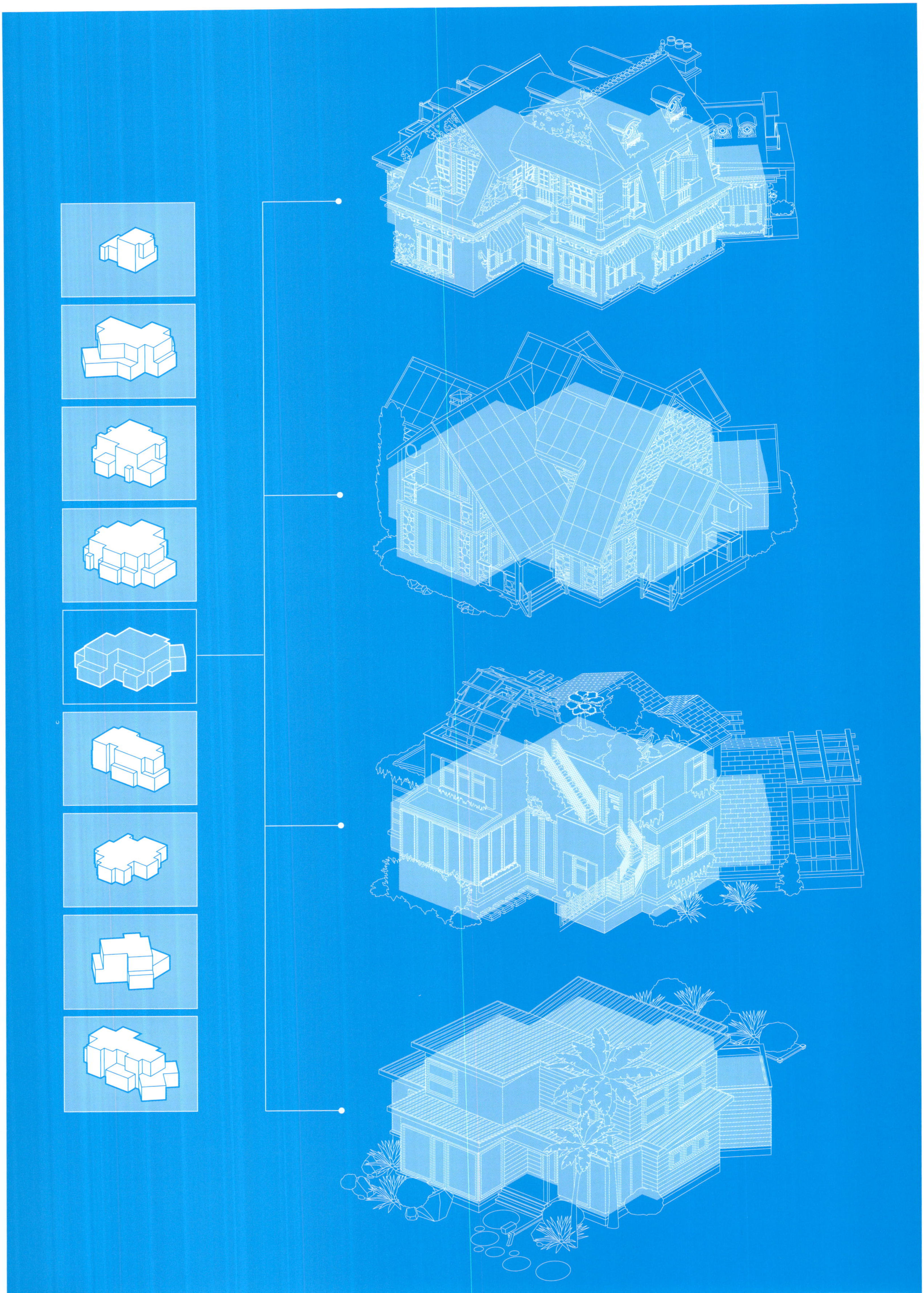

[Fig.04]

11.3
BORROWING BLUEPRINTS

The Sims 4's build system comprises of an architectural design tool for modular construction, with options to build either from scratch using the components offered, or by downloading ready-made lots and rooms via the Gallery as a starting point for further customization. Organized into categories – including roof sculptures, roofs, foundations, walls, trims, stairs, columns, spandrels, doors, windows, wall sculptures, fences and gates, as well as landscaping features – players have a relatively detailed scope to engage with the most fundamental components of a building. By compiling these elements together into a taxonomy of architectural forms, we can see that the base game's palette is constrained to a North American suburban style, blending modern and traditional trends that emphasize the game's familiar and neutral agency [Fig.05]. When placed, components snap to a grid (with each grid square translating to approximately 0.8 m / 2.6 ft in real world scale), which imposes limitations in the density and sizing of objects, leading to the popularity of move cheats, as previously discussed. Players can build up to four levels above ground, and two below, further reinforcing the low-rise low-density nature of the game. Try as we might, it appears impossible to fully escape suburbia while designing our Sims' worlds.

For all its component-based intricacy, the structural logic of *The Sims 4* remains relatively primitive, with walls, floors and roofs assuming the same implied thickness, regardless of their location or materials. The game 'flattens' this level of architectural detail into one value, making it difficult to understand the structural or 'real-world' implications of different material choices. American suburban development, for example, was predicated on the rapid construction of timber frame houses, in contrast to different construction methods using materials like brick, concrete or earth across the globe. As such, materiality is fundamental to understanding vernacular styles of housing. While this information isn't necessary for buildings to stand up in the game, it removes a degree of realism from the architecture, which is noted by its players. User libra00 posts on Reddit about variable wall thicknesses,[14] in order to accurately replicate the plan of a house that has heavy external walls with niches, and thinner internal walls. User Sharp_Replacement789 advises to 'always build for gameplay',[15] to avoid throwing the house dimensions off if modelling from a real-world plan. By drawing a Sims house how it might actually be constructed, using a timber framing system typical in North American housing construction, we can see variation across the form of the building, which would remove the homogenous material thicknesses that we witness in the game [Fig.06]. If we were to realize a similar domestic building in brick, concrete blockwork or rammed earth, the structural differences would become even more obvious.

Building houses from real-world architectural blueprints has always been a common trend in The Sims, for both accuracy and nostalgia. User ulrick7 replicates Sears Modern Homes – a popular residential building typology sold via mail order in the first half of the 20th century in North America – as templates for renovation challenges. This is another form of user-created build challenge, where a house is uploaded by one player, and renovated by others. While the use of Sears homes in *The Sims 4* is not exclusive to ulrick7, they take this a step further by presenting these houses as dilapidated ruins located in Detroit, echoing the real-world fate of the suburban dream that Sears homes faced due to their decline during the Great Depression. Embellishing these builds with overgrown landscaping, graffiti, rubbish piles and chain-link fencing, they serve as emotive templates for other players to restore to their former picture-perfect glory [Fig.07].

[Fig.05] PAGES 246–7

Catalogue of architectural elements available to players in the base game's build mode, including roof sculptures, roofs, foundations, walls, trims, stairs, columns, spandrels, doors, windows, wall sculptures, fences and gates.

[Fig.06] PAGE 248

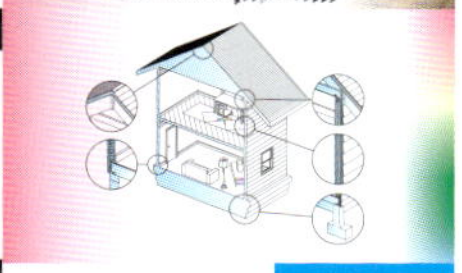

Revealing the 'flattening' of architectural detail in *The Sims 4*, by speculating on how different material junctions in the game might actually be constructed.

[Fig.07] PAGE 249

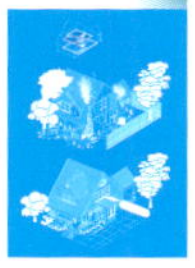

In 'fixer upper' challenges, players create dilapidated houses for others to renovate. User ulrick7 bases his designs on fictional abandoned Sears houses in Detroit, using suburban templates from the physical world.

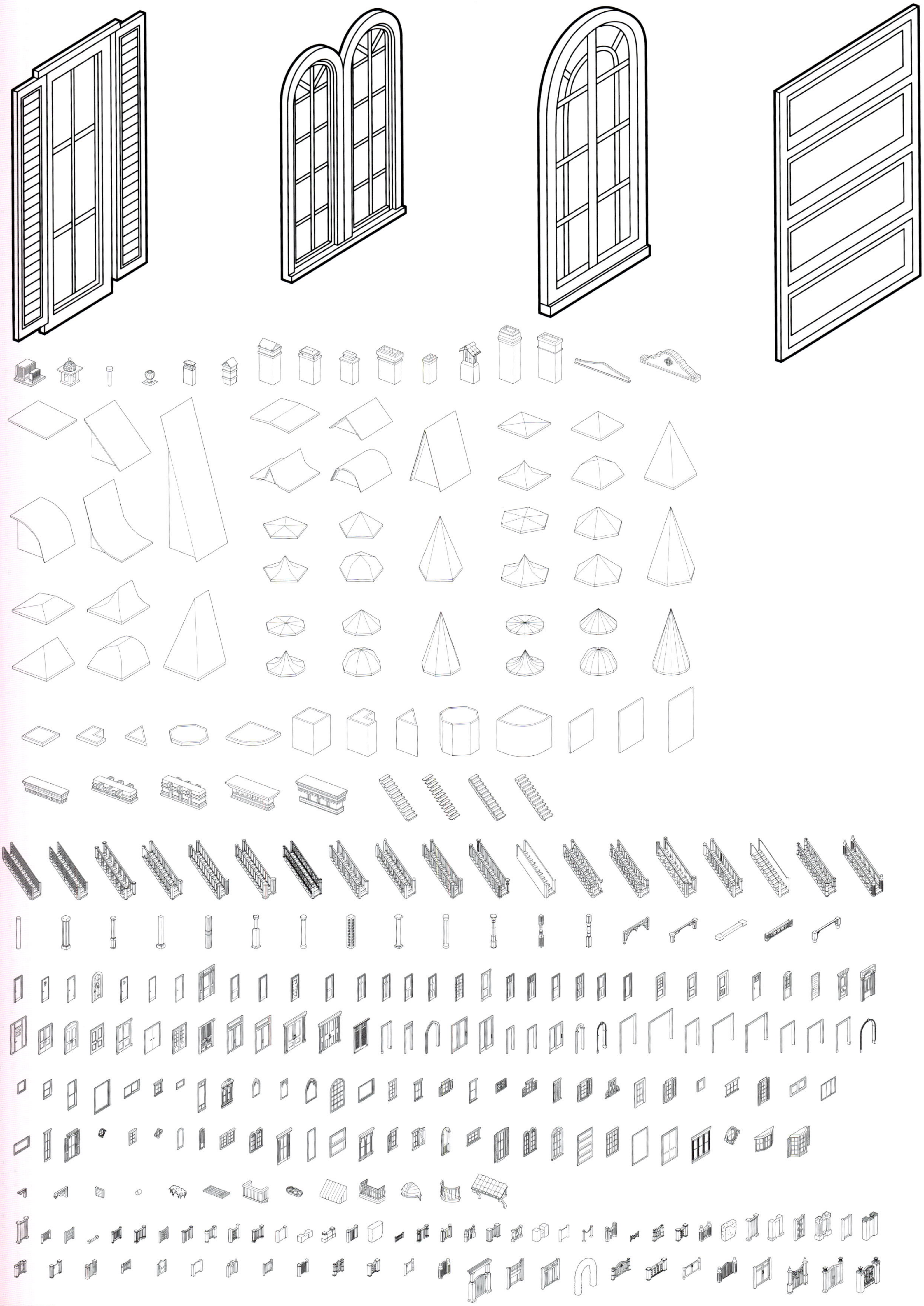

[Fig.05]

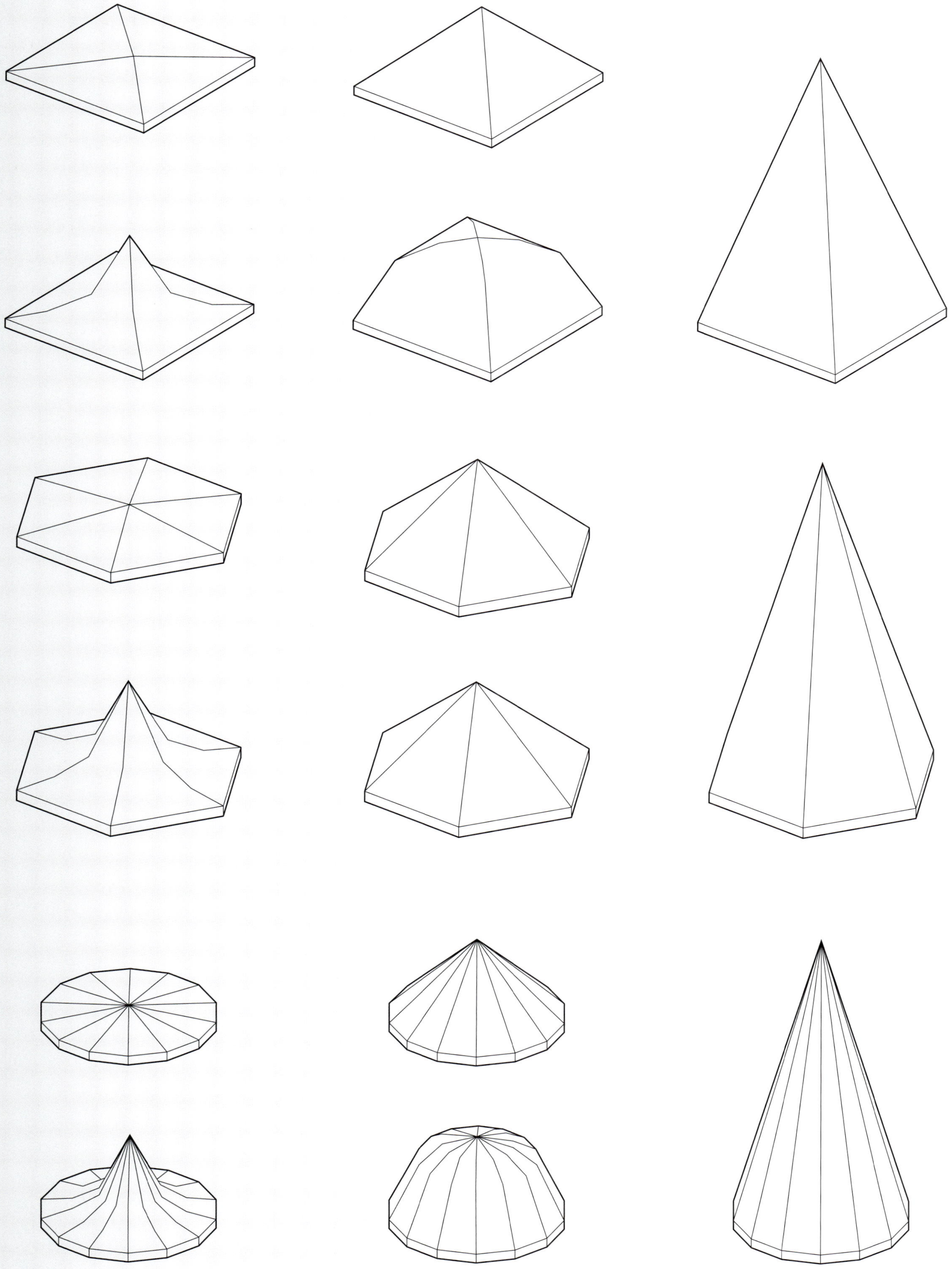

[Fig.05] Detail

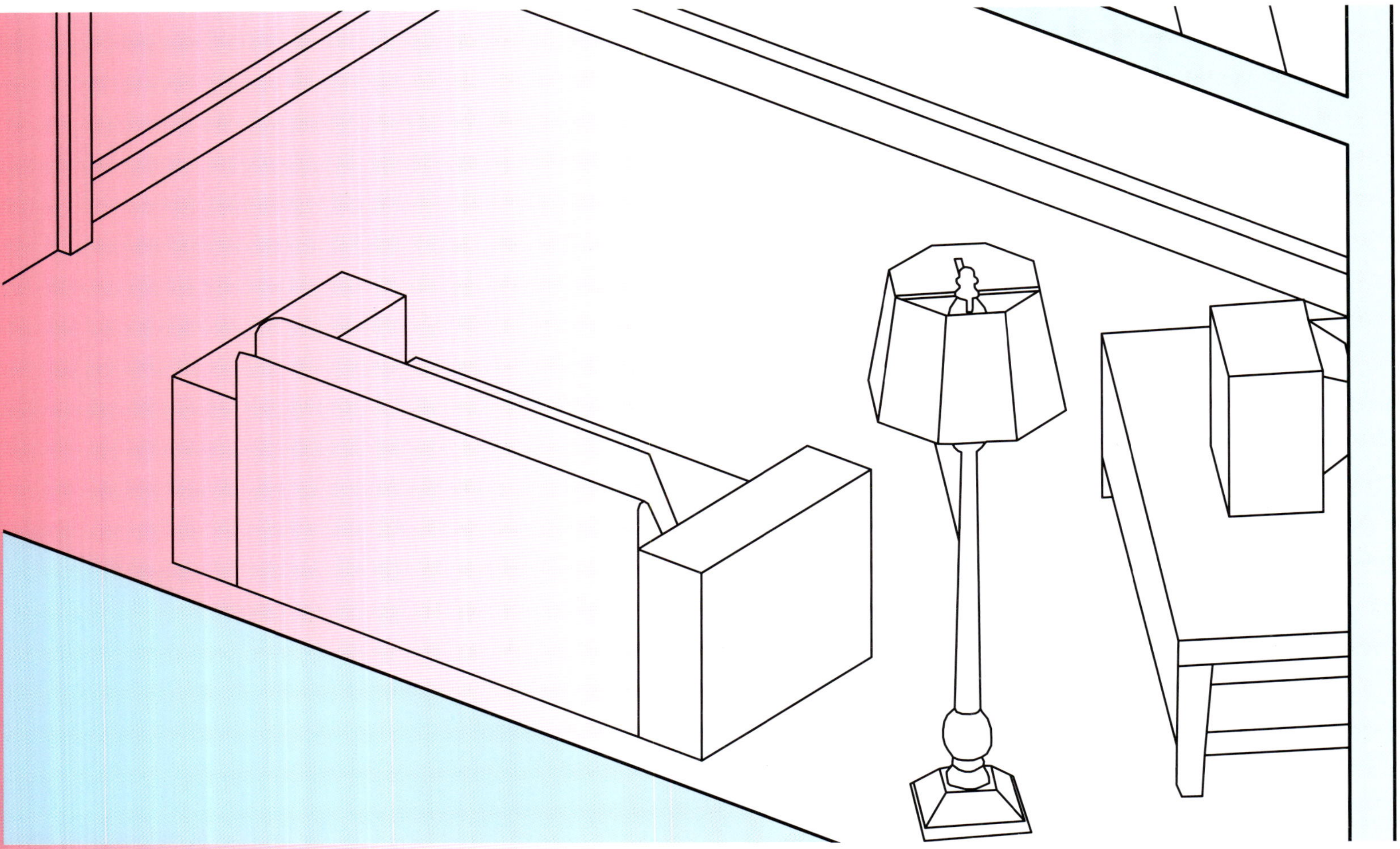

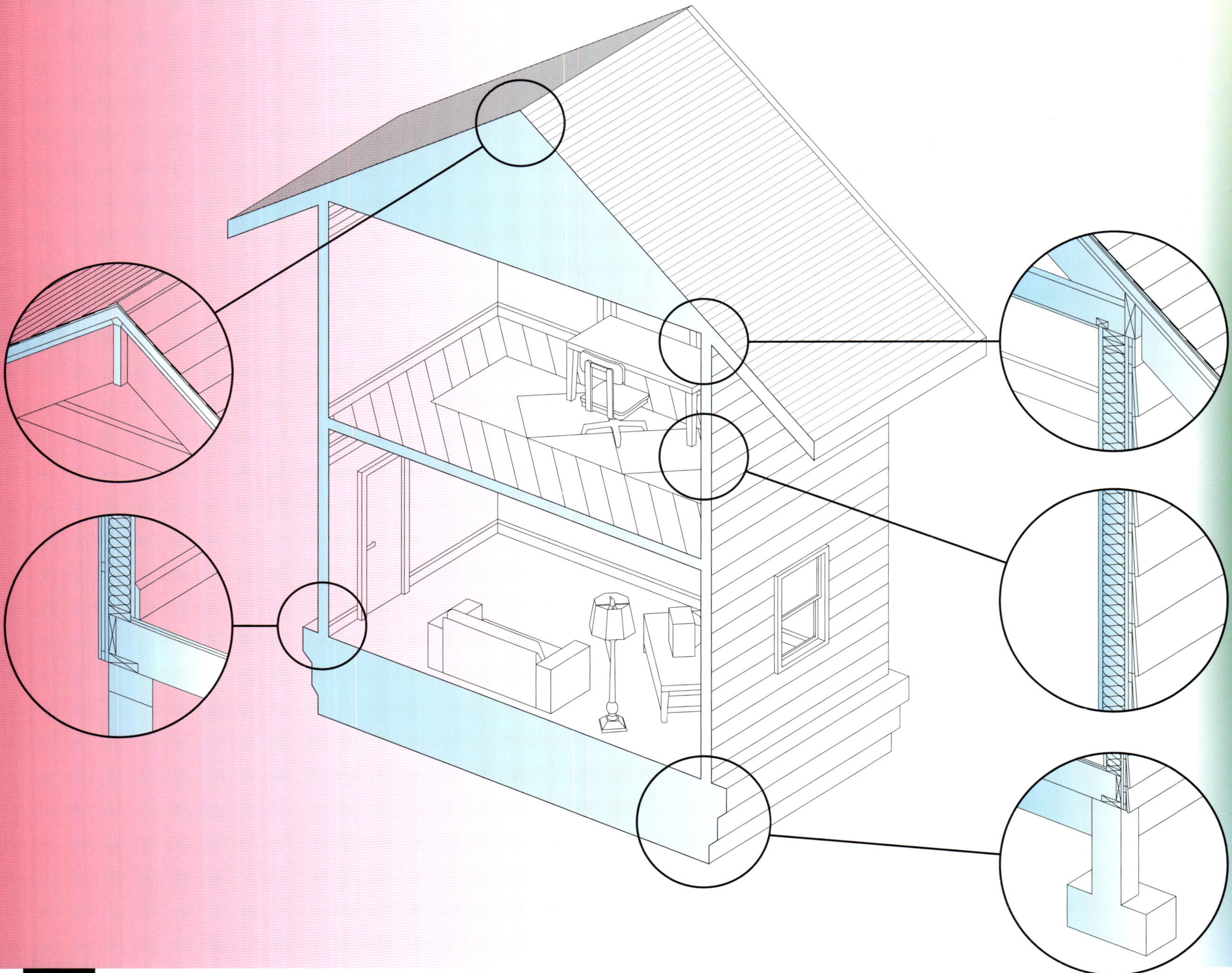

[Fig.06]

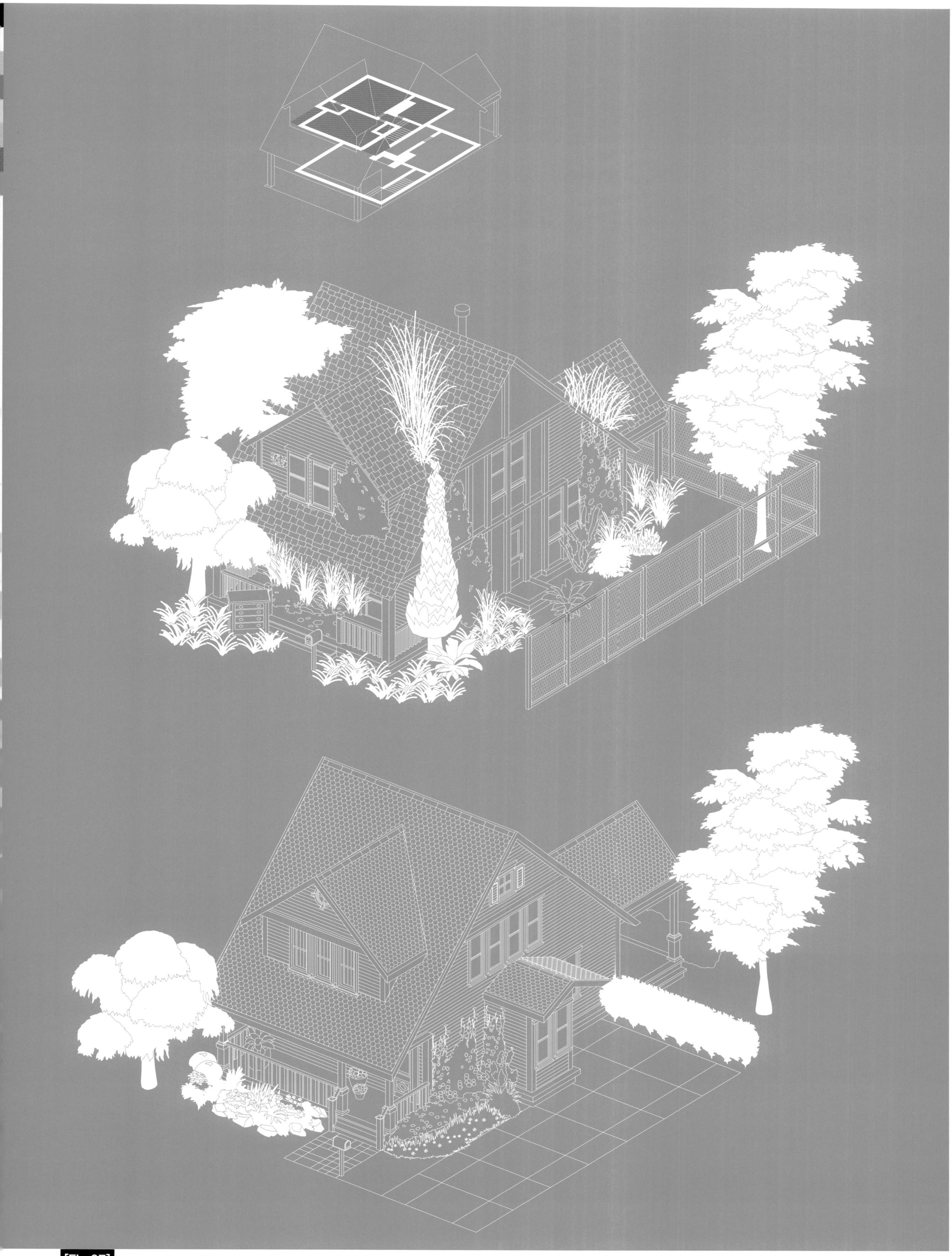

[Fig.07]

11.4 DIGITAL VERNACULARS

Property development in *The Sims 4* takes on several forms, from moving into an existing 'starter home' or buying an empty site, to bulldozing what previously existed to flatten the terrain [Fig.08]. Wiping the slate clean in the game echoes real-life property development in suburban areas of America such as Lake Las Vegas in the Nevada desert, which ceased construction when the 2008 recession hit, leaving partially-completed lots abandoned in the desert.[16] This emphasizes the American landscape as a speculative suburban dream, and a blank canvas to reiterate these different dreams upon. Further creative freedom can be achieved using cheats like 'bb.enablefreebuild', which allows players to build outside of the constraints of a lot, creating higher density neighbourhoods. Decorative lots – those that aren't playable and inhabit the outskirts of a neighbourhood – cannot be as freely deleted without third-party mods and therefore continue to define the architectural characteristics of the area, as aesthetic backdrops to the player's intentions.

The initial release of *The Sims 4* in 2014 provided players with only two contrasting world maps, the New Orleans-inspired Willow Creek, and the Southwestern/Californian desert of Oasis Springs, followed a year later by the modern suburbia of Newcrest. Since then, expansion packs have been released annually, adding new worlds and providing players with further possibilities for spatial exploration. Alongside new worlds, the expansion packs also introduce new inventory items for building and decorating houses in line with the new architectural theme, extending the design possibilities. The worlds include the dense, high-rise city of San Myshuno; the tropical archipelago of Sulani; the Japanese-inspired mountain resort of Mt. Komorebi; and the quaint English countryside of Henford-on-Bagley, amongst others. Within each world is a series of neighbourhoods with different residential lots – empty, starter home or occupied – and different commercial lots with buildings that include museums, nightclubs, gyms, libraries, bars, parks and lounges [Fig.09]. By mapping the plans of these worlds, we can see that the typical form of suburban drift starts to be challenged, allowing for new architectural influences to shape the player's designs.

Across these suburbs, the most commonly occurring commercial typology is the bar, which appears in fourteen worlds and provides a communal social point for gathering. Ironically, the prevalence of the bar as a social space in *The Sims 4* might challenge recent research that shows drinking cultures have shifted even in the globe's thirstiest cultures, with the number of UK pubs[17] and Japanese izakayas seemingly declining.[18] By collecting all these bars into a typological drawing, we can see how each building is adapted to fit with its corresponding world, taking on new forms depending on the location, reflected in its identity [Fig.10]. At the same time we can track how common details are preserved across these varying buildings, namely that their design is always centred around the space of the bar, providing a social hub for the inhabitants of the world.

Each of these worlds is different, starting to more accurately represent the diversity of living conditions beyond the American suburbs. Seen through screenshots, some of these worlds start to appear complex in a way that was not possible in earlier iterations of the game or its predecessors. The biggest and most densely populated world in *The Sims 4* is Windenburg, released as part of the *Get Together* expansion pack in 2015, presenting a quaint, coastal town inspired by European gothic architecture, 'full of history, steeped in mystery.'[19] The world comprises four neighbourhoods, including the architecturally distinct Olde Platz, densely packed with half-timbered buildings that create a unique, village feel [Fig.11]. While, as previously mentioned, these buildings do not possess the real 'fachwerk'[20] timbering of the structures that inspired them, the European-scale density of their relationship provides quite a different context for observing the life of Sims, especially the social relationships of some of Windenburg's more idiosyncratic inhabitants, including a DJ, a pair of bros and a successful criminal, whose wife has mysteriously disappeared.

[Fig.08]
PAGES 252–3

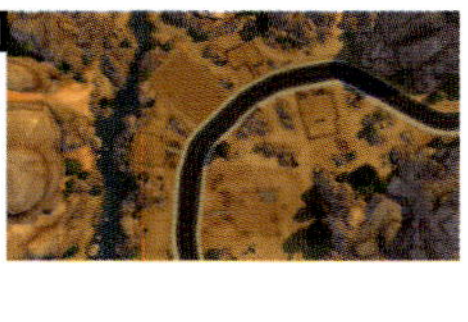

Plan of empty and demolished lots in Oasis Springs, awaiting further development.

URBAN MORPHOLOGIES OF ALL TWENTY-SEVEN WORLDS IN THE GAME, INDICATING PLAYABLE, OCCUPIED AND COMMERCIAL LOTS ACROSS DIFFERENT NEIGHBOURHOODS.

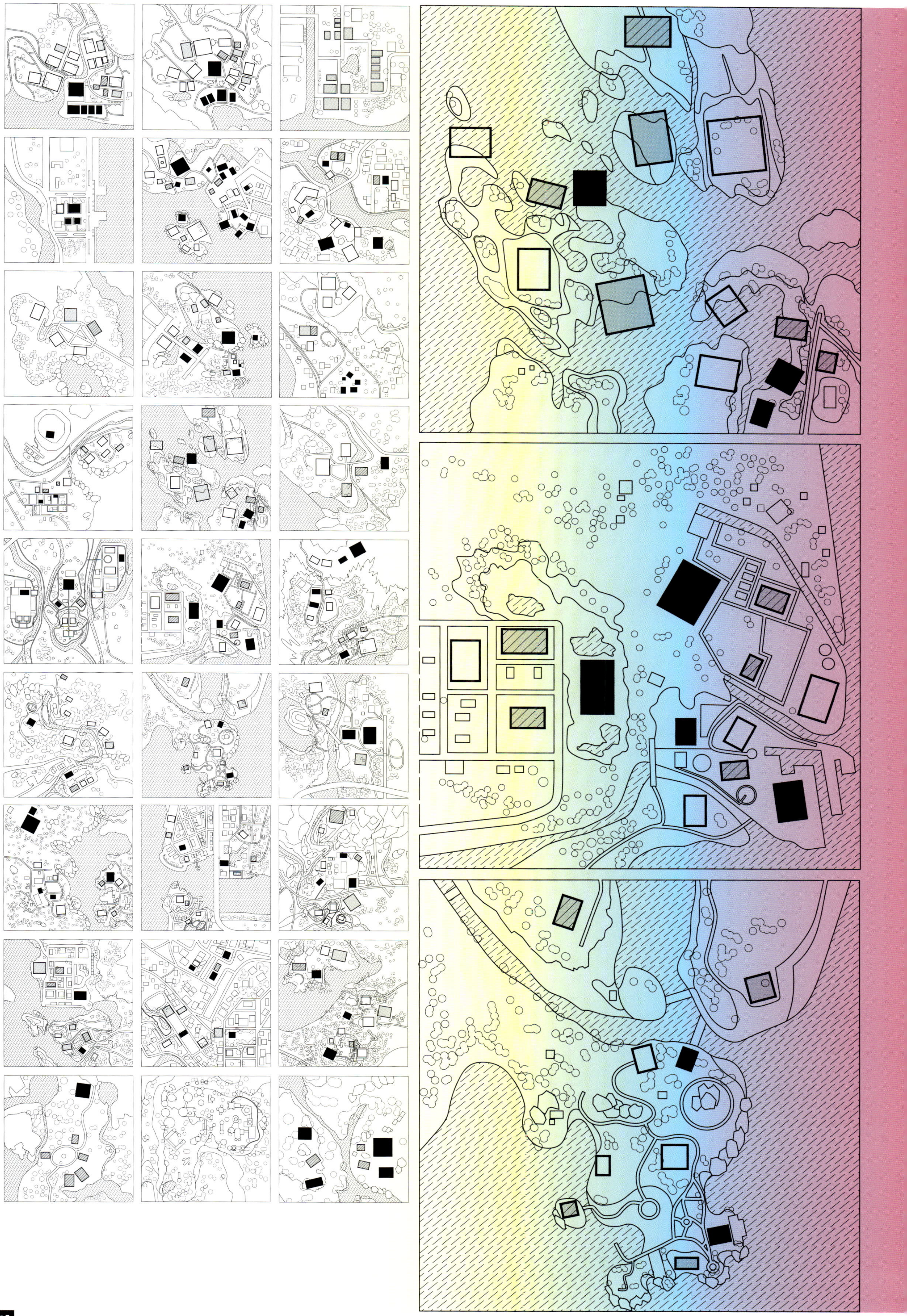

[Fig.09]

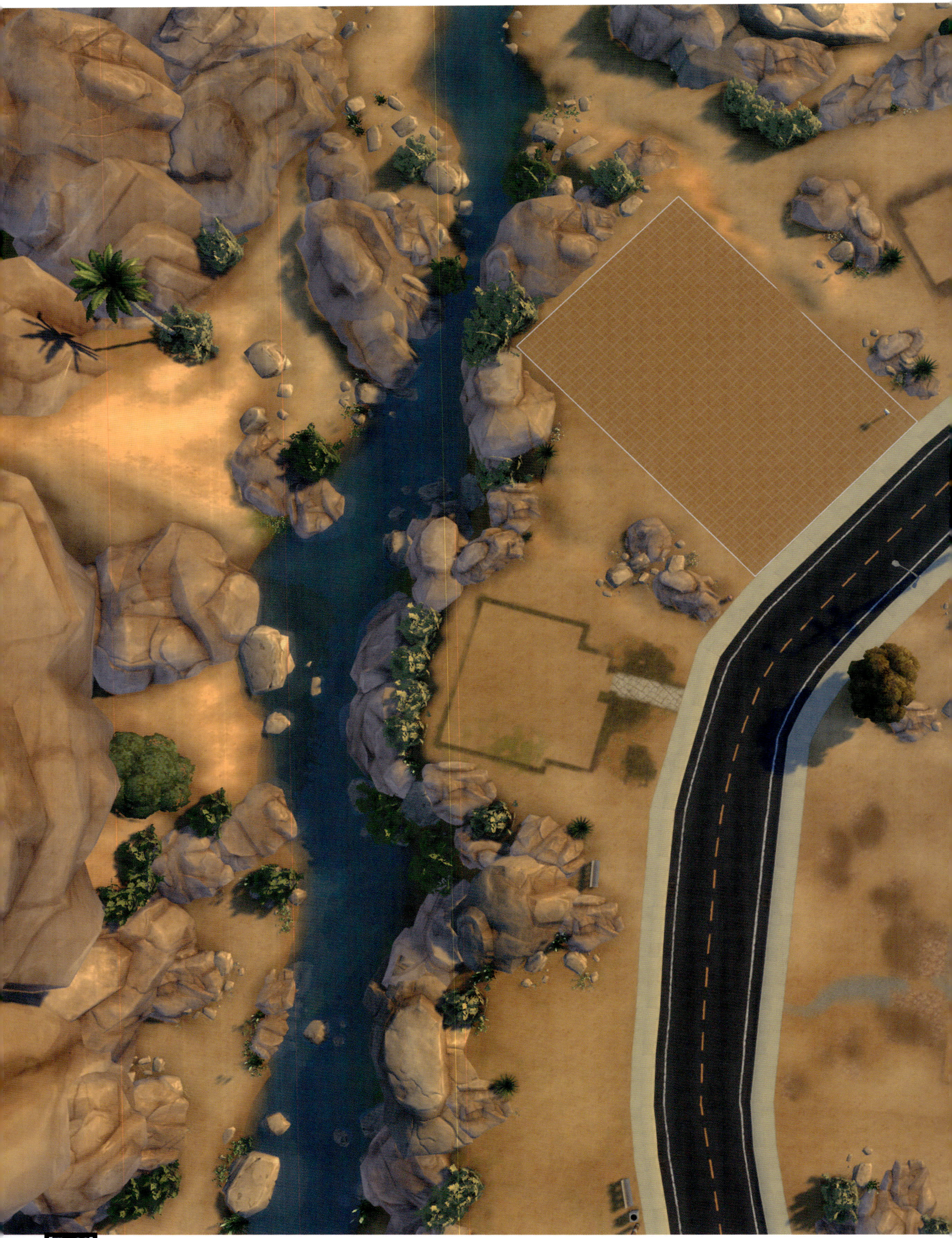

[Fig.08]

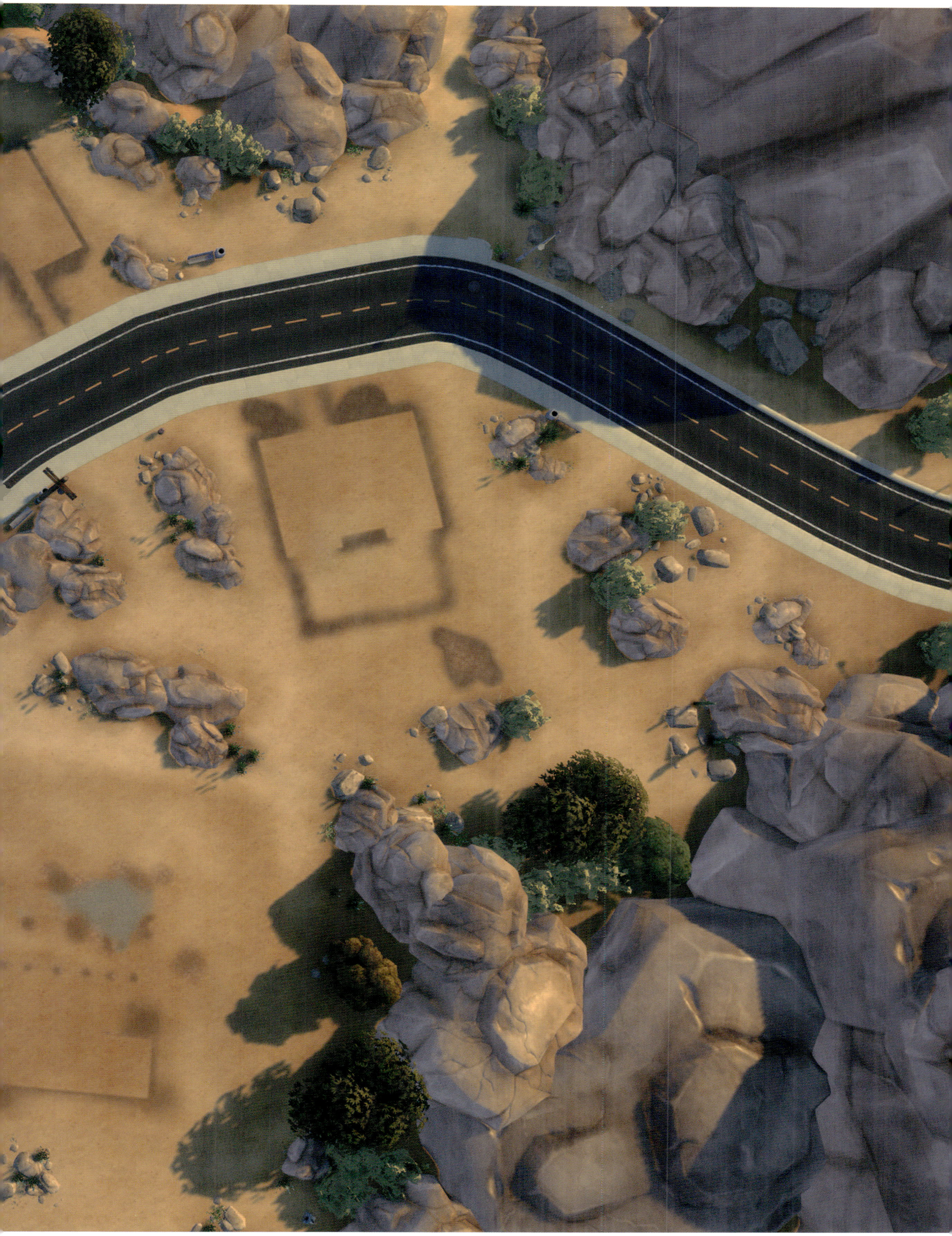

TRACKING THE BAR AS THE MOST COMMONLY OCCURRING COMMERCIAL BUILDING TYPOLOGY ACROSS DIFFERENT WORLDS IN THE GAME, ANALYSING THE LOCALIZATION OF STYLE WITHIN EACH WORLD.

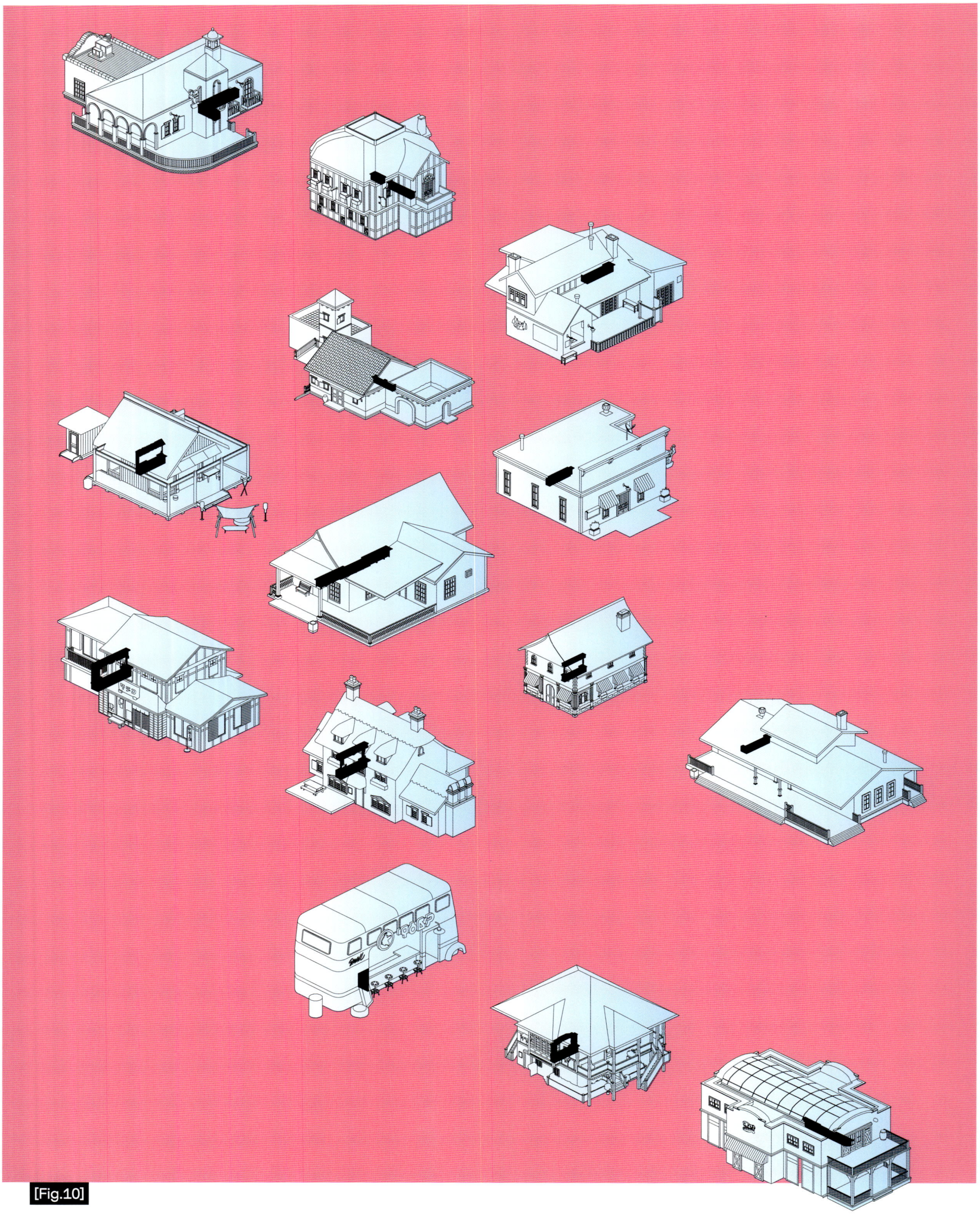

[Fig.10]

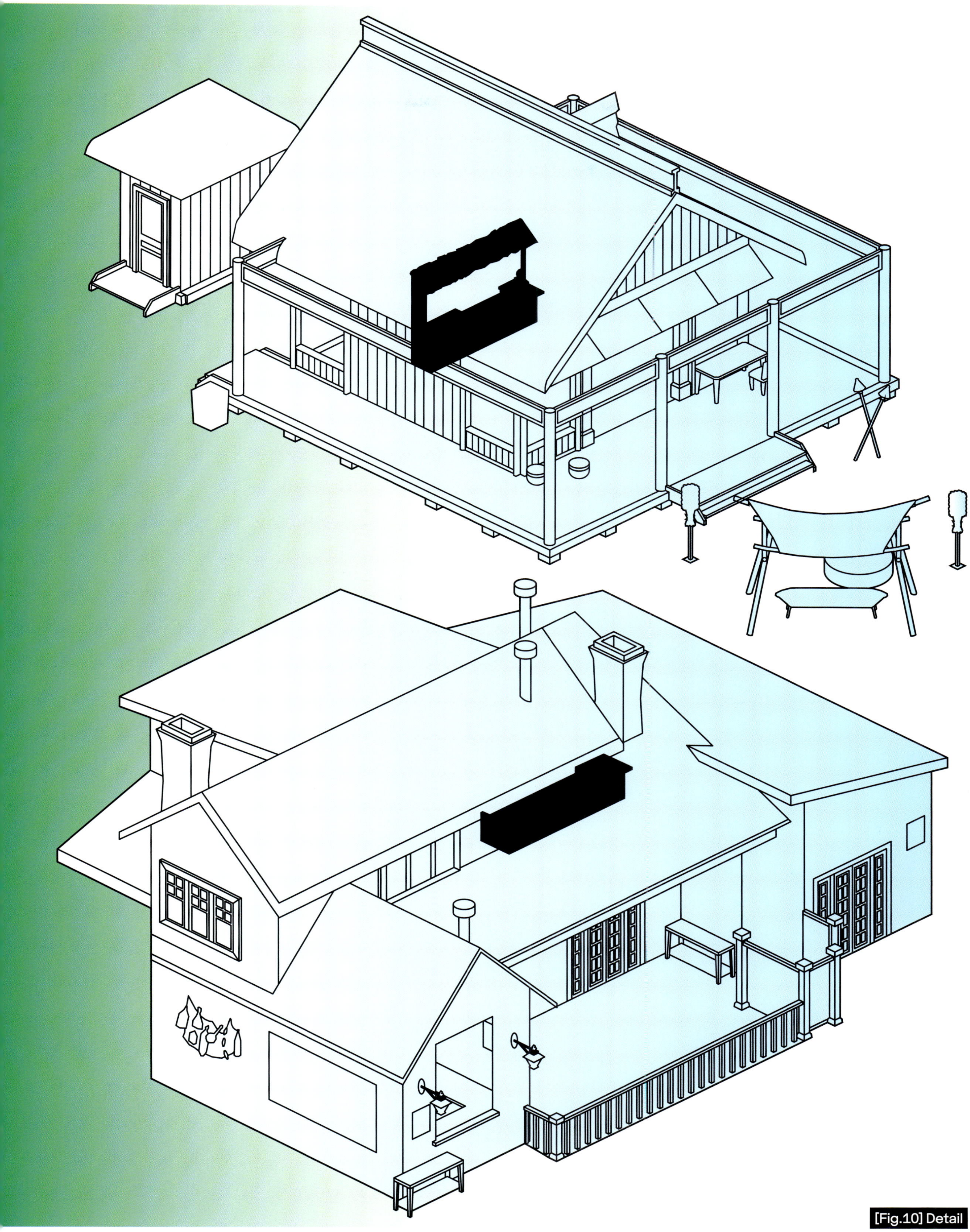

[Fig.10] Detail

[Fig.11]
PAGES
256–7

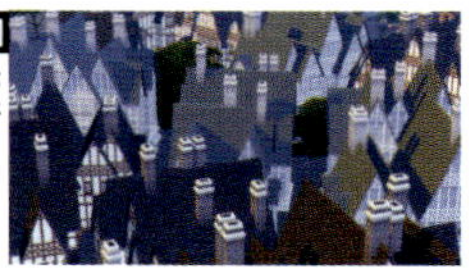

Windenburg roofscape, showing the density of traditional timber-framed houses that are emblematic of its German architectural influence.

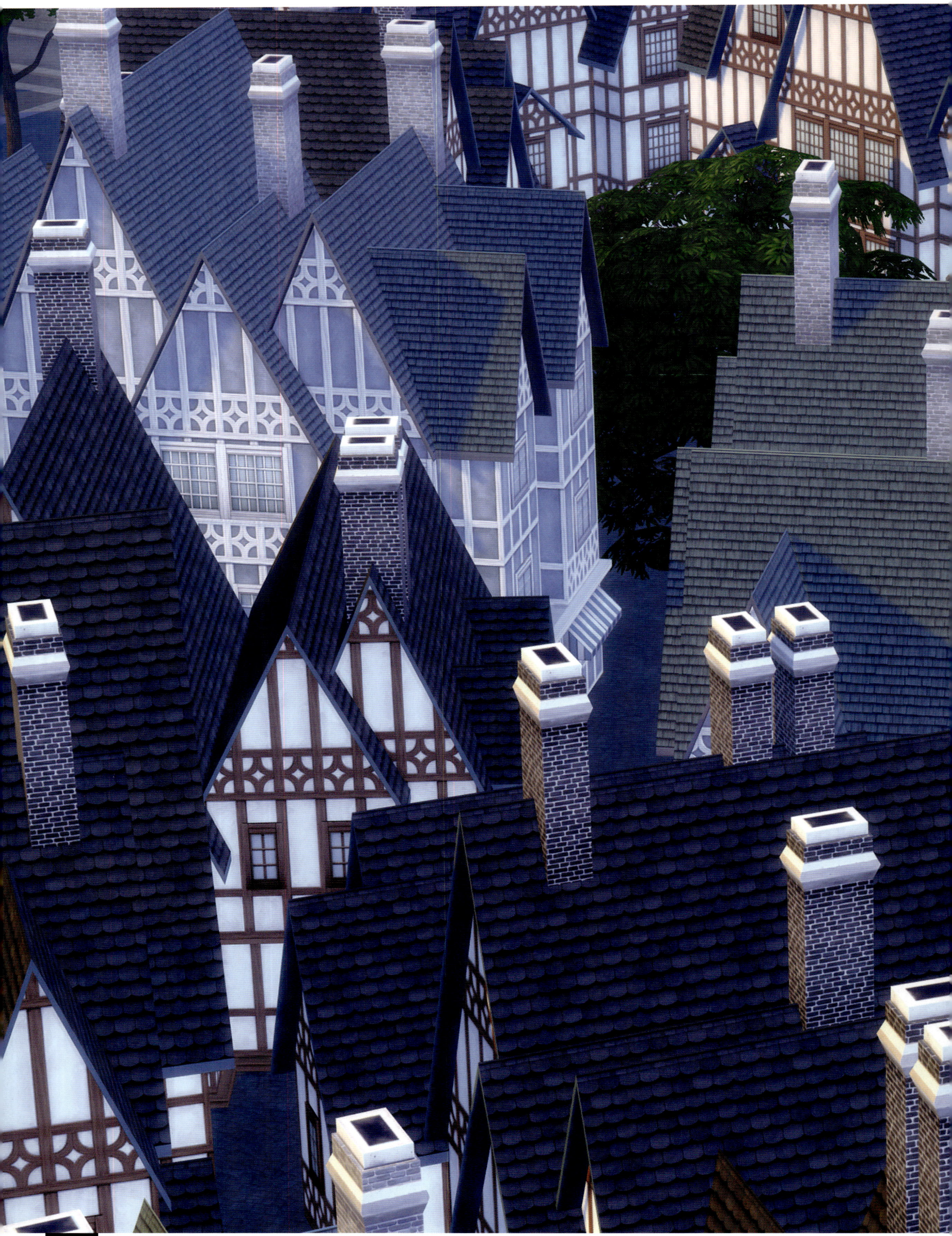

[Fig.11]

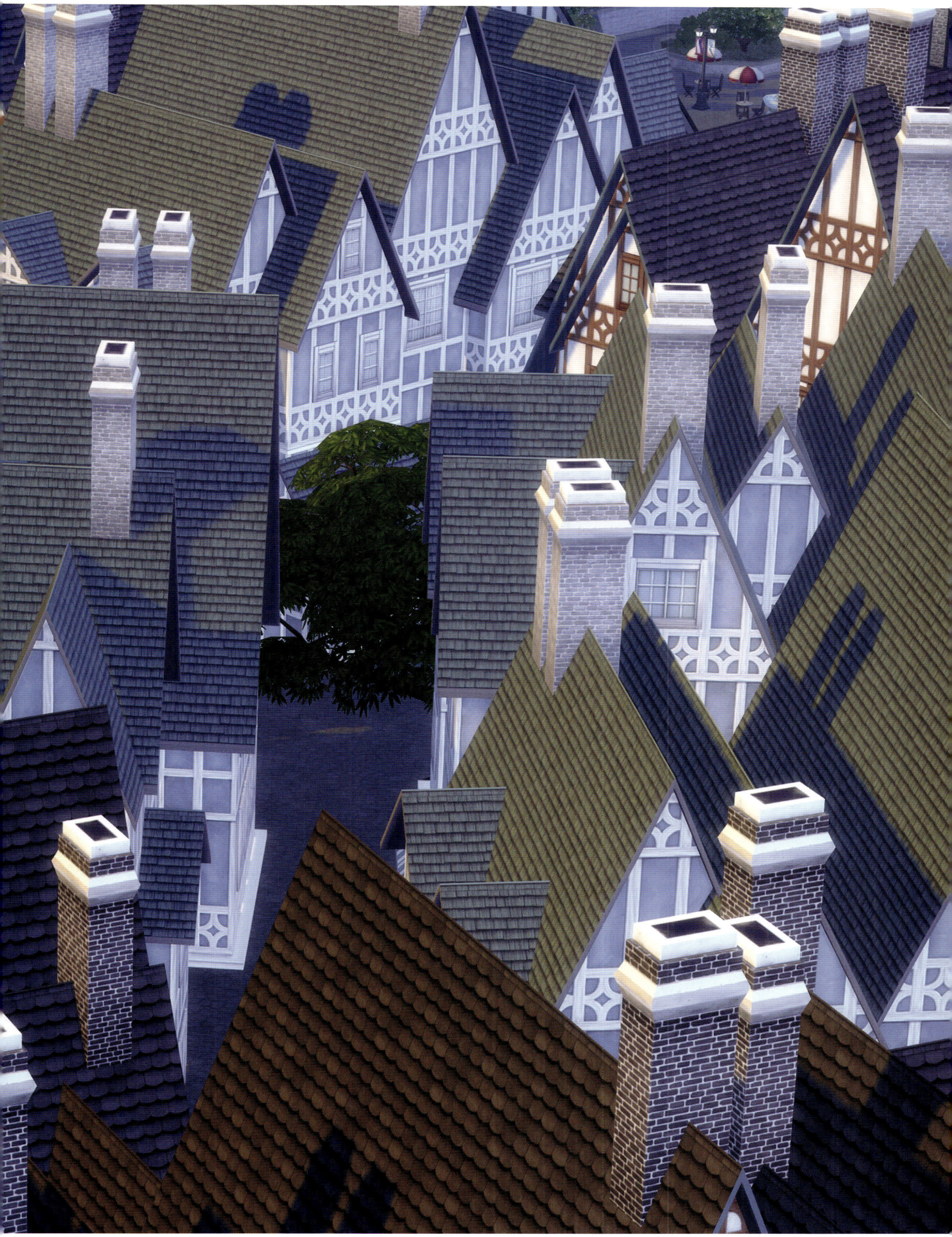

11.5

A SOCIAL SIMULATION

In the social lives of Sims, sexual relations are the most intimate and private, with the game using the euphemism 'WooHoo' to describe two Sims hooking up. Yet Sims still have the ability to choose weird and wonderful places for these encounters to occur. Through a typological drawing collecting some of the most prominent WooHoo spots (to date), we can see how the game offers a wide variety of different possibilities for pleasure [Fig.12]. These range from the more vanilla double bed to a bush, waterfall or even a dumpster. Experimental Sims with certain traits can find themselves WooHooing in a rocket ship or a coffin, as players watch fireworks and tiny heart icons float across the screen.

For all its aesthetic glory, it is easy to forget that *The Sims 4* is centred around the wellbeing of the Sims themselves, reacting to the environment the player has created around them. The architecture of *The Sims 4* goes beyond a static backdrop to function as a dynamic tool for shaping action within the game. The built environment is deliberately constructed to influence how Sims navigate the world and respond to it. The architecture and objects within it are 'mood-altering', provoking different emotional reactions from the Sims – transforming these into responsive sites for storytelling. But more than this, the architecture of *The Sims 4* has produced social spaces *around* the game, in online communities and social media. While players love to observe their Sims and become voyeurs of their lives, they also love to share their strange designs, curious solutions and spicy challenges. This leads them to explore the meaning, function and symbolism of domestic space, in an environment where anyone's uploaded building could become as ubiquitous as a Sear's catalogue house, repeated in millions of worlds, but perhaps always slightly different.

[Fig.12] Detail

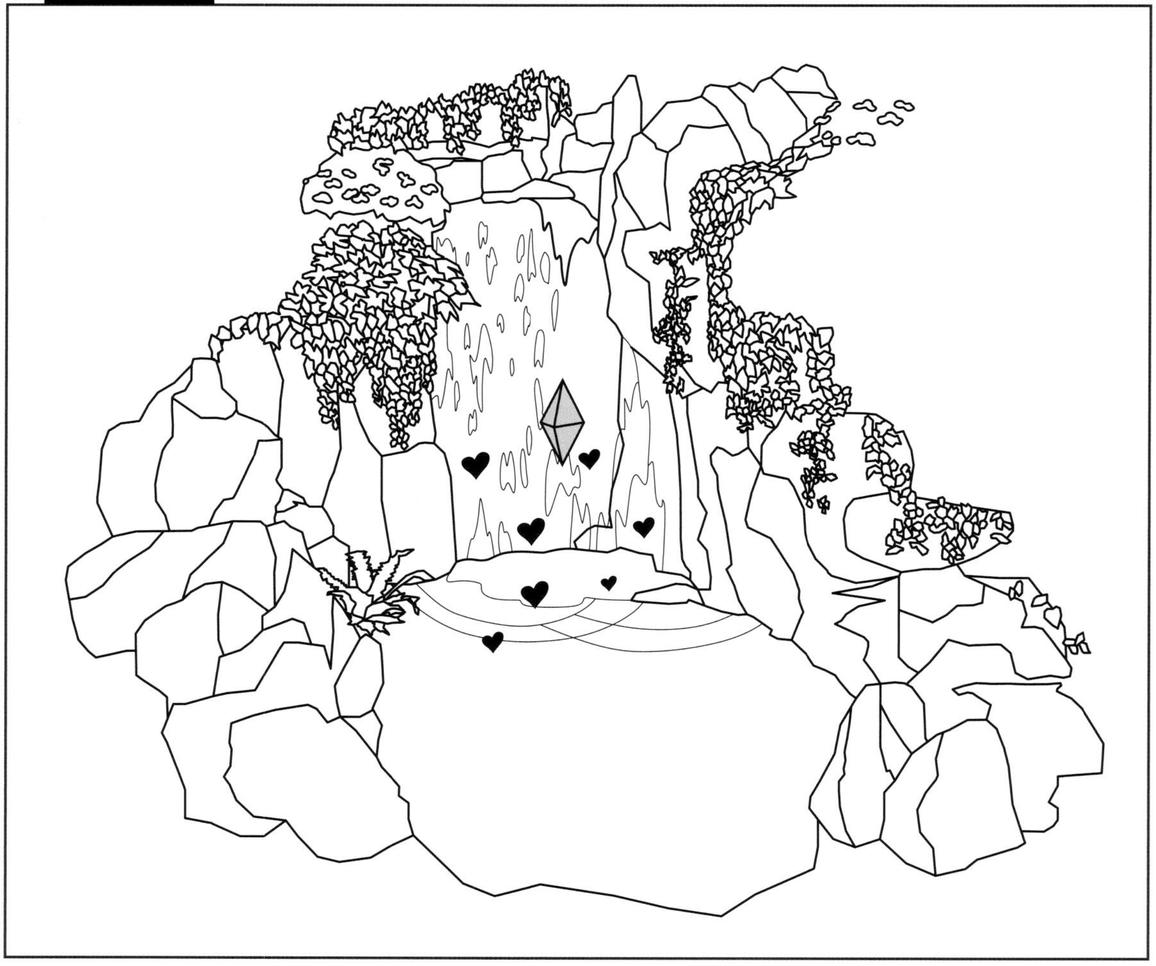

WooHoo locations are prominent mood-altering places within the game, commonly sought after by players as social catalysts of expression.

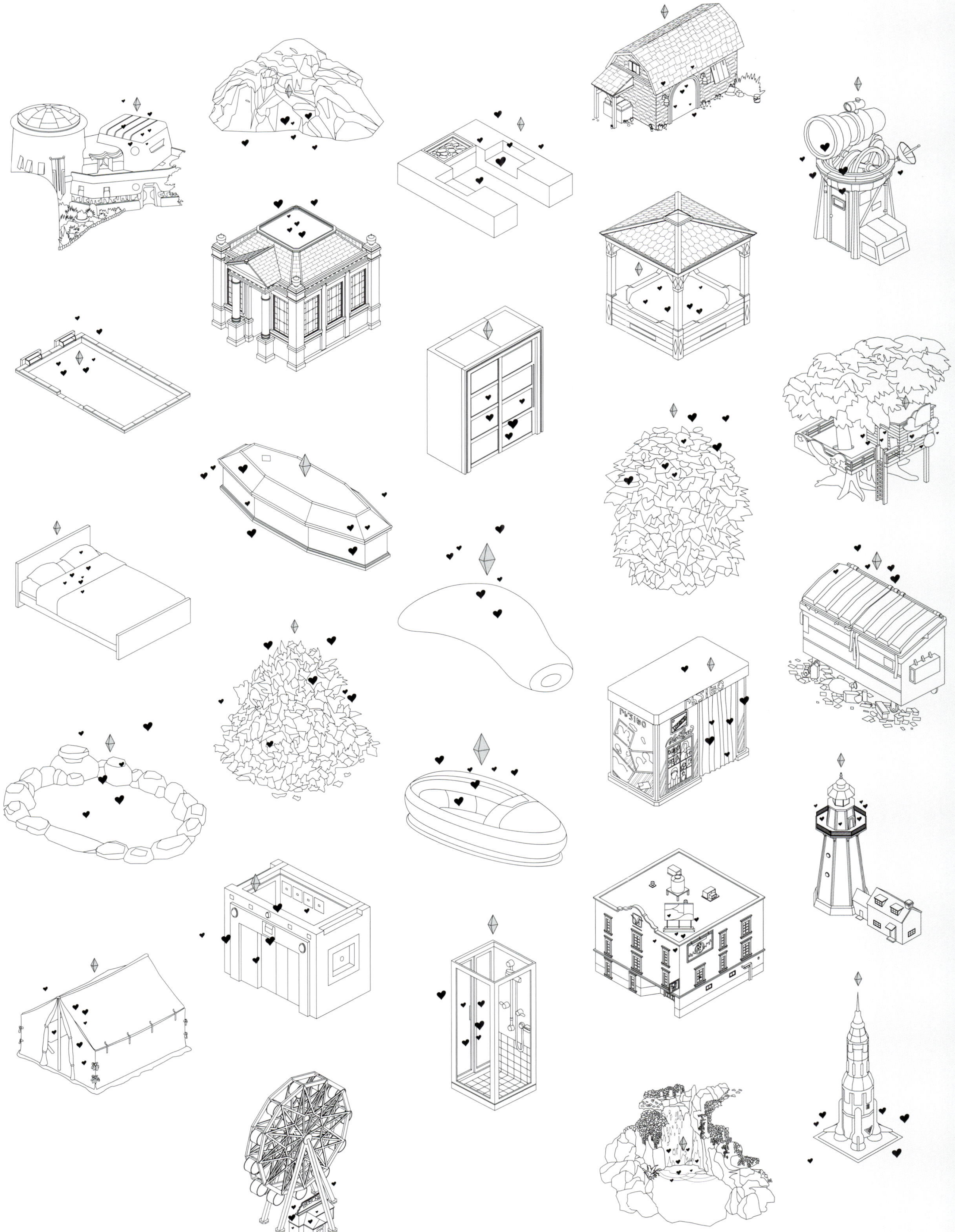

[Fig.12]

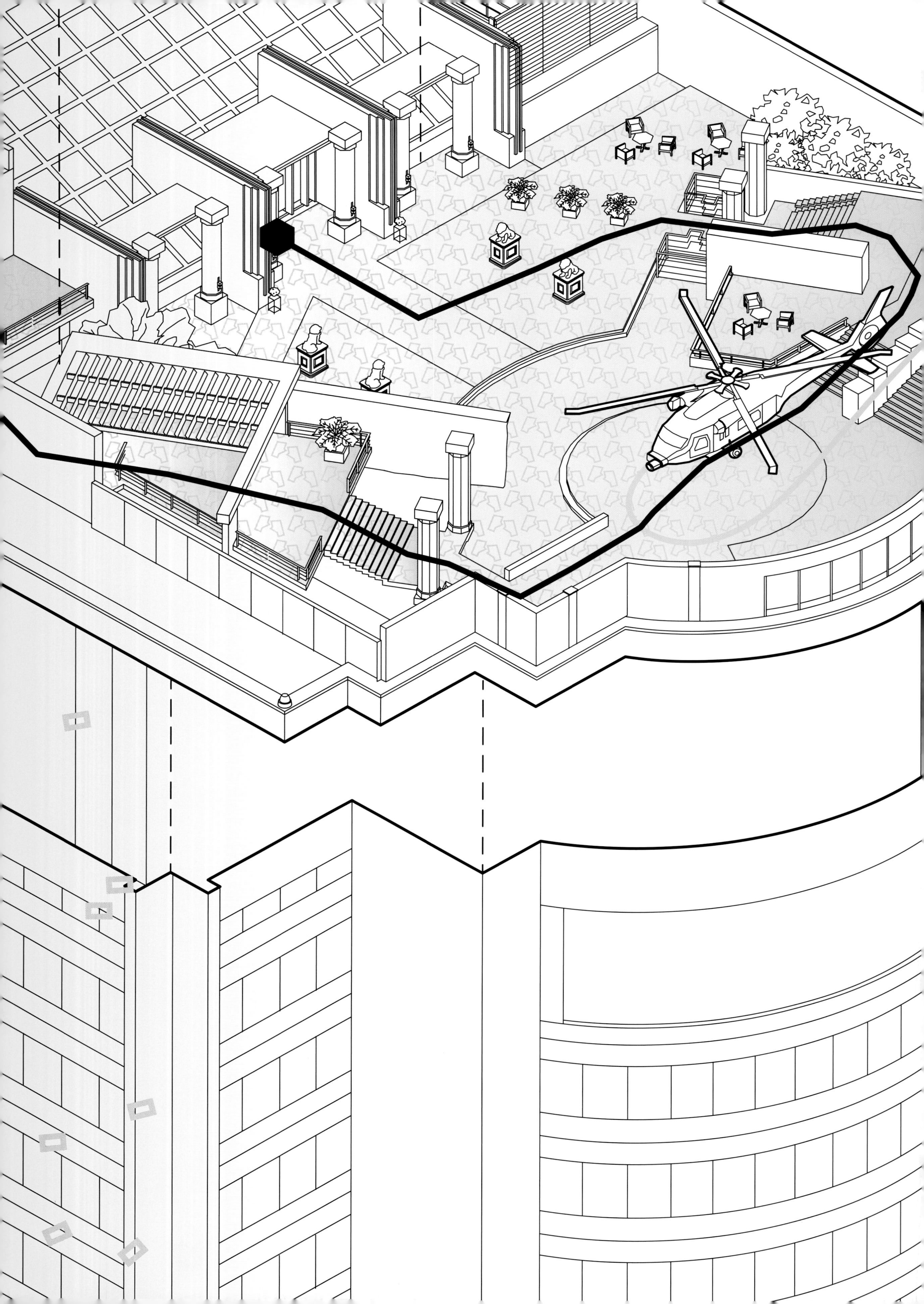

CHAPTER 12

YAKUZA KIWAMI

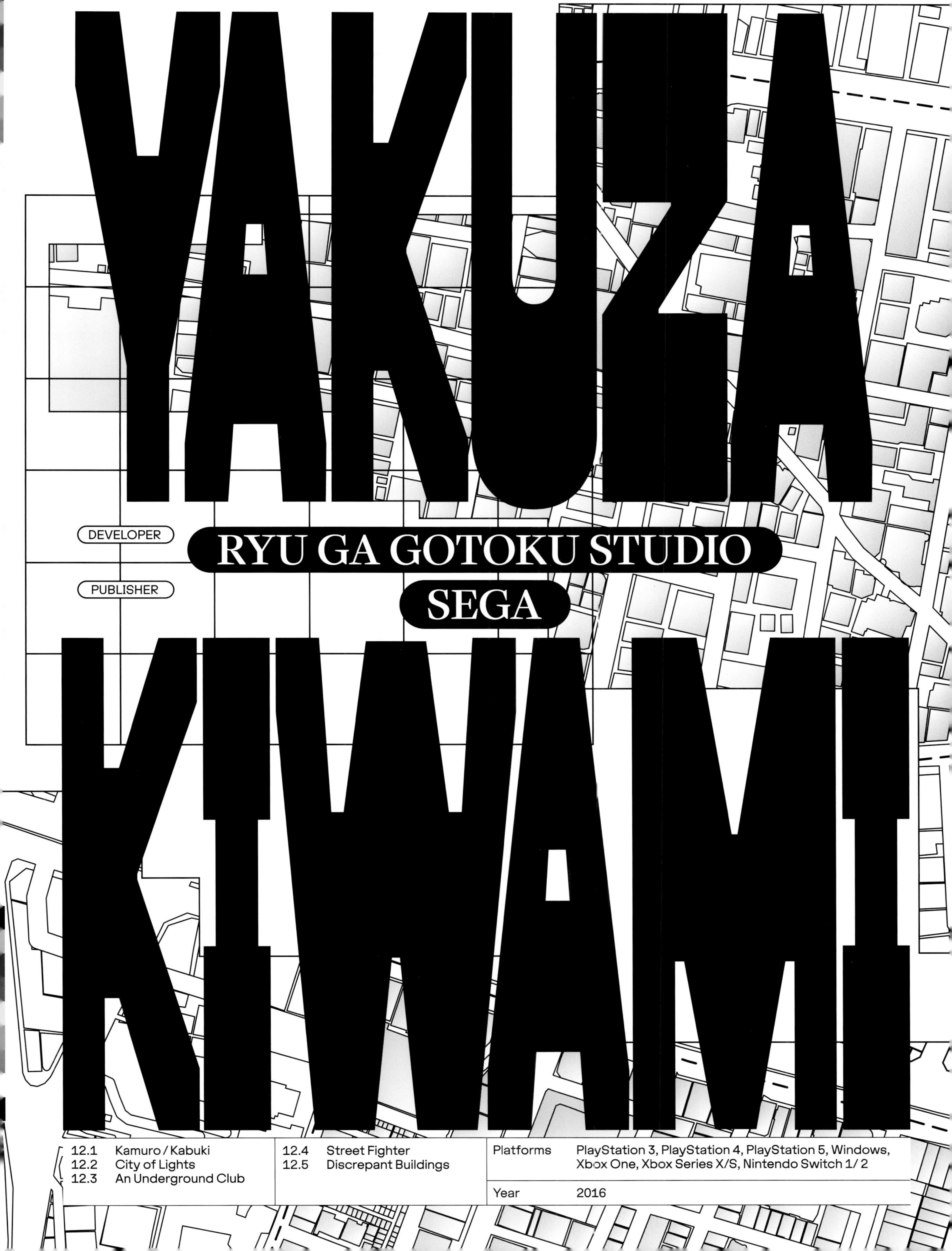

DEVELOPER: RYU GA GOTOKU STUDIO

PUBLISHER: SEGA

Platforms	PlayStation 3, PlayStation 4, PlayStation 5, Windows, Xbox One, Xbox Series X/S, Nintendo Switch 1/ 2
Year	2016

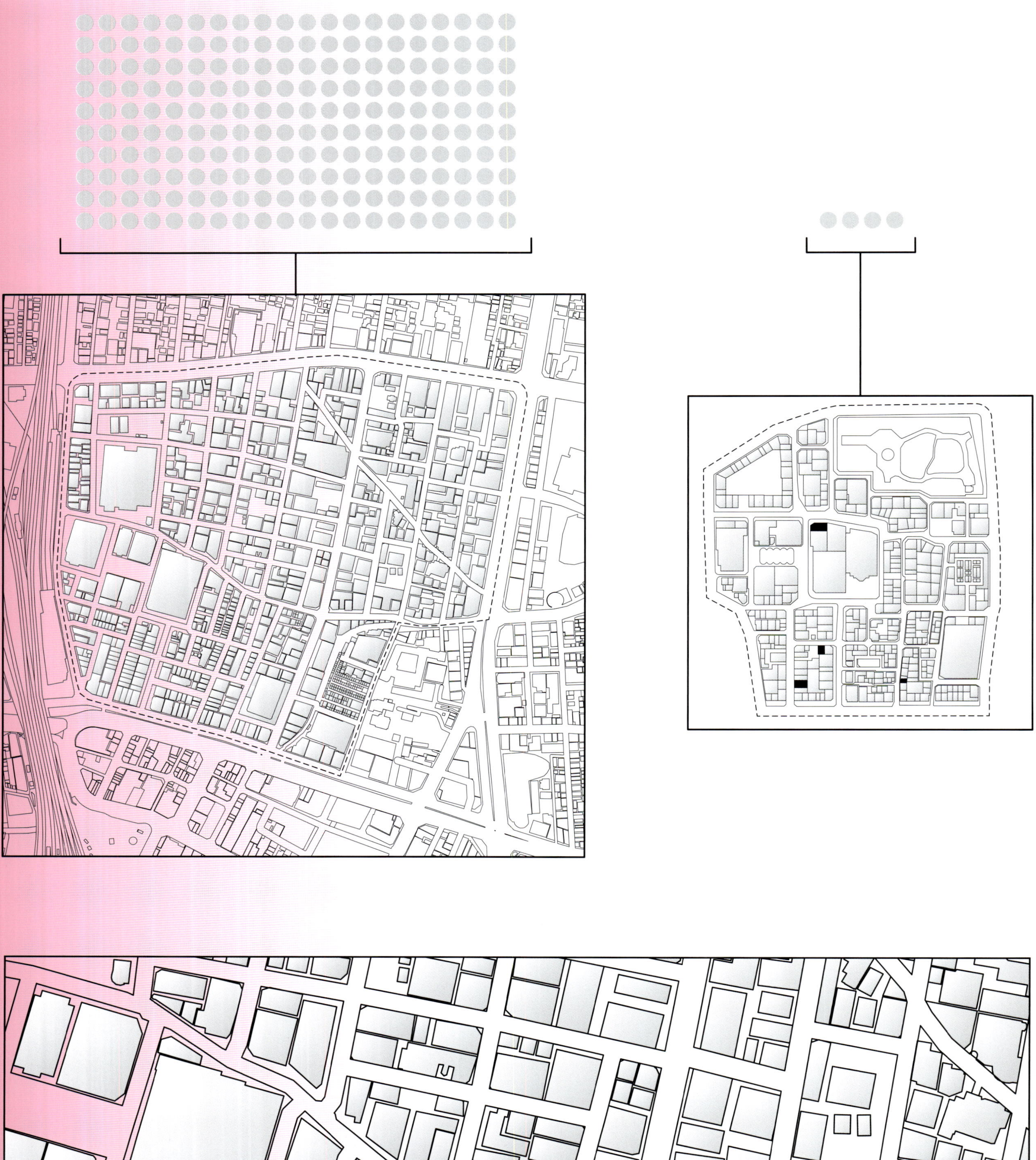

[Fig.01]

値引でオトク

12.1

KAMURO / KABUKI

The Yakuza series of games is well-known for its emphasis on the seedier aspects of Japanese urban life. They repeatedly revisit a real-world location that changes over time, in both subtle and wilder ways. *Yakuza Kiwami* is a 2016 remake of 2005's original *Yakuza* game, centred around the fictional area of Kamurochō, a close approximation of Tokyo's Kabukichō, the famous red-light district in Shinjuku that is now a global tourist destination. Kabukichō grew from the late 1940s, first planned as a theatre and entertainment district before embracing the red-light economy, cabarets and eventually host and hostess clubs as a key driver of its success.[1] Kamurochō, as Kabukichō once was, is a spatial synonym for yakuza control, showing a world governed by organized crime, patrolled by thugs and gangsters. These criminals regularly start fights with our protagonist, Kazuma Kiryu, a former yakuza who has returned to Tokyo following a prison sentence, only to find himself set up for the shooting of his mentor. While *Kiwami* is an open-world game, the relatively compact scale and granular detail of Kamurochō offers a density and sensorial overload that is intoxicatingly close to the real thing.

By comparing the size of the Kabukichō district to the extents of Kamurochō's map using OpenStreetMap data, it is clear that there is a divergence in scale, with Kamurochō's area comprising approximately 51% of its real-world counterpart (12.7 hectares to 24.7) [Fig.01]. This is something we might expect, particularly considering the game is based on a much older original, made at a point where such rich and detailed worlds were technically harder to achieve. What the developers have managed to retain, and even perhaps enhanced through this compression, is the essential spirit of Kabukichō, its density and the overwhelming constellations of signs and adverts that beckon visitors into mysterious entrances. Trickier to represent is the vast number of real-world pleasure businesses and sites of illicit activity. In his study *Black Market, Chinatown, and Kabukichō*, Timothy Yun Hui Tsu estimates that in the early 2000s (when *Kiwami* is set), Kabukichō 'boasted some eight thousand' entertainment venues and eateries, alongside 'two hundred yakuza offices.'[2] As our mapping shows, the presence of clearly marked criminal facilities in Kamurochō is much lower, with only four yakuza family and loan shark offices accessible to Kiryu. Having such places clearly marked is not unusual for yakuza because 'as a *non-secret* criminal organization, they can afford to have offices and headquarters officially registered' and they even 'turned visibility into a key feature of their public image.'[3] Despite this, the sheer number of other yakuza Kiryu encounters on the streets suggests there may be many more offices unknown to us.

[Fig.01] A MAP COMPARING THE SIZE OF THE REAL-WORLD KABUKICHŌ (LEFT) WITH THE KAMUROCHŌ DISTRICT (RIGHT). DOTS REPRESENT THE DENSITY OF YAKUZA OFFICES OBSERVED IN TOKYO AT THE TIME OF THE GAME'S SETTING.

Kamurochō also portrays key buildings within Kabukichō, some of which have subsequently been demolished but others can still that can be located in the real-world district twenty years later. Community-made camera tools[4] reframe these structures in new ways, allowing us to compile the four most notable real-world reference points into a drawing that explores their relationship as iconic elements within the cityscape. In doing so, these buildings become visual landmarks, tying the design of the world together and being instantly recognizable to anyone who has visited [Fig.02]. The hulking Humax Pavilion Shinjuku, becomes the Power building, with its ground floor arcade replaced by a larger Club Sega game centre promoting the game's publishers' own arcade brand. Other less obvious, but still significant landmarks are portrayed, such as the Yoshida Batting Center – an altered version of Kabukichō's Shinjuku Batting Center – and the large billboards surrounding a parking lot on Hanamichi-dori Street. These advertising hoardings are a popular tourist photo spot and depict the many coiffured hosts and hostesses that one may encounter at Kabukichō's clubs. The similarity in ostentatious fashion and big hairstyles between *Kiwami*'s 2005 version of the area, and Kabukichō two decades later suggests that the area's sense of style may be slow to change. Finally, the infamous real-life Don Quijote store makes an appearance in the game, allowing Kiryu to buy gifts or snacks, although there are somewhat fewer novelty items, cheap souvenirs and overwhelmed tourists than we might find in reality. One key building that no longer remains is the famous Shinjuku Koma Theater, which was demolished in 2009, four years after the game is set.

[Fig.02] Detail

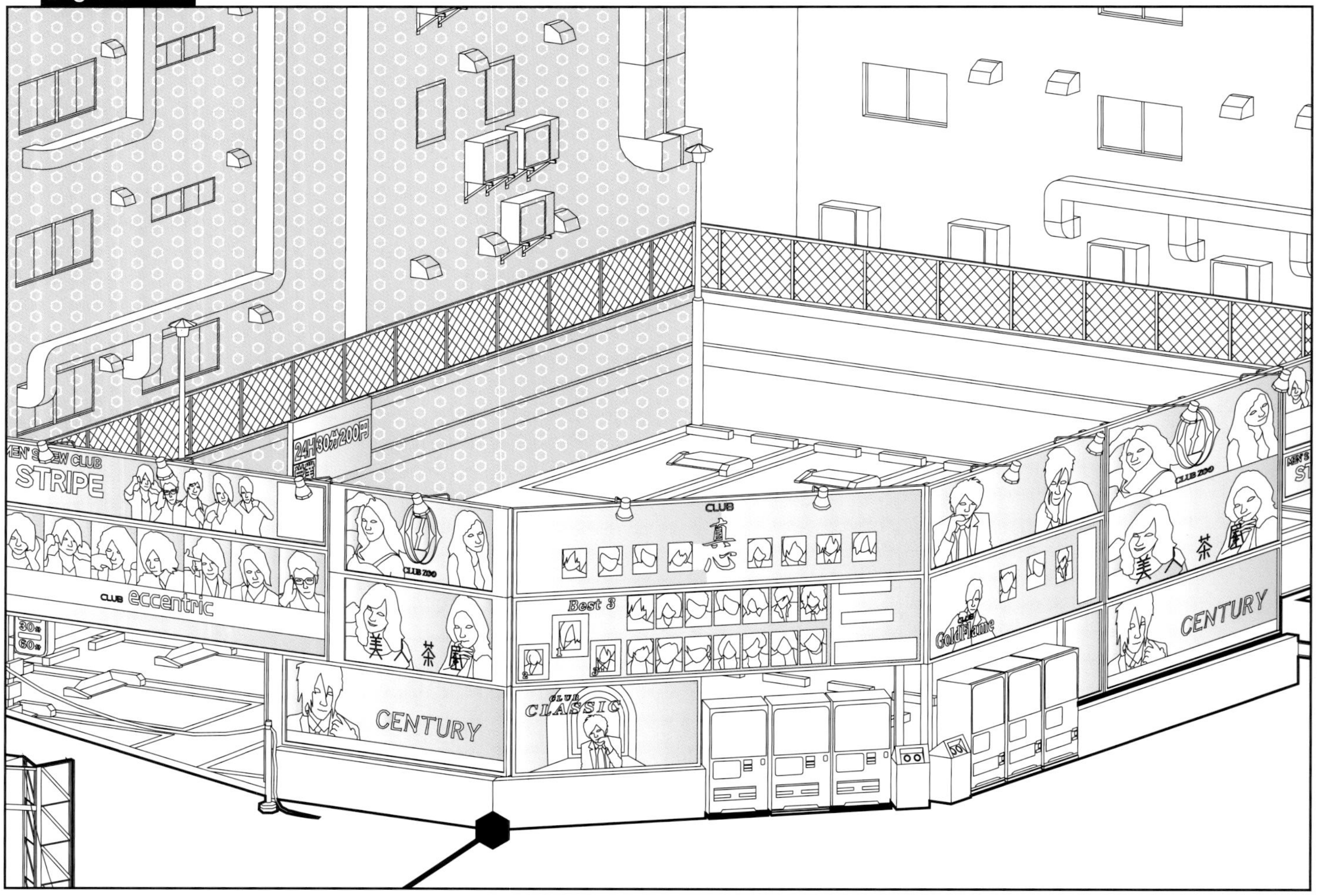

[Fig.02] DRAWING COMBINING SOME OF THE KEY BUILDINGS FOUND IN KABUKICHŌ THAT ARE PORTRAYED IN THE GAME, FROM THE HUMAX PAVILION TO THE FAMOUS CAR PARK HOARDINGS ADORNED WITH PORTRAITS OF HOSTS AND HOSTESSES.

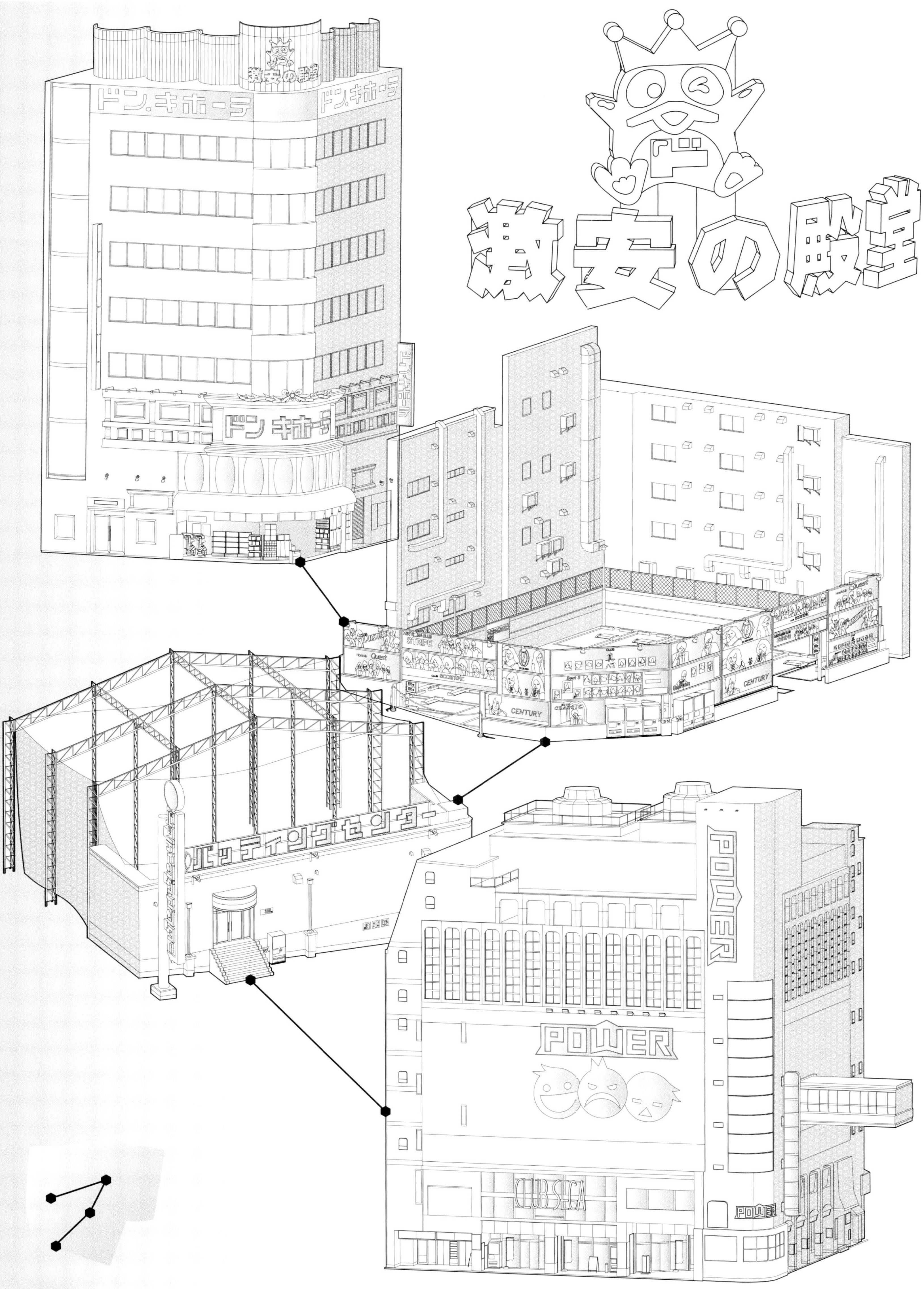

[Fig.02]

12.2

CITY OF LIGHTS

At the heart of Kamurochō's streetscape are the small businesses that give Kabukichō its density and visual language. Shops compete through flashing signs, unusual names, over-the-top entrance designs and heavily photoshopped portraits of the attractive companions within. By taking our own photographic recordings of real-world Kabukichō entrances, we performed the same action using camera tools in *Yakuza Kiwami*, allowing us to draw comparative street elevations from both the real world and the game world, to see the common visual languages between them [Fig.03]. Shared principles include the unwritten rule that there is no such thing as *too much* ornamentation, clearly demonstrated in the façade of the StarDust host club. The actual front door to clubs should be out of view, hidden either up or down a staircase, or at least behind a row of *noren* fabric dividers. Signs and architectural details are also composed in a *laissez-faire* manner, where any symmetrical form is usually broken by another detail placed in front or behind it. Materials are also applied on a building-by-building basis, and it is hopeless trying to find much continuity between two adjoining structures. Another small detail we find replicated in Kamurochō is the narrow gaps between many buildings – too small to constitute alleyways, but just the right size for collecting nightlife rubbish.

As screenshot photography of Kamurochō shows, the density of the streets and signage has the effect of creating a glowing landscape at night [Fig.04]. The radiance of the nighttime street also mirrors that of Kabukichō, where architectural researchers have found that the general illuminance level of the district is 2.5 times the Japan Industrial Standard for lighting design.[5] Interestingly, despite the area's seedy reputation, this research argued that the sheer number and variance of lights from businesses was found to be beneficial to its security and safety. We can also see from the columns of signage running up the side of buildings the verticality that is key to the density of Japanese cities. Kiryu is barely allowed to wander beyond the first or second floor of buildings, and so we are left to wonder at what lies above us.

[Fig.03]

ELEVATION DRAWINGS DEMONSTRATING THE VISUAL LANGUAGE OF KAMUROCHŌ'S BAR AND CLUB ENTRANCES (LEFT) COMPARED TO THOSE FOUND ON THE STREETS OF KABUKICHŌ (RIGHT).

[Fig.04] PAGE 268

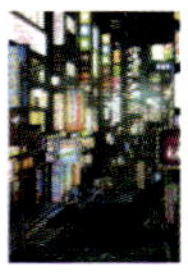

A view showing the lighting levels of Kamurochō's streets at night, regulated by the extremely high density of glowing signs.

SMART 無料案内所

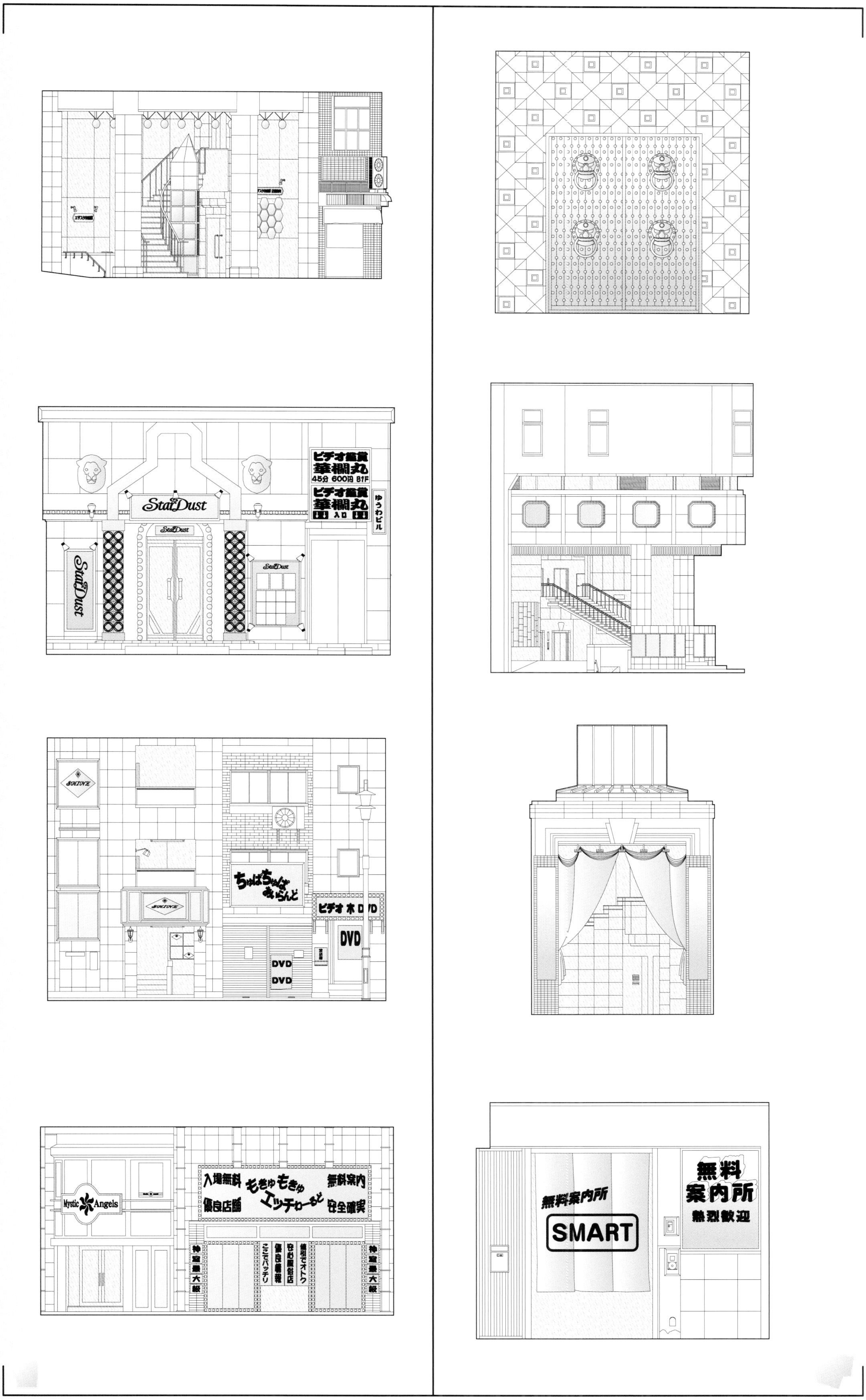

[Fig.03]

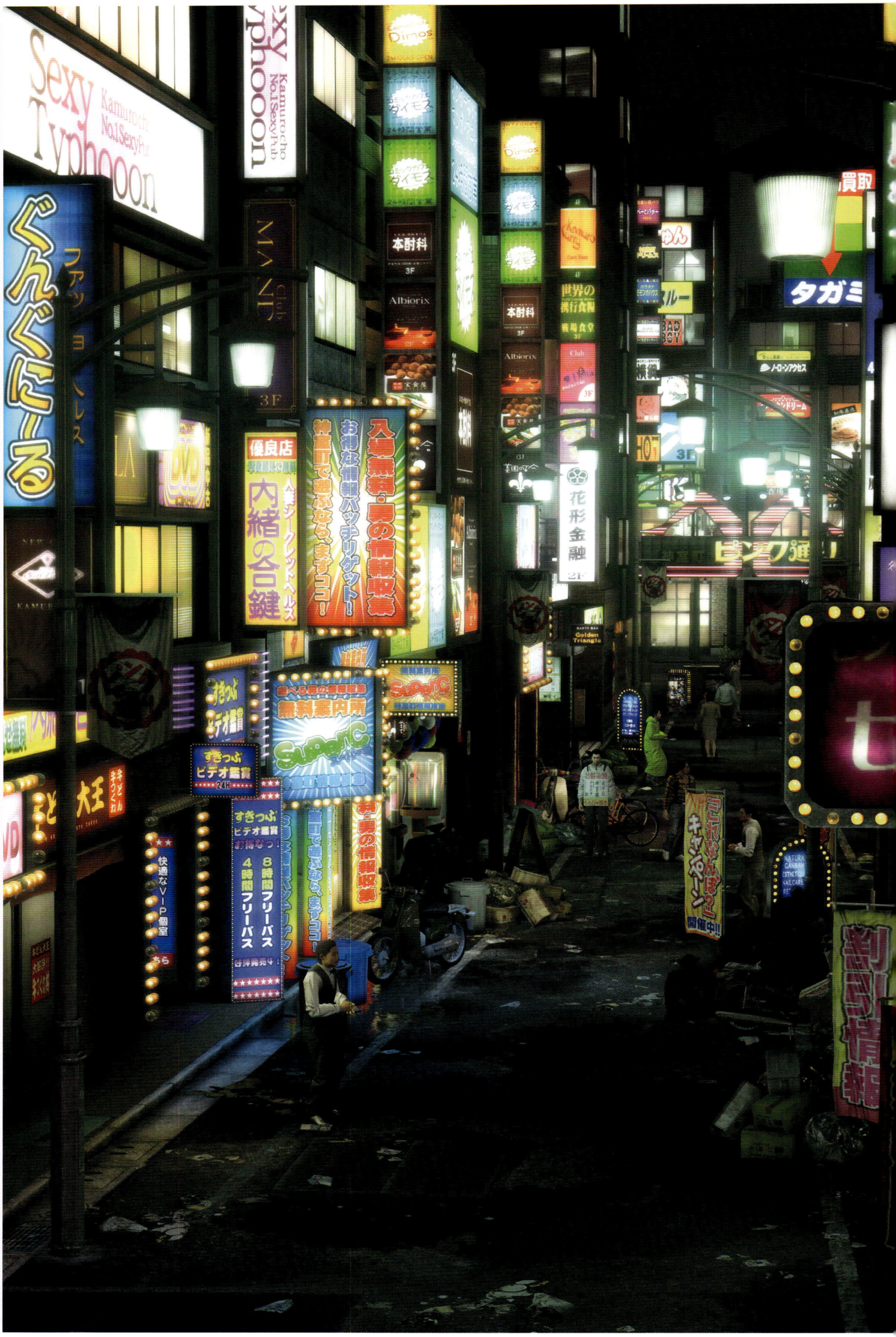
Sexy Typhooon
Kamurocho No.1 Sexy Pub
ぐんぐにーる
Dinos
本酎料
Albiorix
優良店
内緒の合鍵
入場無料・男の情報収集
お得な情報バッチリゲット！
神室町で遊ぶなら、まずココ！
花形金融
タガミ
買取
ピンク通り
無料案内所
すきっぷ
ビデオ鑑賞
24H
快適なVIP個室
8時間フリーパス
4時間フリーパス
これなんぼ？
キャンペーン
開催中!!
割引情報

[Fig.04]

As with Kabukichō, these signs and entrances use a visually striking language to entice their clientelle into more private and secluded spaces. *Kiwami* does not quite allow us to have the full experience of shuffling up a tiny stairwell to an 8th-floor cocktail bar, but drinking establishments and host and hostess clubs are key parts of the world. These are where meetings and fights take place, and where Kiryu can flirt and refresh himself ahead of the next battle. Mapping the key bars and clubs from *Kiwami* shows how they also represent the full range of interior experiences Kabukichō offers, from the Golden Gai's tiny bars (Bar Shellac in the game's Champion District) to the flamboyant hostess clubs Shine and JeweL [Fig.05]. In her book on hostess bars in Tokyo, anthropologist Anne Allison, who worked as a hostess for her research, describes how 'a person who walks into [a hostess bar] for the first time will be struck by the sumptuous materials and arrangements.'[6] Club Shine, where Kiryu meets hostess Rina, has large red wraparound sofa booths separated by ornate ballustrades and an ornamental plant arrangement at its centre. Allison describes how such bars focus on making 'an area that accommodates a luxurious number of luxurious things,' producing a space that wows customers 'by dressing, and overdressing, the part.'[7]

We can consider all of *Kiwami*'s bars to be dressing the part, allowing us to peer behind the curtain of Kamurochō, into a sleazy cabaret bar, through the dark wood and marble of Kiryu's favourite haunt New Serena, or the gold and glitz of the host club StarDust. Although Kamurochō is dense, spatial concessions are required to allow the third-person camera to move. This means that the true intimacy of some real-world spaces cannot quite be replicated. Bar Shellac is around four metres (13 ft) wide to allow Kiryu to navigate the space, despite the real-world Golden Gai district accommodating two or even three tiny bars in the same floorplan.

[Fig.05] Detail

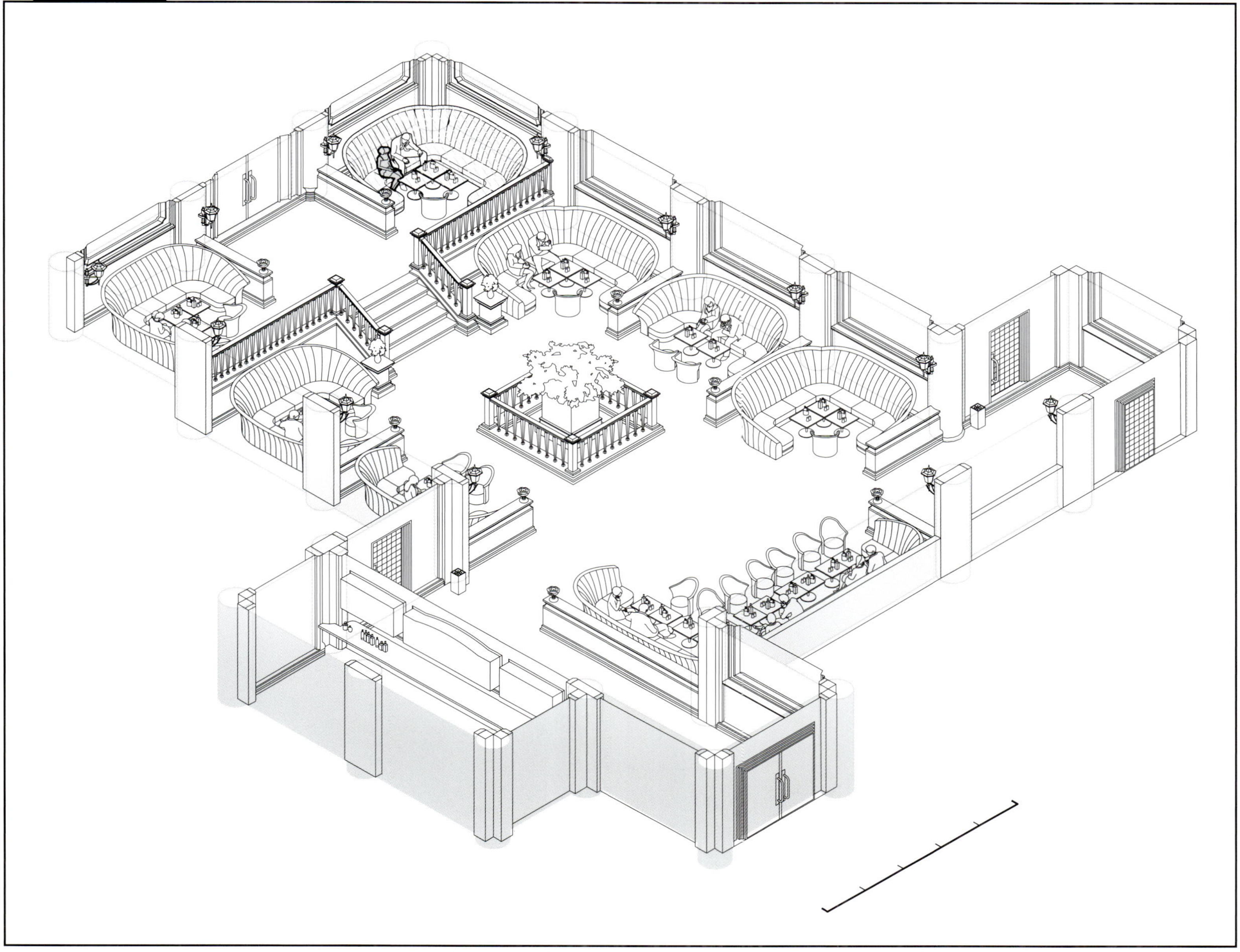

[Fig.05]
PAGES 270

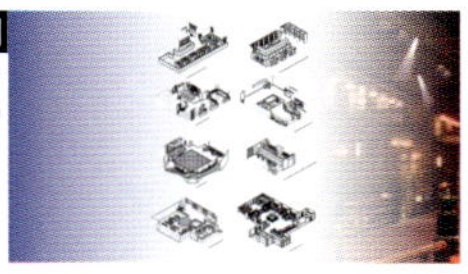

Isometric studies of the main bars in the game, showing the places and people Kiryu interacts with and how their architectural language closely follows real Kabukichō styles.

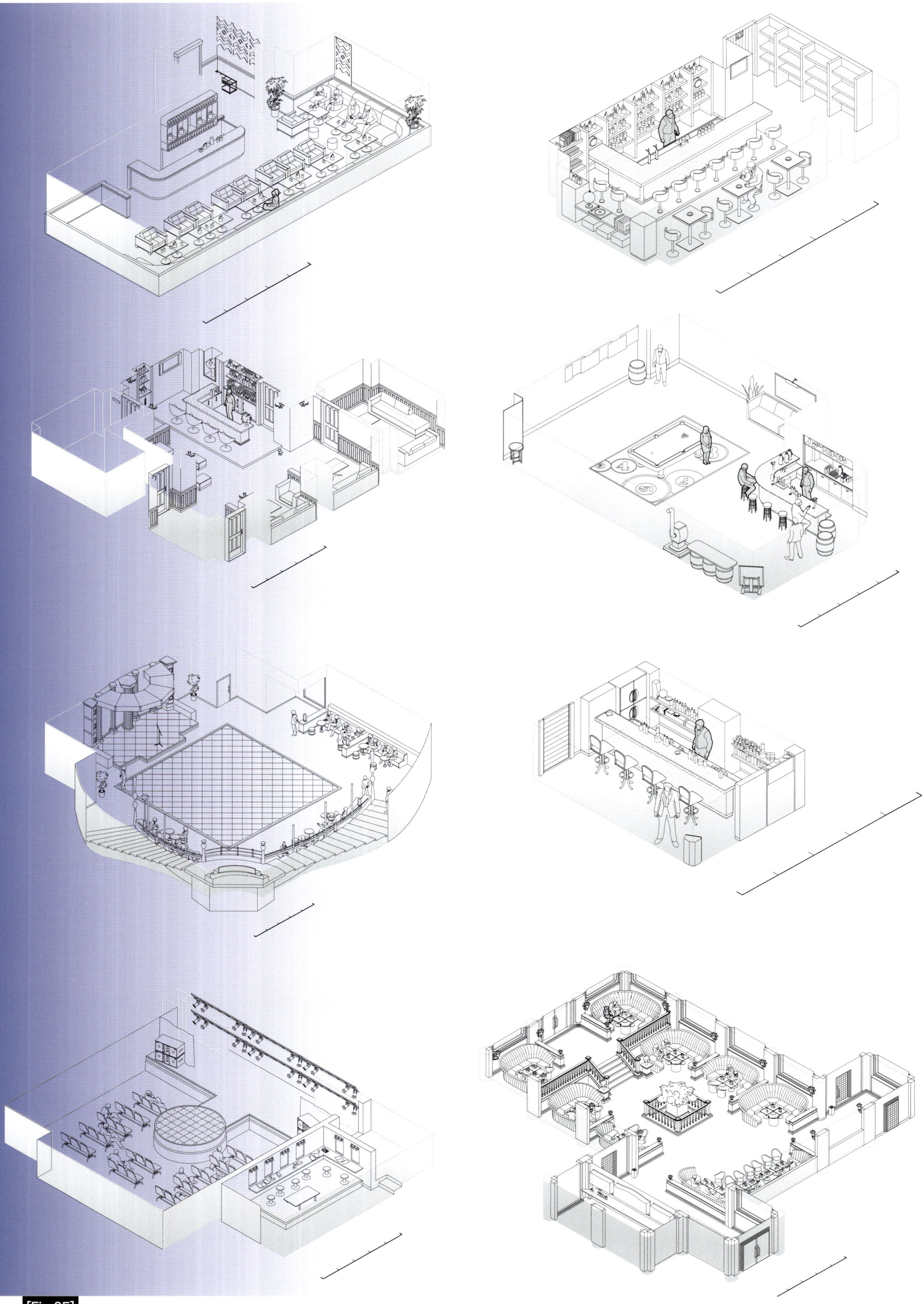

[Fig.05]

12.3

AN UNDERGROUND CLUB

Despite Kabukichō already offering a rich set of precedents for underground bars and clubs, in *Kiwami* the developers go further by creating a whole subterranean world of illicit gambling, fighting and prostitution. This area, called Purgatory, is located in the abandoned Kamurochō Station in West Park, a dilapidated public park now occupied by the homeless. Here players meet the 'Florist of Sai', who explains how he employs the homeless to surveil Kamurochō. Being watched by the homeless is an ironic inversion of reality, where the government installed a network of fifty-five cameras across Kabukichō in 2002[8] to push both the yakuza and the homeless out of the district. To understand how Purgatory might possibly exist, we mapped it against Kamurochō Station's most likely real-world inspiration, Higashi-Shinjuku station at the northeast corner of Kabukichō, completed five years before the game is set [Fig.06]. The entrance to the virtual station most closely corresponds to the 'A1' gate in the real-world, so by combining the in-game geometry with the official subway station plan of Higashi-Shinjuku,[9] Purgatory appears to occupy the east-west Toei Ōedo Line platform on the B3F floor, which corresponds to the orientation of the in-game map. As the entrance to Kamurochō Station displays a sign very similar to the Toei subway logo, it is fair to presume this is indeed based on one of Toei's lines. By analysing the hollowed-out cave at the centre of Purgatory that is the home to the Florist's base, it appears to be around 32 metres (105 ft) in height. While Higashi-Shinjuku does have a maximum depth of 35.4 m (116 ft) at the B6F floor,[10] this occurs on another line, meaning that while this is not completely unfeasible given the real-world station engineering in the area, the developers have played around with the station's geometry in order to convincingly realize this subterranean pleasure district.

This playfulness is seen in little incidental details: signs on both the east and west platforms of the station indicate that either direction of travel leads to the same destination, Shin-Kamurochō Station. But this also extends into the design of Purgatory itself, as seen through our screenshot photography [Fig.07], where it appears the subway tunnel has been flooded before a set of traditional store fronts and vernacular Japanese *machiya* buildings[11] has been constructed. Women sitting behind fences, like those of 19th-century *yūkaku* red light districts, beckon towards Kiryu. This reference to earlier forms of architecture has a rich spatial symbolism as Tokyo is a city almost literally built on top of its predecessor, Edo. Jinnai Hidenobu describes how 'Edo provided the basic design upon which, layer by layer, the modern and present-day cities of Tokyo were built.'[12] In a similar way, Purgatory's traditional pleasure district aesthetic is built into the very underpinnings of Kamurochō above it. The flooded tunnel also recalls Tokyo's G-Cans facility,[13] a giant cathedral of water drainage, demonstrating the huge unseen infrastructure that keeps a city functioning.

DVD 神室最大級 隠引真 StarDust 45分 600円 B1F DVD

[Fig.06] PAGE 272

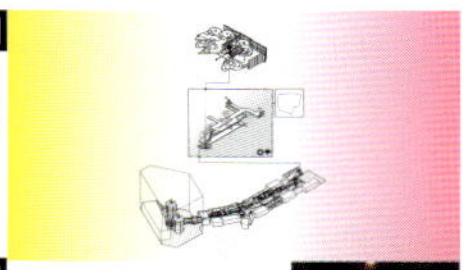

Mapping how the fictional Kamurochō station, leading to the Purgatory underworld, might be located within the real-world Higashi-Shinjuku station on the Toei Ōedo Line platform.

[Fig.07] PAGE 273

Looking through the Purgatory area, showing how this illicit underworld is built into the concrete infrastructure of a flooded metro tunnel.

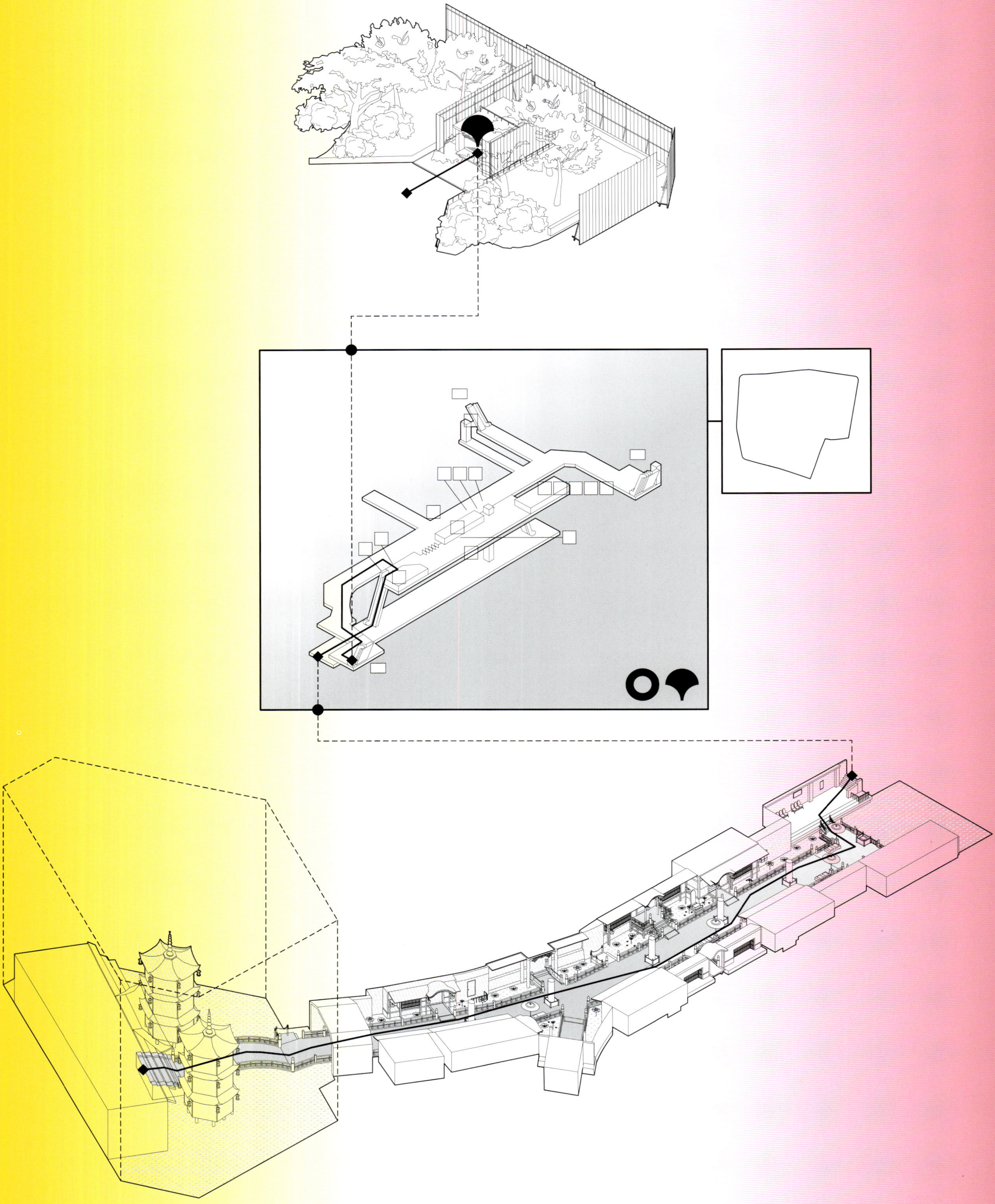

[Fig.06]

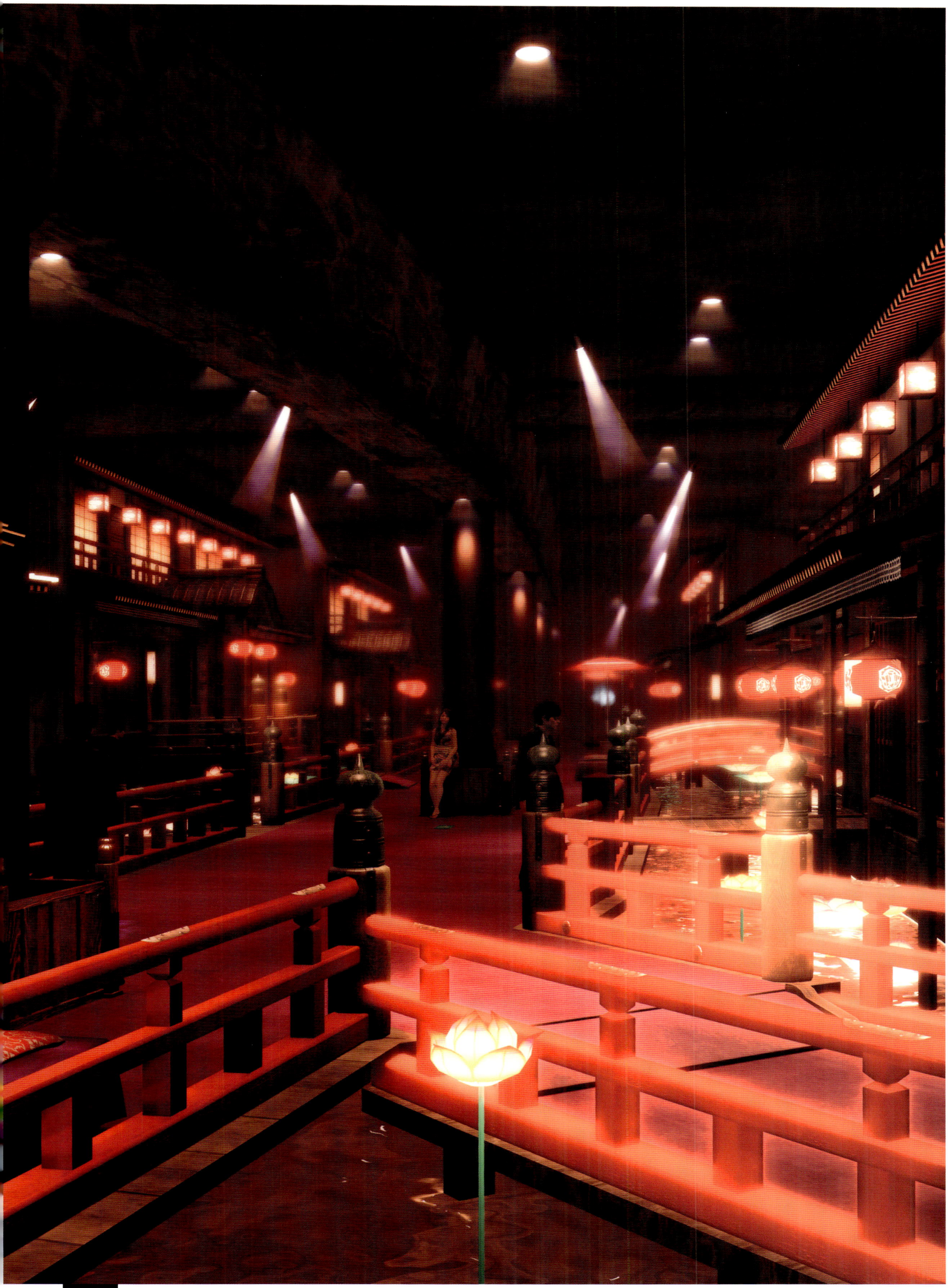

[Fig.07]

12.4 STREET FIGHTER

When Kiryu is not drinking, slurping ramen or chatting up hostesses, he is usually fighting. Kamurochō provides a perfect setting for this, with large numbers of angry yakuza and other thugs roaming the streets. Following anti-yakuza *Bōtaihō* legislation in the 1990s, 'the void left by the yakuza in places like Kabukichō seems to have paved the ground for the emergence of a new type of crime, more loosely and flexibly organized'[14] which is known as *hangure*. The game's story also covers the emergence of gangs that have less respect for the strict codes of the yakuza, turning Kamurochō's streets into an active battleground. When Kiryu enters a fight, the streets close off as pedestrians going about their day become a willing audience, clapping and cheering him on. Mapping one of these fights demonstrates how people suddenly shuffle into position to create a temporary battleground in the street, running to form human walls and ensure Kiryu cannot escape [Fig.08]. These encirclements last for fleeting moments, until the last thug has been knocked out cold and the streetscape resets. As Elizabeth Grosz argues, 'space itself…requires and entails a mode of time, timeliness, or duration.'[15] In *Kiwami* these temporary moments in time transform the street from a lifelike slice of urban Tokyo into a more chaotic but also more tightly-bound space.

Once Kiryu is in a fight, Kamurochō comes alive as traffic cones, bikes, signs and trash cans become objects he can grab, swing and hurl at assailants. Long regarded as one of the grimier parts of the usually spotless Tokyo, Kabukichō and all the elements that accompany nightlife represent a perfect streetscape of objects to hit burly gangsters with. Taking a view down one of the main streets in Kamurochō, we can see quite how many elements are designed to be grabbed and thrown [Fig.09]. As objects are removed from their context in the street to be wielded by Kiryu, their former meaning becomes less important than the specific number of blows to enemies that they can provide before breaking. This emphasis on the importance of objects placed on the street is reminiscent both of anthropologist Kon Wajiro's 'modernology' drawings of domestic objects in Japanese homes,[16] and Austrian architect Hans Hollein's declaration that 'Alles ist Architektur' (everything is, and could be, architecture).[17] Here we can see that these objects form not only visual scenes reminiscent of the real Kabukichō, but also create a game-specific space where things being bounced off the heads of thugs is arguably their truer form.

[Fig.08]

MAP OF A TEMPORARY FIGHTING TERRITORY CREATED BY PEDESTRIANS, PORTIONING OFF THE STREET AS THEY GATHER TO CHEER ON KIRYU WHILE HE BATTLES THUGS AND OTHER YAKUZA.

[Fig.09]
PAGE 276

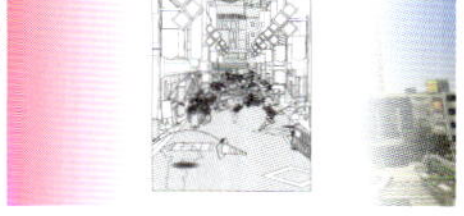

A view down one of Kamurochō's streets, showing the many pieces of street furniture that Kiryu can pick up, turning the objects that define Shinjuku's party district into weapons.

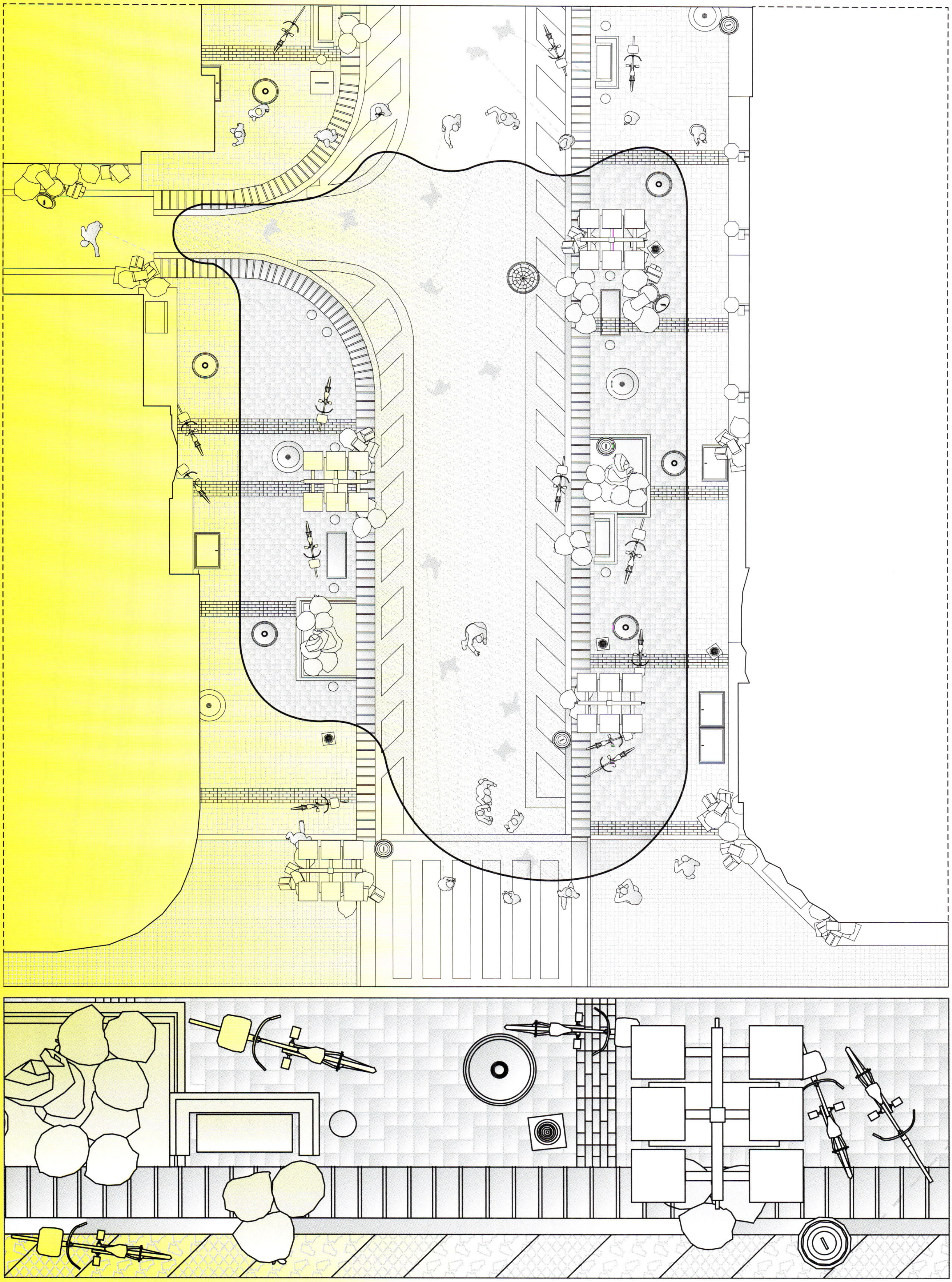

[Fig.08]

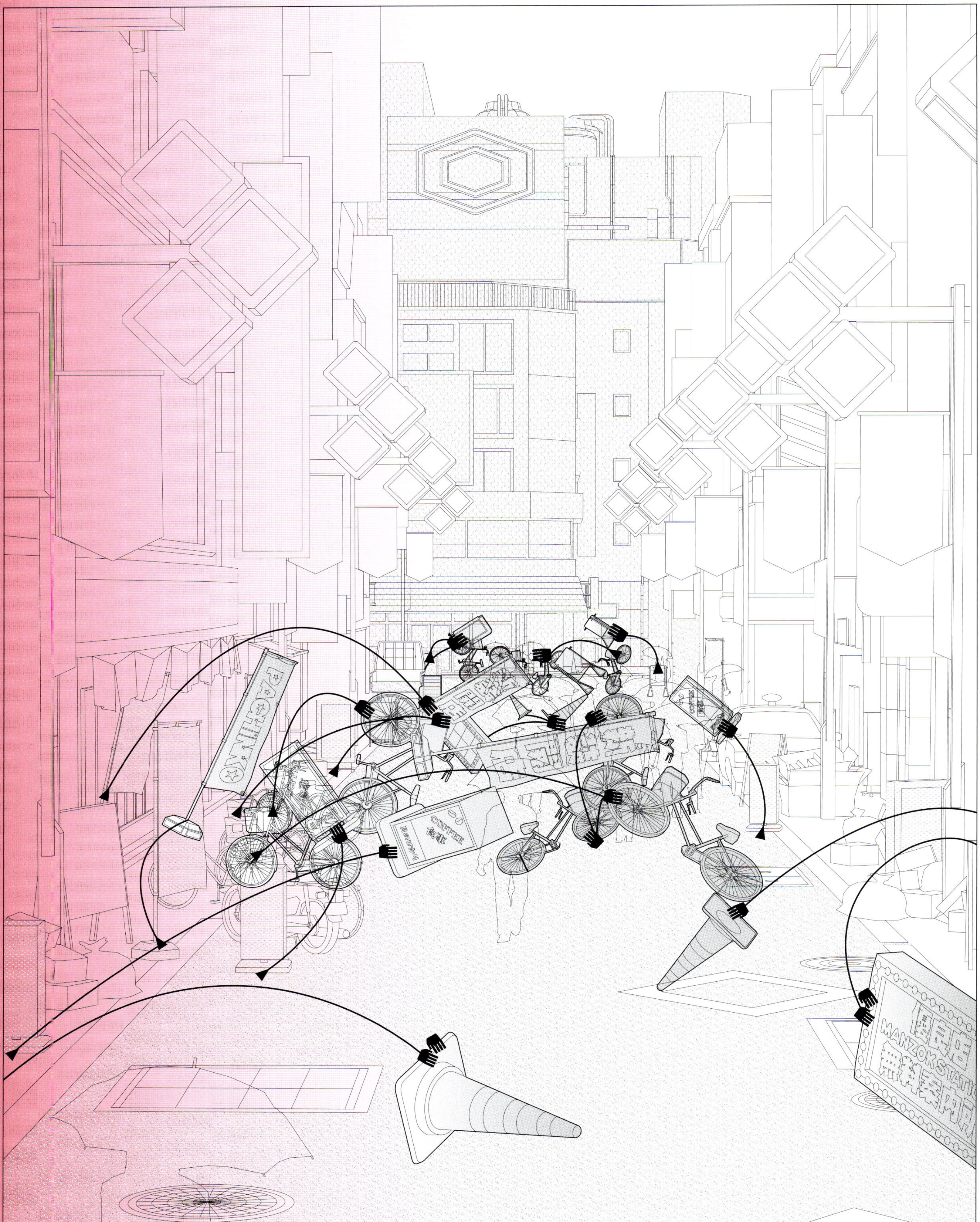

[Fig.09]

12.5

DISCREPANT BUILDINGS

Kamurochō is a thorough and meaningful recreation of Kabukichō, but it is not without certain, sometimes large, slippages between fact and fiction, where the designers have taken artistic license with the city. In one of the game's larger battle sequences, Kiryu fights his way through an abandoned building, trying to reach his friends Shinji and Reina. The external form of this building is placed near to a love hotel that exists in the real Kabukichō, giving it appropriate context. By comparing the exterior of the building to the interior maps, it appears that they broadly match, apart from some stairwells that protrude further than expected. Yet once we emerge onto the roof of the building for the climactic battle, everything has changed [Fig.10]. Surrounding buildings are taller and more densely packed than before, and the single building we entered has now become four smaller rooftops that Kiryu needs to jump across. This is a rare moment when the contextual relationship between Kamurochō and Kabukichō is clearly severed to create a more interesting space for the player to overcome.

The largest discrepancy is also the most notable architectural invention of Kamurochō, the Millennium Tower, a building which does not and has not existed in the real world, yet serves as a repeated setting in the Yakuza series [Fig.11]. While social media users who visit Kabukichō find the Tokyu Kabukichō Tower to be a reasonable real-world approximation (drawing the attention of the game's developers),[18] this building was not completed until 2023, almost two decades after the original game. While the Tokyu tower serves as a convenient proxy, Reddit users have identified a potential alternative inspiration from an unlikely origin, the visually similar Millennnium Tower in Rotterdam,[19] which was completed in 2000 and thus a possible inspiration for the original game. By counting rows of windows and atrium heights from the in-game building we can estimate it at around forty-two storeys in total height, with the tower itself rising around thirty-two storeys. Rotterdam's tower rises thirty-four storeys while the modern Tokyu tower is significantly taller at forty-eight floors, suggesting that these online theories may not be too wide of the mark.

The Millennium Tower is key to *Kiwami*'s story, and central to the last moments of the game. We have mapped this journey as Kiryu fights his way through the tower's lower atriums, eventually reaching the rooftop bar Ares – appropriately the most luxurious drinking establishment in the game [Fig.12]. Camera tools show us how the rooftop of the building is disembodied from the rest of the structure, fully encased in a skybox depicting Tokyo's nighttime cityscape complete with its iconic flashing red warning lights. Connecting it back to the rest of the building reveals the entire form of the tower, showing how the battle against Kyohei Jingu continues all the way up to the tower's helipad. Returning to Ares, Kiryu must face off with his former friend Akira Nishikiyama, in a fight where both the protagonists survive, but the same cannot be said for the bar's interior furnishings. Finally, once all the punching is done, Nishikiyama triggers an explosion that rains a stash of ten billion yen in embezzled money down over the streets of Kamurochō, onto the heads of the district's citizens.

[Fig.10] PAGE 278

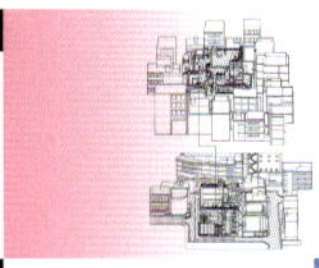

Oblique drawing comparing the contextual exterior of an abandoned building that Kiryu fights through to the very different roofscape onto which he emerges in the later stages of the mission.

[Fig.11] PAGE 279

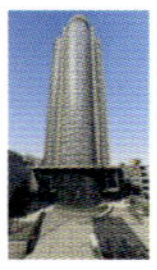

A view of the Millenium Tower, an icon of Kamurochō which unlike other notable buildings in the game, does not have an exact real-world counterpart.

[Fig.12] PAGES 280–1

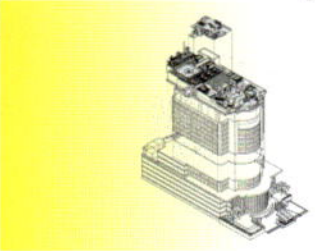

Isometric analysis of Kiryu's ascent of the Millennium Tower in the game's closing stages, fighting all the way to the helipad and leading to an explosion that rains stolen money down onto the streets below.

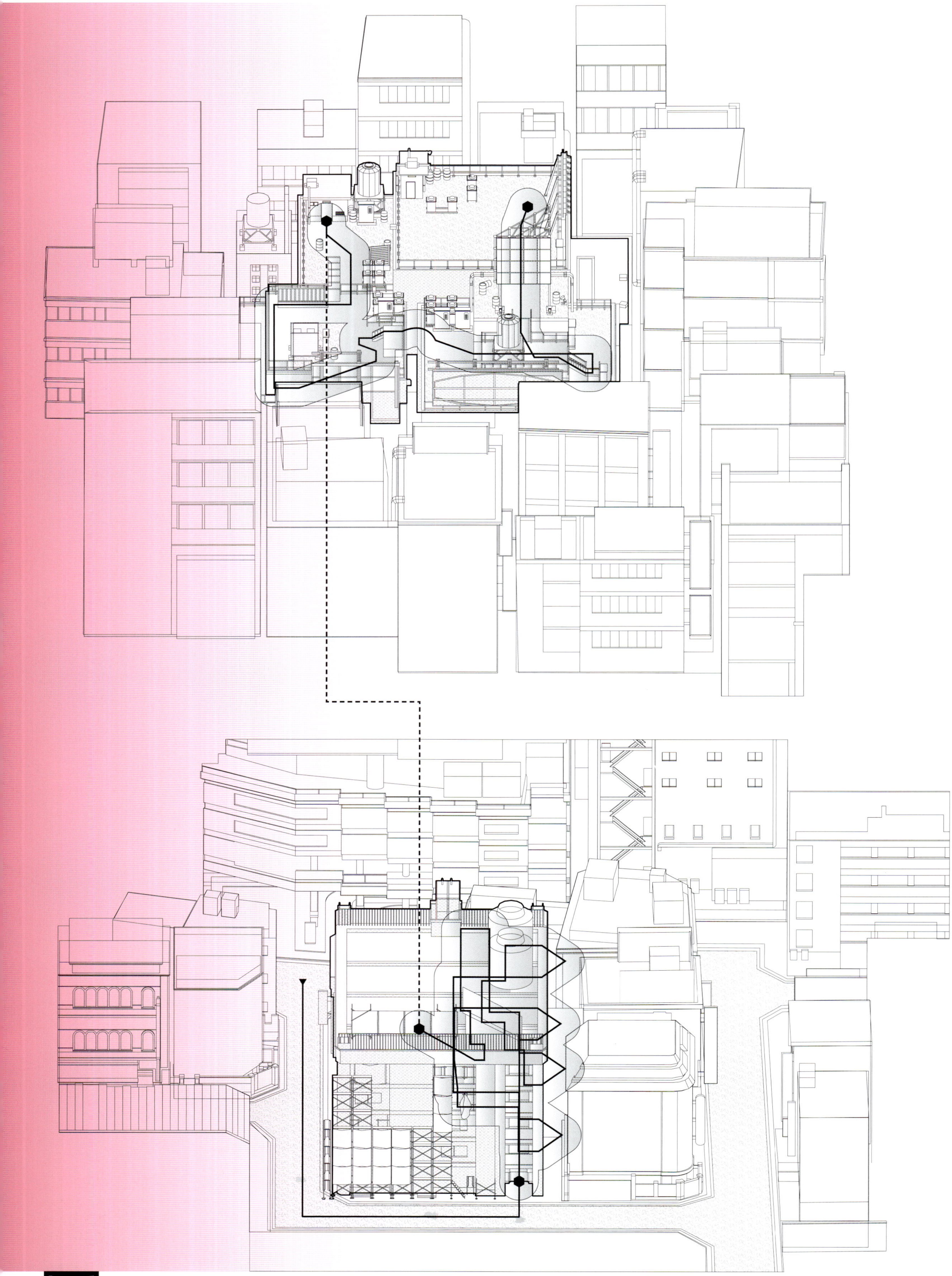

[Fig.10]

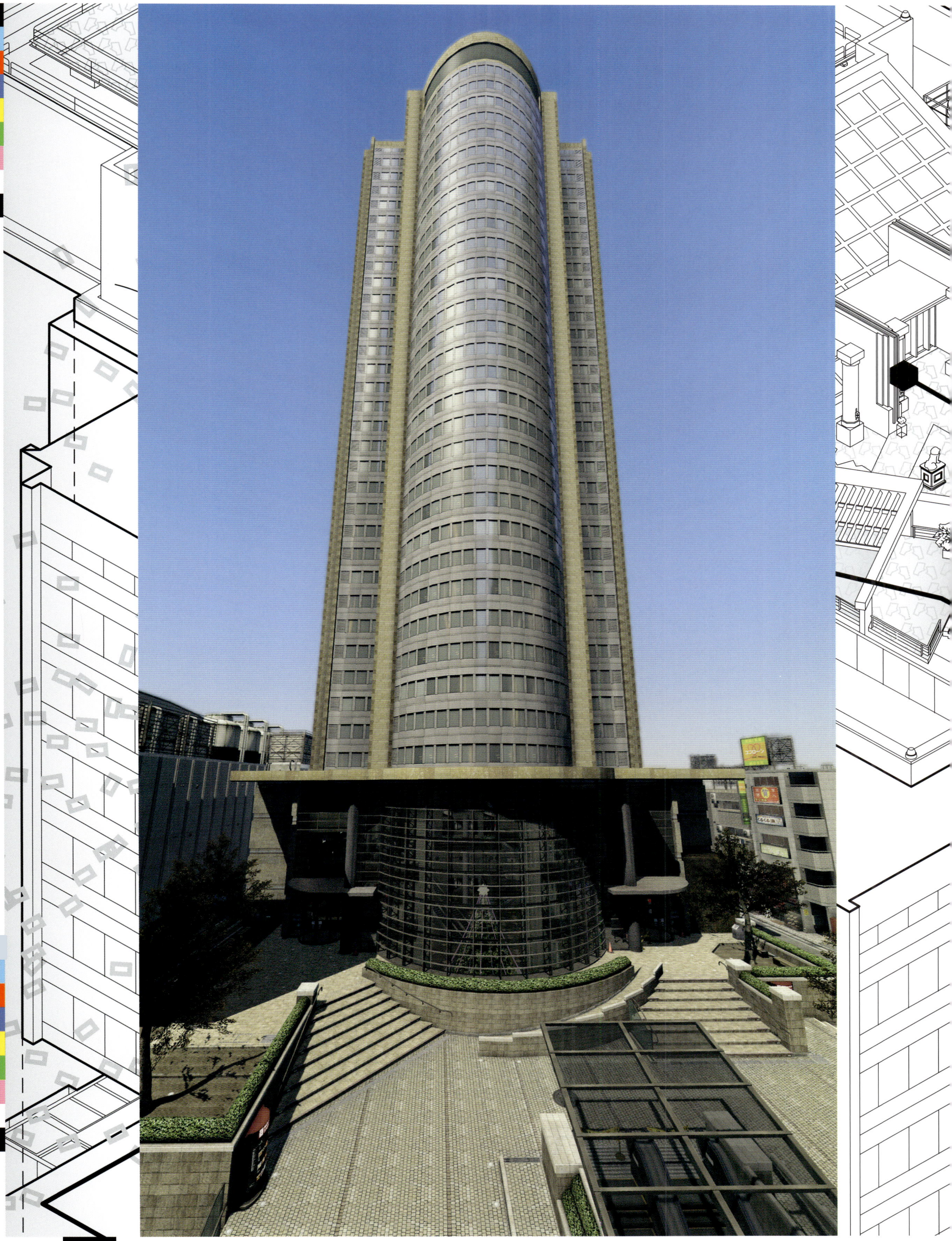

[Fig.11]

This event concludes the first game in the *Yakuza* series while setting up stories for subsequent returns to Kamurochō. As we learn in *Yakuza 4*, the explosion that blew money down onto the streets was a catalyst for another key character, Shun Akiyama, to grab a million yen in cash, overcome his homelessness and rebuild his life. Through these interconnected stories and repeated visits to Kamurochō over the years, players can come to know the area so well that navigating real-world Kabukichō may feel like second nature. Of course, both the virtual and physical areas have changed over the years. But some things remain constant, like the bouffant hairstyles of hosts, the chime of the minimart entrance or, in Kamurochō at least, never being more than a few seconds away from another dust-up.

[Fig.12] Detail

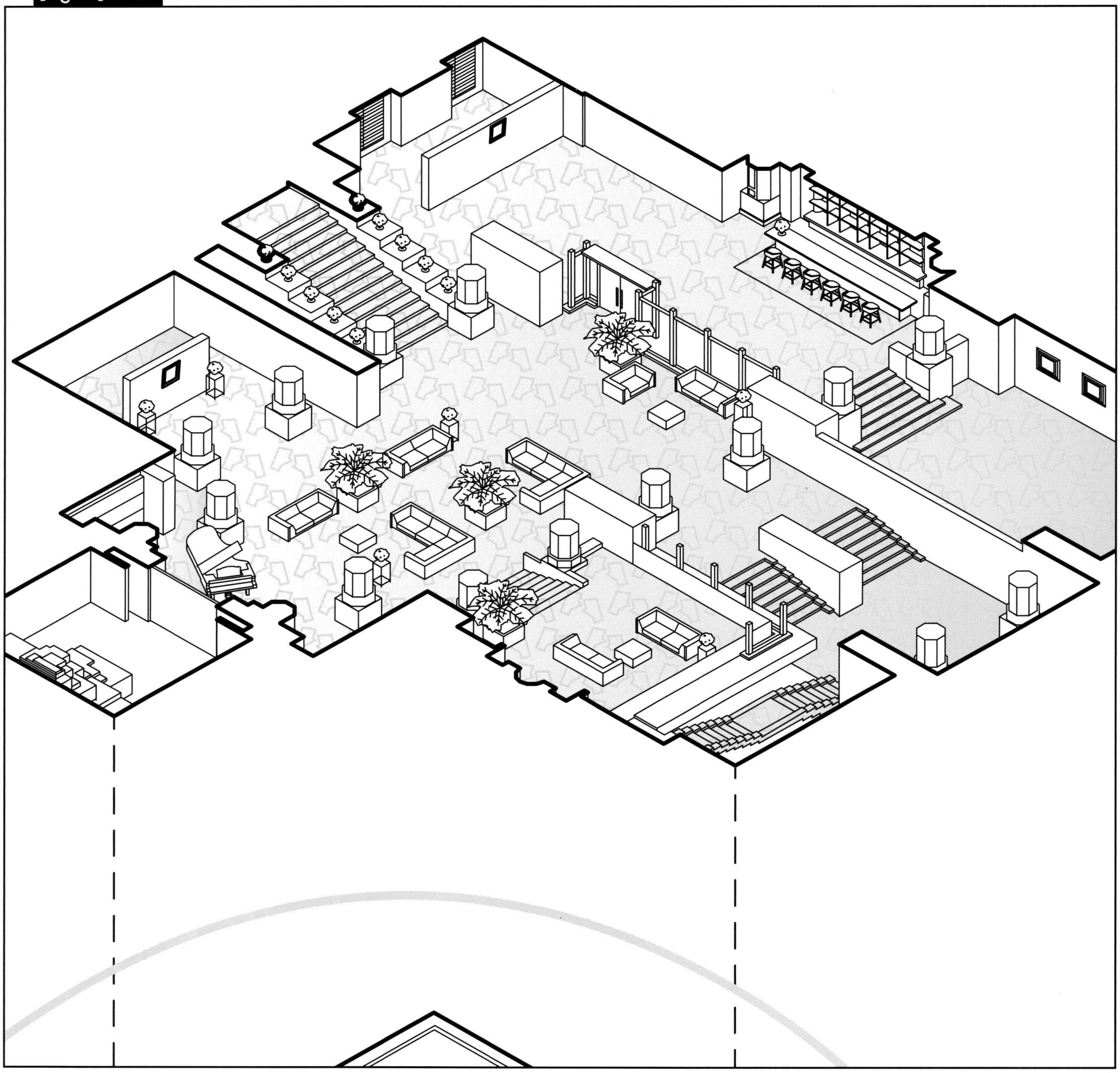

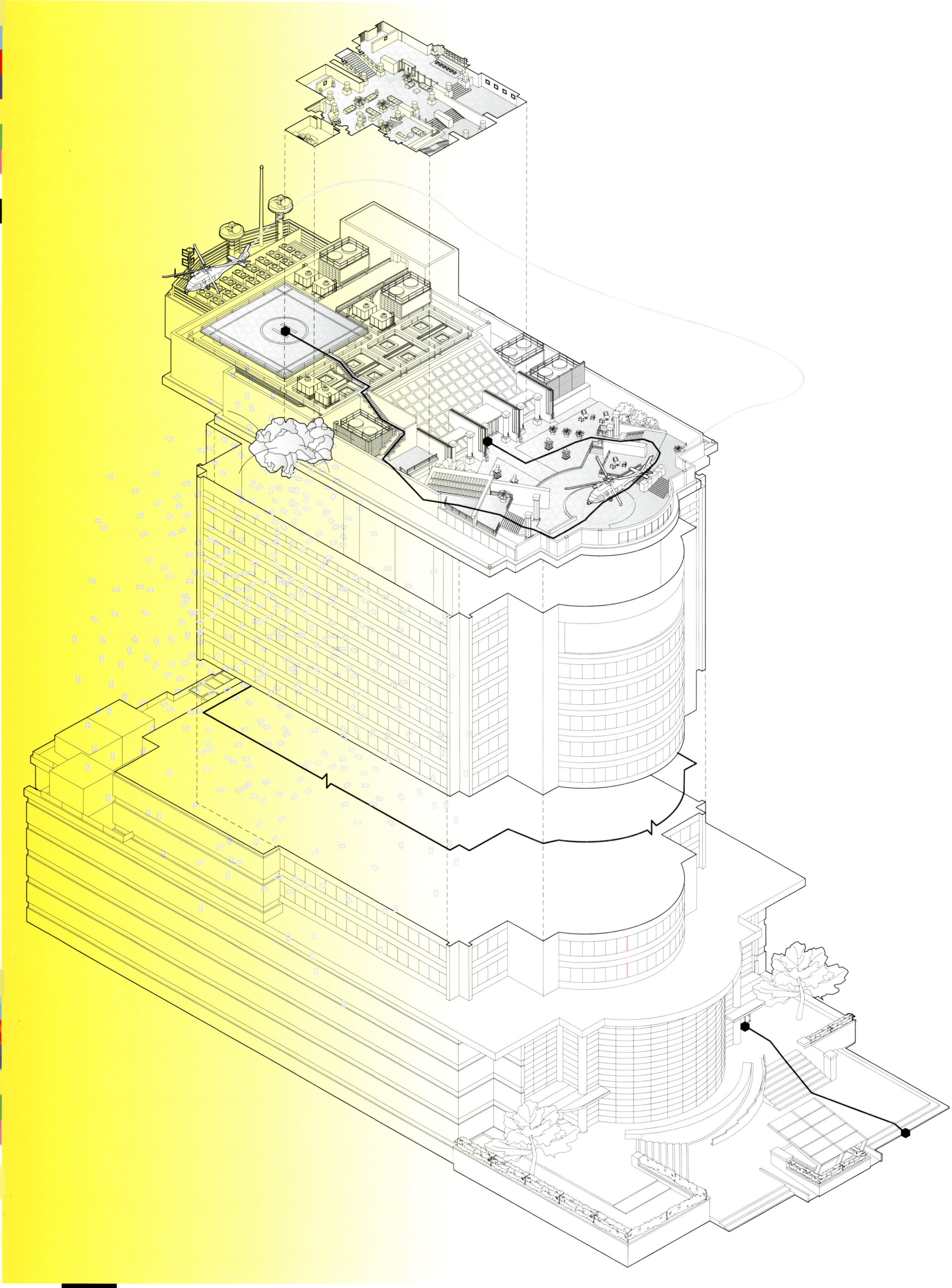

[Fig.12]

EPILOGUE

IF YOU BUILD IT, THEY WILL PLAY

Across the twelve chapters in this book, we have used architecture as a framework to uncover new knowledge about the design and construction of game worlds. The countless drawings and screenshots we have produced refer to different ways of understanding and representing space that have existed for centuries, and our methods run from the very old to the very new. This could be as simple as a considered walk through the world, or as complex as data analysis of a game's coded systems. Colliding the fields of architecture and games creates new understandings of both disciplines. The cities and landscapes of *Videogame Architecture* challenge the orthodoxy of the 'built environment' that we experience in our everyday lives. Weather, material lifespan, structural integrity and even gravity can be contested in these worlds, through the *deviations* we discuss at the start of this book. As a result, each of the games we have studied, whether old or new, has something deeper to say about our relationship to place and culture. As with physical buildings, videogame architecture is designed by people, for people, with specific ideas of how they will inhabit and use the space. But unlike 'real-world' structures, games can push architecture into places where the impossible becomes possible in the service of exploring novel stories and mechanics.

Throughout this book our methods have attempted to extract, represent and interrogate what these worlds might mean, and how gameplay and spatial design are in a constant relationship. In *Gravity Rush 2*, for example, we found architectural styles collected from around the world, carefully composed to mirror a political structure while simultaneously promoting the freeform movement of a character who literally falls in and out of society. This is a world formed by a complex set of requirements and forces. We can say similar for every other game we have analysed. In fact, we can extend this to many other games that we have not been able to include in this study, such is the breadth and variety of videogame architecture.

The amount of detail we have been able to uncover through our analysis is testament to the deep and layered qualities of these game worlds. By establishing ways of looking at the world that players may not have encountered before, this is also a call to play games differently, to explore them in new ways and to question some of the assumptions we may have about the worlds they represent. All games provide a relationship between the depicted world and the agency we are afforded within that environment. But while for many titles that might imply the ability to fight or jump our way through space, there are countless other forms of agency possible – even if they may require a mod or two to unlock. Asserting our position as virtual surveyors, we exercise the ability to stop and look, to escape the world and gaze back upon it. The act of drawing – transcribing these worlds and their logic into the flat pages of this book, allows us to place ourselves both within and outside these environments and explore them from this unique vantage point.

This process has allowed us to speak about games we all love in a new way, understanding them in more analytical terms and proving that they represent a discipline of spatial design that is increasingly intertwined with architecture. Developing innovative ways of comprehending these places is important because of the millions that find meaning in these worlds – whether they are the latest viral smash, or a low-poly place we remember from our youth. As we have shown throughout this book, *Videogame Architecture* is no mere environmental backdrop, subservient to the actions of the player – it is a main character.

COMMUNITY RESOURCES

CH 01 BALDUR'S GATE 3

→ Baldur's Gate 3 Wiki: https://bg3.wiki
→ Fextralife Baldur's Gate 3 Wiki: https://baldursgate3.wiki.fextralife.com/Baldur's+Gate+3+Wiki
→ Forgotten Realms Wiki: https://forgottenrealms.fandom.com/wiki/Main_Page
→ Greyscale, 'Iron Throne 100% – The Smart and Easy Way,' Steam Community: https://steamcommunity.com/sharedfiles/filedetails/?id=3041431809
→ Mapgenie: https://mapgenie.io/baldurs-gate-3
→ Northalix, 'Having a Chat with the Architect of Moonrise Towers in the House of Hope,' YouTube: https://www.youtube.com/watch?v=JP-EvaMhR_c
→ Otis_Inf Photomode Mods: https://opm.fransbouma.com/Cameras/bg3.htm
→ Reddit: https://www.reddit.com/r/BaldursGate3/
→ RPG Division, 'Save Everyone & Loot Everything in Iron Throne – Baldur's Gate 3,' YouTube: https://www.youtube.com/watch?v=IkgXJQsTzMQ

CH 02 BIOSHOCK

→ BioShock Wiki: https://bioshock.fandom.com/wiki/BioShock_Wiki
→ Reddit: https://www.reddit.com/r/Bioshock/
→ ShoddyCast, 'The TECH! How Close Are We to Creating BioShock's Rapture?,' YouTube: https://youtu.be/YUVCSjM5Yvc
→ SpacePak, 'Could Rapture Exist? – BioShock Science Ep. 1,' YouTube: https://youtu.be/_ergF-jmrsY
→ UE Viewer (formerly UModel), Konstantin Nosov (Gildor): https://www.gildor.org/en/projects/umodel

CH 03 DISCO ELYSIUM

→ Fandom Disco Elysium Wiki: https://discoelysium.fandom.com/wiki/Disco_Elysium_Wiki
→ FAYDE Playback Experiment: http://fayde.co.uk
→ Reddit: https://www.reddit.com/r/DiscoElysium/
→ Wikimedia Commons, 'Soviet-era Street Lights in Estonia': https://commons.wikimedia.org/wiki/Category:Soviet-era_street_lights_in_Estonia

CH 04 DOOM

→ Ashes 2063: https://www.moddb.com/mods/ashes-2063
→ Brutal Doom: https://www.moddb.com/mods/brutal-doom
→ Classic Doom: https://classicdoom.com/
→ CountryCide (ModDB): https://www.moddb.com/mods/trench-foot-wip/downloads/countrycide
→ decino, 'Showcasing Doom's Line Specials,' YouTube: https://www.youtube.com/watch?v=0s4DpRTZenw
→ Doom Launcher: https://github.com/nstlaurent/DoomLauncher
→ Doom Wiki: https://doomwiki.org/
→ Doomworld: https://www.doomworld.com/
→ Doom 3: The Golden Souls: https://batandy.itch.io/goldensouls3
→ Ian Albert, Doom Maps: https://ian-albert.com/games/doom_maps
→ IMX Doomer, Tumblr: https://imx-doomer.tumblr.com
→ Reddit: https://www.reddit.com/r/Doom/
→ Sandwedge: 'INSANELY DETAILED Doom Map Has 65K Linedefs! INSATANITY by Man With Gun,' YouTube: https://www.youtube.com/watch?v=y876PjjUZf0
→ The Level Design Book, 'Doom Metrics': https://book.leveldesignbook.com/process/blockout/metrics/doom
→ Ultimate Doom Builder: https://ultimatedoombuilder.github.io/
→ ZDoom: https://zdoom.org/downloads

CH 05 ELDEN RING

→ Otis_Inf Photomode Mod: https://opm.fransbouma.com/Cameras/eldenring.htm
→ Reddit: https://www.reddit.com/r/Eldenring/
→ Smithbox Modding Tool: https://www.nexusmods.com/eldenring/mods/4928
→ Tarnished Archaeologist, YouTube: https://www.youtube.com/@TarnishedArchaeologist
→ UXM Selective Unpacker: https://github.com/Nordgaren/UXM-Selective-Unpack
→ VaatiVidya, YouTube: https://www.youtube.com/@VaatiVidya
→ WitchyBND ('ivi' et al.): https://www.nexusmods.com/eldenring/mods/3862

CH 06 GENSHIN IMPACT

→ Genshin Asriel, 'Azure Cottage – Liyue Serenitea Pot,' YouTube: https://www.youtube.com/watch?v=RPaINExBW4Q
→ Genshin Asriel, 'White Manor – Fontaine Serenitea Pot,' YouTube: https://www.youtube.com/watch?v=pMxs8sdxe0I
→ Genshin Impact Interactive Map: https://genshin-impact-map.appsample.com/
→ Genshin Impact Wiki: https://genshin-impact.fandom.com/wiki/Genshin_Impact_Wiki
→ 竹壺 taketsubo, 'Genshin Small Swimming Pool Resort | Serenitea Pot Design,' YouTube: https://www.youtube.com/watch?v=0swF50yg_hM
→ Vineet Kumar Naik, 'Genshin Impact Astral Puzzle Solution for Mona's Domain,' Sportskeeda: https://www.sportskeeda.com/esports/genshin-impact-astral-puzzle-solution-mona-s-domain

CH 07 GRAVITY RUSH 2

→ Jace, 'Storybook Islands: Errands as Worldbuilding in Gravity Rush,' Medium: https://medium.com/@pizzasheets/storybook-islands-errands-as-worldbuilding-in-gravity-rush-c70a8d778b72
→ Kill Screen: https://www.killscreen.com/
→ MoeGamer: https://moegamer.net/2017/06/08/gravity-rush-the-franco-belgian-tradition-via-japan/
→ Reddit: https://www.reddit.com/r/GravityRush/
→ ResetEra: https://www.resetera.com/threads/is-jirga-para-lhao-gravity-rush-2-the-most-visually-distinct-open-world.28972/

CH 08 GRIM FANDANGO REMASTERED

→ Fandom Grim Fandango Wiki: https://grim-fandango.fandom.com/wiki/Special_Features
→ fSpy: https://fspy.io/
→ Grim Fandango Art, Tumblr: https://grimfandangoart.tumblr.com/
→ Grim Fandango Network: https://grimfandango.network/
→ MobyGames: https://www.mobygames.com/game/70792/grim-fandango-remastered
→ Reddit: https://www.reddit.com/r/grimfandango/
→ ScummVM: https://www.scummvm.org/
→ The Department of Death: http://www.grim-fandango.com/

CH 09 HALF-LIFE 2

→ Blender Source Tools: https://developer.valvesoftware.com/wiki/Blender_Source_Tools
→ Combine OverWiki: https://combineoverwiki.net/
→ Crafty, Nem's Tools: https://nemstools.github.io/pages/Crafty.html
→ Nathraichean, 'City 17 Confirmed to Be in Sofia, Bulgaria,' Imgur: https://imgur.com/a/hl-city-17-confirmed-to-be-sofia-bulgaria-DeF7XWS
→ NFKRZ, 'Where Is City 17 Really Located?,' YouTube: https://www.youtube.com/watch?v=bOg59e23QPM
→ Noclip: https://noclip.website/
→ Reddit: https://www.reddit.com/r/HalfLife/
→ Say Hi to Atlas, 'Aoyama Technical College Building': https://www.sayhito-atlas.com/article/aoyama-technical-college-building-tokyo-japan-by-makoto-sei-watanabe
→ SourceIO Blender Importer: https://github.com/REDxEYE/SourceIO
→ Source Engine Blender Collection: https://github.com/hisprofile/blenderstuff/blob/main/Creations/Source%20Engine%20Blender%20Collection.md#half-life-2

CH 10 THE LAST OF US PART 1

→ Andrew Levitt, 'The Last of Us Locations in Real Life,' YouTube: https://www.youtube.com/watch?v=pVSXHNdz32w
→ Giant Bomb Wiki: https://giantbomb.com/wiki/Games/The_Last_of_Us
→ Otis_Inf Photomode Mod: https://opm.fransbouma.com/Cameras/tlou1.htm
→ Reddit: https://www.reddit.com/r/thelastofus/
→ SmooviesTV, 'Salt Lake City – Game vs Real Life Comparison,' YouTube: https://www.youtube.com/watch?v=py4nsfSQGPo
→ SmooviesTV, 'UEC / Silver Lake / Boulder – Game vs Real Life Comparison,' YouTube: https://www.youtube.com/watch?v=DuvahVlKU8Q

CH 11 THE SIMS 4

→ Blue Moon NoCC, 'Cayrees': https://www.ea.com/en-gb/games/the-sims/the-sims-4/pc/gallery
→ Deligracy, 'I Built the Goths a New House,' YouTube: https://www.youtube.com/watch?v=Gf9Aia0066Y
→ Devon Bumpkin, 'I Renovated the Goth Family Home,' YouTube: https://www.youtube.com/watch?v=p50Bw_1_lEU
→ Eco Sanctuary, 'a-winged-llama': https://www.ea.com/games/the-sims/the-sims-4/pc/gallery
→ Just Nora Gaming, 'I Tried to Renovate the Goth House,' YouTube: https://www.youtube.com/watch?v=SIsros6d7kA
→ Reddit: https://www.reddit.com/r/Sims4/
→ lilsimsie, 'Touring Your Incredible Builds,' YouTube: https://www.youtube.com/watch?v=1cq8OffRNrE
→ mewbuilds, TikTok: https://www.tiktok.com/@mewbuilds
→ SatchOnSims, 'Testing Viral Sims 4 Life Hacks!,' YouTube: https://www.youtube.com/watch?v=Y-rmTFwNjcI
→ Syd Mac, 'Building a House Using TikTok Hacks,' YouTube: https://www.youtube.com/watch?v=r3CVRfHCQHE
→ Syd Mac, 'Testing Sims 4 TikTok Hacks,' YouTube: https://www.youtube.com/watch?v=F5SD4pP6J3c
→ The Gamer, 'All WooHoo Spots and Where to Find Them': https://www.thegamer.com/sims-4-all-woohoo-locations-found/
→ The Sims Wiki: https://sims.fandom.com/
→ Teoalida, 'The Sims 4 Worlds': https://www.teoalida.com/thesims/the-sims-4-worlds/

CH 12 YAKUZA KIWAMI

→ Adventures of Chris and Tifa Wiki: https://adventures-of-chris-and-tifa.fandom.com/wiki/Millennium_Tower
→ Reddit: https://www.reddit.com/r/yakuzagames/
→ Yakuza Freecam: https://github.com/etra0/yakuza-freecam
→ Yakuza Wiki: https://yakuza.fandom.com/wiki/Yakuza_Wiki

NOTES

INTRODUCTION

1. Luke Pearson and Sandra Youkhana, *Videogame Atlas: Mapping Interactive Worlds* (Thames & Hudson, 2022).
2. Robert Venturi, Denise Scott Brown and Steven Izenour, *Learning from Las Vegas: The Forgotten Symbolism of Architectural Form* (MIT Press, 1976).
3. Karal Ann Marling, *Designing Disney's Theme Parks: The Architecture of Reassurance* (Flammarion, 1997).
4. François Blanciak, *Tokyoids: The Robotic Face of Architecture* (MIT Press, 2022).
5. Oxford Languages definition of 'folksonomy': 'a user-generated system of classifying and organizing online content into different categories by the use of metadata such as electronic tags.'

CH 01 BALDUR'S GATE 3

1. Ed Greenwood, Matt Sernett and Steve Winter, *Murder in Baldur's Gate* (Wizards of the Coast, 2013).
2. Elliot Gardner, 'How Baldur's Gate III Devs Are Crafting the Definitive Dungeons & Dragons Video Game', *TechRadar*: https://www.techradar.com/news/how-baldurs-gate-iii-devs-are-crafting-the-definitive-dungeons-and-dragons-video-game
3. Wizards of the Coast, *Baldur's Gate: Descent into Avernus* (Wizards of the Coast, 2019), p.159.
4. Ed Greenwood, Matt Sernett and Steve Winter, *Murder in Baldur's Gate* (Wizards of the Coast, 2013), p.126.
5. Stimona Milanova (Larian Studios), 'Combining Environmental Storytelling and Level Design in Baldur's Gate 3', Sofia Game Jam lecture, YouTube, 2024: https://youtu.be/2x8eQOZUu9A
6. Kevin Lynch, *The Image of the City* (MIT Press, 1960).
7. Otis_Inf Photomode Mods: Baldur's Gate III: https://opm.fransbouma.com/Cameras/bg3.htm
8. Bernard Rudofsky, *Architecture Without Architects: An Introduction to Non-Pedigreed Architecture* (Museum of Modern Art, 1964).
9. Ibid.
10. Larian Studios, *Artwork from Baldur's Gate 3* (Wizards of the Coast, 2023), p.33.
11. Stimona Milanova (Larian Studios), 'Combining Environmental Storytelling and Level Design in Baldur's Gate 3', Sofia Game Jam lecture, YouTube, 2024: https://youtu.be/2x8eQOZUu9A
12. Kiyoshi Matsumoto, 'MA – The Japanese Concept of Space and Time', *Medium*: https://medium.com/@kiyoshimatsumoto/ma-the-japanese-concept-of-space-and-time-3330c83ded4c
13. Chiara Testoni, 'From Rialto to Bjarke Ingels: The Evolution of the Inhabited Bridge Through Fifteen Examples', *Domus*: https://www.domusweb.it/en/architecture/gallery/2023/10/11/inhabited-bridges-with-buildings-ponte-vecchio-rialto-italy-world.html
14. Chris Van Hayden, 'History of the Old London Bridge: The Original Bridge over the River Thames', *Guide London*: https://www.guidelondon.org.uk/blog/around-london/history-of-the-old-london-bridge
15. Larian Studios, *Artwork from Baldur's Gate 3* (Wizards of the Coast, 2023), p.89.
16. u/TheFoodAtHome42, 'How the Heck Is Baldur's Gate Still Standing?', *Reddit*: https://www.reddit.com/r/BaldursGate3/comments/1aj6ewj/how_the_heck_is_baldurs_gate_still_standing/
17. Izabela Cardoso and Fernando Teixeira, 'The Mysterious Inverted Tower Steeped in Templar Myth', *BBC Travel*: https://www.bbc.com/travel/article/20200220-the-mysterious-inverted-tower-steeped-in-templar-myth
18. Larian Studios, *Artwork from Baldur's Gate 3* (Wizards of the Coast, 2023), p.19.
19. RPG Division, 'Save Everyone & Loot Everything in Iron Throne – Baldur's Gate 3', YouTube: https://www.youtube.com/watch?v=IkgXJQsTzMQ
20. Nick Compton, 'Cave Man: Inspecting Atelier Van Lieshout's Transcendental Work', *Wallpaper*: https://www.wallpaper.com/art/cave-man-inspecting-atelier-van-lieshouts-transcendental-work
21. Northalix, 'Having a Chat with the Architect of Moonrise Towers in the House of Hope', YouTube: https://www.youtube.com/watch?v=JP-EvaMhR_c

CH 02 BIOSHOCK

1. Ayn Rand, *Atlas Shrugged* (Random House, 1957).
2. The location as given by Fontaine in the note to Jack is 63° 2' N, 29° 55' W.
3. General Bathymetric Chart of the Oceans (GEBCO), global bathymetric terrain data: https://www.gebco.net/
4. ShoddyCast, 'The TECH! How Close Are We to Creating BioShock's Rapture?', YouTube: https://youtu.be/YUVCSjM5Yvc
5. Acceleration and distance travelled calculated using Omni Calculator: https://www.omnicalculator.com/physics/acceleration
6. Hugh Ferriss, *The Metropolis of Tomorrow* (Princeton Architectural Press, 1986).
7. Rem Koolhaas, *Delirious New York: A Retroactive Manifesto for Manhattan* (The Monacelli Press, 1994), p.281.
8. *Edge*, 'The Making of BioShock': https://web.archive.org/web/20130123122432/https://www.edge-online.com/features/making-bioshock/
9. Konstantin Nosov, *UE Viewer (UModel)*: https://www.gildor.org/en/projects/umodel
10. Starr Charles, 'The Chrysler Building Is "A Perfect Example" of the Art Deco Style', *Dezeen*: https://www.dezeen.com/2025/03/04/chrysler-building-art-deco-centenary/
11. Eric Nash, *Manhattan Skyscrapers* (Princeton Architectural Press, 1999), p.3.
12. Bridget Elliott and Michael Windover, 'What's the Use of Style? The Case of Art Deco', *The Routledge Companion to Art Deco* (Routledge, 2019), p.3.
13. Eric Nash, *Manhattan Skyscrapers* (Princeton Architectural Press, 1999), p.31.
14. John Shirley, *BioShock: Rapture* (Titan Books, 2011), p.121.
15. SpacePak, 'Could Rapture Exist? – BioShock Science Ep.1', YouTube: https://youtu.be/_ergF-jmrsY
16. 'New Aquarium in China Sets Five World Records', *Practical Fishkeeping*: https://www.practicalfishkeeping.co.uk/fishkeeping-news/new-aquarium-in-china-sets-five-world-records/
17. John Shirley, *BioShock: Rapture* (Titan Books, 2011), p.92.
18. Ibid., p.111.
19. Kingspan, 'What Is Thermal Bridging?': https://www.kingspan.com/gb/en/knowledge-articles/what-is-thermal-bridging/
20. Sven Schmalfuss, 'Authentic Bodies Genome(s) vs. Gender Norms in Oryx and Crake, The Year of the Flood, and BioShock', in Wolfgang Funk, Florian Groß and Irmtraud Huber (eds.), *The Aesthetics of Authenticity: Medial Constructions of the Real* (Transcript Verlag, 2012), p.94.
21. Roger Travis, 'BioShock as Plato's Cave', Luke Cuddy (ed.), *BioShock and Philosophy* (Wiley-Blackwell, 2015), p.69.
22. Paul Virilio, *Open Sky* (Verso, 1997), p.40.
23. Sandra Cohen-Rose, 'The Evolution and Role of Art Deco Societies and World Congresses in the Preservation and Popularization of Art Deco', in Bridget Elliott and Michael Windover (eds.), *The Routledge Companion to Art Deco* (Routledge, 2019), p.340.

CH 03 DISCO ELYSIUM

1. Robert Kurvitz, *Sacred and Terrible Air* (ZA/UM, 2013).
2. Helen Hindpere interviewed by Konstantinos Dimopoulos, 'Disco Elysium: Designing the City of Revachol', *Film Stories*: https://filmstories.co.uk/features/disco-elysium-designing-the-city-of-revachol/
3. N. S. Parthasarathy and Vela Murali, *Engineering Drawing* (Oxford University Press, 2015), p.538.
4. Ray Lucas, *Drawing Parallels: Knowledge Production in Axonometric, Isometric and Oblique Drawings* (Routledge, 2019), p.70.
5. John Hejduk, *Mask of Medusa: Works 1947–1983* (Rizzoli, 1985), p.50.
6. Michał Kłosiński, 'The Object Gives Rise to Thought: Hermeneutics of Objects in Disco Elysium', *Baltic Screen Media Review*, Vol. 9 (2021), p.58.
7. ZA/UM, *Disco Elysium Digital Artbook* (iam8bit, 2021), p.49.
8. Helen Hindpere interviewed by Konstantinos Dimopoulos, 'Disco Elysium: Designing the City of Revachol', *Film Stories*: https://filmstories.co.uk/features/disco-elysium-designing-the-city-of-revachol/
9. Maris Mändel, 'Welcome to the Free World! Building Materials in Post-Soviet Estonia in the 1990s', in João Mascarenhas-Mateus and Ana Paula Pires (eds.), *History of Construction Cultures Volume 1* (CRC Press, 2021), p.346.
10. Ibid., p.347.
11. Cedric Price and Joan Littlewood, *Fun Palace* promotional brochure (1964).
12. David Huber, 'The Story of the 1960s Mass-Produced Modular Design That Actually Went into Production', *ArchDaily*: https://www.archdaily.com/806346/the-story-of-the-1960s-mass-produced-modular-design-that-actually-went-into-production
13. Ewan Wilson, 'How the Stanley Kubrick Carpet Is Invading Video Games', *The Face*: https://theface.com/life/stanley-kubrick-the-shining-video-games-disco-elysium-control
14. u/amused-confused, 'Turns Out Martinaise Architecture Is Much More Detailed/Meaningful Than I Thought It Is', *Reddit*: https://www.reddit.com/r/DiscoElysium/comments/vig1tx/turns_out_martinaise_architecture_is_much_more/
15. Annette Tietenberg, 'The Pattern Which Connects', in Petra Schmidt, Ralf Wollheim and Annette Tietenberg (eds.), *Patterns in Design, Art and Architecture* (Birkhäuser, 2007), p.8.
16. Lebbeus Woods, *Radical Reconstructions* (Princeton Architectural Press, 2001), p.18.
17. ZA/UM, *Disco Elysium Digital Artbook* (iam8bit, 2021), p.33.
18. Forensic Architecture: https://forensic-architecture.org/about/agency
19. ZA/UM, *Disco Elysium Digital Artbook* (iam8bit, 2021), p.35.
20. Ibid., p.101.
21. Robert Venturi, *Complexity and Contradiction in Architecture* (Museum of Modern Art, 1966), p.86.
22. ZA/UM, *Disco Elysium Digital Artbook* (iam8bit, 2021), p.31.

CH 04 DOOM

1. Benjamin Turner, 'Creating DOOM: Romero Remembers', *GameSpy*: https://web.archive.org/web/20111119234156/http://archive.gamespy.com/articles/december03/doom/romero/
2. John Romero, interviewed by Luke Caspar Pearson and Sandra Youkhana, 16 February 2026.
3. Ibid.
4. Ibid.
5. Double Fine, '"Devs Play" S01E05 – Doom (Part 2 – Map 1 Hangar) 60fps [2/10]', YouTube: https://www.youtube.com/watch?v=rV6HIBa88js
6. John Romero, interviewed by Luke Caspar Pearson and Sandra Youkhana, 16 February 2026.
7. David Kushner, *Masters of Doom* (Random House, 2003), p.182.
8. Robin Evans, *Translations from Drawing to Building* (MIT Press, 1997), p.56.
9. John Romero, interviewed by Luke Caspar Pearson and Sandra Youkhana, 16 February 2026.
10. Andrew Kovacs, Floor Plans: https://o-k-o-k.net/floor-plans
11. John Romero, interviewed by Luke Caspar Pearson and Sandra Youkhana, 16 February 2026.
12. Doom Wiki, 'Map Unit': https://doomwiki.org/wiki/Map_unit
13. Jasper Carmack, '[FOUND] Doom Sky Source Files', *Doomworld*: https://www.doomworld.com/vb/doom-general/85756-found-doom-sky-source-files/
14. Stephen King and f-stop Fitzgerald, *Nightmares in the Sky: Gargoyles and Grotesques* (Viking Press, 1998).
15. John Romero, quote on Twitter/X: https://x.com/romero/status/542617231650091008
16. John Romero, interviewed by Luke Caspar Pearson and Sandra Youkhana, 16 February 2026.
17. Ibid.
18. Ibid.
19. Alban Janson and Florian Tigges, *Fundamental Concepts of Architecture: The Vocabulary of Spatial Situations* (Birkhäuser, 2014), p.244.
20. John Romero, interviewed by Luke Caspar Pearson and Sandra Youkhana, 16 February 2026.
21. Catherine Ingraham, *Architecture and the Burdens of Linearity* (Yale University Press, 1998), p.50.
22. decino, 'Showcasing Doom's Line Specials', YouTube: https://www.youtube.com/watch?v=0s4DpRTZenw
23. Eddie Lohmeyer, *Unstable Aesthetics: Game Engines and the Strangeness of Modding* (Bloomsbury Academic, 2023), p.60.
24. John Romero, interviewed by Luke Caspar Pearson and Sandra Youkhana, 16 February 2026.
25. Ibid.

CH 05 ELDEN RING

1. Frontline Gaming Japan, 'Elden Ring Release Interview with Director Hidetaka Miyazaki (Part 1/2) – Discussing Lore and Field Design': https://www.frontlinejp.net/2022/03/05/elden-ring-release-interview-with-director-miyazaki-part-1/
2. Sam Coons, 'Wayfinding in Themed Design: The "Weenie"', *Theory of Theme Parks*: http://theoryofthemeparks.blogspot.com/2015/08/wayfinding-in-themed-design-weenie.html
3. Deyan Sudjic, *The Edifice Complex* (Penguin, 2005), p.17.
4. Addypalooza, 'How Big Is the Architecture in Elden Ring? (Real World Comparisons)', YouTube: https://www.youtube.com/watch?v=leQArPFGBtg
5. Smithbox, by Vawser et al.: https://www.nexusmods.com/eldenring/mods/4928
6. 'Lengths of the Principal Rivers in the World; Heights of the Principal Mountains in the World': https://dc.library.northwestern.edu/items/48c7105b-bbcf-4bf4-825b-1cc18e8e7144
7. Beaux-Arts was an architectural teaching method emerging in 19th-century Paris at the École des Beaux-Arts.
8. J. F. Harbeson, *The Study of Architectural Design: With Special Reference to the Program of the Beaux-Arts Institute of Design* (Pencil Points Press, 1926).
9. Alban Janson and Florian Tigges, *Fundamental Concepts of Architecture: The Vocabulary of Spatial Situations* (Birkhäuser, 2014), p.144.
10. u/Middle-Sprinkles-165, 'Does Anyone Know What Is That Substance Coming from the Doors on Lyndell?', *Reddit*: https://www.reddit.com/r/Eldenring/comments/znep6x/does_anyone_knows_what_is_that_substance_coming/
11. Duomo di Milano, 'The Terraces', *Duomo di Milano*: https://www.duomomilano.it/en/art-and-culture/the-terraces/
12. The Lore Hunter, 'Elden Ring Lore | The History & Architecture of Stormveil Castle', YouTube: https://www.youtube.com/watch?v=qFQNbdALu5E
13. Massimo Scolari, *Oblique Drawing: A History of Anti-Perspective* (MIT Press, 2012), p.6.
14. Otis_Inf Photomode Mods: Elden Ring: https://opm.fransbouma.com/Cameras/eldenring.htm
15. Jonathan Hill, *The Architecture of Ruins* (Routledge, 2019), p.62.
16. Florence Smith Nicholls and Michael Cook, 'The Dark Souls of Archaeology: Elden Ring', *FDG '22* (Athens, 2022).
17. u/[deleted], 'The Architecture of *Elden Ring*', *Reddit*: https://www.reddit.com/r/Eldenring/comments/wzz9mi/the_architecture_of_elden_ring/
18. Matt Kim, 'Two Years After Elden Ring, Miyazaki Trusts the Players to Figure It All Out', *IGN*: https://www.ign.com/articles/elden-ring-shadow-of-erdtree-director-hidetaka-miyazaki-look-back-interview-profile
19. Towneley Hall, Lancashire, UK, cited in: Michael Hodgetts, *Secret Hiding Places* (Pear Branch Press, 2024), p.138.
20. 'Nox Monk Hood' item description in *Elden Ring*.
21. Michelle Miller, 'AD Classics: Cenotaph for Newton / Étienne-Louis Boullée', *ArchDaily*: https://www.archdaily.com/544946/ad-classics-cenotaph-for-newton-etienne-louis-boullee
22. William Shenstone, 'Unconnected Thoughts on Gardening', in *The Works in Prose and Verse of William Shenstone, Esq.*, 2 vols (R. & J. Dodsley, 1764), p.131.

CH 06 GENSHIN IMPACT

1. Marina Wardaya, Gracelyn Elizabeth, Fenie Fedora Wijaya, Lovjoyla Belinda Lennial and Selena Cheryl Willyam, 'Genshin Impact's Role in Preserving Chinese Cultural Heritage', *ULTIMART: Jurnal Komunikasi Visual*, 17, No. 2 (December 2024), pp.205–215: https://www.researchgate.net/publication/387674543_Genshin_Impact's_Role_in_Preserving_Chinese_Cultural_Heritage
2. Théophile Larcher, 'Architecture of France: Fake Paris Façades Cover Up Pollution Secret', *The Connexion*: https://www.connexionfrance.com/magazine/architecture-of-france-fake-paris-façades-cover-up-pollution-secret/131191
3. Christina M. Spiker, 'The Dichotomy of Inside and Outside: Exploring Architectural Space in Genshin Impact', *MediaCommons*: https://mediacommons.org/imr/content/dichotomy-inside-and-outside-exploring-architectural-space-genshin-impact
4. Beerevity, 'Fontaine City Is Confusing', YouTube: https://www.youtube.com/watch?v=2TNUHE0-q3Y
5. Xinhua, 'Archaeological Findings Reveal Evolution of Ancient Chinese City', *XinhuaNet*: https://english.news.cn/20220928/f4a511a022d94e8aab6a9de7aa017d52/c.html
6. Juhani Pallasmaa, *The Eyes of the Skin: Architecture and the Senses*, 3rd edition (Wiley, 2012), p.45.
7. Haoyu Cai, 'Genshin Impact: Crafting an Anime-Style Open World', *GDC Vault*: https://www.gdcvault.com/play/1027539/-Genshin-Impact-Crafting-an
8. Ibid.
9. Lifeng Han, 'Communicating Civilization Through Rituals: Mount Tai Pilgrimages in Song China, 960–1279', *Journal of Chinese Humanities*, 1, No. 2 (2015), p.352: https://doi.org/10.1163/23521341-01010018

10. u/displacedindavis, 'Per My Cursory Calculations, There's Been More Than 3.5 Days' Worth of Voiced Content in Genshin', *Reddit*: https://www.reddit.com/r/Genshin_Impact/comments/zeak7i/per_my_cursory_calculations_theres_been_more_than
11. Long Qin and Hong-li Liu, 'The Main Colors of the Forbidden City', *Sociology Study*, Vol. 13, No. 4 (2023), p.208: https://doi.org/10.17265/2159-5526/2023.04.005
12. Genshin Impact Wiki, NPC/List: https://genshin-impact.fandom.com/wiki/NPC/List
13. Matthew James Adams, 'Tech Otakus Save the World? Gacha, Genshin Impact, and Cybernesis', *British Journal of Chinese Studies*, Vol. 12, No. 2 (2022), p.188–208: https://doi.org/10.51661/bjocs.v12i2.199
14. Gwendolyn Yap, 'Assessing Genshin's Soft Power: Impact on Southeast Asia', *Sojourn: Journal of Social Issues in Southeast Asia*, 39, No.3 (2024), p.520: https://www.jstor.org/stable/27352225
15. Rui Zhong, 'As It Adds New Regions, Genshin Impact's Politics Only Get Messier', *Polygon*: https://www.polygon.com/23380882/genshin-impact-sumeru-update-inazuma-stereotype

CH 07 GRAVITY RUSH 2

1. Alejandro Jodorowsky and Jean Giraud (Moebius), *The Incal* (Humanoids, 2014).
2. Gareth Damian Martin, 'Falling Through 100 Million Stories in Gravity Rush: Remastered', *Killscreen*: https://www.killscreen.com/falling-through-a-100-million-stories-in-gravity-rush-remastered/
3. Gareth Damian Martin, 'Gravity Rush 2's City Turns the Player from Tourist to Traveller', *Killscreen*: https://www.killscreen.com/gravity-rush-2s-city-turns-player-tourist-traveller/
4. Corey Brotherson, 'Gravity Rush 2: Bigger Worlds, Little Details, Silly Side Quests', *PlayStation.Blog*: https://blog.playstation.com/2016/06/24/gravity-rush-2-bigger-worlds-little-details-silly-side-quests/
5. Amy Kulper and Diana Periton, 'Introduction: Explicating City Air', *The Journal of Architecture*, Vol. 19, No. 2 (2014): https://www.tandfonline.com/doi/abs/10.1080/13602365.2014.918637
6. Rebecca Maksel, 'The Soviet City in the Sky', *Smithsonian Magazine* (2016): https://www.smithsonianmag.com/air-space-magazine/soaring-city-180957990/
7. Michael Wolf, *Architecture of Density: Hong Kong (new edition)* (Buchkunst Berlin, 2022).
8. Peter Popham, 'Introduction', in Greg Girard and Ian Lambot, *City of Darkness: Life in Kowloon Walled City* (Watermark, 2009), p.13.
9. Christian Nutt, 'GDC 2012: Defining the "Living Background" of *Gravity Rush*', *Gamasutra*: https://web.archive.org/web/20210823233321/http:www.gamasutra.com/view/news/165355/GDC_2012_Defining_the_living_background_of_Gravity_Rush.php
10. Donald Kunze, 'Architecture as Reading; Virtuality, Secrecy, Monstrosity', *Journal of Architectural Education*, Vol. 41, No. 4 (1988), p.30: https://www.tandfonline.com/doi/pdf/10.1080/10464883.1988.10758499
11. Susan Sontag, *On Photography* (RosettaBooks electronic edition, 2005), p.6–7.
12. Ibid.
13. Tim Barringer, *Empire and the Origins of the Panorama*, Yale University Press: https://yalebooks.yale.edu/2021/01/14/empire-and-the-origins-of-the-panorama/
14. Gareth Damian Martin, 'Falling Through 100 Million Stories in Gravity Rush Remastered', *Killscreen*: https://www.killscreen.com/falling-through-a-100-million-stories-in-gravity-rush-remastered/
15. Marie Thébaud-Sorger, 'Thomas Baldwin's *Airopaidia*', in Mark Dorrian and Frédéric Pousin (eds.), *Seeing from Above* (I.B. Tauris, 2013), p.54.
16. Zaha Hadid, quoted in Simon Hattenstone, 'Master Builder', *The Guardian*: https://www.theguardian.com/artanddesign/2003/feb/03/architecture.artsfeatures

CH 08 GRIM FANDANGO REMASTERED

1. Tim Schafer, designer diary originally published on GameSpot, *Grim Fandango Network*: https://grimfandango.network/features/designer-diaries/monday-june-28-1995
2. Francisco Mújica Díez de Bonilla, *The History of the Skyscraper* (Archaeology & Architecture Press, 1929).
3. Luis E. Carranza and Fernando Luiz Lara, *Modern Architecture in Latin America* (University of Texas Press, 2014), p.56.
4. Colin Williamson, 'Scoop! Your First Look at ... Grim Fandango', *PC Gamer*, May 1998 (Imagine Media, 1998), p.41.
5. Mark Cooke, quoted in Double Fine, 'The Making of Grim Fandango Remastered: Episode 2', YouTube: https://www.youtube.com/watch?v=s-LSMCYjHow
6. ScummVM: https://www.scummvm.org/downloads/
7. Peter Chan, Eric Ingerson, Bret Mogilefsky, Tim Schafer and Peter Tscale, *Grim Fandango Puzzle Document* (LucasArts Entertainment Company, 1996).
8. Renée Tobe, *Film, Architecture and Spatial Imagination* (Routledge, 2017), p.62.
9. fSpy by Stuffmatic: https://fSpy.io/
10. Grasshopper script by 3DBeast.
11. Jo Ashburn, *Grim Fandango: Prima's Official Strategy Guide* (Prima Publishing, 1998), p.82.
12. Double Fine, '450 Sutter': https://www.doublefine.com/news/450-sutter
13. Marjorie I. Ingle, *The Mayan Revival Style: Art Deco Mayan Fantasy* (Peregrine Smith Books, 1984), p.75.
14. George Oakley Totten, *Maya Architecture* (The Maya Press, 1926).
15. Marjorie I. Ingle, *The Mayan Revival Style: Art Deco Mayan Fantasy* (Peregrine Smith Books, 1984), p.58.
16. Edward Dimendberg, *Film Noir and the Spaces of Modernity* (Harvard University Press, 2004), p.4.
17. NeoGamer – The Video Game Archive, 'Grim Fandango – 1997 Tim Schafer Interview [Behind the Scenes]', YouTube: https://youtu.be/kePpoQyT6vA
18. Marjorie I. Ingle, *The Mayan Revival Style: Art Deco Mayan Fantasy* (Peregrine Smith Books, 1984), p.75–76.
19. Steven Izenour, Denise Scott Brown and Robert Venturi, *Learning from Las Vegas: The Forgotten Symbolism of Architectural Form* (MIT Press, 1976).
20. Tom Wolfe, 'The Kandy-Kolored Tangerine-Flake Streamline Baby', *Esquire*, November 1963, p.118.
21. Edward Dimendberg, *Film Noir and the Spaces of Modernity* (Harvard University Press, 2004), p.7.
22. Francisco Mújica Díez de Bonilla, *The History of the Skyscraper* (Archaeology & Architecture Press, 1929), p.19.
23. Renée Tobe, *Film, Architecture and Spatial Imagination* (Routledge, 2017), p.33.

CH 09 HALF-LIFE 2

1. Michael Hebbert, 'Figure-Ground: History and Practice of a Planning Technique', *Town Planning Review*, Vol. 87, No. 6 (Liverpool University Press, 2016), p.715: https://www.liverpooluniversitypress.co.uk/doi/10.3828/tpr.2016.44
2. Valve, *Half-Life 2: Raising the Bar* (Prima Games, 2004), p.186.
3. Ibid., p.256.
4. Ibid., p.168.
5. NFKRZ, 'Where Is City 17 Really Located?', YouTube: https://www.youtube.com/watch?v=bOg59e23QPM
6. Valve, *Half-Life 2: Raising the Bar* (Prima Games, 2004), p.195.
7. Christine Varga-Harris, *Stories of House and Home: Soviet Apartment Life during the Khrushchev Years* (Cornell University Press, 2015), p.26.
8. Makoto Sei Watanabe, *Aoyama Technical College* (1990): https://www.makoto-architect.com/aoyamaTC.html
9. Lebbeus Woods, *War and Architecture*, Pamphlet Architecture 15 (Princeton Architectural Press, 1993), p.21.
10. Valve, *Half-Life 2: Raising the Bar* (Prima Games, 2004), p.180.
11. Jim Korkis, 'The Origin of the Disneyland Wienie', *Mouse Planet*: https://mouseplanet.com/the-origin-of-the-disneyland-wienie/5245/
12. Roland Barthes, *The Eiffel Tower and Other Mythologies* (University of California Press, 1979), p.3.
13. Ibid., p.4.
14. As suggested by Valve developer Marc Laidlaw: https://combineoverwiki.net/wiki/Citadel
15. u/Rscreamroad, 'Half-Life – The Citadel's Height (Strikes Back)', *Reddit*: https://www.reddit.com/r/gaming/comments/o8z4hu/halflife_the_citadels_height_strikes_back/
16. Valve, *Half-Life 2: Raising the Bar* (Prima Games, 2004), p.238.
17. Reyner Banham, *Los Angeles: The Architecture of Four Ecologies* (University of California Press, 2009), p.195.
18. Valve, *Half-Life 2: Raising the Bar* (Prima Games, 2004), p.277.
19. Gerald Farca, *Playing Dystopia: Nightmarish Worlds in Video Games and the Player's Aesthetic Response* (Transcript Verlag, 2018), p.104–105.
20. Dimitris Dalakoglou, *The Road: An Ethnography of (Im)mobility, Space, and Cross-Border Infrastructures in the Balkans* (Manchester University Press, 2016), p.9.
21. Both buildings featured in Frédéric Chaubin, *CCCP: Cosmic Communist Constructions Photographed* (Taschen, 2022).

CH 10 THE LAST OF US PART 1

1. Sarah McCreedy, '"There Is No Other Choice Here" – New Naturalism in Naughty Dog's The Last of Us', *Studies in American Naturalism*, Vol. 17, No. 2 (University of Nebraska Press, 2022), p.225.
2. *The Oxford Dictionary of Phrase and Fable* (Oxford University Press, 2005).
3. Jonathan Hill, *Architecture of Ruins: Designs on the Past, Present and Future* (Routledge, 2019), p.294.
4. Melissa Kagen, *Wandering Games* (MIT Press, 2022), p.123.
5. James Wines, cited in Fabrizio Gallanti, 'A Cut, a Move, a Forest', *Harvard Design Magazine*: https://www.harvarddesignmagazine.org/articles/a-cut-a-move-a-forest/
6. John Patrick Leary, 'Detroitism: What Does "Ruin Porn" Tell Us About the Motor City?', *Guernica*: https://www.guernicamag.com/leary_1_15_11/
7. Kevin Lynch, *The Image of the City* (MIT Press, 1960), p.78.
8. Ibid., p.78–81.
9. Emma Fraser, 'Awakening in Ruins: The Virtual Spectacle of the End of the City in Video Games', *Journal of Gaming & Virtual Worlds*, Vol. 8, No. 2 (Intellect, 2016), p.189.
10. Andrew Levitt, 'The Last of Us Locations in Real Life', YouTube: https://www.youtube.com/watch?v=pVSXHNdz32w
11. John Macarthur, *The Picturesque: Architecture, Disgust and Other Irregularities* (Routledge, 2007), p.88.
12. Ibid., p.85.
13. Enea Bianchi, 'Aesthetics at the End of the World', in Charles Joshua Horn (ed.), *The Last of Us and Philosophy: Look for the* Light (Wiley, 2024), p152.
14. Sears, Roebuck and Company, *Catalog No. 157: Fall and Winter 1928–29* (Sears, 1928): https://archive.org/details/sears-roebuck-catalog-157-fall-1928/
15. u/theinternetisnice, 'I Tried to Reason with Them', *Reddit*: https://www.reddit.com/r/thelastofus/comments/1gcnu1k/i_tried_to_reason_with_them
16. Melissa Kagen, *Wandering Games* (MIT Press, 2022), p 125.
17. Codex Gamicus, 'Chest-High Wall': https://gamicus.fandom.com/wiki/Chest-high_wall
18. Jonathan Hill, *The Architecture of Ruins: Designs on the Past, Present and Future*, p.294.
19. Amy M. Green, 'The Reconstruction of Morality and the Evolution of Naturalism in The Last of Us', *Games and Culture*, Vol. 11, Nos. 7–8 (Sage Journals, 2016), p.755.

CH 11 THE SIMS 4

1. Jesper Juul, 'Just What Is It That Makes Computer Games So Different, So Appealing?': https://www.jesperjuul.net/text/justwhatisit.html
2. Beatriz Colomina, 'Learning from Levittown: A Conversation with Robert Venturi and Denise Scott Brown', in Andrew Blauvelt (ed.), *Worlds Away: New Suburban Landscapes* (Walker Art Center, 2008).
3. Savannah Goth, 'The History & Evolution of Goth Manor in The Sims', YouTube: https://www.youtube.com/watch?v=JJeJEGIsd6w
4. Just Nora Gaming, 'I Tried to Renovate the Goth House in The Sims 4', YouTube: https://www.youtube.com/watch?v=SIsros6d7kA
5. Deligracy, 'I Built the Goths a New House', YouTube: https://www.youtube.com/watch?v=Gf9Aia0066Y
6. Devon Bumpkin, 'I Renovated the Goth Family Home | The Sims 4', YouTube: https://www.youtube.com/watch?v=p50Bw_1_IEU
7. TheIgnoredAnomaly's Sims 4 House Tours, 'Exploring Gallery Homes: BLUE MOON NOCC by Cayrees – The Sims 4 House', YouTube: https://www.youtube.com/watch?v=Ic5XDmRptjs
8. Petrana Radulovic, '18 Years Later, The Sims 2 Fandom Is Thriving on TikTok', *Polygon*: https://www.polygon.com/23013857/the-sims-2-tiktok
9. MewBuilds, TikTok: https://www.tiktok.com/@mewbuilds
10. Jennifer Bonner / MALL, *Domestic Hats*: https://jenniferbonner.com/03-Domestic-Hats
11. Amanda M. May, 'Random Build Challenges and Vital Materialism in The Sims 4: Influences, Innovations, and Improvisations', *Computers and Composition*, Vol. 65 (2022), article 102723: https://doi.org/10.1016/j.compcom.2022.102723
12. lilsimsie, 'Touring Your Incredible Builds in The Sims 4 (Shell Challenge)', YouTube: https://www.youtube.com/watch?v=1cq8OffRNrE
13. Robert Venturi, *Complexity and Contradiction in Architecture* (Museum of Modern Art, 1966), p.71–72.
14. u/libra00, 'Variable Wall Thickness?', *Reddit*: https://www.reddit.com/r/Sims4/comments/10qv78d/variable_wall_thickness/
15. u/UnstableUnicorn666, 'Why Real Life Houses Are Off in Sims', *Reddit*: https://www.reddit.com/r/Sims4/comments/1arcw9k/why_real_life_houses_are_off_in_sims/
16. Zoe Loftus-Farren, 'Remnants of the American Dream', *Earth Island Journal*: https://www.earthisland.org/journal/index.php/magazine/entry/remnants_of_the_american_dream/
17. Julia Kollewe, 'Number of Pubs in England and Wales Falls Below 39,000 for First Time', *The Guardian*: https://www.theguardian.com/business/2024/dec/30/number-of-pubs-in-england-and-wales-falls-below-39000-for-first-time
18. Justin McCurry, 'Last Orders? Soaring Costs and Declining Demand Take Toll on Japan's Legendary Izakaya', *The Guardian*: https://www.theguardian.com/world/2025/jan/18/japan-legendary-izakaya-closing-costs-declining-demand
19. The Sims, 'The Sims 4 Get Together: Come to Windenburg!', YouTube: https://www.youtube.com/watch?v=50KNNqCR8gI
20. Marta Heine-Geldern, 'Places & Spaces: Germany's Fairytale Fachwerk Houses', *Cabana Magazine*: https://cabanamagazine.com/blogs/travel/places-spaces-germanys-fairytale-fachwerk-houses

CH 12 YAKUZA KIWAMI

1. Kouichi Teratani, 'A Town Is Its People', *Kabukicho*: http://www.kabukicho.or.jp/history.php?lang=en
2. Timothy Yun Hui Tsu, 'Black Market, Chinatown, and Kabukichō: Postwar Japanese Constructs of "Overseas Chinese"', *Positions: Asia Critique*, Vol.19, No. 1 (Duke University Press, 2011), p.143.
3. Martina Baradel and Jacopo Bortolussi, 'Under a Setting Sun: The Spatial Displacement of the Yakuza and Their Longing for Visibility', *Trends in Organized Crime*, Vol. 24 (Springer, 2020), p.210.
4. Sebastián Aedo and Jessica Stokes, *Yakuza Freecam Tool* (Rust): https://github.com/etra0/yakuza-freecam
5. Young-hwan Lee, Haruhiko Goto, Chang-ho Lee and Hiroyuki Fukutake, 'Influence of Various Types of Lightings in the Night-Cityscape of Commercial District: The case study in Kabukicho, a commercial area of Shinjuku', *Journal of Architecture and Planning*, Vol. 70, No. 598 (AIJ, 2005), p.108.
6. Anne Allison, *Nightwork: Sexuality, Pleasure, and Corporate Masculinity in a Tokyo Hostess Club* (University of Chicago Press, 1994), p.40.
7. Ibid.
8. Hidefumi Nishiyama, 'Crowd Surveillance : The (In) Securitization of the Urban Body', *Security Dialogue*, Vol. 49, No. 3 (January 2018), p.210.
9. Toei Transportation, Higashi-Shinjuku Station: https://www.kotsu.metro.tokyo.jp/eng/subway_stations/higashi-shinjuku.html
10. Japanese History, '10 Deepest Tokyo Underground Stations: Tokyo Metro & Toei Subway Lines', YouTube: https://www.youtube.com/watch?v=YL_osxxGGlI
11. Machiya Inns & Hotels, 'What Is a Machiya?', *Machiya Magazine*: https://www.machiya-inn-japan.com/blog/what-is-a-machiya-a-brief-history-on-traditional-japanese-townhouses-2/
12. Hidenobu Jinnai, *Tokyo: A Spatial Anthropology* (California University Press, 1995), p.5.
13. The Metropolitan Area Outer Underground Discharge Channel: https://gaikaku.jp/
14. Martina Baradel and Jacopo Bortolussi, 'Under a Setting Sun: The Spatial Displacement of the Yakuza and Their Longing for Visibility', *Trends in Organized Crime*, Vol. 24 (Springer, 2020), p.219.
15. Elizabeth Grosz, *Architecture from the Outside: Essays on Virtual and Real Space* (MIT Press, 2001).
16. Izumi Kuroishi, 'Urban Survey and Planning in Twentieth-Century Japan: Wajiro Kon's "Modernology" and Its Descendants', *Journal of Urban History*, Vol. 42, No. 3 (Sage Journals, 2016).
17. Hans Hollein, 'Alles ist Architektur' (1968), discussed in: https://socks-studio.com/2013/08/13/hans-holleins-alles-ist-architektur-1968/
18. Sayoko Narita, 'Tokyo's New Skyscraper Resembles Yakuza's Millennium Tower', *Automaton*: https://automaton-media.com/en/news/20230410-18419/
19. u/Accomplished_Guide93, 'I Didn't Know This Until Just Now but Apparently There's a Building Called the Millennium Tower in Rotterdam and It's the Actual Millennium Tower', *Reddit*: https://www.reddit.com/r/yakuzagames/comments/oqc4zq/i_didnt_know_this_until_just_now_but_apparently/

Luke Caspar Pearson is an Associate Professor at the Bartlett School of Architecture, University College London (UCL) where he is Co-director of the Cinematic and Videogame Architecture MArch course. He is co-founder of the architectural design studio You+Pea. Luke has written widely on the relationship between architecture and games and holds a PhD in the subject. Luke is the co-author of *Videogame Atlas: Mapping Interactive Worlds* (Thames & Hudson, 2022). His other books are *Architectural Design: Re-Imagining the Avant-Garde* (Wiley, 2019) and *Drawing Futures: Speculations in Contemporary Drawing for Art and Architecture* (UCL Press, 2016). Luke has also consulted for industry and cultural institutions internationally.

Sandra Youkhana is an Associate Professor at the Bartlett School of Architecture, UCL where she is Director of Short Courses, and is a registered architect. She is co-founder of the architectural design studio You+Pea and teaches the Cinematic and Videogame Architecture MArch at UCL. Sandra is the co-author of *Videogame Atlas: Mapping Interactive Worlds* (Thames & Hudson, 2022). Sandra has consulted for game developers, technology companies, and city planners, and is undertaking a PhD at UCL. Her research explores videogames as a tool for decolonization, creating experimental videogame works that challenge Iraq's representation through videogame media.

Together Sandra and Luke founded the architectural design studio You+Pea, based in London. Their work explores the integration of videogame technologies into architectural design, leading conversations on how games can engage new participants in the design of cities. You+Pea's work operates between the design of architectural interventions and virtual environments, developing critical theory that underpins their connection. They create and analyse virtual, interactive game spaces to provoke conversations about the physical world.

John Romero is an award-winning designer whose career spans over five decades, encompassing over 100 games. A co-founder of id Software, he is best known for his level design, programming and direction on the genre-defining first-person shooters *Wolfenstein 3D* (1992), *DOOM* (1993) and *Quake* (1996). He has helped found ten game studios, including Romero Games, which he runs with his wife and fellow designer Brenda Romero. With over 100 industry honours to his name, he is also the author of the memoir *Doom Guy: Life in First Person* (Abrams, 2023).

Picture Credits:
Baldur's Gate 3 (pp14, 20–21, 28): © Larian Studios, 2023; *BioShock* (pp36–37, 44–45, 52–53): © 2K Games, 2007; *Disco Elysium* (pp60–61, 66, 71): © ZA/UM, 2019; *DOOM* (pp84, 87, 92–93): © id Software, 1993; *Elden Ring* (pp100–101, 106, 114): © FromSoftware / Bandai Namco Entertainment, 2022; *Genshin Impact* (pp124–125, 131, 136): © miHoYo, Shanghai Miha Touring Film Technology Co., Ltd. / HoYoverse, 2020; *Gravity Rush 2* (pp148–149, 155, 160–161): © Japan Studio / Sony Interactive Entertainment, 2017; *Grim Fandango Remastered* (pp176–177, 182–183, 188–189): © Double Fine Productions, 2015; *Half-Life 2* (pp196, 202–203, 208): © Valve Corporation, 2004; *The Last of Us Part 1* (pp216, 223, 230): © Naughty Dog / Sony Interactive Entertainment, 2022; *The Sims 4* (pp240–241, 252–253, 256–257): © Maxis / Electronic Arts, 2014; *Yakuza Kiwami* (pp268, 273, 279): © Ryu Ga Gotoku Studio / Sega, 2016.

On the cover: original illustrations by Luke Caspar Pearson and Sandra Youkhana, inspired by the virtual architecture of *BioShock*, *Disco Elysium*, *Elden Ring*, *Grim Fandango Remastered* and *The Sims 4*.

First published in the United Kingdom in 2026 by Thames & Hudson Ltd, 6–24 Britannia Street, London WC1X 9JD

First published in the United States of America in 2026 by Thames & Hudson Inc., 500 Fifth Avenue, New York, New York 10110

Designed by Alex Dujet – Type System Corp

You+Pea Production Baby: Ida Nene
Research Assistants: Ness Lafoy and Xiaojun (Katrina) Lin

Research Assistants funded by the Architecture Research Fund of the Bartlett School of Architecture, UCL.

EU Authorized Representative: Interart S.A.R.L.
19 rue Charles Auray, 93500 Pantin, Paris, France
productsafety@thameshudson.co.uk
interart.fr

A CIP catalogue record for this book is available from the British Library

Library of Congress Control Number 2026936982

ISBN 978-0-500-02970-1
01

Printed in China by RR Donnelley

FSC www.fsc.org MIX Paper | Supporting responsible forestry FSC® C144853